# Documentary Culture and the Laity in the Early Middle Ages

Many more documents survive from the early Middle Ages than from the Roman Empire. Although ecclesiastical archives may account for the dramatic increase in the number of surviving documents, this new investigation reveals the scale and spread of documentary culture beyond the Church. The contributors explore the nature of the surviving documentation without preconceptions to show that we cannot infer changing documentary practices from patterns of survival. Throughout Late Antiquity and the early Middle Ages – from North Africa, Egypt, Italy, Francia and Spain to Anglo-Saxon England – people at all social levels, whether laity or clergy, landowners or tenants, farmers or royal functionaries, needed, used and kept documents. The story of documentary culture in the early medieval world emerges not as one of its capture by the Church, but rather of a response adopted by those who needed documents, as they reacted to a changing legal, social and institutional landscape.

WARREN C. BROWN is Professor of History at the California Institute of Technology.

MARIOS COSTAMBEYS is Senior Lecturer in History at the University of Liverpool.

MATTHEW INNES is Professor of History at Birkbeck, University of London.

ADAM J. KOSTO is Professor of History at Columbia University.

# Documentary Culture and the Laity in the Early Middle Ages

*Edited by*
Warren C. Brown, Marios Costambeys,
Matthew Innes and Adam J. Kosto

CAMBRIDGE
UNIVERSITY PRESS

CAMBRIDGE UNIVERSITY PRESS
Cambridge, New York, Melbourne, Madrid, Cape Town,
Singapore, São Paulo, Delhi, Mexico City

Cambridge University Press
The Edinburgh Building, Cambridge CB2 8RU, UK

Published in the United States of America by Cambridge University Press, New York

www.cambridge.org
Information on this title: www.cambridge.org/9781107025295



First published 2013

Printed and bound in the United Kingdom by the MPG Books Group

*A catalogue record for this publication is available from the British Library*

*Library of Congress Cataloguing in Publication data*
Documentary culture and the laity in the early Middle Ages / edited by Warren C. Brown, Marios Costambeys, Matthew Innes and Adam J. Kosto.
pages cm
Includes bibliographical references and index.
ISBN 978-1-107-02529-5
1. Middle Ages – Sources. 2. History – Sources. 3. Europe – History – 476–1492 – Sources. 4. Civilization, Medieval – Sources. I. Brown, Warren C. II. Costambeys, Marios. III. Innes, Matthew. IV. Kosto, Adam J.
D113.D627 2012
302.2′2440940902 – dc23 2012017771

ISBN 978-1-107-02529-5 Hardback

# Contents

# Figures and tables

## Figures



## Tables

# Contributors

BROWN, WARREN C., Professor of History, Division of the Humanities and Social Sciences, California Institute of Technology

CONANT, JONATHAN P., Assistant Professor, Department of History, Brown University

COSTAMBEYS, MARIOS, Senior Lecturer, School of History, University of Liverpool

EVERETT, NICHOLAS, Associate Professor, Department of History, University of Toronto

HUMMER, HANS, Associate Professor, Department of History, Wayne State University

INNES, MATTHEW, Professor, Department of History, Birkbeck College, University of London

INSLEY, CHARLES, Senior Lecturer, School of Arts, Languages and Cultures, University of Manchester

KOSTO, ADAM J., Professor, Department of History, Columbia University

SARRIS, PETER, University Senior Lecturer, Faculty of History, University of Cambridge

SENNIS, ANTONIO, Lecturer, Department of History, University College, University of London

# Acknowledgements

This book is less a traditional edited volume than one result of a highly fruitful process of collaborative research. What began as a discussion over a pint in Princeton in November 2000 grew into an ever-widening e-mail exchange spanning eight time zones, and then a panel at Leeds (2002); formal workshops in London (2003), Pasadena (2004), Vienna (2005), Canterbury (2006) and Cambridge (2007); a panel at the Medieval Academy in Vancouver (2008); and finally – for the four editors – a remarkable series of group writing sessions, from which the introduction and conclusion emerged and the various parts were woven into a whole. From the beginning, the ten members of the Lay Archives Working Group, as we came to be called, were all frustrated by the increasingly outcomes-driven framework of much research in the humanities. We therefore banned all discussion of a collective publication until several years into the undertaking; our goals were, rather, undirected exploration of our common theme and intellectual exchange among a transatlantic network of younger scholars, most of whom did not know each other well or at all when we began. Various members did publish work separately as we progressed, but only when it became clear that we as a group had something potentially important to say did we turn to work on the present volume. This long process (punctuated by the arrival of eight children!) lies behind what we hope will be seen as a very well-integrated publication – not a set of papers, but a book with a collective voice and a common argument.

So as not to succumb to groupthink, from early on we invited other scholars to sit in on our workshops, and it is their probing questions, collegial suggestions and encouragement of our collective approach that we have the pleasure to acknowledge first: Rosamond McKitterick and Christina Pössel at London; Patrick Geary, Jason Glenn and Claudia Rapp in Pasadena; Walter Pohl, Peter Erhart and Bernhard Zeller in Vienna; and Geoff Koziol and Barbara Rosenwein, who served as commenters on the Vancouver panel. Koziol went on to serve as an extraordinarily incisive reader of our manuscript for Cambridge University

Press. He pressed us to clarify our thinking and ultimately helped us to strengthen our collective argument. We also thank the other (anonymous) reader for that press, as well as readers for what was an unsuccessful grant application along the way.

Our meetings received institutional support from Birkbeck College, University of London; the California Institute of Technology; the Huntington Library; the Institut für Mittelalterforschung (Vienna); the Austrian Academy of Sciences; and Cambridge University – not to mention the home institutions of the individual authors that paid for much of the transatlantic travel. Funding from the British Academy (via an International Network Award) and the Leverhulme Trust (via some of the funding awarded as a Philip Leverhulme Prize) proved vital in getting the project off the ground.

We dedicate this book to our mentors, formal and informal, who taught us to value collaboration over competition.

# Abbreviations

**Series**

| | |
|---|---|
| CSEL | Corpus scriptorum ecclesiasticorum Latinorum (Vienna, 1866–) |
| CCSL / G | Corpus Christianorum series Latina (Turnhout, 1953–); series Graeca (Turnhout, 1977–) |
| MGH | Monumenta Germaniae historica |
| AA | Auctores antiquissimi |
| Capit. | Capitularia |
| Const. | Constitutiones et acta publica imperatorum et regum |
| DD | Diplomata |
| Epist. | Epistolae |
| Libri mem. n.s. | Libri memoriales et necrologia, nova series |
| LL | Leges (in folio) |
| LL nat. Germ. | Leges nationum Germanicarum |
| SrG [n.s.] | Scriptores rerum Germanicarum [nova series] |
| SRL | Scriptores rerum Langobardicarum et Italicarum |
| SRM | Scriptores rerum Merovingicarum |
| MGH Formulae | *Formulae Merowingici et Karolini aevi*, ed. K. Zeumer, MGH Legum sectio V (Hannover, 1886) |
| *Form. Andec.* | *Formulae Andecavenses* |
| *Form. Arvern.* | *Formulae Arvernenses* |
| Marculf | *Formulae Marculfi* |
| Marculf [Supp.] | *Marculfi formulae [Supplementum]* |
| *Form. Marc. Kar.* | *Formulae Marculfi aevi Karolini* |
| *Form. Tur.* | *Formulae Turonenses vulgo Sirmondicae dictae* |
| *Form. Tur. Add.* | *Additatmenta e codicibus formularum Turonensium* |

| | |
|---|---|
| *Form. Bitur.* | *Formulae Bituricenses* |
| *Form. Sen.* | *Formulae Senonenses* |
| *Cart. Sen. [App.]* | *Cartae Senonicae [Appendix]* |
| *Form. Sen. Rec.* | *Formulae Senonenses recentiores* |
| *Form. Sal. Big.* | *Formulae Salicae Bignonianae* |
| *Form. Sal. Merk.* | *Formulae Salicae Merkelianae* |
| *Form. Sal. Lind.* | *Formulae Salicae Lindenbrogianae* |
| *Form. Sang. Misc.* | *Formulae Sangallenses miscellaneae* |
| *Coll. Sang.* | *Collectio Sangallensis Salomonis III. tempore conscripta* |
| *Form. Salz.* | *Formulae Salzburgenses* |
| *Coll. Flav.* | *Collectio Flaviniacensis* |
| *Coll. Flav. Add.* | *Collectio Flaviniacensis [Additamenta]* |
| *Form. Vis.* | *Formulae Visigothicae* |
| PL | Patrologiae cursus completus, series Latina, ed. J.-P. Migne, 221 vols. (Paris, 1845–6) |
| PG | Patrologiae cursus completus, series Graeca, ed. J.-P. Migne, 161 vols. in 166 (Paris, 1857–66) |

## Charters

| | |
|---|---|
| *ChLA* | *Chartae latinae antiquiores*, ed. A. Bruckner *et al.* (Olten, 1954–) |
| *CDL* | *Codice diplomatico longobardo*, ed. L. Schiaparelli *et al.*, 5 vols. in 7 (Rome, 1929–2003) |
| *Cluny* | *Recueil des chartes de l'abbaye de Cluny*, ed. A. Bernard and A. Bruel, 6 vols. (Paris, 1876–1903) |
| *RF* | Gregory of Catino, *Regestum Farfense*, ed. I. Giorgi and U. Balzani, *Il Regesto di Farfa*, 5 vols. (Rome, 1879–1914) |
| Rio, *Formularies* | A. Rio, trans., *The Formularies of Angers and Marculf: Two Merovingian Legal Handbooks* (Liverpool, 2008) |
| *TF* | *Die Traditionen des Hochstifts Freising*, ed. T. Bitterauf, 2 vols. (Munich, 1905–8) |
| Tjäder | J.-O. Tjäder, *Die nichtliterarischen lateinischen Papyri Italiens aus der Zeit 445–700*, 3 vols. (Lund, 1954–82) (documents cited volume in Roman, number in Arabic [I:3]; commentary cited volume in Arabic: page in Arabic [1:3]) |

| | |
|---|---|
| *TP* | *Die Traditionen des Hochstifts Passau*, ed. M. Heuwieser (Munich, 1930) |
| *TW* | *Traditiones Wizenburgenses: Die Urkunden des Klosters Weissenburg: 661–864*, ed. K. Glöckner and A. Doll (Darmstadt, 1979) |
| Wartmann | *Urkundenbuch der Abtei Sanct Gallen*, ed. H. Wartmann, 6 vols. in 7 (Zürich, 1863–1931) |

**Law**

| | |
|---|---|
| *CE* | *Codex Euricianus*, ed. A. d'Ors (Rome, 1960); *Liber iudiciorum sive Lex Visigothorum*, ed. K. Zeumer, MGH LL nat. Germ. 1:3–32 |
| *CIC* | *Corpus iuris civilis*, 16th/11th/6th edn, ed. P. Krüger *et al.*, 3 vols. (Berlin, 1954) |
| *CJ* | *Codex Iustinianus*, ed. P. Krüger, *CIC* 2 |
| *CTh.* | *Codex Theodosianus*, ed. P. Krüger, T. Mommsen and P. M. Meyer, 2 vols. (Berlin, 1905) |
| *Dig.* | *Iustiniani Digesta*, ed. T. Mommsen and P. Krüger, *CIC* 1 |
| *Epit. Aegid.* | *Epitome Aegidii*, ed. G. Haenel, in *LRV* |
| *ER* | *Edictus Rothari*, ed. G. H. Pertz, MGH LL 4:3–90 |
| *ETh.* | *Edictum Theodorici regis Italiae*, ed. F. Bluhme, MGH LL 5:145–68 |
| Gaius, *Inst.* | Gaius, *Institutiones*, ed. F. de Zulueta, 2 vols. (Oxford, 1946–53) |
| *Inst.* | *Iustiniani Institutiones*, ed. P. Krüger, *CIC* 1 |
| *J.Edict* | *Iustiniani XIII Edicta quae vocantur*, ed. R. Schöll and W. Kroll, *CIC* 3 |
| *J.Nov.* | *Iustiniani Novellae*, ed. R. Schöll and W. Kroll, *CIC* 3 |
| *LV* | *Liber iudiciorum sive Lex Visigothorum*, ed. K. Zeumer, MGH LL nat. Germ. 1:33–456 |
| *LRV* | *Lex Romana Visigothorum*, ed. G. Haenel (Leipzig, 1847) |
| *Nov.* | Valentinian III, Marcian, Maiorian: *Novellae*, ed. T. Mommsen and P. M. Meyer, in *CTh.* 2. |
| Leo III: | Leo III: *Novellae*, ed. C. E. Zachariae a Lingenthal (Leipzig, 1857) |
| *Peira* | Eustathios Romaios, *Peira*, ed. C. E. Zachariae a Lingenthal (Leipzig, 1857) |
| *PSent.* | *Pauli sententiae*, ed. M. Bianchi Fossati Vanzetti (Milan, 1995) |

## Papyri

| | |
|---|---|
| *CPR* | *Corpus papyrorum Raineri* (Vienna, 1895–) |
| *P.Bad* | *Veröffentlichungen aus den badischen Papyrus-Sammlungen*, 6 vols. (Heidelberg, 1923–38) |
| *P.Ital.* | = Tjäder |
| *P.Marini* | *I papiri diplomatici*, ed. G. Marini (Rome, 1805) |
| *P.Oxy* | *The Oxyrynchus Papyri* (London, 1898–) |
| *PSI* | *Papiri greci e latini* (Florence, 1912–) |

## Studies

| | |
|---|---|
| Brown, 'Documents' | W. Brown, 'When Documents Are Destroyed or Lost: Lay People and Archives in the Early Middle Ages', *EME*, 11 (2002), 337–66 |
| Classen, 'Fortleben' | P. Classen, 'Fortleben und Wandel spätrömischen Urkundenwesens im frühen Mittelalter', in *Recht und Schrift*, 13–54 |
| Costambeys, *Power* | M. Costambeys, *Power and Patronage in Early Medieval Italy: Local Society, Italian Politics and the Abbey of Farfa, 700–900* (Cambridge, 2007) |
| Davies, *Acts of Giving* | W. Davies, *Acts of Giving: Individual, Community and Church in Tenth-Century Spain* (Oxford, 2007) |
| Geary, *Phantoms* | P. Geary, *Phantoms of Remembrance: Memory and Oblivion at the End of the First Millennium* (Princeton, NJ, 1994) |
| Hummer, *Politics* | H. Hummer, *Politics and Power in Early Medieval Europe: Alsace and the Frankish Realm, 600–1000* (Cambridge, 2005) |
| Innes, *State and Society* | M. Innes, *State and Society in the Early Middle Ages: The Middle Rhine Valley, 400–1000* (Cambridge, 2000) |
| Kosto, 'Laymen' | A. J. Kosto, 'Laymen, Clerics, and Documentary Practices in the Early Middle Ages: The Example of Catalonia', *Speculum*, 80 (2005), 44–74 |

| | |
|---|---|
| *Les cartulaires* | O. Guyotjeannin, L. Morelle and M. Parisse (eds.), *Les cartulaires: Actes de la table ronde organisée par l'École nationale des chartes et le G.D.R. 121 du C.N.R.S.* (Paris, 1993) |
| *Les tranferts* | 'Les transferts patrimoniaux en Europe occidentale, VIII$^{e}$–X$^{e}$ siècle (I): Actes de la table ronde de Rome, 6, 7, et 8 mai 1999', *Mélanges de l'École française de Rome: Moyen âge*, 111 (1999), 487–972 |
| McKitterick, *Carolingians* | R. McKitterick, *The Carolingians and the Written Word* (Cambridge, 1989) |
| *Recht und Schrift* | P. Classen (ed.), *Recht und Schrift im Mittelalter* (Sigmaringen, 1977) |
| Rio, *Legal Practice* | A. Rio, *Legal Practice and the Written Word in the Early Middle Ages* (Cambridge, 2009) |
| Rosenwein, *Saint Peter* | B. H. Rosenwein, *To Be the Neighbor of Saint Peter: The Social Meaning of Cluny's Property, 909–1049* (Ithaca, NY, 1989) |
| *Settlement of Disputes* | W. Davies and P. Fouracre (eds.), *The Settlement of Disputes in Early Medieval Europe* (Cambridge, 1986) |
| *Uses of Literacy* | R. McKitterick (ed.), *The Uses of Literacy in Early Medieval Europe* (Cambridge, 1990) |
| Wickham, *Framing* | C. Wickham, *Framing the Early Middle Ages: Europe and the Mediterranean, 400–800* (Oxford, 2005) |

## Journals

| | |
|---|---|
| *EME* | *Early Medieval Europe* (Harlow, 1992–) |
| *TRHS* | *Transactions of the Royal Historical Society* (London, 1872–) |

## Varia

| | |
|---|---|
| Amm. Marc. | Ammianus Marcellinus, *Rerum gestarum libri*, ed. W. Seyfarth, 2 vols. (Leipzig, 1978) |
| BnF | Paris, Bibliothèque nationale de France |
| *CIL* | *Corpus inscriptionum Latinarum*, 18 vols. (Berlin, 1862–1989) |

| | |
|---|---|
| *CLA* | *Codices Latini antiquiores*, ed. E. A. Lowe, 11 vols. (Oxford, 1934–71) |
| Niermeyer, *Lexicon* | J. F. Niermeyer, *Mediae Latinitatis lexicon minus* (Leiden, 1976) |
| Settimane | Settimane di studio del Centro italiano di studi sull'alto medioevo (Spoleto, 1953–) |

# 1 Introduction

In 1928, archaeologists working along the Tunisian-Algerian border uncovered an earthenware jar containing forty-five wooden panels. When deciphered, the scraps were found to contain the texts of thirty-four Latin documents from the last decade of the fifth century: tables of calculations, a record of a dowry and several documents of sale. Most of the latter concern small plots of olive, fig and nut trees; one deals with a slave. The properties and individuals involved appear to have been associated with a single rural estate, the Fundus Tuletianos.[1]

The episcopal archive in Pisa preserves a simple list of eighty-eight documents given by Teuspert to Ghittia and her daughters. No reason can be given for its composition, but it can be dated to between 768 and 774. It inventories different kinds of documents, many of them rare among the large numbers of complete documents that survive in Italian ecclesiastical archives, but here catalogued and classified with care. In over half of the various charters (*cartae*), notes (*breves*), judgements (*iudicati*), letters (*epistolae*) and precepts (*praecepta*), neither party to the transaction was expressly associated with the Church. Ghittia herself was a nun, but her collection includes documents from a wide variety of her kin and contacts in which she is not implicated; forty-four of the documents in her list, for example, concern the layman Alahis.[2]

A formula collection from Gaul compiled towards the end of the seventh century contains a model letter from a king to an unfortunate who has had his house destroyed by fire. Among the things he lost were all of his documents, particularly those that recorded his title to property. According to the text, the man provides written testimony to the king verifying his property claims; the king then issues this letter confirming his property rights. Late in the ninth century – two centuries

[1] *Tablettes Albertini: Actes privés de l'époque vandale (fin du V^e siècle)*, ed. C. Courtois *et al.*, 2 vols. (Paris, 1952); see below, 40.

[2] *ChLA* XXVI 808; *CDL* II 295; see below, 239.

later – a Bavarian formula collection includes the same text word-for-word, save that the house in which the documents had been stored is now a monastery.[3]

A monk at the monastery of Sahagún in León in the early twelfth century, transcribing charters into a codex for his institution, copied a document that listed in abbreviated form twelve sales of land concerning a property called Melgar de Foracasas. These transactions, which did not involve the monastery, dated from between 945 and 954. In 959 Melgar de Foracasas was donated to the monastery by its peasant proprietors, Iscam and Filaura, along with the document. The total value of the twelve parcels was 133 *solidi*, 22 measures of wheat, a small plot and a red cow.[4]

For much of the modern period, a deeply embedded commonplace held that in Europe and the Mediterranean world in the early Middle Ages (AD 400–1000) documents were produced, used and preserved primarily by, and according to the needs and interests of, churchmen and monks. A corollary belief maintained that the surviving evidence for early medieval society so completely depended on the Church for its production and preservation that the investigation of such things as secular practices of landowning and conflict resolution, as opposed to the strategies used by the Church to pursue its interests, was impossible. Any effort to look beyond the confines of ecclesiastical institutions and reconstruct the workings of society as a whole would necessarily be indirect because of the nature of the surviving evidence.[5]

Yet, each of the examples given above shows laypeople using and storing documents. Many other examples like these survive, mostly – though not exclusively – scattered among and embedded in ecclesiastical and monastic archives. In the last several decades, early medievalists interested in how the written word was used in their period have begun to explore the implications of this evidence, namely that the early medieval laity may in fact have used and relied on writing to carry on the business of their lives to a considerable degree. Their efforts have begun to transform dramatically our understanding of writing practices in the period.[6]

[3] Marculf 1.33; *Form. Marc. Kar.* 22. See the discussion by Brown, 'Documents'.

[4] *Colección diplomática del monasterio de Sahagún (siglos IX y X)*, ed. J. M. Mínguez Fernández (León, 1976), nos. 94, 162, 164; see below, 279–80.

[5] See Kosto, 'Laymen', 47nn10–12; M. Clanchy, *From Memory to Written Record: England, 1066–1307*, 2nd edn (Oxford, 1993), 32.

[6] In addition to the work of the scholars represented in this volume, see two decades of publication on the subject by Cambridge University Press, from McKitterick, *Carolingians* to Rio, *Legal Practice*. French and Italian projects centre on the École française de

This transformation has not, however, taken hold in the non-specialist literature, either in the work of early medievalists not themselves directly concerned with writing practices or in the assumptions about the early Middle Ages perpetuated by those working on the high and late medieval periods. The reason, we think, has to do with scale. Each specialist working on document use among the early medieval laity has tended to focus on the examples with which he or she is familiar. Their insights have, therefore, been restricted to particular times and particular regions. This may well have created or reinforced an impression in the wider scholarly world that their examples were exceptional rather than typical. Though as a group the specialists now have a sense that the laity used writing more than was earlier believed, they have not yet put all of their individual pieces together to form a broad picture of how early medieval laypeople used documents or how their use of documents developed over time from the end of the Roman period through the turn of the first millennium. Nor have they been able to describe in anything like a comprehensive fashion exactly how laypeople in the period used writing, how we can discover this from sources whose survival in the main has been mediated by ecclesiastical and monastic archives and interests, or how this information might change our understanding of early medieval history in general.

This book represents an effort by a group of scholars who work on late antique and early medieval documentary culture to put their pieces of the puzzle of lay documentary use together and to see what picture emerges. We examine, directly and across a broad range of space and time, the scattered but nevertheless significant evidence for the use of documents by laypeople – that is, men and women who were not officials or functionaries of a church or members of a religious community, in transactions that did not involve ecclesiastical institutions – as well as the factors determining the survival or not of lay documents. We also explore the similar evidence for the existence of what can only be called 'lay archives'; that is, collections or dossiers of documents kept and used

Rome: *Les Transferts*; F. Bougard, L. Feller and R. Le Jan (eds.), *Dots et douaires dans le haut moyen âge* (Rome, 2002); F. Bougard, C. La Rocca and R. Le Jan (eds.), *Sauver son âme et se perpétuer: La transmission du patrimoine au haut moyen âge* (Rome, 2005); L. Feller and C. Wickham (eds.), *Le marché de la terre au moyen âge* (Rome, 2005). The German and Dutch projects are the Sonderforschungsbereich 231: Träger, Felder, Formen pragmatischer Schriftlichkeit im Mittelalter (Universität Münster, 1986–99), reported on in *Frühmittelalterliche Studien* from 1988 on; and the Pionier Project Verschriftelijking (Universiteit Utrecht), published in the series Utrecht Studies in Medieval Literacy (Turnhout, 1999–).

by laypeople.[7] In other words, we address the degree to which laypeople were not just using documents, but regarding them as important enough to store and make retrievable. Some of the evidence for these lay practices survives more or less independently of ecclesiastical institutions. However, much of our discussion uses indirect evidence that, for example, ecclesiastical archives took over or incorporated material which originated outside the Church, or that ecclesiastical institutions served as 'safe deposits' for the secular records of lay landowners. We thus directly question the premise that patterns of current document survival reflect patterns of early medieval access to and control of written documentation, and that clerics writing charters and ecclesiastical institutions storing them did so only to serve narrow sectional interests which were distinct from those of the wider society.[8] Putting all of our pieces together, we will show how laypeople together with clerics and monks participated in what was a common documentary culture, and how we can begin to integrate the experiences they recorded in their documents into our histories of the early Middle Ages.

## The laity

To begin with our main category of analysis: the laity, as opposed to Christian clergy and monks, is not a group whose existence or characteristics we can take for granted or whose unchanging distinctiveness we can automatically assume. Lay is a relational category that can exist only in dialogue with categories of the clerical. This relationship shifted radically in the course of the first millennium. It is only in the late second and early third centuries, for example, that sources begin to mention laity (*laikos/laicus*) at all. Laypeople begin then to be identified as such by clerics, even while clerics admitted their own origins in the laity. Fourth- and fifth-century councils insisted on the distinctiveness of the priesthood, to the extent that ascetics who took a monastic vow were classified as laymen.[9] In the eighth and ninth centuries, as the Carolingians tried to delineate more sharply the distinctions between lay and clerical, monks came to join the ranks of the 'clergy' – the classical tripartite theory of social functions, so very different from earlier patristic models, merged what had previously been two distinct orders into 'those

[7] For the issue of definition, see below, 12–15.
[8] See already H. Fichtenau, *Das Urkundenwesen in Österreich vom 8. bis zum frühen 13. Jahrhundert* (Vienna, 1971), 79.
[9] P. Siniscalco, *Laici e laicità: Un profilo storico* (Rome, 1986); Siniscalco, 'I laici nei primi secoli', in *Il laicato nella Bibbia e nella storia* (Rome, 1987), 91–105.

who pray'.[10] By the twelfth century, the reciprocity implicit in such theorizing was contested, as clerics attempted to define themselves as a new and self-conscious power elite; it was precisely in this period that they also attempted to define themselves as *literati*, the lettered class, thus encouraging the identification of the remainder of society as unlettered, illiterate.[11]

As our work will make clear, for much of our period the distinction between lay and clerical does not help us understand how documentary culture developed. Nevertheless, it remains necessary for our discussion. The terms 'lay' and 'clerical', of course, form the frame of reference within which modern discussions of early medieval writing have taken place, and they thus perforce form the framework for our enquiry. More important, however, is the fact that they have real, though changing, referents; our sources use them. In many times and places, people identified by our sources as lay, or not explicitly identified as clerics and monks, can be seen using documents in ways similar to those called clerics or monks and for similar purposes. However, these same sources tell us that laypeople were not the same as clergy. The interests of both were often shaped by the differing contexts in which they lived and acted and by the interests of those for whom they worked; these interests in turn helped determine what documents they used and how and where they stored them. Furthermore, there comes a point towards the end of our period when, as a result of a particular combination of cultural and political circumstances, the distinction between clerical and lay does begin to affect documentary culture in Europe on a large scale.

## Laypeople, documents and the Church

Direct evidence that laypeople in Late Antiquity and the early Middle Ages used documents survives in significant amounts: for example, in

[10] On clerical identity in the Carolingian centuries, see, e.g., L. Coon, 'What Is the Word If Not Semen? Priestly Bodies in Carolingian Exegesis', in L. Brubaker and J. Smith (eds.), *Gender in the Early Medieval World: East and West, 300–900* (Cambridge, 2004), 278–300; M. de Jong, *In Samuel's Image: Child Oblation in the Early Medieval West* (Leiden, 1996); F. Prinz, *Klerus und Kreig im früheren Mittelalter* (Stuttgart, 1971). On early medieval/Carolingian 'three orders' theory and its mutation, see O. G. Oexle, '*Tria genera hominum*: Zur Geschichte eines Deutungsschemas der sozialen Wirklichkeit in Antike und Mittelalter', in L. Fenske *et al.* (eds.), *Institutionen, Gesellschaft und Kultur im Mittelalter: Festschrift für Josef Fleckenstein zu seinem 65. Geburtstag* (Sigmaringen, 1984), 483–99, and D. Iogna-Prat, 'Le "baptême" du schema des trois ordres functionnels: L'apport de l'école d'Auxerre', *Annales ESC*, 41 (1986), 101–26.

[11] R. I. Moore, *The First European Revolution* (London, 2004); H. Grundmann, '*Litteratus–illitteratus*: Der Wandel einer Bildungsnorm vom Altertum zum Mittelalter', *Archiv für Kulturgeschichte*, 40 (1958), 1–65.

the 45 per cent of documents from a sample of some 2,000 charters from tenth-century Catalonia that record transactions involving only laymen and laywomen; in discrete groups of lay documents from the eighth- and ninth-century Frankish and Lombard worlds that later found their way into monastic archives; and in collections of documents that have survived on unusual (to us) material, such as the wooden tablets from fifth-century North Africa, or slates from seventh-century Iberia.[12] Because this evidence is scattered in time and place and often embedded in complex ways in the ecclesiastical sources, its extent and importance has been easy to overlook.

It is important because it allows us to confront pressing issues in the history of medieval writing from a new perspective. Chief among these is the question of institutional change: the effect of the end of Roman rule on ways of structuring and recording landholding; the fate of late Roman strategies of record-keeping in the successor states; the development of post-Roman institutions and their demands; and the methods whereby ecclesiastical institutions in particular attempted to control time and space through documents and archives. These changes in the institutional landscape and in documentary practices prompted broader transformations in the relationships between those who produced documents, the places in which documents were preserved and the uses to which documents were put.

One aspect of this process of change turns on the development of the early medieval Church and in particular of ecclesiastical archives. Specifically ecclesiastical archives cannot be taken as given. It is necessary to ask when and why churches and monasteries felt it necessary to store and organize their documents in a manner distinct and separate from other social actors and institutions. The balance between churches and other loci of documentary production, preservation and archival activities is historically contingent and tied to specific political contexts as well as to long-term developments. There may also be a problem of historical perspective. Did churches and monasteries ever *in general* come to dominate the preservation and production of documents for everyone, and, if so, when, where and why? Or, rather, have we privileged certain ecclesiastical institutions whose impact on document preservation has been especially durable? How did the practices of churches relate to other forms of record-keeping, which in some areas predated the dominance of the Church but in others piggybacked on ecclesiastical institutions? When, where and why did ecclesiastical documentary practice become

[12] See, e.g., Kosto, 'Laymen'; *Tablettes Albertini; Documentos de época visigoda escrita en pizarra, siglos VI–VIII*, ed. I. Velázquez Soriano (Turnhout, 2000); below, Chapters 3 and 4.

qualitatively different from those of other social institutions and groups, and what implications did this have for cultural and social practice?

The documentary and archival practices of churches and monasteries were influenced by those of the laypeople with whom they were intimately connected. As a rich seam of recent work has emphasized, the connection between churches and monasteries and the families that founded and patronized them was a two-way street.[13] The needs and interests of patron families shaped the formation and organization of churches and monasteries, and vice versa. Documentary and archival practice was as crucial to the formation of both institutional and family identity as was the movement of property. How did the inclusion of a core set of documents concerning the family of a monastery's founder affect the formation and future development of that monastery's archive? Why do so many of the documents contained in these embedded lay archives structure transfers of property *within* families? What role did women play in the ownership and transmission of property beyond making the donations to churches and monasteries that dominate the ecclesiastical records in which they appear as primary actors?

Asking these questions forces us to recognize that documents themselves played a role in social and institutional development rather than simply bearing witness to them. Early medieval archival documents are not always routine and descriptive; they can themselves be narratives subject to the same instrumental or strategic manipulation as texts more traditionally called 'narrative'.[14] The archives in which they were stored also reflect the differing interests and needs of the individuals, families or institutions that created them. Documents and archives, therefore, must themselves be treated as subjects of theoretical and historical enquiry, and must be understood in their specific historical contexts. A proper understanding of the ways in which the documentary record has been filtered, by the creation of the documents themselves and by historically contingent processes of archive formation, is necessary to understand the relationship of the surviving source material to the society it records.

When seen in this full context, our material shows that laypeople were full and conscious participants in early medieval societies that regarded

[13] Classically, Rosenwein, *Saint Peter*; see now, e.g., A.-J. Bijsterveld, *Do ut des: Gift Giving, Memoria and Conflict Management in the Medieval Low Countries* (Hilversum, 2005); Davies, *Acts of Giving*; Hummer, *Politics*; Costambeys, *Power*.

[14] E.g. W. Brown, 'Charters as Weapons: On the Role Played by Early Medieval Dispute Records in the Disputes They Record', *Journal of Medieval History*, 28 (2002), 222–48; P. Geary, 'Monastic Memory and the Mutation of the Year Thousand', in S. Farmer and B. H. Rosenwein (eds.), *Monks and Nuns, Saints and Outcasts* (Ithaca, NY, 2000), 19–36.

documents as important. As a rule, we have been unable to identify consistent formal differences – in script, layout or formula – between documents used by laypeople and those written by and for clerics in any of our samples, although patterns of preservation are in places distinct. The comparisons we draw between the patterns of document use and storage by laypeople and ecclesiastical institutions dissolve the picture of an impermeable divide between a literate clerical and an illiterate/oral lay culture.[15] Breaking down this divide opens up a new line of questions that can only be answered by analysing 'ecclesiastical' and 'lay' documents together, in the context of what was a common documentary culture.

## Literacy and the use of documents

Our sources consist principally of documentary records; that is, written texts generated primarily for pragmatic purposes.[16] These might be records of legal transactions: conveyances of property for the most part, but also testaments, or records of dispute settlements. But they also include a small but significant number of letters and formulaic models for drafting letters, and accounting documents. Alternative sources for our questions in our period scarcely exist. Scholars of the high and late Middle Ages have a number of resources beyond documentary records or letters for studying the use of writing among a broad swath of the laity, such as, for example, texts written for entertainment, texts written in the vernacular, university texts or religious texts written explicitly for a lay market. The very small number of such non-documentary texts from the early Middle Ages that can help illuminate written culture outside the Church (such as, for Carolingian Francia, the letter of the aristocratic woman Dhuoda to her son William, or the *Histories* of the equally aristocratic Nithard) reflect the activities, needs and interests of the very highest members of the elite; moreover, they have already been thoroughly explored.[17] Documentary texts thus provide challenging but potentially fruitful material with which to expand our picture of early medieval documentary culture beyond the elites.

15 The 'impermeable divide' model has recently been critiqued from other materials, most notably as regards intellectual and religious culture: see, e.g., J. M. H. Smith, *Europe after Rome: A New Cultural History 500–1000* (Oxford, 2005). Cf. T. Reuter, 'Gifts and Simony', in E. Cohen and M. de Jong (eds.), *Medieval Transformations: Texts, Power and Gifts in Context* (Leiden, 2005), 157–68, for eleventh-century change.

16 As in the title of the Münster project (above, n. 6), 'pragmatische Schriftlichkeit'.

17 E.g. the essays collected in P. Wormald and J. L. Nelson (eds.), *Lay Intellectuals in the Carolingian World* (Cambridge, 2007).

As noted above, the number of lay documents that survive from the early Middle Ages, while significant, appears very small when compared to the tens of thousands of documents that concern the business of churchmen and monks.[18] After the twelfth century, the archival and documentary practices of the laity become much more visible, and they have therefore been studied directly.[19] One important product of the scholarship on this later period has been a new willingness to push past the constraints of the concept of 'literacy' – defined as the ability to read and to write – by allowing for the study of practices beyond these abilities and therefore beyond the clerical elites most likely to possess them. Drawing on a new historiography that has emphasized the collective contexts – whether sociable or pragmatic – of premodern reading, these medievalists have felt more confident in presenting the peasant listening to the reading of a biblical text[20] and the landowner who hires a scribe to redact a charter as nevertheless 'using literacy'.[21]

When this work has looked back to the early Middle Ages, it has assumed – quite naturally given the views held until recently by many early medievalists – that the vast majority of early medieval people relied exclusively on oral communication.[22] Both Michael Clanchy and Brian

18 See Kosto, 'Laymen'; M. Garrison, '"Send More Socks": On Mentality and the Preservation Contexts of Medieval Letters', in M. Mostert (ed.), *New Approaches to Medieval Communication* (Turnhout, 1999), 49–99.

19 The path-breaking work is Clanchy, *From Memory to Written Record*. For case studies, see, e.g., R. Berkhofer, *Day of Reckoning: Power and Accountability in Medieval France* (Philadelphia, 2004), and, for aristocratic as opposed to ecclesiastical record-keeping: J. Freed, *The Counts of Falkenstein: Aristocratic Consciousness in Twelfth-Century Bavaria* (Philadelphia, 1983); *Littere baronum: The Earliest Cartulary of the Counts of Champagne*, ed. T. Evergates (Toronto, 2003); *Feudal Society in Medieval France: Documents from the County of Champagne*, ed. T. Evergates (Philadelphia, 1993); A. J. Kosto, 'The *Liber feudorum maior* of the Counts of Barcelona: The Cartulary as an Expression of Power', *Journal of Medieval History*, 27 (2001), 1–22; and K. Heidecker (ed.), *Charters and the Use of the Written Word in Medieval Society* (Turnhout, 2000).

20 In any case, as Geoffrey Koziol pointed out to us in his review of an early draft of this volume, the stereotype of the 'illiterate' peasant is in many ways, at least in the later Middle Ages, an ideological or constructed trope. See S. Teuscher, 'Textualizing Peasant Enquiries: German *Weistümer* between Orality and Literacy', in Heidecker (ed.), *Charters*, 239–53; P. Biller and A. Hudson (eds.), *Heresy and Literacy, 1000–1530* (Cambridge, 1994).

21 Smith, *Europe after Rome*, 13–50, for a synthesis. For the historiography, see L. Melve, 'Literacy-Aurality-Orality: A Survey of Recent Research into the Orality-Literacy Complex of the Latin Middle Ages', *Symbolae Osloenses*, 78 (2003), 141–97; M. Clanchy, 'Introduction' and M. Mostert, 'New Approaches to Medieval Communication', in Mostert (ed.), *New Approaches*, 3–14, 15–40; and work cited above, n. 6.

22 A view still defended by Michael Richter: *The Formation of the Medieval West: Studies in the Oral Culture of the Barbarians* (Dublin, 1994); '"Quisquis scit scribere, nullum potat abere labore": Zur Laienschriftlichkeit im 8. Jahrhundert', in J. Jarnut and U. Nonn (eds.), *Karl Martell in seiner Zeit* (Sigmaringen, 1994), 393–404.

Stock, for example, argue that the eleventh century witnessed a fundamental transition from orality to literacy.[23] However, Rosamond McKitterick has extended the study of literate practices back before the eleventh century, documenting their extent in law and administration, property transactions and manuscript culture in eighth- and ninth-century Francia, and describing a society 'largely dependent on the written word for its religion, law, government and learning'. She argues specifically for the substantial involvement of laypeople in this culture of writing.[24] McKitterick and others have also hypothesized that the use of writing among the laity extended well below the level of the elites.

We recognize the dangers of reifying as 'literacy' a variety of activities which may have been distinct in their medieval manifestations and which may not fit with modern assumptions about what 'literacy' entails – especially the assumption that it is tied to the ability to read and write. We will therefore use the phrases such as 'documentary practices' or 'documentary use' rather than 'literacy', in order to capture the full range of ways that early medieval people might have interacted with documentary culture.[25]

Documents produced and used by early medieval laypeople survive in a very limited number of contexts. Some texts, like Ghittia's, exist as single sheets of parchment; others, like those from the Fundus Tuletianos, were written on papyrus, wood or slate. In the case of wood and slate, they are only preserved when and where they were deposited under conditions that have allowed for their physical survival and rediscovery. Still other lay documents were copied in the early Middle Ages as formulas, such as those concerning burned archives. Letters survive in a few letter collections, but more often because they were likewise incorporated as model texts into formula collections. Most stand-alone lay documents, however, whether on papyrus or parchment, have been transmitted to us along with surviving parts of the ecclesiastical or monastic archives into which they were later incorporated. Furthermore, a large proportion of our sources survives not individually, but because they were copied in the ninth to thirteenth centuries, along with other contents of ecclesiastical

23 Clanchy, *From Memory to Written Record*; B. Stock, *The Implications of Literacy: Written Language and Models of Interpretation in the Eleventh and Twelfth Centuries* (Princeton, NJ, 1983).

24 See McKitterick, *Carolingians* (quotation at p. 2); *Uses of Literacy*; and, for a sense of some of the directions of subsequent debate, Walter Pohl and Paul Herold (eds.), *Vom Nutzen des Schreibens: Soziales Gedächtnis, Herrschaft und Besitz im Mittelalter* (Vienna, 2002).

25 Cf. D. Ganz, '*Temptabat et scribere*: Vom Schreiben in der Karolingerzeit', in R. Schieffer (ed.), *Schriftkultur und Reichsverwaltung in der Karolingerzeit* (Opladen, 1996), 13–33.

or monastic archives, into books (*codices*) called cartularies; this technology, first used by the churches of the newly conquered and Christianized regions of the Carolingian Empire east of the Rhine in the ninth century, was adopted by major ecclesiastical institutions right across Europe in the course of the tenth and eleventh centuries, and by the twelfth century the first aristocratic landowners were likewise compiling cartularies.[26] The survival of this class of text therefore directly depends on choices made by medieval archivists (and, as we shall see, early modern antiquarians).

Classical diplomatics would classify the sorts of documents that we are interested in as 'private charters' – technically, legal documents not issued by a public authority (emperor, king, pope).[27] However, fundamental analytic categories such as 'public charter' and 'private charter' have been to a significant degree conditioned by nineteenth-century (and earlier) historiographical concerns with their characteristically reified notion of legimate public authority and, more to the point, the then current demands of archival organization and editing. These categories have had – and continue to have – huge value for particular kinds of scholarship, but there is nonetheless a danger of their forming a barrier between modern historians and the evidence, and of their importing anachronistic assumptions. We do not deny that there may be real generic differences – evident, for example, in the categories used in Ghittia's inventory, or in the script and layout of surviving originals – between a document issued by a king and one prepared for an otherwise undistinguished landowner. But we prefer to examine these differences by considering how documents were actually used – as physical objects and legal proofs – rather than judging their meaning uncritically according to the categories of traditional diplomatics. And their use and meaning includes more than their role as carriers of information. To illustrate the distinction: the study of charters in recent decades has taken two overlapping but distinguishable paths. One focuses on the human

26 On cartularies, see Geary, *Phantoms*, 81–114; G. Declercq, 'Originals and Cartularies: The Organization of Archival Memory (Ninth–Eleventh Centuries)', and L. Morelle, 'The Metamorphosis of Three Monastic Charter Collections in the Eleventh Century (Saint-Amand, Saint-Riquier, Montier-en-Der)', both in Heidecker (ed.), *Charters*, 147–70, 171–204; B. Resl, 'Nutzen des Abschreibens: Überlegungen zu mittelalterlichen Chartularen', in Pohl and Herold (eds.), *Vom Nutzen des Schreibens*, 205–22; A. J. Kosto and A. Winroth (eds.), *Charters, Cartularies and Archives: The Transmission and Preservation of Documents in the Medieval West* (Toronto, 1999); *Les cartulaires*.

27 H. Bresslau, *Handbuch der Urkundenlehre für Deutschland und Italien*, 2nd edn, 2 vols. (Leipzig, 1912–31), I, 3–4; O. Redlich, *Die Privaturkunden des Mittelalters* (Munich, 1911), vi; A. de Boüard, *Manuel de diplomatique française et pontificale*, II, *L'acte privé* (Paris, 1948), 7–11; A. Giry, *Manuel de diplomatique* (Paris, 1894), 823.

networks and interactions revealed in the charter evidence – for example, those that determine the mechanisms of dispute settlement or patterns of witnessing.[28] This path necessarily treats documentary evidence principally as repositories of information about these networks. In contrast, the second path explores the way that charters and especially cartularies reflect and even constitute processes of identity and memory formation. Thus many early cartularies have been shown to be documents aimed consciously at commemorating pious donors as well as their estates.[29] It is on insights of this kind in particular that we draw as we stress the historicity of documents themselves as parts of the processes they purport to describe.

## Archives

The study of documentary culture and practice is inseparable from the study of how documents are stored and transmitted to us; that is, from the study of archives and their history.[30] Archives are not unproblematic presences; they are not sites from which theoretically minded scholars can mine facts before subjecting them to a preferred model of interpretation. Nor are they places where empiricists can simply lock themselves away, safely quarantined from the distractions of anthropology, sociology or critical theory, and find out 'what happened'. If archives are fundamentally the conduit whereby the past is transmitted to the present, then *their* history and historiography determine the range of possible histories and historiographies. They therefore deserve a place at the heart of attempts to understand historical writing. Moreover, the actual contents of an archive – the raw materials of history – are themselves products of historical processes that shaped what was produced, how it was transmitted, and how it was presented to modern scholars. Archives and documents

[28] *Settlement of Disputes*; W. Brown and P. Górecki (eds.), *Conflict in Medieval Europe: Changing Perspectives on Culture and Society* (Aldershot, 2004).

[29] Geary, *Phantoms*; Geary, 'Entre gestion et *gesta*: Aux origines des cartularies', in *Les cartularies*, 13–26.

[30] A. Blair and J. Milligan, 'Introduction' [to the special edition entitled 'Towards a Cultural History of Archives' of], *Archival Science*, 7 (2007), 289–96, as well as the articles contained in the rest of the issue; F. X. Blouin and W. G. Rosenberg (eds.), *Archives, Documentation, and Institutions of Social Memory: Essays from the Sawyer Seminar* (Ann Arbor, MI, 2006); A. Burton (ed.), *Archive Stories: Facts, Fictions, and the Writing of History* (Durham, NC, 2005); A. J. Behne, 'Geschichte aufbewahren: Zur Theorie der Archivgeschichte und zur mittelalterlichen Archivpraxis in Deutschland und Italien', in P. Rück (ed.), *Mabillons Spur: Zweiundzwanzig Miszellen aus dem Fachgebiet für historische Hilfswissenschaften der Philipps-Universität Marburg* (Marburg an der Lahn, 1992), 277–97; and below, Chapter 11.

are shaped by power relations in *both* past and present and *between* past and present, and by the institutions through which power is mediated.

If archives are first and foremost artefacts of power, then their history is fundamentally a history of changing experiences and practices of power. For critical theorists inspired by Jacques Derrida, this has become an article of faith. Using an oddly early medieval etymological logic, Derrida thought that the derivation of a name reflected the nature of the phenomenon. The word 'archive', he argued, was derived from the Greek *archon* ('magistrate'), and so archives have at their heart an 'archonitic principle': they are places where documents are subject to the physical and the interpretative control of a ruling elite.[31] By this logic, archives are thus, on the one hand, fundamentally public institutions whose visibility is essential for them to bestow legitimacy on their holders, while, on the other hand, they simultaneously subject their contents to processes of classification and organization accessible only to those with specialist knowledge and so embed the particular interests of a power elite. This model has allowed scholars to write a story of 'modernization', in which the action moves seamlessly from the city states of classical Greece to the rising nation states of classical modernity. The nineteenth century, unsurprisingly, stands as a turning point in this narrative, when states both organized 'public archives' in the form of cultural institutions that propagated an agreed national story, and developed more robust systems to classify and store the information necessary to govern society, an entity newly defined as a separate and separable subject upon which the state could act.[32]

This model of the archive and its development is fundamentally bound up with discussions of the modern state and its development. It does not necessarily work well in late antique and early medieval contexts in which the imperatives driving document production and storage were diverse, in which patterns and loci of record-keeping were changing, and in which the existence or nature of 'states' themselves is controversial.[33] The modern expectation that archives are primarily tools with which to classify and record official data is arguably misplaced here, even for the most heavily bureaucratized polities; concerns about commemoration and notions of identity are more relevant than modern assumptions about reference literacy. For example, late antique states were indeed direct heirs of the rich archival heritage of the ancient Near East and eastern

31 J. Derrida, *Archive Fever: A Freudian Impression*, trans. E. Prenowitz (Chicago, 1996), 1–3.
32 See the articles in *History of the Human Sciences*, 12 (1999).
33 S. Airlie, W. Pohl and H. Reimitz (eds.), *Staat im frühen Mittelalter* (Vienna, 2006).

Mediterranean; hence, in the central bureaus of Byzantium – and the Islamic Caliphate and its provinces – records sprawled in their own dedicated spaces. But the arcane lore of record-keeping appears to have served to define the group identity of particular sections of the palace officialdom, as John Lydus' sixth-century tract on the magistracies of the Byzantine state indicates. Lydus' mandarin mindset reminds us that archives in this context might have had limited use as a practical tool of government.[34] In the post-imperial West, for all the fundamental influence of Roman precedents on social and political practice, the scale and character of such central bureaus altered. Kings, inspired by Roman advisers and expectations, issued documents and laws whose content and form demonstrated a continuous evolution from established practice.[35] But the institutions responsible for producing and preserving documentary material underwent significant changes: by Carolingian times, for example, the royal writing office had been subsumed into the king's household chapel and was manned by clerics.[36] Recent scholarship has underlined the effort and resources expended by Carolingian kings in making available copies of royal directives and instructions to bishops and counts across the realm, and there are references to dedicated archives, for example, at the palace in Aachen in Charlemagne's last years.[37] But to expect these archives to fulfil identical functions to those described by John Lydus, or to judge them against the benchmark of the nation states of nineteenth- and twentieth-century Europe, is to take them out of context.[38]

[34] On the ancient background, see M. Brosius (ed.), *Ancient Archives and Archival Traditions: Concepts of Record-Keeping in the Ancient World* (Oxford, 2003). On John Lydus, see: *De magistratibus populi Romani libri tres* (ed. A. C. Bandy [Philadelphia, 1983]); M. Maas, *John Lydus and the Roman Past: Antiquarianism and Politics in the Age of Justinian* (Oxford, 1992); and C. Kelly, 'Later Roman Bureaucracy: Going Through the Files', in A. K. Bowman and G. Woolf (eds.), *Literacy and Power in the Ancient World* (Cambridge, 1990), 161–76.

[35] See; classically, Classen, 'Fortleben', and P. Wormald, '*Lex scripta* and *verbum regis*: Legislation and Germanic Kingship from Euric to Cnut', in P. Sawyer and I. Wood (eds.), *Early Medieval Kingship* (Leeds, 1977), 105–38; more recently, e.g., P. Heather, 'Literacy and Power in the Migration Period', in Bowman and Woolf (eds.), *Literacy and Power*, 177–97; M. Innes, 'Land, Freedom and the Making of the Early Medieval West', *TRHS*, 6th ser., 16 (2006), 39–74; and below, Chapter 4.

[36] D. Ganz and W. Goffart, 'Charters Earlier than 800 from French Collections', *Speculum*, 65 (1990), 306–32; D. Ganz, 'Bureaucratic Shorthand and Merovingian Learning', in P. Wormald *et al.* (eds.), *Ideal and Reality in Frankish and Anglo-Saxon Society: Essays Presented to J. M. Wallace-Hadrill* (Oxford, 1983), 58–75; J. Fleckenstein, *Die Hofkapelle der deutschen Könige*, I, *Die Karolinger* (Stuttgart, 1966).

[37] E.g. McKitterick, *Carolingians*, 23–75; Schieffer (ed.), *Schriftkultur*.

[38] C. Pössel, 'Authors and Recipients of Carolingian Capitularies (779–829)', in R. Corradini *et al.* (eds.), *Texts and Identities in the Early Middle Ages* (Vienna, 2006), 253–74; M. Innes, 'Charlemagne, Justice and Written Law', in A. Rio (ed.), *Law and Custom in Late Antiquity and the Early Middle Ages* (London, 2011), 155–203.

We need to understand archival practice in terms of its own logic rather than to view record-keeping as an inherently rationalizing tendency lacking any specific cultural and political context. This is true of central record-keeping, whether at Constantinople or Aachen; it is vital in making sense of the documentary practices of landowners that are the primary focus of this book. Does a collection of documents kept in a chest by an individual or a family even qualify as an archive if it lacks organization and public accessibility? To what degree is such a collection fundamentally any different from the church and monastic archives of ninth-century Francia, which – though often extremely well organized and geared for retrieval – were equally 'private' and primarily concerned with property rights and privileges? Does it even make sense for us to tie our definition of 'archive' to a distinction between public and private functions? If so, when and under what circumstances?

The essays in this volume collectively engage these questions. However, they will place their understandings of the term 'archive' in particular contexts that will produce related but nevertheless different understandings of what the word means. These understandings will reflect not only the different contexts in which document production and storage took place but also the different needs and interests that documents and archives satisfied in each time and place.

We aim to revise our understanding of how documentary practices developed across Latin Europe as a whole, with evidence drawn from the late antique and early medieval Mediterranean to expand our picture of the late Roman backdrop. Our effort has been shaped to a large degree by imperatives imposed upon us by our evidence. We have found major regional and chronological differences in documentary and archival practices. Some areas, notably Italy after the eighth century and Iberia in the tenth, possess voluminous stocks of original, single-sheet parchment documents, many offering direct evidence of lay practices. Egypt enjoys a continuous documentary tradition from the Roman period (and earlier) onwards; a similar pattern of continuity can be implied for other regions of the East Roman world. In still other areas, such as Francia, the early medieval evidence for lay practices has been transmitted principally through later copies in ecclesiastical cartularies, or indirectly, as, for example, in formularies; moreover, much of it consists of references to lost documents (*deperdita*), relegated to the appendices and footnotes of nineteenth-century editions but in many ways invaluable in widening our perspective on document use.

We thus begin with the practices of the Roman and immediately sub-Roman world, examined here in North Africa (the Roman provinces of Egypt and 'Africa'), Italy and Iberia. We then study the transformation of these practices in the eastern Mediterranean and the emergence of what are often seen as new documentary cultures in Francia, Iberia and Italy. We interrogate the regional differences and chronological transformations underlying these contrasts. Many areas of the broader early medieval world are left out, but their stories are very different. At present, northern and eastern Europe appear to lack a documentary culture prior to the eleventh century, while the impact of Islam renders moot the entire question of lay documentary practice and its legal and institutional underpinnings.[39] Nevertheless, the connections between the North African wooden panels, Ghittia's inventory, the Frankish formulas and the sales of Spanish peasants, tell us a great deal about the culture of documentary practice in the early Middle Ages.

[39] For northern, eastern and central Europe, see, e.g., A. Adamska, 'The Introduction of Writing in Central Europe', in Mostert (ed.), *New Approaches*, 165–92; A. Adamska, '"From Memory to Written Record" in the Periphery of Medieval Latinitas: The Case of Poland in the Eleventh and Twelfth Centuries', and I. Hlavacek, 'The Use of Charters and Other Documents in Premyslid Bohemia', both in Heidecker (ed.), *Charters*, 83–100, 133–46; L. Wolverton, *Hastening Towards Prague: Power and Society in Medieval Czech Lands* (Philadelphia, 2001); A. Nedkvitne, *The Social Consequences of Literacy in Medieval Scandinavia* (Turnhout, 2004). Islamic documentary papyri in former Roman provinces (above all, Egypt), for long an overlooked or ignored source, are now proving to be an invaluable and voluminous source for the late antique and early medieval transformation: see particularly the work of P. Sijpesteijn: 'Landholding Patterns in Early Islamic Egypt', *Journal of Agrarian Change*, 9 (2009), 120–33; 'The Archival Mind in Early Islamic Egypt: Two Arabic Papyri', in Sijpesteijn *et al.* (eds.), *From al-Andalus to Khurasan: Documents from the Medieval Muslim World* (Leiden, 2006), 163–87; and *Shaping a Muslim State: The World of a Mid-Eighth-Century Official* (Oxford, forthcoming).

# 2 Lay archives in the Late Antique and Byzantine East: the implications of the documentary papyri

*Peter Sarris*

*A survey of documentary practices in the eastern Mediterranean raises many of the key themes that we will be following throughout the book. Among these are issues of definition, such as of archive, or lay and clerical, or public and private; issues of the institutional contexts for document production and preservation, such as the shifting nature of the late Roman state and its organs, the early institutional Church, or structures of property ownership; and issues of documentary culture, such as the phenomena of destruction and dossierization, the symbolic function of documents, and intentionally ephemeral documents.*

## The ancient archive from Babylon to Byzantium

According to the Book of Ezra, in the fifth century BC, the governor of the Achaemenid province of Abr-Nahrain wrote a letter to the Persian Great King, Darius I. The purpose of the letter was to check whether, as they claimed, the empire's Jewish subjects had formerly been granted leave by Darius' predecessor, Cyrus, to rebuild the Temple in Jerusalem. The letter requested:

> Now therefore, if it seem good to the king, let there be search made in the king's treasure house, which is there at Babylon, whether it be so, that a decree was made of Cyrus the king to build this house of God at Jerusalem, and let the king send his pleasure to us concerning this matter. (Ezra 5:17)

The account goes on to relate how:

> Then Darius the king made a decree and search was made in the house of the rolls, where the treasures were laid up in Babylon. And there was found at Achmetha, in the palace that is in the province of the Medes, a roll. And therein was a record thus written: In the first year of Cyrus the king the same Cyrus the king made a decree concerning the house of God at Jerusalem, Let the house be builded, the place where they offered sacrifices, and let the foundations thereof be strongly laid. (Ezra 6:1–3)

Two points of considerable interest emerge from the passage above. First, it alerts us to how deeply rooted techniques of archival record-keeping were in the world of the Near Eastern Fertile Crescent. By Darius' day they had already been in existence for thousands of years, dating back to the third millennium BC.[1] Second, these ancient archival techniques were not necessarily quite as efficient as some have imagined: it is worth noting that the initial search in Babylon for what a civil lawyer would call Cyrus' rescript proved fruitless. Eventually, the document was found, but it was found in the wrong place.[2]

Just as the Roman Empire of the fifth century AD was heir to the 'palace culture' of the civilizations of the ancient Near East,[3] so, too, was it heir to their archival culture, or rather, cultures. The voluminous collections of documentary papyri from Egypt demonstrate that the late Roman world was awash with paperwork, and that the late Roman state in particular relied heavily on written instruments, especially written legal instruments, for its administration and cohesion.[4] The significance of the written word was both practical and symbolic: imperial pronouncements and laws issued to the provinces of the Roman Empire were, as we might imagine, read out by court officials (typically the *quaestor*) and circulated to provincial governors, but they were also displayed in public before the eyes of the emperor's subjects, often in the form of monumental inscriptions.[5] As Patrick Wormald reminded us, the association between *Romanitas* and the written word as a symbol of authority was one of which post-Roman *duces et reges* in the West remained keenly aware.[6] Yet, as in Achaemenid Persia, no one archive, not even a central state archive, could be regarded as entirely reliable. When, for example, in the 420s, a law commission was set up in Constantinople to codify imperial constitutions in the form of the *Codex Theodosianus*, we see the commissioners adopting two distinct strategies in relation to the legal texts which they needed. It appears to have been decided that, with respect

1 M. Brosius, 'Ancient Archives and Concepts of Record-Keeping: An Introduction', in Brosius (ed.), *Ancient Archives and Archival Traditions: Concepts of Record-Keeping in the Ancient World* (Oxford, 2003), 1–16, at 1.

2 A. Millard, 'Aramaic Documents of the Assyrian and Achaemenid Periods', in Brosius (ed.), *Ancient Archives*, 230–40, at 237.

3 F. Dvornik, *Early Christian and Byzantine Political Philosophy: Origins and Background*, 2 vols. (Washington, DC, 1966).

4 See most recently F. Millar, *A Greek Roman Empire* (Berkeley, CA, 2006).

5 Classical Greek origins: J. K. Davies, 'Greek Archives: From Record to Monument', in Brosius (ed.), *Ancient Archives*, 323–43. Sixth-century Byzantine practice: R. Scott, 'Malalas and Justinian's Codification', in E. and M. Jeffreys and A. Moffatt (eds.), *Byzantine Papers* (Canberra, 1981), 12–31.

6 P. Wormald, '*Lex scripta* and *verbum regis*: Legislation and Germanic Kingship from Euric to Cnut', in P. Sawyer and I. N. Wood (eds.), *Early Medieval Kingship* (Leeds, 1977), 105–38.

to laws issued after 398, the imperial archive in Constantinople could be relied upon. For laws issued before that date, however, much greater use was to be made of the archives of provincial governors, either because the laws the commissioners sought were not preserved in the imperial capital, or because they wished to check the text of laws recorded there for authenticity.[7]

Such unreliability on the part even of state archives could be the result of a number of factors. First, archives and archival documents could be lost or destroyed by accident – the cause of numerous legal disputes recorded in the papyri.[8] Second, archives were vulnerable to deliberate vandalism. It is instructive that during the so-called 'Nika' riots that erupted in Constantinople in the year 532, the *praetorium* of the praetorian prefect of the East, along with its associated archive containing taxation and other financial records, was purposefully destroyed by the rampaging mob.[9] Such disturbances were far from uncommon in late Roman cities such as Constantinople, Alexandria and Antioch.[10] Given the enormous practical and symbolic importance of the written word to the imperial system, it should come as no surprise that uprisings on the part of the urban mob were often associated with the wanton destruction of governmental and gubernatorial archives.

Indeed, it is worth noting that the deliberate destruction of archival and documentary materials can also be seen to have been a feature of periods of heightened social tensions and political conflict in both the post-Roman West and the post-Roman East. In 579, for example, Gregory of Tours records how the citizens of Limoges 'rose up against the new taxation of King Chilperic and burnt the *libri discriptionum*'.[11] Likewise, the papyrological record of early Islamic Egypt preserves 'an eighth-century papyrus listing prisoners among whom some who had set fire to a fiscal register'.[12] In the opening years of the tenth century, as the Tulunid regime in Egypt teetered on the brink of collapse before the advancing Ikshidids, 'Tulunid chancellery officials . . . made sure

7 A. M. Honoré, *Law in the Crisis of Empire 379–455 A.D.: The Theodosian Dynasty and Its Quaestors* (Oxford, 1998), 128.

8 W. Clarysse, 'Tomoi Synkollesimoi', in Brosius (ed.), *Ancient Archives*, 344–59, at 344–5.

9 G. Greatrex, 'The Nika Riot: A Reappraisal', *Journal of Hellenic Studies*, 117 (1997), 60–87, at 75.

10 See Greatrex, 'The Nika Riot', for discussion and bibliography.

11 Wickham, *Framing*, 10, discussing Gregory of Tours, *Libri historiarum* 5.28 (MGH SRM 1.1:240).

12 P. M. Sijpesteijn, 'The Archival Mind in Early Islamic Egypt', in Sijpesteijn *et al.* (eds.), *From al-Andalus to Khurasan: Documents from the Medieval Muslim World* (Leiden, 2007), 163–86, at 165, referring to text no. 1.13 in F. Morelli, 'Dalle prigioni dell'Arsinoite', in H. Harrauer and R. Pintaudi (eds.), *Gedenkschrift Ulrike Horak* (Florence, 2004), 185–95.

[as they fled] . . . to take their tax registers with them, since they knew how crucial these documents were to the effective running of Egypt. But in doing so they thereby ensured, unfortunately, their loss.'[13] In short, the 'logocentric' always risked inciting the 'logoclastic'.

## The typology of the ancient archive

What do we mean by 'archive'? In English the term signifies two distinct but related subjects. As Maria Brosius has written:

> Archives are first a physical space within a public space (palace or temple complex, public archive) or within a private building or private complex of buildings, and second a collection of stored documents . . . Since the point of an archive was to provide access to documents, the material must have been stored in such a way as to allow those consulting the archive to retrieve the information according to some practical rationale.[14]

It is this imposition of order on documentary materials so as to render their contents more readily retrievable that sets or set apart the 'archive' properly understood from a mere storeroom or assemblage of documents. From our earliest records we see documents being organized archivally into dossiers, typically by theme and often according to a chronological framework. Thus, in the surviving 'economic' documentation, in the form of inscribed tablets, from the third millennium BC (our earliest extant archival materials),

> distinctions were made by subject matter . . . such as grain, wool, fruit, cattle, metal, labour payments . . . The contents of individual receipts were eventually transferred to weekly, monthly, and annual accounts . . . Clearly, tablets were stored according to different types and labelled containers were marked to denote the 'dossiers' they contained.[15]

These techniques of 'dossierization' discernible in what we might choose to term the ancient Near Eastern 'tablet cultures' (so dubbed by virtue of the medium on which they wrote) were continued in the papyrus documentation of the Greco-Roman period down to the fourth century AD in the form of the *tomos synkollesimos*, by which papyrologists mean a series of separate documents or sheets (*kollemata*) pasted together to form a single roll (*tomos*) – a form of documentation used at every level of imperial government and administration and emulated in private documentary practice too.[16] The use of the *tomos synkollesimos*, however, appears to have died out in the Roman Empire some time around the middle of

[13] Sijpesteijn, 'The Archival Mind', 164.
[14] Brosius, 'Ancient Archives', 10–12.
[15] Brosius, 'Ancient Archives', 14–15.
[16] Clarysse, 'Tomoi Synkollesimoi', 346.

the fourth century, a phenomenon that has baffled those papyrologists who have sought to address the subject.[17] Yet the explanation for the disappearance of the 'pasted roll' is perhaps disarmingly simple. Papyrus in antiquity was never cheap, and many of the *tomoi synkollesimoi* were evidently both massive and unwieldy. A normal, shop-bought papyrus roll ordinarily consisted of about twenty sheets, pasted together in the factory, and would have been about 4 m in length from end to end.[18] By virtue of the system of 'sheet numbering' we encounter on certain of the papyrological fragments, we know that many *tomoi* were over a hundred sheets in length. We even hear of one, recording a series of *libelli* of the emperor Decius, that contained no fewer than 433 sheets.[19] We should not be surprised to discover, therefore, that the disappearance of the *tomos synkollesimos* from the papyrological records coincides very closely with the more widespread dissemination of the *codex*.[20] Certainly, in the sixth century, we find the *codex* being used in imperial contexts where, in the third century, we might have expected a pasted roll.[21]

## Lay archives in the early Byzantine period: problems of definition

Attempting to distinguish private lay archival materials from other archival types encountered in the documentary record of the early Byzantine period of, say, the fourth to the seventh centuries AD, is not entirely straightforward. The only region of the late antique or early Byzantine world for which large numbers of private documentary sources survive is Egypt, where the dry sands have preserved hundreds of papyrological fragments and texts ranging from the theological and the literary, to private letters, estate accounts and receipts.[22] Many of the documents that we encounter are inevitably difficult to classify. As shall be seen shortly, from the fifth to the seventh century AD, for example, much of the land around the Middle Egyptian city of Oxyrhynchus was owned by members of a single local family, the Flavii Apiones.[23] A large number of documents from this family's archive survive. Yet much of the documentation that may be associated with this archive looks distinctly official and public

17 Clarysse, 'Tomoi Synkollesimoi', 356–8.

18 Clarysse, 'Tomoi Synkollesimoi', 352.

19 Clarysse, 'Tomoi Synkollesimoi', 349–50.

20 E. Turner, *The Typology of the Early Codex* (Philadelphia, 1977).

21 Note the imperial *monobiblon* referred to by Malalas (Scott, 'Malalas and Justinian's Codification', 21) and the *demosios ptyx* (emendavit Rea) referred to in *J.Edict* 13.15.

22 Although see now L. Koenen, 'The Carbonized Archive from Petra', *Journal of Roman Archaeology*, 9 (1996), 177–88.

23 R. Mazza, *L'archivio degli Apioni* (Bari, 2001); P. Sarris, *Economy and Society in the Age of Justinian* (Cambridge, 2006).

in character. By the sixth century, members of the Apion household were clearly obliged to assist in the collection of imperial taxes for the region around their hometown, by virtue of the head of the family's possession of the title of *pagarch*, and we have documentation concerned with this: letters to and from imperial officials, accounts of payment of arrears and so on.[24] Are these documents 'public' or 'private'? Does their existence within the archive affect its character? Likewise, many of those whom the Apion household employed as estate managers, or from whom the household demanded sureties with respect to its workforce, held ecclesiastical rank (and from the reign of Constantine the Christian clergy had acquired a distinct legal status signified by their exemption from civic *munera*).[25] Is a contract made between an Apion-employed artisan and an Apion-employed deacon a purely 'lay' document? What of the documentation concerned with Apion payments to local churches?

This picture is further complicated when we start looking beyond Oxyrhynchus. For the mid-to-late sixth century (as we shall see), we possess a number of documents and texts belonging to the private archive of the Psimanobet family, a sort of yeoman farmer/gentry family from the village of Aphrodite (more commonly known in English as 'Aphrodito' – the name given it after the Arab conquest of the seventh century).[26] Probably in the 530s, one member of this family, a certain Apollos, founded and retired to a monastery, in which the family thereafter maintained an active interest. How are we to classify documents contained in the Psimanobet family archive concerned with the administration of Apollos' monastery (known, after its founder, as Apa Apollous)? A parallel problem emerges with respect to the (mostly Coptic) papyri and *ostraca* that survive from the sixth to the eighth centuries from the Egyptian village of Jeme. While many of the documents from Jeme were found in the houses of those who had owned them, it is clear that many lay members of local society entrusted their personal documentary archives to the safe keeping of the Church, which probably began to fulfil this function as soon as it acquired 'legal personality' under Constantine in the fourth century.[27]

24 Sarris, *Economy and Society*, 149–76.

25 C. Rapp, *Holy Bishops in Late Antiquity* (Berkeley, CA, 2005), 238.

26 H. I. Bell, 'An Egyptian Village in the Age of Justinian', *Journal of Hellenic Studies*, 64 (1944), 21–36; L. MacCoull, *Dioscorus of Aphrodito: His Work and World* (Berkeley, CA, 1988); T. Gagos and P. van Minnen, *Settling a Dispute: Toward a Legal Anthropology of Late Antique Egypt* (Ann Arbor, MI, 1994).

27 T. G. Wilfong, *Women of Jeme: Lives in a Coptic Town in Late Antique Egypt* (Ann Arbor, MI, 2002).

This phenomenon requires a certain degree of explanation. In earlier periods of the history of Roman Egypt (and most probably into the sixth century), there almost certainly continued the traditional Greek and Hellenistic practice whereby private papers, especially those pertaining to relations between individuals and the state, could be stored in an officially run governmental or gubernatorial archive (a *grapheion* or suchlike) in the local city.[28] However, the fifth and sixth centuries in Egypt, as elsewhere in the East Roman Empire, witnessed a gradual emasculation of the structures and institutions of municipal government as local society came increasingly to be dominated by aristocratic magnate households, such as that of the Flavii Apiones.[29] While the state sought to harness the social authority and clout of these magnate households through investing them with public obligations that had hitherto been delegated to civic *curiae*, the net result was inevitably a certain measure of 'privatization' of functions that had formerly been the preserve of municipal institutions. As part of this process, the use and maintenance of 'public' archives seemingly went into decline, even with respect to documents pertaining to public responsibilities and affairs. In a law of 535, for example, the emperor Justinian noted that 'the public registration of property transactions was no longer taking place because cities lacked archives where the documents might be kept'.[30] Increasingly, it would appear, the private archives of great estates and especially the archival resources of the Church came to replace the *archivum publicum* referred to in the Justinianic constitution.

Perhaps the best way to get around the problems of definition occasioned by these evolving circumstances is simply not to worry about them too much and instead to fall back upon 'the primacy of practical reason'. That a family's private papers happened to be stored in a church or monastery, for example, as seems to have occurred at Jeme, reveals a great deal about the role of the Church in local society, but it does not really affect the lay character of the papers themselves. Likewise, that the Apion archive may have contained papyri of an official provenance, or papyri concerned with dealings between the family and local ecclesiastical institutions, does not of itself alter the fact that the family archive was privately run for the Apion household, by the household and its secretariat, irrespective of what other documents were acquired and preserved along the way.

[28] Brosius, 'Ancient Archives'. [29] Sarris, *Economy and Society*, 149–99.

[30] J. H. W. G. Liebeschuetz, *The Decline and Fall of the Roman City* (Oxford, 2001), citing *J.Nov.* 15 praef.: 'cum nullum habeant archivum, in quo gesta apud se reponant'.

## Problems of language

The identification of private lay archives in the early Byzantine period is further complicated, especially with regard to the public/private distinction, by a linguistic feature of those papyri (the majority) written in Greek. Here, once again, the problem may be most clearly exemplified with respect to the Apion archive.

In the Greek documentary papyri that make up the Apion archive, we often find employed a terminology and vocabulary that bears very close resemblance to that used by the imperial authorities in public and administrative contexts. As a result, documents that are entirely 'private' in character, may be read as if they are 'public' or official. This linguistic feature of the Apion papyri is, however, entirely explicable both lexically and sociologically in a way that may also have implications for how we read post-Roman Western Latin documentation written within or emergent from the late Roman tradition. Members of early Byzantine aristocratic families, such as the Apiones, typically enjoyed high-ranking careers in the imperial bureaucracy and army. The same was also true of many of those employed as their estate administrators and overseers.[31] It would only have been natural for such individuals to deploy, with regard to their private economic transactions, techniques and terminological forms derived from their experience of imperial administration, thereby (to modern eyes) giving them something of an official appearance or quality. We should also remember that many of the documents we possess were written by men whose native tongue is likely to have been Coptic, individuals who may have had a natural tendency, when writing Greek, to fall back upon well-known phrases, clichés and formulas. Accordingly, many of the documents we possess from the Apion archive, such as petitions to the head of the family drafted by individuals bearing Coptic names, for example, have a distinctly stilted quality about them. In many ways their linguistic register resembles the formulaic tone at times evident in modern sub-continental (Indian) English, itself a hangover from the verbosity of Victorian and Edwardian 'officialese'. As a result, we must be careful not to be misled by the linguistic register of a document into misidentifying its provenance or character, or even the 'private', as opposed to 'official', nature of its subject matter.

To a great extent, just such a misapprehension underlies the hypothesis of the distinguished French papyrologist Jean Gascou, who has argued, in a highly influential and stimulating work, that the large estates of

[31] Thus the estates recorded in *P.Bad* IV 95 were administered by estate employees bearing the official imperial title of *comites* or 'counts'.

early Byzantine Egypt, such as that of the Apiones, were primarily 'semi-public' bodies created by imperial *fiat* to meet the needs of the imperial government in Constantinople.[32] In its *étatisme*, this is a splendidly Parisian stance, albeit one that is not entirely supported by a closer reading of the evidence. At the core of Gascou's argument, for example, is the assertion that the 'rents' (Greek *phoroi*) collected by the managers of the Apion estates around Oxyrhynchus from the inhabitants of the estates' labour settlements (*epoikia*) represented not the private income of the Apion family, but rather a 'rent-tax' much of which was destined for imperial coffers. Yet the papyrological support for this assertion is very thin. The Apion estate accounts are careful to distinguish between rents (*phoroi*) and taxes (*demosia* or the *synteleia kephales*) collected from estate employees.[33] While the latter were handed over to the imperial authorities, the former tended to be spent on the internal requirements of the household, from funding the extension of cultivated land to the hiring of dancing girls. The important point to note from our perspective, however, which may be of significance to the reading of the Western Latin sources, is that tone and style of language are not always clear indicators of documentary or archival 'type'. In the West, in short, an 'official' Latin vocabulary derived from the workings of the Roman state could have continued to be used in private contexts long after the fiscal and administrative structures of empire had faded away – a point with considerable implications for the work of both Jean Durliat and Walter Goffart.[34]

## Documentation, 'archivalization', and social and economic relations in the early Byzantine world

The earliest archival evidence we have, dating from the third millennium BC, is represented by the 'economic documentation' of inscribed tablets referred to earlier. The economic focus of this documentation is important for alerting us to the fact that much of the impetus to create, store and systematize the collection of documentary evidence was, from the very beginning, generated by relations of economic dependence

[32] J. Gascou, 'Les grands domaines, la cité, et l'état en Égypte byzantine', *Travaux et mémoires*, 9 (1985), 1–90. For a detailed critique, see Sarris, *Economy and Society*, 149–76.

[33] E.g. *P.Oxy* LV 3804 line 93, distinguishing between payments made for the poll tax and for rent on sheep, or the pasturing thereof, by the inhabitants of the settlement of Luciu.

[34] E.g. W. Goffart, *Barbarian Tides: The Migration Age and the Later Roman Empire* (Philadelphia, 2006); J. Durliat, *Les finances publiques de Dioclétien aux Carolingiens (284–889)* (Sigmaringen, 1990).

and inequality and by the urge to enforce or contest rights over property and person. By 'clarifying the potentially contestable', documents and archives served to frame social and economic relations and tensions.[35] As a result, it should not surprise us that, just as archivalized documentation continued to be central to the workings of the late Roman state in the early Byzantine East, so, too, did it remain central to the operation and workings of society beyond the state, especially the concerns of landowners and those who interacted with them. So, for example, almost all of the papyrological evidence we have comes 'from the viewpoint of the propertied classes of the cities of Egypt, the *metropoleis* and nomes', and even the village archives we possess (from Karanis, Theadelphia and Aphrodito) can be seen to have largely been concerned with and determined by the demands of the Roman state and relations with members of the locally dominant landed elite, who also tended to reside in the region's cities.[36]

For the period from the third to the sixth centuries, the main extant private archives recorded in the documentary papyri (excluding those held by churches) can be summarized as follows. For the third century, we possess the 'Heroninos' archive from Theadelphia in the Arsinoite nome. For the fourth century, there exist the archive of Apollonios from the Hermopolite nome, the archives of Theophanes and Aurelia Charite and her son from the city of Hermopolis itself, and that of Ammon scholasticus from Panopolis, alongside the archive of Leonides, and that of Papnoutis and Dorotheos from Oxyrhynchus. For the fifth century, the main non-ecclesiastical archive is that of Taurinos from Hermopolis, while the sixth century preserves two related archives (of Dioscorus and Phoibammon) from the town of Aphrodito, and that of the Apiones from Oxyrhynchus.[37] Of these, by far the most important is that of the Apion family, whose members we can trace in imperial service from the early fifth century through to the early seventh.[38] The Apion archive is of inestimable value, for the papyri provide illuminating insights into the day-to-day realities of life in what was, economically, the most important, productive and highly developed region of the entire Eastern Empire. The documents permit us to begin to come to terms with the

35 Sijpesteijn, 'The Archival Mind', 163.

36 R. Bagnall, *Egypt in Late Antiquity* (Princeton, NJ, 1993); I have not yet had an opportunity to consult Bagnall, *Everyday Writing in the Graeco-Roman East* (Berkeley, CA, 2011).

37 P. van Minnen, 'The Other Cities in Later Roman Egypt', in R. Bagnall (ed.), *Egypt in the Byzantine World 300–700* (Cambridge, 2007), 207–25, at 215.

38 Although the *stemma* is now obsolete, for a general sense of the family's history and that of the archive, see Sarris, *Economy and Society*, 10–28.

extent and character of the economic resources that underpinned the social authority and political role of members of the late antique imperial aristocracy. Crucially, they also enable us to see a late antique archive 'at work'.[39]

The economic details concerning the day-to-day management of the Apion estates, the condition and organization of labour, and the chains of command and responsibility within the Apion household that we can reconstruct on the basis of the papyri are not the primary concern here and have been set out in detail elsewhere.[40] What is more significant is that each and every one of these aspects generated a great deal of paperwork, which was gathered in at a central Apion bureau in Oxyrhynchus: there the documentation was often filed in its own right in a retrievable form. This is particularly evident with respect to documents of receipt and other legally enforceable contracts: so, for example, *P.Oxy* LXXI 4835 records a loan of money on the part of an employee of the Apion household to the inhabitant of a labour settlement or *epoikion*. The receipt for the loan was then stored in the archive with the inscription on its verso 'receipt of Phoibammon from the *epoikion* of Peneb'.[41] Likewise, in *P.Oxy* I 134, 135 and 136, we have respectively a contract of employment between the Apion household and a stonemason, a contract of surety guaranteeing the residence on an estate labour settlement of an agricultural labourer, and the work contract of an estate overseer or *pronoetes*. On the verso of each of these, we find a label describing the nature of the document, indicative of its having been filed away within the archive in case of any need for future reference.

Alternatively, the details required from a document could be extracted and archivalized, the original document then being reused as scrap: such, for example, was evidently the fate of the annual accounts of receipt and expenditure submitted by the estate overseers or *pronoetai* employed by the Apiones' Oxyrhynchite managers to supervise the collection of revenues in kind and coin from the various estate *epoikia*. These documents essentially conformed to a pattern of 'charge–discharge' accounting, permitting the ready identification through historical comparison of unexpected or unexplained shortfalls in estate income from one year to the next (on which see more below). Accordingly, it would appear that once in the hands of the managers of the Oxyrhynchite bureau, the documents' contents were entered into some sort of central ledger or codex, a copy of which was then probably sent to a higher level of estate management

[39] For a detailed account of the contents of the archive and the uses to which they can be put, see Sarris, *Economy and Society*, 29–89.

[40] Sarris, *Economy and Society*, 29–80.

[41] *P.Oxy* LXXI 4835 verso.

in Alexandria, with the verso of the original annual accounts then being used for jottings, mathematical calculations and the like.[42] On the verso of the annual estate accounts of a *pronoetes* published as *P.Oxy* LV 3804, for example, we find (published as *P.Oxy* LV 3805) details and sums pertaining to various financial transactions from throughout the region of the Oxyrhynchite, totally unrelated to the contents of the accounts themselves: rents received, for example, on an urban warehouse and a synagogue, and a payment made by agricultural workers with respect to hunting rights associated with an estate demesne or *autourgia*.[43] Similarly, on the verso of the estate accounts published as *P.Oxy* XIX 2243 (a), we find – published as *P.Oxy* XIX 2243 (b) – a list of contracts of employment again unconnected to the contents of the accounts. In addition to estate accounts, receipts for loans in coin or kind and other legal contracts such as contracts of employment or leases, the archive also included petitions addressed to the head of the Apion family and letters concerning estate business or official affairs, although here the evidence for archivalization as such is more meagre and we may simply be encountering chance survivals.[44]

## Documentation, credit arrangements and control

One of the most conspicuous features of the Apion papyri is the 'paper trail' created by credit arrangements and associated economic transactions and by attempts to subject to careful scrutiny and control the activities of estate employees. So, for example, when collecting payments, be they fiscal or rental, from members of the estate workforce, the Apion *pronoetai* were meant to operate according to an annual schedule of demands or *apaitesimon*. When collecting such revenues, the overseers were supposed to issue the estate workforce with receipts styled *entagia*, which the peasant could, if need be, bring forth as proof that he had met his personal obligations. The sums collected and dispensed by the overseer were then meant to be worked up into the annual set of accounts sent off to the Oxyrhynchite office.[45] Any act of fraudulence or theft engaged in by the *pronoetes* would thus have been readily identified by the estate accountants or *chartoularioi* in Oxyrhynchus by means of checking the

42 For the existence of an Alexandrian office, see Sarris, *Economy and Society*, 46.
43 E.g. *P.Oxy* LV 3804 and 3805 lines 16–17.
44 Sarris, *Economy and Society*, for details, examples and discussion of each of these categories.
45 Each one of these features can be seen in the overseer's contract of employment: *P.Oxy* I 136.

revenues collected against the schedule of demands issued and, if necessary, the receipts held by the estate's workforce.[46] Moreover, the estate accounts and contracts of employment record that wages were frequently issued to estate employees in the form of credit notes or chitties termed *pittacia*, which could then in turn be cashed in with estate managers and cashiers styled *enoikologoi* and *trapezitai*.[47] Certain of these survive from other contemporary estates in a papyrologically identifiable form.[48]

Further evidence concerning credit arrangements emerges from the deeds of receipt contained within the archive, which generally bear the designation of *cheirographiai*. These documents often consist of statements made by workers bearing the legal status of *enapographoi georgoi* or *coloni adscripticii* acknowledging that they had received items of irrigational machinery from the household. As such, the documents reveal that while the *georgoi* of the Apion labour settlements frequently owned their own agricultural tools and livestock, the household provided major capital requirements for agriculture, especially for mechanically irrigated cultivation.

*P.Oxy* XXXVI 2779 may be taken as a simple example of the *cheirographia*-type.[49] The deed is dated to 530, and was made on behalf of a certain Aurelius Epimachus, 'also called Apima', from the *epoikion* of Panguleeion.[50] Apima declares:

> Having now had occasion to require one axle for the landowner's water-wheel under my charge which is called 'five arouras' and supplies water to vine-land and arable land, I went up to the city and asked your magnificence to order the said axle to be provided for me. And at once your magnificence, having regard to the state of your property, gave me the said axle through Moison, *oiketes* of the said most magnificent man, a new one, serviceable, suitable for irrigation and satisfactory. I received it as completion of all the irrigation implements this very day . . . The old axle was brought in and given to the great household of the landowner. In declaration of the receipt I have made this deed (*cheirographia*) which is valid written as a single copy and in reply to the formal question I gave my assent.[51]

Among the more fragmentary deeds found within the Apion archive are three – *P.Oxy* I 137, XVI 1988 and XVI 1989 – which reveal how the parallel system of credit notes in the form of *pittakia* was then interleaved into this practice.[52] *P.Oxy* I 137, dating from 584, consists of an acknowledgement given by a *georgos* named Aurelius Ptollion that he had received an axle for a waterwheel. The document stands out from that detailed

[46] Sarris, *Economy and Society*, 52. [47] Sarris, *Economy and Society*, 56, 67, 75, 77, 88.
[48] Especially *CPR* VII 23. [49] *P.Oxy* XXXVI 2779.
[50] *P.Oxy* XXXVI 2779 lines 1–9. [51] *P.Oxy* XXXVI 2779 lines 9–24.
[52] *P.Oxy* I 137; *P.Oxy* XVI 1988–9. Note also *P.Oxy* XVI 1990.

above, however, in terms of the information it provides as to the procedure whereby the new axle was issued, for Ptollion states that the price of the wheel was 'credited to me in the cheques (*pittacia*)'.[53] Ptollion was thus provided with the wherewithal to buy the axle by the Apion household. The *pittakion* was presumably handed over by Ptollion to whoever was responsible for issuing or selling the machinery. *P.Oxy* XVI 1988, dating from 587, also acknowledging the receipt of a water-wheel axle, records that the *georgos* in question had purchased a replacement and that 'its price was credited to me in my *pittakia*'.[54] The same procedure is recorded in *P.Oxy* XVI 1989, dating from 590×1.[55] The use of estate cheques or credit notes evidently extended well beyond the mere issuing of wages.

The contractual papyri thus reveal the highly formalized character of dealings between the Apion household and its employees, and the household's extraordinary dependence upon written legal instruments, and written documentation in general (accounts, *entagia*, *apaitesima*, *pittakia*, etc.). Certainly, this feature is indicative of the highly standardized and professional character of household estate management. On another level, however, as with relations between state and subject, the evidence would suggest that the written word also played an important symbolic, and – it might be inferred, intimidatory – role in relations between master and servant, especially given how often, in the contractual papyri, the latter is described as unlettered.[56] Even in this highly documentary society the use of archivalized knowledge and information was 'functional' in a variety of ways.

The other archival collections that survive from the sixth and seventh centuries from elsewhere in early Byzantine Egypt reveal a similar concentration on economic transactions, credit arrangements, loans and documents establishing or associated with legal obligations or rights. Two particularly important thematically and chronologically distinct papyrological dossiers survive from early medieval Aphrodito, for example. The later of these, dating from the Umayyad period, is derived from the bureau of a local Arab governor, Qurra b. Sharik (r. 709–14), and it reveals much of the character of early Islamic rule as the Islamic

[53] *P.Oxy* I 137 line 19. [54] *P.Oxy* XVI 1988 lines 23–5.

[55] *P.Oxy* XVI 1989 lines 17–18 – only here the word used for cheques is *entakia*. For the interchangeability of these words, see E. R. Hardy, *The Large Estates of Byzantine Egypt* (New York, 1931), 98. That this practice was not uniform, however, is established by *PSI* I 60 (a. 595).

[56] For literacy rates and levels in late Roman Egypt, see the discussion in Bagnall, *Egypt in Late Antiquity*, 230–60.

government began to lay for itself firmer administrative foundations.[57] For the earlier period, encompassing much of the sixth century, as noted above, the extant papyrological record preserves part of the archive of one of Aphrodito's most prominent families, the descendants of a certain Psimanobet – 'the goose-herd's son' – more commonly known as the 'Dioscorus archive'.[58] Although, as this name would suggest, the origins of the family would appear to have been relatively humble, by the early sixth century, its male members had risen into the elite of the local village headmen or *protokometai*. As a result, the Dioscoran materials preserve not only accounts and leases concerned with the family's own direct economic interests and dealings, but also documents concerning the village's relations with the 'outside world'. Chief among these is a series of petitions and verse *encomia* by which the village lawyer and man-of-letters, Dioscorus, sought to protect the settlement's independent fiscal status (*autopragia*) against the encroachments of local landowners and imperial officials.[59] A focus on economic interests, legal rights and especially credit arrangements is also evident from the seventh- and eighth-century papyri that survive from the town of Jeme.[60] The documents safeguarded in the church in Jeme were overwhelmingly legal in character, detailing dispute resolutions and suchlike. The primary extant archive beyond that held by the church, interestingly, consists of pottery sherds or *ostraca* associated with the business activities of the local moneylender, a woman by the name of Koloje.[61]

## The seventh century and beyond

In the year 616, the conquering armies of the Sassanian Shah Khusro II entered imperial territory in Egypt, and by 619 Alexandria had been wrested from East Roman control. Although the Persian occupation was eventually reversed, Egypt was not to be restored to Roman rule for long. In 639, the Muslim general Amr Ibn al-As pursued retreating Byzantine forces out of Palestine and initiated the Arab conquest of the region. Accordingly, we lose sight of the one area of the Byzantine world from which extensive lay archival documentation survives. That a culture of archival record-keeping remained a feature of lay society in what survived of the East Roman Empire, however, seems clear. For irrespective

[57] See especially *Greek Papyri in the British Museum*, IV, *The Aphrodito Papyri*, ed. H. I. Bell (London, 1910). I am indebted to Dr Petra Sijpesteijn for discussion of the Arabic papyri.
[58] Gagos and Van Minnen, *Settling a Dispute*, 19, 131 (family tree).
[59] Sarris, *Economy and Society*, 96–114.
[60] Wilfong, *Women of Jeme*. [61] Wilfong, *Women of Jeme*, 117–50.

of how much territory was lost to the Arabs in the seventh century, and no matter how much damage was done to the urban infrastructure of Anatolia, Asia Minor and Greece, a bureaucratic political culture and a bureaucratic class survived in Constantinople.[62] Moreover, although the Byzantine aristocracy beyond Constantinople became increasingly militarized, it remained profoundly literate. Thus, in the eleventh century, we see the retired general John Cecaumenos advising a young man, 'When you are free and not busy with a commander's duties, read books, both histories and church writings. Do not say, "What benefit is there for a soldier from ecclesiastical books?", for you will profit greatly from them.'[63] There is no reason to suppose that middle Byzantine imperial government was any less reliant on the written word than was late antique imperial government. Nor is there any reason to suppose that middle Byzantine landowners made any less use of written instruments. In the eleventh-century accounts of legal proceedings known as the *Peira* of Eustathius the Roman, for example, we find both great landowners and independent peasant farmers producing written documents, agreements, settlements of claims and contracts at court, so as to advance or protect their interests against one another.[64] That so little documentary material survives is not the point. As ever, absence of evidence should not be confused for evidence of absence.

Moreover, it is interesting to note that when documentary evidence does begin to become more abundant in the Byzantine world, especially from the eleventh century onwards, the documents that surface bear striking terminological similarity to their late antique antecedents in a way that cannot be explained entirely in terms of the survival of legal and literary traditions from Late Antiquity through to the middle Byzantine period. Rather, the same terms are used to describe the same – often quite technical – features of agrarian social relations and relations of production. For example, the directly administered 'demesne' of the aristocratically owned bipartite estates recorded in the early Byzantine papyri such as those found in the Apion archive was, as we have seen, commonly known as the *autourgia*. The same term is used to designate the same category of land in our late Byzantine sources.[65] It is striking that the contents both of the eighth-century *Farmer's Law*, detailing regulations concerning village life, and the eleventh-century *Peira* make

62 M. Whittow, *The Making of Orthodox Byzantium* (London, 1996).
63 Cited in C. Mango, *Byzantium: The Empire of New Rome* (London, 1980), 239.
64 E.g. *Peira* 7.6, concerning a private settlement of claims or *dialysis*.
65 P. Sarris, 'Economics, Trade, and Feudalism', in L. James (ed.), *A Companion to Byzantium* (Oxford, 2010), 25–42.

sense only when placed in the semantic context of our late antique Greek documentary sources – the Egyptian papyri. This apparent continuity of both managerial tradition (with respect to the *autourgia*) and vocabulary (with respect to the *Farmer's Law* and *Peira*) is perhaps suggestive of a high degree of survival of specific documentary traditions.

## Conclusions and implications

The early Byzantine evidence, seen in the context of the history of archival culture as a whole in the Near East back to the world of the third millennium BC, has a number of potential implications for students of the early medieval West. Certainly, the survival of archival and documentary cultures in Byzantium is likely to have been much facilitated by the survival of a bureaucratic class in Constantinople and of a strong tradition of elite literacy. In this respect, Byzantium arguably stands in marked – some would insist *very* marked – contrast to the world of the post-Roman and early medieval West, although only in very few instances can state structures and elite literacy be seen to have disappeared absolutely. But perhaps the evidence of archival cultures in the round would suggest that too narrow a concentration on bureaucracies and elites rather misses the point. As this chapter has hopefully indicated, and as those by Conant and Everett certainly do, the late Roman world was a world in which the use and archivalized storage of written instruments were deeply embedded and are discernible at a range of social levels. The documents on slate from early medieval Spain clearly indicate that such traditions were sufficiently embedded to have been more than capable of survival at the level of village society and within the context of agrarian social relations.

We are thus dealing with post-Roman societies in the West where people were used to dealing with the written word and were perfectly aware of its utility. Moreover, as we have seen, the impetus first to document and then to 'archivalize' information was to a very great extent generated by economic transactions and concerns – in particular, relations of dependence, actual or anticipated coercion, and structures of extraction and exploitation. Credit relations, in particular, were especially inclined to leave behind them an extensive paper trail. This is important, in that systems of credit would appear to have been central to the operation of rural patronage in the late Roman and very early medieval (that is, fifth-century) West, where, as in the East, well-connected patrons would offer credit to their potential peasant clients in return for their labour or in return for acquiring ownership of their plots of land.[66] It may well have been similarly generative of archivalized documentation.

Most crucially of all, however, hardly any (and perhaps none at all) of the societies that emerged from late Roman conditions in the fifth- and sixth-century West were egalitarian or classless societies. Anglo-Saxon England has perhaps the strongest claim to have been the exception that proves the rule, yet even here such a characterization of early medieval society is highly contestable.[67] James Campbell, for example, has argued that the England of Bede in the seventh to eighth centuries was 'a rich place with a booming export trade in cloth'.[68] Likewise as Mark Whittow has noted:

> We know almost nothing of an Anglo-Saxon leather industry, but since half a million people wore shoes and belts it must have existed. Monkwearmouth-Jarrow was a lavishly-furnished monastery . . . the resources required to sustain it must have been substantial. We now know that Monkwearmouth-Jarrow was not alone: Bede's England was full of monasteries. Multiplied out the resources required to sustain this culture will have been immense.[69]

Certainly on the continent, and perhaps even to some extent in Britain, the Roman Empire bequeathed what Jairus Banaji has described as a 'legacy of oppression' that continued to weigh heavily on elements of the peasantry, most obviously in terms of an inherited tradition of direct management of estates.[70] In Gaul and Italy, such continuity is clearly discernible.[71] Even in lowland Britain, where such continuity is more unlikely, one should note the striking and highly suggestive correlation between late Roman villa sites and places of high-status Anglo-Saxon

[66] B. Sirks, 'The Farmer, the Landlord, and the Law in the Fifth Century', in R. W. Mathisen (ed.), *Law, Society, and Authority in Late Antiquity* (Oxford, 2001), 256–61; see also the classic account of fifth-century rural patronage in Salvian of Marseilles, *De gubernatione Dei* (MGH AA 1.1).

[67] See esp. M. Whittow, 'Beyond the Cultural Turn: Economic History Revisited?', *Journal of Roman Archaeology*, 20 (2007), 697–704, esp. 701–3 (review of Wickham, *Framing*).

[68] J. Campbell, 'Production and Distribution in Early and Middle Anglo-Saxon England', in T. Pestell and K. Ulmschneider (eds.), *Markets in Early Medieval Europe: Trading and Productive Sites, 650–850* (Macclesfield, 2003), 12–19.

[69] Whittow, 'Beyond the Cultural Turn', 703.

[70] J. Banaji, 'Aristocracies, Peasantries and the Framing of the Early Middle Ages', *Journal of Agrarian Change*, 9 (2009), 59–92.

[71] As argued in P. Sarris, 'The Origins of the Manorial Economy', *English Historical Review*, 119 (2004), 279–311. The survival of actual patterns of great landowning is also acknowledged, but with very different emphasis, in Wickham, *Framing*, 195 and 299; see P. Sarris, 'Continuity and Discontinuity in the Post-Roman Economy', *Journal of Agrarian Change*, 6 (2006), 400–13.

settlement.[72] The survival and (in certain instances) continuity of tradition of relations of dependence, coercion and exploitation in the early medieval West would have given both the powerful and the vulnerable a strong incentive to record and to store evidence pertaining to their respective rights, obligations and claims, and is likely to have favoured the survival of documentary and archival cultures. Any such tendency would have been further intensified by what Wickham has characterized as the legacy from the Roman Empire to much of the post-Roman West of the concept of there being 'a public sphere of power' in which rights could be asserted, challenged and either vindicated or dismissed.[73] Social and economic relations of inequality perhaps provide the key to the existence and perpetuation of archivalized documentation in the early Middle Ages, not the broader cultural contexts and categories to which attention can too easily be drawn.

72 Private communication with Dr R. Faith.

73 Wickham, *Framing*, 57.

# 3 Public administration, private individuals and the written word in Late Antique North Africa, *c.* 284–700

*Jonathan P. Conant*

*North Africa was also a place where the civil administration drove documentary use, even through changes in regime. Here, however, we also see the particular importance of the military. In addition, the nature of the surviving documents draws attention to the deep penetration of documentary culture well below the level of the elite, as well as to the importance of documents that were not intended to be preserved for long periods. This evidence also indicates how crucial the interests of individuals, or of collectives outside the apparatus of the state, were to the persistence of documentary culture. The distinction between laypeople and clergy is visible, but did not determine how documents were used or preserved.*

Egyptians were not the only inhabitants of the late antique Mediterranean to make extensive use of written documents. To be sure, outside Egypt, comparatively few sources have been preserved through which to study documentary practice in Late Antiquity; but what evidence we do have seems to suggest that the scattered documents that survive from the western Mediterranean barely scratch the surface of what was once produced there. Together with occasional references to documents that once existed but have subsequently been lost or destroyed, these fragments raise important questions as to the nature and extent of documentary practice throughout the late Roman and early medieval West.

Such questions are particularly acute in the case of the Roman Empire's African provinces, because they have never been explored synthetically in this region. Yet, Africa has preserved a remarkable range of materials that allow us to assess the role of documentation in local society. By the late antique period, an agricultural regime based on the cultivation of olive trees and cereals had extended even into marginal regions of the North African countryside, where arid conditions are favourable to the preservation of the organic materials with and on which ancient documents were written. As a result, a small but significant amount of written documentation survives from Africa: at least three assemblages of wooden tablets and – though otherwise rare – over twenty collections of Latin *ostraca*, ranging from single finds to a large group of over 140 sherds. Not all of this material has yet been published, but these scattered remnants combine with references to other similar texts in the historical, legal, homiletic and other literary sources to suggest that Africa was once characterized by a vibrant culture of record-keeping, in both the private and the public spheres. Indeed, as in Egypt, much of the documentation generated in Africa was produced to satisfy the demands of the late Roman fiscal, judicial and military administration (and its successors in the Vandal and Byzantine periods); but a reliance on the written word to facilitate the practical aspects of property ownership, estate management and trade also seems to have percolated quite deeply into secular society in general and to have survived there until at least the mid sixth century, and quite possibly beyond.

## Private documentation

There can be little question that African society relied heavily on written documentation in the late antique period. To judge from the texts that survive to us, estate management – or what Chris Wickham has referred to as 'accounting' – seems to have been a major aspect of that documentary culture.[1] Extant tables of calculation indicate that this could involve the computation of income and expenditures, reckoned either in coin or in real terms. Thus, for example, in the late fifth century on a *fundus* in the hill country of eastern Algeria, someone tallied up the money that members of a local family had spent buying various small parcels of land.[2] Three *ostraca* from the same general area list a series of names, each followed by a sum; the largest sherd adds a total and the phrase *partis dominice*, suggesting that the numbers represent the income that a local landowner received either in rents or from labour services on his or her 'demesne'.[3] Such income also seems to be recorded in a collection of five Vandal-era *ostraca* discovered in an earthenware jar near Bir Trouch, again along the edges of the eastern Algerian highlands.[4] At least three

1 Wickham, *Framing*, 266.

2 *Tablettes Albertini: Actes privés de l'époque vandale (fin du V^e^ siècle)*, ed. C. Courtois *et al.*, 2 vols. (Paris, 1952) (henceforth *TA*, with act no. in Roman, volume and page in Arabic numerals), XXXIII, 1:299.

3 E. Albertini, 'Ostrakon byzantin de Négrine (Numidie)', in *Cinquantenaire de la Faculté des lettres d'Alger (1881–1931)* (Algiers, 1932), 53–62, at 62; see also R. Cagnat, in *Bulletin archéologique du Comité des travaux historiques et scientifiques* (henceforth *BCTH*) (1908), ccxlvii–ccxlix. On the 'demesne' in Africa and the late Roman world, see Wickham, *Framing*, 273–80.

4 J.-P. Bonnal and P.-A. Février, 'Ostraka de la région de Bir Trouch', *Bulletin d'archéologie algérienne*, 2 (1966–7), 239–49. See also the discussion of these documents in Wickham, *Framing*, 266.

of these documents involve the same individual, a certain *Massiese*, and all of them appear to concern two different holdings under simultaneous cultivation, one in a place called *Viginti Boguli* and another at *Adeudaci*. The five texts follow a standard formula; the fullest of them reads:

*annu nonu cartaginis / domni nostri regis Gunta/mundi accessit Massiese / in xx boguli parte dominica / ordei m(ensuras) iii tres tam/tum.*[5]

In the ninth year of Carthage of our lord king Gunthamund [AD 492×3] *Massiese* accepted 3 three measures of barley only on the lord's portion at *Viginti Boguli*.

Though this is the only example to specify that the measures in question were of barley, the others also involve *mensurae*, presumably of some agricultural product. Taken together, these five *ostraca* likely represent accounts of rents or labour services generated as a product of the internal management of a local estate. Yet another document, this one undated, survives from Ksar Koutine in southern Tunisia and is addressed to a certain Severus *conductor*, probably the chief tenant of a local estate, but perhaps a collector of customs duties.[6]

Other documents from North Africa suggest that the issuing of receipts was probably also fairly widespread in Late Antiquity. For example, a collection of eight *ostraca* survives from Maknassy in the highlands of southern Tunisia (on the road between Sfax and Gafsa); five contain texts that are legible in varying degrees and which for the most part appear to be receipts for payments in kind of sheep meat and wine. Fragmentary references to the Roman calendar –*Kal(endas) mai(i), id(us) iulias, august* – indicate that these records were originally dated, but none can now be assigned to a precise year. However, one of the *ostraca* seems to be dated according to a king's reign, and therefore probably belongs to the period of Vandal or Moorish ascendancy in this region. This document is addressed by a certain Sylvester to one *Africanus Tu. . . .rus*, while two or perhaps three of the other texts were written by or addressed to a woman named Urbanilla. All five indicate that they were once subscribed, though the names of the subscribers have been lost.[7]

Other excavations, surveys and chance finds in Tunisia and Algeria have turned up a handful of additional Latin *ostraca* from Late Antiquity, and though they are even more difficult to interpret, many may also plausibly be connected with the economic life of rural estates. One of

5 Bonnal and Février, 'Ostraka de Bir Trouch', 241.
6 A. Merlin, in *BCTH* (1913), ccxxxii, no. 2. On the term *conductor*, see A. H. M. Jones, *The Later Roman Empire, 284–602: A Social, Economic and Administrative Survey*, 2 vols. (Oxford, 1964), 417–19 and 788–92, but also 430.
7 P. Delattre and M. Héron de Villefosse, in *BCTH* (1912), cclviii–cclx.

the *ostraca* found at Henchir bou Gornine in southern Tunisia contains a highly abbreviated text dating to 359 that relates to a farm known as the Fundus Villa Magna. The text on a second sherd from the same site is not fully intelligible, but seems to concern the repayment of a debt.[8] At least two of the four late antique *ostraca* from Henchir el Abiod, Algeria, are associated with a place called Casae Nigrensium, and, of these, one also refers to a Fundus Puteos. A third renders an account of goats and sheep.[9] One of the eleven *ostraca* found at Henchir el Maïz, Algeria, makes reference to a Thrasamund (presumably the sixth-century Vandal king of that name) and seems to have to do with oil production on a local estate.[10]

It is worth observing, though, that estate managers were not the only individuals to employ written documentation in late antique North Africa. Evidence of its commercial use in the late fourth or early fifth century is provided by thirty-two recently published *ostraca* from the island of Jerba, many of which are in Greek but some of which are in Latin. The texts concern places as far distant as Rhodes, the Troad and perhaps Thrace; they include a letter and records that appear to be orders, receipts, loans or notes; and they mention a slave trader, murex dye and olive oil, as well as some unspecified commodity or commodities measured in discrete units.[11]

North Africans also appear regularly to have recorded sales and other transfers of property in written documents. On 24 January 494, for example, a certain Julius Restitutus and his wife Donata sold a scrap of land with a single almond tree on it – together with the water rights associated with the property – to another local landholder by the name of Geminius Felix. The whole package sold for 100 *folles* in cash. The parties involved secured the services of a local writer familiar with the formulas necessary to draw up a legal deed of sale (probably the local schoolteacher Quadratianus), and he enumerated, among other details, the owners of the properties that bounded this small holding in three directions.[12]

8 A. Merlin, in *BCTH* (1915), cxcii–cxciii. On the use of *ostraca* by Koloje the Moneylender and her family to record loan agreements in late antique Egypt, see T. G. Wilfong, *Women of Jeme: Lives in a Coptic Town in Late Antique Egypt* (Ann Arbor, MI, 2002), 117–28.

9 Cagnat, *BCTH* (1908), ccxlvii–ccxlix.

10 *CIL* VIII 22646.20. Wickham, *Framing*, 266n10, advocates reading the abbreviation *pd* in this text as expandable once again to *pars dominica*.

11 Z. Várhelyi and R. S. Bagnall, 'Ostraka', in E. Fentress, A. Drine and R. Holod (eds.), *An Island Through Time: Jerba Studies*. I. *The Punic and Roman Periods* (Portsmouth, RI, 2009), 334–44.

12 *TA* XIX, 1:274; for Quadratianus as the scribe, see 1:54. On the value of these transactions, see P. Grierson, 'The *Tablettes Albertini* and the Value of the *solidus* in the Fifth and Sixth Centuries A.D.', *Journal of Roman Studies*, 49 (1959), 73–80.

The instrument that records this transaction is one of the Albertini Tablets, a remarkable collection of thirty-four documents preserved on forty-five wooden panels that were discovered in 1928 along the Tunisian-Algerian border in the region of Djebel Mrata. The panels include one of the tables of calculations mentioned above, as well as a dowry and various deeds of sale concerning a slave, an olive press and numerous small plots of olive, fig and nut trees, most of which were associated with a rural estate known as the Fundus Tuletianos.[13] These tablets reveal something of the significance of written documentation on the pre-desert frontier of post-Roman Africa. The texts that they contain were written by and for the rural smallholders that made up the Tuletianos community, and in selecting friends, neighbours, patrons and clients to witness their purchases and sales of property, local landholders seem to have shown a preference for individuals who could read and write. The fact that the wood on which the instruments were written appears to have been imported into the Djebel Mrata region shows the importance that members of this community attached to having a written document to record their property transactions. So, too, the fact that landholders like Restitutus, Donata and Felix were willing to pay scribes to draw up deeds for relatively small-scale transactions like the sale of a single almond tree and its water rights – though, to be sure, a selling price of 100 *folles* was not an insignificant sum in the Fundus Tuletianos community: the same amount could buy six olive trees, and for somewhat less one could buy two fig trees.[14] As important as it appears to have been to document a sale on the Fundus Tuletianos, tablets that (for whatever reason) had outlived their usefulness were scraped down and reused to hold the texts of new instruments. This seems to have happened with some regularity. Though not all of the documents in the assemblage can be precisely dated, those that can were all written between 493 and 496, in the final years of the reign of the Vandal king Gunthamund. The production of so substantial an amount of written documentation in a restricted region in such a short period of time may even suggest frequent archival culling.[15]

[13] See above, n. 2.

[14] Six olive trees: *TA*, XVIII, 1:271; see also *TA* IX, 1:246 (90 *folles*). Two fig trees: *TA* XVI, 1:269.

[15] J. P. Conant, 'Literacy and Private Documentation in Vandal North Africa: The Case of the Albertini Tablets', in A. H. Merrills (ed.), *Vandals, Romans, and Berbers: New Perspectives on Late Antique North Africa* (Aldershot, 2004), 199–224; note, however, that the sermon attributed there (p. 1) to Augustine (*Sermo* 303 [PL 39:2324–8]) is in fact pseudo-Augustinian: L. Dossey, 'Christians and Romans: Aspiration, Assimilation, and Conflict in the North African Countryside', unpublished Ph.D. thesis, Harvard University (1998), 371.

The examples that we have considered so far all come from the highland or pre-desert fringes of the North African countryside, but they are probably a guide to the practices of the region's agricultural and urban centre as well. At least, the documentary culture of late fifth-century western Byzacena that is revealed in the Albertini Tablets seems to mesh seamlessly with that of the diocese of Hippo Regius evoked by Augustine nearly a century earlier. Here, too, the use of written deeds (*instrumenta* or *tabulae*) to record sales and gifts of property appears to have been a familiar practice. In one of his sermons, Augustine tells the story of a man named Barnabas who received a piece of land as a gift from a certain Eleusinus. Barnabas was later ordained a priest and a monastery was built on the land, whereupon 'he changed the *instrumenta* so that [the land] was held in the name of the monastery'.[16] The implication, though, is that at the time of the original gift Barnabas received a written document transferring ownership of the property. It is also worth emphasizing that at that point Barnabas was still a layman, and that he had retained the deed until he needed to alter it once again to reflect the new change in ownership entailed by his subsequent donation of the land to the monastery. In another sermon, Augustine indicates that in his day deeds of title typically specified the neighbours whose landholdings bordered on a property.[17] As we have seen, in the Vandal period, too, the writers of the Fundus Tuletianos documents continued to list the members of the local community whose properties bordered on a landed sale to the north, south, east, west, north-west, south-west and toward the sea.[18] As in Augustine's day, in the closing years of the fifth century the use of instruments was not restricted to landed property.[19] Indeed, the highest-value sale in the Tuletianos dossier concerns a young slave boy named Fortinis.[20] Another tablet records the movable goods with which a certain Januarius endowed his future bride, Geminia Januarilla.[21] Januarilla's dowry is also evocative of – though not a direct parallel to – the *tabulae matrimonialae* that Augustine tells us were read aloud to brides at their weddings.[22] In short, then, the Albertini Tablets seem to have functioned in a world of

16 Augustine, *Sermo* 356.15 (PL 39:1581): 'mutavit instrumenta, ut nomine monasterii possideatur'.

17 Augustine, *Sermo* 358.2 (PL 39:1587): 'quomodo solent instrumentis quaeri possessores, inter quos sint affines'.

18 *TA* III–XXIV, 1:218–83.

19 Augustine, *Confessiones* 9.9.19 (ed. J. J. O'Donnell, 3 vols. [Oxford, 1992], I:112) and *Sermo* 37.7 (CCSL 41:454).

20 *TA* II, 1:216–17.

21 *TA* I, 1:215.

22 Augustine, *Confessiones* 9.9.19 (ed. O'Donnell, I:111–12); see also Augustine, *De Genesi ad litteram* 11.41 (CSEL 28.1:376), and E. Meyer, *Legitimacy and Law in the Roman World: Tabulae in Roman Belief and Practice* (Cambridge, 2004), 277n76.

documentary practice that was recognizably the same as it had been in Augustine's day. Unfortunately, no other documents from late antique North Africa have yet been published that unambiguously record dowries or private sales. Still-unedited wooden tablets, such as those found at an ancient well in Bir Trouch or those from Guert, Algeria, may contain such documents; the same may be true of some of the Latin *ostraca* from North Africa which have so far proven too difficult either to read or to interpret.[23] Even so, private individuals in late antique Africa seem to have demanded, produced and made use of a considerable amount of practical written documentation.

## The late Roman administration and its successors

The culture of private documentation in late antique North Africa was underpinned and informed by the practices of the late Roman state and its successors, in both the civil and the military spheres. Indeed, in seeking to control the empire, the later Roman bureaucracy demanded the production of a truly extensive amount of written documentation. In the records that survive to us, this official reliance on the written word is particularly visible at the highest levels of the late Roman administration in Africa. The praetorian prefects, vicars and proconsuls of Roman Africa of course received frequent rescripts from the imperial centre concerning the region's civil, ecclesiastical and military affairs.[24] The vicar of Africa, in turn, had written instructions from the emperor to send along reports from subordinate provincial officials that required imperial

[23] Unpublished wooden tablets: Bonnal and Février, 'Ostraka de Bir Trouch', 239; Marseille, Archives Départementales des Bouches-du-Rhône, 100 J 19 (Archives de P.-A. Février: Tablettes du Guert), with photos in Y. Duval and P.-A. Février, 'Procès-verbal de déposition de reliques de la région de Telergma (VII$^{e}$ s.)', *Mélanges d'archéologie et d'histoire* (École française de Rome), 81 (1969), 257–320, Figures 44–5 (my thanks to Mark Handley for this reference).

[24] Praetorian prefect: e.g. *CTh.* 1.5.12; 1.15.10, 14, 17; 7.4.2, 3, 33; 7.6.1; 7.13.21, 22; 11.1.31; 11.7.8; 11.13.1; 11.28.8; 12.6.4; 12.12.1; 13.4.1; 13.6.10; 15.14.13; 16.2.31; 16.5.37. Vicar: e.g. *CTh.* 1.12.6; 7.8.9; 7.15.1; 9.26.3; 11.1.30; 16.2.29, 34; 16.5.35. Proconsul: e.g. *CTh.* 1.3.1; 1.12.6, 8; 4.22.6; 6.28.7; 6.29.9; 7.8.7; 8.4.23; 8.5.64; 8.10.3, 4; 9.26.2; 9.39.3; 9.40.19; 10.1.13; 10.9.3; 10.10.27–8; 11.1.24, 28, 32, 34; 11.5.1; 11.7.19–21; 11.8.2; 11.17.2; 11.28.6; 11.30.53, 60, 62, 64–5; 12.1.95, 141–5, 149, 166, 174, 176, 185–6; 12.5.3; 12.6.27, 28, 29, 31; 13.1.8, 18; 13.5.25, 30; 16.5.39, 41, 44, 54–5; 16.10.17–18; 16.11.1, 2. Rescript system: T. Honoré, *Emperors and Lawyers*, 2nd edn (Oxford, 1994), 1–70. Composition of the *CTh.*: J. Harries and I. Wood (eds.), *The Theodosian Code* (Ithaca, NY, 1993), esp. 17–67; T. Honoré, *Law in the Crisis of Empire, 379–455 A.D.: The Theodosian Dynasty and Its Quaestors* (Oxford, 1998), 123–53; J. Matthews, *Laying Down the Law: A Study of the Theodosian Code* (New Haven, CT, 2000); A. J. B. Sirks, *The Theodosian Code: A Study* (Friedrichsdorf, 2007). Responsibilities of these officials: P. S. Barnwell, *Emperor, Prefects, and Kings: The Roman West, 395–565* (Chapel Hill, NC, 1992), 58–67.

attention.[25] The proconsul of Africa – who was outside the vicar's jurisdiction – similarly forwarded such cases to the emperor, and furthermore submitted his own reports.[26] At least on occasion, we also hear of less exalted African officials sending written appeals to the emperor for his consideration. Thus, for example, the leading citizens of Tripolitania sent envoys to Valentinian I (364–75) in the late fourth century who carried written *decreta* intended to inform the emperor of the severe and widespread devastation that their province had experienced at the hands of Moorish raiders.[27] Similarly, though his missives were intercepted before they reached the emperor, the Mauretanian general and future rebel Firmus sent written letters to the imperial court to defend himself against the spurious accusations of one Romanus, who was then the supreme commander of the Roman forces in Africa, or *comes Africae*.[28] However, legislation of Constantius II (337–61) sought to ensure that such direct exchange of letters between lower-ranking officials and the emperor was the exception rather than the rule. When the governor of Numidia wrote to Constantius to present a matter for the emperor's consideration, he was rebuked and informed that he should have first submitted the issue to the vicar of Africa.[29]

The role that the vicar and proconsul of Africa played in relaying important cases to the emperor also hints at the volume of written exchange that probably took place laterally between the province's civil and military officials. The nature of our sources is such that we are not often able to see such communications, though some light is shed on them in the context of the coordination of military action. Thus, for example, if the hostility of the local population made it impossible for the civilian authorities to apprehend those who had committed 'outrages' against priests, a provincial governor was permitted to request military support from the *comes Africae* by sending him a letter that included a copy of an imperial rescript approving the use of troops for such purposes.[30] Similarly, when Constantius II sent a certain Gaudentius to Africa to prepare the province for war against the emperor's upstart nephew and junior colleague Julian, the imperial representative discharged his task by writing letters both to the *comes Africae* and to the region's other military commanders.[31] The Mauretanian rebel Firmus likewise sent a letter that sought to explain and justify the reasons for his revolt to the Roman military commander charged with the pacification of Africa.[32] When the commanding officer of the recalcitrant Christian centurion Marcellus sent the soldier to be

[25] *CTh*. 1.15.2. [26] *CTh*. 9.19.3. [27] Amm. Marc. 28.6.9.
[28] Amm. Marc. 29.5.2. [29] *CTh*. 1.15.3; see also 1.15.2; contrast *CJ* 1.33.1.
[30] *CTh*. 16.2.31. [31] Amm. Marc. 21.7.4. [32] Amm. Marc. 29.5.8–9.

tried for refusing to continue to serve in the imperial army, he, too, sent a letter to the court officials detailing the man's actions.[33] Letter-writing of this sort appears to have remained important to the functioning of the army in Africa into the Byzantine period: we have at least fourteen lead seals struck in the names of sixth- or seventh-century *duces* and *magistri militum* from Africa that would originally have been attached to written documents issued by these military officials, and in the late sixth century Gregory the Great wrote a letter recommending the Suevic commander Droctulf for military service in Africa under the Byzantine exarch Gennadius.[34]

The use of documentation in the civil and military administration of Africa was not confined to the writing and circulation of letters. A sense of the notarial sophistication of which the imperial administration in Africa was capable can be gleaned from the documentation generated over the course of the conference held in Carthage in 411 to resolve the long-running rivalry between the region's contentious Catholic and Donatist Churches.[35] The conference was convened on the order of the Western emperor Honorius (395–423) and presided over by the imperial legate Flavius Marcellinus; the secretarial team that oversaw the recording of the conference's proceedings was headed by two scribes (*scribae*) and four stenographers (*exceptores*) attached to Marcellinus' staff and to those of the proconsul, the vicar of Africa and the *curator* of Carthage. The official stenographers recorded the proceedings of the conference in shorthand, as did two teams of ecclesiastical notaries, one from each of the rival African Churches. Under the supervision of one of the two *exceptores* from the proconsul's office, the opposing parties checked the resulting transcripts against each other and resolved any discrepancies before a finalized text was written out in longhand. The rival Catholic and

33 *Passio S. Marcelli Tingitani* 4 (ed. H. Delehaye, in 'Les Actes de S. Marcel le centurion', *Analecta Bollandiana* 41 (1923), 257–87, at 262 (M) and 265 (N)).

34 Seals: P. Delattre and P. Monceaux, in *Bulletin de la Société nationale des antiquaires de France* (henceforth cited as *BSNAF*) (1908), 164 (no. 1) (= *Revue archéologique*, 4th ser., 12 [1908], 449 [no. 184]); (1912), 331–2 (no. 1); (1913), 316 (no. 1); (1914), 284 (nos. 1 and 2); P. Monceaux, 'Enquête sur l'épigraphie chrétienne d'Afrique', *Revue archéologique*, 4th ser., 2 (1903), 59–90, at 75–6 (nos. 15–16); J. Nesbitt and N. Oikonomides (eds.), *Catalogue of Byzantine Seals at Dumbarton Oaks and in the Fogg Museum of Art*. I. *Italy, North of the Balkans, North of the Black Sea* (Washington, DC, 1991), no. 6.1; G. Zacos and A. Veglery, *Byzantine Lead Seals*, I/3 (Basel, 1972), nos. 2885, 2898a–b; F. Icard, 'Sceaux et médailles de plomb trouvés à Carthage', *BCTH* (1917), 1–18, no. 33; F. Icard, 'Sceaux et plombs marqués découverts à Carthage', *BCTH* (1927), 479–87, no. 1; and A. Merlin and P. Monceaux, in *BSNAF* (1915), 300 (no. 1); V. Laurent, *Les sceaux byzantins du médaillier vatican* (Vatican City, 1962), no. 92. Letter of recommendation: Gregory I, *Registrum epistularum* 9.9 (CCSL 140A:570); on this Droctulf's career, see also Paul the Deacon, *Historia Langobardorum* 3.18–19 (ed. L. Capo [Milan, 1992], 148–50), and *CIL* XI 319.

35 *Gesta conlationis Carthaginiensis, anno 411* (CCSL 149A:1–257).

Donatist speakers were asked to confirm the accuracy of their recorded statements by writing in their own hands the word *recognovi* ('I have recognized' or 'I have recalled') after the words attributed to them, and only rarely does the surviving account indicate dissent on the part of a participant.[36]

The conference of Carthage, of course, was something of an exceptional case; but even so, down to at least the early fifth century it was standard procedure in Africa for court recorders to keep transcripts of municipal sessions and legal proceedings held before local officials, eventually including Christian bishops.[37] On at least one occasion we hear of a proconsul asking that these records be read back to him before he passed sentence on the accused.[38] Moreover, sentences were themselves typically read aloud from writing tablets.[39] For Augustine, too, the *gesta proconsularia* and *gesta municipalia* were not only the tribunals where individuals could be attacked or interrogated, and where the *traditores* had surrendered the scriptures and liturgical instruments of the Church; they were also the written records left behind by such legal actions, records that could be accessed and read aloud to prove or disprove what the bishop of Hippo perceived as the Donatists' partisan allegations.[40] Record-keeping of the sort employed by state officials at the conference of 411 seems to

36 Composition of the *acta*: E. Tengström, *Die Protokollierung der Collatio Carthaginensis: Beiträge zur Kenntnis der römischen Kurzschrift nebst einem Exkurs über das Wort scheda (schedula)* (Göteborg, 1962), 7–30; *Actes de la conférence de Carthage en 411*, ed. S. Lancel, 4 vols. (Paris, 1972–91), I, 337–53. Oral qualities of the surviving text: *Actes*, I, 289–327, esp. I, 309–27. Objections: e.g. *Gesta conlationis Carthaginiensis* 1.67 (CCSL 149A:90).

37 *Passio sanctorum Scilitanorum* (ed. F. Ruggiero, *Atti dei martiri Scilitani: Introduzione, testo, traduzione, testimonianze e commento* [Rome, 1991], 71–4); *Acta proconsularia sancti Cypriani* (ed. R. Reitzenstein, *Die Nachrichten über den Tod Cyprians: Ein philologischer Beitrag zur Geschichte der Märtyrerliteratur* [Heidelberg, 1913], 12–17); *Passio S. Maximiliani* (ed. P. Siniscalco [Turin, 1974], 159–61); *Passio s. Marcelli Tingitani* (ed. Delehaye, 260–4 [M] and 264–7 [N]); *Passio sanctae Crispinae* (ed. P. Franchi de' Cavalieri, *Nuove note agiografiche* [Rome, 1902], 32–5); *Gesta apud Zenophilum* (CSEL 26:185–97); *Acta purgationis Felicis episcopi Autumnitani* (CSEL 26:197–204); Augustine, *Contra Fortunatum disputatio* (CSEL 25.1:81–112); Augustine, *Contra Felicem* (CSEL 25.2:799–852); C. Humfress, *Orthodoxy and the Courts in Late Antiquity* (Oxford, 2007), 248–52; and, in general, G. Lanata, *Gli atti dei martiri come documenti processuali* (Milan, 1973).

38 *Passio s. Crispinae* 2 (ed. Franchi de' Cavalieri, 35).

39 *Passio ss. Scillitanorum* 14 (ed. Ruggiero, 73–4); *Acta proconsularia s. Cypriani* 2 (ed. Reitzenstein, 16); *Passio S. Maximiliani* 3 (ed. Siniscalco, 160); *Passio s. Crispinae* 2 (ed. Franchi de' Cavalieri, 35).

40 Tribunal: Augustine, *Epistulae* 76.2–3, 108.5.14, 114 (CSEL 34:327–8, 627, 660); *Contra litteras Petiliani* 1.21.23, 2.15.35 (CSEL 52:18, 40); *De unitate ecclesiae* (= *Epistula ad Catholicos de secta Donatistarum*) 18.46, 19.50 (CSEL 52:291, 297). Documents: Augustine, *Epistulae* 88.11 (CSEL 34:418); *Contra litteras Petiliani* 2.20.45, 2.58.132 (CSEL 52:45, 93); *De unitate ecclesiae* 12.31 (CSEL 52:270); *Contra Cresconium grammaticum et Donatistam* 3.47.51, 3.48.53, 3.56.62, 3.72.84 (CSEL 52:458, 460–1, 468–9, 489); *De unico baptismo* 17.31 (CSEL 53:32); see also *Epistulae* 108.5.14 (CSEL 34:627) and *De unitate ecclesiae* 12.31 (CSEL 52:270) ('gesta forensia').

have been very much a part of the legal and judicial culture of late Roman Africa.

Writing in general and letter-writing in particular appears to have been so central to the conduct of the late Roman and Byzantine administration of Africa that its misuse was the focus of a certain amount of official anxiety. In part this surrounded the treasonous thoughts or sentiments which state officers or their correspondents might commit to writing. In the fourth century, for example, the introduction as evidence at his trial of the 'more private papers' (*secretiores charti*) of Hymetius, a former proconsul of Africa, revealed an embarrassing note written in the man's own hand inveighing against the avarice and ferocity of the reigning emperor.[41] The papers of Romanus, a contemporary of Hymetius and the commanding general of Africa, included a letter that hinted at some of the plots in which the officer was implicated.[42] Much later, in the seventh century, imperial officials would accuse Maximus the Confessor of having written a similarly treasonous letter to the Byzantine military commander of Numidia, urging him not to take part in the defence of Egypt against the Islamic invasion.[43] In part, however, such anxieties surrounded the dangers of forgery. By 367 the script employed by the writing office of the proconsul of Africa had come to imitate that of the imperial chancery so successfully that the emperor Valentinian I began to worry that provincial officials might be tempted to forge imperial commands. The emperor ordered that thenceforth communications from the proconsul's office be written in 'common letters' (*litterae communes*).[44] Similarly, in 641, George, the praetorian prefect of Byzantine Africa, received a letter in support of some Monophysite nuns that had been written in the name of the empress Martina and which (for his own reasons) the prefect rejected as a forgery.[45] But it was not only letters that aroused such suspicions. Early in the fourth century, Constantine had fretted that African provincials might try to dupe local fiscal officials by faking tax receipts.[46]

Forgeries of the latter sort could potentially have far-reaching ramifications. Indeed, in all probability the most prominent way in which the bureaucratic apparatus of the late Roman state made itself felt in the lives of the vast majority of Africans would have been through the

[41] Amm. Marc. 28.1.20. [42] Amm. Marc. 28.6.26.

[43] *Relatio factae motionis inter domnum Maximum monachum et socium eius coram principibus in secretario* (CCSG 39:15, lines 30–7).

[44] *CTh.* 9.19.3.

[45] Maximus Confessor, *Epistulae* 12 (PG 91:460–509, esp. col. 460); on this George, see also *Epistulae* 1, 16, 18, 44–5 (PG 91:364–92, 576–80, 584–8, 641–9), and J. R. Martindale, *The Prosopography of the Later Roman Empire, III, A.D. 527–641* (Cambridge, 1992), s.n. 'Georgius 50'.

[46] *CTh.* 11.1.2.

extraction of revenue in the form of taxes. The sources that survive to us suggest that this process must originally have generated an enormous amount of documentation, most of which has subsequently been lost or destroyed. At a minimum this would have included the census lists and tax assessments generated by imperial officials, and the tax receipts that landholders were expected to deposit with the public registrars.[47] On occasion, however, the process would have generated far more in the way of paperwork. In 365, for example, the new emperor Valentinian I instituted an elaborate system to ensure the payment of delinquent taxes by absentee landowners resident in Rome but with property holdings in Africa. The staff of the vicar of Africa was to draft annual briefs (*breves*) indicating the amounts that such landholders owed; representatives of the urban prefect of Rome and the prefect of the annona were to travel to Africa to record how much these proprietors had paid; and copies of the resulting documentation were to be filed with both the praetorian prefect and the emperor himself.[48]

Whatever else changed in Africa with the coming of the Vandals, the regular extraction of revenue certainly continued, at least for a time. To be sure, the Vandal ruling class was said to have been granted hereditary tax-free allotments; but Procopius tells us that the property of the Vandals' Romano-African subjects continued to be heavily taxed.[49] Before his conversion to the monastic life the future bishop of Ruspe, Fulgentius, had enjoyed a successful career in the Vandal civil service as a *procurator* or tax collector.[50] Victor of Vita indicates that during the persecution of 484, provisions and wages (*annonae et stipendia*) were denied to Catholics serving in the Vandal administration; this would seem to imply that under normal circumstances African office-holders continued to receive both, and that the system for procuring them was still in place.[51] The *fiscus*

47 *CTh.* 11.1.2, 28, 32; 13.5.12. Tax collection in late Roman Africa: C. Saumagne, 'Un tarif fiscal au quartième siècle de notre ère', *Karthago*, 1 (1950), 105–206; J. T. Peña, 'The Mobilization of State Olive Oil in Roman Africa: The Evidence of Late 4th-c. *Ostraca* from Carthage', in J. H. Humphrey (ed.), *Carthage Papers: The Early Colony's Economy, Water Supply, a Public Bath, and the Mobilization of State Olive Oil* (Portsmouth, RI, 1998), 117–238, at 153–65.

48 *CTh.* 11.1.13.

49 Victor of Vita, *Historia persecutionis Africanae provinciae* 1.13 (CSEL 7:7), with Procopius, *De bello Vandalico* 1.5.12–15 (ed. J. Haury [Leipzig, 1962], 333–4). Nature of these allotments: Y. Modéran, 'L'établissement territorial des Vandales en Afrique', *Antiquité tardive*, 10 (2002), 87–122; A. Schwarcz, 'The Settlement of the Vandals in North Africa', in Merrills (ed.), *Vandals, Romans, and Berbers*, 49–57. Transformative effect on early medieval society: M. Innes, 'Land, Freedom and the Making of the Medieval West', *TRHS*, 6th ser., 16 (2006), 39–74.

50 Ferrandus, *Vita S. Fulgentii episcopi Ruspensis* 1 (ed. G.-G. Lapeyre [Paris, 1929], 13).

51 Victor of Vita, *Historia persecutionis* 2.10 (CSEL 7:27).

also seems to have continued to function under the fifth-century Vandal regime, and one of the few surviving edicts of the Vandal king Huneric (477–84) refers to the existence of a *domus regia* and a decurial order as well.[52] This edict is modelled on earlier Roman anti-Donatist legislation, and therefore cannot necessarily be taken to reflect contemporary social reality; but taken as a whole the constellation of evidence would seem to suggest both that many of the fundamental elements of the late Roman tax system survived for at least the first sixty or so years of Vandal occupation, and that they were redirected to serving the interests of Africa's new rulers.[53]

After his reconquest of the Vandal kingdom, the Byzantine emperor Justinian (527–65) similarly arranged for a new census to be taken in Africa.[54] The region's much-lauded wealth had been a major factor in motivating the emperor's African venture, and down to at least the reign of Constantine IV (668–85), Justinian's successors continued to take a close financial interest in the province. An overwhelming number of the lead seals that survive from Byzantine Africa concern the region's financial administration. Many of them date to the seventh century. These include the seal of a certain Stephen, honorary consul and *dioecetes provinciarum*, as well as those of three *sacellarii* and perhaps sixteen *commerciarii*.[55] In addition, a sixth- or seventh-century funerary inscription from Carthage records the burial of one Redemptus '*arcarius* of the fifth region' (*ar[car]iu[s r]egi/onis qui[ntae]*).[56] The combination of a census, taxes and tax officials empowered to issue sealed documents implies tax records as well.

The fiscal impositions of the late Roman state probably also provide the context in which we should understand a Latin *ostracon* discovered at Ksar Koutine, north-west of Médenine in southern Tunisia. The text describes itself as a chitty (*pittacium*) issued on 17 July 419 in connection with the assessment of some 1,800 *folles* on olive oil that was to be

52 Victor of Vita, *Historia persecutionis* 2.23, 3.11 (CSEL 7:33, 77); J. H. W. G. Liebeschuetz, '*Gens* into *regnum*: The Vandals', in H.-W. Goetz, J. Jarnut and W. Pohl (eds.), *Regna and gentes: The Relationship Between Late Antique and Early Medieval Peoples and Kingdoms in the Transformation of the Roman World* (Leiden, 2003), 55–83, at 75; but see also Wickham, *Framing*, 636–7.

53 See, however, Wickham, *Framing*, 89–92, who makes a strong case for the deterioration of the classical city-based tax system in the later Vandal period.

54 Procopius, *De bello Vandalico* 2.8.25 (ed. Haury, 455).

55 P. Delattre and A. Merlin, in *BCTH* (1924), ccxx–ccxxi (no. 7); C. Morrisson and W. Seibt, 'Sceaux de commerciaires byzantins du VII^e^ siècle trouvés à Carthage', *Revue numismatique*, 6th ser., 24 (1982), 222–40; *CIL* VIII 22656.25; and Monceaux, 'Enquête sur l'épigraphie chrétienne', 73 (no. 11). We hear in addition of John, *sacellarius* of the general of Numidia in *Relatio factae motionis*... (CCSG 39:15, lines 28–9).

56 *L'année épigraphique* (1986), 259 (no. 717).

sold.[57] In all probability, the document is a receipt for the payment of customs duties at a local town or rural market.[58] However, our best evidence for what tax records looked like in the late Roman period comes from a group of thirty-two Latin *ostraca* discovered on the Admiralty Island in Carthage's circular harbour, recently the subject of a magnificent edition and commentary by J. T. Peña. The *ostraca* all seem to date to the year 373 and form two distinct groups, one concerned with the receipt and inspection of olive oil shipments sent to Carthage, and the other concerned with the weighing and storage of oil to be exported from Carthage as part of the region's tax levies. The *ostraca* were made from locally produced amphorae and most were cut to a fairly standard size and shape, with the result both that the sherds could be held firmly in the palm of one hand and that they could be easily archived.[59] These *ostraca* provide a vivid glimpse of the mundane bureaucratic functioning of the late Roman state. The group concerned with the receipt of oil shipments for the most part give the date, the name of the shipmaster or the owner of the vessel delivering the oil, and the amount of oil accepted and rejected, all on one side of the sherd; on the other side, much the same information is provided in more summary form, though with the addition of the name and title of the official receiving the oil shipment. The group of *ostraca* concerned with the weighing and storage of oil to be exported similarly provide (with some variation) the date, the names of oil-weighers and amounts of weighed oil, the aggregate sum of these figures, plus a 'to do' (*fieri*) list with estimates of further quantities of oil. As with the records of delinquent taxes that Valentinian I ordered to be drawn up, copies of these records (or a summary of them) were presumably sent to the appropriate imperial authorities.[60]

## Shaping African documentary practice

The heavy reliance of the late Roman administration and its successors on written records probably shaped African documentary practice in a

[57] Merlin, in *BCTH* (1913), ccxxxi (no. 1): 'pc dd nn honorio xii / et theudosio octies / xvi kal aug aurel . . . / et iu..ntes sasucthani / constitui estinasse ex pre/tium olei quod uendes / perienslume folles / mille octingentas tnt. es (?) / estum pitacium / emisi'.

[58] Jones, *Later Roman Empire*, 429–30, 825–6. Rural markets in North Africa: B. Shaw, 'Rural Markets in North Africa and the Political Economy of the Roman Empire', *Antiquités africaines*, 17 (1981), 37–83; L. de Ligt, *Fairs and Markets in the Roman Empire: Economic and Social Aspects of Periodic Trade in a Pre-Industrial Society* (Amsterdam, 1993), 119–22, 134–5, 155–96; D. Kehoe, *Investment, Profit, and Tenancy: The Jurists and the Roman Agrarian Economy* (Ann Arbor, MI, 1997), 209–13.

[59] Peña, 'Mobilization of State Oil', 120–2, 128, 130.

[60] Peña, 'Mobilization of State Oil', 122–52.

number of important ways. Local African aristocrats pursued careers in service to the imperial and, later, Vandal regimes; and though we have less evidence for the Byzantine period, it seems likely that at least the lower-level functionaries who staffed the administration were generally of local origins.[61] Thus, as Peter Sarris has argued for Egypt, the language and techniques of the bureaucracy will also have provided high-status Africans with their most natural means of expression. As a result, in Africa, too, it can be difficult to distinguish in the surviving sources between 'public' and 'private' documents. For example, an early Byzantine-era *ostracon* from Négrine, Algeria, reads:

*anno XVI domni / nostri iustiniani in/peratori extima/tus fuit laudeti in / portione dominica / oliariu arcariu / unu tantum.*[62]

In the year 16 of our lord emperor Justinian [AD 542×3] one oil *arcarius* only was assessed at *Laudeti* on the lord's portion *(in portione dominica)*.

The text thus records the assessment of oil on the *portio dominica* of a local estate. This reference to assessment might suggest that the document is a tax receipt, but to judge from the *ostracon*'s dating formula it is probably not an official document. The Négrine text is dated according to Justinian's regnal year only; but in 537, five years before this record was composed, the emperor had mandated that documents also be dated according to the consular year, indiction, month and day.[63] To be sure, the choice of a small (but carefully manufactured) 5.5-cm-wide *ostracon* and the decision to write the text of the Négrine document without abbreviations made the inclusion of the other imperially mandated dating elements impractical; but these same decisions probably also imply that this document was private in character.

It is worth emphasizing, however, that the production and use of documents was hardly the exclusive preserve of the administrative elite. Indeed, the physical act of writing was not a high-class pursuit in the later Roman world.[64] The scribes who drew up the surviving African documents engaged in a diverse array of professions, and though some of them probably figured among the notables of their local communities, none appear to have been of particularly elite status. Between nine and eleven writers produced the Albertini Tablets. They included the local priest, Saturninus, as well as two *magistri*, probably local schoolteachers – both of them humble occupations in the later Roman

[61] M. Overbeck, *Untersuchungen zum afrikanischen Senatsadel in der Spätantike* (Kallmunz, 1973), 23–40, 55–74, 83–8.
[62] Albertini, 'Ostrakon byzantin de Négrine', 54, with commentary at 54–8.
[63] *J.Nov.* 47.1. [64] Jones, *Later Roman Empire*, 515.

countryside.[65] A fourth scribe, named Donatianus, identified himself simply as a 'citizen' (*cibis*) of Cappraria, probably another estate neighbouring the Fundus Tuletianos. Together with a certain Saturninus, this Donatianus was the co-owner of a 6-year-old slave boy, who was sold to Geminius Felix, 'citizen of Tuletianos' (*cibis tuletianensis*), on 5 June 494.[66] Yet another of the scribes, Paul, was at least a moderately well-off smallholder whom we meet selling a plot of fifteen olive and fifteen fig trees.[67] The remaining writers are, at best, little more than names to us. The scribes who wrote up the contemporary Bir Trouch *ostraca* are not even that. The *Massiese* that they mention seems not to have drawn up these documents himself, though, or at least not all of them. Indeed, these five *ostraca* appear to have been written by five different scribes: though the writing on all of the sherds is similar, no two texts seem to have been written by the same hand.[68] Significantly, at least two of these scribes were active in the same year.[69] The responsibility for drawing up texts of this sort would thus appear to have been shared between numerous writers, presumably estate officials of some sort. The Jerba *ostraca*, too, seem to have been written up by numerous different scribes, though these texts otherwise betray little about those who wrote them up.[70] Soldiers also show up as writers in a number of cases. In the third century Roman military recruiters in Africa appear to have kept written lists of recruits, and the fourth-century Admiralty Island *ostraca* seem to have been drawn up by individuals with military training.[71] The same, of course, was true of the voluminous daily reports, lists and letters produced at local garrisons like that at Bu Njem – despite some of the Punic-speaking recruits' apparently low levels of literacy and imperfect command of the Latin language.[72]

[65] See Conant, 'Literacy and Private Documentation', 203–4, 223–4, but also L. Dossey, *Peasant and Empire in Christian North Africa* (Berkeley, CA, 2010), 260n153 (on *magister* as 'schoolmaster'). Status of rural priests and schoolteachers: Jones, *Later Roman Empire*, 908–9, 997.

[66] *TA* II, 1:217; the name is common in Africa, but he could conceivably be the same Donatianus who had a field on the Fundus Tuletianos: *TA* XXIV, 1:283.

[67] *TA* XXVI, 1:288.

[68] Bonnal and Février, 'Ostraka de Bir Trouch', 246.

[69] Bonnal and Février, 'Ostraka de Bir Trouch', 239–42 (nos. 1–2).

[70] Várhelyi and Bagnall, 'Ostraka', 341, 343.

[71] *Passio S. Maximiliani* 3 (ed. Siniscalco, 160): 'Sterne nomen eius'; J. Godfrey, 'Who Wrote the Ostraka from the Ilôt de l'Amirauté, Carthage?', in Merrills (ed.), *Vandals, Romans, and Berbers*, 181–98.

[72] R. Marichal, *Les* ostraca *de Bu Njem* (Tripoli, 1992), with J. N. Adams, 'Latin and Punic in Contact? The Case of the Bu Njem Ostraca', *Journal of Roman Studies*, 84 (1994), 87–112, and, in general, Adams, *Bilingualism and the Latin Language* (Cambridge, 2003), 213–30; however, see also Adams, 'The Poets of Bu Njem: Language, Culture, and the Centurionate', *Journal of Roman Studies*, 89 (1999), 109–34.

The individuals who used the documents that these scribes produced also appear to have represented a wide range of social statuses. Our best evidence naturally concerns the more prosperous elements of late antique society. These would include the merchants for whom the Jerba *ostraca* were produced. The *Massiese* from the Bir Trouch *ostraca* may well himself have been an estate owner, and, as we have seen, the Severus to whom a southern Tunisian *ostracon* was addressed was a *conductor.*[73] The Albertini Tablets similarly seem to preserve what remains either of an estate archive or of the private dossier of Geminius Felix and his family; the Geminii may have run the Fundus Tuletianos, and in any case they were likely kinsmen of the estate's owner, the civic priest Flavius Geminus Catulinus.[74] However, the use of documents also seems to have extended deeper into society than these relatively elevated examples would suggest. The peasant cultivators of the Fundus Tuletianos certainly appear to have been familiar, even comfortable, with the culture of written documentation that surrounded them. In addition to the nine or more scribes that the community produced, at least four of the twenty-five men who sold land or other property in this community were able to sign a document with an autograph formula indicating that a sale had taken place and that the selling price had exchanged hands. This is not a high number, in either absolute or proportional terms; but in the same area, twenty-four local witnesses could be found to authenticate such a document in their own hands.[75] Moreover, if the Albertini Tablets constituted a family rather than an estate archive, then there may also be some slight evidence to suggest that both buyers and sellers of property received a copy of the deed of sale: a number of these *instrumenta* are palimpsests, and in one or two cases documents in which one of the Geminius brothers was a seller were scraped down and reused to draw up acts in which another of the brothers was the buyer.[76] In this case, the Albertini Tablets may simply have been the most extensive (and best preserved) of dozens of similar dossiers maintained in the Djebel Mrata region by estate owners, managers and tenants alike.

Thus, service in the imperial (or royal) civil administration was only one of the many factors that will have shaped documentary practices

[73] *Massiese:* Wickham, *Framing*, 266. Severus: see above, n. 6.

[74] D. J. Mattingly, 'Olive Cultivation and the Albertini Tablets', in Attilio Mastino (ed.), *L'Africa romana: Atti del VI convegno di studio* (Sassari, 1989), 403–15, at 404.

[75] Conant, 'Literacy and Private Documentation', 203–10.

[76] *TA*, tablets 1a and 18a, 1:215, 245, where the position of the names near the beginning of the act suggests that they were sellers, not buyers. Brothers: Cresconius and Felix were both sons of Fortunus: *TA*, XV, 1:266 (Cresconius); *TA* II, III, XXIX, XXXI, 1:217, 218, 293, 295 (Felix).

in late antique North Africa. Military service was another; interaction with officialdom and its expectations of written documentation was a third. As Wickham has pointed out with respect to the late Roman West in general, it seems likely that 'the main stimulus, and model, for private accounting was always the record-keeping that taxation depended upon'.[77] It is worth pointing out, though, that African officials imposed other documentary expectations on their region's inhabitants as well. As part of the Vandal kings' efforts to secure the conversion to Arianism of their kingdom's Catholic subjects, for example, those Africans who consented to be rebaptized were issued with written certificates attesting to their actions. These documents functioned as passports that allowed their bearers to travel without molestation within the territory of the Vandal kingdom. By contrast, those who refused rebaptism and thus lacked the appropriate certificate were by necessity forced to avoid the public roads in their movements; if they were discovered, they could be subjected to beatings and other indignities.[78]

Finally, the production, keeping and use of documents in Africa were probably encouraged by the region's legal culture. An inscription from Timgad (mod. Thamugadi, Algeria) dating to the reign of the emperor Julian (360–3) sets out the schedule of fees that local litigants could expect to pay to court stenographers, among other officials, in pursuit of their cases. The fees included 5 *modii* of wheat (or the equivalent) to draw up a formal legal claim (*postulatio simplex*); 12 for the presentation of the litigant's case in court (*contradictio*); and 20 for a 'finished case' (*definita causa*), which presumably included a transcript of the argument as well as the final judgement. Litigants also had to pay for the papyrus (*carta*) used to write up these documents, and in order to limit expenses the quantities were restricted to one large roll for the *postulatio simplex*, four for the *condradictio* and six for the *definita causa*.[79] Moreover, as was increasingly the case throughout the later Roman world, written documentation could also be entered into evidence in the course of a trial or official hearing in Africa.[80] At the centurion Marcellus' trial during the reign of Diocletian, for example, a letter from his regimental commander was read out detailing the officer's refusal (as a Christian) to continue

77 Wickham, *Framing*, 268.

78 Victor of Vita, *Historia persecutionis* 3.47 (CSEL 7:95); Ferrandus, *Vita Fulgentii* 6 (ed. Lapeyre, 35–9).

79 *CIL* VIII 17896; Jones, *Later Roman Empire*, 497; A. Chastagnol, *L'album municipal de Timgad* (Bonn, 1978); J. Harries, *Law and Empire in Late Antiquity* (Cambridge, 1999), 100; C. Kelly, *Ruling the Later Roman Empire* (Cambridge, MA, 2004), 138–42.

80 Harries, *Law and Empire*, 108–9.

serving in the Roman army.[81] At a hearing in 320 before an official named Zenophilus, no fewer than seven letters were read out as evidence, as were the formal records (*acta*) of an earlier enquiry held before the *curator* of Cirta (mod. Constantine, Algeria).[82] The *acta* of another case, this one tried in Carthage in 314, were read out at the legal proceedings that vindicated Bishop Felix of Aptunga of the charge of having been a *traditor* during the Great Persecution.[83] Of course, such written documents could also be doctored, as – under threat of torture – a certain clerk by the name of Ingentius admitted to having done to these very *acta*.[84] The comment of a Catholic advocate named Apronianus, who was present for Ingentius' confession, suggests that altering official documents was a familiar problem in early fourth-century Africa. 'It is not new to do this,' he remarked – adding, as a barb, 'for them,' by which he meant Donatists and their supporters.[85] Apronianus was scoring a rhetorical point in what was both a legal and a sectarian debate; but given the persistent fear of forgery that we encounter in Late Antiquity, his allegation may not have been entirely unfounded.[86]

## Record-keeping and archives

If public records could not entirely be trusted, Africans may have considered it all the more essential to retain their own copies of documents that they deemed to be particularly valuable. It is worth stressing that these never seem to have been the only kinds of documents generated in the region: even as late as the mid seventh century, for example, we hear of an African who 'wrote down on a leaf of parchment' ('*egrapsen en chartēi*') the directions that people gave him to a particular church that he wanted to visit in Constantinople.[87] However, the *ostraca* and wooden tablets that survive to us from late antique Africa seem for the most part to involve either substantial amounts of money or property of some significance. Though individual acts in the Albertini Tablets could involve fairly small-scale transactions, the surviving assemblage as a whole establishes title to 178 olive, 61 fig, 4 almond and 2 pistachio trees; an olive press; a dowry worth at least 750 olive trees and a slave worth another

81 *Passio s. Marcelli Tingitani* 4–6 (ed. Delehaye, 262 [M] and 265 [N]).
82 *Gesta apud Zenophilum* (CSEL 26:186–8, 189–92).
83 *Acta purgationis Felicis episcopi Autumnitani* (CSEL 26:199–200).
84 *Acta purgationis Felicis episcopi Autumnitani* (CSEL 26:203).
85 *Acta purgationis Felicis episcopi Autumnitani* (CSEL 26:203): 'nec nouum est illis hoc facere'.
86 See above, nn. 44–6, and also *CJ* 4.21.20.
87 *Miracles of St Artemios* 4 (ed. and trans. V. S. Crisafulli and J. W. Nesbitt [Leiden, 1997], 82–4).

65.[88] To judge from a table of calculations jotted down on the back of one of the extant acts, other now-lost tablets once existed that recorded purchases of another 3 *solidi*, 3,155 *folles* worth of property, or, in real terms, the equivalent of between 262 and 290 additional olive trees.[89] By contrast, D. J. Mattingly notes that 'the vast majority of modern Tunisian peasant families specialising in olive cultivation has owned between only 20 and 100 olive trees'.[90] It is harder to assess the value of the barley mentioned in the Bir Trouch *ostraca*, though the quantities involved varied widely from year to year: in 485×6, for example, the holding at *Viginti Boguli* yielded 26 measures, but seven years later it produced only 3.[91] At 1,800 *folles*, however, the Ksar Koutine *ostracon* (which probably records a customs payment on olive oil to be sold at an early fifth-century town or rural market) also involved a considerable sum. Though the value of the *follis* was severely undermined by the inflation of the bronze coinage over the course of the fourth and fifth centuries, in early fifth-century Africa 1,800 *folles* would perhaps have been the equivalent of a little over 1 gold *solidus*.[92] If the text does represent a customs payment, and if that payment was levied at the canonical rate of 2 to 2½ per cent, then the total value of the oil to be sold may have been as much as 90,000 *folles*, or upwards of 50 *solidi*.[93] In this case, the figures involved would doubtless have made the chitty valuable enough for the vendor to retain, at least for a time.

Of course, valuable documents – both private and public – needed to be stored somewhere. Most institutions in Africa appear to have maintained their own files in archives of one sort or another. The African countryside was peppered with municipalities of widely varying sizes, and, as we have seen, major ones (at least) like Carthage, Cirta and Timgad maintained records of their official acts. Augustine clearly had access to such *gesta municipalia*, and he assumed that his adversaries did as well.[94] The bishop of Hippo also makes numerous references to public archives (*archiva publica*) in general, and to the proconsular archive (*archivum proconsulis* or *archiva proconsularia*) in particular. Such

[88] In the Tuletianos community, olive trees normally sold for about 15–16 *folles* each: Grierson, 'The *Tablettes Albertini*', 74. The slave Fortinus was sold for 1 *solidus*, 700 *folles* (*TA* II, 1:217); Januarilla's dowry was valued at 12,000 *folles* (*TA* I, 1:215).

[89] *TA*, XXXIII (tablet 29b), 1:299 written on the back of *TA* XV (tablet 29a), 1:267. The sum of 3 *solidi*, 3,155 *folles* does not include the sums from *TA* XXXIII lines 5–7, 10–11, 15, 19–20, or 22, which appear to record transactions recorded in the extant acts.

[90] Mattingly, 'Olive Cultivation', 407n19.

[91] Bonnal and Février, 'Ostraka de Bir Trouch', 239–41, 244–5 (nos. 1, 4).

[92] A. H. M. Jones, 'The Origin and Early History of the Follis', *Journal of Roman Studies*, 49 (1959), 34–8, esp. 37 for early fifth-century Africa.

[93] Jones, *Later Roman Empire*, 825.

[94] See above, n. 40.

repositories, he wrote, were full of Catholic protests against Donatists' acts of violence, and of course they also contained records of the accusations levied and court cases tried before the proconsul.[95] In addition, the public archive preserved Constantine's judgement in favour of the controversial appointment of Caecilian as bishop of Carthage.[96] At the conference at Carthage in 411, the Catholic bishops cited a report (*relatio*) from the proconsul Anulinus to the emperor Constantine dating to 313; when the Donatist bishop Petilianus asked whether it came from a public or private cache of documents, Augustine first tried to avoid the question, and then claimed that this text, too, could be found in the proconsular archive.[97] Elsewhere, when quoting part of the fourth-century decision of the proconsul Aelianus exonerating Felix of Aptunga of the charge of *traditio*, Augustine told his readers, 'If you want to read the whole *gesta*, get it from the archive of the proconsul.'[98] Thus, in addition to the province's tax accounts and the imperial edicts and rescripts sent to its leading officials, the state archives in late Roman Africa would appear to have contained copies of important communications sent to the emperor, records of court trials held before the proconsul and other legally significant documents. On the orders of Constantine, the latter were to include samples of illicit defamatory writings circulated in Africa, which the offices of the proconsul and the vicar were to keep on file.[99] In 414, three years after the disputation between the leading Catholic and Donatist bishops at Carthage, the emperor Honorius indicated in a rescript to the proconsul of Africa that the proceedings of that council were deemed to have permanent validity and that they, too, had been transferred to the public records (*publica monumenta*).[100]

In the centuries following the Vandal conquest, the impression that such public record-keeping leaves in our sources becomes fainter. In the midst of the Vandal king Huneric's persecution of the Catholics in 484, for example, a local bishop by the name of Habetdeum is said to have told his Arian tormenters that he had drawn up a *gesta* against them in his heart, which would seem to suggest that Africans continued to be familiar with the concept of transcribing judicial procedures.[101] Whether the

[95] Augustine, *Epistulae* 129.4 (CSEL 44:36–7); Augustine, *Contra Cresconium* 3.45.49, 3.61.67 (CSEL 52:455–6, 473–4).

[96] Augustine, *Contra partem Donati post gesta* 16.20 (CSEL 53:118–20).

[97] *Gesta conlationis Carthaginiensis* 3.216–20 (CCSL 149A:232–3); Augustine, *Breviculus conlationis cum Donatistis* 3.7.8 (CCSL 149A:276). Augustine cited the same *relatio* earlier in his letter to the Donatist bishop Januarius: *Epistulae* 88.2 (CSEL 34:408).

[98] Augustine, *Contra Cresconium* 3.70.80 (CSEL 52:485): 'si tota gesta uis legere, ex archiuo proconsulis accipe'.

[99] *CTh.* 9.34.2. [100] *CTh.* 16.5.55.

[101] Victor of Vita, *Historia persecutionis* 3.46 (CSEL 7:94–5).

practice continued to be characteristic of Vandal-era realities is less clear, though it seems plausible. To be sure, Habetdeum's claim, 'I have drawn up a *gesta* in the headquarters of my heart' (*in praetorio cordis... gesta confeci*), is likely to be a play on the widespread concept that one could bear beliefs or memories in that same organ (*in corde gestare*); but, perhaps significantly, the distinctive turn of phrase that the bishop was said to have employed does not appear to have been proverbial in late ancient Latin.[102] In either case, the old state archives likely continued to function for as long as the Vandals extracted taxes from their Roman subjects. Victor of Vita certainly had access to the texts of the only three Vandal royal laws that survive to us, though, of course, copies of these could just as well have been preserved in the archives of the Carthaginian Church.[103] More telling is the fact that the specific provisions of Huneric's edict of persecution were modelled on the western emperor Honorius' rescript of 412 ordering the suppression of Donatism. This strongly suggests that, over seventy years on, the bureaucrats who staffed the Vandal royal writing office not only continued to maintain old Roman imperial laws on file, but also were still able to access them when necessary.[104] In the Byzantine period, Justinian deplored the state of provincial archives in general, but at a minimum the newly reimposed fiscal regime would probably have required a functioning method of storing and retrieving tax records in Africa, and it is difficult to believe that the new flow of imperial rescripts to the province would not also have been preserved locally.[105]

The need to access important documents probably also meant that it was not unusual for private individuals to maintain personal or family dossiers in late antique North Africa. We have already seen that the proconsul Hymetius and the general Romanus kept private papers that

[102] *In corde gestare*: see, e.g., Augustine, *Enarrationes in psalmos* 34.2.8, 34.2.11, 51.11, 80.10, 88.1.7, 90.2.9 (CCSL 38:318, 319; CCSL 39:631, 1125, 1225, 1276); Augustine, *Sermo* 24.3, 199.1.2, 288.4 (CCSL 41:327; PL 38:1027, 1306). See also (*corde gestare*), e.g. Augustine, *De doctrina christiana* 1.13.12, 2.18.28 (CCSL 32:13, 53); Augustine, *De sermone domini in monte* 2.2.5 (CCSL 35:95); Augustine, *In Iohannis evangelium tractatus* 3.2 (CCSL 36:20); Augustine, *Sermo* 37.7, 62.1.1, 169.13.16, 187.3 (CCSL 41:454; PL 38:415, 925, 1002).

[103] Laws: Victor of Vita, *Historia persecutionis* 2.3–4, 2.39, 3.3–14 (CSEL 7:25, 39, 72–8). On African ecclesiastical archives: Augustine, *Breviculus collationis* 3.17.31–2 (CCSL 149A:296–7) and Augustine, *Contra partem Donati post gesta* 15.19 (CSEL 53:117). A single, much-abraded *ostracon* written in a fourth-century cursive found in the basilica at Skhira, Tunisia, may be the only document to survive from such an archive: M. Fendri, *Basiliques chrétiennes de la Skhira* (Paris, 1961), 56–7.

[104] Victor of Vita, *Historia persecutionis* 3.3–14 (CSEL 7:72–8); *CTh.* 16.5.52. On the symbolic importance of written law to early Germanic kingship, see P. Wormald, '*Lex scripta* and *verbum regis*: Legislation and Germanic Kingship, from Euric to Cnut', in P. H. Sawyer and I. N. Wood (eds.), *Early Medieval Kingship* (Leeds, 1977), 105–38.

[105] *J.Nov.* 15 praef.; see also 36–7 and App. 2, 3, 6, 9 (rescripts to Africa).

included their correspondence; the legislation of Valentinian III (425–55) assumed that fifth-century African landowners kept records detailing their property holdings, though the emperor also imagined that such documentation might have been lost or destroyed in the disorder of the Vandal invasion.[106] Nearly a century later, Justinian thought it entirely plausible that the descendants of African refugees living in the East might still have access to the documents they would need to prove their title to lands expropriated by the Vandals.[107] In Gigthis, four unedited *ostraca* have been found in a private house neighbouring on the forum, and they may well hint at a private archive that was once much larger.[108] As we have seen, the Albertini Tablets and the Bir Trouch *ostraca* would seem to represent portions, at least, of similar assemblages. The latter two collections also provide valuable evidence that, in times of disorder, Africans did what they could to protect their documents: both the *ostraca* and the tablets were found in earthenware jars, where they had presumably been stashed for safe keeping.[109] At least, the presence of dorsal notes on the Albertini Tablets, summarizing the acts contained on the polyptychs' interior faces, would seem to suggest that these documents were not normally kept in a pot.[110]

Barring disorder, documents could be maintained for wildly variable periods of time. Even when the later Roman emperors remitted tax arrears, they continued to lay claim to what was owed the state from on average the previous five or six years, suggesting that the fiscal authorities generally maintained good records for at least that long.[111] These general numbers correspond well with the specifically African evidence: in 410 the western emperor Honorius remitted all delinquent taxes for the region down to 405, and in 414 he forgave African *navicularii* what they owed down to 409.[112] As was often the case in instances of this sort, Honorius' rescript of 410 also ordered the destruction of old *chartae* rendered obsolete by his remission.[113] Similarly, neither of our two datable collections of private records from late antique Africa suggests that such documents were preserved for more than a decade. As we have seen, some of the Albertini Tablets were scraped down and reused in as little as two years, and the extant assemblage as a whole spans only the three

106 Valentinian III, *Nov.* 12, esp. 12.2.
107 *J.Nov.* 36.1. 108 P. Gauckler, in *BCTH* (1903), ccvi.
109 Bonnal and Février, 'Ostraka de Bir Trouch', 239.
110 Conant, 'Literacy and Private Documentation', 215.
111 *CTh.* 11.28.3, 9, 16; Marcian, *Nov.* 2; Valentinian III, *Nov.* 1.1, 3; Maiorian, *Nov.* 2; *J.Nov.* 147.1, 148.1; and Jones, *Later Roman Empire*, 467.
112 *CTh.* 11.28.6, 8. 113 *CTh.* 11.28.6; see also (in general) *CTh.* 11.28.2, 3, 14.

years between 13 March 493 and 21 April 496.[114] The Bir Trouch *ostraca* collectively cover only eight years.[115] On the other hand, it would seem that at least some privately held documents could enjoy a considerably longer life: a rescript of Honorius addressed to the praetorian prefect of Africa tried to put an end to lawsuits against shipmasters based on 50-year-old documents.[116]

Finally, in late antique Africa, writing of a different sort was also often on what was probably intended to be undying public display. In the late Roman period, the Christian emperors imagined that their written edicts – especially those on the unity of the faith – would be posted in prominent, heavily frequented places throughout the African provinces.[117] In the immediate wake of the Byzantine reconquest of Africa, new or restored fortifications were dedicated with inscriptions in both Latin and Greek. Both such uses of writing served to project imperial power; the bilingual military inscriptions also made a potent statement about the permanence of Justinian's reintegration of Africa into the Roman *respublica*.[118]

Even before the Byzantine reconquest, though, late antique Africa had been enormously productive of inscriptions. After Rome itself, more inscriptions survive from Carthage than from any other city in the West; indeed, the African metropolis alone has preserved nearly as many inscriptions as has the whole of Gaul. Provincial towns such as Hadrumetum (mod. Sousse, Tunisia), Ammaedara (mod. Haïdra, Tunisia) and Altava (mod. Ouled Mimoun, ex-Lamoricière, Algeria) also produced epigraphic corpora whose surviving elements run into the hundreds.[119]

114 Scraped down: see above, n. 76, and in general Conant, 'Literacy and Private Documentation', 212–13. Earliest act: *TA* XVI, 1:269 (13 March 493). Latest act: *TA* XXIV, 1:283 (21 April 496).

115 The earliest dates to Gunthamund's second regnal year; the latest two, to his ninth: Bonnal and Février, 'Ostraka de Bir Trouch', 239–42, 244–5 (nos. 1–2, 4).

116 *CTh.* 13.6.10.

117 *CTh.* 16.5.37, 16.11.2. That few survive has to do with the fact that texts of this sort were generally inscribed in bronze, much of which was subsequently melted down: e.g. S. Hornblower and A. Spawforth (eds.), *The Oxford Classical Dictionary*, 3rd edn (Oxford, 1996), s.n. 'epigraphy, Latin' (at p. 544); G. Woolf, 'Literacy', in A. K. Bowman, P. Garnsey and D. Rathbone (eds.), *The Cambridge Ancient History. XI. The High Empire, A.D. 70–192* (Cambridge, 2000), 875–97, at 886–7.

118 J. Durliat, *Les dédicaces d'ouvrages de défense dans l'Afrique byzantine* (Rome, 1981), 7–91; D. Pringle, *The Defence of Byzantine Africa from Justinian to the Arab Conquest: An Account of the Military History and Archaeology of the African Provinces in the Sixth and Seventh Centuries* (Oxford, 1981; repr. 2001), 315–32.

119 M. A. Handley, *Death, Society, and Culture: Inscriptions and Epitaphs from Gaul and Spain, AD 300–750* (Oxford, 2003), 18. See, however, R. Duncan-Jones, *The Economy of the Roman Empire: Quantitative Studies*, 2nd edn (Cambridge, 1982), 360–2, on the rate of inscription survival.

Many of these inscriptions are epitaphs commemorating secular members of the regional elite: men and women of senatorial status, lawyers, doctors, goldsmiths, ships' captains and other local notables and their families.[120] Such inscriptions are revealing of the documentary culture of Africa in two particular ways. First, occasional mistakes – like that in an epitaph from Hippo Regius which reads, 'here lies the body of the boy (to be named)' *Hic iacet corpus pueri nominandi* – would seem to indicate that funerary inscriptions were produced by workshops working from model books.[121] Second, such inscriptions indicate the importance with which prominent secular families continued to regard the commemoration of their beloved departed in writing. This public display does not necessarily imply anything about the ability of African provincials, either individually or collectively, to read or write; but it does say something meaningful about the ways in which the written word was used to express power, authority, social prominence and a sense of imperial and family permanence in Africa, and indeed throughout the late Roman world.

## Conclusions

Of course, Africa, like the eastern Mediterranean, is something of a special case. Here, too – in marked contrast to the situation in much of the early medieval West – a bureaucratic class survived down to *c.* 700, and on the face of it, it seems likely that the strength of Africa's documentary culture owed something to this survival. Yet the very contrast between Africa and the north-western Mediterranean (let alone north-western Europe) raises two closely related questions about developments in documentary practice in the early medieval West in general. First, Africans made use of the written word to record a remarkable array of social activities. These included estate management and bookkeeping; the sale, gift and endowment of property; the entering into and discharging of debt; paying taxes; appealing to the emperor; contracting marriages, recording rebaptisms and choosing epitaphs; pursuing legal claims; recommending protégés to official appointments; and getting directions. A Byzantine-era inscription from the military installation at Thabraca (mod. Tabarka, Tunisia) even reserves a horse for the use of a certain Michael, a courier of the *cursus publicus*.[122] What is more, Punic appears to have been used

120 Handley, *Death*, 37. Lawyers: G. Charles-Picard, in *BCTH* (1950), 74–89, at 88 (= *Revue archéologique*, 6th ser. 37 [1951], 173–4 [no. 45]); *CIL* VIII 25837 (= *Inscriptiones Latinae selectae*, ed. H. Dessau, 3 vols. [Berlin, 1892–1916], 2.1:414 (no. 5731]).

121 *Revue archéologique*, 4th ser., 34 (1931), 367 (no. 112); Handley, *Death*, 26.

122 Pringle, *Defence*, 338 (no. 56), with discussion at 230–1.

alongside Latin in the third-century Bu Njem *ostraca*, and the language was also employed in *ostraca* from Silin and Wadi el-Amud in Libya as well as from Henchir Khanefi, on the borderlands south-west of Gabès, Tunisia. Punic was also used as an epigraphic language in late antique Tripolitania, as, for example, in the fourth-century Christian catacombs at Sirte.[123] This, in turn, would seem to suggest that a culture of written documentation had penetrated African society to such an extent that it had even transcended the most 'Romanized', Latin-speaking segments of the population in Late Antiquity. Indeed, recourse to written instruments was so deeply embedded in local society that, as late as the 490s, it is still discernible at a range of social levels, from the wealthy elite to the prosperous rural peasantry. The use of documents, in other words, appears to have been all-pervasive in late antique North Africa – which raises the question of whether the same was true elsewhere in the West.

Second, Africa's documentary culture was underlain and probably strengthened by the practices of the late Roman state and its successors, which required or assumed the use of the written word not only at the highest levels of the civil administration, but also in the army, in the courts and – critically – in the extraction of taxes. This culture was thus built on complex foundations whose component parts reinforced one another, with the result that the edifice as a whole could probably survive the weakening of one or another individual element, at least for a time. Just how long is not completely clear, but references to the indiction in the Négrine and Henchir el Abiod *ostraca* show that on some level the use of documents in estate management survived in Africa into the Byzantine period.[124] The fact that the imperial collection of taxes continued in this region well into the seventh century – and in fact seems to have intensified late in the reign of the emperor Constans II (641–68) – probably provided African landowners with an incentive to document how much produce they got out of their estates all the way

123 Marichal, Ostraca *de Bu Njem*, no. 146, with Adams, 'Latin and Punic', 88–9; P. Berger and P. Gauckler, in *BCTH* (1902), clxxvi; R. Bartoccini, 'Scavi e rinvenimenti in Tripolitania negli anni 1926–1927', *Africa italiana*, 2 (1928), 187–200, with K. Jongeling and R. M. Kerr (eds.), *Late Punic Epigraphy: An Introduction to the Study of Neo-Punic and Latino-Punic Inscriptions* (Tübingen, 2005), 71–4 (Sirte) and, in general, 105–6. The most important collections of late Punic inscriptions include R. G. Goodchild, 'La necropoli Romano-Libica di Bir ed-Dréder', *Quaderni di archeologia della Libia*, 3 (1954), 91–107; F. Vattioni, 'Glosse Puniche', *Augustinianum*, 16 (1976), 505–55, at 536–55; and the material cited in J. M. Reynolds and J. B. Ward-Perkins, *Inscriptions of Roman Tripolitania* (Rome, 1952), 10–13.

124 Albertini, 'Ostrakon byzantin de Négrine', 54; Cagnat, *BCTH* (1908), ccxlviii.

down to the Islamic conquest.[125] Yet, without the fiscal, administrative, military and legal imperatives of the late Roman state, a culture of written documentation is likely to have survived in the West only for as long as merchants, property owners, soldiers, litigants and possibly even rural tenants found it to be useful. How long that was will be the subject of the rest of this book.

125 Collection of taxes in seventh-century Africa: see above n. 55; M. McCormick, *Origins of the European Economy: Communications and Commerce, A.D. 300–900* (Cambridge, 2001), 102.

# 4 Lay documents and archives in early medieval Spain and Italy, *c*. 400–700

*Nicholas Everett*

*Late Roman governmental institutions and imperatives had a profound impact on documentary culture in the West, as well as on the nature of our evidence. Changes in these institutions and imperatives – driven to a large degree by fiscal needs but also by changes in the nature of the empire itself – made documents more important and encouraged their use by individuals both lay and clerical. The traces left by these developments can be seen particularly well in late and post-Roman Italy and Spain, where the legal and documentary inheritance of the late Roman Empire, adapted to meet local conditions, remains visible at all levels of society. Visigothic Spain demonstrates how late Roman legal imperatives concerning documents were adopted and developed in a barbarian kingdom, as well as providing a model for reckoning with our loss of surviving evidence elsewhere. Surviving papyri from Ravenna show how barbarians and Romans cultivated documentary norms and rituals, such as registration in municipal archives, quite beyond the requirements of Roman law; they also reflect, however, immediate political circumstances and the growth of a powerful church whose interests had become intertwined with those of secular government.*

## From late Roman diocese to barbarian kingdom

The peninsulas of Spain and Italy, under Roman rule since the Second Punic War, shared the similar fate in Late Antiquity of two highly urbanized Roman dioceses, once central to Rome's imperial power, that fell to rule by barbarian peoples in the fifth century. Undeniably, the demise of the Roman Empire in these regions was a blow to governmental use of documents, and to the literate traditions that supported it: a liberal arts education focused on rhetoric, and a bureaucracy to facilitate communication across a vast stretch of territory. But at the level of individual laypeople, developments in late Roman law had increased the importance and frequency of documents for private transactions. The barbarian governments of Spain and Italy were direct heirs of legal traditions that privileged writing as a form of proof, and made it mandatory to exercise juridical authority. That 'barbarian' governments in Spain and Italy embraced the legal traditions of the late empire, and developed them to suit their more regionally compact kingdoms, certainly upsets our conventional picture of the 'fall of Rome' and 'barbarian invasions'. But neither the history of literacy, nor of technology (in this case, writing), need subscribe to periodizations based on value-laden views of political change. Instead, the rich evidence of the use of documents in barbarian Spain and Italy demonstrates that documents continued to be valued as a superior form of proof for claims to title, and as a source of authority, whatever their format: whether written out by a professional scribe on papyrus, by a friend on parchment, or by a neighbour scratched onto slate.

In examining the use of documents at this level of private transactions, this chapter focuses on certain issues raised by the evidence, rather than attempting to survey it. For these issues go to the heart of understanding how the end of the Western Roman Empire affected documentation in post-Roman Europe, and may serve as historical background for many of the later chapters in this volume. The word 'may' is operative here, as the arguments put forward here are not ones with which all historians of the period would agree, and stem from research on the issue of literacy, which often provides a different perspective from, say, legal or economic history. These arguments are best signalled here and now, and reflect the order of the discussion.

Firstly, I argue that changes in late Roman law increased the importance of writing, as proof to claims, and as part of court procedure, a development buoyed by political and cultural developments, such as the expansion of late Roman bureaucracy and the conversion to a religion of the book. Our two peninsulas under barbarian rule were direct heirs of late Roman legal culture, and subsequently inherited the emphasis upon written proofs and the use of documents in courts of law.

Secondly, the evidence of the papyri of Ravenna is discussed with a particular focus on the registration of documents in municipal archives (known as *gesta municipalia*), for Ravenna provides us with the only surviving examples of this practice. It is argued that *gesta municipalia* were a short-lived creation of the late Roman state for fiscal purposes, and their survival in Ravenna reflects not only that city's role as an administrative capital but also the influence of a powerful metropolitan church that effectively functioned as an arm of the state. The *gesta municipalia*, and the registration of documents, are therefore something of a distraction for understanding wider currents of document production and preservation. If the Ravennate *gesta* provide any sort of model for understanding developments outside Ravenna, it is that of how churches engaged in registration as they merged with local *curiae* and assumed their functions, echoes of which are found in formula collections. Moreover, many of the *gesta* documents from Ravenna demonstrate peculiarities that reflect a particular historical context – that of a political capital, for both imperial and barbarian rulers, in a period of fundamental change and regional instability.

Thirdly, the discussion turns to the legislation of Visigothic Spain, and measures its copious references to documentary practices against the evidence of the *Formulae Visigothicae*, the few surviving scraps of parchment, and above all the extraordinary documents written on slate. It is argued that not only does such evidence dispel reasonable doubts about the applicability of Visigothic legislation on documents, but also that Visigothic legislation typifies the development of Roman law mentioned in the first section, and as such provides a model for how documents continued to be valued in post-Roman Europe.

Finally, to respect the chronology posted in the title and as a fitting conclusion, I shall briefly point to the main issues concerning the use of documents in seventh-century Lombard Italy.

In concentrating on private transactions between lay individuals, I leave out some subjects that might well be considered pertinent. State documents and archives are considered where relevant to issues raised by the papyri of Ravenna and Visigothic law; Cassiodorus' *Variae*, although a rich source for the production of state documents and chancery traditions in Ostrogothic Italy, is referred to only on occasion, as uncertainty surrounds the date of its contents and its publication. Similarly, the close alliance between the Church and the Visigothic monarchy in the seventh century meant that legislation in Church councils was also considered law, but I have not included that legislation here: it would not change the argument anyway. Finally, an aspect of ecclesiastical influence which affects all documentation in this period is the emphasis on the oath as a legal instrument and its effect on legal procedure, both in Roman and in barbarian law, but the subject is too large to tackle here, and awaits thorough treatment.[1]

[1] On the *Variae* (MGH AA 12:1–385), see: G. Vidéu, *The Roman Chancery Tradition: Studies in the Language of the Codex Theodosianus and Cassiodorus' Variae* (Gothenburg, 1984) (chancery traditions); R. Macpherson, *Rome in Involution: Cassiodorus' Variae and Their Literary and Historical Setting* (Poznań, 1989) (historical setting); A. Gillett, 'The Purposes of Cassiodorus' *Variae*', in A. C. Murray (ed.), *After Rome's Fall: Narrators and Sources of Early Medieval History: Essays Presented to Walter Goffart* (Toronto, 1998), 37–50 (publication). Visigothic councils: R. Stocking, *Bishops, Councils, and Consensus in the Visigothic Kingdom 589–633* (Ann Arbor, MI, 2000). Oaths: *Settlement of Disputes*; N. Everett, 'Diritto tardo romano e alfabetismo giuridico nell'Europa alto-medievale', in *Scrivere e leggere nell'alto medioevo*, Settimane 59 (Spoleto, 2012), 213–46; Everett,

## From tablets to charters and late Roman 'popular law'

The 'late antique' period (traditionally AD 285–632, from the emperor Diocletian to the death of the prophet Mohammad) witnessed a revolution in the use and importance of the written word which greatly affected legal documentation. The momentous changes behind this revolution encompassed ideological and practical developments which overlapped: a more centralized and more bureaucratic Roman Empire; its highly rhetorical education system that prized literary knowledge and convoluted literary expression as evidence of the right to rule; the dominance of a religion of the book; the shift from roll to codex, and from papyrus to parchment; and new forms of script and page layout that facilitated reading for a wider audience of less experienced readers.[2] Legal developments were an integral aspect of this revolution. The first, large collections of Roman law were compiled in this period, from the two privately commissioned codes under Diocletian (*c.* 290s), to the Theodosian Code (438) and Justinianic Code (529), plus a host of legal compilations comparing Roman, Greek and even Mosaic law. Born from aspirations of imperial unity, these collections primarily served the practical need to supply condensed and organized repositories of legal precepts in an accessible and

'Paulinus of Aquileia's *Sponsio episcoporum*: Written Oaths and Ecclesiastical Discipline in Carolingian Italy', in W. Robbins (ed.), *Textual Cultures of Medieval Italy* (Toronto, 2011), 167–216. There is still much in H. Brunner, *Zur Rechtsgeschichte der römischen und germanischen Urkunde.* I. *Die Privaturkunden Italiens; das angelsächsische Landbuch; die fränkische Privaturkunde* (Berlin, 1880).

2 For a survey of these developments, see N. Everett, 'Literacy from Late Antiquity to the Early Middle Ages', in D. Olson and N. Torrance (eds.), *Cambridge Handbook of Literacy* (Cambridge, 2009), 362–85. Education: R. A. Kaster, *Guardians of the Language: The Grammarians and Society in Late Antiquity* (Berkeley, CA, 1988); M. Irvine, *The Making of a Textual Culture: 'Grammatica' and Literary Theory, 350–1100* (Cambridge, 1994); R. Browning, 'Education in the Roman Empire', in A. Cameron, B. Ward-Perkins and M. Whitby (eds.), *The Cambridge Ancient History,* XIV, *Late Antiquity: Empire and Successors, A.D. 425–600* (Cambridge, 2000), 855–83; R. Cribiore, *Gymnastics of the Mind: Greek Education in Hellenistic and Roman Egypt* (Princeton, NJ, 2001); Cribiore, *The School of Libanius in Late Antique Antioch* (Princeton, NJ, 2007). Bureaucracy: H. C. Teitler, *Notarii and Exceptores: An Inquiry into the Role and Significance of Shorthand Writers in the Imperial and Ecclesiastical Bureaucracy of the Roman Empire from the Early Principate to c. 450 A.D.* (Amsterdam, 1985); C. M. Kelly, 'Later Roman Bureaucracy: Going Through the Files', in A. K. Bowman and G. Woolf (eds.), *Literacy and Power in the Ancient World* (Cambridge, 1994); C. M. Kelly, 'Emperors, Government and Bureaucracy', in A. Cameron and P. Garnsey (eds.), *The Cambridge Ancient History,* XIII, *The Late Empire, A.D. 337–425* (Cambridge, 1998), 138–88; C. M. Kelly, *Ruling the Later Roman Empire* (Cambridge, MA, 2004). Rhetoric: P. Brown, *Power and Persuasion in Late Antiquity: Towards a Christian Empire* (Madison, WI, 1992). Books: L. Hurtado, *The Earliest Christian Artifacts: Manuscripts and Christian Origins* (Grand Rapids, MI, 2006); A. Grafton and M. Williams, *Christianity and the Transformation of the Book* (Cambridge, MA, 2006); W. Klingshirn and L. Safran (eds.), *The Early Christian Book* (Washington, DC, 2007).

reference-ready format: parallel developments can be witnessed in other fields of literature, including history, medicine and, of course, religion, wherein careful scrutiny of texts and debate over their meaning formed the basis for formulating and establishing orthodoxy.[3]

But another motive for the legal compilation was the need to define exactly what was Roman law in the aftermath of Caracalla's Antonine Constitution of 212, which extended Roman citizenship and, as a consequence, the application of Roman law to all inhabitants of the empire.[4] The explosion of juristic activity that resulted grappled with an influx of new ideas and concepts from provincial legal practices, which often could not be reconciled with the subtleties and distinctions of classical Roman law, nor with its requisite formal and ceremonial niceties. This process has been distastefully labelled the 'vulgarization' of Roman law, particularly in regard to property law, though 'popularization' is perhaps the better term.[5] But it was precisely this 'vulgar'/'popular' Roman property

[3] Codification: J. Matthews, *Laying Down the Law: A Study of the Theodosian Code* (New Haven, CT, 2000); A. D. Lee, 'Decoding Late Roman Law', *Journal of Roman Studies*, 92 (2002), 185–93; C. Humfress, 'Judging by the Book: Christian Codices and Late Antique Legal Culture', in Klingshirn and Safran (eds.), *The Early Christian Book*, 141–58. Religious texts: B. D. Ehrmann, *The Orthodox Corruption of Scripture: The Effect of Early Christological Controversies on the Text of the New Testament* (New York, 1993); K. Haines-Eitzen, *Guardians of Letters: Literacy, Power and the Transmitters of Early Christian Literature* (Oxford, 2000). History: G. B. Greatrex, 'Lawyers and Historians in Late Antiquity', in R. Mathisen (ed.), *Law, Society and Authority in Late Antiquity* (Oxford, 2001), 148–61. Medicine: V. Nutton, *Ancient Medicine* (London, 2004), 292–309; N. Everett, *The Alphabet of Galen: Pharmacy from Antiquity to the Middle Ages* (Toronto, 2011).

[4] On the (fragmentary) text: A. Lukaszewicz, 'Zum Papyrus Gissensis 40 I 9 (*Constitutio Antoniana*)', *Journal of Juristic Papyrology*, 20 (1990), 93–101. Effect: P. Garnsey, 'Roman Citizenship and Roman Law in the Later Empire', in S. Swain and M. Edwards (eds.), *Approaching Late Antiquity: The Transformation from Early to Later Empire* (Oxford, 2004), 133–55, and, for a revisionist account, R. Mathisen, '*Peregrini*, *Barbari*, and *Cives Romani*: Concepts of Citizenship and the Legal Identity of Barbarians in the Later Roman Empire', *American Historical Review*, 111 (2006), 1011–40.

[5] The term 'vulgar law' was first coined by Brunner, *Zur Rechtsgeschichte*, 113–19, but the concept was fully articulated by E. Levy: *West Roman Vulgar Law: The Law of Property* (Philadelphia, 1951); *Pauli sententiae: A Palingenesia of the Opening Titles as a Specimen of Research in West Roman Vulgar Law* (Ithaca, NY, 1945); 'Vulgarization of Roman Law in the Early Middle Ages', *Mediaevalia et Humanistica*, 1 (1963), 14–40. A different interpretation was offered by F. Wieacker, *Vulgarismus und Klassizismus im Recht der Spätantike* (Heidelberg, 1955). The concept of 'vulgar law' has been heavily criticized by Tony Honoré ('Conveyances of Land and Professional Standards in the Later Empire', in P. Birks (ed.), *New Perspectives in the Roman Law of Property: Essays for Barry Nicholas* (Oxford, 1989), 137–52, at 151; 'Roman Law 200–400: From Cosmopolis to Rechtsstaat?', in Swain and Edwards (eds.), *Approaching Late Antiquity*, 109–32), but it is still a useful concept. Overview of debates and implications for post-Roman law: J. B. Sirks, 'Shifting Frontiers in the Law: Romans, Provincials and Barbarians', in R. Mathisen and H. Sivan (eds.), *Shifting Frontiers in Late Antiquity* (Aldershot, 1996), 146–57; cf. T. Charles-Edwards, 'Law in the Western Kingdoms Between the Fifth and

law that was transmitted to the barbarian kingdoms of Spain and Italy as the basis of their own property law, and in particular the treatment of documents as legal instruments. Leaving aside the complicated shifts in legal theory associated with this vulgarized Roman law, one practical aspect of the change was clear: writing – and documentation – became more important than it had been in classical law – as proof, as testimony to correct procedure followed, and as a source of authority. This is particularly true for the courts, as is clear from Constantine's decree (320) that all accusations now had to be in writing, and a later decree of 374 which mandated that all judges 'in the provinces' must read their judicial decisions from a written statement: any oral pronouncement that was not a *recitatio scripti* was invalid, a precept we hear echoed in our barbarian codes and law courts of Spain and Italy.[6]

Moreover, a wider range of forms and formats of documents became acceptable. Romans and Roman law had privileged *tabulae*, inscribed wooden tablets embodying 'unitary' acts in steeply formalized language, as *the* authoritative legal instrument until the third century AD But the Antonine Constitution, and an increasingly eastern-oriented empire, demanded that other forms of documentation be recognized, particularly Greek and Egyptian practices; thesse used papyrus, were much less formal in style and were more epistolary.[7] Caracalla's chief legal adviser, the jurist Ulpian (d. 228), noted the change when he remarked that a will, that most traditional of Roman documents and customarily written upon tablets amidst solemn rituals and formalized speech, should now be valid 'when written on any kind of material, whether it be on bound tablets, or papyrus, or parchment, or on the skin of any kind of animal'.[8] A century later, the emperor Constantine, who created a new capital in the East and introduced many eastern 'vulgarisms' into Roman law, opened up the format of the will to include simplified language:

> in the execution of last wills, the requirement of formal speech is hereby removed, and those who desire to dispose of their own property can write their wills upon any kind of material whatsoever, and are freely permitted to use any words which

the Seventh Centuries', in Cameron, Ward-Perkins and Whitby (eds.), *The Cambridge Ancient History*. XIV. *Late Antiquity*, 260–87.

6 *CTh.* 9.1.5; 4.17.1. Also *CTh.* 11.3.40. Repeated in *ETh.* 64 (see below, n. 39) (cf. Cassiodorus, *Variae* 11.38 (MGH AA 12:351–2; according to *Variae* 6.3.3 (MGH AA 12:176), praetorian prefects were exempt), and *LV* VIII.1.1.5, IV.1.2, II.3.4 (see below, n.74). On *recitatio* in the imperial period: E. Meyer, *Legitimacy and Law in the Roman World: Tabulae in Roman Belief and Practice* (Cambridge, 2004), 88–99. See also Classen, 'Fortleben', 14–15, 51–2.

7 A full account is given by Meyer, *Legitimacy and Law*, with references to earlier literature.

8 *Dig.* 37.11.1 (Ulpian).

they may desire . . . and it makes no difference whatever what grammatical forms of the verbs indicate in his will, or what way of speaking pours out.[9]

Specific forms, language or format did not matter, so long as the document was clear in its intent and was rooted in a social context (in this case, the use of witnesses) that could be examined if contested. No matter where we look in late Roman law – whether in the realm of sales, donations, wills or different types of agreements between consenting parties – the victory of documentation over other forms of proof is a recurring theme, even if this meant simplification of legal concepts, such as a reduction in the number of different types of donation, or the collapse of contract and conveyance into a single, dispositive act for sales.[10] By 472, Emperor Leo declared that any document recording any transaction (sales, loans, private agreements), even if not subscribed by the interested parties or even witnessed, was to have the full force of those that had enacted these measures.[11] Justinian, particularly in his *Novels* (largely unknown in the West), was forced to concede to similar precepts, despite his efforts in the *Codex* and *Digest* to turn back the clock and reintroduce classical concepts and formalities centred on oral procedures.[12]

The supremacy of written documents as proof, therefore, was one of the most important aspects of late Roman law that fundamentally shaped the legal landscape of barbarian Spain and Italy, and the role of documents within those kingdoms. Both the Visigothic and the Ostrogothic kingdoms were direct heirs of Roman legal traditions, and barbarian kings relied directly on Roman legal advisers to repackage Roman law with a royal imprimatur: the *interpretationes* to the Visigothic king Alaric's compilation of Roman law, the *Breviarium* (published 506), are directly paralleled in the precepts of the near-contemporary *Edict* of King Theoderic the Ostrogoth.[13] The Lombards took a different legislative route, but they

[9] *CJ* 6.23.15 + 6.37.21 + 6.9.9.

[10] Levy, *West Roman Vulgar Law*; R. Zimmerman, *The Law of Obligations: Roman Foundations of the Civilian Tradition* (Oxford, 1996).

[11] *CJ* 8.17.11.

[12] Everett, 'Diritto tardo romano', 223–4 (documentary practices in the *Novels*); S. Puliatti and A. Sanguinetti (eds.), *Legislazione, cultura giuridica, prassi dell'impero d'Oriente in età giustinianea tra passato e futuro: Atti del Convegno, Modena, 21–22 maggio 1998* (Milan, 2000); C. Humfress, 'Law and Legal Practice in the Age of Justinian', in M. Maas (ed.), *The Cambridge Companion to the Age of Justinian* (Cambridge, 2005), 161–84; Levy, *West Roman Vulgar Law*.

[13] *Interpretationes* to the *Breviarium*: Matthews, *Laying Down the Law* and 'Interpreting the *interpretationes* of the *Breviarium*', in Mathisen (ed.), *Law, Society, and Authority*, 11–32. Similarity to provision in the *ETh.*: S. Lafferty, 'The *Edictum Theoderici*: A Study of a Roman Legal Document from Ostrogothic Italy', unpublished Ph.D. thesis, University of Toronto (2010), ch. 2.

were also heavily reliant on late Roman property law and its documentary norms for security of title and the administration of justice.

Before we turn to examine the evidence, three points should made concerning the late Roman legal heritage and its effect on documentation in barbarian Spain and Italy:

(1) In late Roman law as in the barbarian laws that followed, who actually wrote the document did not matter. The validity of the document resided in its concordance with the law and, where relevant, the subscriptions of witnesses who attested to the document's contents as the intent of the person who requested its redaction. One could certainly hire a professional notary or *tabellio*, as was the case in nearly all of our documents from Ravenna, and as is hinted at in one Visigothic law mentioning 'public notaries', but this had no effect on the document's legal validity, which was a (much) later medieval development.[14]

(2) Under classical Roman law, tampering with documents or forgery constituted a less serious delictal act of fraud (*dolus*). In late Roman law and barbarian law, forgery is elevated to the crime of *falsum*, forgery proper, on a par with counterfeiting money and other crimes considered to be *lèse majesté* or against the state itself.[15] The far heavier penalties for forgery, including amputation and capital punishment, further illustrate the increased importance of documents in the eyes of both barbarian and Byzantine successor states.

(3) With the questionable exception of the *gesta municipalia* (see below), people were responsible for preserving their own documents, and there was no insistence on archival practice of any sort for the validation of documents or for determining the superiority of one kind of document over another. Let us now turn to the Italian evidence, which forces us to confront the issue of archives head on.

## The papyri of Ravenna and *gesta municipalia*

The small corpus of fifty papyrus documents dating to the period AD 455–700 and collected in an edition by the Swedish scholar Jan-Olof Tjäder[16] constitutes the only surviving documentary evidence from Italy

[14] N. Everett, 'Scribes and Charters in Lombard Italy', *Studi Medievali*, 41 (2000), 39–83, at 42–5. Ravennate scribes: Everett, 'Scribes and Charters', 56–9. Visigothic law: *LV* VII.5.8, and below, 85.

[15] Delict: *Dig.* 4.3.1 (Ulpian), based on the Cornelian law: cf. *PSent.* 5.7.2. Constantine extended the definition and added capital punishment: *CTh.* 9.19.1, 2; 9.21.9; 9.22.1.

[16] Hereafter cited as *P.Ital* (papyri), and Tjäder (will be cited by volume and page numbers [vol.:pp.]) (commentary). Tjäder's edition can be difficult to obtain: the papyri can also be consulted in the relevant volumes of *ChLA*, many of which Tjäder also edited; the

in this period, which witnessed the end of the Roman Empire and the establishment of three successive barbarian kingdoms in Italy (that of King Odovacar 476–93, the Ostrogoths 493–535 and the Lombards 568–774). Most are associated with the city or church of Ravenna in some way, in terms of their production or preservation, but not all. The documents include sales (eleven documents), donations (sixteen), wills (seven), a few ecclesiastical leases (from the seventh century), a number of inventories of Church property, part of an inventory of the praetorian prefect's archive (*c*. 510–50) and a few court proceedings. They are fascinating artefacts in a number of ways: full of convoluted legal formulas in rough Latin written by professional scribes in cursive scripts, and containing transactions and subscriptions of laity – bankers, soldiers, silk-makers, soap-makers, trouser-makers, shipbuilders, grammarians and so on; some used Greek characters for their Latin, while some Gothic clergy wrote in Gothic, and a barbarian king scrawled 'hello, keep well' on a charter. A dozen of these papyri comprise the only surviving examples of *gesta municipalia*, or proceedings of the city council (*curia*), in which documents are presented by citizens to the council for inspection, recitation, confirmation and registration in the city archives, with copies of the transcript of these proceedings given out to the citizens.

These *gesta* documents have exercised a considerable amount of influence on our understanding of late Roman and post-Roman documentary practices, for some scholars saw them as representing a dividing line between the 'public' documentary practices of Late Antiquity and the 'private' documentary world of the early Middle Ages.[17] Hence it is thought that the eclipse of municipal *curiae* sometime in the sixth century (no one is sure when, and it depends on where) explains why our private charters only seem to survive in decent numbers from the seventh century onwards, and likewise records of court cases (*placita*), as though these somehow filled a void left by the collapse of public archives. There is no need to rake over how and why such theories appealed to scholars in the *Rechtsschule* tradition, or how a few templates for such documents in Merovingian and Visigothic formularies,[18] combined with

largest number (sixteen) are preserved today in the Vatican (*ChLA* XX–XXII), with other libraries (Paris, Padua, Naples, Florence, Vienna, Venice) possessing only a few each. Cross-references to *ChLA* are given when individual papyri are discussed.

[17] B. Hirschfeld, *Die Gesta municipalia in römischer und frühgermanischer Zeit* (Hamburg, 1904); Classen, 'Fortleben', 48–9; W. Bergmann, 'Untersuchungen zu den Gerichtsurkunden der Merowingerzeit', *Archiv für Diplomatik*, 22 (1976), 1–186, at 105–6.

[18] Merovingian evidence for *gesta*: Rio, *Formularies*, 255–8; Rio, *Legal Practice*; A. Murray, 'Review Article: The New MGH Edition of the Charters of the Merovingian Kings', *Journal of Medieval Latin*, 15 (2005), 246–58. The rich array of documents: Brown, 'Documents'. *Formulae Visigothicae*: below, n.54 and n.73. *Rechtsschule* scholarship: *Settlement of Disputes*, 2–4; P. Wormald, *The Making of English Law: King Alfred to the*

the Ravennate examples and references in late antique legislation, have helped contribute to a false picture of thriving registration throughout the late empire.

As a creation of the late Roman state, the *gesta municipalia* are indeed another reflection of the increased importance of writing in Late Antiquity, particularly for disputes in court.[19] But the primary purpose of registration of common transactions between laypeople, such as sales and donations in the *gesta municipalia*, was not, as is often suggested, the creation and storage of an 'authoritative' document, but rather a means by which the late Roman government kept track of property ownership for taxation; as such, it was largely restricted to wealthy, landowning elites, particularly the senatorial and decurion classes.[20] That registrations of sales and donations only survive from Ravenna, and not, say, Egypt, which provides an abundance of evidence for official documents and formal notifications of transfer of title (and tax obligations) to the local council,[21] suggests that Ravenna may in some ways be an exception. But Ravenna was no ordinary late antique city. From AD 400 onwards, it was the imperial, administrative capital of the West, and home of a powerful metropolitan church that became inextricably entwined with secular administration upon the resumption of imperial control from 540 onwards, the period from which most of *gesta* papyri date (up to 557, then a gap until the last in 625), nearly all of which concern the church.[22] In fact, there are only three purely 'secular' documents in

*Twelfth Century*. I. *Legislation and Its Limits* (Oxford, 2001), 11–12. The few formulaic references to *gesta* in the Merovingian material invite theories of institutional continuity, most recently in J. Barbier, 'Testaments et pratique testamentaire dans le royaume franc (VIe–VIIIe siècle)', in F. Bougard, C. La Rocca and R. Le Jan (eds.), *Sauver son âme et se perpétuer: Transmission du patrimoine et mémoire au haut moyen âge* (Rome, 2005), 7–79, and Barbier, 'Pouvoirs et élites dans le monde franc (VIe–XIe siècle): Matériaux pour servir à l'histoire des élites des cités (VIe–IXe siècle): Le dossier des *gesta municipalia*, étude n° 2', unpublished mémoire d'HDR, Université de Paris I–Panthéon-Sorbonne (2009) (though only parts have been made available); Barbier argues that *gesta* continued in Francia into the ninth century. Such theories, to my mind, misunderstand the function of *gesta* in the late Roman world (as described here), and the ecclesiastical nature of the Merovingian evidence – see the explanation offered below, at nn. 33–5.

19 R. Lim, *Public Disputation, Power and Social Order in Late Antiquity* (Berkeley, CA, 1995); J. Harries, *Law and Empire in Late Antiquity* (Cambridge, 1999), 70–6 and *passim*; C. Humfress, *Orthodoxy and the Courts in Late Antiquity* (Oxford, 2007).

20 As is clear from *CTh*. 2.29.2; 5.15.20.1; 6.2.18; 8.1.9; 8.2.2; 11.1.3; 11.28.13; 12.1.173; 12.6.20; 13.10.8; 13.11.2, 13 – and the references cited below.

21 E.g. *P.Oxy* LIV 3754, 3756, and esp. 3758 (a compilation), containing petitions addressed to or proceedings before a *logistes* (*curator*), *c*. 320s; also *P.Oxy*. I 126. See above, Chapter 2, and R. Bagnall, 'Papyrus Documents in Egypt from Constantine to Justianian', in R. Pintaudi (ed.), *Miscellenea papyrologica* (Florence, 1980), 12–23; R. Bagnall, *Egypt in Late Antiquity* (Princeton, NJ, 1993).

22 Only three are pre-540: *P.Ital* 10–11 (a. 489, Odovacar), 12 (a. 491, church donation), 29 (a. 504, cleric). Last: *P.Ital* 21 (a. 625), donation of cleric to the church. Church

*gesta* format among the Ravennate collection, and two of these were originally registered elsewhere: one is a complicated donation made by King Odovacar in 489 on the eve of his demise, which was registered in Syracuse, where the property was located; the other records a court case concerning a Gothic widow in the town of Rieti in 557, where it was registered (but our copy is from elsewhere), and which reflects social tensions caused by the Gothic wars in Italy.[23] The document registered in Ravenna itself also reflects political change: a purchase by the Ostrogothic king Witigis' personal notary in the inauspicious year of 540, on the eve of Ravenna's reconquest by imperial forces.[24] Several other (non-*gesta*) documents also reflect 'this barbaric time' (as declared in a donation by yet another Gothic widow – as we shall see, there are several) of conflict in sixth-century Italy and troubles for Goths, which raises suspicions of selection behind what survives – an aspect of this corpus that has largely gone unnoticed.

This is not to say that registration was unimportant – in fact, it seems to have been more important to Ravenna's ruling classes, barbarian or otherwise, than it was to contemporary emperors, for we find Ravenna's citizens registering transactions beyond the requirements of imperial law. There is no need to review in detail the imperial legislation that maps the rise and decline of *gesta municipalia*, but a few salient points should be made to explain Ravenna's unique position, and the character of its surviving papyri. Constantine introduced the requirement (in 316) that all donations of immovable property be registered 'in the acts (*acta*) before a *iudex* (that is, a provincial governor) or a magistrate' (of the municipality), but legislation towards the end of the century seems to restrict such measures to senatorial patrimonies, and to forced sales of land by town councillors (decurions). Moreover, although magistrates were given the right to create their own records in 366, thirty years later it was declared that they could do so only with three members of the *curia* and one public secretary (*exceptor publicus*) present, 'so no opportunity for fraud should arise'.[25]

and state administration: T. S. Brown, 'The Church of Ravenna and the Imperial Administration in the Seventh Century', *English Historical Review*, 94 (1979), 1–28, and T. S. Brown, *Gentlemen and Officers: Imperial Administration and Aristocratic Power in Byzantine Italy, A.D. 554–800* (Rome, 1984). The city as capital: D. Deliyannis, *Ravenna in Late Antiquity* (Cambridge, 2010).

23 See below, 80–82.

24 *P.Ital* 10–11; 7; 31. 'tempore hoc barbarici': *P.Ital* 13. See Everett, 'Scribes and Charters', 68.

25 Donations, confirmed in 341: *CTh.* 8.12.1, 6. Senatorial: *CTh.* 2.29.2. Councillors: *CTh.* 12.3.1. *ius actorum conficiendorum*: *CJ* 1.56.2. Three *curiales* and *exceptor*: *CTh.* 12.1.151 = *CJ* 10.32.47. This last was addressed to the vicar of Spain, where no evidence of registration survives, save for templates in the *Formulae Visigothicae* (*Form.*

It is worth reflecting that this type of registration before the *curia*, which we find in the Ravenna papyri, was decreed on the eve of the Western empire's destruction. Over the next thirty years the territories of Gaul, Spain and Africa fell to barbarian rule. True, city councils continued to collect taxes in many places, even rapaciously – hence the quip of Salvian of Marseilles (writing *c.* 439–50), 'What cities are there, and not only cities but even towns and villages, in which the councillors (*curiales*) are not so many tyrants?'[26] Barbarian governments maintained the existing tax system where they could, but it became increasingly marginal, and revenues were collected through royal officials, military officers and local bishops. By 444, a desperate Valentinian III introduced the requirement that all sales of land be registered in the *gesta municipalia*: the purpose was to collect a new sales tax, the *siliquaticum* (that is, 1 *siliqua* or 1/24 per *solidus*) from both buyer and seller, a tax he also extended to all sales of movable property – an impossible scenario, even for late Roman legislative ideals.[27] Most later compilations or commentaries on Roman law, including Valentinian's own later edicts, fail to mention it. In any case, Valentinian's law could aim only at what was left of the Western empire, namely Italy; hence, it is not surprising that it is only in Ostrogothic Italy that we find evidence for the survival of the *siliquaticum*, a tax which 'antiquity ordained', according to Theoderic (via Cassiodorus), though he struggled to collect it, and granted several exemptions.[28]

Yet everywhere else we see a retreat from government archives at the local level. In 479, the emperor Zeno had declared that donations without

*Vis.* 21, 25): see below, 82–93. Registration laws: Everett, 'Scribes and Charters', 73–9. Postclassical legislation on registration is collected in S. Tarozzi, *Ricerche in tema di registrazione e certificazione del documento nel periodo postclassico* (Bologna, 2006). Fees for documents: Harries, *Law and Empire*, 122–4; Kelly, *Ruling the Later Roman Empire*, 74–6, 153, 163; Teitler, *Notarii and Exceptores*, 27–37.

26 Salvian, *De gurbernatione Dei* 5.4(18) (MGH AA 1.1:58), cited in A. H. M. Jones, *The Later Roman Empire, 284–602: A Social, Economic and Administrative Survey*, 2 vols. (Baltimore, MD, 1986), II, 756, who surveys the evidence for councils, II, 737–63; updated by Wickham, *Framing*, 596–602. Arguing for continuity in Spain, at least in terms of local prestige and identity, is M. Kulikowski, *Late Roman Spain and Its Cities* (Baltimore, MD, 2004), 42–9.

27 Valentinian III, *Nov.* 15.1.3. As desperate taxation: Jones, *Later Roman Empire*, 205, 435, 826. In the context of Valentinian III's legislation: T. Honoré, *Law in the Crisis of Empire, 379–425 A.D.: The Theodosian Empire and Its Quaestors* (Oxford, 1998), 259–74. The use of *gesta municipalia* is part of a jumble of measures to collect the tax: special *praepositi* were appointed in each province to attend personally to each transaction, collect the tax and issue a receipt; this required that city councils designate specific market days for different classes of goods.

28 Cassiodorus, *Variae* 4.19 (MGH AA 12:122–3), exempting sales of corn, wine and oil 'to stimulate trade'. Its collection was paired with another, *monopolium*: *Variae* 2.4, 12, 26, 30; 3.25–6; 5.31 (MGH AA 12:49, 52, 61, 63, 92–3, 160).

registration, or even made without any documents, were valid, and we can trace similar sentiments in legislation of fifty years earlier.[29] Justinian limited registration to donations and gifts over 500 *solidi* in value, did not countenance registration for sales anywhere in his legislation, and even allowed sales without any document.[30] Moreover, his attempt to restore the dignity of the office of *defensor civitatis*, another late antique bureaucratic invention (*c.* 368), which he bemoaned as having become 'an insult rather than distinction', reveals the poor state of city archives across the empire. In 535, Justinian conceded that:

> When documents are drawn up by them [*defensores*] in the first place, they only do this for money; and then, as there are no archives in which these documents can be deposited, they are lost; and no monuments of former times are ever found in the possession of those who receive them.[31]

Such comments suggest that Ravenna, and its functioning curial archives, may have been exceptional. A glimpse at the fragments of Ravenna's praetorian prefect's archive – or more precisely, an archival index – preserved among our papyri shows an effective system at work. Two fragments provide forty-four lines (entries) that list documents preserved with the *arcarius* (treasurer) sometime between 510 and 550, but most likely in the Ostrogothic period. I quote a few entries to give something of its flavour:

> Notice [*brevis*] between Stefan, Peter and Iacob from the collection in Liguria [*de colligatione Liguria*].
>
> Guarantee [*cautio*] of Macedonus made out to Peter for 1,250 *solidi* in the year after the consulship of the *uir clarissimus Paulinus* [499].
>
> Guarantee, again of Macedonus, and in Greek, made out to Peter for 1,100 *solidi*.
>
> Guarantee of Verissimus, assistant in the accounting office [*numerariorum*], made out to Peter for 4 *solidi* in the year after the consulship of Paulinus [499].
>
> Promissory note [*pittacium*] of Stefan, *vir spectabilis*, made out to Peter, for 4 *solidi* and 2 tremisses.

29 *CJ* 8.53.31.1, looking back to *CJ* 8.53.29 (a. 428). In contrast, note *CJ* 8.53.31pr., that there is no need for witnesses 'cum publica monumenta sufficiant'. Note also *CJ* 8.53.32 (Anastasius, a. 496), dismissing *CJ* 8.53.30.2 (a. 459).

30 *Inst.* 3.23. Note also the casual process of redacting a document. Registration of donations was abolished altogether by Leo III (717–41), *Nov.* 50.

31 *J.Nov.* 15.5.1–2; see M. Frakes, 'Late Roman Social Justice and the Origins of the *Defensor Civitatis*', *The Classical Journal*, 89 (1994), 337–48, and A. Dietl, *Defensor civitatis: Der Stadtpatron in romanischen Reliefzyklen Oberitaliens* (Munich, 1998).

Letter of notice [*epistula praecaturia*] made by Nonno, Asclepius and Aelius concerning 4,000 *solidi*.

Likewise [by Nonno?], a document folder made of soft leather which was found here bound with a [ . . . ] [possibly *br(evis)*]

The archive is organized by name rather than dates and the amounts vary greatly, from 2 to 4,000 *solidi* (a considerable sum). The list also refers to other collections, such as the soft leather folder mentioned above but also a 'fascicle . . . of promissory notes', an 'accounting document of the envoy's office' of *Picenum* (Ancona), a 'chest in which there are found different documents concerning 152 *solidi*' and – notably using a Latinized Gothic word – 'twelve little lists' (*listula duodecim*).[32]

I should like to suggest here that changes to the office of *defensor civitatis* and the city council in the early fifth century may explain our *gesta* evidence from elsewhere, and much of that from Ravenna. Legislation of 409 and 413 granted the local bishop and his clergy important roles in councils, including the election of the *defensor civitatis* and the right of bishops and *defensores ecclesiae* to sit beside a judge during a trial, offer him advice and enter his private chambers – that is, direct access to and involvement with council procedures.[33] We may suspect that our evidence for registration from Merovingian and Visigothic formula-books, all displaying ecclesiastical origin, stems from such changes and the increasing power of the Church in local governance. For we see the same in Ravenna: a *gesta* document dating between 552 and 575 records how Ravennate clerics (two *defensores ecclesiae* and two chief notaries) presented before the 'praetorian prefect of Italy' accounts of the opening of six wills which had taken place before the *curia*, the earliest dating to 480, the latest to 552, held before a *defensor civitatis*. That is, these clerics were re-registering *gesta* documents which had already been registered.[34] The

[32] *P.Ital* 47–9 (aa. 510–50) (= *ChLA* XXV 792, XXIX 870). Ostrogothic period: the 'Peter' mentioned in twenty-two documents (out of around sixty), and apparently titled *arcarius* in no. 18, is possibly the *arcarius* of Cassiodorus, *Variae* 12.20 (*c.* 536) (MGH AA 12:376–7); Venantius *conrictor Lucaniae et Brittiorum* of no. 22 appears in *Variae* 3.7–8 and 46 (all a. 507×11) (MGH AA 12:83–4, 101–2). Leather: *adlatum chartarium alutacium*. Picenum accounting document: *ratiocinia leagturae*. Prefecture: secured by 'de suffragio praefecturae' and titles in the list (*cursor, strator scolaris*, all *inlustris potestatis*, plus two *adiutores numeriorum*, and a *consularis Flaminiae*).

[33] *CJ* 1.55.8; *CTh*. 6.26.16. *Defensores ecclesiae* and the *ius sedendi*: C. Humfress, 'A New Legal Cosmos: Late Roman Lawyers and the Early Medieval Church', in P. Linehan and J. Nelson (eds.), *The Medieval World* (London, 2001), 557–75.

[34] *P.Ital* 4–5 (= *ChLA* XVII 653 + XXIX 878). Notaries: *primicerius* and *secundocirius notariorum*. Dates: Tjäder 1:200–3. The *defensor civitatis* appears in the last will of 552. Other donations registered by *defensores ecclesiae: P.Ital* 14–15 (a. 572), 21 (a. 625, the last known *gesta*) (= *ChLA* XXIX 889, XXII 720). Note another will benefiting the church of Ravenna in 575: *P.Ital* 6 (= *ChLA* XXI 714).

wills, of laity and clergy, all benefited the church in some way; hence, we can only assume that the church was engaged in some sort of archival reorganization – or perhaps we witness here a glimpse of how the city and church archives merged. One lay will among these, that of Georgius, a silk-maker (*olosiricoprata*), shows that the testator dictated his will from his deathbed to his 'known friend' the scribe (*forensis*) Deusdedit, 'in accordance with civil or praetorian law or even the new laws recently given', a phrase that resonates with the Visigothic material, just as the term *defensores* constantly appears in the Merovingian evidence, the bulk of which concerns the registration of wills.[35] Georgius adds a plea 'that any charters [of his] written on parchment or any other material' remain inviolable, suggesting that he does not ordinarily register documents, and his last words in the will reveal why it was registered: 'You, holy mother Catholic church of Ravenna, in which the entire Christian people worship for the forgiveness of sins, I decree to be heir for a tenth of my property.'

The Ravennate church encouraged registration to secure its gains, but the laity of Ravenna faced legal and cultural imperatives to register due to Ravenna's role as the administrative capital of Italy. The legal imperatives stemmed from the maintenance of a robust system of taxation and fiscal surveillance. Nearly all of our surviving *gesta* papyri record the vendor's request to the *curia* to 'remove my name from the public tax list (*de polypticis publicis*) and write the name of the abovementioned buyer in its place'.[36] Many *gesta* documents included (or alluded to including – most are fragmentary) copies of a letter of conveyance (*epistula traditionis*), an instrument designed to inform the council of transfer of title. Yet, these 'letters of conveyance', too, took the opportunity to relieve tax obligations, as is clear from one letter that survives in its original format (as opposed to being a *gesta* copy), in which the brothers Milanius and Gerontius inform the *curia* of nearby Faenza in 540 (again that auspicious date!) that they have sold a property to Laurentius, *uir strenuus* (a soldier), in Ravenna:

> but because the land is in your territory, and still corporal conveyance has not yet taken place, therefore lords and senior cultivators of the law, may Your Praiseworthiness accept this letter, so that when the abovementioned buyer and his men arrive to take up solemn conveyance as is customary, you have the letter read out and inserted into your records (*acta*), and that you also hasten to advise the tax

[35] *Form. Vis.* 21 ('ad ius praetorium et urbanum'), 25, both concerning wills. Cf. Marculf 2.37, *Form. Arvern.* 1, *Form. Andec.* 1, *Form. Tur.* 3, etc. See Rio, *Formularies*, and Rio, *Legal Practice*, with references cited.

[36] *P.Ital* 31 (= *ChLA* XX 707). Others use *vasaria publica*, from which the *tributa fiscalia* are known (*P.Ital* 10–11 [= *ChLA* XX 703]), or similar terms: Tjäder 2:26–7.

collector of your city (*tabularius civitatis*) concerning the amount of taxable land (*cespitis iugationem*) for this property, which has been recorded in the documents mentioned above, and likewise that you order the buyer and his agents to be designated [for the liabilities], so that he might be aware of everything owed from the third indiction to the time of his ownership.[37]

Despite the fact that the letter was written in the year Belisarius captured Ravenna, the revenue system was still fully operational, even rapacious, as it was certainly reputed to have become under Justinian.[38]

While emperors had largely revoked or simply given up on registration in city archives by the end of the fifth century, the barbarian king Theoderic, who lavished patronage upon Ravenna after he assumed rule there in 493, and who maintained the trappings of late Roman civilian bureaucracy, maintained and even extended registration, if the *Edictum Theoderici* was really his.[39] The *Edict* stipulated that it was necessary to register donations of 'rural or urban estates' before three councillors (*curiales*) and either a magistrate or *defensor civitatis*. But a following provision admits the difficulty of finding a magistrate or *defensor* and so offers the alternative of three councillors 'provided that corporal conveyance is carried out with neighbours knowing about it (*uicinis scientibus*)', a much more casual process. Indeed, the papyri show a more casual *curia*, in terms of personnel, as the sixth century progresses.[40] Following a Novel of Valentinian (451), the *Edict* required that a free man who defiled a virgin slave and wished to marry her must acknowledge her owner's consent and his own loss of freedom in the *gesta*. A provision against forgery of

[37] *P.Ital* 32 (a. 540) (= *ChLA* XX 708). The letter was dictated to a *notarius*, an unusual title for Ravenna's scribes, suggesting it may have been written elsewhere, and was signed by three witnesses.

[38] See references in Brown, *Gentlemen and Officers*; P. Sarris, *Economy and Society in the Age of Justinian* (Cambridge, 2006); and J. F. Haldon, 'Economy and Administration: How Did the Empire Work?', in Maas (ed.), *The Cambridge Companion to the Age of Justinian*, 28–59.

[39] On the *ETh.*, see now the work of Sean Lafferty: 'The *Edictum Theodorici*' (above, n. 13); 'Law and Society in Ostrogothic Italy: Evidence from the *Edictum Theodorici*', *Journal of Late Antiquity*, 3 (2010), 377–404; 'Italy in the Twilight of Empire: The Decline of Roman Law and Culture Under Theodoric the Great, *c.* 493–526', *Canadian Journal of History*, 45 (2010), 457–84. Lafferty proves beyond doubt that the *ETh.* derives from Italy, and argues convincingly for Theodoric's paternity; I reserve the possibility that it was drawn up under Odovacar. Others, particularly G. Vismara (*Edictum Theoderici* [Milan, 1967]), have argued for King Theuderic II of the Visigoths; this has been persuasive, though rejected early: H. Nehlsen, '*Edictum Theoderici*', *Zeitschrift der Savigny-Stiftung für Rechtsgeschichte*, Germanistische Abteilung, 86 (1969), 246–60. Others have dismissed it as forgery (e.g. B. Paradisi, 'Critica e mito dell'editto teodericano', *Bollettino dell'Istituto di diritto romano*, 68 [1965], 1–47).

[40] *ETh.* 52, modelled on *CTh.* 8.12.8; *ETh.* 53, modelled on *CTh* 8.12.8.2, is likewise concerned about location, but does not water down official presence. Fewer *curiales*: Brown, *Gentlemen and Officers*, 16–19.

documents includes tampering with *gesta*, an addition to the passage in the *Pauli Sententiae* upon which it was based. And anyone who receives a man claiming to be freeborn (*ingenuus*) must lead him before the *gesta*, where he may publicly declare his status, that way protecting the receiver in case the self-proclaimed freeborn turns out to be a fugitive slave; there seems to be no precedent in Roman law for this.[41]

We also see a penchant for registration in some of the Ravenna papyri that went beyond Roman laws. In 491, while Theoderic was besieging the city (490–3), the *defensores* of the Ravennate church registered before the *curia* a charter and an *epistula donationis* recording the donation of the widow Maria, *femina spectabilis* (suggesting that her deceased husband was a military officer), to the church. Maria's *epistula* mentions that while she and her husband had drawn up a charter, his death meant 'that we could not register it (*eam allegare*), so now it has been necessary for me to write this letter in my own name' to reiterate the donation.[42] But it was not necessary: the only purpose for Maria's letter should have been to advise the *curia* to remove her name from the tax register (it may have done so, as the letter is fragmentary). Registration was the *defensores*' responsibility as the new owners, as Maria's charter rightfully indicates by containing the necessary 'permission to register' (*licentia allegandi*) formula that appears in all donations. That this same formula appears in sales after 540 further suggests Ravenna's enthusiasm for registration, which Tjäder noted.[43] The political uncertainty of the times, or the fact that the donation included the condition that Maria and her husband be buried inside the church of S. Lorenzo, may both have played a role. Either way, registration for Maria was a cultural imperative, not a legal one, just as it was not legally required for sales in Justinianic law.[44]

41 Marrying a slave: *ETh.* 64; cf. Valentinian III, *Nov.* 31.5, where the man keeps his free status but cannot leave. Forgery: *ETh.* 90, 'testamentum, codicillum, tabulas, rationes, gesta, libellos, cautiones, epistolas'; cf. *PSent.* 5.25.1–5, 'instrumenta, epistolae, cautiones, chirographa', though both laws also concern counterfeit money; *ETh.* 80, 'ut eum ducat ad gesta, et se profiteatur ingenuum'.

42 *P.Ital* 12 (a. 491) (= *ChLA* XXV 791). Theoderic's siege: J. Moorhead, *Theoderic in Italy* (Oxford, 1992), 24–5. *Spectabilis*: Jones, *Later Roman Empire*, 143, 282, 528–9.

43 Tjäder 2:26–7 (for the receiver's benefit, not for the state). On changes in the formula *c.* 600, see Everett, 'Scribes and Charters', 75n118.

44 Instances of the *licentia allegendi* formula aside, three sales were registered: *P.Ital* 29 (a. 504), for only 18 *solidi* (the purchaser was an acolyte of the Roman church, and the land in question bordered that of the Ravennate church (lines 11–12); this explains why it was registered); *P.Ital* 31 (a. 540), for 40 *solidi* (Montanus *vir clarissimus*, Witigis' notary, purchases land in Faenza from a local layman, Domnicus); *P.Ital* 33 (a. 541), for 20 *solidi* (Minulus, a Gothic cleric; see below, n.46).

It should not be surprising that the citizens and church of Ravenna were steeped in civic rituals and practices that proclaimed their Romanness and the capital status of their city. But is it a coincidence that these rituals keep appearing in papyri that date to periods of conflict, and include Goths? A year before Belisarius took the city, a Gothic widow, Thulgilo and her children sold land in Faenza to a soldier (*vir strenuus*) named Pelegrinus for 110 *solidi*: the witnesses were all officials or nobles associated with the palatial administration, including Julian the banker, and more official names were dropped in the description of the land. While the charter was not registered, Thulgilo states that she has properly drawn up a letter of conveyance (*dyploma vacuole*), and that the sale was 'performed with the customary imperial *nummus* and with Serapio *vir strenuus* acting as scale-holder [*libripens*] and Opilio *vir strenuus* as the special witness [*antetestator*], both of whom are present to sign below as witnesses'. Perhaps this Gothic widow really did perform the ancient Roman emancipation ceremony, striking a set of scales with a bronze coin and announcing, according to Gaius, 'These things I declare to be mine by Quirinary right.'[45] We have already mentioned King Witigis' personal notary registering his purchase in 540: surely he was aware of the political winds that could sweep away his property rights. Another *gesta* from the next year, after the conquest, records a sale of land by a Gothic cleric, Minnulus, to Isaac, a soap-maker in Classe; Isaac promptly brought the charters to the *curia* of Ravenna and asks for their registration 'for the protection of my ownership' (*ad munimen dominii mei*).[46] That the words *munimen* (protection, defence) and *monumen(tum)* (monument, record, document) become semantically fused together in the Ravennate papyri (and continue so in Lombard Italy) further highlights the association of documents with security of title. And it seems significant that this phrase appears only in 540 and after, replacing the older, pre-Justinianic formula that first requested the judge to change the tax records, and then requested registration.[47]

45 *P.Ital* 30 (a. 539) (= *ChLA* XX 706). Witnesses: Serapio *v.s. de scrinio cursorum*; Opilio *strator inlustris potestatis*; Candidianus *vir laudabilis*; Petrus *collectarius*, etc. Neighbours: *dromonarius, scutarius, praepositi dromonariorum*, etc. Gaius, *Inst.* 1.119.

46 *P.Ital* 33 (a. 541) (= *ChLA* XXV 973). A fragmentary text (*P.Marini* 118) that used the same formula may date a year earlier: see Tjäder 2:40–5. In *P.Ital* 20 (*c.* 590×602), another Gothic widow cites 'de sexu femineo Belliianus senatusconsultus'; that is, the *senatusconsultus Velleianum*, probably dating from the mid first century AD; see H. Vogt, *Studien zum Senatus Consultum Velleianum* (Bonn, 1952).

47 *P.Ital* 14–15 (a. 572), 31 (a. 540): missed by Niermeyer, *Lexicon*, 771, who cites Lombard charters, the *Liber diurnus* and other slightly later Italian documents for the fusion of meaning. Pre-Justinianic formula: *P.Ital* 10–11 (a. 489), 12 (a. 491); see Tjäder 2:67.

Finally, our longest and most complete *gesta* papyrus by far (107 lines, four pages of printed text) also seems to reflect Byzantine–Gothic conflict. It records a hearing in 557 before the *curia* in Rieti (290 km south of Ravenna), in which the Gothic widow Gundihild *(inlustris femina)* requests the appointment of a legal guardian (*tutor*) for her two sons, Lendarit and Landarit, who were still minors and unable to defend their property against three Gothic soldiers (Adiud *inlustris uir*, Rosemud and Gundirit *uir magnificus*) who had begun to encroach upon it. Gundihild's husband, Gudehals (*uir inlustris*), had died only days before, but had previously been defending the property in court. Gundhild herself was not present at court; her well-drafted and somewhat moving request (*petitio*) is read out before the *curiales*, who order it entered into the *gesta*. What follows is the record of a protracted process, in very formulaic speech, of interrogating the guardian, named Flavianus, and then his guarantor (*fideiussor*), Liberatus, about whether they fully understand and accept their obligations.[48] Gundihild's choice of a tutor and guarantor with Roman names was probably wise: sometime between that year (557) and 565, Justinian ordered that all property belonging to the Goths, 'not only in the cities, but also in suburban villas and hamlets', be confiscated and given to the Ravennate church. Another of our surviving papyri documents this process: the *fiscales* of the state presented to the archbishop (Agnellus, 557–70) a list of rents owed from the properties and the taxes due from these.[49] As it happens, yet another court case survives from 557 (not in *gesta* format): the Goth Gundila tried to regain property in Nepi (near Viterbo, north of Rome), lost in the war with Byzantine forces in the 530s, by converting to Catholicism. Pope Vigilius and a Gothic bishop intervened and ordered that Gundila's property be restored to him, but the Gothic resurgence under Totila (540s) meant Gundila lost it again to a Gothic count, who gave it to his sons.[50] And a papyrus charter of 551 records how the clergy of the Arian church of St Anastasius sold their neighbouring swamplands to the *defensor* of the Ravennate church,

[48] *P.Ital* 7 (a. 557) (= *ChLA* XX 712). It seems the copy we have is that of the tutor, which he obtained from a Constantine, '*vir devotus* and *comitiacus*', and which Constantine obtained 'from originals' (*ex autentico edidi*). *Comitiacus* seems to have been a military office: Cassiodorus, *Variae* 2.10, 5.6, 6.13, 7.31 (MGH AA 12:51, 147, 186–7, 218); Jones, *Later Roman Empire*, 253–5. The copy was written crosswise, rather than lengthwise, and without columns, and hence not in regular *gesta* format.

[49] *P.Ital* 2 (a. 565×700); Brown, 'The Church of Ravenna', 7. Confiscation: Agnellus, *Liber pontificalis ecclesiae Ravennatis* 85–6 (MGH SRL 334–5). Taxes: Jones, *Later Roman Empire*, 820–1; Wickham, *Framing*, 64–6.

[50] *P.Ital* 49 (a. 557) (= *ChLA* XXIX 885). Date and reconstruction of events: P. Amory, *People and Identity in Ostrogothic Italy, 489–554* (Cambridge, 1997), 321–5, 382–3.

Peter, in part to pay back a loan they had taken from Peter sixteen years earlier.[51]

That so many of the Ravennate papyri record the demise of the Goths in Italy says more about their preservation than about their production: if Goths or Byzantines registered or simply recorded transactions in times of trouble it is further proof that such practices were common and considered secure. But the regional and chronological arc of these papyri is narrow. It makes sense that the Ravennate church would preserve together (perhaps in a soft-leather folder) documents for ex-Gothic property, particularly since it was the direct beneficiary of Justinian's seizure of Gothic lands between 557 and 565. Their dispersal might be blamed on the fire that burned the church archives around 700, in which 'the flames consumed many documents, while many were seized and hidden by wicked men', who subsequently faced angry clerics hurling anathemas at them in the local tavern to give the documents back.[52] For clearly Ravennati valued documents, and the traditions which produced them, as is clear from the almost exclusive use of public scribes (*tabelliones/forenses*), who always qualified themselves as 'of the city of Ravenna' and maintained a 'college of scribes' (*schola forensium*).[53] The use of *gesta municipalia* to register transactions was another such tradition, but their use in Ravenna was limited to lay and ecclesiastical elites of a capital city that clung to Roman identity during a period of change and conflict, as barbarian kings and the Byzantine generals who replaced them promoted that identity to provide a veneer of continuity. The *gesta* among the Ravennate papryi should not be used as evidence for such practices elsewhere: the non-*gesta* documents in that collection provide the better guide.

## Visigothic Spain: legislation, formularies and slate

Visigothic Spain provides a startling array of evidence for lay uses of documents in the legislation of Visigothic kings and in a formula-book, but almost nothing of it survives in terms of the documents themselves, with the exception of five fragmentary documents on parchment and, extraordinarily, about 160 texts written on slate from the central western regions of the peninsula (mainly Avila, Segovia and

51 *P.Ital* 34 (a. 551) (= *ChLA* XX 704).

52 Agnellus, *Liber pontificalis* 134 (MGH SRL 365–6). Ravennate archepiscopal archive: Tjäder 1:17–27.

53 *P.Ital* 24 (*c.* 650) (= *ChLA* XXIX 865): 'primicerius schola forensium civitatis Ravennae seo Classis'; Everett, 'Scribes and Charters', 57–9.

Salamanca).[54] The following seeks to highlight some of the more illuminating references to the production and preservation of documents in the law, and to correlate those with surviving examples in the *Formulae Visigothicae* (thought to date *c.* 615–45), on parchment and on slate. Topics addressed (in order) are forgery, wills, court documents, sales, family law and finally estate management with reference to the slates. The discussion is framed by two wider points being made: firstly, the reliance of Visigothic law on late Roman legal tradition shows how the latter's preference for written proofs continued to be developed in a post-Roman political order, and as such provides a model for understanding the importance of documents elsewhere in early medieval Europe; secondly, the explosion in the number of surviving documents in Spain from the ninth century onwards,[55] which match the templates of the *Formulae Visigothicae* and cite precepts from Visigothic law, reflects improved methods of preservation, rather than greater appreciation of the use and value of documents, which have secure precedent in this earlier period.

Caution is needed in using the Visigothic law code as evidence, for the political or ideological element of royal legislation always demands consideration, and this is particularly true for the seventh-century Visigothic kings. Each promulgation of the law code known as the *Book of Judgements* (*Liber iudiciorum*), in 654, 681 and 692, coincided with a period of crisis for the monarchy, and there are large chronological gaps (up to 75 years) between legislative efforts. Moreover, Karl Zeumer's critical edition of the laws published in the MGH (1902) was established on principles that no longer seem secure against the advances of modern research on the manuscript traditions.[56] Nonetheless, Visigothic

54 Charters: *ChLA* XLVI 1398–1402 (referred to individually below). A contemporary copy of Visigothic law survives: Vatican City, Biblioteca Apostolica Vaticana, Reg. lat. 1024 (= *CLA* 1.111; s. VII). Slate texts: *Las pizarras visigodas: Edición crítica y estudio*, ed. I. Velázquez Soriano (Murcia, 1989); reissued with same numbering and better commentary as *Documentos de época visigoda escritos en pizarra (siglos VI–VIII)*, 2 vols. (Turnhout, 2000); reprinted as *Las pizarras visigodas entre el latín y su disgregación: La lengua hablada en Hispania, siglos VI–VIII* (Burgos, 2004) (hereafter Pizarra # [no.]). Formulary: *Form. Vis.*; also in J. Gil, *Miscellanea Wisigothica* (Seville, 1972). A tenth-century Catalonian collection may contain earlier material: M. Zimmermann, 'Un formulaire du X$^{\text{ème}}$ siècle conservé à Ripoll', *Faventia*, 4 (1982), 25–86. Following convention, and because of the problems mentioned below, I refer to 'Visigoth law' (*LV*) rather than *Liber iudiciorum*.

55 R. Collins, 'Literacy and the Laity in Early Medieval Spain', in *Uses of Literacy*, 109–33; A. J. Kosto, *Making Agreements in Medieval Catalonia: Power, Order, and the Written Word, 1000–1200* (Cambridge, 2001); Kosto, 'Laymen'.

56 Y. García López, *Estudios críticos y literarios de la 'Lex Wisigothorum'* (Alcalá de Hernares, 1996), who also provides a new edition of the laws of Egica and Wittiza; R. Collins, *Visigothic Spain, 409–711* (Oxford, 2004), 223–39.

Spain produced the most voluminous and comprehensive legislation of all the barbarian successor kingdoms, and it is replete with references to the use of documents (usually termed *scriptura* or *instrumenta*) among the laity. As one law makes clear, 'Whatever is set out in writing in contracts or agreements shall have full validity (*plena firmitas*)', thus echoing the sentiment of Emperor Leo cited earlier, and bestowing authority on writing well beyond the Roman laws on which this precept was based.[57]

The late Roman roots of Visigothic legislation are hidden by the 'nationalist' sentiment of seventh-century kings, often taken at face value by modern scholarship with nationalist preoccupations of its own. The *Book of Judgements* promulgated by King Recceswinth in 654 claimed to have abrogated all previous versions of the law, but in reality it built on a long tradition of royal legislation extending back to King Euric (466–84) and possibly his father, King Theoderic (419–51), and continuing through the kings Leovigild (569–86), Reccared (586–601), Sisebut (611–20) and Chindaswinth (643–53). Their legislation (with the exception of fragments of Euric's code) survives only in Recceswinth's *Book*, which attributes laws to only four kings (Recceswinth 88 laws, Chindaswinth 99, Reccared 3, Sisebut 2), while the greater part (some 315 laws) are simply called 'ancient' (*antiqua*), so their date is often impossible to determine. Legislation continued under later kings, so that the *Book* was updated by Ervig (681), Egica (692) and Wittiza (702–10). Most of the *Book of Judgements* resembles late Roman law because Visigothic kings adopted it as their own quite early, as is clear from a surviving section of Euric's Code (about one-sixth of the original text) preserved in a sixth-century manuscript.[58] Admittedly, this section covers areas in which Roman law excelled (entitled 'On deposits and loans', 'On sales', 'On donations', 'On inheritances'), but this has not stopped scholarly imagination concerning the missing 'Germanic' elements of Euric's Code, based on the comment of Isidore of Seville (writing a century and half later) in his *Historia Gothoroum* that under Euric the Goths 'began to have ordinances of the laws in writing, for before this they were bound by customs and habit'. Evidence within Euric's Code and elsewhere would deny that, and given what we now know about the accommodation of (small numbers of) barbarians within the military framework of the late empire, the fluidity of both Roman and barbarian ethnic identity, and the stereotypes of late Roman ethnography, there is no need to look for

[57] *LV* II.5.5, based on *LRV* II.9.1, and in turn *CTh.* 9.19.
[58] BnF lat. 12161 (= *CLA* 5.626).

'Germanic' traits anywhere in Visigothic Spain, let alone the laws: likewise for Ostrogothic Italy.[59]

Moreover, Roman law was officially embraced by King Alaric II (485–507) when he published in 506 his *Lex Romana Visigothorum* (or *Breviarium*, as it was dubbed in the sixteenth century), an abridgement of the Theodosian Code with later fifth-century imperial rescripts and excerpts from earlier juristic texts such as the *Pauli Sententiae* and Gaius' *Institutes*. Alaric ordered that copies be given to all counts (*comites*, presumably Gothic) and that no other law be used in their courts: if Goths did use a separate law, they were a small percentage of the population, which at this point included most of southern Gaul. As mentioned earlier, Alaric II's use of Roman legal advisers also to draw up a commentary on the laws, in the form of clarifications and modifications called *interpretationes*, continued the tradition of Roman praetorian prefects adapting law for their provinces, as we saw in the *Edict* of Theoderic.[60] Reliance upon Roman models of governance and legal traditions is evident in the *Book of Judgements* also, neatly organized into twelve books (probably imitating Justinian's Code; the Twelve Tables have also been suggested as a model), which are subdivided into chapters and numbered laws (called *eras*), and containing almost no element of identifiable 'Gothic' tradition or custom. One (undated) law against forgery of royal documents reveals a society steeped in traditions of written law, as we shall see in other spheres:

> many not only write out royal orders themselves, but also promulgate them, and publish documents confirmed by the signatures of notaries, whereby many things have been introduced into the laws of our kingdom, and many provisions have been written, or attempted to be added, which have not received the sanction of our authority.[61]

The law goes on to warn royal, official and, surprisingly, 'public notaries' (*notarii publici*), who are not mentioned anywhere else in our sources, not

59 Isidore of Seville, *Historia Gothorum* 35 (MGH AA 11:281). Evidence of previous legislation in *CE* 277, and Sidonius: Collins, *Visigothic Spain*, 227–9. The tenacity of the Roman–German dichotomy is evident in P. D. King, *Law and Society in the Visigothic Kingdom* (Cambridge, 1972), 8–9, who, despite defending the territoriality of Euric's Code, believes there were parts 'exclusively Germanic', citing Levy, *West Roman Vulgar Law*, 125–6, but these traits are found in *PSent.* and similar sources. Ethnography: Amory, *People and Identity*. 'Germanic': Collins, *Visigothic Spain*, 239–46 and *passim*.

60 Matthews, 'Interpreting the *interpretationes*'; R. Collins, *Early Medieval Spain: Unity in Diversity, 400–1000*, 2nd edn (London, 1995), 24–32; M. Rouche and B. Dumézil, *Le Bréviaire d'Alaric: Aux origines du Code civil* (Paris, 2008).

61 *LV* VII.5.9. Undated: *LV*, p. 308n2 (neither *antiqua* nor Recceswinth). An *antiqua* law (*LV* VII.5.1) on the same subject, which quotes *PSent.* 5.25 on Cornelian law, distinguishes between *honestiores*, who lose half their property, and *humiliores*, who lose their hand; cf. Lombard King Rothari, *ER* 243.

to write decrees without royal approval. One of our (five) surviving parchment fragments from this period appears to be a royal decree, revealing traces of an otherwise unattested Visigothic chancery script, unless it is clever forgery of the sort complained about above.[62] King Chindaswinth complained that new laws on forgery were needed because forgers kept inventing new means of deception. Interestingly, one fragmentary slate text contains two separate inscriptions, one mentioning that king's name ('Cindasuindus dominus') and possibly imitating a royal decree, immediately followed by a writing exercise that addresses 'assembled citizens, senators and prefects', before mixing phrases from the *Disticha Catonis* and the Bible in some type of moralizing letter. The alliance between Roman rhetoric and Visigothic kingship, so evident in the laws, extended to scratching on slate in rural Diego Álvaro (Ávila), 120 km from royal Toledo.[63]

The issue of forgery reveals how valued, and how common, documentation was, for the Visigoths not only punished forgery severely but also employed palaeographical analysis as part of court procedure to detect forgery, even coining a new legal term for this practice (*contropatio*). Forgery of royal documents (as above) incurred the penalty of 200 lashes, a scalping and amputation of the thumb, whatever the social rank of the forger. Forging, suppressing or tampering with any (non-royal) documents automatically incurred 100 lashes, and additional punishments were inflicted according to social rank: the upper ranks (*potentiores*) lost a quarter of their property; lower and poorer classes (*humiliores sane vilioresque*) had to 'sign a profession to the effect . . . that they shall forever be the slaves of those they deceived'.[64] The stakes were high, for as we saw earlier, written contracts were considered to have *plena firmitas*. This even extended to doctors and their patients, who, after the initial diagnosis was given, signed an agreement on the method of healing and the price to be paid – or not paid, if the patient did not survive (fortunately no such cases do).[65] Doubts about the authenticity of documents could be resolved in court by palaeographical analysis (*contropatio*), best described in a law concerning documents of deceased persons:

All documents (*omnes scripturae*), where he who made them and the witnesses to the same are dead, and in which the signature of the former and the attestation of the witnesses appear, when brought into court to be verified, may be proved by comparison of their seals and signatures with those of other documents; and the proof shall be sufficient in this investigation, if the seals and signatures of three

[62] *ChLA* XLVI 1399, s. VII$^{in}$. The script is similar to that of Merovingian royal charters.
[63] *LV* VII.5.8 (Chindaswinth). Pizarra #59, and *Las pizarras* (2004), 105–10.
[64] *LV* VII.5.1, 9 (royal); VII.5.2.
[65] *LV* XI.1.3–4. Note also the specified fees for training apprentices (5) and removing cataracts (7).

or four other documents, when introduced, shall be evidently those of the parties in question.

Recceswinth clarified further that documents (*instrumenta chartarum*) for the comparison are to be found in the household archives (*in scriniis domesticis*) of the deceased; if these proved insufficient, other examples of *similitudo scripturarum* were to be found, or the case fell.[66] This is the only mention of lay archives in the laws, but their existence is clearly assumed, and we know now that their format extended to chunks of slate.[67] The importance of signatures is confirmed by the spectacle of King Wamba (*c.* 679) forcing rebels to confirm their handwriting on oaths of loyalty signed at his election, and then showing the written oaths the rebels later signed to support the usurper Paul.[68] Soon after (681), King Ervig mandated that every converted Jew sign a written oath or 'profession' abjuring his past faith, the text for which was provided in the laws, and then place it upon an altar with his own hands before the local bishop, who preserved it the archives of the church.[69]

The laws against forgery were particularly concerned with wills, another sphere in which the Visigoths borrowed heavily from late Roman legislation. Persons over 14 years of age could dispose of their property as they wished, though there were some limits and reservations, and the law envisaged four types of written will that reflect different degrees of literacy or ability among the testator and/or witnesses: one with subscriptions by the testator and witnesses; one with only the mark (*signum*) of the testator, guaranteed by the subscription of a witness, who later was forced to swear to its authenticity; one used when (presumably because of illness) the testator could not even make a mark, requiring a special representative and witnesses to swear before a judge; and finally, a holograph will, written and subscribed by the testator in the absence of witnesses, probate of which required comparison of the handwriting in the will with at least three specimens of the alleged testator's script before

[66] Quotation: *LV* II.5.15 (Chindaswinth). Recceswinth: II.5.17. See also I.2.23; II.4.3, 5.15. *Contropatio* (from *contrapactio*), can also mean compensation: cf. III.1.5, IV.5.3, VI.1.5; K. Zeumer, 'Zum westgotischen Urkundenwesen. I: *Subscriptio* und *signum*. II: Die Schriftvergleichung *contropatio*', *Neues Archiv der Gesellschaft für ältere deutsche Geschichtskunde*, 24 (1899), 13–38.

[67] The only other archives mentioned are an *archivum ecclesiae* (for Jewish professions to a priest: *LV* XII.3.28; for examples given in the code, see below, n. 69), and *arca publica* (V.4.19) for the state treasury.

[68] See J. Martínez Pizarro (trans.), *The Story of Wamba: Julian of Toledo's Historia Wambae regis* (Washington, DC, 2005), 237–8. Oaths in Visigothic law: King, *Law and Society*, 113–15.

[69] *LV* XII.3.14–15. On this despicable 'twelfth book', see Collins, *Early Medieval Spain*, 132–4; King, *Law and Society*, 130–45.

a judge or a bishop, who then validated the will by adding his subscription. The casual prescription for the will's contents reads very much like that of Constantine mentioned above: 'Let the testator write out how he wishes to dispose of things, and let it be especially noted who he wishes to act as executor, and what of his property he chose to give to whom.' The only formal requirement for a will of whatever type was that it record the exact date of production (day and year). Even an oral will needed to be confirmed in court by witnesses, who swore to its veracity and then subscribed their oaths before a judge.[70]

Visigothic courts operated on the assumption that documents would be provided and produced, not only to resolve cases but also to introduce them. Summons to court required a letter impressed with a judicial seal and delivered to the defendant in the presence of a witness.[71] In a case where torture (*quaestio*) might be employed, the Visigoths took over the late Roman practice of *inscriptio*, whereby an accuser presented to the judge a subscribed statement in which he promised to suffer the same penalties as his opponent if he failed to prove his case. Moreover, the accuser had to submit secretly to the judge a written account of the events of the crime, which the judge would then compare to the confession obtained under torture.[72] As with Roman law, there were considerable disincentives for an accuser or a judge to turn to torture. Nonetheless, these safeguards revolved around the use of documents, and the acquitted left the court armed with documents issued by the judge to prevent the case from being reopened. In important cases the judge himself was compelled by law to write out and subscribe two identical accounts of the proceedings and his verdict, one for each party. In fact, an example of this survives in the *Formulae Visigothicae*, which also records that one party cited Visigothic law by book, chapter and verse (*eras*).[73] In all cases, however, the judge's decision was required to be written out, and the judge was to keep a copy for himself; otherwise, the decision was considered invalid – a late Roman law we find also in the *Edict* of Theoderic.[74]

In lesser cases, the parties received a sworn protocol of the evidence of the witnesses of the victorious side; indeed, one of our longest slate texts

[70] Wills: *LV* II.5.1–17; also IV.2.20; II.5.10, 12 (oral); King, *Law and Society*, 244–8.

[71] Summons: *LV* II.1.19–20; King, *Law and Society*, 93–6.

[72] *Inscriptio: LV* II.3.4, IV.1.2, VIII.1.1.5. Late Roman *inscriptio*: Harries, *Law and Empire*, 101, 120–2.

[73] *LV* II.1.24; *Form. Vis.* 40: 'sententias legis libri ill[e] protulit, legam illam, qui est sub titulo illo, era illa'. Finish: 'ad singula decernentes in hanc iudicii paginam inseruimus, quatenus futuris temporibus iustitiam habens congaudeat'.

[74] *LV* II.1.25; *CTh.* 4.17, 11.3.40; *ETh.* 64.

appears to be such a document. It is entitled *Conditiones sacramentorum*, and its format is replicated in a formulary template with the same title. The slate records a dispute over an exchange of horses in which a certain Lolus was ordered by four judges and two *vicarii* to swear an oath accepting the terms of their decision. The oath itself is directly mirrored in the formulary template and is in strict accordance with Visigothic law: in the absence of evidence or witnesses, the judge was to administer an evidentiary oath, which seems to be exactly what happened in this case. In taking the oath, Lolus emerged as the victor and departed from the court with a written copy of it as insurance against future prosecution.[75] In another slate recording a court case (*placitum*) held before at least two *vicarii*, a certain Gisadus took an oath in which he pledged a pig as a security for the debt he had incurred to Aninaus and Teudoteus for 10 *solidi*. Again the terms used and the general framework of the case reflect two provisions on securities in Visigothic law, and other fragmentary slates recording court cases also reflect the legal language of Visigothic law or the Roman sources on which they are based.[76] Two parchment fragments further reflect court activity: one seems to be the order of a count called Medema, in handsomely executed cursive script (unfortunately, his seal was removed), instructing judges to obtain an oath in court (*c.* 697); the other is an oath concerning agricultural goods (*c.* 704).[77]

While it is true that for sales, exchanges and donations writing was not absolutely essential and witnesses were considered equally valid, it is often stated throughout the laws that writing offers greater security, couched in expressions such as *firmitas/dignatas/veritas scripturae, veridica/stabilis scriptura* and so on.[78] Recceswinth even legislated against people using documents to camouflage conditions that were illegal.[79] Euric's Code had already determined that 'a sale contracted through writing has full

75 Pizarra #39, *Form. Vis.* 39; cf. *LV* II.1.12–13.

76 Gisadus: Pizarra #92; cf. *LV* V.6.3–4. The property to be pledged should be decided by a judge or three respectable persons (*trium honestorum uirorum*); the slate is fragmentary but may refer to three or four *vicarii* present. Other *placita*: Pizarra #12–14 (*CE* 285, *PSent.* 1.12.3; *LV* III.4.10, V.4.14, etc.), 18, 43 (*Form. Vis.* 2, 6, 38).

77 *ChLA* XLVI 1398, at the petition of a deacon and priest; *ChLA* XLVI 1400 (i.e. the superior script of the royal decree mentioned above), reread and signed by the actor (Cixa) and several witnesses.

78 I omit here (for reasons of space) discussion of manumission, which likewise could be performed *per scripturam* or among witnesses with equal validity (*LV* IV.2.18, 5.12; V.1.13–14, 6.6–7, 7.1–20, etc.), though V.7.14 addresses the use of a document to stipulate the terms of the freedman's *peculium*. The templates for manumission in the formulary (*Form. Vis.* 1–6) show ecclesiastical influence, and no examples survive in the slates (though some fragments might be such) or parchments.

79 *LV* II.5.10, 'scripturas conficit amplius quam lex iubet'; cf. III.1.5, IV.5.1. *Firmitas*: e.g. *LV* V.4.3. Sales with *scriptura* have *plena firmitas*, dating back to *CE* 286. Written and oral evidence: King, *Law and Society*, 105–11.

validity', and we see similar statements privileging writing in the *Formulae Visigothicae*: one template quotes and then updates a precept of the *Pauli Sententiae*: 'Granted that "written instruments of sale are not essential in contracts of sale and purchase defined in good faith" (= *PSent.* 2.18.10 *interp.*), however, it confers security for the buyer if the specific terms (*definitio ipsa*) are confirmed with the solidity of writing.' Other templates for sales make similar statements.[80] Moreover, many examples of sales can be found among the slate texts, and these repeat the legal language for such transactions found in the formulary and in Visigothic law. Unfortunately, most of these are very fragmentary, but the small sums of money and property they record show that even minor transactions were considered worthy of scratching into slate and preserving.[81]

One slate in particular shows how they were used for archival purposes. On one side the slate preserves a charter recording the sale of land by Gregorios to his 'lord and nephew' Desiderius; the other side preserves a document entitled *Professio de seruitudine*, in which a certain Unigildus testifies that he arrived in the area to initiate a lawsuit relating to fraud, and had adduced Froila as a witness at the house of Desiderius. Froila then, we are told, led Unigildus to another house, where he was set to work 'in the strawberry fields' (*in fragis*), and received in return certain objects from Desiderius.[82] It seems that Desiderius, by recording the testimony of Unigildus, could prove that he paid for the work that Froila had performed by proxy, thereby avoiding legal problems that might arise once Unigildus had left the area. Here one slate has functioned as the record of two different transactions that could be used by Desiderius in court to verify his claims.

Before turning to the issue of documents for estate management raised by these slates, it is worth noting that Visigothic law excelled other barbarian legislation in the use of documents in family law, particularly for marriage and divorce. Donations, either *causa mortis* or *inter vivos*, could be made with or without documentation, but documents were absolutely

[80] *CE* 286 (*plena firmitas*); *Form. Vis.* 13. Sales and writing: *Form. Vis.* 12 ('ut scripturae firmitas emittatur'), 27 (*cartula commutationis*, 'per scripturae conscribere tramitem'), 28 ('licet mutuo . . . consensu . . . sed ad posteritatis memoriam reservandam adicitur testimonium literarum'); cf. *Form. Vis.* 11, only 'iuratione confirmo'.

[81] Sales: Pizarra #8 (land for 3 *solidi*), 19, 30 (wine), 41, 66 (wine), 107 (wine), 121, etc.; too fragmentary are #9, 15–17, 22, 26, 37–8, 44, 60–1, 64–5, 70, 72B, 73, 80, 94, 98, 112, 122, 126, 130, 136–8, 142, 144, 150. A fragmentary sale or exchange of cows is also preserved on parchment (*ChLA* XLVI 1402, s. VII$^{ex}$), as is a *cartola commutationis vel resepenationis* subscribed by no fewer than six different hands, none giving any qualification, hence they are presumably laymen (*ChLA* XLVI 1401, *post*-687).

[82] Pizarra #40; the charter uses language similar to *Form. Vis.* 11. My thanks to Graham Barrett for sharing with me his observations on this text and the slates in general.

necessary for donations between husband and wife.[83] A formal betrothal (*disponsatio*), the second stage of marriage proceedings after the suit (*petitio*) and before the wedding (*nuptiae*), involved legal obligations of establishing the 'dowry' – not the traditional Roman type, but rather one conveying property from the groom's side to the bride, common to late Roman society (*donatio ante nuptias*) and Germanic traditions ('bride-price', 'morning gift'). This needed to be witnessed, either in writing or by the delivery of a ring as pledge, but the benefits of a dowry contract (*dotale scriptura*, or *dotale tabula*) ensured 'future conjugal dignity'.[84] Indeed, the templates for several such contracts survive in the *Formulae Visigothicae* (and Merovingian formularies also), including one in verse form for a Goth marrying a girl 'from senatorial stock' and another that cites 'Papean, Popean and Julian law about the statutes of marriage', which date back to Augustus.[85] While divorce was only acceptable on certain grounds (mainly adultery), the law notes that 'reckless men' try to obtain divorce by producing false documents or coercing their wives into signing them.[86]

We have discussed how slate texts were used in the legal contexts mentioned above, but a final word needs to be said about their role as documentation for estate management and their place in the history of documentation.[87] The use of slate for texts is known in a few other places (such as tenth-century Ireland and fifteenth-century England), but can be compared to the use of birch bark at Novgorod or wood and *ostraca* in Africa as constituting a locally convenient medium for preserving information. Nearly all of our slate texts come from the northern Meseta region, from around forty-two different sites located along the Salamanca-Ávila border, most in contexts – apparently from villas or walled *castros* – without any obvious ecclesiastical presence, such

83 Husband–wife: *LV* V.2.7. Visigothic donations: Levy, *West Roman Vulgar Law*, 138–42, 164–6.

84 *LV* III.1.9 (possibly Ervig); also III.1–8.

85 *Form. Vis.* 14–20.14: 'ex lege Papeam Popeam et ex legem Iulianum quae de maritandis ordinibus'. *Lex Papia Poppaea* (*c.* AD 9), was a supplement to the *Leges Juliae* of 18 and 19 BC concerning marriage and adultery: S. Treggiari, *Roman Marriage: Iusti Coniuges from the Time of Cicero to the Time of Ulpian* (Oxford, 1993); the same laws are alluded to (though not named) in Marculf 2.15 (see MGH Formulae 85n1). *Form. Vis.* 20: 'ex stirpe senatus', also suspiciously mentioning a *morgincap*. Cantabria maintained a council called a 'senate', and the term appears in other places: King, *Law and Society*, 46n5; Wickham, *Framing*, 94, 223. Pizarra #67 may be a marriage contract.

86 *LV* III.6.1–3. King, *Law and Society*, 235, suggests divorce by mutual consent, but III.6.2 denies it.

87 As the editions of Velázquez Soriano replaced previous attempts, so does her accompanying commentary on the slates. A succinct overview is Collins, *Visigothic Spain*, 170–3.

as that of Diego Álvaro, which has yielded the largest number (fifty-three slates).[88] Despite the different archaeological contexts, the slates display striking similarities of form and content, and nearly all date from the period 560–700, pointing to a shared literate culture of legal norms and estate management removed from any major urban or ecclesiastical centre. Why they cease with the Visigothic kingdom is difficult to answer: the Arab conquest (711), which turned the Meseta into a frontier zone for two centuries, and which reconnected Spain to a wider world in which papyrus and eventually paper could be imported, may be part of the explanation. The argument that they were primarily taxation records that had no purpose after the eclipse of the Visigothic kingdom has no weight.[89]

As is known, the slates comprise a range of different purposes and texts besides those mentioned above, including educational and religious texts (alphabets and writing exercises; prayers and talismans), and, of course, many slates have little or no writing at all, merely recording numbers alongside names or types of produce, such as a 'record of cheeses' (*notitia de casios*) or 'record of sheep' (*notitia de ueruices*). These probably concerned rents, as suggested by other slates with phrases such as 'he has paid', 'I keep back', 'I have given firewood', and so on, or other estate business that needed to be recorded ('John paid 33 *modii* for the horses'), or lists of animals recording their age and sex.[90] Contemporary confirmation that these practices were routine for lay landowners is found in the seventh-century *Life of St Fructuosus*, which records how the saint's father visited his estates in Bierzo (200 km from the slate finds) to receive reports on his flocks, reports that probably looked like our numerical slates, whatever material was used.[91]

While the spelling and grammar of the slates is far from classical and well on its way to proto-Romance (even more so than the Ravennate

88 Five find sites (yielding twenty-four slates altogether) contain archaeological traces of a chapel (e.g. La Aceña de la Fuente and Navahombela), but they may be villas with a private chapel, as was common in late antique Spain, or villas later reused as churches: *Las pizarras visigodas* (2004), 23–41. The archaeology and architecture of Visigothic Spain is notoriously difficult and in need of serious revision: Collins, *Visigothic Spain*, 174–222.

89 I. Martín Viso, 'La sociedad rural en el suroeste de la Meseta del Duero (siglos VI–VII)', in Martín Viso and G. del Ser Quijano (eds.), *Espacios de poder y formas sociales en la edad media* (Salamanca. 2007), 171–88. Spain and trade: O. R. Constable, *Trade and Traders in Muslim Spain: The Commercial Realignment of the Iberian Peninsula, 900–1500* (Cambridge, 1994), 30–2.

90 Cheese: Pizarra #11. Sheep: #97. *Exprendit, recondo* and horses: #5. *Dedi licias*: #125. Animals: #53–4, 75–7.

91 *Vita sancti Fructuosi* 2 (ed. M. C. Díaz y Díaz [Braga, 1974], 82; trans. A. T. Fear, *Lives of the Visigothic Fathers* [Liverpool, 1997], 124).

papyri and Lombard charters), they reveal a degree of practical literacy in the remote countryside that was difficult to imagine before their discovery (in the 1940s and 1950s) and subsequent publication. We have seen this in the legal texts mentioned above, but it is also apparent in a handful of letters on slate relating to estate management. By far the most complete letter (fourteen lines of text on both sides of a slate *c.* 89×168 mm) is that of Faustinus, who writes to a 'Lord Paul' to request that he gather the olive harvest in the customary manner (*ut comodo consuetudinem*), warn him of potential fraud by his slaves or tenants (*mancipii*), ask him to verify the receipt of certain goods with his seal-ring (*sigilla de tuo anula*), and transfer certain dependants (all named) to different locations. Even more striking than the mention of a seal-ring (referred to several times in Visigothic law) is the impression of an administrator telling a lord (*dominus*) what to do and how to do it.[92] Another letter, unfortunately very fragmentary, also appears to be a report to a landowner, perhaps one who resides in or holds office in Toledo, for it mentions the city (the only location named among all the slates), money (*tremisses*) and even a Gothic loanword for profit (*gannatione*), along with a list of names and quantities in the manner of the *notitiae* mentioned above.[93]

## Conclusion: towards Lombard Italy

Lombard Italy presents problems of evidence that are similar to those of Visigothic Spain: legislation and other evidence offer strong indications that there was a considerable amount of documentary activity going on, but hardly a scrap of it survives.[94] Our surviving charters begin in the eighth century, which tally over 370, and the numbers double, even triple in some places, in the ninth century. Yet, twenty years after their initial conquest of north and central Italy, and once monarchic rule was secured (568–90), Lombard kings adopted late Roman trappings of court culture, issued royal charters in chancery style, and engaged in diplomatic correspondence with Rome, Ravenna and Constantinople. The *Edict* of King Rothari, published in 643, on the eve of an aggressive (and successful) campaign against the Byzantines, contained far fewer references to documents than Recceswinth's *Liber iudiciorum* (654), but it, too, adopted much of late Roman property law, and was clearly intended to be used

92 Pizarra #103. Seal-rings: *LV* VI.6.2 (royal); II.1.19, 20, etc.; King, *Law and Society*, 94n3. Other letters: Pizarra #61, 68, 111–12, 134–5.

93 Pizarra #75.

94 What follows is fully documented in N. Everett, *Literacy in Lombard Italy* (Cambridge, 2003); Everett, 'Scribes and Charters'; Everett, 'Literacy and the Law in Lombard Government', *EME*, 9 (2000), 93–127.

in courts, as it certainly was in our eighth-century evidence, along with later legislation, most notably that of King Liutprand (712–44), which contains many references to the use of documents. There is no doubt that Rothari's *Edict* is full of Lombard customs that derive from a more Germanic world – wergelds, compositions, oath-helpers (a type of character witness) – and glosses of crimes, practices and legal categories with Old High German words (*plotraub*, *fulcfree*, *gairethinx*, etc.). There is plenty here for the strain of historiography that highlights Lombard difference, or argues that their kingdom represents a complete break from the Roman past, unlike Odovacar or the Ostrogoths. True, Rothari envisages oral procedures (pledges, oaths, sureties) for most transactions, but his few references to documents are telling: two laws, one insisting on documentation for leased land (for later use in court if needed), and another prescribing amputation of the hand for forging charters, book-end a section concerning property, and immediately before this Rothari recommends the use of a charter to secure manumissions performed with the 'four roads' ceremony, a ritual involving a whip and arrow, and described with six Old High German words.[95] The use of such terms and practices was undoubtedly in part ideological: Liutprand introduced Germanic words where Rothari was content to use Latin, yet his legislation was far more Roman in character. In any case, the eighth-century evidence, both legislation and documents, shows that Lombard elites adapted to written forms of administration and legal instruments quickly. To illustrate, let us end with an archive: a list of documents belonging to a Lombard officer, Alahis *vir magnificus*, active in Tuscany *c.* 720–30, mentions about fifty charters, a dozen of which were royal diplomas of Liutprand.[96] That we only know about this archive because it was later preserved by a nun (and her daughter), and then by the bishop of Pisa, is the same pattern of preservation we have seen in Ravenna, and see everywhere else in early medieval Europe, as the chapters in this volume amply show.

[95] *ER* 227 (*libellus* for leases), 243 (amputation), 224 (manumission). Royal charters: *CDL* III 197. Private charters: *CDL* I–II.

[96] Alahis and Pisan list: *CDL* II 295 (= *ChLA* XXV 808); on the date, Everett, 'Scribes and Charters', 39–40, 80.

# 5 The *gesta municipalia* and the public validation of documents in Frankish Europe

*Warren C. Brown*

*The degree of continuity or change in documentary practices after the disappearance of the western Roman Empire is a question raised with particular force by continued references to the* gesta municipalia. *Although their core fiscal function had vanished along with the Roman state, references to the* gesta *continue to be found in Frankish formularies – that is, collections of models for different kinds of legal document – dating from the late eighth and ninth centuries, and referring to procedures undertaken between the late sixth and the ninth. The deliberate inclusion, and sometimes adaptation, of* gesta *formulas in manuscripts of formula-books, and references in charters, show that even though now used by different institutions in different contexts, the* gesta*'s established language and procedures continued to be adopted, as one among several options for the pubic validation of transactions and their documents.*

For students of documentary practices in the early medieval West, the *gesta municipalia* have long been an important touchstone.[1] As Everett notes, the disappearance of these civic document registers has been linked in particular to a putative transition from a public to a private documentary culture as Roman Late Antiquity gave way to the early Middle Ages.[2] Pushing against this narrative, Everett shows us that the *gesta* reflected a very particular context. They were never intended to

[1] H. Cancik and H. Schneider (eds.), *Brill's New Pauly: Encyclopaedia of the Ancient World*, 16 vols. (Leiden, 2002–10), s.v. *gesta* (V, 827–8); P. Johanek, 'Gesta municipalia', in *Lexikon des Mittelalters*, 10 vols. (Munich, 1980–99), IV, 1408; B. Hirschfeld, *Die Gesta municipalia in römischer und frühgermanischer Zeit* (Marburg, 1904), 8–15; O. Redlich, *Die Privaturkunden des Mittelalters* (Munich, 1911), 8–10; P. Classen, *Kaiserreskript und Königsurkunde: Diplomatische Studien zum Problem der Kontinuität zwischen Altertum und Mittelalter* (Thessaloniki, 1977), 33, and Classen, 'Fortleben', 42; I. Wood, *The Merovingian Kingdoms 450–751* (London, 1994), 204, and Wood, 'Disputes in Late Fifth- and Sixth-Century Gaul: Some Problems', in *Settlement of Disputes*, 7–22, at 12–14. Of J. Barbier, 'Pouvoirs et élites dans le monde franc (VI$^{e}$–XI$^{e}$ siècle). Matériaux pour servir à l'histoire des élites des cités (VI$^{e}$–IX$^{e}$ siècle): Le Dossier des *gesta municipalia*, étude n$^{o}$ 2', unpublished mémoire d'HDR, Université de Paris I–Panthéon-Sorbonne (2009), only Part I, ch. 3, and Part II were available to me at the time this volume went to press.

[2] Above, 71.

serve, nor did they serve, as public document repositories, on which document users depended to safeguard their documents and through which, therefore, document use was mediated. Their *raison d'être* was fiscal; they represented, above all, efforts by successive imperial governments to keep track of properties that could be taxed and of those who were responsible for the tax burdens.[3] As the late Roman state dissolved, the *gesta* lost their reason for being. They remain visible in Ravenna into the early seventh century only because Ravenna was a centre of late Roman and Romanized barbarian administration and power in a time when uncertainty drove both Roman and Gothic elites to cling to Roman traditions, and because Ravenna's correspondingly powerful church preserved records of *gesta* protocols in which it had been involved.[4]

The *gesta municipalia* have nevertheless left us with a puzzle that needs to be solved in order to understand why our evidence for documentary culture in the post-Roman West looks the way that it does. The *gesta* left a *Nachklang* that resonated in the West for centuries, especially in the Frankish kingdoms north of the Alps. References to the *gesta* in Frankish sources are abundant and surprisingly persistent; they stretch from the Merovingian period deep into the Carolingian period and beyond. These references appear in a variety of sources, including wills and charters.[5] The most numerous and detailed, however, are to be found in the Frankish formula collections.[6] These are albums of document forms; that is, collections of texts that could serve as complete templates for documents and letters, or as sources for language. Some of them were obviously created as models for typical or frequently needed documents. Others were apparently drawn from actual documents that had some interesting or important characters or features; they were turned into formulas by having some or all of their case-specific information removed. The formula collections survive in manuscripts ranging in date from the eighth through the tenth centuries that span the entire Frankish world both east and west of the Rhine. The document forms in them for the most part stem from roughly the same period, but many can be traced back to the seventh and even the sixth centuries.[7]

[3] Above, 64, 72. See also Everett, 'Scribes and Charters in Lombard Italy', *Studi Medievali*, 41 (2000), 39–83, at 43–4, and Wickham, *Framing*, 70.

[4] Above, 64–5, 72–82. [5] Barbier, 'Pouvoirs et élites', Part II, pp. 114–97.

[6] Edited by K. Zeumer as MGH Formulae.

[7] Rio, *Legal Practice*; R. Buchner, *Deutschlands Geschichtsquellen im Mittelalter*, Beiheft, *Die Rechtsquellen* (Weimar, 1953), 49–55; Classen, 'Fortleben', 15; *Settlement of Disputes*, 271 (glossary, s.v. 'Formula and Formulary'); McKitterick, *Carolingians*, 25; I. Wood, 'Administration, Law and Culture in Merovingian Gaul', in *Uses of Literacy*, 63–81, esp. 64–5; C. Lauranson-Rosaz and A. Jeannin, 'La résolution des litiges en justice durant le haut *moyen âge*: L'exemple de l'*apennis* à travers les formules, notamment celles d'Auvergne et d'Angers', in *Le règlement des conflits au moyen âge: XXXI$^{e}$ Congrès de la S.H.M.E.S. (Angers, juin 2000)* (Paris, 2001), 21–33, esp. 23–5; Brown, 'Documents'.

Some of the formulas that refer to the *gesta* do so only in short, formulaic phrases, as, for example, when a formula for a transaction mandates that the record be submitted to the *gesta*.[8] Others, however, represent complete *gesta* protocols that describe the entire process of submitting a document to the *gesta* in detail. These latter formulas give a very late antique impression; that is, they refer specifically to such things as a city's municipal assembly or *curia*, to officials bearing late Roman titles and so forth. Most of them describe transactions by laypeople (or at least people who are not explicitly identified as clerics) for the benefit of laypeople. Only a few concern transactions in which a layperson gave, or might have given, something to a church or monastery.[9] On the surface, then, they would indeed seem to reflect tradition-minded Frankish scribes carrying forward relics of late Roman documentary culture into a world to which they no longer applied.

And yet, these formulas kept getting copied, and recopied, for a very long time. Though many of them were originally Merovingian, they all survive in manuscripts from the Carolingian period: from the late eighth century in a few cases, in most cases from the ninth. If the *gesta municipalia* themselves were by this point dead, and if the context that had produced them and the culture of lay document use of which they were a part had disappeared, why did anyone go to the (often significant) effort to copy complete *gesta* protocols into the surviving manuscripts? Tradition might explain the persistence of formulaic phrases, and the formulas in general are indeed rife with phrases that clearly represent vestigial memories of long-vanished practices.[10] But for Frankish scribes to go to the effort to copy and recopy complete formulas for this particular document type over such a span of time suggests to me that they were motivated by more than tradition.

Their efforts can be explained by going back to late antique Italy and looking more closely at how the *gesta* served the needs and interests not only of the late Roman and Gothic authorities but also of the people who brought their documents to the *gesta* for registration. If the authorities used the *gesta* to keep track of tax obligations as property changed hands, those who came to the *gesta* achieved something equally valuable: they had their legal transactions validated and secured by having the

8 See, *inter alia*, *Form. Andec.* 41: 'gestis municipalis sit oblegatum'; *Form. Tur.* 20: 'et adhuc mihi inserere placuit, ut hoc mandatum civitate illa cum curia publica, ut mos est, gestis municipalibus facias alligari'.

9 What I mean by 'might have given': three formulas give churches or monasteries as options; that is, a person N gave property to the church N, or to his nephew N, or to his bride N.

10 For example, the tag *stipulatione subnixa* at the end of charter formulas, or the references to manumitted persons enjoying the freedoms of Roman citizens, both of which are discussed below, 133, 135.

documents in which those transactions were recorded publicly ratified by the civic authorities and by receiving from the authorities a document saying that the necessary steps had been carried out.

The Frankish *gesta* formulas, and especially the evidence of their manuscript transmission, suggest strongly that a desire to secure transactions in this way persisted in the Frankish kingdoms even after the late Roman state that had created and maintained the *gesta* had dissolved. Accordingly, some of the procedures that had been associated with the *gesta* persisted there as well. Many people in both Merovingian and Carolingian Europe continued to resort to what alongside the civic document registers had always formed an essential part of the *gesta*, namely, public, ceremonial procedures, carried out in an authority-bearing forum, that validated documents recording legal transactions. That these procedures were descended from those associated with the *gesta municipalia* is revealed by the fact that in some places in Frankish Europe, even in the ninth century, formulas describing the *gesta* process were still considered the right and proper way to capture these legal rituals in writing.

Among those who chose to validate and secure their documents this way were laypeople as well as monks and clergy. This tells us that members of both groups still saw written documents as important. When we compare the *gesta* formulas to actual surviving transaction records from both the Merovingian and the Carolingian periods, it becomes clearer how and why documents were important. A legacy of late Roman documentary culture remains clearly visible in the Frankish West: many people, both lay and clerical, still believed that recording their transactions in writing and having the resulting documents publicly validated in an authority-bearing forum was a powerful way to secure them.

## The *gesta municipalia* in the Italian papyri

Despite substantial variation in their subjects and in the formulaic language that they use, the papyri from fifth-, sixth- and early seventh-century Italy give a fairly consistent picture of the *gesta municipalia*.[11] The picture begins with someone who wants to carry out some sort of legal transaction, such as making a new will or verifying the validity of an old one, giving or selling property, acknowledging receipt of a debt

[11] The relevant texts are Tjäder I 4–5, 7, 8, 10–11, 14–15, 18–19, 21; II 29, 31, 32, 33. Following Tjäder's lead, I have chosen to label the papyri under discussion here as 'Italian' rather than 'Ravennate' because, although most of them were undeniably produced in Ravenna or mediated through the archives of the city's cathedral church, there is some uncertainty about whether all of them were. See Tjäder 1:21–3.

payment, or setting up a ward for a minor.[12] This person draws up the appropriate document, or has it drawn up by a scribe, in the presence of witnesses who then add their signatures to it. Occasionally, the document will include a clause asking that it be submitted to the *gesta* (*gestis municipalibus allegare*).[13] Next, either the originator of the transaction or a representative, or the intended beneficiary or a representative,[14] goes with the document to the city whose authorities had jurisdiction over the transaction by virtue either of where the principals lived or where the property at issue was located. There they bring the document to an assembly headed by one or more authority figures. In most cases the assembly can be identified as the city's municipal council.[15] The assembly heads are generally called 'magistrate' (*magistratus*), or occasionally 'advocate' (*defensor*);[16] an exalted exception is the praetorian prefect who headed an assembly in Ravenna in the middle of the sixth century.[17] The papyri also mention officials or functionaries, such as notaries or record keepers (*exceptor*, *notarius*, *chartarius*).[18]

Once the petitioners come before the assembly, the magistrates ask them what they wish. The petitioners reply that they would like their document taken up, read out loud and entered into the records (*acta*, *gesta*). The heads of the assembly then order the document to be taken up, displayed openly and read out loud. In some cases, the original witnesses are present and testify to their role in the document's creation.[19] If the principal responsible for drafting the document is not present, the assembly heads accept the document from his or her representatives and, at their request, order a delegation sent to the principal to verify orally that he or she was responsible for creating it, that it said what he or she wanted it to say, and that he or she had gathered the witnesses whose signatures were on it; in this situation the witnesses also sometimes testify

12 In the sequence given, Tjäder I 4–5, 14–15; II 29; I 8, 7.

13 Tjäder I 8. See Everett, 'Scribes and Charters', p. 75.

14 Originator/representative: the embedded wills in Tjäder I 4–5, 7; beneficiary/representative: Tjäder I 8, 10–11.

15 The members of the assembly are referred to variously as *curiales*, *principales* (or *principales viros*) or *municipes*. See G. W. Bowersock, P. Brown and O. Grabar (eds.), *Late Antiquity: A Guide to the Postclassical World* (Cambridge, MA, 1999), s.vv. 'councils' and 'curiales'.

16 *Magistratus*: throughout the collection; the occasional modifier *quinquennalis* simply means a magistrate serving for a 5-year term. *Defensor*: e.g. Tjäder II 31 (section II, line 6); see C. T. Lewis and C. Short, *A Latin Dictionary* (Oxford, 1879), s.v. *defensor*; Cancik and Schneider (eds.), *Brill's New Pauly*, s.v. *defensor*.

17 Tjäder I 4–5.

18 *Exceptor*: e.g. Tjäder I 10–11 (section II, line 8). *Notarius*: e.g. Tjäder I 10–11 (section II, line 11). See Bowersock, Brown and Grabar (eds.), *Late Antiquity*, s.v. *notarii*. *Chartarius*: see, for example, Tjäder I 10–11 (section III, line 6); Niermeyer, *Lexicon*, s.v. Chartarius.

19 See the will validations embedded in Tjäder I 4–5.

in person.[20] When the delegation has returned with positive answers, the document is taken up by the assembly, read out and entered into the record.

Once all this is done, the assembly heads ask the petitioners what more they wish. The petitioners ask for an official record of the proceedings (*gesta*) 'as is the custom' (*ex more*). The assembly heads order this done. Though it is not always possible to tell for certain, it appears that in most if not all cases it is these *gesta* records given to the petitioners, or later copies, that we have in the papyri. In several examples, the text then concludes with validating statements by the members of the assembly and/or the officials involved.[21]

This broad template covers various kinds of transactions, and various kinds of principals, both lay and ecclesiastic. A sub-deacon gives property to the church at Ravenna.[22] A lay couple gives half of their property to the church at Ravenna.[23] A cleric from the Gothic (that is, Arian) church in Ravenna sells property to a soap-maker from a nearby town;[24] a banker sells an acolyte from Rome some property in Ravenna.[25] The ward for a minor who has inherited property from a man who has died gives a security for the receipt of the property to the dead man's widow.[26] In Rieti, a Gothic woman appoints a ward for her two children to handle the lawsuits in which their dead father was involved.[27]

The *gesta* records include the texts of the original transaction documents they were intended to validate, as well as the texts of any attachments, such as a property list.[28] They can also contain the records of other *gesta* processes. The most spectacular example, from 489, comes from Syracuse. This document represents the last stage in a gift of property in the territory of Syracuse, from the king Odovacar, who had in 476 seized power in Italy from the western emperor Romulus Augustulus, to his faithful follower Pierus. Odovacar's original gift document is embedded within the record of that document's validation before an assembly in Ravenna and its entry into the Ravenna *gesta*. The texts of both of these documents are embedded in the text written on the actual surviving papyrus, which is the copy (*gesta*) issued to Pierus' representatives of the record written up by the *curia* in Syracuse recording the gift's entry into the *gesta* of Syracuse, the formal transfer of the property (*traditio*) and the change of the owner of record in the tax rolls (*polypthicis publicis*).[29]

This last example makes explicit the fact that the late Roman state used the *gesta municipalia* to keep track of people's tax obligations. The

[20] See Tjäder I 14–15. [21] See, for example, Tjäder I 7, 14–15, or 31.
[22] Tjäder I 21. [23] Tjäder I 14–15. [24] Tjäder II 33. [25] Tjäder II 29.
[26] Tjäder I 8. [27] Tjäder I 7. [28] E.g. Tjäder I 8. [29] Tjäder I 10–11.

papyri accordingly highlight the entry of documents and the record of the proceedings into a central, official register. But the *gesta* also served their petitioners; those who submitted their documents to the *gesta* had reasons for doing so that went beyond simply responding to the state's imperatives. First, they obtained the legal validation (*firmitas*) of their transactions. Second, they had an entry in the city's official records (*acta* or *gesta*) made that contained the text of their original transaction documents and stated that the actions necessary to validate them and thus secure the transaction had taken place. Third, they received an official copy of this record to take with them.[30] They would presumably have kept this copy with the original transaction document to protect their rights should their transaction ever be challenged. These ends are captured by a statement appearing towards the end of several of the papyri, made by the petitioners to the officiating magistrate(s) at the end of the process, that runs more or less as in the following example: 'Since everything that pertains to the validation of these documents of sale and letter of transfer has been properly carried out in sequence, I therefore ask your Excellency, highest magistrate, that you order the *gesta* to be issued to me, for my defence, by the responsible official according to custom.'[31]

The *gesta* records demonstrably did what they were supposed to do. Sometime between 552 and 575, some notaries from the church of Ravenna wanted for some unknown reason to re-establish their church's claims to properties that had been willed to it.[32] So they came before an assembly in Ravenna headed by the praetorian prefect of Italy. There the *gesta* documents recording the relevant wills' validation were read out and entered anew into the city's records.[33] The result is another set of nested documents; the original *gesta* records containing the texts of the original wills (albeit truncated), and recording their opening, verification, validation and entry into the city records, were copied into a new *gesta* document that in turn recorded their revalidation and entry into the record.

[30] That this latter copy had an official character emerges from a comment at the end of one of the papyri, from 557, which notes that it was produced from an 'authentic' original ('ex authentico editum'): Tjäder I 7.

[31] 'Quoniam omnia ordine suo, que ad firmitatem ipsorum instrumentorum venditionum vel epistule traditionis rubor pertinebat, rite ademplita sunt . . . ut gesta mihi propter monimen meum a conpetenti officio edi iubeatis ex more': Tjäder II 31. Cf. Everett, 'Scribes and Charters', 43–4, and above, 80 (on *monimen*).

[32] Tjäder I 4–5. Cf. above, 76–7.

[33] Since the beginning of this text is missing, it is impossible to say for sure whether these *gesta* records were brought from the church, that is, that they were the church's copies, or were pulled from the city's archives. Tjäder (1:200) assumes the latter, though without giving a reason.

The papyri place officially sanctioned written records at centre stage in the making and securing of legal transactions. They also, however, tell us that much more was involved. The transactions described in the papyri were first set down in writing, and then they were witnessed and signed (and in some cases sealed). The documents were then taken to a public, authority-bearing forum, openly displayed and read aloud by an official attached to that forum. The creator of the document orally verified that its contents matched his or her wishes and that the witnesses whose marks were on it were those that he or she had gathered. In some cases the witnesses themselves also orally verified the contents of the document and their participation in its creation. The document was then copied into an official record along with a written description of the ritual acts surrounding its verification. The final act in the process had the petitioners, in the last of a series of ritual actions, asking for and receiving an official written description of all of the steps, written, oral and ritual, that had been taken to validate their transaction. In short, to submit documents to the *gesta municipalia* meant to go through this entire process, in which written records, speech, memory and public ceremony were combined and interdependent.[34] The process produced two records, one in the city's official register, and one that went home with the petitioner(s), presumably to be kept with the original transaction documents.

## The Frankish formulas describing the submission of documents to *gesta municipalia*

Eight surviving manuscripts from Frankish Europe contain formulas describing the submission of documents to *gesta municipalia*.[35] As noted above, these manuscripts stem from the Carolingian period; that is, the eighth (mostly the late eighth) and ninth centuries. Their geography is a bit harder to pin down because not all of them have been localized precisely. They all, however, come from the regions west of the Rhine. Those whose place of origin has been determined more precisely stem from areas on the Loire.[36] The formula texts themselves appear to cover

[34] On the tradition of publicly performing transactions, visible in late Roman legislation from Constantine on, see Everett, 'Scribes and Charters', 52 and 60.

[35] Fulda (Hessische Landesbibliothek) D1; Leiden (Universiteitsbibliothek) BPL 114; BnF lat. 2123, 4409, 4627, 4697, 10756; Warsaw (Biblioteka Uniwersytecka) 1.

[36] Fulda D1: s. VIII$^{ex}$, Angers or Tours; Leiden BPL 114: Bourges?, s. VIII$^{ex}$ or s. IX$^{in}$; BnF lat. 2123: W. Francia, possibly Burgundy, s. VIII$^{ex}$ or s. IX$^{in}$; BnF lat. 4409: N. Francia, s. IX$^{ex}$; BnF lat. 4627: Tours?, s. IX (possibly soon after 818); BnF lat. 4697: Francia, s. IX; BnF lat. 10756: the relevant part is Burgundian, s. VIII (727?);

a much broader span of time.[37] They have been dated from the late sixth century to the early ninth century. They too are West Frankish. Most stem from cities located on the Loire and southwards, except for one from eastern Neustria and two from Sens.[38]

The *gesta* formulas all describe more or less the same sequence of events. First, someone carries out a transaction of some kind (such as a property gift, a dowry grant, an inheritance arrangement, etc.) and has a charter written that describes it; this charter is witnessed. Then, the person responsible for the transaction gives another person a written mandate to take the charter to a nearby city and submit it to the *gesta municipalia* (*gestis municipalibus allegare* or *prosequere*). The mandate bearer (from this point on often called the *prosecutor*) duly appears before the *curia* of the city, which is headed by a *defensor*. He asks the *defensor* and *curia* to have the public books (*codices publici*) opened to him because he has something that ought to be submitted to the *gesta municipalia*. The *defensor* replies that the public books lie open to him and that he should do what he wishes. In response, the *prosecutor* offers first his written mandate from the original donor, then the original charter to the assembly, and asks that they be read out loud. The documents are accepted by the assembly and read out, most often by a notary (*amanuensis*).[39] The documents having been read, the *curia* recognizes them as valid. At the *prosecutor*'s request, the *curia* then issues a written document (that is, this formula) to the *prosecutor* saying that all this has been done. Finally, in some cases we get a note from the *prosecutor* back to the original donor saying that he had done what he was supposed to do.

Although the *gesta* formulas all outline the same procedure, and in some places use virtually identical language, they are not all the same. They are not derived from a single source or even much related to each other beyond their essential content. For one thing, each deals with a different kind of transaction.[40] Most of the transactions involve only

Warsaw 1: Tours, s. IX$^{1/2}$. See Rio, *Legal Practice*, 241–71 ('Appendix: A Handlist of Manuscripts'), and the literature she cites in the entry on each manuscript.

37 Using Zeumer's names and numbering, the formulas are as follows: *Form. Andec.* 1abc; *Form. Arvern.* 2ab; *Form. Bitur.* 6 and 15abcd; Marculf 2.37–8; *Cart. Sen.* 39–40; *Cart. Sen. App.* 1abcd; *Form. Tur.* 2–3; *Form. Tur. Add.* 4–5 = *Coll. Flav.* 9–10.

38 *Form. Andec.* (Angers, s. VI$^{ex}$); *Form. Arvern.* (Clermont, s. VIII$^{med}$); *Form. Bitur.* (Bourges, *c.* 800); Marculf (St-Denis or Meaux?, s. VII$^{2/2}$); *Cart. Sen.* (Sens, 768×74); *Cart. Sen. App.* (Sens, s. VIII?); *Form. Tur.* (Tours, s. VIII$^{med}$); *Form. Tur. Add.* (Tours or Flavigny, s. VIII$^{ex}$ or s. IX$^{in}$?); *Coll. Flav.* (Flavigny, s. VIII$^{ex}$ or s. IX$^{in}$). See Rio, *Legal Practice*, 67–101, 111–26.

39 Bowersock, Brown and Grabar (eds.), *Late Antiquity*, s.v. *notarii*; Niermeyer, *Lexicon*, s.v. *amanuensis*.

40 Very little of the formula evidence for the *gesta*, Merovingian or Carolingian, deals with the registration of wills. See also J. Barbier, 'Testaments et pratique testamentaire dans

laypeople: husbands make dotal gifts to their brides,[41] a mother gives power of attorney to her son,[42] a man donates property.[43] One case deals with a husband who never quite got around to giving his wife her morning gift or *dos*, so that their children were legally illegitimate; the transaction has him passing property to his children anyway.[44] Three formulas include churches as optional parties: one man makes a donation to a church, a monastery, or an illustrious man;[45] another either gives property to a church or makes a dotal gift to a woman;[46] a third gives property either to a church or to his grandson.[47] The formulas' structure also varies. Some present each element of the procedure in distinct parts, in the following order: the original donation charter, the mandate, the procedure before the *curia*, and the mandate bearer's notification to the original donor. Others present the pieces in the order in which they would have taken place before the *curia*. That is, we start with the *prosecutor* appearing before the *curia*; then, as the mandate and original transaction charter are read out, their texts are given; then we close with the ending of the *gesta* procedure. Still others compress some or all of these parts together, or stop halfway through with the procedure incomplete. Finally, the length and detail vary from formula to formula; some present all of the elements I have described; others are truncated to a greater or lesser degree. In other words, these formulas appear to reflect a set of assumptions about the *gesta municipalia* procedure that was common to several areas in the central regions of Gaul. Nevertheless, they represent independent formula traditions; they were not all derived from a single source.

Many of these formulas do share one other feature in common, however: it is very hard to understand how a central document register fits into the process they describe. As noted above, all of the formulas start out by referring to a set of public books (*codices publici*). The *prosecutor* asks the assembly and its heads to have the public books opened because he has something that he wishes to submit to them;[48] the *defensor* then

le royaume franc (VI^e–VIII^e siècle)', in F. Bougard, C. La Rocca and R. Le Jan (eds.), *Sauver son âme et se perpétuer: Transmission du patrimoine et mémoire au haut moyen âge* (Rome, 2005), 7–79, at 31n129. Many of the references to the *gesta* outside the formulas, however, do come in the context of testaments; see Barbier, 'Pouvoirs et élites', Part I, Chapter 3, *passim*; compare above, 77 and n.35.

41 *Form. And.* 1abc; *Form. Bitur.* 15abcd. 42 *Form. Arvern.* 2ab.

43 *Form. Tur.* 2–3; *Form. Tur. Add.* 4–5 = *Coll. Flav.* 9–10. 44 *Cart. Sen. App.* 1abcd.

45 Marculf 2.37–8. 46 *Cart. Sen.* 39–40. 47 *Form. Bitur.* 6.

48 E.g. *Form. Andec.* 1a: 'utique coticis puplici patere iobeatis, qua habeo, quid apud acta prosequere debiam'; Marculf 2.37: 'ut mihi codices publicus patere iubeatis, quia habeo aliquid, que gestis prosequere debeam'; *Form. Tur.* 3: 'ut mihi codices publicos patere iubeatis, quia inluster vir ille per hunc mandatum ad me speravit, ut donationem illam,

replies that they are open. But in most of the formulas, these public books then drop out of sight; they take no further part in the proceedings and leave behind no hint of how they were used. Only at the end of one example from Tours do they make another appearance; the *prosecutor*, after his documents have been read out before the assembly, asks that the public records (*publica momenta = monumenta*) be taken up, and that once the books have been opened (*patefactis codicibus*) he be given a copy of the *gesta*.[49] This vague request implies that the copy was to be produced from the public books.

In only two formulas does a central, written register maintained by the *curia* play a clear and coherent part in the process. Both derive from the same source, namely the formula collection of the monk Marculf, compiled in eastern Neustria sometime in the second half of the seventh century. One appears in Marculf's collection itself; it is titled '*Gesta* according to the custom of the Romans, how donations or testaments should be read'. The other was drafted either in Tours or in Flavigny, but it lifts the relevant language directly from Marculf.[50] In both, we start as usual with the opening dialogue about the public books. As the process unfolds, the *defensor* orders that the original donation charter be read out and then inserted into the public *gesta* (*gestis publicis*). At the end, he directs that a written copy of the proceedings (*gesta*) be given to the prosecutor and that the *gesta* be preserved in the public archives to be remembered (*ut in arcipibus publicis memoranda servetur*). It appears that Marculf drew on a documentary tradition, which he quite consciously thought of as Roman, in which central records and archives were important. The Tours or Flavigny copyist picked this tradition up from Marculf.

These two formulas are, however, exceptions. In the other *gesta* formulas, it is very difficult to tell what part centrally maintained written records

quem de rebus suis proprietariis de loca nuncupantia illa, sitas in pago illo, partibus illius per sua legittima strumenta confirmavit, gestis municipalibus cum curia publica et defensore prosequere et alligare deberem'; *Form. Bitur.* 15c: 'uti mihi codicis publicae paterae praecipiatis, que abeo, gestorum alegatione cupio roborarae'.

49 *Form. Tur.* 3: 'rogo, ut publica momenta suscipiat, et, patefactis codicibus, gesta, cum a vobis fuerit subscripta, mihi nobilitas vestra, ut mos est, tradi precipiat'.

50 Marculf 2.37–8; *Form. Tur. Add.* 4–5. These last two formulas appear only in the two surviving manuscripts of a formula collection from Flavigny, called by Zeumer the *Collectio Flaviniacensis*; they are *Coll. Flav.* 9 and 10. Because they blend material from Marculf with formulas that clearly come from a Tours formula collection, and because in one of the manuscripts they were incorporated *en bloc* with the rest of the Tours collection into the Flavigny collection, Zeumer apparently concluded that they had come from Tours and published them as *Form. Tur. Add.* 4 and 5. However, there is no compelling reason to conclude that they come from Tours; they may just as easily have been created and copied in Flavigny. Cf. Rio, *Legal Practice*, 117–21.

are playing.[51] The opening references to 'public books' suggest that central records did once form an important element of the *gesta municipalia* tradition in the areas where these formulas were produced. However, as the formulas present them, the references appear to be vestigial. The public books are disconnected from events; they remain peripheral to the action and their purpose is unclear.

One standard for judging whether or not a piece of formulaic language in a formula text had any real connection to the world of the scribe who copied it might be whether it makes any sense within the formula's internal logic. In the *gesta* formulas that stand outside the Marculf tradition, the references to a central written record do not make this kind of sense; they have no essential connection, or at best a vague one, to the process being described.

Yet the *gesta* formulas do describe a process with a recognizable logic whose purpose we are able to grasp. In this process, a petitioner secured a transaction by having the original transaction document ratified by a public assembly that had the authority to ratify it. The document was ratified by having it read out loud before the assembly and by having the assembly publicly acknowledge that it was valid. The assembly then produced for the petitioner a document saying that all this had been done. This comprises only part of what we saw in the Italian papyri. There the *gesta* process had two elements: on the one hand, the central written register, and, on the other, the public display of documents, oral performance, human memory and final issuing of a document that supported the central register and validated the petitioners' transactions. In the Frankish formulas that fall outside the Marculf tradition, the part of the process having to do with the central written register has become incoherent. The other part, however, remains in focus.

Within the picture created by these formulas, then, it appears that to submit a document to the *gesta municipalia* essentially meant to secure a transaction (*gesta*) by having the original charter with which it was carried out (*gesta*) read out in a public, authority-bearing forum (*gesta*

[51] In the oldest of the *gesta* formulas, from sixth-century Angers, the *prosecutor*, at the end of the process, says, 'Gracias agere magnitudine vestrae quod dotem sua scripta quem prosequio gestis municipalibus ut abuit karitas vestra alegassetis.' It is very hard to tell what exactly this means; that is, whether the prosecutor is thanking the *curia* for having taken up the dotal gift that he (i.e. the prosecutor) had submitted to the *gesta*, for having taken up the dotal gift before the *gesta* (i.e. the assembly) which they had held, or for having inserted it into the *gesta* as a central written register, i.e. the *coticis puplici* (*sic*) with which the formula sequence opens. Rio, *Formularies*, 49–50, indeed translates the passage in the latter sense. The point to take away here, however, is that it is not at all clear.

*municipalia*) and recognized as valid; the security thus given the transaction by this procedure was embodied in the document (*gesta*) produced at the forum saying that this had been done. In other words, what the original donor cared about – what he wanted to have done and have a record saying had been done – was the public reading and ratification of his charter in an authority-bearing forum. The most important thing for his representative the mandate-bearer/prosecutor to do was not to insert a document into a *gesta municipalia* as a central, written record, but rather to take away a document from a *gesta municipalia* as an authority-bearing public assembly describing what that assembly had done.

Supporting this argument is some language that appears in examples from Bourges and from Sens. Here the original donor writes to the mandate-bearer: 'do not delay to write me back about the proceeding that was celebrated' (*de caelebrata prosecutione mihi rescriberae non tardaris*).[52] In other words, for the donor it was the public ceremonies, the public declaration and confirmation of the transaction, that lay at the heart of the matter.

## The manuscripts

There is no way to tell by looking at these formulas by themselves that they were not, for all of their individual variation, just late antique fossils carried forward in time by conservative and tradition-bound (or uncomprehending) compilers and copyists. To say something firm about how these formulas might have connected to some early medieval reality, we have to look at the manuscripts.

Some manuscripts reveal little or nothing about the history of the formula collection they contain. For example, the Angers formulas, which have been dated to the late sixth century, survive only in one late eighth-century manuscript from the Angers/Tours region.[53] There is no way to tell what processes of choice or selection (or lack thereof) might have led this collection to include a *gesta municipalia* sequence,[54] or when these processes might have taken place. It is possible that the eighth-century copyist simply transcribed a group of late antique formulas whole,

52 *Form. Bitur.* 15b (see also *Form. Bitur.* 15d; *Cart. Sen. App.* 1b and d). Note the earlier use of *celebrari* in Tjäder I 7.

53 Fulda D1; Rio, *Legal Practice*, 67–80, and Rio, *Formularies*, 37–101, 248–54; Bergmann, 'Formulae Andecavenses'; Bergmann, 'Verlorene Urkunden'; B. Bischoff, *Die südostdeutschen Schreibschulen und Bibliotheken in der Karolingerzeit*. I. *Die bayrischen Diözesen*, 2nd edn (Wiesbaden, 1960), 258.

54 *Form. Andec.* 1abc.

without concerning himself too much about what was in it or about anachronistic language.

Other formula manuscripts, however, show clearly that the formula collections they contain had histories and that formula collections could evolve over time. The people who compiled and copied out these manuscripts constructed their formula collections by deliberately selecting, adding or dropping individual formulas or groups of formulas from older sources, sources which themselves sometimes reflect similar processes. The most direct example that applies to the *gesta municipalia* is a codex, now kept in Paris, which consists of pieces from several other codices sewn together.[55] The interesting piece for our purposes is a fragment of an eighth-century manuscript containing some formulas from Bourges. The formula collection represented by this fragment must have originally contained at least fifteen formulas, but the first ten formulas were somehow lost; the quire begins with a formula numbered 11 and continues through number 15. These formulas formed part of a unified collection; they were written out in one go, with the same page layout, in a single eighth-century hand.[56] They stop at the top of the recto side of a folium. Then comes a short hymn text in Tironian notes, in a different hand and in a different ink. The remaining half of this recto side originally contained some sort of drawing involving circles that is now too faint to make out. Written over the drawings, squeezed tightly into the available half-page, and in yet a different (but still eighth-century) hand, is a *gesta municipalia* formula from Bourges (see Figure 5.1).[57] Specifically, it is the text of a *gesta* procedure whereby a man, acting on behalf of (and bearing the mandate of) his brother, comes before a civic *curia* and its *defensor* to submit a property gift made by his brother to the *gesta municipalia*.[58] On the top of the following page is something completely different: a calendar. In short, this Bourges *gesta* formula was not part of the original formula collection of which this quire formed a part. It was later added deliberately by someone who thought it important enough to squeeze it into the space left at the end of this page and on top of the original drawing.

The *gesta* formulas could not only be selected; they could also be modified and adapted. The best evidence for this comes from two manuscripts containing a formula collection from the abbey of St Praeiectus in

[55] BnF lat. 10756; Rio, *Legal Practice*, 259–60.

[56] BnF lat. 10756 fols. 62–4; Rio, *Legal Practice*, 111; MGH Formulae 166 (notes to *Form. Bitur.*); H. Mordek, *Kirchenrecht und Reform im Frankenreich: Die Collectio Vetus Gallica: Die älteste systematische Kanonessammlung des Fränkischen Gallien: Studien und Edition* (Berlin, 1975), 107n43.

[57] BnF lat. 10756 fol. 64r.

[58] *Form. Bitur.* 6.

Flavigny.[59] Sometime in the late eighth century or early ninth, monks at the abbey mixed formulas from Marculf together with a formula collection from Tours and with formulas derived from documents and texts in their own archive and library to create a new formula collection. The original manuscript of this collection has been lost, but it must once have existed, for its two surviving manuscripts derive from a common exemplar.[60]

Early in the Flavigny collection comes a large group of formulas about property gifts, sales, inheritances, benefices, etc., that reproduces the Tours formula collection in almost the same order that it appears in other manuscripts.[61] The exceptions come at the beginning. Right after Tours 1 are inserted two formulas from Flavigny.[62] Then, after the two Flavigny formulas, come Tours 2 and 3. Except that they are not really Tours 2 and 3. The original Tours 2 and 3 are a *gesta municipalia* sequence. Tours 2 represents a mandate given by a property donor to another man to go to the city, submit the donation to the *gesta muncipalia* and return word that he had done so. Tours 3 describes the actual *gesta* process, held in the city of Tours, in which the mandate bearer carries out his mandate before the *defensor* and *curia* of the city. In the Flavigny collection, what we find in place of Tours 2 and 3 are two similar formulas, – likewise, a mandate formula and a *gesta* formula. But they have been constructed by blending sections lifted from Tours 2 and 3 with pieces of the Marculf *gesta* formulas; I mentioned them above when noting the language about central document registers and archives that they borrowed from Marculf.[63] The blending has a substantive impact. For example, the revised mandate leaves out a line from the Tours original in which the property donor asks the mandate bearer to report back about what he has done. The revised *gesta* formula leaves out the original's specific reference to the city of Tours. The revised *gesta* is also more detailed than its Tours counterpart; the extra detail comes from Marculf.

In short, the compiler of the Flavigny formula collection wanted to have a *gesta municipalia* sequence in the spot where this group of Tours formulas would have had one. However, he did not like what the Tours

59 *Coll. Flav.*: Copenhagen, Kongelige Bibliotek, Coll. Fabr. 84; BnF lat. 2123.

60 Rio, *Legal Practice*, 96–9; P. Depreux, 'La tradition manuscrite des "Formules de Tours" et la diffusion des modèles d'actes aux VIII$^{e}$ et IX$^{e}$ siècles', *Annales de Bretagne et des pays de l'Ouest*, 111 (2004), 55–71, at 61–3. See the more extensive discussion of this collection in the next chapter.

61 I.e. Zeumer's *Form. Tur.* 1–32.

62 Zeumer's *Coll. Flav.* 7 and 8.

63 *Coll. Flav.* 9–10. Cf. Rio, *Legal Practice*, 179–80.

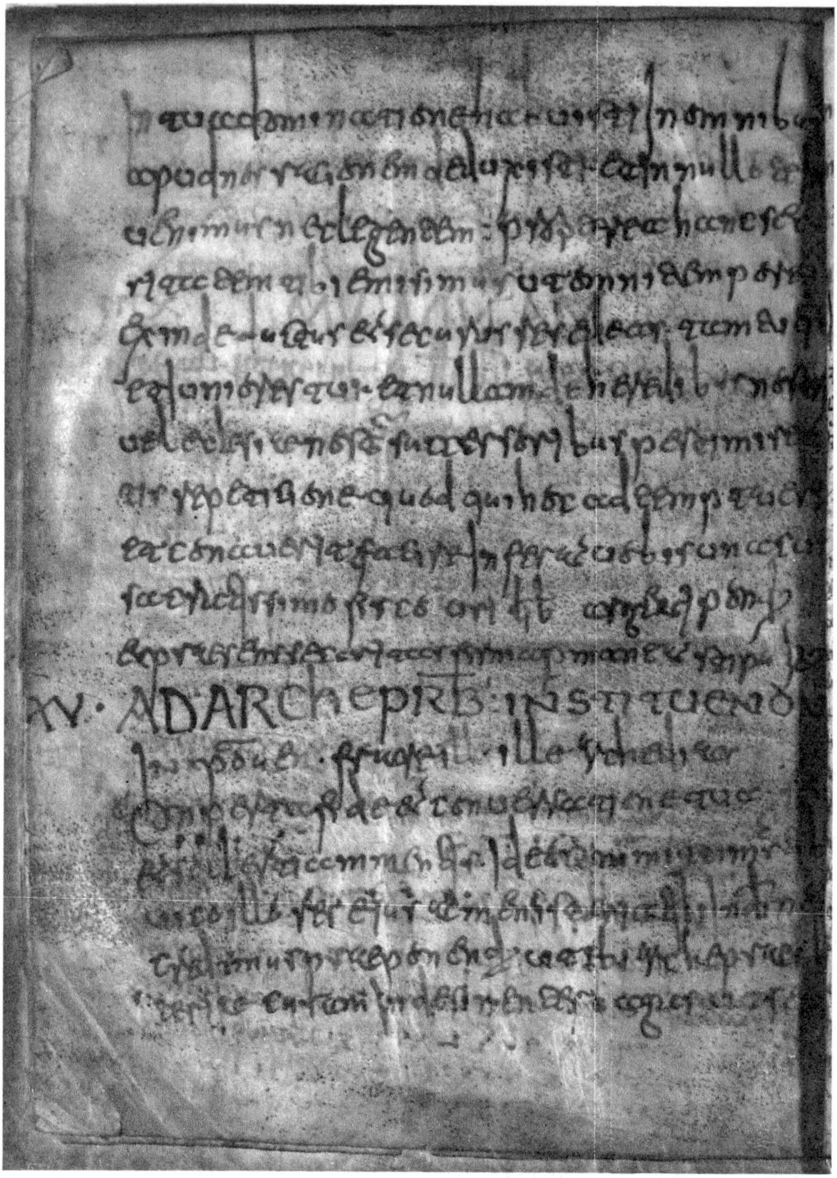

Figure 5.1 BnF lat. 10756, fol. 63v: fragmentary formula collection from Bourges, no. 15.

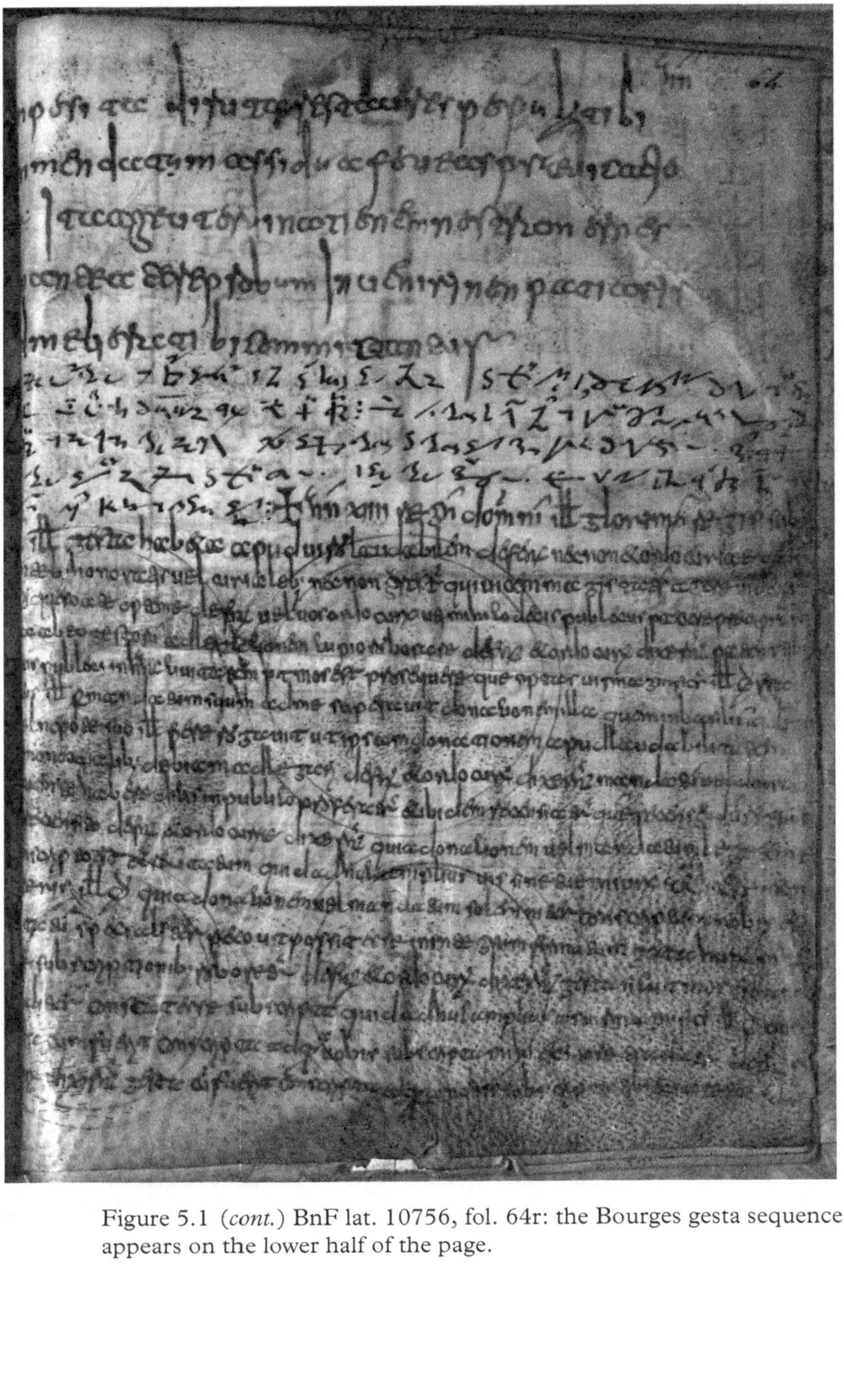

Figure 5.1 (*cont.*) BnF lat. 10756, fol. 64r: the Bourges gesta sequence appears on the lower half of the page.

collection offered, so he modified the Tours formulas by blending them with the corresponding Marculf formulas. Later on, the Flavigny collection reproduces a great deal of Marculf Book II, albeit in a different order from the original and with several formulas left out. Among the formulas left out, of course, are the Marculf *gesta* formulas, from which the compiler had borrowed to make his replacements for Tours 2 and 3.

Finally, the text of at least one of the surviving *gesta* formulas indicates that it was actually used in a document at about the time the manuscript containing it was put together. A ninth-century manuscript, which was most likely put together in Bourges, contains in its last quire one of the most detailed and complete of all the *gesta* sequences in the formulas.[64] It starts with a very long and ornate charter by which a man gives property in the *pagus* of Bourges to his betrothed. Then comes the mandate, in which the donor asks a friend to take the charter to Bourges and have it submitted and affirmed. Then comes the *gesta*, in which the friend submits the charter to the city's *defensor* and to the public *curia*. The *gesta* starts with the following dating clause: 'in such-and-such a month, on such-and-such a day, in the thirty-fourth year of the reign of our lord Charles and five years from when, with the aid of Christ, he took up the imperial rule'. This dating clause can refer only to Charlemagne. It is, therefore, virtually certain that this formula was derived from an actual document; the copyist removed the names of the people involved, but failed for some reason to remove the specific date. So, somewhere in the area around Bourges, in 805 (that is, five years after Charlemagne was crowned emperor), someone used this series of *gesta* formulas to record an actual property transaction. The record was then used as the basis for the Bourges *gesta* formulas.

## Evidence for the *gesta* outside the formulas

This last example connects immediately to some corresponding evidence from outside the formula collections, namely a sequence of charters preserved in the *Liber Aureus* of the monastery at Prüm. This codex was put together starting in the last decade of the ninth century to record the monastery's property holdings in the wake of Viking attacks in the 880s. It contains a property catalogue (*Urbar*) and a series of charter transcriptions. A first group of transcriptions was complete by 919. The codex

[64] Leiden BPL 114; *Form. Bitur.* 15abcd; Rio, *Legal Practice*, 245–6.

remained in this form until the twelfth century, when more transcriptions were added.[65]

Transmitted in this twelfth-century section of the *Liber Aureus* is a fully articulated *gesta municipalia* sequence.[66] First comes a property gift, which according to the text was carried out in the city of Angers in April of the fourth year of Charlemagne's imperial rule: a man named Harwic gave property in the territory (*pagus*) of Angers to the monastery of the Holy Saviour at Prüm. After the donation, comes a *traditio*; that is, the formal legal handover of the property, carried out according to the dictates of Roman law, which repeats the terms of the donation. The *traditio* was likewise carried out in Angers and bears the same date as the donation. Then comes the mandate, dated to the same place and day: the donor gives one Aganbert a mandate to go to Angers and submit the gift charter to the *gesta municipalia*. Then comes the *gesta* itself: the by now familiar blow-by-blow account of the procedure by which Aganbert carried out his mandate before the *defensor* and *curia* of Angers. Here, as in the Marculf formulas, a civic document register plays a comprehensible role in the proceedings. The *amanuensis* reads out the mandate, and then he takes up the donation that is to be inserted into the *gesta* (*gesta inserendi*) and reads it out. Once this is done, the *defensor* orders that the donation be inserted into the *gesta* (*gestum* [sic] *inserere iubeatur*). Finally, Aganbert asks that once the proceedings (*gesta*) have been written up and subscribed by the *curiales*, he be given a copy.

It seems safe to assume that the Prüm copyists of the twelfth century copied this text into the *Liber Aureus* because they wanted to preserve the record of this property gift. Why in this case they included the entire *gesta* procedure rather than just the original donation charter remains unclear. The scribe copied the sequence as a whole rather than in distinct parts; it is possible, therefore, that he thought it was all the donation charter (the complete text of the entire sequence in the *Liber Aureus* ends with the comment in large letters: *Carta quam Hariuuicus Fecit*). It is also possible that he thought all of the pieces were necessary for this particular charter to be valid, or that they would somehow strengthen it.

I have no reason to think that the text is not a verbatim transcript of the original or that it is a forgery, so I will take it at face value. It tells us that, in 804, someone in Angers used formulas for the *gesta* sequence to record a gift of property to Prüm. The place where the gift was carried out is

[65] *Das 'Goldene Buch' von Prüm (Liber aureus Prumiensis): Faksimile, Übersetzung der Urkunden, Einband*, ed. R. Nolden (Prüm, 1997), 8–9.

[66] *Das 'Goldene Buch' von Prüm*, fols. 97b–99b, trans. pp. 276–80. See also *Urkundenbuch zur Geschichte der, jetzt die Preussischen Regierungsbezirke Coblenz und Trier bildenden mittelrheinischen Territorien*, vol. I, ed. H. Beyer (Coblenz, 1860), nos. 41–2.

important; while this is the only *gesta* sequence preserved in the Prüm *Liber Aureus*, it is also the only donation recorded in the *Liber* that was carried out in Angers. So perhaps the tradition of using these document forms had survived in Angers where it had not in the other areas from which Prüm received property. The sequence does not, however, match the *gesta* sequence that survives in the Angers formula collection, which is much more vague and deals with a dotal gift. Nor does it follow any of the other extant *gesta* formulas; while it shares the basic elements of the *gesta* sequence and procedure with them, in its details it is unique (most noticeably in its inclusion of a separate *traditio*, which does not appear in any other *gesta* sequences).[67] So, evidently, a tradition for writing these documents survived in Angers in 804 that was independent both of the Angers formula collection and of all the other formula traditions that we know about.

Earlier writers on the *gesta municipalia* have already noted this sequence in the Prüm *Liber Aureus*. These scholars have disagreed with each other, sometimes sharply, about its implications. Some have taken an optimistic view, to the point of arguing that, in Angers in 804, a *gesta municipalia* on late antique lines was still functioning.[68] Others argue that it represents an archaic charter tradition and that it says nothing about what really took place.[69]

In my opinion, the Prüm *gesta* sequence does connect in an important way to the reality of early ninth-century Angers, though not in the way that the argument for absolute continuity would have it. My reason for thinking so has to do with the fact that there were people involved in the transaction, and that these people had names. The witnesses to the donation, the *traditio* and the mandate all overlap (more or less – one or two drop out here and there); it was essentially the same group of people who witnessed all three.[70] But the people involved in the *gesta* are entirely different, indicating that it was a distinct assembly.[71] The

[67] See Classen, 'Fortleben', 44–5, for a discussion of the formulas, or pieces of formulas, that this text echoes.

[68] Staab, *Untersuchungen*, 137–8.

[69] Hirschfeld, *Die Gesta municipalia*, 86–7; H. Aubin, 'Vom Absterben antiken Lebens im Frühmittelalter', *Antike und Abendland*, 3 (1948), 88–119, at 94; Classen, 'Fortleben', 44–5.

[70] Donation: *vicarius* Godald, Dilidran, Gedulf, Agisbert, Ramirtran, Gaginhard, Adialhard. *Traditio*: Godald, Dilidranus, Tedulf, Agisbert, Ramirtan, Cacinhard, Adalhard. Mandate: Godald, Dilidran, Thedulf, Agisbert, Ramirtan, Cacinhard.

[71] Count Nono, *curator* Risclen, *vicedomus* Uuigfred, Hermedran, Gendrad, *centenarius* Letbaud, Gerald, Saidris, Srodald, David, Lethard, *centenarius* Stabul. Classen, 'Fortleben', 45, argues that *Protokollierung* before the *gesta* has become part of the gift

*gesta* itself presents us with a familiar cast of characters, namely the *curia* of the city of Angers, the *defensor*, the court notary (*amanuensis*) and the mandate bearer. What is striking is that the last three are named: the *defensor*, Uulfred; the notary, Leodegar; and the mandate bearer, Aganbert, as noted above.[72] At the end we get the list of witnesses: Count Nononus; a municipal official of some sort (*curator*)[73] named Riscleno; an administrative assistant, possibly to the count (*vicedomus*), named Uuigfred;[74] then Hermedranus and Gendradus; then a regional officer under the count's authority (*centenarius*)[75] named Letbaud; then a Gerald, a Saidris, a Srodaldus, a David and a Lethard; and, finally, another *centenarius* named Stabulus. This list starts off with a count; the titles for the other office-holders it names are unequivocally Carolingian. One might be tempted to say, therefore, that this was not in fact a 'real' *gesta municipalia*, but rather a typical Carolingian comital court of the early ninth century wrapped up in the archaic language of the *gesta*. However, the *defensor* Uulfred, who heads the assembly, and the notary Leodegar are not on the witness list; they occupy their own separate position in the proceedings.[76] Count Nononus appears only in the witness list. If it had been a comital court that a tradition-bound scribe had tried to capture with an archaic formula, I would have expected him to name the count, rather than Uulfred, as the person heading the assembly.

The point is that the scribe who drafted this text was able, apparently without any strain, to fit named people into each of the slots required by the *gesta* formula. This does not mean that a *gesta* process took place exactly as described by the text.[77] We do not need to argue that the men

charter itself, that there was no longer a *curia* in Angers, and that we are therefore faced here with an attempt to convey some sort of judicial legitimacy by couching the transaction in old forms. While I agree with the third statement, for reasons that will become clear below, the difference in the witnesses indicates that the parts of the transaction were distinct and that some sort of separate legitimating assembly had in fact gathered in Angers.

72 Staab, *Untersuchungen*, 137n569 assumes from the address in the mandate ('domno in christo fratri Aganberto') that the mandate bearer Aganbert was a monk of Prüm. However, *frater* appears frequently throughout the formulas in contexts indicating that it can also serve as a general form of address.

73 Niermeyer, *Lexicon*, s.v. *curator*.

74 F. L. Ganshof, *Frankish Institutions under Charlemagne*, trans. B. and M. Lyon (Providence, RI, 1968), 33.

75 Ganshof, *Frankish Institutions*, 32–3.

76 Here I disagree sharply with Hirschfeld, *Die Gesta municipalia*, 87, who, in order to see the assembly as a Carolingian court, arbitrarily decided that the *defensor* Uulfred and the *vicedomus* Uuigfred were the same person.

77 Here I differ with Staab, *Untersuchungen*, 138, who apparently thought that it meant just this.

listed at the end of the text thought of themselves as *curiales*, although the text refers to them as such, to think that they most likely represent the members of the assembly; we do not need to think that Uulfred saw himself acting as a *defensor* in the late antique mould as he headed the assembly, if he were even aware that this is what the text called him. Nor can we say whether the documents involved were actually entered into a civic document register. But it does seem that something took place that was more or less equivalent to what the text says took place. I would suggest the following: the original donor Harwic had the donation, the *traditio* and the mandate drawn up (or drew them up himself? In the witness lists to these three, we read *Haruuicus hanc donatione/traditionem/mandatum a me facta*) and witnessed. He then gave them to his mandate-bearer Aganbert. Aganbert took them to an assembly that had the authority to ratify them, that was composed of the signatories listed at the end, and that was presided over by Uulfred. The notary for the assembly, Leodegar, used the *gesta* formula to capture the ratification process, and copied the other associated documents along with it. According to our text, a signed copy of the *gesta* written by Leodegar was given to the mandate bearer Aganbert. Count Nononus, as the city's leading secular authority, would naturally have been present at such an assembly, but it does not appear that he presided over it.

## Beyond the *gesta municipalia*

I would argue that the compilers of our formula manuscripts copied *gesta municipalia* formulas into their collections because such formulas were actually used in the Carolingian period. This is emphatically not to suggest that real, live *gesta municipalia*, exactly as the formulas describe them, were still operating in the same way and in the same form. However, I do think it is safe to say that there was a perceived need in the late eighth and ninth centuries, on the part of at least some people, to secure transaction charters by having them read out at and ratified by a public assembly that was understood to have some authority to ratify them, and to have the assembly issue a document saying that this had been done. This process was sometimes, or even often, carried out by a surrogate – hence the mandate. That the need for this procedure and the procedure itself derived from the tradition of the Roman *gesta municipalia* is indicated by the fact that the *gesta municipalia* formulas were used to record what had happened. The details of what these formulas said, or the terminology that they used, may not have been important, but it is evident from the ways that they were selected, copied and used that they were considered to be the right and proper way to record the ratification process.[78]

The belief that documents ought to be ratified in this way evidently covered transactions among laypeople only, as well as transactions involving clerics and churches. Hence, these formulas provide evidence from the eighth and ninth centuries for a public (in the sense covered by the German *öffentlich* rather than *staatlich*) system of validating documents in which laypeople as well as clerics participated, a system that was, moreover, not anchored in churches (as was, say, the practice of validating a charter by placing it on a church altar). The formulas reflect, therefore, a general world of document use comprising both lay and clerical members of the upper crust of Carolingian society (by which I mean those people propertied enough to be involved in the kind of transactions covered by the formulas).

The *gesta* formulas were used to record the public validation of documents in the western parts of the Frankish world. The practice appears to have been most at home in cities on the Loire and southwards,[79] but it is also visible elsewhere in West Francia. This is, of course, precisely where one would expect to find Roman-style documentary practices and a Roman institutional legacy surviving the longest. No formulas like this stem from East Francia, despite the fact that important formula collections have survived from Bavaria and Alemannia.

However, the documentary practices that lay at the heart of the *gesta municipalia* formulas are visible over a much wider area.[80] I have argued that from the point of view of those carrying out transactions, what was most important about the *gesta municipalia* was public ceremony; people thought it important to secure their transactions by having their transaction documents read out loud before an assembly or forum that had the authority to ratify them and that could produce another document saying that it had done so. The two formula sets from the Marculf tradition, as well as the actual charters from Poitiers and Angers/Prüm, do

[78] Cf. Rio, *Legal Practice*, 180–2; Rio, *Formularies*, 257–8. Cf. Barbier, 'Pouvoirs et élites', Part I, ch. 3, esp. pp. 106–8. Barbier infers from references to the *gesta* in other kinds of sources (i.e. diplomas, testaments and charters, but also Marculf 2.3) that real *gesta municipalia*, with central document registers, persisted in some places up to the beginning of the ninth century (though she does suggest that the *gesta* evolved in the eighth century away from central archiving and increasingly stressed public reading and validation of documents). The surviving *gesta*, she argues, reflected an ongoing interest on the part of civic elites in controlling local property arrangements and preventing or resolving property disputes. Her argument, however – at least as it appears in the chapter that was available to me – is speculative and depends on meagre and ambiguous evidence that could be (and has been) interpreted differently.

[79] Cf. Wickham, *Framing*, 110–11.

[80] For the framework of what follows, see below, Chapters 8–9.

integrate the civic document register intelligibly into the *gesta* process. They survive, however, alongside a greater number of formulas in which references to such registers appear to be vestigial. What remains in focus in all of the formulas is what consumers of the *gesta* had been getting out of the process ever since Late Antiquity: public ceremonial validation of their transaction documents and a written record of that validation.

To achieve this essential result, one did not have to go to a *gesta municipalia*. One simply needed to find an authority-bearing and public venue where one could present one's documents for validation and which could issue a document saying that the necessary public steps had been taken. One could, for example, go to a king and his court. In a formula from the so-called Marculf Supplements, a king writes to a count to say that a man (or the man's *missus*) came before him and reported that he had bought property from another.[81] The buyer had apparently brought with him the original document of sale, for next the seller stepped forward, confirmed the document's contents, and acknowledged that he had received payment. The king then confirmed the transfer of ownership with this document (*per presentem . . . preceptum*). This scenario also appears in several Merovingian diplomas. In an example from 596, a priest *vir inluster* and a nun founded and endowed a chapel dedicated to St Martin in Le Mans *per eorum strumenta*. They then went to see King Theuderic II and asked him to confirm the transaction. After the *epistola donationis* had been viewed, the king did so.[82]

The same end result was likewise achieved in the so-called *Scheinprozesse*, or 'staged disputes' from the Merovingian period. These were cases brought up before a royal judicial hearing, or *placitum*, in which one party charged another with unjustly holding its property, the defendant conceded without a defence, and the plaintiff received a document confirming his rights.[83] At a *placitum* headed by King Childeric III in 710, the *inluster vir* Ragnesind declared that he had purchased property from one Sicland and his wife Dinan, that they had accepted the purchase price from him, and that a document of sale had been drawn up. Ragnesind held up the charter to be read, and it was read.[84] Sicland, who was present, confirmed Ragnesind's account. Accordingly, the king together with his leading men ordered that, the document of sale having been

81 Marculf [Supp.] 2 = *Coll. Flav.* 105.

82 MGH DD Mer. 1, no. 25; see also nos. 22, 28, 32, 75.

83 See P. Fouracre, 'Disputes in Later Merovingian Francia', in *Settlement of Disputes*, 26 and n. 13.

84 Presumably out loud: 'et ipsa vindicione in presente ostendedit relegienda relicta [*sic* = relecta?] ipsa vindicione'.

examined, Ragnesind be confirmed in his possession of the property; the order was written up in the form of a royal judgement.[85]

People similarly resorted to kings to validate their documents in the Carolingian period. In Pavia in 774, for example, Charlemagne confirmed an exchange of property between Bishop Merol of Le Mans and Abbot Rabegaud of St-Calais. The parties produced the original exchange document to be read; from the detail given, it appears that it was substantially copied into the royal diploma confirming the exchange, of which the king ordered two identical copies made.[86]

This kind of document validation process also shows up in the East. A Salzburg manuscript of the late ninth century contains an only superficially altered version of the Marculf Supplement formula discussed above.[87] Other examples appear in the charters of St Gall. According to one, in Worms in 780, Charlemagne confirmed an agreement made between Bishop Sidonius of Constance and Abbot John of St Gall about the dues owed by the monastery to the bishopric.[88] The two men had reached the agreement at some earlier point, and had fixed it in writing in two identical copies. When they came before the king, they displayed the documents for reading.[89] Thereupon Charlemagne ordered this charter produced, confirming their contents. In Frankfurt in April 875, Charlemagne's grandson Louis the German similarly issued a diploma confirming an exchange between Abbot Hartmot of St Gall and the royal vassal Widpert. The exchange had originally been carried out by means of documents affirmed 'by the hands of good men'; the pair displayed these documents before the king to be read out.[90]

Kings were not, however, the only authorities to which one could resort. Some people in Bavaria and Alemannia carried out their transactions before a comital court, or *mallus*. This achieves the same result as the *gesta* procedure, but compresses it. The transaction and the ceremonial ratification before an authority-bearing assembly are all wrapped up in one public process; at the end, the principal or principals come away with a document saying that the necessary public steps had been taken. A formula from the same Salzburg formula manuscript discussed above, for example, has a man and his wife appear at a public *mallus* and give

85 MGH DD Mer. 1, no. 158; see also nos. 136, 143, 153, 155, 187.

86 MGH DD Kar. 1, no. 79; see also nos. 130, 136, 161, 206.

87 *Form. Marc. Kar.* 28 = Munich, Bayerische Staatsbibliothek, Clm 4650 fols. 57v–58v (no. 51).

88 Wartmann I 92.

89 'eorum manus roboratus uno tenore conscriptas nobis ostenderunt relegendas'.

90 Wartmann II 586. For the original exchange charters, see Wartmann II 576; see also 454, 479, 587, 588, 694, 716.

property to God and Sts Peter and Rupert (the patrons of the monastery of St Peter in Salzburg); the gift would take effect after both had died. The transaction is witnessed and confirmed by people who have been given the power to witness by the typical Bavarian practice of ear-pulling (*testes per aurem tracti*).[91] Actual charters that describe more or less the same thing survive in the St Gall archive. Among them are three recording transactions carried out on the same day before a *mallus* held in Egg, just south-east of Zurich, sometime between 841 and 872.[92]

Examples such as these reveal a continuum of procedures for validating and securing transactions. All of these procedures involve public enactment;[93] in all of them ritual, oral and written forms of communication and memory mutually reinforce each other, and in all of them documents were produced at the end saying that the necessary steps had been carried out. Venues range from a central place on the property that was being donated or sold (such as a villa or a church) to courts and to churches (especially the atria of churches) that were not themselves the subjects of transactions. In these latter cases, it would seem that God himself and/or the patron saint of the church or monastery was serving as the necessary authority figure.[94] In Bavaria before the Carolingian conquest, several transactions were carried out before Agilolfing dukes (Odilo or Tassilo III) and/or in a location called a *castrum*, implying that it embodied ducal authority.[95] In cases that do not explicitly assign any special authority to the venue, the witness lists sometimes contain office-holders, such as counts, tribunes or *centenarii*, suggesting that the assembly may have had some authority-bearing character.[96]

In her well-known 1989 work on the St Gall charters, Rosamond McKitterick identified a loose hierarchy of such venues. Some transactions recorded in the charters were carried out locally, on the site of the property concerned, in front of local witnesses; in these cases, nothing suggests that anything more than simple publicity was involved in carrying out and securing them. However, McKitterick also identified

[91] *Form. Salz.* 4 = Clm 4650 fols. 64v–65v (no. 58).

[92] Wartmann II 565–7. See also Wartmann I 11, 297, 321; II 643.

[93] On publicity in the sense of the German *Öffentlichkeit* in this context, see Fichtenau, *Das Urkundenwesen in Österreich vom 8. bis zum frühen 13. Jahrhundert* (Vienna, 1971), 80.

[94] Cf. Fichtenau, *Urkundenwesen*, 77–8, and Barbier, 'Pouvoirs et élites', Part I, ch. 3, pp. 94–8.

[95] *TF* 1, 2, 7, 12.

[96] But one does need to be careful; sometimes office-holders were present because they were related to the principals in the transactions. In assemblies explicitly called a *mallus*, the witness lists often do not mention any counts; conversely, the presence of a count in the witness list does not mean that the transaction was carried out at a *mallus*.

places to which people went regularly and repeatedly to take care of legal and judicial matters, places that they evidently perceived as having the necessary authority and offering the necessary public visibility to secure transactions, and at which documents could be produced saying that the necessary steps had been taken. The assemblies held at these places are not always labelled as courts (that is, as a *mallus* or *placitum*), but their locations were independent of the properties concerned in the transactions that came before them. McKitterick has also documented what she calls, following Rolf Sprandel, 'witness leaders'. These were landowners who show up in the charters heading witness lists at several locations; they appear to have acted as local authority figures who headed assemblies before which transactions were carried out. Following McKitterick, one can imagine that, depending on the wealth and importance of the parties involved, and the size or symbolic importance of the property involved or the legal matter at hand, there was a corresponding loose hierarchy of public venues and authorities to which people went to carry out their business, and from which they took home a document saying that they had done so.[97]

Even at this local level, some Eastern records describe two-stage processes that closely resemble those of the *gesta municipalia*. In the winter of 804, for example, a man named Starcholf and his son Hitolf came to Bishop Atto of Freising in Bavaria.[98] They asked him for a benefice, namely a church in Assling, in exchange for other property in Assling as well as in Steinkirchen, and annual payments in kind and in silver. The father and son then pledged or enacted somehow their end of the bargain.[99] Next, a Freising archpriest named Ellanod, acting as Bishop Atto's *missus*, travelled together with Starcholf and Hitolf to a public *mallus* headed by Count Cundhart in Steinkirchen. There Ellanod, *coram omnibus*, pledged to give Starcholf and his son the benefice that they had asked for. Starcholf and Hitolf in turn pledged again to give what they had promised. At the end, the document describing the process was subscribed by witnesses. In 884, one Moyses gave property to St Gall. In the charter recording the gift, just before the witness list, comes the line: 'Carried out publicly at this monastery, in the presence of those whose names are contained here.' Then we read: 'Afterwards this charter was lifted up in the public *placitum* before a multitude of the people and once more affirmed, with those agreeing whose signatures are noted

97 McKitterick, *Carolingians*, 98–115. 98 *TF* 195.

99 'pro qua (i.e. the benefice) spoponderunt se daturos usum beneficii. Quod ita et fecerunt.'

below.'[100] In other words, the transaction was first carried out by the two parties involved at St Gall; then, the charter was taken to a judicial assembly and publicly reaffirmed. Another St Gall charter, recording an exchange of unfree dependants between St Gall and one Chadaloh, suggests the same two-step process with the line, 'Carried out and lifted up in the *pagus* of *Munteriheshuntere* in the villa of Dieterskirch, affirmed and accomplished in the *pagus* of Eritgau, in the place called Bussen, publicly in the atrium of [the church of] St Laudegarius'.[101] Still other St Gall charters include two separate lists of witnesses given as present in different locations (and sometimes segregated into clerical and lay), or a statement that a transaction was carried out first before one office-holder and then another.[102]

## Conclusions

The *gesta municipalia* did not simply disappear from the Frankish world. Instead, they were gradually transformed, at different rates and in different ways in different places, into a set of varied but related practices, as the decline of late Roman civic and fiscal institutions made municipal document registers largely irrelevant. The *gesta* papyri from late antique Italy still emphasize storing copies of records in central registers or record books because, at the time they were written, a state still existed in Italy that had an interest in keeping track of its own fiscal rights and its subjects' tax obligations. Nevertheless, they also record a series of public ceremonies, including the very formal public ceremony that took place when a transaction was secured in the *gesta*. What the *gesta* papyri provided for those who received copies of them was a written guarantee that the public ceremonies necessary to validate and thus secure their transaction documents had been properly carried out. In Frankish Gaul from the sixth century on, it appears that many people who bought, sold, exchanged or gifted property continued to believe that it was essential to securing transactions to record them in writing, to have the records publicly ratified by an authority-bearing body and to get another written record saying that this had been done. This belief is reflected in the survival, copying and continued use of the *gesta* formulas. Where *gesta*

[100] Wartmann II 639: 'Postea vero in publico placito sub frequentia populi levata atque iterum firmata est haec eadem carta, astipulantibus his, quorum hic signulacula subnotatur.'

[101] Wartmann II 684: 'Acta et levata in pago Munteriheshuntere in villa Diethereskiriha, firmata et perpetrata in pago Eritgeuve, in loco, qui dicitur Pusso, in atrio sancti Laudegarii puplice.'

[102] Wartmann I 87, 92, 115, 144; II 486.

formulas were copied or used as the basis for real documents, they were copied or used because the people involved thought that they were the proper way, or at least one valid way, of recording how documents were validated and that they thus were, or might be, useful. In other words, the formulas still had some perceived relationship to reality. But in many places the language in them that had to do with central civic registers or archives dissolved, along with the institutions that had inspired that language, until it became incoherent. Outside Frankish Gaul, in areas where Roman institutional and municipal traditions were weak or non-existent, people nevertheless handled and ratified documents in a way consonant with the *gesta* tradition. They simply found different venues and authority figures to fulfil the same purpose.

It has been suggested that, as the eighth century progressed, churches came to take over the role of the *gesta municipalia*. The evidence behind this suggestion lies in explicit references to storing documents in church archives, such as that in the Flavigny will formula discussed above, as well as in the undeniable number of transactions that were carried out at churches and recorded by church scribes.[103] To assign to churches the role formerly played by the *gesta*, however, is to assume that the *gesta* served primarily as archives where both the civic authorities and those who carried out transactions could store copies of transaction documents for safe keeping and later reference. Our evidence indicates that even in Late Antiquity this was only part of the *gesta*'s purpose, and that as time passed its importance waned. The *gesta municipalia* served to record transactions in a central register for the purposes of the late Roman state; for their users, they guaranteed that their transactions were valid through public ceremonies, document readings and the issuance of an official document. What was important to the users were the official documents that they took with them, with their lists of authority figures and witnesses, that said that they had gone through the necessary public steps to validate their transactions. They kept these records with their others at home, or sometimes (over time and in some places) in churches or monasteries because churches and monasteries offered the security of better buildings and divine protection.[104] Churches kept their own documents for the same reason everyone else did. By the Carolingian period, no one any longer had any institutional or fiscal interest in preserving registers of property transactions that recorded everyone's transactions, or better, the transactions of those wealthy enough to matter, in the way

[103] Rio, *Legal Practice*, 181; McKitterick, *Carolingians*, 89; Fichtenau, *Urkundenwesen*, 70. Cf. above, 76–7.

[104] Brown, 'Documents', 351–2; below, 371.

that the *gesta municipalia* in late antique Italy had.[105] The official document registers compiled and kept as part of the late antique *gesta* process served the interests of the late Roman state; they served the interests of users only in so far as they protected them from getting in trouble for not registering, and provided a backup source of documentation.

If we choose to see the *gesta muncipalia* as primarily central document registers or archives, we can say that they died as the institutional infrastructure of the late Roman state died, at different rates in different regions. But if we focus on the part of the *gesta* that had most interested its users, that is, on the public, ceremonial validation of documents, then they lived on, at least in spirit. The vigour of the *gesta* tradition is attested in the *gesta* formulas that continued to be copied. It is equally strongly attested in the other venues that people found for accomplishing the same purposes. Churches did number among those venues; they were, however, but one such among several possible.

As the early Middle Ages progressed, institutional change or transformation altered the landscape of available venues to which people could resort to have their transactions and documents validated. Where and while the fiscal infrastructure of the Roman state persisted, the *gesta municipalia* in something like its old form endured. But when that infrastructure withered, or when documentary practices spread to (or were revived in) areas where they had never or had hardly existed, other venues were found that combined the publicity, the authority and the ability to produce written documents that had characterized the *gesta*.

[105] Cf. the suggestion by Barbier (above, n. 78) that local civic elites may have had such an interest.

# 6 Laypeople and documents in the Frankish formula collections

*Warren C. Brown*

*The surviving Frankish collections of legal formulas demonstrate in the round how documents were used at the time when the manuscripts were written, at the (usually earlier) time when the identifiable collections were originally compiled, and at the time when individual formulas were first composed; and they therefore also show how documentary practices changed over time. The three collections examined here – that of Marculf, and those from Tours and Flavigny – were first put together in, respectively, the late seventh, mid eighth, and late eighth centuries. While the majority of their formulas are for laypeople's documents, all three collections were made in ecclesiastical milieux, and some formulas responded to the distinct needs of the clergy. These collections therefore suggest that in the Carolingian period the clergy were taking responsibility for producing documents for both themselves and the laity.*

The Frankish formula collections addressed in the previous chapter are not just a useful source for the history of the *gesta municipalia*. They are perhaps the richest source available for studying the ways that laypeople used documents in Frankish Europe.[1] They contain a great many examples of documents or document types that do not survive in extant charter or letter collections. Heavily represented among these are documents in which none of the actors involved, including the issuer and recipient, are clerics or monks, and in which there is no apparent role played by ecclesiastical institutions.

These formulas presumably represent document or letter types that were useful in some way, or at least comprehensible, to the people who copied them. There is, as we saw before and will see again in the specific case study below, simply too much evidence that they were deliberately selected and crafted by their compilers to think otherwise.[2] If they were

[1] Edition: MGH Formulae. Basic literature: R. Buchner, *Deutschlands Geschichtsquellen im Mittelalter*, Beiheft, *Die Rechtsquellen* (Weimar, 1953), 49–55; Rio, *Legal Practice*.

[2] See also Rio, *Legal Practice*, 63–6, 238–40; W. Brown, 'Die Karolingischen Formelsammlungen – warum existieren sie?', in P. Erhart, K. Heidecker and B. Zeller (eds.),

intended to serve as templates for complete documents, then they represented documents that could conceivably have been needed and that therefore captured transactions or behaviours that could conceivably have happened. If they were intended to be sources of language, then they contained language or phrases that might conceivably have been useful. If they were intended to be practice models for student scribes, or cases for them to study, then they represented document types or procedures that students might need to know, or at least profit from knowing about. The formulas for lay documents, therefore, can tell us something about the situations in and purposes for which laypeople might have used documents, or at least about the range of possibilities for which their compilers felt they needed to be prepared or for some reason wanted to have a record of.

The formulas present a somewhat fractured or blurred picture of lay documentary culture, however, because their transmission histories are complicated. As we saw previously, individual formula collections often include documents or formulaic passages that are older, even centuries older, than the manuscripts in which they survive. Sometimes these older formulas were updated to match contemporary Latin norms or to render the incomprehensible understandable; sometimes they were not.[3] Later formula collections not infrequently took formulas from older collections, mixed them together, altered them, and added new texts to produce a new collection that differed in content and emphasis from its sources. As a consequence, it can be difficult or impossible to pin down a given formula in time and space.

Nevertheless, by untangling the transmission history of given formula sets, particularly those that draw on older formula collections, we can use the formulas to say some things about the ways that laypeople interacted with documents at several points along a continuum: at the time the earliest formulas or language in a given collection must have originated; at the time(s) earlier formula collections from which that collection drew were compiled; at the time the collection itself was put together; and at the time when the extant manuscript was copied out. Moreover, by looking at

*Die Privaturkunden der Karolingerzeit* (Dietikon, 2009), 95–101. An exception might be the Angers formula collection, whose texts probably stem from the late sixth century but which is preserved in the late eighth-century manuscript Fulda, Hessische Landesbibliothek, D1; since this is the only copy of this group of very old documents, we can only guess at possible processes of selection or adaptation involved in its creation. It remains possible, therefore, especially since it is copied together with a (poor) copy of the *LRV*, that it represents an antiquarian compilation. But cf. Rio, *Legal Practice*, 77–80.

3 See, for example, Munich, Bayerische Staatsbibliothek, Clm 4650, which contains a version of some of Marculf's formulas that were updated to reflect Carolingian political realities (*Form. Marc. Kar.*); Rio, *Legal Practice*, 104–5.

the formulas in the context of the entire manuscript in which they survive, we can say some things about the needs and purposes behind their final copying out, and thus about the cultural and institutional context in which lay documents were being copied, studied and produced.

To draw one such picture of lay documentary practices in Frankish Europe, I will discuss one manuscript: BnF lat. 2123. This codex encompasses a continuum covering Neustria, the Touraine and Burgundy from the late sixth through the early ninth centuries. The formula collection it contains offers rich evidence for a culture of document use in which laypeople actively participated; in this envelope of time and space, laypeople, both men and women, both high status and low, regarded documents as important and used them. They interacted through the medium of documents not only with churches and monasteries but also directly with each other. Although clerics and monks were institutionally, legally and vocationally distinct enough from laypeople that they sometimes needed their own versions of common documents, in general laypeople and clergy used similar kinds of documents in similar ways for similar things.

The relationship between lay documentary culture and ecclesiastical institutions along this continuum, however, was not static. Our manuscript points to a second process of institutional change that followed the disappearance of the late Roman civic institutions that had originally lain behind the *gesta municipalia*. Over the course of the late Merovingian period, but especially in the Carolingian period, churches and monasteries began to fit into the societies around them in new ways such that they became focal points for the production of documents, to the point that they compiled collections of formulas allowing them to study and produce documents for laypeople alongside those they needed for their own purposes. By the ninth century, at least some ecclesiastical institutions had developed if not a monopoly on, then a significant and perhaps dominant role in, the production and use of documents in their regions.

BnF lat. 2123 was most likely copied out in Burgundy at the end of the eighth century or the beginning of the ninth.[4] It is primarily an ecclesiastical reference book; its contents include church council acts, sermons, an epitome of the *Liber Pontificalis*, and religious writings and letters by such figures as Gennadius of Marseilles, Leo the Great and Theodore of

[4] Rio, *Legal Practice*, 252; P. Depreux, 'La tradition manuscrite des "Formules de Tours" et la diffusion des modèles d'actes aux VIII$^{e}$ et IX$^{e}$ siècles', *Annales de Bretagne et des pays de l'Ouest*, 111 (2004), 55–71, at 61; L. Kéry, *Canonical Collections of the Early Middle Ages (ca. 400–1140): A Bibliographical Guide to the Manuscripts and Literature* (Washington, DC, 1999), 54–5.

Canterbury. Towards the end it contains an extensive collection of formulas, briefly discussed in the previous chapter, that can be traced, on internal evidence, to the abbey of St Praiectus at Flavigny. This collection was edited by Karl Zeumer for the MGH as the *Collectio Flaviniacensis*.[5] The Flavigny formula collection predates the manuscript. It survives in one other manuscript, now in Copenhagen,[6] that differs from our Paris manuscript in ways indicating that they both stemmed from a common model.[7] This common model can be dated on internal evidence to the second half of the eighth century.[8]

The Flavigny formula collection is a hybrid.[9] It blends some formulas from Flavigny itself with formulas from two earlier collections: a mid-eighth-century collection from Tours, and the collection of Marculf from the latter part of the seventh century.[10] It thus holds embedded within it layers of time, layers that contain interlocking images of lay documentary practices. Not only does it offer its own image but also its two major sources (that is, the Tours and Marculf collections) each provide theirs. These sources in turn contain fragmentary images inherited from a still deeper past. I will begin by working through the images of lay documentary practice offered by the Marculf and Tours collections. Then I will explore how those images were combined into the image projected by the Flavigny collection. Finally, I will examine the Paris manuscript itself. The information offered by the manuscript does not change the picture of documentary culture that the formulas provide. However, it does tell us something about how and why the Flavigny collection was put together in the form in which it survives.

## Marculf

Marculf's formula collection comprises ninety-two formulas,[11] divided into two sections: Book I, containing *praeceptiones regales* or royal documents, and Book II, containing *cartas pagenses* or non-royal documents. The collection is unusual in that it leads off with a prologue that says

[5] *Coll. Flav.*

[6] Copenhagen, Kongelige Bibliothek, Coll. Fabr. 84 (Francia, s. IX$^{med}$); Rio, *Legal Practice*, 243–4.

[7] See below, n. 87. [8] See below, n. 84. [9] See above, 108–9.

[10] *Form. Tur.*; Marculf. On the former, see Rio, *Legal Practice*, 112–17; Depreux, 'La tradition manuscrite'; on the latter, see Rio, *Legal Practice*, 81–101. A. Jeannin, 'Formules et formulaires: Marculf et les praticiens du droit au premier *moyen âge* (V$^{e}$–X$^{e}$ siècles)', unpublished Ph.D. thesis, Université Jean Moulin–Lyon 3 (2007), was not available to me.

[11] Not counting the Supplements.

who its author was and how that author understood its purpose.[12] The monk Marculf, by his own testimony 70 years old or more, states that he had compiled the collection at the behest of a certain Bishop Landeric as a resource to begin the training of young boys (*ad exercenda initia puerorum*). The jury is still out on the precise time and place in which Marculf put the collection together; the various arguments depend on different identifications of Bishop Landeric, on different interpretations of the kinds of documents Marculf chose to include, and on the ways that his formulaic language compares, or does not, with that of extant documents. The two chief possibilities are somewhere near Paris around the 650s, or in the area of Meaux closer to 700. None of the arguments are conclusive; the safest statement is that Marculf compiled the collection somewhere near Paris or in eastern Neustria, sometime in the second half of the seventh century, though some significant evidence would tend to push the date towards the end of the century.[13]

Even leaving aside the testimony of the preface, there is no question that Marculf's collection once existed; it is not, unlike others of the formula collections published in the MGH, an editorial fiction.[14] It survives in more or less identical form in two manuscripts, and in varying stages of completeness and alteration in five more.[15] The documents that Marculf selected reflect what the old monk thought were important examples or possibilities. They were, therefore, comprehensible and relevant to his world and presumably to that of his imagined students as well. Nevertheless, his collection captures impressions of Frankish life over a span rather than at a single point in time. Given his age, Marculf drew on experience that may have covered up to half a century. Furthermore, some of the documents he chose contain echoes of language and procedures that can be traced back to Late Antiquity.

Book I contains the royal documents. Fully half of this book's forty formulas do not in any way involve clerics or monks. They therefore project writing as an instrument of late Merovingian royal power that embraced and worked through laypeople as well as ecclesiastics.[16] We see kings confirming property grants or property arrangements made by their predecessors;[17] we see kings making property arrangements themselves (including granting benefices and taking property from rebels and handing it out to others).[18] We see kings helping people to divide property;[19] we see them settling disputes and overseeing *placita*.[20] We also see them

[12] Marculf, prologue (MGH Formulae 36–7). [13] Rio, *Legal Practice*, 85–8.
[14] Rio, *Legal Practice*, *passim*. [15] Rio, *Legal Practice*, 92–101.
[16] Marculf 1.8, 9/10, 13, 17, 18, 20–1, 25, 28–32, 33/34, 37–40.
[17] Marculf 1.17, 31. [18] Marculf 1.13, 30, 32.
[19] Marculf 1.20. [20] Marculf 1.25, 38.

appointing people to office,[21] assigning advocates to people,[22] issuing orders and summoning people to show up at court.[23] An example of the latter, specifically titled *Indecolum* [*sic*] *ad laicum*, has a *fidelis* complaining to a king that someone had attacked him on the road, beaten and wounded him, and stolen his property. The king in this letter therefore commands the accused either to make amends, or, if he wished to contest the charge, appear at court to give a legal response.[24] Some royal communications were, however, evidently too detailed or important to entrust to writing, for two formulas represent letters between kings authenticating oral messages carried by their bearers.[25]

Marculf's Book I projects an image of a world in which, as far as the royal use of documents was concerned, clergy and laity hardly differed from one another; kings used the same sorts of documents in the same way for the same things regardless of whether they were dealing with clergy (or their institutions), laypeople or both. This impression is strengthened by the formulas that provide options allowing users to choose either ecclesiastical or lay actors. A king confirms a property arrangement whereby a childless lay couple could let property pass either to a monastery or to their relatives as they wished.[26] A formula for a royal property gift comes with different prologues that couch the gift as going either to a layperson, as a reward for loyal service, or to a monastery.[27]

These 'two-way' formulas, however, also tell us that in Marculf's world there was a difference between clergy and laity; one sometimes needed to have separate versions of the same document for each. A king's confirmation of a gift to a bishop's church by one of his predecessors is followed by language for the case that the king was confirming a gift made to an *inluster vir*.[28] Two formulas titled *indecolum ad episcopo* regarding charges of unjust property seizure are followed by the *indecolum ad laicum* that deals with essentially the same situation.[29] In short, a cleric was not a layperson, and in some situations this distinction was important enough that Marculf provided for it.

While Book I of Marculf's formulas is focused on kings, it does occasionally indicate that the use, and storage, of documents extended beyond the royal courts. A letter to a king from a group of *pagenses* documents the fact that one of their lay neighbours had lost all of his documents in a fire; it is followed by a formula that has the king confirming the layman

[21] Marculf 1.8. [22] Marculf 1.21. [23] Marculf 1.28–9, 37, 39–40.
[24] Marculf 1.29. [25] Marculf 1.9–10. [26] Marculf 1.12.
[27] Marculf 1.14a–c. See also 1.23, a royal precept crafted to fit either a layman or an ecclesiastic.
[28] Marculf 1.16–17. [29] Marculf 1.26–7, 29.

in his property rights.[30] Another royal formula states that some people were reported to have given property to a church or monastery 'by means of their charters' (*per eorum instrumenta*).[31] A group of laypeople demonstrate their rights before the king by displaying charters.[32] A king gives a man a precept in which he makes the man one of his military retainers (*antrustion*) and raises his wergeld accordingly; the recipient would surely want to keep such a document.[33] So, too, would two disputing parties whom a king orders be given copies of a precept regulating how their dispute was to be handled.[34]

However, by far the best evidence in Marculf's collection for lay document use outside the arena of the royal courts comes in Book II, containing the *cartas pagenses*. More than half of these – thirty-two out of fifty-two – qualify as 'lay' formulas according to the criteria used above.[35] A good number of them deal with inheritance, marriage or other intrafamilial property arrangements.[36] Others concern dispute settlements or judicial procedures that required documents.[37] We find here securities for debts and receipts for debts paid,[38] and manumission charters and other documents relating to serfs and to free or unfree status.[39] We find formulas for letters of commendation and for letters asking for intercession.[40] Some particularly striking examples speak volumes about the society that produced them. A father declares that the usual custom, according to which only sons should inherit, is impious and that he will not follow it; he therefore gives his daughter a share in the family inheritance equal to that of her brothers.[41] A man has forcibly married a girl without her parents' consent. The formula gives two options for the girl herself: the marriage occurred either with her consent or without it. In either case, the man is in danger of his life until, with the intercession of priests and other good men, he agrees to make the required prenuptial property gift.[42] Members of a kindred write to a man who had killed their brother, to say that the man had paid the agreed-upon wergeld and should henceforth remain free from trouble about the matter.[43] A man got in some sort of trouble for which he was unable to pay compensation. His lord stepped forward and paid the compensation for him; in return, the man agrees to become the lord's *servus*.[44] A marriage has been marked not by God's charity but by discord to the point that the man and wife can

[30] Marculf 1.33–4. [31] Marculf 1.36. [32] Marculf 1.17.
[33] Marculf 1.18. [34] Marculf 1.38.
[35] Marculf 2.9–19, 21–2, 24–38, 41, 50–2 (a companion to 1.39). Note that in 2.16 and 18 priests are mentioned as among the intercessors in a dispute among laypeople.
[36] Marculf 2.9–17. [37] Marculf 2.16?, 30–1, 41. [38] Marculf 2.18, 25–7, 35.
[39] Marculf 2.28–9, 32–4. [40] Marculf 2.50–1. [41] Marculf 2.12.
[42] Marculf 2.16. [43] Marculf 2.18. [44] Marculf 2.28.

no longer talk to each other; as a consequence, the couple agree to get divorced.[45]

None of these lay formulas in Book II represent documents that a church or monastery would have needed because they dealt with transactions among laypeople in which a church or monastery had an interest, for example, because some of the property involved belonged to it. The collection does cover such a case, but with its own specific formula: two men exchange villas, but one has to get a bishop's permission to do so, presumably because the bishop's property interests were somehow involved.[46] In short, these lay formulas represent documents for which a church or monastery would have had no direct use.

Like Book I, Marculf's Book II tells us that there was no difference between laypeople and ecclesiastics as far as getting involved in matters that could produce or require documents was concerned. Another 'two-way' formula secures property arrangements between a childless couple in case one survives the other. One version allows the surviving spouse to include a church among his or her heirs, while another specifies that the property pass undiminished to the couple's legitimate heirs.[47] Two of the formulas summarized above, the stolen bride formula and the receipt for a wergeld payment, have priests as well as laymen involved in bringing about the settlements concerned.[48] If Marculf is any guide, ecclesiastics wrote more letters, though laypeople did on occasion as well.[49]

Nevertheless, by presenting clergy and laity as options, Marculf once more recognizes the distinction between lay and ecclesiastical. Clerics and monks, monasteries and churches, were in his world qualitatively different from laypeople and lay kindreds, and therefore sometimes needed their own documents, even if the transactions involved were of the same sort that laypeople carried out by themselves. For their part, laypeople did some things with documents that clerics did not, like get married or divorced, pass property to children, pay wergeld for homicide, etc. The formulas covering these situations strongly support the conclusion that laypeople in Marculf's world sometimes used writing in spheres and for purposes different and separate from those of the churches and monasteries.

While I have argued so far that our picture of lay document use reflects Marculf's world of the late seventh century (or at least the world of possibilities that Marculf imagined for students), his formulas contain echoes of lay documentary culture that go back much further in time. As noted in the previous chapter, Marculf included in his collection a

[45] Marculf 2.30. [46] Marculf 2.23. [47] Marculf 2.7–8.
[48] Marculf 2.16, 18. [49] See Marculf 2.52.

pair of formulas that carry forward the language and procedures associated with the late antique *gesta municipalia*, presumably because these formulas were still useful for recording processes by which documents were publicly validated.[50] A formula for a testament similarly evokes a procedure visible in the Italian papyri for validating a will. The couple concerned have a notary draw up their testament; a specified number of days after their deaths, specified legates were to take the will before the *gesta municipalia* and – after the seal had been recognized and the cord binding the document roll had been cut as the authority of Roman law declared – have it validated.[51] Several of the Marculf formulas end with the tag *stipulatione subnexa*. This is a fossilized vestige of the Roman *stipulatio Aquiliana*, a clause attached to transaction documents that declared both parties to be free from claims by one party against the other.[52] None of this is to say that in Marculf's world Roman procedures and institutions were still functioning as they had in Late Antiquity. But people were apparently still doing things similar enough to Roman precedents that Marculf considered formulas using the old language and describing the old procedures to be the proper way to record them.[53]

## Tours

The formula collection from Tours is another that survives in several manuscripts and whose manuscript tradition points to the existence of an original 'ur-collection'. Although some manuscripts contain more formulas, and some less, the core of the collection comprises thirty-three document texts, some of which refer directly to the monastery of St Martin in Tours[54] or to the city of Tours itself.[55] It was most likely assembled in the eighth century, possibly during the reign of the sons of Charles Martel as mayors of the Frankish palace.[56]

The first thing to note about the Tours collection is that very little of it could have been of direct use to the monks of St Martin – only three formulas, to be specific: one for a donation to a church, one for a precarial grant, and one in which the poor on the alms rolls of the

[50] Marculf 2.37–8; see above, 105. [51] Marculf 2.17; see above, 98–102.

[52] Marculf 2.1, 3–4, 6–7, 9–11, 14, 19, 22–4, 29, 32, 36, 39, 52. *Stipulatio*: R. Zimmermann, *The Law of Obligations: Roman Foundations of the Civilian Tradition* (Cape Town, 1990; repr. Oxford, 1996), 757; F. Sturm, *Stipulatio Aquiliana: Textgestalt und Tragweite der Aquilianischen Ausgleischsquittung im klassischen Römischen Recht* (Munich, 1972).

[53] See also above, Chapter 5. [54] *Form. Tur.* 1b, 11. [55] *Form. Tur.* 3, 28–9.

[56] Rio, *Legal Practice*, 113, 116–17; Depreux, 'La tradition manuscrite', 55–9, 67–70.

monastery (*matricularii*) find an abandoned infant and locate someone to adopt it.[57] A couple of others record transactions that tangentially involve a monastery or a church: a layperson sells to another layperson land that lay within the boundaries (*termini*) of a monastery, and the manumission of a *servus* takes place before the altar and clergy of a church.[58]

The overwhelming majority of the Tours formulas do not involve a church or monastery, or clerics or monks, at all. We see laypeople giving each other power of attorney to handle their affairs[59] and having documents validated by the civic authorities.[60] We see them giving or receiving property or benefices to/from each other and exchanging property;[61] we see them selling property to each other[62] (including selling themselves into someone else's service)[63] and freeing *servi*.[64] We see them making property arrangements in advance of a marriage,[65] kidnapping (or eloping) with brides and settling the resulting disputes,[66] regulating inheritance arrangements and legal powers within their families and adopting heirs,[67] and getting divorced.[68] We see judges giving orphans to people to be raised and educated;[69] we see people having their property rights confirmed by a king after their documents had been destroyed[70] and settling conflicts over everything from seizure of property to homicide and assault on the road.[71] One of these latter dispute formulas has a man coming before a judicial assembly in Tours and charging another with having unjustly seized his property. The formula has an optional variant prologue in case the suit concerned homicide rather than property.[72]

Like their counterparts in Marculf, some of the Tours formulas suggest strongly that these were documents that laypeople would take home and keep. A letter by which a judge assigns a guardian for an orphan specifies that two copies of the document be made, one for the guardian and one for the person who would serve as guarantor for the arrangement.[73] A man who had lost his archive because he had feared the approach of a marauding army and had buried it, only to find later that the documents had rotted and were ruined, receives a copy of the charter confirming his property rights from the civic authorities.[74] The *servus* freed by his master would plausibly want to keep the document recording his manumission, even if he could not read it; more likely, the master would

57 *Form. Tur.* 1a, 7, 11.
58 *Form. Tur.* 8, 12; see Depreux, 'La tradition manuscrite', 58.
59 *Form. Tur.* 2. 60 *Form. Tur.* 2–3. 61 *Form. Tur.* 4, 6, 13, 26.
62 *Form. Tur.* 5, 8, 9. 63 *Form. Tur.* 10. 64 *Form. Tur.* 12. 65 *Form. Tur.* 14–15.
66 *Form. Tur.* 16, 32. 67 *Form. Tur.* 17–18, 20–3, 25. 68 *Form. Tur.* 19.
69 *Form. Tur.* 24. 70 *Form. Tur.* 27–8. 71 *Form. Tur.* 29, 30–1, 33.
72 *Form. Tur.* 29. 73 *Form. Tur.* 24. 74 *Form. Tur.* 27–8.

want to keep it as evidence for his position as the newly freed person's benefactor.[75]

Other Tours formulas indicate that documents were 'out there' filtering through society in the world beyond the collection. The lost archive case just mentioned lists a number of possible kinds of documents that the victim could have had in his possession: documents recording property gifts from kings, as well as property sales, gifts, grants and exchanges.[76] A *post obitum* gift of property to the monastery of St Martin explicitly blocks anyone from trying to undermine the arrangement by showing up with a charter that the donor had not personally approved.[77]

Also like Marculf, the language used by the Tours collection echoes a culture of document use going back to Late Antiquity. Many of the Tours formulas refer to Roman law, some citing specific passages from the Theodosian Code or the *Lex Romana Visigothorum*.[78] The tag *stipulatio subnixa* likewise shows up frequently. One formula even recalls the tag's origins; in a formula describing a property arrangement between a husband and wife, the penalty clause actually says that the two copies of the document to be produced should remain firm *cum stipulatione Aquiliana*.[79] As discussed in the previous chapter, several of the Tours formulas assume that the transactions they record would be validated by the local *gesta municipalia*;[80] others have their transactions carried out in the presence of the civic *curia*.[81] The manumission charter mentioned above guarantees the newly freed *servus* the right 'to lead a free life just like other Roman citizens' (*et sicut alii cives Romani vitam ducat ingenuam*).[82] As with the similar language in the Marculf collection, it is impossible to tell to what degree, if at all, this language might have been relevant or comprehensible to those who might have used the Tours formulas as a basis for real documents in the course of real transactions. Nevertheless, as far as the compilers of the collection were concerned, it apparently still formed part of the process of drafting these documents in the proper way. The monks may have understood some of the references to Roman law or procedures that they copied; others may have been traditional but less comprehensible. Nevertheless, the Tours monks regarded the old

[75] *Form. Tur.* 12; compare above, 130–1. [76] *Form. Tur.* 27. [77] *Form. Tur.* 1b.

[78] Cf. *Form. Tur.* 11 (*CTh.* 5), 14 (*LRV*), 15, 16 (*LRV*, *Epit. Aeg.*), 17 (*LRV*), 19–21 (all *LRV*), 22, 24, 25, 29–30 (both *LRV*), 32. Those that do not specifically quote the law contain general phrases such as 'secundum legem Romanam' or 'lex Romana constringit'. On the continued use of Roman law in the region, especially among churchmen, see P. Stein, *Roman Law in European History* (Cambridge 1999), 38–41.

[79] *Form. Tur.* 17.

[80] *Form. Tur.* 2–3, 17, 20, 23; see above, 105, 109. [81] *Form. Tur.* 23.

[82] *Form. Tur.* 12. See also the (albeit transformed) echoes of the late antique *appennis* procedure in *Form. Tur.* 27–8.

language as necessary to the document models that they wanted to have on hand.

The fact that the Tours collection refers directly to the monks of St Martin, but that most of the formulas it contains would have been of little direct use to the monks, suggests that in mid-eighth-century Tours the scribes of St Martin were generating – or at least wanted to know about – documents needed by the laypeople around them, of all social stripes.[83] This too, then, was a world in which laypeople of all kinds were actively using and keeping documents, and producing them for examination when necessary. Like Marculf, the compilers of the Tours collection dragged with them a great deal of far older language and references to older procedures. It appears, therefore, that in the older world or worlds from which the Tours monks drew their documentary traditions, laypeople had actively used documents as well.

## Flavigny

Sometime in the second half of the eighth century, and possibly towards the very end of the century, monks at the Burgundian abbey of St Praeiectus at Flavigny compiled a formula collection of their own. They took much, though not all, of Marculf's collection, added substantial pieces from the Tours collection, and filled in the blended collection that resulted with a small number of unique formulas that came directly from their own archive and library.[84] There is no doubt that the collection was put together at Flavigny; among the documents that the monks pulled out of their abbey's archive to make formulas were two, a property gift and a testament, written by the abbey's founder, Widerad. How the Flavigny monks got hold of the Marculf and Tours formula collections is not clear. Philippe Depreux has speculated quite plausibly that the Tours collection made its way to Flavigny through the good offices of, or the connections inspired by, Alcuin, who was abbot of Tours and, after 797, simultaneously abbot of Flavigny.[85]

83 But it is possible that the collection was not put together by the monks of St Martin at all, but rather by someone working outside the monastery, but who included some potentially useful documents from the monastery.

84 Rio, *Legal Practice*, 117–21. The collection includes two formulas for testaments that its scribes derived from testaments by Flavigny's founder, Widerad; these testaments were most likely written in 717 and 719. However, the incorporation of the mid-eighth-century formula collection from Tours pushes the *terminus post quem* for the collection up to that point. If the Tours collection reached Flavigny through connections inspired by Alcuin (see below, at n. 85), then the Flavigny collection would have been put together some time during Alcuin's simultaneous tenure as abbot of Tours and of Flavigny, i.e. after 797.

85 Depreux, 'La tradition manuscrite', 61–2.

The original manuscript of this Flavigny collection has been lost. It must have once existed, however, because the collection survives in two manuscripts, one now in Copenhagen[86] and the other our Paris manuscript BnF lat. 2123, that differ enough from each other to indicate that both stemmed from a common model rather than one from the other. Though the Copenhagen manuscript reproduces the formulas in a different order from the Paris manuscript, the Paris manuscript is assumed to reproduce the ordering of their common source because it gives its versions of the Marculf and Tours formulas in more or less their original order. Some of the formula texts given in the Paris table of contents are missing from the Paris manuscript; nevertheless, they can be reconstructed with the aid of the Copenhagen version.[87]

The Flavigny collection is numbered through from 1 to 117.[88] Its compilers cast a wide net in their search for models. The collection starts off with five late antique texts, four letters and a speech, drawn from the Acts of S. Sylvester and from the Latin translation of the sixth-century Greek *Historia tripartita* of Theodorus Lector. These include letters between the Roman emperor Constantine and his mother Helena, a letter from the emperor Constantius to Bishop Athanasius, part of a letter from Pope Julius to the clergy and people of Alexandria, and a short fragment of a speech purportedly given by Emperor Valentinian II on the election of Bishop Ambrose of Milan. All of the names and specific details were left in the texts and/or titles, making them easy to identify. Nevertheless, it does appear that they were intended to be models or sources for language. None of the five are set off or in any way distinguished from the rest of the formula collection. The last of the five consists only of three sentences. Though we can identify it as part of an imperial speech said to have been given in a specific context,[89] this brief excerpt makes no mention of that context. It consists only of general exhortations and is titled in a way – *de ordinando episcopo. Valentinianus imperator ad episcopos ait* – that generalizes it into something that could be generically useful as an example of an imperial letter on the ordination

[86] Copenhagen 84 (Francia, s. IX$^{med}$); Rio, *Legal Practice*, 243–4.

[87] The scholarship now assumes a stemma that starts with the original and proceeds to a copy from which both the Copenhagen and Paris manuscripts stem; another, reordered exemplar must have lain between this copy and the Copenhagen manuscript. See Rio, *Legal Practice*, 118; Depreux, 'La tradition manuscrite', 63; K. Zeumer, 'Die Lindenbruch'sche Handschrift der Formelsammlung von Flavigny', *Neues Archiv der Gesellschaft für ältere deutsche Geschichtskunde*, 14 (1889), 589–603, at 593–603.

[88] Thus the table of contents in BnF lat. 2123. The manuscript includes five more formulas after no. 117, some of which may have been part of the original Flavigny collection; see below, n. 123.

[89] The speech is reported by Theodoret, as transmitted in Cassiodorus-Epiphanius, *Historia ecclesiastica tripartita* 7.8 (CSEL 71:394).

of bishops.[90] The impression that the compilers of the collection were treating these antique texts as formulaic models is strengthened by some letter fragments from a similar source that appear at the end of the collection. The table of contents titles the very last entry, Flavigny 117, as 'letters made in different ways' (*Indicolos diversos modos factos*). This entry consists of twelve openings for letters addressed by bishops to a variety of recipients, the first few of which are simply headed *item alio*. The last two of the twelve, titled *Dionisius episcopus ad Romanos* and *Item ad imperatorem* respectively, have been identified as coming from Rufinus' translation of Eusebius' *Ecclesiastical History*.[91] The first of these two retains in the title the name of the person who wrote it. Nevertheless, the texts themselves are very short excerpts – two and three sentences respectively – that mention no names; they are completely subsumed within Flavigny 117 as examples of *Indicolos diversos modos factos*.[92]

The bulk of the Flavigny collection consists of large pieces of the Marculf and Tours collections interspersed with formula texts taken from the Flavigny archives that all involve clerics, monks or ecclesiastical affairs. The Tours and Marculf sections are for the most part copied in their original order and with very few changes (though most of the specific references to St Martin's in Tours have been dropped);[93] they therefore pick up and reproduce the priorities of their original compilers. These copies of the Tours and Marculf formulas were, however, by no means blind; the Flavigny scribe or scribes did not simply copy them out of antiquarian interest or a respect for the old that was disconnected from the realities of their world. On the contrary, they copied with a visible intent to put together a collection that fitted their needs.

The first evidence for this comes right away with the sixth formula. This formula represents a *post obitum* gift to a church; it is taken from Tours 1.[94] The scribe did not move immediately on to Tours 2, however. Instead, he followed Tours 1 with a Flavigny formula, taken neither

[90] Rio suggests that the names were left in these texts because the protagonists were prestigious; she also suggests that esp. no. 5 'is very much the sort of thing one would expect to find in such a [formula] collection'; Rio, *Legal Practice*, 119.

[91] MGH Formulae 498–9 (*Coll. Flav.*), marginal notes to 117l and 117m.

[92] It is possible to question whether Flavigny 1–5 and 117 belonged to the original Flavigny collection; they appear only in the Paris manuscript. Because they are listed in the Paris table of contents, however, which is presumed to follow the exemplar being copied by the compilers of the Paris manuscript, it seems justified to assume that they did form part of the original collection. If they did not, then the comments here about their use as formulas apply to their inclusion in the Paris manuscript, where they are presented physically, and treated in every way, as organic parts of the larger formula collection.

[93] The exceptions are *Coll. Flav.* 35–6 = *Form. Tur.* 28–9, which preserve the specific references to the *civitas* of Tours.

[94] *Coll. Flav.* 6ab.

from Tours or Marculf, that represents a gift to a church or monastery *a die presente*.[95] He thus created a matching pair of gifts, one *post obitum*, the other *a die presente*. Next comes a testament, in which a cleric leaves property to a church.[96] The text was adapted from the testament of Flavigny's founder, Abbot Widerad. However, the beginning of the formula was taken from the corresponding formula for a will in Marculf.[97] The Flavigny copyist took with the Marculf excerpt its late antique language mandating the will's validation before the *gesta municipalia*. He modified the Marculf text, however, so that a copy of the will would also be stored in a church archive (*in archivis basilice sancti illius*). In other words, he stitched together exactly the text he wanted.

Just as telling are the next two formulas. These are the two Flavingy *gesta municipalia* formulas discussed in the previous chapter.[98] First is the mandate from a property donor to a *magnificus frater*, asking him to go in his place to the city, have the donation validated by the *gesta municipalia*, and return with confirmation that he had done so. The second is the blow-by-blow description of the mandate bearer carrying out his task before the *gesta* assembly.[99] Both the Tours and the Marculf collections contain formulas for such documents: Tours 2–3 and Marculf 2.37–8. One would expect that, having led off this group of formulas with Tours 1, the Flavigny copyist would have simply used Tours 2–3. He did not. What he did was to make up new formulas by mixing pieces from Tours 2–3 with pieces of Marculf 2.37–8.[100] In short, despite their late antique language and descriptions of procedure, the compiler of the Flavigny collection understood these formulas. He also knew what he wanted, and he knew how to blend pre-existing but apparently not completely right material together to get what he wanted. He must, therefore, have considered these formulas to be not only relevant to his world but also important enough to be worth putting in the effort to get them right.

The twenty-nine formulas that follow, Flavigny 11–39, are copies, in order, of Tours 4–32. They therefore reproduce the order, contents and priorities of the Tours collection, including its view of lay participation in documentary culture. Flavigny 39, however, contains an interesting wrinkle; someone working on the text changed it to fit his preconceptions. In the original Tours version of this formula, a couple eloped without permission from the girl's parents but also without objection or complaint from either the parents or the girl. The crucial sentence explaining the situation reads as follows: 'accusabat aliquo homine nomine illo, eo

[95] *Coll. Flav.* 7. [96] *Coll. Flav.* 8. [97] Marculf 2.17.
[98] Above, 109. [99] *Coll. Flav.* 9–10. [100] Into Zeumer's *Form. Tur. Add.* 4–5.

quod aliqua femina nomine illa iam anno expleto sine diffinicione parentum vel sine eius clamore aut vociferatione eam volentem rapuisset atque in coniugio sibi malo ordine contra legem et iustitiam sociasset'. In both the Copenhagen and the Paris manuscripts of the Flavigny collection, the meaning of this sentence has been altered. Instead of 'eam volentem rapuisset', we read 'eam violenter rapuisset'.[101] It is impossible to tell exactly when this change took place. It may have been present already in the exemplar from which the Flavigny copyist was working; it may have happened when the Flavigny version was compiled, when the exemplar that served as the common source for the Copenhagen and Paris manuscripts was copied out, or at some point in between. It is also impossible to say whether the change was conscious or unconscious. Whatever the case, the original Tours language did not fit the assumptions of whoever made the change. It made more sense to him, or he automatically assumed as he was writing, that any *raptus*, that is, in this context any carrying off of a girl for the purpose of marriage, would have been carried out forcefully or impetuously, and would have been a violation of right, regardless of what the girl or her parents thought about the matter.[102]

The last formula in this Tours section, Flavigny 40, brings evidence of unequivocally deliberate change. It has the title of Tours 33, *iudicium evindicatum*, but it has different content. The Tours original was a directive from a king to a count; a plaintiff had come to the king saying that a man of the count's *pagus* had beaten him up on the road, taken his property and seriously injured him. The accused had been summoned to a *placitum* but had failed to show up. The king therefore ordered the count to constrain the accused and force him to make adequate amends. The Flavigny copyist[103] evidently felt that he needed to include a formula like this in his collection, but that the most likely judicial scenario would be different. So he altered the text to turn the charge into one of unjust property seizure rather than assault and robbery; the king ordered

[101] Turning *eam* from part of an accusative absolute into a direct object. See Copenhagen 84 fol. 28v, and BnF lat. 2123 fol. 122v.

[102] The word *violenter* in this period does not necessarily mean 'violently' in the modern sense; it has the more specific connotations of acts carried out with forcefulness or impetuosity, or of a violation of boundaries. See W. C. Brown, *Violence in Medieval Europe* (London, 2010), 6–7 and nn. 25–6.

[103] It is possible that this change was introduced not by the Flavigny copyist, but by whoever wrote the exemplar from which he was working. Given that this alteration is not present in any other extant manuscript of the Tours collection, however, and given the other evidence for intervention in these texts by the Flavigny copyists, I have concluded that this change was most likely made when the Flavigny collection was compiled.

that since the defendant had failed to attend the *placitum* and swear an oath to his rights, the plaintiff's possession of the disputed property be confirmed.[104]

From here we move into a section of the Flavigny collection dominated by formulas from Marculf's Book I. As with the group taken from Tours, at first we get some additions. Three unique formulas are inserted right after Marculf 1.1. Then come Marculf 1.2–4, then another formula is inserted and, after Marculf 1.5–7, yet another.[105] The last two inserted formulas appear in other Marculf manuscripts.[106] They must have come from the manuscript of Marculf that the Flavigny copyist had in front of him. Seen as a whole, this newly constructed group of formulas is not random, but rather has an identifiable logic; it deals with episcopal rights and privileges, especially immunity. Its last three formulas cover all the steps involved in appointing a new bishop, from the initial royal command that the bishop take up his post, to the royal request to another bishop to consecrate him, to the letter from the citizens of the city formally requesting that the new bishop be installed.

What follows is the rest of Marculf Book I, complete. The Flavigny compiler(s) thus reproduced the preoccupations, and assumptions about lay document use, of this part of Marculf's collection. Next, we move into the material drawn from Marculf Book II; here the Flavigny compiler(s) did a great deal more selection and reordering. The selection and reordering were again not random. A number of formulas from Marculf Book II were left out, apparently because they were redundant.[107] They are either covered by formulas from Tours or Flavigny that appear earlier in the collection, or they offer variations on other material from Marculf, variations that the Flavigny compiler(s) must have thought unimportant. The formulas that the Flavigny compiler(s) did take from Marculf Book

[104] Note that a similar Marculf formula, 1.29, is also in the Flavigny collection, as no. 74. It is not a duplicate of *Form. Tur.* 33 = *Coll. Flav.* 40, however. It represents a different stage in the proceedings; rather than a royal order to constrain someone who had ignored a summons to a *placitum*, this formula represents the original command to the accused that he attend the *placitum*.

[105] *Coll. Flav.* 41–52.

[106] Marculf Supp. 1, 6.

[107] It is possible that these formulas were already missing from the Marculf manuscript from which the Flavigny copyists were working. However, the fact that they would have been redundant specifically in the context of the Flavigny collection, where what was copied was arranged in coherent groups (see below), and that their content was covered in part by formulas from Flavigny, suggests to me that they were dropped as the Flavigny collection was compiled. An alternate scenario would have the Flavigny copyists, faced with a Marculf manuscript in which these formulas were missing, working with what they had to fill in the gaps and fill out their groupings. If this were the case, then someone earlier, compiling a now lost recension of Marculf, engaged in the process of evaluation and decision-making that led to these formulas being dropped.

II were gathered together and reordered to make new groups of formulas. For example, Flavigny 86–90 takes Marculf 2.1, 3, 5, 39–40 and 41 and groups them into a set of formulas dealing with donations of property and with benefice arrangements. The missing formulas Marculf 2.2, 4 and 6 are covered by formulas from Tours or Flavigny, or by other Marculf formulas.[108] Then comes a group of formulas for property arrangements within families that was streamlined compared to the similar section in Marculf.[109] Then, a security for a wergeld payment is followed by property sales, more securities and debt payments, and one power of attorney.[110] A set of formulas dealing with unfree status[111] is followed by a mixed bag: a royal confirmation of a sale, a letter from a mayor of the palace to a bishop, and a letter from a bishop to his mother,[112] all of which segue easily into a group of letters to bishops, kings and queens to be sent at Christmas and Easter.[113] The section ends with letters of supplication and commendation.[114]

To sum up: the compiler(s) of the Flavigny formula collection selected their formulas to meet their abbey's needs for model documents as they understood those needs. They drew their texts from the Marculf and Tours collections, and from their own archives and library, and deliberately selected and arranged them. Although the Flavigny additions all concern clerical/monastic affairs, the Flavigny collection as a whole retains a large number of forms for documents that would only be useful to laypeople. The way these lay formulas are arranged reveals the same kind of evidence of conscious selection, arrangement and modification as do the clerical formulas, indicating that the compiler or compilers understood what they were doing when they copied them.

The collection that resulted projects assumptions about lay participation in documentary culture in the area around Flavigny in the later eighth century that are essentially the same as those projected by the earlier Tours and Marculf collections. The fact that the Flavigny compilers chose to copy the formulas that they did indicates either that they felt a need to know about and study, or to teach young scribes about, lay documents in addition to those their abbey would need for its own

[108] Marculf 2.2 is a variant prologue for the same kind of donation to a church given by Marculf 2.3; Marculf 2.4 is roughly equivalent to *Coll. Flav.* 7; Marculf 2.6 is roughly equivalent to *Form. Tur.* 1b.

[109] *Coll. Flav.* 91, 92–5 = Marculf 2.11–12, 14–15.

[110] *Coll. Flav.* 96–101 = Marculf 2.18, 19–22, 25–7, 35, 28, 31.

[111] *Coll. Flav.* 102–4 = Marculf 2.29, 32–4, 36.

[112] *Coll. Flav.* 105–7 = Marculf Supp. 2–4.

[113] *Coll. Flav.* 108–10 = Marculf 2.42–4.

[114] *Coll. Flav.* 111–16 = Marculf 2.46–51.

purposes, or that they needed the lay document formulas because they would be producing documents for laypeople.

## BnF lat. 2123

All of the threads that we have been following come together in a surviving physical object: our manuscript. This manuscript reveals some things about how formula collections were created. Equally important, it embeds the Flavigny formulas in a particular context that tells us more about why our formulas for lay documents might have been copied and kept.

BnF lat. 2123 has, with varying degrees of precision, been dated to the end of the eighth century or the beginning of the ninth, to 795×816, or even to 814×16.[115] It most likely originated somewhere in Burgundy.[116] The codex now comprises 156 folia; a few of its original folia are missing. Its texts are written out in two columns, in a pre-Caroline minuscule, which might indicate a date of the very end of the eighth century rather than the ninth.[117] We even have a named scribe; on fol. 91 is the comment *Walefredus me fecit.*[118]

The codex appears to be an ecclesiastical reference book. It contains, in addition to the Flavigny formulas, excerpts from Church council acts and papal letters, an incomplete copy of Gennadius of Marseilles's *De ecclesiasticis dogmatibus*, some pseudo-Augustinian sermons, the Cononian epitome of the *Liber pontificalis*, Polemius Silvius' *Laterculus*, the *Dicta* of Theodore of Canterbury, the canon law collection known as the Herovalliana, a *computus* of the ages of the world up to the reign of Charlemagne, and the sections from Isidore of Seville's *Etymologies* on weights and measures.[119] It was conceived as a whole and executed with some care; it is written out in the same way throughout, with the same kinds of (often rather nice) rubrics and capitals (and occasional drawings in the margins), by if not the same scribe then scribes with very similar hands, with no visible breaks across the various texts.

115 See the literature cited above, n. 4.

116 Attributions to Flavigny itself appear to rest too much on its copy of the Flavigny formulas.

117 Rio, *Legal Practice*, 252.

118 At the bottom of fol. 75r, the name *Hathulfus* is written next to the name *Walefredus*; at the bottom of fol. 65v, the name *Hathulfus* appears by itself. This suggests that there were perhaps two scribes involved in writing the codex. If so, their hands are very similar. On fol. 52r, a later hand (s. X–XI?) continues the list of popes, which had originally ended with Hadrian I, from Leo III to John IX.

119 Rio, *Legal Practice*, 252.

The Flavigny formula collection starts on fol. 105v. The scribe began with a spectacular initial and capitals for the title *Incipit praefacio libri huius*. Following the title comes the prologue to Marculf's formula collection; it has been adapted here as a preface for the Flavigny collection. The prologue preserves Marculf's self-attribution and his explanation for the collection's purpose. There is one change, however: Bishop Landeric has become Bishop Aeglidulf.[120] It has proven impossible to identify Aeglidulf. It is also impossible to say whether this change was made when this manuscript was compiled, or at some earlier stage in the history of the Flavigny collection.[121] Nevertheless, someone – either our scribe or an earlier one – used Marculf's prologue essentially as a formula in its own right, by simply plugging in the name of the appropriate bishop.[122]

After the prologue comes a lengthy table of contents. The table of contents does not entirely match the actual contents of the formula collection. Five formulas are written on fols. 151–153v that are not listed in the table of contents; these concern property donations, precarial and prestarial grants to and from a monastery, and a monk who had fled his monastery.[123] Moreover, as noted earlier, several of the formulas given in the table of contents are missing from the manuscript. That they formed part of the original Flavigny collection is ensured by the other (Copenhagen) manuscript of the collection.[124] Their absence here is not due to missing folia. It appears to have been due to simple scribal error; the text moves seamlessly from one formula to the next but skips one or more formulas listed in the table of contents, including their numbers. For example, on fol. 148r, we continue smoothly, in the middle of a column, from Flavigny 96 to Flavigny 98 with no visible change of hands.[125]

Nevertheless, the manuscript offers considerable evidence that care was taken with the formula collection, that at least some level of oversight went into its production, and that the person or people doing the work understood what he or they were doing and made some effort to get it right. This applies to the lay formulas as well as to those in which clergy were involved. Words found to be missing were inserted along with

120 BnF lat. 2123 fol. 105v.

121 The Marculf preface is not in the Copenhagen 84 version of the Flavigny collection.

122 Rio, *Legal Practice*, 60.

123 These formulas were edited by Zeumer as *Coll. Flav. Add.* 1–5; Rio, *Legal Practice*, 118–19. The beginning of Add. 1 has been lost along with the folium on which it was written.

124 See Rio, *Legal Practice*, 118, 243.

125 See also fol. 140r, skip from *Coll. Flav.* 80 to 86; fols. 147v–148r, skip from *Coll. Flav.* 94 to 96; fol. 148v, skip from last formula of *Coll. Flav.* 98 group to *Coll. Flav.* 100; fol. 150v, skip from *Coll. Flav.* 104 to 111.

insertion marks to show where they belonged. For example, on fol. 122v, when copying out Flavigny 39 = Tours 32 (the formula discussed above in which a man ran off with a girl *violenter* instead of *eam volentem*), the scribe, when he reached the sentence explaining the situation, skipped all the way from *sine diffinicione* to *eam violenter rapuisset.* Catching his error, he placed a sign at the end of *diffinicione* and a corresponding sign in the bottom margin of the page, where he wrote the missing text: *vel sine eius clamore aut vociferacione* (though he still left out the *parentum* that should have followed *diffinicione*).[126] Mistakes were marked with rows of dots underneath or above the affected lines, which told readers to ignore them. For example, on fol. 138r, in the middle of the second column, in the text of Flavigny 77 = Marculf 1.32 (in which a king gives property confiscated from rebels to some *viri inlustri*), the words *mixti fuerunt* are supposed to appear twice; the first time in the phrase, 'qui cum eodem mixti fuerunt, ex hoc conprehensum adduxerunt', and the second time in the phrase, 'qui cum illo mixti fuerunt, nec ab heredes eorum'. After the scribe wrote the first *mixti fuerunt*, he let his attention wander and skipped to the *nec ad heredes* that followed the second. Realizing his mistake after writing these three words, he marked them as an error with a row of dots underneath, and then continued correctly with *ex hoc conprehensum adduxerunt.*[127]

The most spectacular mistake tells us something about how the formula collection in this manuscript was put together; the scribe had in front of him separate leaves or quires from his sources, leaves or quires that could get mixed up. On fol. 147r, in the middle of the second column, Flavigny 91 = Marculf 2.9 ends (see Figure 6.1). Then comes the title of Flavigny 92 = Marculf 2.11. Instead of the opening line of this formula, however, we get, complete with a nicely decorated capital,

[126] See also fol. 137rb middle (in *Coll. Flav.* 73 = Marculf 1.28 the missing 'mo' in 'cum omnibus modis' is written in above the line with an insertion mark); fol. 115rb, two-thirds of the way down (a missing 'quis suum' inserted in the text of *Coll. Flav.* 18 = *Form. Tur.* 11); fol. 144va, bottom (in the opening lines of *Coll. Flav.* 117a, the missing 'moda' inserted for the phrase 'salutem vobis multimoda').

[127] See also: fol. 135v, in *Coll. Flav.* 67 = Marculf 1.22: dots mark a missing 't' in 'aut sua'. Fol. 136r: in the same formula text, dots mark mistaken letters copied between 'titulum' and 'a iugo'. Fol. 145v: at the beginning of *Coll. Flav.* 117e, the scribe skipped part of a line and wrote a few words that should have come later; he made a mark, blocked off the incorrect text with two dots over and under the offending words at either end, made a second mark, and then started again where he made the mistake but this time wrote correctly. Fol. 146v: in *Coll. Flav.* 117i, the scribe wrote 'dign&tis' instead of 'dignastis', so he crossed out the '&', marked it with dots above and below, and wrote the letters 'as' above it. Fol. 147v, at the beginning of *Coll. Flav.* 93 = Marculf 2.12, the scribe wrote, instead of 'ut de terra paterna', 'ut d& erna', so he put dots above and below between the 'e' and 'r' of 'erna', and simply placed the missing letters 'ra pate' above, to create 'ut d& er[ra pate]rna'.

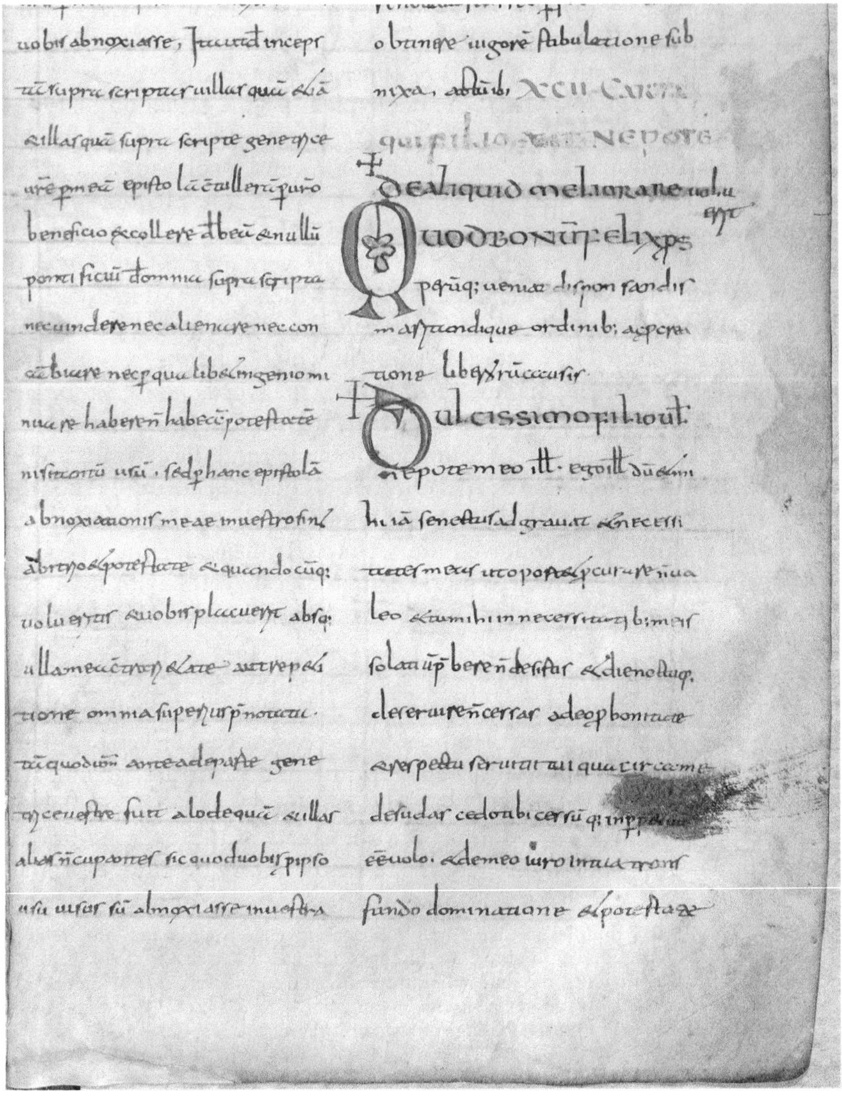

Figure 6.1 BnF lat. 2123, fol. 147r detail: the opening line of Marculf 2.15 written by mistake between the title and first line of Flavigny 92, with cross-marks to guide the reader around it.

the line, 'Quod bonum filex prosperumque veniat disponsandis maritandisque ordinibus ac procreatione liberorum causis'. At the beginning of this line, the scribe placed a cross-mark; at the end, he did so again. Next comes the proper opening line of Flavigny 92, which represents a property gift from a grandfather to a dutiful grandson. The line in between the title and the correct text turns out to be the beginning of Marculf 2.15, in which a man about to be a father-in-law makes a dotal gift to his son's betrothed; according to the table of contents, this formula was supposed to appear in the collection farther down as Flavingy 95. The scribe apparently had leaves or quires of his exemplar of the Flavigny collection in front of him but got them mixed up; after he copied the beginning of Flavigny 95 = Marculf 2.15, he realized his mistake and made a note for readers to skip over the abortive copy to the correct beginning of Flavigny 92. As it happens, Flavigny 95 is one of the formulas that got left out of the manuscript; when he got there, the scribe skipped straight from 94 to 96. When he came to copy it, he must have thought he had copied it already, or had misplaced his exemplar, or had simply forgotten about it.

The care taken to show readers how to get around mistakes indicates that this was indeed a codex intended to be used as a practical reference. More evidence to this effect is provided by scattered efforts to demarcate formula texts proper from instructions for using formulaic options and from shorthand references to common formulaic phrases. While the scribe concerned did not do this consistently, on a few occasions he marked such words or passages by suddenly shifting from the pre-Caroline minuscule that dominates the codex into a flowery chancery-like script. On fol. 121va, eight lines from the bottom, for example (see Figure 6.2), we come to the place in the judicial formula Flavigny 36 = Tours 29 where an optional prologue is provided for the case of homicide; the direction, 'Et si de homicidio accusacio facta fuerit', stands out clearly from the rest of the text by virtue of its suddenly more flowery script.[128]

Then there is some internal cross-referencing. On fol. 120r, the scribe copied Flavigny 34 = Tours 27, which is a royal confirmation of the property rights covered by a lay archive lost to a fire. Next to the title, he wrote, 'alibi require sub hera lxxviii'; that is, 'for another one see number 78'. Sure enough, Flavigny 78 = Marculf 1.33 is another royal precept confirming the contents of a lost lay archive. On fol. 136v, at the bottom of the first column, the end of the royal *placitum* prologue Flavigny 70 = Marculf 1.25, we find inserted the line, 'require in hera lxxxiii'; that is, 'see number 83'. Flavigny 83 is another one of the formula texts that got left out, but, according to the table of contents, it was to have been the royal judicial precept Marculf 1.38. Since Flavigny 70 is just a prologue, it looks like the scribe wanted to refer searchers to another royal judicial text that had more content (his note also, by the way, gives further evidence

[128] See also fol. 114rb, line 4: 'facta loco'; fol. 149rb: 'et si voluntaria servo accipit dicis'.

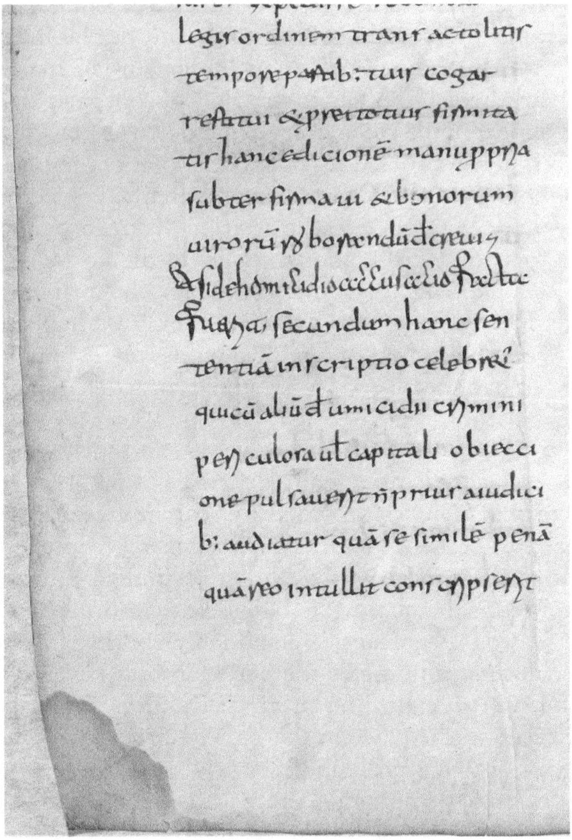

Figure 6.2 BnF lat. 2123, fol. 121va, detail: directions for use of an optional prologue are written in a different script.

that the missing Flavigny 83 was supposed to be included but was left out by mistake).

The choice of the word *hera* (or *hira*) for 'chapter' or 'number' in this context is interesting. It is used three times in this copy of the Flavigny collection in the same way to make cross-references.[129] In general, this word is rare in the formula collections, but it is used in the Herovalliana

[129] See also fol. 142r, at the end of *Coll. Flav.* 88a = Marculf 2.5 (a precarial grant): 'et reliqua sicut in hira'. There is no number given for this one. Zeumer (MGH Formulae 484) seems to indicate that it refers back to *Coll. Flav.* 87 = Marculf 2.3, which is the prologue for a donation to a church. However, it makes little sense for the ending of a precarial grant to be completed by referring upwards to the beginning of a donation.

collection of canons, which appears earlier in this manuscript. Apparently, the scribe who used the word in the formulas was influenced by its use in the canon law collection – another sign that the same person or same team was involved in producing other parts of the manuscript.[130]

## Conclusions

In the end, this manuscript offers us evidence across an envelope of space and time for a culture of document use in the heart of the Frankish world that included laypeople. The envelope extends from the mid or late seventh through the early ninth century and covers the Touraine, Neustria and Burgundy. Echoes from formulaic language take the evidence for lay documentary culture back even earlier.

At each stage of the timeline that culminated in our manuscript, the formulas indicate that laypeople as well as clergy were using documents for a variety of transactions and legal processes that involved personal rights and privileges as well as property. The people involved ranged from the powerful (kings and counts, bishops and archbishops), to the powerless (that is, the unfree or those falling into unfreedom). Some of these transactions and processes connected laypeople and clergy but many did not; they involved only laypeople, or only clergy.

At least in the worlds of possibility imagined by those who compiled the formula collections, laypeople and clerics or monks did similar things with similar kinds of documents; both thought documents were important and when necessary went to some effort to get them and to keep them. The only distinction that we can really draw is this: clerics and monks sometimes needed their own versions of common documents, or engaged in kinds of transactions that were unique to them and their institutions; to that degree, the formula collections treat laypeople and clergy differently. The fact that formula scribes felt compelled at times to include specifically clerical versions of common documents, however, is good evidence that the specifically lay versions were important in their own right, rather than simply sources or models for documents that clergy needed. Moreover, the care with which our scribes collected, selected, arranged and sometimes altered or combined formulas indicates that they were all, lay as well as clerical, comprehensible and important to them.

However, it is very important to note that monasteries played a fundamental role in collecting and preserving the model documents contained

[130] H. Mordek, *Kirchenrecht und Reform im Frankenreich: Die Collectio Vetus Gallica: Die älteste systematische Kanonessammlung des Fränkischen Gallien* (Berlin, 1975), 122n66.

in our manuscript. Marculf was a monk who compiled his collection for students at the behest of a bishop. The monastery of St Martin in Tours compiled its own formula collection. Copies of both the Marculf and Tours collections made their way to the abbey at Flavigny. If Philippe Depreux is right, it was no less a man than Alcuin as lay abbot of both Tours and Flavigny who was at least indirectly responsible for the Tours collection coming to Flavigny. The monks at Flavigny took these collections, added material from their own library and archives, and made their own collection. It is impossible to say for sure where the manuscript BnF lat. 2123 itself was put together. However, its contents point unmistakably to an ecclesiastic or monastic milieu.

Clearly, some monasteries from the end of the seventh, but especially from the middle of the eighth through the first decades of the ninth century, were strongly interested in preserving and maintaining access to models for documents that were potentially of use to a wide range of people, lay as well as clerical, high born as well as low. By implication, then, they felt they needed to be able to generate such documents, or at least that their scribes and students needed to know about them, and probably both. The question is, why?

The answer to this question lies in looking at all of the formula manuscripts, not just at BnF lat. 2123, as well as at the other kinds of evidence for early medieval documentary culture that is discussed elsewhere in this volume. Here I will make some preliminary suggestions. All of the extant manuscripts containing collections of formulas date from the eighth century through the early tenth; the overwhelming majority of them come from the ninth century.[131] Some of the formula collections contained in these manuscripts are indeed older; Marculf wrote in the late seventh century, while the content of the Angers collection strongly suggests that at least the documents in it stem from the late sixth. Even so, however, most of the ur-collections that have been reconstructed from later manuscripts, or that exist only in single copies, date from after the middle of the eighth century.[132] The majority of these formula collections project an essentially similar picture of a common documentary culture, shared and participated in by both clergy and laity, to what we have seen here; moreover, they extend the picture to cover not only Francia but also Alemannia and Bavaria.[133] They appear in a wide variety of

[131] Rio, *Legal Practice*, 241–71; Brown, 'Die Karolingischen Formelsammlungen'.

[132] Rio has pointed out that all seven Marculf manuscripts date from the Carolingian period and could thus be called 'Carolingian versions' of Marculf: Rio, *Legal Practice*, 59.

[133] See the geographical range of the collections given in Rio, *Legal Practice*, 67–164.

manuscript contexts: in collections of canon law and secular law (that is, Roman and/or Germanic law, Carolingian capitularies, etc.), schoolbooks and miscellanies and by themselves in their own codices. We can directly trace the origins of only some; we can infer the possible origins of others from their contents. Many of those whose origins we can trace or at least surmise point to monasteries or cathedral churches. Some betray in addition evidence of direct involvement by the Carolingian court.

The Carolingian world of the late eighth and early ninth centuries was one in which secular authority and ecclesiastical authority are difficult if not impossible to separate. It was a world in which very powerful people wore both secular and ecclesiastical or monastic hats, and in which churches and monasteries were being used as instruments of government and power to an unprecedented degree. It was a world in which writing itself was also being used as an instrument of government and power to an unprecedented degree, and in which churches and monasteries, as well as those overseeing the royal fisc, were being encouraged by the court to make and keep written records of their properties and incomes. The formula evidence suggests that, in this context, churches and especially monasteries were, consciously or unconsciously, taking responsibility for producing documents for everyone. They therefore needed to create and to keep collections of models that covered the range of possible documents that people might need, and that their scribes might need to draw on or study.

# 7 Archives, documents and landowners in Carolingian Francia

*Matthew Innes*

*We have just seen how in the Frankish world the needs of ecclesiastical institutions generated a set of sources – formula-books – that give us an indirect picture of the broader documentary culture in the period following the atrophy of late antique institutions. In this chapter, we see directly how these same needs play out with real documents and real archives. In particular, we see how church and monastic archives filtered and reshaped the documentary record in response to their own needs, warping our view of the broader documentary culture. Peering through this filter we can see traces of the wider world of document use and how some of these traces got into churches and monasteries in the first place. Clerical and monastic documentary practices were not* sui generis, *but rather reflect assumptions about and practices surrounding records and record-keeping in the local societies of which they were a part.*

## Evidential horizons and their historiographical repercussions

Histories of written law and legal documentation in the early medieval world are inevitably framed in terms of the Roman inheritance to the western Empire's successor states.[1] Assessing the nature of that inheritance is difficult, however, on account of the different profiles of the evidence for the Roman and immediately post-Roman centuries on one

[1] Law: P. Wormald, '*Lex scripta* and *verbum regis*: Legislation and Kingship from Euric to Cnut', in P. Sawyer and I. Wood (eds.), *Early Medieval Kingship* (Leeds, 1977), 95–138. Charters: Classen, 'Fortleben'; McKitterick, *Carolingians*, esp. 77–134; essays in *Settlement of Disputes*, esp. Nelson; and, in the wider context of written law, P. Wormald, *The Making of English Law. I. Legislation and Its Limits* (Oxford, 2001), 30–108, all now supplemented by a range of regional studies; for a fresh appraisal, see Rio, *Legal Practice*, esp. 9–27, and G. Koziol, *The Politics of Memory and Identity in Carolingian Royal Diplomas: The West Frankish Kingdom (840–987)* (Turnhout, 2011), ch. 1. I am grateful to the Lay Archives Working Group; to Peter Erhart, Karl Heidecker, Geoffrey Koziol, Wendy Davies and Charles West for their comments; and to Jon Jarrett for work undertaken as a research assistant paid by Birkbeck College and the Leverhulme Trust, in which capacity he identified 'lay' documents embedded within cartularies and also undertook analysis of surviving dispute-settlement (*placita*) texts.

hand, and the eighth to eleventh centuries on the other. In Francia, our understanding of the documentary and legal culture of the fifth and sixth centuries – and to a significant degree the seventh century also – rests on normative sources such as law codes, with some contextualization from hagiographical and historiographical narratives.[2] It is only as we progress towards the end of the seventh century that we begin to find a steady trickle of documentary texts, mostly transmitted through later copies, from which to work; the compilation and copying of collections of model documents in formularies relates to a similar time horizon and in important ways was a response to the same processes that determined the vectors of documentary transmission.[3] Once we move into the eighth and ninth centuries, the new or refounded ecclesiastical institutions closely associated with the 'Carolingianization' of the Frankish world, particularly its eastern regions, offer a much fuller supply of documents, mostly in the 'books of traditions' compiled by these newly founded and heavily patronized churches; and from a handful of institutions we get a steadier trickle of originals, particularly of royal diplomas.[4]

The changing nature of the documentation thus immediately sets up major interpretative problems in handling change over time. For we view the successive phases of Frankish documentary culture through different sources accessed via contrasting historiographies. In dealing with Merovingian documentary culture, we adopt historiographical strategies and interpretative techniques familiar to scholars of Roman legal practice, nuancing an idealized normative picture against isolated and indirect hints at a more varied practice in narrative and normative texts. Such a historiography poses questions about the extent to which the agendas

[2] E.g. I. N. Wood, 'Dispute Settlement in Late Fifth- and Sixth-Century Gaul: Some Problems', in *Settlement of Disputes*, 7–22, and Wood, 'Administration, Law and Culture in Merovingian Gaul', in *Uses of Literacy*, 63–81.

[3] Surviving original documents (overwhelmingly transmitted from a single archive, St-Denis, for reasons discussed below, 317–19, with a significant stream from the Carolingian period from St Gall, discussed below, 155–64) are in *ChLA*; D. Ganz and W. Goffart, 'Charters Earlier than 800 from French Collections', *Speculum*, 65 (1990), 906–32. Royal documents are edited by T. Kölzer (MGH DD Mer.); see A. C. Murray, 'The New MGH Edition of the Charters of the Merovingian Kings', *Journal of Medieval Latin*, 15 (2005), 246–78. There is no systematic collection or study of the late seventh- and early eighth-century documents transmitted in cartulary copies. Formularies: above, Chapter 5; Rio, *Legal Practice*.

[4] Carolingian cartularies: below, Chapter 8. Transmission via high medieval cartularies and compilations: below, Chapter 11. *ChLA* is now expanding its scope into the ninth century; for original documents from the ninth and tenth centuries, below, 313–20, with references to the ARTEM database. Even in the ninth century, transmission in the original is dominated by three archives (St-Denis, St Gall and Cluny), with a handful of others that preserve some important royal and founding documents as originals (e.g. Hersfeld, Murbach).

of rulers and their agents to regulate society could be put into practice, but it does not allow the presentation of alternative visions of social practice from those implicit in the normative discourses of the time. For the historian of the Carolingian and post-Carolingian periods, the interpretative disjuncture is more severe, with the appearance of a sizeable body of evidence directly relating to legal practice on the ground. The brute fact of the dominance of ecclesiastical archives in our evidence for legal practice is difficult to avoid, and skews our perspective on practice; and the fact that we know so much more about practice in the later period makes us all the more aware of the problems of interpreting normative sources. In fact, it produces an interpretative paradox. Scholars dealing with the immediately post-Roman period of Merovingian Gaul, because they have little or no surviving practical documentation but a range of hints at social practice, do not rub against concerns about ecclesiastical monopolization on the documentary record and so feel confident in drawing inferences about wider documentary cultures. In contrast, students of the Carolingian world, acutely aware of the wealth of traditions transmitted through ecclesiastical archives in copy and original, and the overwhelming dominance of documents directly establishing the interests of the Church in those traditions, feel apologetic or defensive in attempting to recreate the legal and tenurial practices of lay landowners.

This chapter deals directly with the issues raised by the changing profile of the evidence and the interpretative problems these create. Explaining changes in the nature of the sources, and the relationship of these changes to social processes, is the first job of the historian. What follows argues that the ecclesiastical archives of the Carolingian world not only define our evidential horizons but also were themselves an important product of cultural, legal and political change. These processes are elucidated through a detailed case study of the biggest surviving collection of original documents from the early Middle Ages, those from St Gall. Because the St Gall material is preserved as originals with notations and markings, it offers a priceless opportunity to see inside the archive of an early medieval ecclesiastical institution and reconstruct the concerns and techniques underpinning documentary classification and preservation; it therefore sheds light on the parallel processes feeding into the production of ninth-century 'books of traditions' elsewhere in the eastern regions of the Carolingian world. At St Gall, it is clear that the institutional archival practices which produce such a dramatic upsurge in documentary texts do not represent the totality of Carolingian documentary culture: they need situating amidst a wider documentary culture, many of whose features can be reconstructed. Moving beyond St Gall, its unique transmission of originals and its particular political context, we can trace hints of a similar variety of practices elsewhere; the estate of Perrecy in Burgundy provides an example, for a region with a very different history, topography and society.

## Charters and their transmission at Carolingian St Gall

Archives – even ecclesiastical archives – are notoriously elusive in Carolingian sources. We have a handful of uses of the Latin *archivum* to refer to the place where documents were stored, amidst a more varied and less specific terminology ('treasury', 'store'). The variety of words used suggests that document storage may not have been defined by a dedicated space with its own specialized rules. It certainly is striking that in their voluminous writings the likes of Einhard and Hincmar nowhere describe archives as a source of authority, nor did the practices of document keeping define the identities of any of the many servants of the Carolingian rulers, in marked contrast to the later Roman and early Byzantine world of John Lydus.[5] To search for a set of institutional spaces with defined public profiles is probably fruitless; we would do better to focus on archival practices – the pragmatics of how and when documents were utilized after their initial production – rather than institutional history. If we do so, can we read archival practices as a means of acquiring physical and interpretative control of the documentary record, as some recent theorists have suggested?[6] The case of the monastery of St Gall in modern Switzerland allows us to reconstruct the mechanisms whereby a major church, as its patrimony reached a certain scale and it acquired a certain degree of institutional self-consciousness, might develop a fixed archival memory of a new kind. The evidence from St Gall also suggests that, prior to reaching this 'critical mass', such an institution might 'piggyback' on pre-existing archival and documentary practices and manage its muniments in a manner familiar to the landowning classes around it.

[5] H. Fichtenau, 'Archive der Karolingerzeit', in Fichtenau, *Beiträge zur Mediäevistik*, 3 vols. (Stuttgart, 1986), III, 115–25; for Lydus, above, 14. I hope to discuss Carolingian royal archives elsewhere. Recent arguments for the systematic central registration of the contents of royal diplomata do not take on board the findings of previous scholarship: cf. D. Bachrach, 'The Exercise of Royal Power in Early Medieval Europe: The Case of Otto the Great 936–973', *EME*, 17 (2009), 389–419; B. and D. Bachrach, 'Continuity of Written Administration in the Late Carolingian East *c*. 887–911: The Royal Fisc', *Frühmittelalterliche Studien*, 42 (2008), 109–46.

[6] See above, 13.

St Gall, famously, provides a potentially unique insight into Carolingian record-keeping, thanks to the preservation of its charters in the original rather than via a cartulary.[7] However, although the abbey has had a continuous history since its refoundation *c.* 720, its archival holdings – for all their transmission in the original – have not. In particular, the early modern period saw the disruption of the archive and the removal of a significant part of its contents following the plundering of the abbey in 1531 – a reminder that systematic post-medieval disruption is a constant in the history of medieval archives. The centuries following 1531 saw recurrent campaigns of restitution, a process which went hand-in-hand with the editing of collections of documents. As a result, although the last known group of surviving documents removed from St Gall in 1531 was only returned to the abbey in 1946, the shape of the surviving charter collection of over 700 original Carolingian documents has been well known since the nineteenth century.[8] While this transmitted material seems to provide a relatively full picture of the abbey's property acquisitions, it is salutary to remember that we have no way of knowing what was destroyed in 1531, or subsequently lost, nor how the processes of dispersal and restitution altered the pattern of surviving documentation.

For all the need to consider the possibility of gaps, the survival of over 700 originals allows us unrivalled insight into a major Carolingian archive, and the work of Peter Erhart and others has used this material to elucidate St Gall's archival practice.[9] By the ninth century, an archiving process seems to have been well established. Scribes often made extensive notes (the so-called *Vorakte*) on the parchments, either prior to a transaction when they were 'commissioned' or as a contemporaneous note at a public meeting; these then informed the working up of a formal

[7] The St Gall charters are published as Wartmann I–VI; those prior to 800 have been edited, with facsimile, in *ChLA* I–II; the ninth-century material is in *ChLA* C–CIII. See also P. Erhart and L. Hollenstein (eds.), *Mensch und Schrift im frühen Mittelalter* (St Gall, 2006).

[8] P. Erhart, 'Dem Gedächtnis auf der Spur: Das frühmittelalterliche Archiv des Klosters St. Gallen', in Erhart and Hollenstein (eds.), *Mensch und Schrift*, 59–66, with references; P. Erhart and J. Kleindinst, *Urkundenlandscaft Rätien* (Vienna, 2004), 24–6.

[9] Erhart, 'Dem Gedächtnis auf der Spur'; Erhart, '*Carta ista amalfitana est et nescitur legere*: The Charters of Cava dei Tirreni and St Gall and Their Evidence for Early Medieval Archival Practice', *Gazette du livre médiéval*, 50 (2007), 27–39; K. Heidecker, 'Les actes privés de la période carolingienne dans les archives de Saint-Gall', *Annuaire de l'École pratique des hautes études (EPHE), Section des sciences historiques et philologiques*, 139 (2008): ashp.revues.org/index570.html.

charter text.[10] The charter was then brought to St Gall, where the individual parchment was folded into a long, finger-like, packet, and a note on the contents (normally the name of the donor and land) was made on the outside. Sometimes this note was written by the actual charter scribe (who when he was a monk seems to have been responsible for archiving his own documents), but sometimes in another hand (presumably that of the monk then responsible for the charter collection). The physical location in which the documents were then stored remains obscure – it is not indicated in the ideal monastery on the so-called Plan of St Gall – but we do know that charter scribes doubled as book scribes and worked in close proximity to the scriptorium. In all likelihood, the scriptorium or the sacristy doubled as the storage place for documents; by the eleventh century the *armarium*, close to the treasury (*thesaurus*), served as the charter store.[11]

Archiving practice – in particular, the annotation of documents – seems to have been motivated by immediate concerns from its very beginnings. The earliest dorsal notices began *c.* 770 and were made by the monk and later abbot, Waldo; the practice of making annotations for reference was subsequently adopted by other monastic scribes and became general by the ninth century. Waldo's moves were in all probability a response to urgent need; he referenced not only documents he wrote himself but also older muniments, including several of the earliest surviving St Gall documents.[12] These documents predated the Carolingian takeover and recorded the gifts to the abbey made by local Alemannian landowners prior to the battle of Cannstadt in 746. They had contemporary significance precisely because so many of these gifts had been subsequently seized by Ruthard and Warin, the Frankish aristocrats who ruled Alemannia with an iron rod in the middle decades of the eighth century. Not only was the establishment of Carolingian rule through Warin and

10 E.g. McKitterick, *Carolingians*, 94–8, and Heideicker, 'Les actes privés'. It seems to me rather odd that some (most famously, M. Richter, '"Quisquis scit scibere, nullam potat abere labore": Zur Laienschriftlichkeit im 8. Jht', in J. Jarnut and U. Nonn [eds.], *Karl Martell in seiner Zeit* [Sigmaringen, 1994], 393–404), have seen the *Vorakte* as indicating a disjuncture between the legal moment of disposition and the written record.

11 On the elusiveness of archival space, see Fichtenau, 'Archive der Karolingerzeit', 117–19; for St Gall, Erhart and Kleindinst, *Urkundenlandschaft Rätien*, 22–3, citing Ekkehard IV, *Casus sancti Galli* 112 (ed. H. F. Haefele [Darmstadt, 2002], 220); also S. Barret, *La mémoire et l'écrit: L'abbaye de Cluny et ses archives (X$^{e}$–XVIII$^{e}$ siècle)* (Münster, 2004), 91–6.

12 The dorsal notices were edited by O. Clavadetscher and P. Stärkle, *Die Dorsualnotizen der älteren St Galler Urkunden* (St Gall, 1970); they are distinct from the *Vorakte*; a good example of the early annotation of significant donations to Otmar comes in *ChLA* I 40, 44 = Wartmann I 8, 9.

Ruthard effected by systematic confiscations and expropriations whose documentary footprint structures the record for the region through the ninth century; it also involved the subjection of St Gall to the bishop of Constance, and the trial, deposition, exile and subsequent death of Abbot Otmar (717–59).[13]

St Gall tradition not only remembered the misfortunes visited by Warin and Ruthard; it also fostered active memories of lost lands that informed long-running attempts at reclamation. In the house histories in which these memories found written reworking, these carefully nursed grievances were often articulated through stories about documents. St Gall's subjection to Constance, for example, was presented as an act of arbitrary seizure encapsulated in a complex tale about the removal of charters and their subsequent incarceration in the treasury (*scrinium*) of Constance cathedral. St Gall's claims here need taking with a pinch of salt. With the benefit of hindsight, the monks claimed that since the time of Pippin they had held privileges that were in fact identical to those systematically granted to royal monasteries in the reign of the current Carolingian, Louis the Pious; indeed, they were successful in mobilizing this version of the past to procure new privileges from Louis. But documents mattered both as symbols of identity – the theft of royal privileges by the bishop of Constance was almost a ritual demonstration of St Gall's humiliating subjection – and practically in eliciting Louis' grant of royal protection and associated rights.[14] Documents such as those Waldo indexed were likewise crucial points of memory, for the lands lost under Warin and Ruthard were the subject of a St Gall campaign for restoration spanning a century and more, a campaign that resulted in a slow but steady trickle of restitutions from the very last years of the eighth century through to the end of the ninth. As the house histories make clear, issues of identity loomed large in the memories of such estates, their donors and their complex histories. But studying and referencing the abbey's documentary resources was also, simultaneously, a practical action with instrumental intentions, not least as confiscated estates might have been subsequently transferred by charter themselves, creating a rival parchment trail to St Gall's. A remarkable pair of royal charters from 790, for example, show Charlemagne dealing with the case of Alemannian estates

[13] For confiscation, expropriation and Carolingian rule in Alemannia, see M. Innes, 'Property, Politics and the Problem of the Carolingian State', in W. Pohl and V. Wieser (eds.), *Das frühmittelalterlichen Staat: Europäische Perspektiven* (Vienna, 2009), 299–314.

[14] Ratpert, *Casus sancti Galli*, esp. cc. 2–3 (MGH SRG 75:151–65); P. Depreux, 'La plainte des moines de Saint-Gall auprès de l'empereur Louis le Pieux (815)', *Zeitschrift für schweizerische Kirchengeschichte*, 94 (2000), 7–16.

that had been confiscated in the aftermath of the Carolingian conquest, and then passed on by Ruthard to private landowners by charter of sale. In both cases, Charlemagne overturned these (now lost) deeds on the grounds that the initial confiscation had been unjust, and returned the land to the abbeys of St-Denis and St Martin at Tours.[15] It would therefore be a mistake to take the relatively laconic *placitum* tradition from this region – which tends not to give detailed accounts of argumentation in court, simply listing witnesses without normally mentioning documents – at face value, and argue that these documents were not used in court: their referencing by St Gall scribes implies otherwise.[16]

The notices show not only continual reference and use but also at least two systematic efforts at archival organization. The first, which saw charters annotated with names of donors and the location of the land, was completed by 815. This may be linked to the compilation of a listing of the monastery's monks, headed by their saintly patron, Otmar, *c.* 802: the same hand is evident at work in both projects.[17] This would confirm the commemorative aspect of such archival activity, evident also in cartulary compilation elsewhere. But this codification of institutional memory was also linked to fundamental changes in the governance of Alemannia and its relationship to the royal court, which made the cult of Otmar, and complaints about the actions of Ruthard, Warin and the first generation of Carolingian agents, politically live issues.[18]

A further systematic reorganization *c.* 840 underlines the relationship between internal archival organization and external social and political changes. This second campaign of reorganization involved the reordering and numbering of the charters, region by region, with each region given – in true Carolingian fashion – its own *capitulum*, with the relevant documents probably stored together in a single drawer. Simultaneously, royal diplomas were differentiated from private charters, creating a contrast which Notker was to play on in appealing to Charles the Fat for further

[15] MGH DD Kar. 1, nos. 166–7. Charlemagne's simultaneous resolution of both cases probably relates to a wider moment in Alemannia's history, and the royal charters likely obscure local compromises: Innes, 'Property, Politics', 307–8.

[16] Cf. T. Reuter, 'Property Transactions and Social Relationships Between Rulers, Bishops and Nobles in Early Eleventh-Century Saxony: The Evidence of the Vita Meinwerki', in W. Davies and P. Fouracre (eds.), *Property and Power in the Early Middle Ages* (Cambridge, 1995), 165–8, at 171–2; or for the classic denial of any dispositive or probative value for this material, Richter, '"Quisquis sit scribere"'.

[17] Erhart, 'Dem Gedächtnis auf der Spur'; Erhart, '*Carta ista*'; Heidecker, 'Les actes privés', with references to the foundational work of Bruckner and Stärkle.

[18] Innes, 'Property, Politics', with M. Borgolte, *Geschichte der Grafschaften Alemanniens in karolingischer Zeit* (Sigmaringen, 1983) for administrative change as reflected in scribal formulas.

privileges.[19] This distinction between royal *praecepta* and *cartae pagenses* dates back at least as far as Marculf's formula-book in the late seventh century, but as a principle of archival organization it is characteristic of Carolingian charter compilations in East Francia, the prototypes for later cartularies right across the post-Carolingian world; they normally list royal documents separately at the beginning, and private charters by geographical region.[20] The St Gall evidence perhaps suggests that these principles of organization reflect an archival system originating in the early ninth century. At St Gall, these archival practices can probably also be linked to the final establishment of a regular network of counties in Alemannia – evident from changing charter formulas, and reflected in the regional organization of the material – and perhaps to the contestation of political power in the area.[21]

Because St Gall's campaigns of archival organization took place through the physical reordering of original documents, rather than the compilation of a 'book of traditions' of copied texts, they can be viewed in an unusual degree of detail. The St Gall experience, indeed, raises issues about the impulses underpinning the copying of collections of deeds in other major churches east of the Rhine. At Freising, where we have the original manuscript of the charter compilation made by the priest Cozroh, we can perhaps sense the practicalities of archival classification interacting with twenty-plus years spent copying deeds into the cartulary.[22] Cozroh's codex consists of three parts bound together, the first two written contemporaneously with each other by Cozroh himself, and the third compiled *c.* 848 under his supervision. The first contains the documents of the four bishops of the Agilolfing period and follows neither a chronological nor topographical order. It does conclude by emphasizing the records of judicial proceedings in the episcopate of Atto (783–811), in which the titles of gifts received prior to the Carolingian takeover were publicly affirmed in court and synod before the agents of the new regime. The second part consists of both documents of gift and sale, and records of litigation, written under Bishop Hitto

19 Notker, *Gesta Karoli* 2.10 (MGH SRG n.s. 12:66–7); for his success in so winning privileges from Charles the Fat, see S. Maclean, *Kingship and Politics in the Late Ninth Century: Charles the Fat and the End of the Carolingian Empire* (Cambridge, 2004), 201–2.

20 Marculf's formula-book is divided into two books on these lines; see Rio, *Formularies*. It is a moot point whether Marculf's distinction was based on an archival scheme.

21 Borgolte, *Grafschaften Alemanniens*, for this context.

22 *TF*. The Cozroh codex is now available in a magnificent interactive facsimile with hyperlinks to Bitterauf's edition and Adelheid Krah's notes at www.bayerische-landesbibliothek-online.de/cozroh. On its compilation, see A. Krah, 'Die Handschrift des Cozroh: Einblicke in die kopiale Überlieferung der verlorenen ältesten Archivbestände des Hochstifts Freising', *Archivalische Zeitschrift*, 89 (2007), 407–31.

(811–35), at whose behest Cozroh made the cartulary; these are organized by imperial year. The third records transactions made under the next bishop, Erchanbert (835–58), up to the year 848. While the ordering of the documents exemplifies the commemorative concerns spelled out in Cozroh's preface, the codex is also an eminently practical artefact; witness the register of property acquisitions under Hitto with which the first part ends and the systematic use of headings and reference marks through the text. This is no surprise, given Cozroh's own extensive work as a scribe and his responsibility for charter production under Hitto. His role most likely extended to include acting as what we would term the 'archivist' for the charter collection and presumably involved assembling written proofs for the recurrent litigation evident through the codex. As Adelheid Krah has shown, there is clearly a complex set of interactions at play between Cozroh's organizational scheme in the cartulary and the classification and physical archiving of the original charters in the Freising cathedral, which was perhaps inspired by Cozroh's own experience of visiting Aachen, noted in the cartulary codex.[23]

Cozroh sought to preserve the memory of benefactors and bishops and order their traditions so as to establish Freising's title to its estates, but he was also aware that the archive from which he worked was far from static. His copies, indeed, were in part motivated by a recognition that many documents had fallen into oblivion, whether wilfully destroyed through malice or lost through carelessness, and a fear that more might be removed in future by those who wished to contest their contents.[24] These fears underline that, as at St Gall so at Freising, the Carolingian takeover fundamentally altered the distribution of property. The Church was left dependent on claiming royal patronage to safeguard its interests, using written proofs to mobilize official support and popular opinion in local assemblies and setting off a cycle of land litigation that reverberated right through the first half of the ninth century.[25] The Cozroh codex, still more than the dorsal notes made by Waldo and his successors at St Gall, encourages us to see an archivist marshalling his charters and awaiting his moment to assert title to this or that property as the political configuration of both the empire and the local landowning community changed. While we cannot see quite so clearly these concerns feeding

23 Krah, 'Die Cozroh Handschrift'.

24 *TF*, pp. 1–2. Cozroh as an author: P. Geary, 'Medieval Archivists as Authors: Archival Memory and Social Memory', in F. Blouin and W. Rosenberg (eds.), *Archives, Documentation and Institutions of Social Memory: Essays from the Sawyer Seminar* (Ann Arbor, MI, 2006), 106–13.

25 Impact of Carolingian takeover: W. Brown, *Unjust Seizure: Conflict, Interest and Authority in an Early Medieval Society* (Ithaca, NY, 2001).

through into the other East Frankish cartularies, we can be clear that what united them was the tenurial and political impact of Carolingian conquest, and its interaction with the rapidly growing landholdings of the newly institutionalized Church in the region.[26]

There can be little doubt that the kind of activity we can see at St Gall or at Cozroh's Freising reflects an archival consciousness, and a concern to structure documentary holdings so as to facilitate their use. But the 'compact and efficient storage system'[27] created at St Gall was only viable in an archive of a thousand or so documents when related to known estates managed by the monks and tied to the commemoration of patrons; one had to know in advance where to look. This was not reference literacy of a modern kind, but the structuring of an archive of a particular size according to a topographical and geographical mnemonic: those concerned with a particular estate would remember the carefully cultivated traditions about its history, and look in the appropriate drawer for the appropriate region to find the documentary record. It is this style of document keeping – in the context of a living tradition of estates and their erstwhile owners – that should form the baseline against which we assess Carolingian archives. It relied on a living memory of the monastery's episodic relationships with its patrons and neighbours.

The surviving originals overwhelmingly consist of property acquisitions by St Gall. Nonetheless, even a cursory look underlines the fact that the monastery's archive was not hermetically sealed or separate from the lay society around it. A handful of documents record transactions in which the monastery was not directly implicated, detailing the prehistory of property later acquired by St Gall.[28] The run of land acquisitions immediately prior to Cannstadt in 746, for example, includes one now-mutilated charter in which Daghilinda sold property at Gebhardswil for 30 *solidi*. A gap in the parchment means that the identity of the buyer is now unknowable, but the document is preserved because the scribe Odo wrote it on the same parchment as the gift of property, also at Gerbhardswil, made by Gauzoin to Abbot Otmar; it was annotated by a ninth-century St Gall hand as 'Agilind's charter concerning Gebhardswil'.[29] Similarly, a fascinating charter from the 850s involves

[26] E.g. for Salzburg, H. Wolfram, 'Die Notitia Arnonis und ähnliche Formen der Rechtssicherung im nachagilolfischen Bayern', in *Recht und Schrift*, 115–30; for Wissembourg, see Hummer, *Politics*; for Fulda, below, Chapter 8.

[27] Erhart, '*Carta ista*'.

[28] Erhart and Kleindinst, *Urkundenlandschaft Rätien*, 21–2; they cite Wartmann I 70 (a. 772), a sale to a local church dedicated to St Gall, which the monks may have misread as a gift to the monastery.

[29] *ChLA* I 40, 44 = Wartmann I 8, 9. This was filed with gifts and purchases by St Gall by the ninth century, with the dorsal note 'car[t]a Agilind de Gaebaratuilari'; if Otmar

Balfred and his wife Evalia selling land to Wacharen and his daughter Odalswind, with the proviso that Odalswind should not sell the land to anyone, Roman or Aleman, other than to Priectus or his offspring, or if she wished to make a gift for her soul to St Gall. Although we have no further documentation concerning Odalswind, a dorsal notation in a St Gall hand from the ninth century labels this the 'charter of Priectus', perhaps indicating that this document was passed on as a title-deed with a later donation.[30] The dorsal notices provide further priceless evidence for the interaction of the monastic archive with a wider documentary culture among the landowning classes. They demonstrate, for example, the existence of pairs of charters, one within and one without the monastery, and they also record the removal of charters from the monastery to a secular household where they might be consumed by fire along with other items of an individual's possessions.[31] We know that the granting of life interests (*precaria*) to donors and their descendants was widespread at St Gall as elsewhere in this period, and that such transactions must have generated a ready flow of parchments between the monks and their patrons. It is also clear that – other than where a donor reserves a life interest in an initial donation charter – such transactions are underrepresented in the surviving charter collection, presumably as written acts recording *precaria* had little value once they had expired.[32] Further indirect evidence for lay documentary practices has been assembled in Rosamond

was the beneficiary, as has been suggested, this would make sense, but there is no real reason to suppose so other than the charter's ending up at St Gall, and it is equally likely that the charter was filed simply because it was attached to a genuine donation at the same place on the same day, and later interpreted by the St Gall archivist as a further acquisition. Note that, bizarrely, the Gauzoin document was also noted as 'carta Aegilinda'. Did the pair of acts have Dagalinda selling land to Gauzoin for him to gift immediately to Otmar? The extreme rarity of sales to St Gall may be relevant here.

30 Erhart and Kleindinst, *Urkundenlandschaft Rätien*, no. 42. The crucial clause is slightly garbled: 'ipse pretius fuit Odolsenda; in tale vero rationem, quod <si> ipsa iure vendidere voluerit, non habeant licentiam nec ad Romanos nec ad Alaemannos, set Priecto vel ad suos infantes; exceptum si pro remedium animae sue voluerint donare ad monasterium sancti Galli licentiam habeant'. I would interpret this as limiting any further transfer of this property other than to Priectus or his offspring, unless Odalswind wished to make a gift to St Gall. In the event, it looks as if the land came to Priectus, who then made a gift to St Gall, with this charter passing on as a title-deed, and doubtless would be of value if the process whereby the land came to St Gall were questioned.

31 See Erhart, '*Carta ista*', citing Clavadetscher and Stärkle (eds.), *Die Dorsualnotizen*, nos. 609, 610, 626 (alluding to paired documents in exchanges, one for the monastery, one for its lay partner), 783 ('priorem cartam illorum cum ceteris rebus suis ignis consumpsit'). Cf. below, Chapter 8, for other East Frankish examples; Brown, 'Documents', for destruction and replacement; and for the Freising and Marseille evidence, above, n. 24, and below, n. 64.

32 P. Depreux, 'L'apparition de la précaire à Saint-Gall' and L. Morelle, 'Les "actes de précaire", instruments de transferts patrimoniaux (France du nord et de l'est, VIII^e^–XI^e^ siècle), both in *Les transferts*, 649–73, 607–47; Hummer, *Politics*, esp. 76–129.

McKitterick's pathbreaking work, which demonstrated the existence of an infrastructure of local scribes, some lay and some priests, supporting a documentary culture among the regional landowning class prior to the foundation of St Gall.[33]

Given this evidence for St Gall's involvement in a wider documentary culture, it would be a mistake to see the relative paucity of surviving lay documents as indicative of original patterns of production and use, rather than the result of the complexities of transmission. Recent research on cartularies has emphasized that they were not copies of an archive's entire contents at a particular moment, so much as a carefully organized selection of documents designed to commemorate benefactors and establish title, which therefore potentially excluded significant tranches of documents.[34] While St Gall had no cartulary, the ninth-century reorganization of the charters into neatly labelled parcels each allocated to the correct *capitulum* may have left little space for documents that now had limited utility. For example, one late ninth-century charter that documents a group of over a dozen landowners giving their shares of a mountain to the church of St Saviour at *Roncalam* only survives because it was used in the thirteenth century for jottings relating to the monastery's accounts.[35] In any case, any secular documents held by the abbey through the Middle Ages are less likely to have been transmitted across the disruptions of the early modern period, not least as after 1531 the abbey had little reason to seek their restoration. Such a conclusion would be supported by the contents of several legal compilations and formula collections made at St Gall, many of which outline documents for which there are no obvious analogues in the surviving charters, and imply the existence of now lost secular documentation. One such document template, for example, records the reconciliation of Otulf and Undolf following a quarrel over a wood which broke into open conflict and was settled by a gift of property. Even if we see the case as fictitious, it still has important implications: that such events needed a documentary record, and that St Gall scribes might provide a legal template for such an eventuality, without leaving a trace in the monastery's archive.[36]

33 McKitterick, *Carolingians*, 77–134; and now K. Heidecker, 'Urkundenschreibern im alemannischen Umfeld des Klosters St. Gallen', in Erhart, Heidecker and Zeller (eds.), *Die Privaturkunden der Karolingerzeit*, 183–91.

34 See further below, Chapters 8 and 11.

35 Wartmann III A10 = Erhart and Kleindinst, *Urkundenlandschaft Rätien*, no. 54. Like the other Rhaetian material, this was excluded from the *capitulum* system – perhaps material not filed in this way was particularly vulnerable to loss or reuse.

36 The famous formula-book of Salomon (*Coll. Sang.*) needs treating carefully on account of its ideological motivation; more practical in orientation is the material edited as

### A locality, its documents and their survival: Rankweil and St Gall

For one locale, it is possible to move beyond these hints of a wider documentary culture and gain direct insight into documentary practices, thanks to a run of fifty-three surviving documents from Rhaetia, the overwhelming majority of which are concerned with Rankweil and surrounding villages high on one of the main passes over the Alps. Of these fifty-three ninth- and tenth-century Rhaetian documents transmitted via the St Gall archive, the abbey is involved in only seven.[37] This collection itself provides clear evidence for the post-Carolingian loss of documents from the St Gall archive, for several of the Rankweil documents came to light in early modern book-bindings, some at St Gall but most recently the fifty-third document at Zurich.[38] Once again, the dorsal notices supply priceless evidence as to the archival and transmission history of the Rhaetian material. In a handful of Rhaetian documents gifting land to St Gall, the dorsal notices indicate that the normal processes of entry into the monastery archive were followed, and even though Rhaetia was excluded from the *capitulum* system (the monastery's holdings there were scarce), some were entered into another 'chapter' on grounds that remain obscure.[39] The bulk of the Rankweil documents, however, came to St Gall not via this standard process of archival entry but as a group at a far later date than their redaction. The dorsal notices on the Rhaetian material from the 800s, 810s and 820s – in which St Gall was not a direct actor – were made in the first instance by the local scribes who wrote the documents. Around half of the Rhaetian material dates from the later part of the ninth century, but a significant number of documents have dorsal notation which does not conform to St Gall practice. Quite when these charters came to St Gall remains unclear: there is a rich seam of Rhaetian charters in which St Gall is not implicated through the 880s and

*Form. Sang. Misc.*, which is actually drawn from four distinct ninth- and tenth-century manuscripts. Otulf and Unolf are *Form. Sang. Misc.* 5.

[37] See now for analysis, texts and facsimiles in Erhart and Kleindinst, *Urkundenlandschaft Rätien*, with P. Erhart, 'Erratische Blöcke am Alpennordrand? Die rätischen Urkunden und ihre Überlieferung', in Erhart, Heidecker and Zeller (eds.), *Die Privaturkunden der Karolingerzeit*, 161–72, and the classic H. Fichtenau, *Das Urkundenwesen im Osterreich vom 8. bis zum frühen 13. Jahrhundert* (Vienna, 1971), 38–53.

[38] *ChLA* CI 178 = Erhart and Kleindinst, *Urkundenlandschaft Rätien*, no. 26.

[39] The following documents bear traces of normal archiving as evident in the other St Gall documents: Erhart and Kleindinst, *Urkundenlandschaft Rätien*, nos. 1 and 2 (as a pair), 40, 42. No. 39 is a donation to St Gall, made at Gams, which lacks dorsal notices or other archiving marks; similarly no. 46, made at Rankweil; no. 53, a swap; and no. 57, a gift; nos. 45 and 51 both have dorsal notices that cannot be definitively linked with St Gall. See further below, 168–71.

890s, with further surviving documents from 920, three from 933 and a final document from 975.[40] What is clear is that at some point, almost certainly in the tenth century, these charters were physically moved from Rankweil – an important judicial and legal centre – to St Gall. Here they remained through the Middle Ages, within the monastery's archive but never integrated into the *capitulum* system, an anomalous group separate from the main classification system documenting St Gall's holdings.[41]

For modern scholars, these documents are associated above all with the career of Folkwine, a minor official active *c.* 820; twenty-seven of the surviving charters document his wheeling and dealing between 817 and 825.[42] Only two documents predate Folkwine's, a pair of *placita* from the first years of the ninth century, when the hold of the prince-bishop of Chur was weakened by Charlemagne and a Frankish count dispatched to wield secular power in Rhaetia.[43] Folkwine was a follower of the new Frankish counts and in all probability an outsider, appointed to act as a local official; in his first surviving charter, he is styled *escultaizo*, a Latinization of the Germanic term *Schultheiss*, a generic vernacular label for a subcomital official, comparable to the catch-all terms *centenarius* or *vicarius* of the normative sources. He was based at Rankweil, a strategically crucial point on the Alpine pass, and one where there was an important royal *villa* that doubled as a base for the new counts.[44] References abound in his documents to his 'good offices', and to the network of favours and obligations he was able to build up in the local community as he fulfilled his fiscal and judicial roles. Folkwine's personal acquisition of a sizeable portfolio of landed property – he is the buyer or recipient of land in all twenty-seven surviving documents in which he features – thus cannot be divorced from his public role, which in any case probably supplied the wherewithal for him to make his purchases. Given the

[40] Fichtenau suggests a possible political context in the tenth century when the county of Rhaetia was combined with the duchy of Swabia; any hypothesis would need to account for the five surviving tenth-century documents from Rhaetia finding their way to St Gall. See below, 168–71.

[41] The exclusion of the Rankweil material from the *capitulum* system does raise the question of whether only documents recording monastic acquisitions were so classified, with material less directly related to the monastery's interests excluded.

[42] In addition to Erhart and Kleindinst, *Urkundenlandschaft Rätien*, esp. 83–90, and Fichtenau, *Urkundenwesen*, 38–53, see K. Bullimore, 'Folqwine of Rankweil: The Local World of a Carolingian Official', *EME*, 13 (2005), 3–17, and Innes, 'Practices of Property', 256–62.

[43] Erhart and Kleindinst, *Urkundenlandschaft Rätien*, nos. 9 and 10; for the politics, Borgolte, *Grafschaften Alemanniens*, 219–29.

[44] See the inventory of royal rights made in 842×3: *Bündner Urkundenbuch*, vol. I, ed. F. Perret and E. Meyer-Marthaler (Chur, 1955), 375–96; Lothar issued a royal charter in Count Hunfrid's villa at Rankweil (no. 44).

political context of Folkwine's activities – the evident tensions caused by the presence of his masters and his arrival in a tight-knit mountain community, and the campaign of appeal and complaint to successive Carolingians waged by the bishops of Chur against the new disposition imposed by Charlemagne – the careful preservation of these documents was a necessity. After all, there was a real possibility of the investigation and overturning of the new order, and at least some of Folkwine's transactions were potentially contestable.[45] Continued interest in the Folkwine charters is indicated by the addition of a further layer of dorsal notices to this material, most made in a single hand of the second half of the ninth century, which undertook the further classification of the *carta Folquini*. As this is not a known St Gall hand, the classification must have taken place prior to the monastery's acquisition of these documents.[46]

What was the agency for the transmission and continued scrutiny of Folkwine's dossier? The key lies in the scribes who sustained the documentary culture that produced it. The texts of Folkwine's documents show a priest, Andreas, bearing official responsibility for their drafting, while occasionally also noting that another clerical scribe – Valerius or Vigilius – actually wrote the charter. A group of four charters from Schlins are drafted under another priest, Bauco. Palaeographical analysis indicates a variety of hands even in those charters where Andreas alone is named as scribe, a phenomenon that has been paralleled in other contexts where a significant body of originals survives. Andreas' role therefore has a public element, as he was an individual bearing responsibility for the documents drafted on his authority, but with a team of other scribes working with him: an important reminder that ultimately charters needed to be publicly trusted.[47] In fact, a series of priest-scribes is responsible for more or less the totality of the Rankweil documentation. Indeed, they appear as actors, neighbours and witnesses throughout it, in some cases perpetuating priestly and scribal dynasties. Andreas and company are almost certainly to be seen as priests serving the church associated

[45] We have no record of any appeal against Folkwine, nor do we know what happened to his land; he is commemorated in the St Gall necrology, suggesting some link with the monks, but the political context, regional and regnal, was fraught, and we know that when an aristocrat fell from grace in this period his property acquisitions and those of his subordinates might well be subjected to scrutiny, as in the case of Matfrid of Orleans. Note also that in the context of the civil strife of the 830s the bishop of Chur was able to move on long-standing grievances and reclaim land seized by the counts of Rhaetia.

[46] Erhart and Kleindinst, *Urkundenlandschaft Rätien*, 26–32, drawing on Fichtenau, *Urkundenwesen*, 45.

[47] Erhart and Kleindinst, *Urkundenlandschaft Rätien*, esp. 54–70; P. Erhart, 'Der Rotulus des Valerius: Das Schreiben von Urkunden im frühmittelalterlichen Rätien', *Geschichte und Region / Storia e regione*, 15 (2006), 38–61; for the Cluny comparison, see below, Chapter 11.

with the comital residence at Rankweil, an important administrative and judicial centre.[48] Tied into the community of local landowners whom they served as priests and scribes, they were allied with and writing for the rulers of the region, not least Folkwine, the local face of a newly intrusive Frankish power. It is their activities that connect the cluster of Folkwine-related documents with the steady trickle of local documentation through the remaining decades of the ninth century and into the tenth. The Rankweil documents, therefore, are best seen as the remnants of a local set of records kept at the church in Rankweil, and connected with the work of the priests as scribes closely tied to the royal officials and the royal estate and villa. The first set of documents, from the earlier part of the ninth century, reflects a need to document contested and contestable activities of the earliest Frankish officials in a context of repeated challenges led by the bishop of Chur. Thereafter, we have priests maintaining their own documents, and holding records of some charters they produced for local landowners, and indeed for other local churches such as St Saviour *ad Roncalem*, of which the priest-scribes were important patrons.

Looking at the interests of the priest-scribes, it may indeed be possible to identify the mechanisms by which their charter collection came to St Gall. The monastery had little property in the area before the middle decades of the ninth century: just the one gift of land at Gebhardswil, from 745, survives prior to this date.[49] By the middle decades of the ninth century, however, parts of the community around Rankweil were becoming implicated in St Gall's patronage network. In 835, Berengar and his wife Imma made a sizeable gift to the monks for the health of their souls, with the right to buy back against a lump sum and annual payment.[50] In 844 or 851, Job and his wife Andustria made a gift to the monastery, where their son Drucio had evidently been oblated; if he became a monk or left the monastery of his own volition, the gift was to stand, but if the monks forced him to leave it was to fall.[51] In 851 or 858, Balfred and his wife Evalia sold land to Wacharen and his daughter Odalswind, who had permission to resell the land only to Priectus, or for the good of her soul to St Gall; a dorsal note recording the archiving of the document at St Gall indicates that the land had been passed on

[48] Erhart and Kleindinst, *Urkundenlandschaft Rätien*, 114–15; the 842×3 inventory lists three royal churches, one of them attached to the *curtis dominica*, which was the comital residence.

[49] Erhart and Kleindinst, *Urkundenlandschaft Rätien*, nos. 1–2, on which see above, 162.

[50] Erhart and Kleindinst, *Urkundenlandschaft Rätien*, no. 39.

[51] Erhart and Kleindinst, *Urkundenlandschaft Rätien*, no. 40.

to St Gall by Priectus.[52] The gift connected with Drucio's oblation was similarly entered into the St Gall archive with the normal dorsal note, and an earlier non-St Gall dorsal note was erased.[53]

The next half century saw four further acquisitions by St Gall: in 864 Valerius made a sale on behalf of Magna to the advocate Onoratus and his *maior* Abraham, both apparently acting for St Gall; in 881 Abraham gave his inherited land to the monks for the good of his and his ancestors' souls; in 884 Hisuanus and his son Isuano travelled to St Gall to make a gift for the soul of another son, Nordolo; in 893 the priest Valerius swapped land with the monks in a charter redacted at Rankweil, giving in return his church of St Victor.[54] None of these transactions bears any sign of St Gall archiving protocols: only the 864 sale and the 884 gift bear any dorsal notices and these read, respectively, 'purchase [by] St Gall from Valerius' and 'charter of Isuano to the benefit of St Gall'.[55] The explicit mention of St Gall as beneficiary in both cases is striking, because dorsal notices associated with the monastery archive rarely felt the need to specify the institution's interest; it was taken as read. While the script of both notices is ninth-century, neither has yet been identified with any known St Gall hand. It therefore appears likely that in both cases the dorsal notices were made not at St Gall, but at Rankweil: other Rankweil charters in which St Gall was not implicated have similar notices, while the charter associated with Drucio's oblation likewise had a non-St Gall dorsal notice erased when the charter was entered into the monastery archive. The explicit noting of St Gall as beneficiary would make more sense in an extra-monastic context. Valerius' gift of 893 is particularly intriguing, for Valerius was a frequent charter scribe and his family and contacts dominate the surviving charters, and in return for land he gave St Gall the proprietary church of St Victor in which he was a priest: was this where the charters were kept?

The startling conclusion, then, is that of the seven ninth-century charters from the Rankweil area in which St Gall directly or indirectly benefited, only two can be definitely shown to have been entered into the St Gall archive in the ninth century. Moreover, in both of these cases (Drucio's oblation and Priectus' passing on of Odalswind's purchase), the route was indirect, with the charter being preserved outside the

52 Erhart and Kleindinst, *Urkundenlandschaft Rätien* no. 42, and see above, n. 30.

53 Erhart and Kleindinst, *Urkundenlandschaft Rätien*, no. 40, with the erased dorsal notice 'traditio de Iobones' (perhaps a local entry prior to the gift being confirmed when Drucio became a monk), replaced with the St Gall hand noting 'traditio Iob de Vinumna' and then 'cap. XV'.

54 Erhart and Kleindinst, *Urkundenlandschaft Rätien*, nos. 45–6, 51, 53.

55 'Conparacio sancti Galli de Val[erio]'; 'Carta de Isuano ad parte sancti Galli'.

monastery for a period until the conditions attached to the prospective gift were met and the charter passed over. While three remaining documents have no dorsal notice – which would in itself be remarkable had they been placed at St Gall immediately on their redaction, so routine were the protocols of archival entry – another two, including the only one of the series actually written at St Gall, have dorsal notices that have more in common with the remainder of the run of non-St Gall Rankweil charters than with the context of the monastic archive. It must be possible, then, that they were not entered into the monastery's charter collection on redaction, but rather stored locally with the other charters of the priest-scribes, perhaps themselves functioning as something approaching local 'agents' for the monastery. Could this ongoing relationship – and the presence at Rankweil of some charters in which St Gall was the direct beneficiary – explain why, at some point in the tenth century, at least part of the Rankweil charter collection was brought to St Gall? Or was it advantageous – and indeed expected – for the monks to piggyback on local archival practices and store documents concerning Rankweil and its hinterland on site?

Whatever the date and reason for their removal from Rankweil to St Gall, there is no doubt that these charters are the relict of a once independent document collection later transferred to St Gall. This collection has a relatively long chronological horizon, reaching back over an arc of a century or more to the immediate aftermath of the imposition of direct Frankish rule in Rhaetia. Although the twenty-seven documents connected with Folkwine's activities dominate and were annotated as a coherent subset, this document collection cannot be explained in terms of the interests of any single individual, institution or family. Could we classify the Rankweil collection as a lay archive? It served a range of actors and has a chronological depth reaching back several generations, while dorsal notices and the folding of the documents attest to some level of organization. Just as at St Gall charter scribes normally indexed and archived their own documents, so at Rankweil the agency of local scribes may have been vital in the storage as well as the production of this material. The fact that these scribes were priests does not mean that they were acting solely as agents of their church, nor that they were divorced from the local community of which they were members and which they served; the fact that storage probably took place in a church does not negate the fact that it was serving as, in effect, a public store for the secular documents of the local community. Just as lay landowners who were patrons might use the monastic archive at St Gall and elsewhere, so even more at Rankweil we should not envisage the local document store as a clearly defined institution. Perhaps its functions were multiple, and its boundaries permeable and porous, with landowners able to deposit and remove their documents as they needed them – hence the *ad hoc* and piecemeal nature of much of its contents.

The contents of the Rankweil material give further precious glimpses of the ways in which landowners kept their documents. Most have short notes, of a similar type to the St Gall dorsal notices and comparable to the headings used to introduce a document in a cartulary, jotted by the original scribe on the reverse and apparently used as a reference tool. In several cases, it is also clear that a single, long piece of parchment was used for several transactions; sometimes the individual 'charters' have been subsequently cut apart, but in a number of cases groups of documents survive on a single parchment. In most identified cases, this seems to be a case of several legal acts that took place on the same day, presumably at the same public meeting. Thus, among Folkwine's records, we have a series of transactions over a six-month period in 820, now cut into several separate 'charters' but from the same parchment, and a roll of four transactions from 821 on a single parchment, used in an early modern bookbinding. From 882 we have a single parchment with two versions (one rough, one fair) of the text of the same purchase by Otulf, his wife and his son; in 883 Otulf, his wife and son similarly made two related purchases from two different vendors and had them recorded on a single parchment. A now fragmentary and undated document from the last two decades of the ninth century takes the form of a roll where at least thirteen different landowners gave their shares of mountain land to the church of St Saviour *ad Roncalem*, while in 933 Magnus and his wife Quintella made their last will and testament and recorded a land purchase on the same parchment.[56] These kinds of linked documents are only known, within the St Gall archive, in the Rankweil documents. Presumably, such practices had little use for the monks, whose archive was organized into geographical 'chapters' and who had developed defined archiving protocols. At Rankweil, however, an individual landowner might keep a series of parchments, uncut and if necessary rolled. The documentary practices of lay landowners remind us of the materiality of the written word as a crucial aspect of its practical use, an aspect all too easily ignored if we approach early medieval documents solely through the expectations of high medieval cartularists, and classical diplomatic and modern printed editions.

The Rhaetian material immediately stands out within the St Gall archive as a regional block. In part, as we saw, this is because of its

[56] Erhart and Kleindinst, *Urkundenlandschaft Rätien*, nos. 16–22, 27–30, 47–50, 54, 58–9; see also nos. 74–9.

different provenance and transmission from the mass of material in the monastery's archive. But Rhaetia itself was a distinct region in the early medieval period: nestled in the Alps, politically and socially relatively self-contained, and linguistically Romance rather than Germanic, it was the last of the great independent bishoprics to be firmly integrated into the Carolingian firmament, by Charlemagne at the beginning of the ninth century.[57] As is demonstrated by the early ninth-century local compilation entitled *Lex Romana Curiensis*, this region enjoyed a continuous legal tradition that had developed from Roman times. Both the *Lex* and the surviving documents indicate that Rhaetian legal practice differed from that of St Gall's Alemannian heartland.[58] It is therefore tempting to see this as an island of *Romanitas* whose exceptional footprint within the St Gall archive is hardly surprising. It certainly is the case that the closest comparisons for the Rankweil material come from south of the Alps, in the charter collections associated with the family of Totone of Campione d'Italia, or (still more) the documents of Peter of Niviano, who was, like Folkwine, a local official (*sculdassius*). These parallels may be no accident given the similarities in post-Roman experience and the close cultural links over the Alps in the pre-Carolingian centuries. Indeed, on a macrohistorical level, the Rankweil charters might be linked to a broader geopolitical process whereby Rhaetia's cultural and political alignment shifted from northern Italy to Alemannia.[59]

As it came into contact with an area like Rhaetia, with its rich documentary traditions, the St Gall archive could not help but suck in some of the charter collections which sustained those traditions; because they formed an exceptional block in an area where St Gall otherwise had minimal interests, it was possible for the Rankweil material thus acquired to remain physically within the St Gall archive but not fully integrated into its systems of classification or internal organization. Presumably, if St Gall had made a cartulary, or the originals had been lost, the Rankweil

57 R. Kaiser, *Churrätien im Frühmittelalter* (Basel, 1998) is the best study of the region.

58 *Lex Romana Curiensis* (ed. E. Meyer-Marthaler, *Die Rechtsquellen des Kantons Graubünden* [Aarau, 1959]) exerted influence on the formulas and legal concepts evident in the Rankweil charters, and the sole surviving manuscript (St Gall, Stiftsbibliothek, Cod. Sang. 722) is the copy of Ursicinus, one of our charter scribes: McKitterick, *Carolingians*, 110. Note that *Lex Romana Curiensis* 12.1 (ed. Meyer-Marthaler, p. 341) equated *gesta* with all charters witnessed by four *curiales*; see Erhart and Kleindinst, *Urkundenlandschaft Rätien*, 33, perhaps linking to a similar post-Roman evolution of public 'registration' as proposed above, Chapter 5.

59 S. Gasparri and C. La Rocca (eds.), *Carte di famiglia: Strategie, rappresentazione e memoria del gruppo familiare di Totone di Campione* (Rome, 2005); F. Bougard, 'Pierre di Niviano, dit le Spolétin, et le gouvernement du comté de Plaisance à l'époque carolingienne', *Journal des Savants* (1996), 291–337; see below, Chapters 9, 12 and (for the Iberian evidence) 10.

collection and with it Folkwine's career would have disappeared without trace. As it was, the Rankweil material was too peripheral to the main interests of the monks to be integrated into their archive, and so paradoxically relatively immune from the periodic pruning and reorganization that shaped it to present needs. The abbey's Alemannian hinterland may not have produced secular collections as rich as that from Rankweil, but, in any case, charters held at St Gall were strictly organized in chapters to document and support the monastery's holdings, meaning, as we have seen, that such secular documents as existed have left only the faintest of footprints. In Alemannia, St Gall clearly did not bring documentary practices into a previously oral society. In fact, the evidence of *placita* and judgements suggests that written records were particularly important precisely because confiscated or seized property might be quickly passed on by charter of sale to establish a 'clean' title and an alternative parchment trail to that held in the monastery.[60] Nonetheless, St Gall rapidly acquired a dominant position as a provider of documentary services, and as a result the traces of lay documentary culture are so much harder to find.

## An estate and its documents: Perrecy in the ninth century

The St Gall evidence may be rich, but it pertains to a very particular regional context of conquest, Christianization and confiscation in the peripheral principalities east of the Rhine in the eighth century, followed by the ninth-century institutionalization of new aristocratic and ecclesiastical hierarchies. These processes were the prime drivers of archive formation and changes in documentary culture in the eastern half of the Carolingian world. The time lag of one or two generations between the eighth-century moment of Carolingian conquest and the horizons of archival reorganization and cartulary compilation underline that the latter were not always an immediate and direct response to the former. But the conquest led to the confiscation and redistribution of the estates of erstwhile opponents of the Caroligians and a major investment in a select handful of ecclesiastical institutions that were definitively aligned

[60] MGH DD Kar. 1, nos. 166–7, discussed above, 158–9; the parallel with Folkwine's careful archiving of written proofs of the 'hot' property he acquired by hook or crook is clear. Carolingian legislation insisting on written judgements was responding exactly to these kinds of escalating and competing written claims: see, e.g., M. Innes, 'Charlemagne, Justice and Written Law', in A. Rio (ed.), *Law, Custom, and Justice in Late Antiquity and the Early Middle Ages* (London, 2011), 155–203.

(and sometimes forcibly realigned) to the Carolingian dynasty. In societies where landholding was characteristically diffuse and scattered, with even aristocrats owning dozens of tiny parcels instead of agglomerated estates, these changes created a veritable parchment trail in ecclesiastical archives as the tensions they set in motion were worked through in succeeding generations.[61]

In the old Merovingian heartlands of western Francia and southern Gaul, the Carolingian impact took a different form. The crucial phase focused on the renegotiation of tenurial arrangements around Church land, but in a context of a publicly acknowledged regalian prerogative to call on and make temporary grants of 'excess' Church land, not of 'raw' conquest and expropriation.[62] These developments took place in a region where the Church enjoyed a continuous and vital post-Roman history and thus had long-established rights and prerogatives, and where landholding at least partially consisted of larger and more compact blocks, especially where the Church and king had been able to consolidate their rights by building on public prerogatives inherited from Roman times. Ecclesiastical institutions had for centuries been interacting with documentary cultures that had evolved from those of the Roman world to safeguard its interests. In the pages of Gregory of Tours, for example, we see a range of individuals and institutions manipulating documents for good or ill, but when Gregory thinks of archives he thinks first and foremost of *gesta episcopalia* recording the prerogatives of churches and the commemorating the activities of bishops.[63] East of the Rhine, where Church property had been rapidly acquired over a few generations and where documentary traditions were thinner in the first place, new archival technologies had been necessary to allow ninth-century prelates to deal with the sharp imperative of working through the consequences of eighth-century tenurial upheaval. In western Francia and southern Gaul, on the other hand, well-established expectations about document collection and use could cope with a tenurial changes that worked to a different rhythm, just as at Rankweil existing techniques of record-keeping were adapted to cope with the dramatic imposition of Carolingian rule and the arrival

[61] For models, see, e.g., M. Innes, 'Kings, Monks and Patrons: Political Identities at the Abbey of Lorsch,' in R. Le Jan (ed.), *La Royauté et les élites dans l'Europe carolingienne* (Lille, 1998), 301–24; Innes, 'Peoples, Places and Power in Carolingian Society', in M. de Jong and F. Theuws (eds.), *Topographies of Power from Late Antiquity to the Early Middle Ages* (London, 2001), 397–437; Innes, 'Property, Politics'.

[62] E.g. G. Constable, '*Nona et decima*: An Aspect of the Carolingian Economy', *Speculum*, 35 (1960), 224–50. Discussion has focused on Charles Martel's attitudes towards Church property rather than the systematic appropriation of rights over 'excess' Church land under Pippin.

[63] I hope to return to discuss this at greater length in future.

of its agents. Thus, when two royal justices (*missi dominici*) visited Marseilles in 780, they heard an incredible story concerning the activities of a *patricius* of Provence earlier in the eighth century, who had seized the charter chest (*arca*) of a local church and burned its contents to facilitate the seizure of property and its redistribution to his followers; the deed recording the gift of the widow Adaltruda and its public validation, so they heard, had survived because a local prelate had hidden it under his robe and secreted it under an altar; witness testimony was then necessary to unravel the complex and contested transactions involving ecclesiastical claims, royal grants, and the activities, licit and illicit, of successive patricians of Provence.[64]

In western Francia and southern Gaul, cartularies were a phenomenon of the eleventh century and beyond. As a result, our access to Carolingian documentary culture is largely obscured by a later archival horizon, and we can only trace the working through of Carolingian rule on the ground indirectly.[65] If we look for documentary responses to this process, we can point to the production first, in the middle decades of the eighth century, of inventories of Church land and then, in the ninth century, of polyptychs documenting the Church's rights over its property and tenants in a wealth of practical detail.[66] Even these were not novel: judging from several of the *gesta abbatum* and *gesta episcoporum* that were such a popular new genre of the Carolingian period, ecclesiastical archives (likewise, potentially, *gesta*) had long been based around inventories of estates and their dues alongside royal privileges and the testamentary depositions recording the heroic piety of past prelates and illustrious benefactors.[67]

[64] *Cartulaire de St-Victor de Marseille*, vol. I, ed. B. Guérard (Paris, 1857), no. 31; this case is also noted by P. Geary, 'Umgang mit Urkunden in frühen Mittelalter', in P. Erhart and L. Hollenstein (eds.), *Mensch und Schrift im frühen Mittelalter* (St Gall, 2006), 11–24, and it deserves full analysis elsewhere; for political context, see Geary, 'Die Provence zur Zeit Karl Martells', in Jarnut and Nonn (eds.), *Karl Martell in seiner Zeit*, 382–92, and Geary, *Aristocracy in Provence: The Rhone Basin at the Dawn of the Carolingian Era* (Stuttgart, 1985), which gives further indications of the rich documentary culture of the region.

[65] For these vectors of transmission, see below, Chapter 11.

[66] E.g. I. Heidrich, 'Das Breve der Bischofskirche von Macon aus der Zeit König Pippins (751–768): Mit Textedition', *Francia*, 24 (1997), 17–37; I. Wood, 'Teutswind, Witlaic and the History of the Merovingian precaria', in W. Davies and P. Fouracre (eds.), *Property and Power in the Early Middle Ages* (Cambridge, 1995), 31–52; for polyptychs, see below, nn. 68–9.

[67] M. Sot, *Gesta episcoporum, gesta abbatum* (Turnhout, 1981). For a model analysis and edition of the instrumental use of Merovingian archival muniments in such material, see M. Weidemann, *Geschichte des Bistums Le Mans von der Spätantike bis zur Karolingerzeit: Actus pontificum Cenomannis in urbe degentium und Gesta Aldrici* (Mainz, 2002); the Carolingian context of controversies over Church property that shaped this material is controversially analysed by W. Goffart, *The Le Mans Forgeries: A Chapter from the History*

Indeed, the nomenclature and conception of the Carolingian polyptychs, if not their function, had its roots in these ecclesiastical collections. In the tenth century, Flodoard of Reims found a continuous tradition of such estate inventories, styled polyptychs, alongside the wills of Merovingian bishops and the voluminous correspondence of their ninth-century successors, while fragmentary survivals from Tours suggest that this was not exceptional.[68] Against such a backdrop, polyptychs could serve as proof of title and of obligation in Carolingian courtrooms.[69]

To understand how inherited documentary cultures might cope with the challenges thrown up by eighth- and ninth-century changes, let us turn to a western case study as a counterpoint to St Gall. The texts of a dozen ninth-century documents concerned with the estate (*villa*) of Perrecy in Burgundy are transmitted via the monastery of Fleury.[70] As at Rankweil, the assembly of this dossier predates the acquisition of these documents by a major church. Perrecy had been willed by Count Eccard of Mâcon to the monks of Fleury in 876, and although his kin had contested this bequest, Perrecy subsequently became an important holding of the monastery and the site of a major priory.[71] A cartulary was compiled at Perrecy *c.* 1014; the collection contained material relating to the

*of Church Property in the Ninth Century* (Cambridge, MA, 1966); see also P. Janin, 'Heiric d'Auxerre et les "Gesta pontificum Autissiodorensium"', *Francia*, 4 (1976), 89–105; I. Wood, 'St Wandrille and Its Hagiography', in G. Loud and I. Wood (eds.), *Church and Chronicle in the Middle Ages: Essays Presented to John Taylor* (London, 1991), 1–16; M. Sot, *Un historien et son église au X^e siècle: Flodoard de Reims* (Paris, 1993).

68 W. Goffart, 'Merovingian Polyptychs: Reflections on Two Recent Publications', in Goffart, *Rome's Fall and After* (London, 1989), 233–53 (orig. *Francia*, 9 [1982], 55–77); for the Tours documents (*ChLA* XVIII 659), see S. Sato, 'The Merovingian Accounting Documents from Tours: Form and Function', *EME*, 9 (2000), 1–19; for Rheims, J.-P. Devroey, 'Les premiers polyptyches rémois', in A. Verhulst (ed.), *La grande domaine aux époques mérovingienne et carolingienne* (Ghent, 1985), 78–97.

69 E.g. J. L. Nelson, 'Dispute Settlement in Carolingian West Francia', in *Settlement of Disputes*, 45–64, esp. 48–51; J.-P. Devroey, 'Libres et non-libres sur les terres de Saint-Remi de Reims: La notice judiciaire de Courtisols (13 Mai 847) et le polyptyque d'Hincmar', *Journal des Savants* (2006), 65–103; Devroey, 'Elaboration et usage des polyptyques: Quelques éléments de réflexion à partir de l'exemple des descriptions de l'église de Marseille (VIII^e–IX^e siècles), in W. Haubrichs, J. Jarnut and D. Hagermann (eds.), *Akkulturation: Probleme einer germanisch-romanischen Kultursynthese* (Berlin, 2004), 436–72. Note also the reference to a polyptych in the Marseille document, cited above n. 64, which predates the surviving *descriptio* of 814.

70 *Recueil des chartes de l'abbaye de St-Benoit-sur-Loire*, ed. M. Prou and A. Viader (Paris, 1903), esp. pp. lviii–lxvii for transmission. For analysis, see B. Kasten, 'Erbrechtliche Verfügungen des 8. und 9. Jahrhunderts: Zugleich ein Beitrag zur Organisation und zur Schriftlichkeit bei der Verwaltung adeliger Grundherrschaften am Beispiel des Grafen Heccard aus Burgund', *Zeitschrift der Savigny-Stiftung für Rechtsgeschichte*, Germanistische Abteilung, 107 (1990), 236–338; Wormald, *The Making of English Law*, 76–91; and Innes, 'Practices of Property', 249–56.

71 *Recueil... St-Benoît-sur-Loire*, no. 25 (Eccard's will), with related nos. 26–8; for his kin contesting this bequest, see no. 30.

priory's complex relationship with Fleury, alongside royal privileges and other documents concerning both Fleury and Perrecy such as Eccard's will, but it began with a run of ten documents from the years 796–876 that predated Eccard's gift of the Perrecy estate to Fleury. Although the Perrecy cartulary is now lost, it was via these copies that the texts of these documents were known at Fleury and so preserved in further cartulary copies.[72]

The documents split into two chronologically and thematically distinct sets. The first, earlier, set consists of seven documents from 796 to 821 which concern the interests of a number of powerful aristocrats holding Perrecy and other nearby parcels of royal land as benefices. The driving force behind this documentation is the activities of the local agents of these aristocratic benefice-holders as they take a succession of named individuals to court and establish their unfree status and therefore their possession as part and parcel of a particular estate. These notices give a rare insight into the use of the public courts to buttress the rights of landlords over the peasantry, especially by adjudging issues of freedom and servitude. In two of these cases, an initial hearing is deferred and a document drawn up recording that deferral, prior to the production of witnesses and the writing up of their testimony, thus creating a paired document. Not all of these cases concern Perrecy itself, although there are clear links explaining their association. For example, the earliest case, from 796, concerns the status of a peasant at Le Jeu, held as a benefice by the Count Hildebrand who appears to hold Perrecy in the remainder of the series.[73] A second case, concerning property at Baugy unjustly held by Amelius and restored to Count Nibelung, who held it as a benefice, relates to an estate that was both earlier and later associated with Perrecy; it may have been a local estate centre whose relationship to the main Perrecy holding changed.[74] Throughout the series, it is local agents rather than the aristocrats who held these benefices who are the main protagonists; often described as 'advocates' of their aristocratic

72 For the context and technique of cartulary compilation in this period, see below, Chapter 11.

73 *Recueil . . . St-Benoît-sur-Loire*, no. 9.

74 *Recueil . . . St-Benoît-sur-Loire*, no. 13. Nibelung was in any case almost certainly a kinsman of Hildebrand. Eccard's will (*Recueil . . . St-Benoît-sur-Loire*, no. 25) tells us that Hildebrand – Eccard's father who had held Perrecy as a benefice – had held Baugy as benefice, but makes Baugy – which Eccard had granted as a benefice to Leutold – an exception to his gifting of Perrecy to Fleury. That is, it acknowledges that it might be seen as an appendage of the larger estate (presumably Eccard's rights at Baugy came from the grants of 836 and 839), but one that was not integrated or integral to that estate; thus Baugy is willed differently from the wider Perrecy estate, going to the monastery of St-Antoine.

masters, these figures should be seen as something like 'estate-managers' recruited locally. Fredelus, for example, who asserts Hildebrand's rights at Perrecy in most of the series, had appeared as a witness in the first document, from 796, where Moses acted as Hildebrand's advocate. Even in the outlier, the reclamation of Baugy, it is one Fulchard who acts as advocate of the benefice-holder Count Nibelung. The parchment trails assembled by Fredelus, Moses and Fulchard as they pursued dependent peasants through the local courts vividly demonstrate the vital importance of procuring publicly affirmed and validated documents to safeguard rights. As they are transmitted via cartulary traditions, not in the original, we can only speculate as to their original appearance and preservation – perhaps in bundles of linked parchments, with contemporaneous or related cases copied beneath each other on a single sheet, as we saw at Rankweil?

The second half of the Perrecy 'dossier' concerns the contestation of control of the estate among the aristocracy in the half-century prior to Count Eccard's gifting it to Fleury. It consists of three documents concerning Count Eccard, which form an obvious prologue to the will and its associated documents in which he gave Perrecy to Fleury. But these documents also imply that from the rebellions of the 830s through the recurrent intradynastic familial conflicts that structured Carolingian politics for the next generation, Perrecy was a plum prize that aristocrats coveted from their royal masters. They comprise the outright gift, in full property, of Perrecy to Eccard by King Pippin of Aquitaine in 836; the subsequent (re)gift of Perrecy, in full property, to Eccard by the emperor Louis the Pious in 839 (after Pippin's death and so presumably reflecting a date where this erstwhile follower of a rebellious royal son had come to terms with the imperial father seeking rapprochment); and finally the incomplete record of a court hearing held between 866 and 877 before two royal justices (*missi dominici*) of King Charles the Bald at the *villa* of Mont, at which Eccard's title to Perrecy was contested by the bishop of Bourges and their cases referred to the testimony of local witnesses.[75]

The Mont notice is a complex and fascinating document, and of particular interest here because within it are references to two further tranches of documents concerning Perrecy that were produced in court but do not survive. Bishop Wulfad of Bourges brought three documents, which

[75] *Recueil. . . St-Benoît-sur-Loire*, nos. 20–1, 24. The Mont case is justly famous thanks to its discussion by Nelson, 'Dispute Settlement', at 53–5. She suggests a date of *c.* 875; the absolute limits remain the ordination of Wulfad to Bourges in 866 and Count Eccard's will in 877.

were read aloud: two Merovingian charters related to Perrecy, and a document from the time of the first Carolingian king in which a previous bishop granted a life interest (*precaria*) in the Perrecy estate to one Nibelung in return for an annual rent of three pounds on the feast of St Mary.[76] The count, Eccard, produced two more recent documents, likewise read aloud: an imperial charter issued by Louis the Pious, and the notice recording a hearing held in a general assembly of the current king, Charles the Bald, in which Eccard recovered property granted to him in the earlier document, against the claims of an otherwise unknown John. While the first of Eccard's documents (Louis the Pious' grant) survives in cartulary copy, the second (the judgement made under Charles the Bald) does not. The use of documents in court was evidently a matter of careful strategic choice: Eccard had first been granted Perrecy by Pippin of Aquitaine in 836, but he chose to base his claims on Louis the Pious' subsequent grant; evidently, a single, 'clean', grant by an emperor was preferable to one made by a rebellious son whose right to make the grant might have been seen as questionable, indeed a troubling precedent given Charles the Bald's recurrent problems with rebellious sons in Aquitaine. Conversely, the court case whereby Eccard was able to prevail before Charles the Bald and thus (re)establish his control of a part of Perrecy, probably after the civil war between Louis the Pious' sons, is omitted from the cartulary dossier, yet it was vital at Mont in showing that the imperial grant by Louis had been previously accepted in a public court and was so 'accredited'. This case shows charters being used as weapons, but they were wielded with a degree of sophistication and precision that is easily overlooked. The surviving notice of the Mont meeting is unfinished, but after relating the documents produced it recites the carefully worded sworn testimonies given by summoned witnesses. It is quite clear from this alone that the hearing was heading in the direction of Count Eccard.

Well-established interpretative traditions have informed the analysis of records of dispute settlement such as the notice of the Mont hearing.[77]

[76] The Merovingian diplomata among the Bourges documents are from the reigns of otherwise unspecified Childebrand and Chilperic; I take the 'precaria ex tempore Pippini regis' to have been issued under the first Carolingian king (751–68), rather than one of the later Pippins who acted as subkings in Aquitaine, given that we know a Nibelung was a crucial backer of the new regime in Burgundy, and that the granting of excess Church land in precaria was a feature of the reign: following Nelson, 'Dispute settlement', 54n38, citing L. Levillain, 'Les Nibelungen historiques et leurs alliances de famille', *Annales du Midi*, 49 (1937), 337–407, at 354.

[77] See W. Brown and P. Górecki, 'What Conflict Means: The Making of Medieval Conflict Studies in the United States, 1970–2000', in Brown and Górecki (eds.), *Conflict in Medieval Europe: Changing Perspectives on Culture and Society* (Aldershot, 2004), 1–36.

Through the nineteenth and much of the twentieth centuries, historians interrogated sources of this kind with a view to weighing the relative value placed on written and oral proof. In doing so, they were influenced by a legal-historical method designed to adduce hierarchies of argument and proof and measure progress towards a 'rational' legal mentality; they thus drew a strong contrast between the use of a written record and sworn testimony as proof. More recent scholarship, on the other hand, has stressed the interaction between the written and the oral in a world where documents were read aloud and their contents tested against the sworn testimony of locals.[78]

In fact, a careful reading of the surviving notice of the Mont hearing underlines the extent to which the documents produced by the two parties framed the questions put and the responses given. Perrecy, it seems clear, had been Bourges' property in the Merovingian period, by royal grant, but in the context of Carolingian takeover in Burgundy, it was deemed 'excess' to Bourges' needs and so granted out for a lifetime to a loyal follower of the Carolingians,[79] with the church retaining ultimate title. By the ninth century, however, Bourges' claims to ultimate ownership were forgotten, and in the context of the struggle between rival Carolingians in the civil strife of the 830s the young Eccard was rewarded with the gift of what was now seen as royal land 'in full property'.[80] When the various witnesses who came to Mont gave their testimony to the royal *missi* who had called the meeting, their words were carefully chosen; they swore not only as to whom they had seen 'holding' the property, but also as to what they had seen and heard said about ultimate

[78] See Nelson, 'Dispute Settlement', 54, on Perrecy: 'oral testimonial proofs . . . were the more necessary where documents conflicted'. For the chronological and geographical variations in the explicit citation of earlier documents in records of dispute settlement, see K. Heidecker, 'Communication by Written Texts in Court Cases: Some Charter Evidence (ca. 800–ca. 1100)', in M. Mostert (ed.), *New Approaches to Medieval Communication* (Turnhout, 1999), 101–26; Heidecker, 'Emploi de l'écrit dans les actes judiciaries: Trois sondages en profondeur: Bourgogne, Souabe et Franconie (VIII$^{e}$–début XII$^{e}$ siècle)', in M.-J. Gasse-Grandjean and B.-M. Tock (eds.), *Les actes comme expression du pouvoir au haut moyen âge* (Turnhout, 2003), 125–37. See also below, Chapter 11, for the ways in which documents might structure court hearings without their being explicitly noted by a *placitum* scribe – another reminder that we should avoid reading *placita* as stenographic transcripts rather than interested representations of dealings in court, as in the salutary warning of W. Brown, 'Charters as Weapons: On the Role Played by Early Medieval Dispute Records in the Disputes They Record', *Journal of Medieval History*, 28 (2002), 227–48.

[79] This Nibelung was none other than the kinsman of the Carolingians who was a key supporter in Burgundy and commissioner of the first set of continuations to the Chronicle of Fredegar, recounting Pippin's reign. On the family (with important information on Perrecy), see Levillain, 'Les Nibelungen historiques'.

[80] Kasten, 'Erbrechtliche Verfügungen', is convincing on the estate's history.

rights of ownership. As it was common ground that Eccard 'held' the estate, particular care was given to the question of his payment of any dues to another, his performance of legal rituals denoting obligations to another, or any other evidence that might constitute a 'mark of *dominium*' over Perrecy. Ultimately, even those whose claims about Bourges' rightful title had precipitated the case could summon no tangible evidence to support the bishop's charters; their claims had been intermittently repeated in the locale, but had never been publicly acknowledged by the local community.[81] The case thus did not turn on any underlying conflict between written and oral proof, or any rule as to the ultimate value of charters of different pedigrees, but rather on a pragmatic approach that tested two competing legal arguments constructed around documents against local public opinion.[82]

Reading the testimony in the context of the charter proofs produced by both sides therefore reveals a structured interrogation of a specific set of legal questions left implicit in the surviving notice. At Mont, both parties produced not only royal diplomas granting them possession of the Perrecy estate but also subsequent documents showing the public affirmation and implicit validation of the claims in those documents. The surviving notice stresses that Bourges' life-grant to Nibelung with its explicit acknowledgement of the bishopric's ultimate ownership was witnessed by many *boni homines*, while Eccard felt the need to supplement his imperial diploma, for all its undeniable charisma, with a notice recording his successful defence of this grant in court.[83] In short, documents needed affirmation, and a demonstration that a document – however ancient or charismatic – had been tested in the public courts and not found wanting added to its value. The Mont notice thus gives us priceless insight into how documents – all bar one now lost – were received, used and understood. Although *deperdita* such as those mentioned in the Mont document are characteristically treated as phantoms and excluded from editorial and historiographical canons, it might be argued that footprints such as these – even where we have no surviving text – have a particular value for some forms of historical analysis, precisely because they reveal use and reception.

81 Following Innes, 'Practices of Property', arguing that the words chosen to record the testimony were carefully selected to distinguish claims of 'holding' from 'ownership'; Nelson's translation tends to see the Latin as less precise in its meaning.

82 This model of 'substantive legalism' ultimately draws on the work of Stephen D. White; e.g. 'Inheritances and Legal Arguments in Western France, 1050–1150', *Traditio*, 43 (1987), 55–103.

83 See below, 249–50, for *ostensio cartae* procedures in Italy, and above, Chapter 5, for the move from formal validation to public recognition in earlier Frankish validation procedures.

It has been suggested that the survival of the Perrecy documents 'implies the existence of a family archive transferred to Fleury on Eccard's death'.[84] In fact, the pattern of surviving documentation cannot easily be reduced to such an institution, and the transmission suggests that it was stored at Perrecy, where it remained. True, the documents establishing Eccard's title to Perrecy might be seen as part of Eccard's personal archive, handed over with his will and associated material to the monks of Fleury. But it is not at all clear that Eccard's documents should be seen as a part of a coherent whole with the documents that preceded Eccard's acquisition of the estate. Although Count Hildebrand, who had held Perrecy to the 820s, was Eccard's father, we do not know that the estate was passed on in direct or seamless succession from them, for Hildebrand had died in 827 and Eccard received his father's former benefice as full property in the scramble for *honores* in the 830s, and in rivalry with other aristocrats. The earlier documents might be seen as a useful set of test cases for the unfree status of certain sections of the local peasantry tied to the Perrecy estates, and thus understood as part of the apparatus of estate management held on site by those locals entrusted with running Perrecy and defending the rights of its owners: hence their preservation at Perrecy right through to 1014 and the compilation of the priory's cartulary.[85] At Perrecy, then, our window on the ninth century is only possible because the Carolingian estate records could be used to underpin the claims of the eleventh-century *seigneurie*, and because they gave Perrecy a history independent of Fleury, and so aided the cartulary compiler in his aims of providing a documentary template for the complex relationship between priory and mother house.[86]

## From Roman public records to Frankish charter collections

How does the documentary culture revealed at Rankweil and Perrecy relate to our inherited models of long-term change? In view of the

[84] Nelson, 'Dispute Settlement', 54, and later Nelson, 'Literacy in Carolingian Government', in *Uses of Literacy*, 258–96, at 276.

[85] Landownership and estate structures at Perrecy: O. Bruand, 'La Villa carolingienne, une seigneurie? Réflexions sur les cas des villas d'Hammelburg, Perrecy-les-Forges et Courçay', in D. Barthélemy and J.-M. Martin (eds.), *Liber largitorius: Études d'histoire médiévale offertes à Pierre Toubert par ses élèves* (Geneva, 2003), 349–73, although there is a teleology implicit in the argument that Perrecy was therefore 'already' a *seigneurie*. I owe this reference to Charles West. Bruand's discussion does provide a clear context for the collection and preservation of documents classifying and controlling unfree dependants. It also makes sense of the Baugy reclamation and the lost case in which Eccard defeated the claims of John, cited at Mont; some of the testimony at Mont also seems to imply the possibility of levels of agency and subjection within the villa.

[86] See above, at n. 70.

problems of organizing complex and changing bodies of source material into a compelling account of change, it is no surprise that historians of documentary practice have developed grand narratives that are fundamentally influenced by and intertwined with familiar historiographical meta-narratives of post-Roman transformation. True, those favoured meta-narratives have freed themselves from notions of cataclysm and decline, in large part because the distant Roman roots of early medieval documentation as it emerges from the end of the seventh century are incontrovertible. But meta-narratives about the shift from public to private power, and from the institutions of the late Roman state to the early medieval Christian Church, have been powerful but often hidden organizing principles in much scholarship. They have allowed historians to pit the inevitable messiness that emerges when we can glean detailed insights into the practical workings of legal documentation after *c.* 700 against the norms that are all that remain from the fifth, sixth and early seventh centuries. The result, unsurprisingly, has been a contrast between the public institutions of Late Antiquity and the variety of interests and institutions involved with written documentation in the Carolingian period. Late antique regulations on the drafting and registration of documents are read as indicating a clearly defined and strictly demarcated set of institutions – public notaries and public archives – whereas surviving charters from *c.* 700 onwards seem to show a variety of scribes and mechanisms for the validation and publication of documents. Similarly, whereas our normative sources from the immediately post-Roman period envisage a wide range of contexts in which documents might be used by private individuals, the actual documentation from later centuries has a narrower range, and is dominated by property transfers to the Church. One important strand of scholarship has seen these shifts as ultimately indicative of a series of wider changes in documentary culture: late antique systems of public notarization and registration gave way to the private production and preservation of documents, with the Church becoming the dominant institution of written record; ecclesiastical scribes and ecclesiastical archives, therefore, both aligned to the particular interests of the Church, marginalized the landowning classes from documentary practice.[87]

Care needs to be taken in moving from the changing profile of our sources to institutional and social practice. After all, where we do have a meaningful volume of documents to elucidate late antique archival and scribal practice, the clearly defined and strictly demarcated public institutions of the normative sources are immediately shot through with the interests of powerful individuals and specific interests, as the Egyptian

[87] Classen, 'Fortleben and Wandel'; Ganz and Goffart, 'Charters Prior to 800'.

and Ravennate evidence demonstrates.[88] The run of over fifty original papyrus and parchment documents from the late Merovingian St-Denis archive – without which we would be clutching at fragments in evaluating seventh-century Frankish documentation – fits only with difficulty into inherited grand narratives, and raises issues paralleled in the run of sixth- and seventh-century papyrus documents of diverse provenance preserved in the archives of the church of Ravenna.[89] It is not a narrowly ecclesiastical *chartrier* as the historiography would have us expect, and it includes a priceless run of royal documents and of private wills of which St-Denis was not a beneficiary. While St-Denis' close links with the late Merovingian court might go some way towards explaining the royal documentation, the range of material makes it difficult not to imagine some wider social function; unlike the Ravenna material, however, none of that from St-Denis uses the template of Roman public registration in the *gesta municipalia*.

In any case, a careful look at Carolingian scribal practices shows some continuing framework of public authority within which a variety of individuals operated, some churchmen who might work for private individuals as well as their own institutions, and some local landowners who might serve patrons, clients and neighbours.[90] The evidence discussed above for practical charter use likewise underlines the importance of formal records of public recognition and validation in 'accrediting' a document; claims, even when recorded in documents, were stronger when they had been affirmed in court and subjected to public scrutiny. In other words, the horizons of our evidence may suggest a clean cut and complete transformation from state registration and regulation to ecclesiastical monopoly, but if we take the care to deal with the surviving documents on their own terms it becomes clear that in fact we are dealing with a shift in understandings of 'the public', no longer so closely tied to the constraints of formal law and regulated state institutions.[91]

In reconstructing these vectors of change, we need to take full account of regional difference within the Frankish world, lest we end up comparing the last gasp of Roman urban civilization south of the Loire in the fifth and sixth centuries with the new ecclesiastical frontier of the provinces east of the Rhine in the eighth and ninth, and ripping our

88 See above, Chapters 2 and 4.

89 I differ here from Ganz and Goffart, 'Charters Earlier Than 800'. On Ravenna, see above, Chapter 4.

90 For the situation as revealed by the Cluny and St Gall originals, see above, 298, 156–7, 167; see also McKitterick, *Carolingians*, 77–134; Innes, *State and Society*, 111–18; and below, Chapter 8.

91 Cf. above, Chapter 5.

evidence from context. When it comes to the history of written law and legal documentation, regional comparisons are normally couched in terms of the differential shading of the Roman inheritance. The pioneer of the study of Roman institutional legacies in Frankish Gaul, Eugen Ewig, even imagined an internal division stretching diagonally, north-west to south-east, across the Merovingian world, starting on the Channel coast, skirting the Loire valley and Burgundy, and reaching the Alps. South of this line, the civic and episcopal institutions preserved Roman practices on a local level into the seventh century and beyond. To the north of this line, Roman institutional survival was at best fragmentary and haphazard; internal acculturation between north and south was vital in the effective revival of the Church in the sixth and seventh centuries and with it a whole spectrum of practices, written documentation not least among them.[92] Inevitably, the details of Ewig's picture need careful nuancing, with a range of other comparisons and variables adding colour to the black-and-white of the original picture. Nonetheless, it is striking that the regional comparison sketched by Ewig seems to map onto the differences in documentary profile evident once we begin to get a meaningful transmission of charters, in the eighth to tenth centuries. Direct continuity of documentary practices through the Merovingian centuries is most marked in those regions south and west of Ewig's line. Rhaetia's history is almost emblematic of the continued evolution of Roman forms on a local level, while the rich documentary traditions evident in Burgundy likewise belong to a region where the documentary habit clearly enjoyed a continuous post-Roman history. Paradoxically, though, in these regions where legal writing enjoyed a continuous post-Roman evolution, the archival horizons are late, with documentary traditions surviving overwhelmingly in post-Carolingian compilations, above all cartularies of the eleventh and twelfth centuries, which cannot be read as providing full or unmediated access into Carolingian documentary culture. One result is a certain tentativeness in scholarly discussion of the extent to which document use extended beyond court and cloister in precisely those regions where documentary traditions enjoyed most continuity through the early medieval centuries.

In Francia north of the Paris basin, and in the East Frankish world beyond the Meuse and Moselle, our archival horizon differs. It is determined by a succession of Carolingian compilations of copied documents

[92] E. Ewig, *Spätantikes und fränkisches Gallien: Gesammelte Schriften*, 3 vols. (Munich, 1976–2009), esp. I, 409–34 ('Das Fortleben römischer Institutionen in Gallien und Germanien', orig. *Relazioni del X Congresso internazionale di scienze storiche*, 6 vols. [Florence, 1955], VI, 561–98).

made by major ecclesiastical institutions. As we have seen, these compilations related to the specific situation of newly conquered and Christianized regions; even at St Gall where – exceptionally – no cartulary was compiled either in the Carolingian period or later, the complexities of the abbey's relationship with central authority led to a coherent system of archival organization being developed very early in the institution's history, a system reminiscent in its underlying principles of contemporary cartularies and one that effectively determined the contours of institutional memory. As a result, for eastern Francia we have far thicker documentary traditions, with a succession of major institutional compilations of hundreds – and sometimes thousands – of documents, and a sense of a far fuller social picture than is possible for much of western Francia.[93] But the sheer weight of this material produces a sense of ecclesiastical dominance – even in regions like the Moselle, the middle Rhineland or the area around Lake Constance, where odd lay documents transmitted within ecclesiastical traditions hint at local documentary traditions prior to the foundation of the great churches of the Carolingian period. Moreover, because our Carolingian cartularies do not appear to have produced a continuous tradition of updating and recopying, in most cases the surviving profile of document transmission tails off dramatically, with the early 'peak' captured in our ninth-century cartularies followed by a thinner tradition dependent on high medieval cartularists. The resulting impression has further encouraged some historians to think in terms of a 'crisis' in the practical use of writing, which gells with received narratives of Carolingian 'failure' and a tenth-century society organized on 'archaic' and 'oral' lines around political ritual.[94]

Ultimately, it is the East Frankish cartularies that dominate our image of Carolingian documentary practice, because of the sheer wealth of evidence; the close association of their producers with the patronage of Carolingian kings; and the degree of economic, social and political detail they offer. Moreover, although our West Frankish cartulary traditions are later and thinner, they develop the basic forms set down by their ninth-century predecessors, thus supporting our tendency to see the cartulary as a default image of the ecclesiastical archive of the Carolingian period. Yet, as we saw in our case studies, cartulary compilation was a product of tenurial and political upheaval as new forms of institutional landholding familiar from the Frankish heartlands spread to the peripheries of

[93] With obvious exceptions such as eastern Brittany, on which see below, 187 at n.95, 320.
[94] For further historiographical discussion, see below, Chapter 11.

the Frankish world.[95] In organizing their records, churches reacted to the patterns of extra-ecclesiastical document use in their hinterlands and to immediate institutional imperatives, and so there were marked differences between regions and between institutions. Crucial factors here were the differing impacts of the Carolingian state, and the degree to which viable archival practices that allowed institutions to cope with the tensions implicit in Carolingian state-formation were already present.

How, then, should we think of the charter collections of eighth-, ninth- and tenth-century landowners in terms of the questions that frame this book: post-Roman continuity and change, the role of ecclesiastical institutions in archival and documentary culture, and the relationship between record-keeping and power? We should, unsurprisingly, allow for regional difference, not only in our period but also within the Roman inheritance. The documentary cultures behind and before the East Frankish cartularies may have developed through internal acculturation, and may increasingly have been sustained through the interplay between aristocratic landowners and the churches they patronized, but they were not wholly confined to the Church, and they need judging against the frontier literacy of the Roman army and its subsequent legacy. The earliest document from early medieval Bavaria, the 'Rottachgau fragment' (written some time between the end of the sixth and the early eighth century), suggests that such practices were remembered even on the peripheries of the Frankish world, while the rich traditions of title-deeds and judgement notices passed on to the Breton abbey of Redon as it acquired property in the ninth century likewise show the adaption of documentary practices by landowning communities on the fringes of the late Roman world in the centuries that followed.[96] We should also acknowledge that, where it is possible to assess the archival and documentary practices that preceded the formation of ecclesiastical archives and the compilation of cartularies, those practices witness a complex post-Roman evolution that cannot be easily contained within the grand narrative of a shift from public to ecclesiastical production or preservation. It is true that at Rankweil, in a context where the sixth to eighth centuries had seen the establishment of an episcopal principality, local

[95] Hence the anomaly of the Redon charters within the West Frankish tradition. See further below, 320.

[96] The 'Rottachgau fragment', transmitted as the first document in the ninth-century Traditionsbuch of Passau: *TP* 1, and see now F.-R. Erkens, '"Actum in vico fonaluae die consule": Das Rottachgau-Fragment und die romanische Kontinuität am Unterlauf des Inns', in U. Ludwig and T. Schilp (eds.), *Nomen et Fraternitas: Festschrift für Dieter Geuenich zum 65. Geburtstag* (New York, 2008), 491–510. For Redon, see above all W. Davies, *Small Worlds: The Village Community in Early Medieval Brittany* (London, 1988).

priests in the service of royal officials played a crucial role in documentary culture, and a royal church is perhaps the most likely physical location for document storage. But, conceptually, these activities seem to have been understood as part of a wider public culture of document use that transcended particular institutional interests, to the extent that even St Gall seems to have operated through these documentary mechanisms in this locale. Meanwhile, in Burgundy, the Perrecy evidence shows a rich documentary culture in which priests and churches doubtless participated, but in which the Church as an institution had no special role in the production or preservation of documents. Had we the space to expand our range of examples, the range of possibilities would be expanded. But in all of these cases, we see a society in which documents were used and stored by landowners without defined public institutions of record, and without the Church enjoying the kind of hegemony as a provider of documentary services that it may have been establishing east of the Rhine in the eighth and ninth centuries. In other words, we need to acknowledge the existence of a complex set of practices that cannot be understood as a mere staging post between the lost late antique world of public archives and the great ecclesiastical charter compilations of the eleventh and twelfth centuries, but needs evoking in its own terms. The notion of 'Roman survival' hardly does justice to the richness of the practices like those we have glimpsed at Rankweil or at Perrecy, which, after all, were managed not by first-order aristocrats but by their local agents. After all, while a military officer or major landowner in late antique Egypt might have left a comparable documentary footprint to Fredelus or Folkwine, we have no evidence that the same is true of their predecessors in the Empire's western provinces. If we are to understand the documentary transformations of the post-Roman world, we must put the endeavours of estate-managers, local officials and small-time landowners to secure their interests centre stage.

# 8 The production and preservation of documents in Francia: the evidence of cartularies

*Hans Hummer*

*Other cartularies from the East Frankish regions show processes of archival reorganization in response to Carolingian expansion similar to those visible at St Gall, but with very different material outcomes. Carolingian expansion also led to the centralization of scribal practice in churches and monasteries; though the Carolingian state was a very different kind of polity from that of Roman Late Antiquity, here, too, the state and its imperatives shaped documentary culture. Most importantly, however, monastic archives in this region appear once again not as timeless givens, but rather institutional creations that emerged in particular contexts for particular reasons – reasons tied to the ways that the Carolingians changed the relationships between ecclesiastical institutions and the people around them.*

In the Frankish realms of the early Middle Ages there existed no lay method or system of archival management to rival that of monasteries and churches. At least, we have no firm evidence of one. Nonetheless, strong circumstantial and vestigial evidence testifies that many individuals routinely kept documentation. Narrative accounts of disputes sometimes refer to the destruction of documents held by laypersons; charter collections compiled by monks include within them on occasion transactions among the laity; donations to a monastery or church might refer to lay records that once lay behind the transaction; and there are several stunning examples of dossiers of records held by lay individuals and taken up into ecclesiastical archives when they had donated their properties.[1] Some of these are quite large, such as the Folkwine dossier, but without exception they cover a few generations at most. They lack the chronological depth that one generally associates with ecclesiastical and monastic archives, whose holdings span centuries. How widespread these dossiers

[1] Brown, 'Documents'; Kosto, 'Laymen', esp. 60–2; H. Fichtenau, *Das Urkundenwesen in Österreich vom 8. bis zum frühen 13. Jahrhundert* (Vienna, 1971), 38–45.

might have been is impossible to say. The surviving examples are limited mostly to deeply Romanized areas, such as Rhaetia and Catalonia, and perhaps speak to the greater importance attached to documentation in particular regions.[2]

Or maybe not. The unusual survival of originals from St Gall and Catalonia might have seen to the preservation of dossiers that otherwise were present, but not included, in cartularies, the codices of property transactions assembled by monks who were preoccupied mostly with donations. We need not jump to the conclusion from this that cartularies were mere reflections of ecclesiastical interests and therefore preclude any insights into the participation of the laity in written culture. For one, the abbots and monks came from many of the same kindreds who patronized the monasteries, so that the ecclesiastical records encompass within them the interests of their patrons. Indeed, donation charters were overwhelmingly represented, not for material reasons *per se*, but because they bore material witness to an individual's or a family's spiritual relationship to the monastic institution. Consequently, the second most common records in cartularies after donations are precarial documents, which document the patrons' requests for the continued use of donated property. In some cases, the donation charter was not included at all, the precarial record sufficing to bear witness to the gift.

Although the monastery was responsible for assembling cartularies, many of the charters therein – even donation charters – were not authored by monks. These documents often originated from beyond the cloister, only later to be gathered up and organized by monastic copyists. Moreover, the notaries responsible for drawing up many of the transactions between patrons and a monastery might have had no formal connection to the monastery at all, an indication of a more dynamic, complex world of document production than one might casually assume. Cartularies, rather, should be thought of as something like a fossil, a static assemblage of bones which, upon forensic examination, reveals clues that allow us to flesh out the processes responsible for the patterns before us. When examined in this light, monastic charters provide tantalizing evidence for the regular participation of the laity in the use, production and preservation of documents.

Crucial to recognize for the present analysis is the distinction between the original production of a document and its subsequent preservation. Cartularies represent acts of preservation. They are made up of copies of charters: a team of monastic scribes made copies of loosely kept charters, either original drafts of transactions, or copies of originals, at a

[2] See above, Chapter 7, and below, Chapter 10.

particular moment in time. This was in some cases only the beginning of a process, the cartulary having been supplemented thereafter for several decades. Cartularies must be distinguished from the records produced at the moment of a transaction. While a cartulary might preserve only one record of a transaction, sometimes the charters reveal that copies were produced for the donor(s) too. As we shall soon see, cartularies in fact do include multiple drafts of the same transaction, including copies which by all accounts had once belonged to the lay patrons. These personal records produced for the donors also represent acts of preservation in that the patrons presumably took these copies away with them from the transaction and kept them. This mode of preservation, however, was mostly ephemeral. Deprived of the institutional structures which might see to their preservation in a coherent way over time, these documents vanished, unlike those kept by the more stable, ecclesiastical foundations.

This chapter will examine the intersections between lay and ecclesiastical record-keeping. It first will attempt to deduce from the evidence the documents that laypersons might have possessed during the early Middle Ages in Francia, and how their records might have come into the possession of a monastery. It then will offer a chronological analysis that will illuminate the formation of enduring ecclesiastical archives out of the multipolar world of late Merovingian documentary culture. The profound and sweeping transformation of monastic archival consciousness in the late eighth century was responsible for the preservation and the shape of much of the evidence that we have before us. Before we launch this investigation, however, it will be helpful to say a few words about the shape and scope of the evidence.

All of the extant early medieval cartularies stem from the eastern regions of Carolingian Francia, having been compiled at the Rhineland monasteries of Wissembourg in Alsace and Fulda in the Rhine–Main region, and at the Bavarian church of Freising.[3] In addition, vestigial collections remain from the Danube-valley bishoprics of Passau, Regensburg and Salzburg, and the monastery of Mondsee.[4] Why these collections should have arisen, by all appearances, exclusively in the east, has

[3] *TF*; *TW*; *Codex diplomaticus Fuldensis*, ed. E. J. F. Dronke (1850; repr. Aalen, 1962) (hereafter *CDF*, with document number); *Urkundenbuch des Klosters Fulda*, ed. E. E. Stengel (Marburg, 1958) (hereafter *UF*, with document number).

[4] *TP*; *Die Traditionen des Hochstifts Regensburg und des Klosters S. Emmeram*, ed. Josef Widemann (Munich, 1943; repr. Aalen, 1988); F. Lošek, '*Notitia Arnonis* und *Breves notitiae*: Die Salzburger Güterverzeichnisse aus der Zeit um 800: Sprachlich-historische Einleitung, Text und Übersetzung', *Mitteilungen der Gesellschaft für Salzburger Landeskunde*, 130 (1990), 5–193; *Das älteste Traditionsbuch des Klosters Mondsee*, ed. G. Rath and E. Reiter (Linz, 1989).

remained a vexed issue. Briefly, they might represent efforts to consolidate proprietary interests in the wake of Carolingian conquest,[5] but, if so, the chronology does not always align well with the surviving patterns. Bavaria, the argument's favourite example, was conquered by Charlemagne in 788, yet the cartulary of Freising, our most complete collection, was assembled in the 820s, over three decades later, and those of Mondsee, Passau and Regensburg even later in the ninth century.[6] Alsace never was 'conquered', and even if one allows that the area was 'taken over' by Carolingian kings, its incorporation took place a good century before the compilation of the cartulary at Wissembourg around 860.[7] While the areas east of the Rhine were conquered in the late eighth century, the cartulary of Fulda again was compiled well afterwards in the 820s.[8] Moreover, we have areas in West Francia subjected to grinding conquest, notably Aquitaine, none of whose monasteries produced a cartulary, so far as is known. On the other hand, we can at least admit a connection to Carolingian reform, itself an expression of Frankish consolidation, which does provide a broader – if more diffuse – explanatory framework for the appearance of cartularies.[9] Indeed, the monasteries that produced cartularies were bound up within the memorial network of monasteries beginning in the latter eighth century and elaborated in the ninth,[10] a manifestation of the Carolingian ideals of Augustinian order, permanence and social stability. This network also included western establishments, none of which, however, bequeathed to posterity a cartulary before the tenth century, although they did produce abbatial or episcopal chronicles which memorialized proprietary holdings within a wider institutional history.[11] Thus, if, early on, cartularies were unknown in West Francia, property records did exist there, suggesting that if the assembling of cartularies was a regional phenomenon, the patterns of lay participation in documentary culture that can be excavated from their contents nonetheless illuminate practices and developments beyond eastern Francia.

If we consider the greater cartularies from Fulda, Freising and Wissembourg, we have about 1,450 extant charters from the period before 900. Six hundred of these hail from Fulda, but represent just two of

5 Geary, *Phantoms*, 88–92.

6 *TF*, pp. xx–xxi; *Traditionsbuch . . . Mondsee*, 36–8; *TP*, pp. xix–xx; *Traditionen . . . Regensburg*.

7 Hummer, *Politics*, 56–75. 8 *UF*, pp. xviii–xxi. 9 Geary, *Phantoms*, 92–3.

10 Karl Schmid, 'Wege zur Erschließung des Verbrüderungsbuches', in *Das Verbrüderungsbuches der Abtei Reichenau* (MGH Libri mem. n.s. 1:lx–ci, at lx–lxv).

11 Michel Parisse, 'Les cartulaires: Copies ou sources originales', in *Les cartulaires*, 503–11, at 506.

the ten books of charters that made up Fulda's original cartulary.[12] A digest of the Fulda cartulary produced in the high Middle Ages reveals that these other eight books contained about 1,200 charters, bringing the original total at Fulda to nearly 1,800.[13] Similarly, the cartulary of Wissembourg possesses 273 charters dedicated to property in the districts to the south and west of the monastery in Alsace, the Saargau and the Saulnois.[14] There are good reasons to believe that Wissembourg produced a cartulary covering only these districts; nonetheless, other records and surveys from the tenth and the thirteenth centuries reveal that during the early Middle Ages Wissembourg lorded over a concentration of mid-Rhine properties to the north and east which probably exceeded those recounted in the extant cartulary.[15] How numerous these might have been is impossible to say, but we know from the testimony of a seventeenth-century Jesuit who examined its now-lost contents that the cartulary of the nearby monastery at Honau contained over a thousand Carolingian-era charters.[16] Thus, the charters in the cartularies of Fulda, Wissembourg and Honau probably numbered at least around 4,000. The cartulary of Freising contributes another 577 charters, but this figure represents only the records in the cartulary compiled by the priest Cozroh between 824 and 848.[17] The scribes of Freising were remarkably industrious, compiling yet other collections of transactions down to 900; these include about another 500 charters, many of them property exchanges, bringing the total at Freising to over 1,000, and our grand total so far to roughly 5,000.

This number can be augmented with the fragmentary or partial collections from Murbach in Alsace, Mondsee, Passau, Regensburg and Salzburg, which run to almost 470 extant charters and whose original scale presumably matched those of the surviving greater collections.[18] And we have not even considered the vestigial records of numerous

[12] *UF*, p. xix, and E. Stengel, *Abhandlungen und Untersuchungen zur hessischen Geschichte* (Marburg, 1960), in particular the articles, 'Über die karlingischen Cartulare des Klosters Fulda (Fuldensia II)' and 'Untersuchungen zur Frühgeschichte des Fuldaer Klosterarchivs (Fuldensia IV)' (147–93, 203–65).

[13] *Der Codex Eberhardi des Klosters Fulda*, ed. H. Mayer zu Ermgassen, 2 vols. (Marburg, 1995–6).

[14] *TW*, pp. 40–4.

[15] Hummer, *Politics*, 181–90; W. Metz, 'Das Kloster Wissembourg und der Vertrag von Verdun', in C. Bauer, L. Boehm and M. Müller (eds.), *Speculum Historiale: Geschichte im Spiegel von Geschichtsschreibung und Geschichtsdeutung* (Freiburg, 1965), 458–68.

[16] C. Wilsdorf, 'Le monasterium scottorum de Honau et la famille des ducs d'Alsace au VIIIe siècle: Vestiges d'un cartulaire perdu', *Francia*, 3 (1975), 1–87, at 11.

[17] *TF*, pp. xx–xxi.

[18] See above, n. 4, and for Murbach, A. Bruckner, *Regesta Alsatiae aevi Merovingici et Karolini (496–918)*, vol. I (Zurich, 1949).

monasteries, which surely amounted to more than now exist; or the roughly 3,000 abbreviated charters from Lorsch, which, unfortunately, because the copyists of the high Middle Ages left out the wider social circle of witnesses and notaries as they abridged the documents, are less useful for the current purposes.[19] Nor have we considered the western establishments, whose records in that more document-rich area probably were more voluminous than now exist, but whose holdings we know of from a smattering of charters included in later medieval collections and from aggregate summaries of property in *res gesta*, rather than cartularies.[20] Let it not be said that early medieval Europe had ever suffered a poverty of records.

These figures, naturally, reflect what monasteries held, and they also reflect particular institutional imperatives; that is to say that collections of charters were not intended to keep track of just any old record having to do with the cloister. Cartularies were devised to memorialize the gifts made to monastic foundations for salvific purposes, and therefore they necessarily bear witness to the network of patrons bound to the eternal 'family of God'.[21] In addition to their deliberate obliviousness to records unrelated to the cloister, cartularies seldom even bother with property records that the monastery surely possessed in some abundance, but which have to be guessed at from notarial formulas or glimpsed in stray entries in cartularies: the monastery's own more purely economic wheeling and dealing for property, the prestarial grants of property in response to patrons' precarial requests (which are more likely to be preserved, but still in numbers much reduced by comparison with donations), the drafts of donation and precarial charters drawn up for patrons, and the sales of property between laypersons. These records of sales between laypersons probably were transferred to the monastery upon the donation of property previously purchased by the donor. Indeed, the donation of property is usually called a 'handing over' (*traditio*) of property, a process which might include ritual actions or the transfer of objects (though these are only intermittently attested in formulas and even less frequently in ordinary charters),[22] and perhaps the simultaneous conveyance of any

[19] *Codex Laureshamensis*, ed. K. Glöckner, 3 vols. (Darmstadt, 1929–36).

[20] Cf. M. Sot, *Gesta episcoporum, gesta abbatum* (Turnhout, 1981).

[21] Cf. Geary, *Phantoms*, 81–114.

[22] These would be the *festuca* (rod), *wadium* (gage) or *andelangus* (handshake?, see F. Staab, *Untersuchungen zur Gesellschaft am Mittelrhein in der Karolingerzeit* (Wiesbaden, 1975), 259n494). They are attested to in Merovingian and Carolingian-era formularies. *Festuca*: Marculf 1.13, 21; 2.14; *Form. Sen.* 7, 29, 34; *Form. Sen. Rec.* 2; *Form. Sal. Merk.* 21, 27–8; *Form. Sal. Lind.* 1. *Festuca* and *wadium*: Marculf 2.18. *Wadium*: *Form. Tur.* 6, 32; *Form. Sal. Merk.* 29; *Form. Sal. Lind.* 19. *Andelagnus* and *wadium*: *Form. Sen.* 50. *Festuca, wadium* and *andelangus*: *Form. Sal. Lind.* 2, 6–8, 12, 14, 16, 18. However,

prior records. For example, in 754 at Thulbach in Bavaria, a certain Timo received the *epistula* of his donation and at the altar handed it over into the hands of Bishop Joseph of Freising.[23] Glimpses like this might explain why the documentary form itself, the *carta donationis*, could also be called a *traditio*.[24] A transfer of documents would, at any rate, explain the otherwise odd appearance of records between laypersons in cartularies.

Let us now turn to particular examples to get a better grasp of the circulation of documentation among laypeople, as we can perceive it through ecclesiastical collections. The few purely lay transactions included in cartularies involve mostly sales. A remarkable example in the Wissembourg corpus involves two drafts of a sale in 736×7 between two laymen, the purchase of property by a certain Rantwig, son of Chrodwig, from the Etichonid duke Liutfrid.[25] These properties, which had been acquired by Liutfrid from several sources – from his father, from a certain Liudulf and by *uendicionis titulum* ('title of sale') from a woman named Ingina – had been granted in benefice by Liutfrid to Rantwig's father. Both copies were made from two different drafts of the sale, which presumably found their way into Wissembourg's monastic archives with Rantwig's impressive donation of property in twenty-nine locations in 742,[26] a gift which included the previously purchased properties. The two drafts of his earlier purchase were then copied into the cartulary when it was compiled around 860.

We might assume that the two drafts of this sale came to Wissembourg within the context of Rantwig's donation in 742, and presumably were copied into the cartulary because of the wealth of the donation, the prominence of its actors, and the knot of feudal, familial and personal claims previously bound to the property. But to whom had these drafts

the *andelangus* appears just twice in the Wissembourg charters: *TW* 233, 237; a *wadium* once in the charters of Passau, *TP* 78, and twenty-nine times out of about 700 charters of Freising, *TF* 91, 185, 195, 197, 227, 235, 251, 258, 288, 299, 324, 328, 338, 345, 351, 358, 364, 378, 390, 400, 412, 435, 470, 502, 507, 509, 543, 549, 704. The *festuca* appears in none of these collections, though it does appear later in the charters of Cluny (see below, 308–9), as does the *andelangus*, albeit rarely; e.g. *Cluny* 738. Neither the *festuca*, the *wadium* nor the *andelangus* appears among the charters in the Fulda cartulary.

[23] *TF* 7: 'Acta haec epistula accepit eam ipse Timo propriis manibus coram testibus seu ceteris adstantibus atque haec consentientibus involuto palleo ipsam epistulam super altare posita tradidit in manus supradicti venerabilis Joseph episcopi.'

[24] Notaries among the Wissembourg charters, for example, use both terms interchangeably. Guntbert says that he 'wrote this charter of donation' ('hanc carta donationis scripsi') in *TW* 171. In *TW* 175, Guntbert substituted *traditio* for *carta donationis*: 'hanc traditionem scripsi'. For good measure, just above this notarial subscription, the donor Erhart says he had 'caused this *carta donationis* to be done and affirmed', thus underscoring that *traditio* in this context was the semantic equivalent of *carta donationis*.

[25] *TW* 35, 162. [26] *TW* 52.

once belonged? Some of the variation in the two copies of Liutfrid's sale to Rantwig can be attributed to the copies made when the cartulary was assembled, but more substantial deviations indicate that each was descended from separate documents made at the time of the sale between Rantwig and Liutfrid.[27] Presumably, one of these had been Rantwig's record of the transaction, which was transferred to the monks upon his impressive donation of 742. But what of the other? Was that Liutfrid's? If so, how had his draft made its way into the monastic archive? And were these records removed from these individuals to the institution, or did the institution have copies made from documents which the individuals continued to keep?

Moreover, what had been the fate of the records of the earlier sale, of the *uendicionis titulum*, between Liutfrid and Ingina, alluded to in the sale between Liutfrid and Rantwig? Presumably because they did not directly impinge on Rantwig's donation of 742, these records never were handed over to the monastery when Rantwig made his donation. Copies apparently would have been held by Liutfrid and Ingina, neither of whom, nor their descendants, would have felt compelled to preserve their *uendicionis titulum* once the properties had been sold to Rantwig. That is, the case points to the one-time existence of *deperdita*, of now-lost records behind the documents we possess, as well as the likely reasons for their ephemerality.

Rantwig's donation, and the details of the earlier proprietary history of some of his lands, which exist only because the monks happened to include Liutfrid's sale to Rantwig, hint at a much busier world of documentary give and take than the surviving materials normally indicate. Rumour of this activity is not limited to the records of the entitled such as Liutfrid; it also reverberates in the donations of less exalted figures who also refer to the earlier purchase of the property from another layperson by 'title of sale'.[28] In addition to sales, a donation charter might exclude properties granted previously to the donor's wife *in libeldote*, an apparent reference to the *libellum dotis* of Frankish dowry

[27] For example, both copies refer to Liutfrid in Merovingian-era usage as *vir inluster*, but *TW* 35, produced by copyist B, who otherwise has a tendency to compress the text, included the title 'dux (Fratri Rantuuigo, uir inluster Liutfridus dux ui[n]de)', whereas the draft produced by copyist A, *TW* 162, left out the ducal title, an unlikely omission considering the fuller style of the document from which the scribe had copied ('Fratre Rantuuigo emptore, vir inluster Liutfridus uenditor'). This kind of deviation indicates that the copies had descended from two separate documents, cf. *TW*, pp. 213–14 and nn. 162a, 35b.

[28] *TW* 232, 233.

formulas.[29] These records have not survived, either because they were present in the monastic archive but not preserved for posterity in the cartulary, or because they remained in the possession of the layperson who lacked the means (or the intention?) to preserve them beyond his or her own lifetime, or the lives of their immediate heirs. That they could survive in abundance can be perceived at the monastery of Cluny, which preserved – independent of its eleventh-century cartulary – a trove of transactions, many of them sales between laypersons, that took place in the century before its foundation in 909.[30]

We can augment these clues about the documents that laypersons must have once possessed with several dozen instances from the codices of Wissembourg, Fulda and Freising, where two drafts, and in two cases three, of particular transactions were preserved.[31] These offer tantalizing clues about documentary practices because, as we have seen with the drafts of Rantwig's purchase, the deviations among pairs or triplicates seem to spring from the separate copies issued to both the monastery and the patron, whose version sometimes made its way back to the monastery and thence into a cartulary. That is, the monks had copied into the cartulary a record which had once belonged to the lay actor. Many of these double drafts from Wissembourg have to do with precarial transactions, whose patron copies perhaps had been returned to the monastery upon the expiration of the lease.[32] If so, this would have required the precarist's heirs to produce the documentation, in some cases many decades later, a process that assumes the keeping of clutches of charters by patrons. However, these lifelong leases were usually – where the evidence permits us to see it – assumed by the precarists' heirs, who presumably would have kept copies for themselves as evidence of their rights, rather than returning the record to the institution. If the monastery did cull precarial records directly from families, we might then assume the persistence of copies of at least precarial documents among the patrons.

We do encounter multiple drafts of donations in the Wissembourg and Freising codices that were made up to a century before their cartularies were compiled. This leaves dangling the question of how the patron's

[29] *TW* 128, 53 = 178; cf. Marculf 2.15. In another case, *TW* 222, a certain Sigoin gave property inherited from his mother, who had in turn received the property 'in dotes [titulum]' from her husband.

[30] See below, Chapter 11.

[31] Wissembourg: *TW* 8/47, 17/159, 26/105, 35/162, 53/178, 110/154, 198/251, 204/254, 205/223/252, 194/224, 218/239, 245/250. Freising: *TF* 45, 76, 121, 127, 184, 193, 232, 251, 418, 464, 568, 680. Fulda: *UF* 24, 86, 163–4, 187, 190, 232, 237, 248, 264, 268, 279, 285.

[32] Or so the editors of the cartulary, Glöckner and Doll, consistently assume; see *TW* 8/47, 17/159, 26/105, 35/162, 53/178, 110/154, 204/254, 205/223/252, 218/239, 245/250.

copy of the donation had been acquired by the monastery. That copies of transactions were handed down within families is possible, though the surviving lay dossiers suggest that a century-long persistence of records, at least as a coherent group, is unlikely. Moreover, the well-established cognaticism and partible inheritance practices of early medieval families presumably would have seen to the dispersal of family records from generation to generation.[33] Exceptions might have been records of transactions with ecclesiastical institutions, particularly, as we have seen, those held in *precaria*. These tenures, rendered indivisible by the very nature of the grant, allowed individuals to hand down and receive blocks of property from generation to generation.[34] Even so, the extant lay dossiers do not show the handing down even of precarial documents over such long periods of time.

It may be that patron copies of charters made their way indirectly into monastic archives through estate or village churches, many of which had been donated, and continued to be controlled as *precariae*, by patron groups. The extant donations make clear enough that many of these local churches had been founded by aristocratic kindreds, were supported with their donations, and then eventually were handed over as gifts to powerful monasteries. Might these parish churches have served as local centres of estate records? The monastery of Schlehdorf in Bavaria is perhaps the most outstanding example. Founded and administered by members of the Huosi family, its records were apparently transferred *en bloc* when the foundation was turned over to the see of Freising.[35]

The experience of the Huosi was replicated by humbler, middling patrons in village churches elsewhere. In 714, a certain Nordolf gave part of his property to the basilica of St Martin in the mid-Rhine village of Edesheim.[36] He then gave half of the basilica to the monastery of Wissembourg and had an 'epistle of donation' made out for both the monastery and the local church ('propterea tibi hanc epistolam donationis fieri rogaui vel ad partem ipsius basilicae'), which he says had been built by his ancestors ('apud antecessores meos constr[u]cta esse

[33] On Frankish kinship, see K. Schmid, 'Zur Problematik von Familie, Sippe und Geschlecht, Haus und Dynastie beim mittelalterlichen Adel', *Zeitschrift für die Geschichte des Oberrheins*, 105 (1957), 1–62, and A. C. Murray, *Germanic Kinship Structure: Studies in Law and Society in Antiquity and the Early Middle Ages* (Toronto, 1983).

[34] See the remarkable case of the Rodoins in Hummer, *Politics*, 71–5, 115–27.

[35] J. Jahn, 'Virgil, Arbeo und Cozroh: Verfassungsgeschichtliche Beobachtungen an bairischen Quellen des 8. und 9. Jahrhunderts', *Mitteilungen der Gesellschaft für Salzburger Landeskunde*, 130 (1990), 201–91, at 251–7. On the Huosi, see W. Störmer, *Adelsgruppen im früh- und hochmittelalterlichen Bayern* (Munich, 1972), 91–112. For the phenomenon, compare below, Chapter 10.

[36] *TW* 41.

uidetur'). The cartulary of Wissembourg also contains several donations made not to the monastery, but directly to one of the monastery's village churches by members of the Ratbald-Wicbald kin group, which possessed an array of properties in northern Alsace and in the mid-Rhine region, as well as connections to Wissembourg's abbot, Ermbert, and the founders of the powerful monastery at Lorsch.[37] In 766, a woman named Richsvind gave a contiguous field marked off by stones 'to the most holy church of St Peter which was built in the mark Uhlweiler, where at this time in the name of God Abbot Ermbert [of Wissembourg] is seen to preside'. Likewise, five years later, her kinsman Sigibald donated a vineyard directly 'to the most holy church that was constructed in honour of St Peter the apostle in the place that is called Uhlweiler'.[38]

A donation to the church of St Mary in the Alsatian village of Dauendorf offers a particularly striking example. In 774, its presiding lord and priest Ado, who was closely connected to the Ratbald-Wicbalds, gave his share of the church to Wissembourg.[39] At some point on either side of Ado's donation, a group of twelve petty patrons made an undated donation to Ado and the church of St Mary.[40] Its editors date the charter to anywhere between 760 and 790, reasoning that Ado had retained control of the church after his donation and so could have been the recipient of any gifts made after 774. As the presiding cleric, he no doubt did, but it seems much more reasonable to assume that any gifts made after 774 would have been addressed to Wissembourg's abbot (as was the case with Richsvind's donation to St Peter's at Uhlweiler), rather than to Ado, which would place the donation prior to 774. Whatever the case, the charter was directed to the parish church and its pastor: 'sacrosancta ecclesia sancta Maria quod est constructus in marcha Dachunheim ubi in dei nomine Ado pres[b]iter preesse uidetur'. This formula looks very much like those we encounter in the gifts to monasteries which dominate the extant record, except that the local church was the recipient of the gift and presumably the charter too, an indication that the records had once been housed in Dauendorf and then later transferred to Wissembourg, presumably after Ado had donated the church.

The donation of property at Berg and Waldhambach on the other side of the Vosges yielded a cluster of documents whose patterns can be explained most easily if one assumes their intermediate preservation at

37 W. Alter, 'Studien zur mittelalterlichen Siedlungs- und Volksgeschichte der mittleren Vorderplatz. II. Teil: Die in den Klosterkodizes genannten Personen, insbesondere die Angehörigen der Familie Ratbald-Wicbald', *Mitteilungen des historischen Vereins der Pfalz*, 57 (1959), 39–135; cf. Hummer, *Politics*, 111–13.

38 *TW* 108, 189. 39 *TW* 71. 40 *TW* 181.

an estate church. On 27 June 717, a certain Chrodoin, son of Peter, confirmed an earlier donation of property to Wissembourg.[41] This donation had included an estate in Waldhambach and the basilica of St Martin at Berg, as well as the presiding priests, who were listed among the serfs as if they were servants. Chrodoin received the properties in *precaria*, as did his descendants for the next three generations down to at least 830, and perhaps longer.[42] This *precaria* was reworked three more times over the next year as Chrodoin elaborated his donation into a more comprehensive will.[43] These revisions reveal that Chrodoin's ancestors (plural) had previously donated property to the church of St Martin at Berg, an indication that the church had been under family control for at least two generations prior to Chrodoin's donation. When we combine Chrodoin's testimony with the trail of records attached to his descendants, we can perceive that the properties had been held for at least six generations, from the late seventh to the mid ninth century.

The drafts of Chrodoin's will suggest that the transaction had generated records for both the family and the monastery. Chrodoin's *precariae* and wills were drawn up by a scribe named Leudoin, who identified himself variously as an *emanuensis* and a *cancellarius emanuensis*. Moreover, Chrodoin's final will exists in two drafts, one made by Leudoin and a second by yet another *cancellarius emanuensis*, Guntbert, neither of whom was a monk of Wissembourg.[44] These two drafts, each produced by a different notary, suggest copies issued separately to Chrodoin and to the monastery. How had a version made for Chrodoin made its way to Wissembourg? That it was returned upon the expiration of the lease, as the editors routinely assume in the cases of other doubles,[45] seems doubtful when we consider the long persistence of this family's precarial control of the properties well into the ninth century. Moreover, the copy in question applies to the will, which was separate and distinct from the *precaria*, which was drawn up several months later. We perhaps need look no further than the church of St Martin at Berg as the repository of Chrodoin's copy of his will, and perhaps some of the earlier workings of the will, especially when one ponders, as we shall soon see, the relative underdevelopment of monastic record-keeping prior to the late eighth century.

In one case, we possess three copies of a transaction: one belonging to the monastery, and the other two to the joint donors. In 699, the brothers Ermbert and Count Otto made an extensive donation of properties to Wissembourg in the Saulnois, in the upper Moselle region just south

[41] *TW* 196. [42] Hummer, *Politics*, 118–20. [43] *TW* 194/224, 195, 227.
[44] *TW* 194/224; on the two notaries, see *TW*, pp. 126–8. [45] See above, n. 32.

of Metz.[46] Three *exemplaria* of this transaction were drawn up by a lay notary named Chroccus,[47] one of which was issued to the monastery of Wissembourg. The other two were dubbed, by the scribes who produced the cartulary over a century and a half later, the 'exemplaria Ottoni atque Eremberti', the copies belonging to Otto and Ermbert. The gift included several basilicas established by their ancestors and dedicated to St Martin, St Hilarius and other saints. These copies might have been acquired by Wissembourg from these 'basilicas', or perhaps from the church at Biberkirch, where some of the donated properties lay and where twenty years later they were received in *precaria* by a Count Adalhard.[48] Again, we encounter a node of documents that cluster around a local church.

Taken together, the examples of the Huosi, Nordolf, Richsvind, Sigibald, Ado, Chrodoin, and Otto and Ermbert strongly hint that charters could be regularly deposited and stored in local churches, where they might be culled both by the locally powerful, who by all appearances had organized themselves around estate churches, and by the parent monastery. I consider it significant that almost all of the charters that come down to us in multiple copies in the codices from Freising and Wissembourg deal with donations of property in villages known to have had a suffragan church.[49] The vestiges of evidence teased out here find vivid elaboration in the astonishing evidence of the Folkwine dossier, which, prior to its transfer to St Gall, seems to have been housed in the local church at Rankweil.[50]

At the monastery of Fulda east of the Rhine, we are confronted with contrasting circumstances. Among the Fulda charters are twenty multiple drafts, all but one of which appear to descend from separate copies produced at the time of transaction.[51] Of these twenty, eight date to

[46] *TW* 223/205/252. [47] *TW*, pp. 118–19. [48] *TW* 267.

[49] Nine of twelve from Wissembourg and eleven of twelve from Freising (cf. above, n. 31); but for the churches associated with properties in *TW* 26/105, 35/162, 204/254, 218/239, see *TW* 52–3, 151, 156, 200. The exceptions are *TW* 8/47, 110/154, 245/250, although the first one was transacted in Durstel, where Wissembourg had a suffragan church (*TW* 198/251), and dealt with properties located near local churches in nearby Modern and Kirrwiller (*TW* 60, 151, 156, 172). The second deals with property in Lembach, where Wissembourg held property from a dense cluster of patrons, which must have had a parish church, if the number of donors is a fair guide (*TW* 29, 49, 71, 76–7, 79–80, 82, 89, 93–6, 98–101, 107, 109–10, 122, 136–7, 144, 148, 154–5, 157, 164, 170). With respect to Freising, a local church does not appear to have been involved in the transmission of *TF* 232, though the two drafts of this transaction record a plea to Charlemagne for the return of property seized by a count, a case that was delegated to the royal *missi*, whose court records might have been the source of a second draft.

[50] See above, 165–73.

[51] *UF* 24, 86, 163/164, 187, 190, 232, 237, 248, 264, 268, 279, 285. For the charters after 802, Dronke's edition must be consulted (*CDF*). However, Dronke did not

between 824 and 876. These later transactions deal with property well east of the Rhine in the Saale basin and were conducted during the time when the cartulary was conceived in the 820s and then periodically augmented throughout the rest of the ninth century. Some of the putative patrons' drafts of these eight transactions could have been derived from local churches, since a local monastery or church was implicated in half of them.[52] On the other hand, because these transactions transpired as the cartulary was being compiled, and because half of them bear no evidence of the involvement of a village church, it could be that these patron drafts were culled immediately upon the transaction and rapidly entered into the codex. That is, the second drafts of these latest eight transactions might have been added directly to the cartulary without the mediation of any local archive.

The remaining twelve cases where we have multiple drafts, however, transpired between 754 and 802, and so date to the period well before the cartulary was conceived. In these cases, the patrons' drafts presumably made their way into the monastic archives indirectly. Two involve property from the Saale basin, one of which records the gift in 795 of property in several locations, among them Nordheim.[53] Although the charter does not mention a church, we know from later records copied into the cartulary that Nordheim served as the locus of several transactions and that its church eventually was handed over in 836 to Fulda.[54] The other involves the property of the suffragan monastery Milz.[55] This nunnery was given to Fulda at Milz in 799 by Abbess Emhilt, and then returned to her as a precarial grant. The donation/*precaria* was recorded in the Fulda cartulary, as was a second draft by the monk Eberhard in the twelfth-century *Codex Eberhardi*. Eberhard had devised his draft from a record of the transaction, whose formulas suggest derivation from a copy

edit duplicates, which still have to be examined in the 'Traditionum Fuldensium Libri Tres', published by Johann Pistorius, *Rerum familiarumque Belgicarum chronicon magnum* (Frankfurt, 1654), 445–588. In the following, charter headings are from Dronke's edition, the numbers in brackets refer to the order in Dronke's edition, and the page numbers are to the location of the duplicates in Pistorius, 'Traditionum Fuldensium': *Traditio Rihbrahti* [562], pp. 495, 496; *Traditio Germunti* [455], pp. 495, 542; *Traditio Egilharti* [598], pp. 495, 587; *Traditio Gotehrammi* [461], pp. 534, 545; *Traditio Egilmari et Meginolti* [462], pp. 534, 545; *Traditio Uuitgeri* [411], p. 543; *Traditio Reginhartes* [588], pp. 566, 489; *Traditio Cunihiltae* [611], pp. 569, 574. Of these, only the *Traditio Rihbrahti* is a verbatim copy.

52 *Traditio Rihbrahti* [562], pp. 495, 496; *Traditio Germunti* [455], pp. 495, 542; *Traditio Egilharti* [598], pp. 495, 587; *Traditio Uuitgeri* [411], p. 543. The first three were transacted at the suffragan monastery of Rore. For the church at Sundheim, see *CDF* 323.

53 *UF* 232.

54 *CDF* 423–5. On the donation of the church at Nordheim, see *CDF* 493.

55 *UF* 264.

separate and distinct from that contained in the cartulary,[56] presumably a version that once had belonged to Milz. Emhilt's precarial request turns out to have been derived from an earlier precarial arrangement she had contracted with Milz in 784, when the nunnery was still an autonomous cloister.[57] As we have seen in cases from Freising and Wissembourg, that this earlier precarial request was directed to Milz indicates that the record had once lain at this modest cloister. Presumably, a copy of Emhilt's *precaria* of 784 was transferred to Fulda from Milz upon Emhilt's donation fifteen years later, or shortly thereafter. Although the case of Milz does not involve a layperson, the fate of the documentation underscores the importance of humbler, local institutions in the production, transfer and preservation of documents.

Of the remaining ten cases where we have multiple drafts of a transaction from Fulda, eight are traceable to the Wormsgau and one to the diocese of Strasbourg; the last deals with property in Alsace but was preserved in a section of the cartulary devoted to transactions in the diocese of Strasbourg.[58] Five of the ten cases appear to have been drawn up by non-monastic notaries: one each at Strasbourg, Mainz and a royal assembly in Paderborn, and two whose records do not reveal the place of transaction.[59] However, because these last two record gifts of property in Mainz in 797 and 802, and because both were drawn up by non-monastic scribes, Mainz would appear, as we shall soon see, to be the likely place of conveyance. The other five were drawn up by monastic notaries: three were conducted at Fulda, while the other two do not reveal a place of transaction, though Fulda would be a likely location, as we shall see later, given their drafting by monastic scribes.[60] Of the three explicitly done at Fulda, two deal with property in Dienheim, near Mainz, where Fulda held an impressive concentration of property, while the other recounted the gift of property located just beyond the walls of Mainz in 791.[61] The remaining two, which do not mention a place of transaction, deal with property in villages near Mainz. In sum, in each of these ten cases, whether the transactions were drafted by monastic or non-monastic notaries, we are dealing with multiple drafts that share a connection to Strasburg or to Mainz and its environs.

56 *UF* 375. 57 *UF* 154.

58 *UF* 24, 86, 163/164 (Strasbourg), 187 (Strasbourg), 190, 237, 248, 268, 279, 285.

59 *UF* 24 (Mainz), 187 (Strasbourg), 163/164 (Paderborn), 248, 285. On the non-monastic origins of the notaries, see *UF*, pp. liii–lix.

60 *UF* 86, 190, 237, 268, 279.

61 *UF* 190, 237, 279; on Dienheim, see U. Weidinger, *Untersuchungen zur Wirtschaftsstruktur des Klosters Fulda in der Karolingerzeit* (Stuttgart, 1991), 124–5.

The records issued to the monastic party at the time of the transaction account for one of the two drafts, but where had the other drafts, apparently those taken away from the transaction by the patrons, lain before they were acquired by Fulda? In none of these ten cases can we identify a local church, as in the cases of Nordheim and Milz. The prominence of non-monastic scribes in half of these cases, and the location of donated properties in Strasbourg and Mainz, or in villages very near them, suggests the mediation of diocesan archives, which certainly existed. This supposition finds support in the close connections between Fulda and Mainz stretching back to the days of Boniface and his disciples Lull and Sturm, a relationship materially attested by the repose of Archbishop Boniface's relics at the monastery. One can imagine any number of scenarios whereby documents could have passed between Fulda and the episcopal church of Mainz. More specifically, the very organization of the cartulary suggests the influence of the diocesan notariate on many of the charters. Edmund Stengel, who edited Fulda's charters, observed that, at least where it pertained to the monastery's Rhineland possessions, the organization of properties according to *Gau*, or district, actually breaks along the underlying diocesan boundaries of Mainz, Worms and Strasbourg. He noticed that the notaries responsible for many of the earlier transactions were not monks and their field of activity was circumscribed by diocesan boundaries.[62] Stengel's observations have since been taken up by Franz Staab, whose more thorough examination of the charters from the mid-Rhine region has identified a Mainz notariate, which operated under the auspices of the archbishop and authored many of Fulda's earliest charters.[63]

We might reasonably posit, then, the agency of diocesan archives – by which I mean either the cathedral archive or the plethora of smaller archives in parish churches subject to diocesan supervision – in the preservation of some of the multiple drafts that once had been issued to patrons. But other possibilities remain. Some of the drafts are within three decades of when the cartulary was begun and could have been acquired directly from families. Yet others might have been housed in villages sophisticated enough to have developed an institutional consciousness, and a local archive to go with it. Dienheim, for example, appears variously in the Fulda charters as an *oppidum*, a trading centre along the Rhine, a *vicus publicus*, the location of a *via publica*, the site of a complex of royal estates, and a place for the performance of transactions.[64]

62 *UF*, p. liv.
63 Staab, *Untersuchungen*, 137–53, esp. 144–52; cf. Innes, *State and Society*, 114–17.
64 *UF* 235, 246; *CDF* 217, 250–1, 264, 281, 328.

One case from Fulda hints at the production of documents to meet a range of constituencies. In 785, an Alsatian lord named Hugo made a donation to Fulda of properties near Ribeauvillé. The gift was transacted at the royal assembly in Paderborn, drawn up by a public notary, and entered into the Fulda codices in three versions.[65] One was labelled an *exemplaria*, in this case meaning a copy of an original charter, presumably the one held by Fulda. Although most copies differ in wording, pointing to the existence of multiple drafts, the other two versions of Hugo's transaction deviate in their substance in ways that speak to different purposes and audiences. By contrast with the *exemplaria*, absent in the two other versions, is a list of the *mancipia* attached to the properties and, among the witnesses, a certain Eberhard, by all appearances Hugo's son, 'who consented and subscribed'. The comprehensive listing of *mancipia* and the assent of Eberhard, the person most likely to challenge the gift, make sense in a copy destined for Fulda. The second and third versions, rather, include provisions for Hugo's man Badurich, which are missing in the first. The third version twice mentions the property Badurich held 'in my benefice'. Was this Hugo's copy? The second, which includes a provision allowing the successors of 'my man Baturic' to retain the benefice, apparently was devised to spell out the conditions for Badurich. Had Badurich retained this copy? Ostensibly, all of these were drawn up at Paderborn, though it could be that the latter two were drafted shortly thereafter to spell out the conditions for Badurich, whose interests perhaps had been overlooked in the original transaction. It might also be that all three of these copies were issued to the monastery as the conditions were fine-tuned, since some notarial formulas claim that duplicates were made so that each party would have a copy, though even that would suggest the production of documents for up to three parties, including perhaps a lowlier henchman.

Whatever the case, these three charters point to a busier and more sedimented process of documentation than normally is assumed from the extant record, dominated as it is by the cartularies. In 820, another Alsatian lord named Hugo, Count Hugo of Tours, exchanged his properties in Niederbronn, Preuschdorf, Walf, Barr and Froscheim for property held by Wissembourg in Dettweiler.[66] The exchange was made in front of Louis the Pious at the imperial assembly in Quierzy and, as befitted a transaction of one of the most powerful men in the empire, was witnessed by a formidable assemblage of counts, abbots, bishops and other notables, presumably members of Hugo's retinue. After this witness list, however, were entered groups of figures from each of the communities

[65] *UF* 163–4. [66] *TW* 69.

who had borne witness to the on-the-spot transfer of possession: 'Now the witnesses who saw the investment of this *traditio*, first in the villa that is called Niederbronn . . . Then in Preuschdorf. . . Then the witnesses concerning Walf. . . At Barr as well as at Froscheim . . . ' At Niederbronn, the document explains that Ratbraht and Uodilo, two figures who appear among the untitled notables at Quierzy, 'gave that investment'; that is, apparently, they had been dispatched by Hugo to supervise the transfer of his property to Wissembourg.[67] It might be that the charter of the transaction conducted at Quierzy had been carted around to these villages by Hugo's agents and supplemented with additional witness lists as the transfer was affirmed by the locals, whose assent apparently was crucial for validating the swap. On the other hand, it seems more likely that brief records of local validation had been drawn up, which were then combined with the record of the transaction at Quierzy and fused into the composite document now visible in the cartulary.

When augmented with the other examples from the charters of Fulda, Freising and Wissembourg, the records generated by the two Hugos of Alsace attest to a much more dynamic documentary culture than the static and binary impression of patron giving and ecclesiastical documentation and preservation given by the extant records. The forensic evidence suggests, rather, a regular flow of documentation among individuals, and between patrons, on the one hand, and local and regional institutions on the other. Let us now consider how the relationship between monasteries and this wider documentary culture unfolded over time.

Record-keeping habits in Francia prior to the eighth century, when monastic scriptoria became dominant, presumably were bound up with the processes of public authentication and documentation mediated by the *gesta municipalia*, at least in some regions. This has to be inferred from admittedly sparse documentation, but the chapters in this volume by Everett and Brown suggest that the documents of both individuals and ecclesiastical institutions were registered through these obscure civic institutions for the purposes of taxation and public validation in Italy and West Francia down to the early seventh century.[68] Brown examines in addition the puzzling references to the *gesta municipalia* in West Frankish formulas from the eighth and ninth centuries; he concludes that these late attestations of *gesta municipalia* probably refer to

[67] Ratbraht appears in the Quierzy witness list as the linguistic equivalent *Ratbert*. The element *-braht* appears variously in early medieval sources as *-bert*, *-berht*, *-breht* and *-brecht*.

[68] See above, Chapters 4 and 5; Barbier, 'Pouvoirs et élites', Part I, Chapter 3, 77–80; Wickham, *Framing*, 110–11.

some sort of public validation ceremonies, if not to the municipal institution of Late Antiquity.[69] This conclusion is strengthened by a surprising reference to the *gesta municipalia* in an actual transaction to the east in the Vosges region. In his will of 735×7 to the monastery of Murbach, Eberhard, the Etichonid count in Alsace, claims to have 'decided by all means and taken care not at all with disregard to enter the present donation into the *gesta muncipalia*, lest anyone at any time should reclaim it on account of this case' ('presentem vero donationem nequaquam vilitate gestis minicipalibus alligare curavimus et omnino decernimus, ne aliquando in eam ob hunc casum quisquam valeat repetere').[70] Horst Ebling, perplexed, surmised that 'the phrase of allegation was taken over only as a formula, which in any case only appears meaningful in Burgundy', where the Etichonid family had originated.[71] Ebling apparently was thinking of the formula from Marculf 2.3: 'We took care and wholly decided by no means to have the present donation entered into the public archive by contemptible decurions, so that no one should be able to gain access to it at any point as a result of this' ('presentem vero donationem nequaquam a curalium vilitate gestis municipalibus alligare curavimus, ne aliquando in eam ob hoc casu quisquam valeat repperire').[72]

This does approximate the phrasing in Eberhard's will, but if the author of Eberhard's charter was familiar with Marculf's formula, he adapted it to his own purposes and times, transforming its meaning so that Eberhard spoke not of avoiding 'contemptible curials', but rather of having taken great care to have the document validated by the *gesta municipalia*. Nor does Eberhard speak of restricting access (*repperire*) to the document, but rather of the threat that someone might attempt to relitigate (*repetere*) the donation. The absence of any reference to curials certainly makes sense in that by the eighth century curials had probably become extinct and land most certainly was no longer subject to formal registration for the purposes of taxation. More positively, donations, which exist

69 Above, Chapter 5. See also Rio, *Formularies*, 255–8; Rio, *Legal Practice*, 177–82.

70 Bruckner, *Regesta Alsatiae*, no. 127. On the Merovingian provenance of Eberhard's will, which survives in a copy made in the fifteenth century, see Wilsdorf, 'Le monasterium scottorum de Honau', 63–4, and C. Wilsdorf, 'Remiremont et Murbach à l'époque carolingienne', in M. Parisse (ed.), *Remiremont, l'abbaye et la ville* (Nancy, 1980), 49–57.

71 H. Ebling, *Prosopographie der Amtsträger des Merowingerreiches von Chlothar II. (613) bis Karl Martell (741)* (Munich, 1974), 131n15.

72 Marculf 2.3; trans. Rio, *Formularies*, 185; J. Barbier, 'Pouvoirs et élites dans le monde franc (VI$^{e}$–XI$^{e}$ siècle): Matériaux pour servir à l'histoire des élites des cités (VI$^{e}$–IX$^{e}$ siècle): Le dossier des *gesta municipalia*, étude n$^{o}$ 2', unpublished mémoire d'HDR, Université de Paris I–Panthéon-Sorbonne (2009), Part I, Chapter 3, 88–94.

in abundance only from the late seventh century on, are replete with anxious clauses about meddlesome relatives. This might explain why, whereas the formula of Marculf goes on to warn both heirs (*heres*) and greedy judges not to interfere with the gift, the author of Eberhard's will expands the circle of potentially troublesome heirs (*heres aut proheres*), elaborates Marculf into a more ferocious warning to those heirs (and to himself), and makes no mention of tax-gouging judges.[73]

The formula for the *gesta municipalia* in Count Eberhard's will, shorn as it was of the fiscal and functional trappings of the putative late antique institution, might allude, albeit with linguistic pretension, to the performance of a high-profile transaction, in the assembly that had gathered to witness the assignment (literally) of this count's impressive chartered endowment – as we discover at the end of the document – '*publice* at the *castrum* Habendum and the monastery of Remiremont'; that is, at a place that was the functional equivalent of a Frankish *vicus publicus*.[74] Thus, if the phrase was mobilized for the purposes of affectation, that affectation was appropriate to the solemnity of the occasion: the fabulous endowment of Murbach made publicly at the fortified, comital hub at Remiremont.

Whatever the particulars of its development might have been, the disappearance or transformation of the *gesta municipalia* meant that over the course of the Merovingian period, especially during the seventh century, the institutions central to the generation and preservation of documentation in Late Antiquity had become obsolete. Consequently, many of the records dependent upon it – ecclesiastical records included – passed with it. This, more than anything else, probably explains the meagre documentation surviving from the seventh century. The phenomenon of ephemerality should be distinguished, however, from the production of documentation at that time. Formulas, wills, allusions to records in narrative and hagiographical accounts, and the smattering of monastic charters that do survive point to the wide and deep circulation of documentation in the seventh century.

The wills of two seventh-century aristocrats of the Paris basin, Ermentrude and the son of Idda, will illuminate the contention. Ermentrude's will directed property to her son, her *nepotes*, and several ecclesiastical

[73] Marculf 2.3, on which see above, 207; Bruckner, *Regesta Alsatiae*, no. 127.

[74] The initial foundation of Remiremont around 620 was probably supported with royal grants (H. Büttner, *Geschichte des Elsaß I*. . . , ed. T. Endemann [Sigmaringen, 1991], 57–8), making it a probable hub of comital authority as early as the seventh century. By the ninth century, it was a preferred stop on the royal hunting itinerary (*Annales regni Francorum*, s.aa. 805, 817, 821, 825 [MGH SRG 6:120, 147, 155, 167]). By 849, a royal palace at Remiremont finally comes into view: MGH DD Kar. 3, nos. 105–6.

institutions.[75] Although the document survives because it was preserved by one of the interested churches, the document itself was addressed in the second person to Ermentrude's son, an indication that a copy of the transaction had been made out for him. We might also infer the one-time existence of copies for the other churches, and probably for her *nepotes*. Similarly, the son of Idda made provisions for the dispensation of property to his wife, Chramnethrude, and several churches.[76] Some of the properties were directed to churches the son of Idda had already donated by now lost *epistolae donacionis*. At the end of the will, the subscribing witnesses verified this *exemplar autenticum*, 'authentic copy', of the charter, an indication that at least one other version had been drafted.

The echoes of erstwhile documentation also reverberate in hagiographical accounts. The *Life of Germanus of Grandval*, composed around 680, informs its readers that sometime in the 630s Abbot Waldebert of Luxeuil persuaded Duke Gundoin to 'make firm those places with his hands and those of good men' for the foundation of a monastery in Grandval, a phrase that finds parallels in Salic donation formulas.[77] Likewise, the *Life* (*c.* 615–20) of Gundoin's daughter, Sadalberga, reveals that after she had founded a monastery at Laon, she became embroiled in a dispute with her brother, who withheld from the foundation 'some villas that she had granted through a series of charters'.[78] After harmony was restored, 'the inviolability of the charters was mutually confirmed' by Sadalberga and her brother. Sadalberga's *Life* also tells us that she earlier had founded a monastery, probably by 640, near Langres 'on her paternal inheritance and succession, which she enriched with revenues from the estates of her paternal, hereditary succession'.[79] In light of the wills above, we might infer a transfer of these family properties to Sadalberga by formal testament, and then grants by her to the foundation by formal *epistolae donacionis*. Moreover, the detailed listing of property in the wills of Ermentrude and the son of Idda, and the reference in the *Life of Sadalberga* to Sadalberga's revenues, would seem to rest on the one-time existence of estate records.

75 *ChLA* XIV 592. 76 *ChLA* XIII 569.

77 Bobolenus, *Vita Germani abbatis Grandivallensis* 7 (MGH SRM 5:36): 'Tunc coepit Waldebertus verbis lenibus mulcere animum eius, ut, si vellet, pro Dei intuitu vel pro remedio animae sue vel absolutione peccaminum suorum firmitatem de ipsis locis manibus suis seu bonorum hominum roboratam manibus exhibeat.' Cf. *Form. Sal. Big.* 10: 'ut per hanc epistolam donacione vel deliberatione nostra, manu mea vel bonorum firmata'; *Form. Sal. Lind.* 6: 'sed magis praesens haec cartola tam a me quam ab aliis bonorum hominum manibus roborata, omni tempore firma et stabilis permaneat'.

78 *Vita Sadalbergae Abbatissae Laudunensis* 29 (MGH SRM 5:66).

79 *Vita Sadalbergae Abbatissae Laudunensis* 12 (MGH SRM 5:56–7).

In any event, these wills and saints' lives testify to clusters of collateral documentation that no longer exist but that, if the casual references to them are indicative, were assumed to be integral to the give and take of property settlements. If we could parachute into the period at any moment, we probably would see that documents were routinely generated and pragmatically preserved by institutions and individuals alike. However, while ecclesiastical institutions obtained records of their transactions, monasteries and churches were not yet decisive for the preservation of documentation because they had developed neither the means nor the will to perpetuate, by themselves, their holdings over long periods of time. And this should not be surprising, since there is nothing self-evident about the collection and preservation of documents. Not even the late Roman state pretended to preserve records of its business for eternity; nor were clerics – despite stereotypes – somehow genetically programmed to hoard charters. From the perspective of millennia, property records – barring a change in the consciousness of the institutions to which they were attached – were bound to pass out of existence. Ultimately, a system centred on ecclesiastical institutions would be elaborated and refined only in the Carolingian period, when monasteries became conduits of central authority and assumed a greater public role. Crucially, this public duty was infused with the radical Carolingian ethos of *memoria*, which for our purposes placed upon monks the obligation to preserve *forever* the records of donations as signs of the eternal, heavenly order on earth.[80]

When Carolingian monks created cartularies in the ninth century, they were at a loss to compile a coherent record of their oldest donations. Wissembourg was founded in the seventh century, although exactly when and by whom is obscure because the parchment trail is so meagre. During the high Middle Ages, when their foundation by a great king or lord became an obsession of monasteries (a defining preoccupation, we might add, of many later cartularies), the monks of Wissembourg manufactured an original endowment in 633 by Dagobert I.[81] In reality, Wissembourg probably was founded around 660 by Bishop Dragobodo of Speyer and Duke Bonifatius, though the charters offer no conclusive proof.[82] The

[80] O. G. Oexle, 'Memoria und Memorialüberlieferung im früheren Mittelalter', *Frühmittelalterliche Studien*, 10 (1976), 70–95; Geary, *Phantoms*, 16–19. The literature on *memoria* is now vast; see Oexle, 'Memoria, Memorialüberlieferung', in *Lexikon des Mittelalters*, 10 vols. (Munich, 1980–99), VI, 510–13.

[81] Bruckner, *Regesta Alsatiae*, no. 32.

[82] F. Staab, 'Noch einmal zur Diplomatik der Weißenburger Traditionen', *Archiv für mittelrheinische Kirchengeschichte*, 44 (1992), 311–22; A. Doll, 'Ist die Diplomatik der Wissembourger Urkunden geklärt?', *Archiv für mittelrheinische Kirchengeschichte*, 45 (1993), 439–47; and Doll, 'Kloster Wissembourg, seine Gründung und deren Zeugen', *Archiv für mittelrheinische Kirchengeschichte*, 44 (1992), 287–309.

earliest charter in the cartulary, Bonifatius' donation of 661, is not a foundation charter per se: it grants the property and mill of the duke's late son Gundebald at Görlingen, yet it does make reference to 'the monastery of lord Peter at Wissembourg, which was built by that bishop' (i.e. Dragobodo). This strongly implies that Dragobodo had made earlier grants for the foundation of the monastery. No records of that act survive, though if the previous examples of Germanus and Sadalberga are an indication, they surely had once existed. Nor do we possess seventh-century charters from the Rodoins, a kin group believed to have been among the nexus of founding families: their putative ancestors, Chrodohari and Chrodoald, stood as witnesses to Bonifatius' donation, and the first recorded abbot of Wissembourg, a certain Chrodoin, apparently another ancestor, received the second oldest donation in 682 from Duke Theotchar.[83] Records of the Rodoins' donations begin only in 717, but, as we have seen, the will of Chrodoin, son of Peter, refers to the prior donation of a church at Berg by his 'ancestors', perhaps an allusion to these otherwise obscure figures. Bonifatius' and Theotchar's donations, and a third charter dated to 693×4, represent the only surviving records of the monastery's first three decades of business.[84] Only from 695 on are transactions more or less continuously represented, an impressive memory to be sure when compared to the other collections, but a paltry account of what must have been wider holdings in the seventh century.

The cartularies of Fulda and Freising were compiled three decades earlier than Wissembourg's, during the 820s.[85] Although Fulda was founded in 744, and thus had less than a century of transactions to remember, the oldest charter in the extant portions of the cartulary dates to 751.[86] A cluster of transactions from the 750s ensues, but very little remains from the 760s. Only from the 770s and 780s does the flow of charters become continuous. At Freising, a see established in the 730s when the Bavarian Church was reformed by Boniface, only one charter from the tenure of Bishop Erembert (73?–48) was remembered, and that was mistakenly listed in the register of the charters transacted during the period of Joseph (748–64), his successor, itself a sparse record.[87] Only from 769 does the cartulary impart a steady stream of records.

83 K. Glöckner, 'Die Anfänge des Klosters Weißenburg', *Elsaß-Lothringisches Jahrbuch*, 19 (1939), 1–46, at 13–20. See *TW* 213 for Theotchar's donation.

84 *TW* 203, 213, 38.

85 *TF*, p. xxi; *UF*, p. xx; cf. H. Hummer, 'A Family Cartulary of Hrabanus Maurus? Hessisches Staatsarchiv, Marburg, Ms. K 424, folios 75–82v', in T. Schilp and U. Ludwig (eds.), *Nomen et Fraternitas: Festschrift für Dieter Geuenich zum 65. Geburtstag* (New York, 2008), 645–64, at 646–7.

86 *UF* 11.

87 *TF* 1, and p. 3.

As seen in the previous chapter, the monks of St Gall in Alemannia never did produce, so far as is known, a cartulary; they bequeathed instead an impressive trove of unbound, original charters. It is perhaps significant then that this collection exhibits many of the same patterns evident in the extant cartularies. Although St Gall was, like Wissembourg, founded in the seventh century by a cluster of aristocratic kindreds,[88] it could recall absolutely nothing of transactions made at that time. Aside from a lone charter in 716, and a few from the 740s, the monks failed to remember much of anything prior to the 760s.[89]

Thus we have a similar pattern in multiple regions: a fragmentary record of monasteries' earliest donations, which becomes continuously represented – with the notable early exception of Wissembourg – only after 770. Positive evidence suggests that the memory of the Merovingian and early Carolingian periods was hazy, not because monasteries did not use or possess documents in these periods, but because they developed a self-sustaining system of archival management and preservation only in the late eighth century. Much of what was recorded before the consolidation of this sharpened archival consciousness passed into oblivion, and the vestiges we do possess we owe to Carolingian-era efforts to reconstruct documentation from this earlier time.

Illuminating is a plea from the monastery of Honau, located on an island in the Rhine and founded in 722 by the Etichonids, the ducal family in Alsace. In 775, its abbot Beatus asked Charlemagne to confirm all the properties that had been given to the monastery by kings and God-fearing men because the charters (*instrumenta chartarum*) had been lost due to neglect.[90] That is a startling statement when one considers that Honau had been in operation a mere fifty years. The abbot's complaint, however, gives voice to patterns visible elsewhere: the rapid loss of charters apparently due to poor records management, as well as to the attempts in the late eighth century to reconstitute them. Testimony emanating from the early modern period indicates that the monks indeed appear to have reconstructed their lost records. A seventeenth-century Jesuit claims to have seen a cartulary from Honau, apparently lost subsequently during the Thirty Years' War, which, he says, contained over a

[88] Or so one can infer from Notker's later complaint, albeit exaggerated, that St Gall was poor because of its traditional dependence upon small-scale donations ('ex privatorum tradiciunculis'), by contrast with the royally endowed foundations, *Gesta Karoli Magni imperatoris* 2.10 (MGH SRG n.s. 12:66–7).

[89] Wartmann I 17–28.

[90] MGH DD Kar. 1, no. 10; for a fuller discussion of the context of this plea, see Hummer, *Politics*, 63–5.

thousand charters spanning the period from Honau's foundation through the reign of Charlemagne (768–814).[91]

So what exactly would this late Merovingian world of document production have looked like? Fortunately, the region of Alsace and neighbouring southern Lotharingia has handed down a fairly tight body of charters from the late seventh and early eighth centuries, permitting us to elucidate the patterns of the production and preservation of documentation in the later Merovingian period, as well as the formation of a new archival consciousness within ecclesiastical institutions by the late eighth century. All told, this region yields nearly a hundred Merovingian-era charters, a veritable flood by the standards of other collections. The mother lode of charters springs from the Wissembourg codex, which mediates eighty-three late Merovingian charters from the period 661–747.[92] As we have seen, the two earliest charters date to 661 and 682, and a steady flow of charters commences only around 695. Of these late Merovingian charters, an impressive total of thirty-nine emanate from the period before 720; that is, they belong to the period before Charles Martel had consolidated Carolingian power, an indication that the phenomenon of their existence, or their survival, cannot adequately be explained by the *deus ex machina* of Carolingian takeover.[93]

Revealing within these charters is the notarial evidence. Generally speaking, only during the latter half of the eighth century did the writing of charters come to be centred on notaries from Wissembourg. Prior to that, most operated as free agents outside the monastery's sphere of authority. Here we must rely on the toilsome work of editors, who have developed diplomatic techniques to distinguish monastic from non-monastic notaries. Briefly, the first clue is whether the notary identifies himself as an *emanuensis*, a *notarius* or a *cancellarius*, often an indication of his personal professional identity. Of these, the term *emanuensis* is held

[91] Wilsdorf, 'Le Monasterium scottorum de Honau', 11. Jodocus Coccius, the Jesuit scholar, claims the cartulary was assembled in 1079 by a monk of Honau named Leon. According to Coccius, the charters were arranged in chronological order, perhaps by the abbot/bishop, and ranged from the reign of Theuderic IV to that of Charlemagne. It is impossible to say more from such slim testimony, but the dates of the charters, and their organizational scheme, suggest perhaps that the cartulary was embedded within a larger survey compiled by Leon, in the way that Cozroh's codex, also a chronological survey, was absorbed into the codex produced at Freising in 1187 by Conrad Sacristan.

[92] *TW* 1–7, 8 = 47, 9–16, 17 = 159, 18, 35 = 162, 36–41, 43–6, 52, 136, 141–3, 146–8, 150, 169, 186–8, 192, 194 = 224, 195–6, 202–3, 205 = 223= 252, 213, 218 = 239, 225–6, 228–9, 231–5, 237, 240–4, 247–8, 256–7, 261–2, 265–7. A smattering of other charters, dating from 722×3 to 749, mostly from Murbach and Honau, can be found in Bruckner, *Regesta Alsatiae*, nos. 100–3, 113, 125, 127, 128, 163, 165, 167.

[93] Cf. Hummer, *Politics*, 66, 68.

to be the most discriminating, since it was rarely used by monks. However, a scribe might not identify himself professionally, or might do so in some cases, but not others. Nor can we assume that the absence of self-identification as a monk or priest necessarily means that the scribe is a layperson because vocational statuses too were not uniformly expressed. That is, the consistency of expression that we might expect, or desire, is frustratingly lacking.

Fortunately, the charters yield other clues that can be brought to bear on the problem. In the absence of any firm declaration of professional and vocational status, one can identify the notary's field of activity – does he ever write at the monastery, or exclusively in locales in a defined region? – as well as his name, which might betray a prosopographical connection to a known kin group, or appear in the lists of monks kept by monasteries, against which his membership can be checked. Additional clues can be found in the formulas employed by the scribe (his *Fassung*), which allude to a notarial training acquired from within the monastery or from somewhere else. Sometimes, we can even find a notary who consistently appears in the retinue of a count or a duke, and who does not write for a particular institution, or in a particular region, but for his lord. At other times we encounter a notary who wrote for more than one institution, revealing his status as an autonomous notary, independent of any single institution.

From all of this, researchers have identified two main classes of notaries, ecclesiastical scribes and those who are traditionally, if perhaps misleadingly, called *offentliche Schreiber*, or public notaries. The former can be divided into monastic and episcopal notaries; the latter, into the so-called *Gauschreiber*, or notaries who operate in particular districts, often with a close connection to particular groups; court notaries, who write for entitled lay lords; and free scribes, who might write for multiple monasteries or groups, yet remain independent of them. These categories need not be overstressed, since a *Gau* or a court notary might be a priest, working on behalf of the kin groups or powerful lords with which he was associated, while a local scribe might be someone whose activity suggests work on behalf of a cloister, yet who was not himself a monk. This investigation will stress the distinction between monastic and non-monastic notaries, whoever they might have been, and how the ratio between the two changed over time so that monastic competency came to dominate.

We begin with a closer look at the patterns of notarial evidence in the Wissembourg codex. When Duke Bonifatius made the first recorded donation to Wissembourg in 661, his transaction was drawn up by the duke's own son, Teodoald, who reveals that he was asked to write 'this *epistola* by my father Bonifatius'.[94] Teodoald's statement occurs before the list of witnesses, after which follows the date and place of the transaction. The dating clause and the witnesses, however, appear to have been added by the scribe Leodobert, who claims at the end of the charter to 'have written at the request of those written above' ('rogatus a suprascripta scripsi'), presumably referring to the parties to the transaction. Leodebert, otherwise unknown, might have been related to one of the witnesses, Ledoald, and to the aforementioned early eighth-century *emanuensis* Leodoin.[95] The hybrid configuration of this charter suggests that a record had been drawn up for the duke by his own son, and a second by a local scribe for Bishop Dragobodo, to whom the charter is addressed.

Duke Theotchar's donation of a lucrative salt pan in 682 was drawn up in the Saulnois by a local scribe, Babo *emanuensis*, who seems to have been one of the duke's neighbours.[96] The third oldest transaction in the cartulary was a donation made in 693 or 694 by a certain Hildifrid on behalf of himself and his two siblings, Managold and Waldswind. It was drawn up by the otherwise unknown *notarius* Uadalgari, who 'wrote, having been asked by those written above' ('rogatus a suprascriptis scripsi'), and who, judging by the elements of his name, might have been a relative of the donors and some of the witnesses.[97] In any event, his use of older formulas and his autonomy *vis-à-vis* the transacting parties suggest that he was no monk.[98]

Around 700, when the number of transactions greatly increases, we encounter a series of charters down to the 760s written up by thirty notaries, only two of whom can with any sureness be identified as monks.[99] A third, Theutgar, might eventually have entered the chapter at Wissembourg, but his style betrays a previous notarial education.[100] Ten others identified themselves as clerics – one as a bishop, and the

94 *TW* 203.

95 Glöckner and Doll speculate that Leodebert probably was a non-monastic notary and perhaps related to the *amanuensis* Leodoin, *TW*, pp. 416, 417n2.

96 *TW* 213. The charter records the people living around the property, one of whom was a man named *Bobo*, a name which, when we take into account the irregularity of medieval orthography, is virtually indistinguishable from *Babo*.

97 *TW* 38. The names of one of the donors, Waldswind, and two of the witnesses, Walthari and Willihari, may point to kinship with Uadalgari. So far as can be inferred from other charters, the witnesses mostly were laymen.

98 *TW*, p. 218.

99 *TW*, pp. 115–51, 629–39 (Table 76). The two monks were Hildifrid (*TW*, p. 128) and Erlabold (*TW* 257).

100 Theutgar appears first in 712. Glöckner and Doll infer from evidence in the witness lists to other charters that he probably became active on behalf of the monastery in the late 730s (*TW*, p. 125).

rest as either deacons or priests; but of these ten, four also formally identified themselves as *emanuenses*, and one possibly was a monk at Wissembourg.[101] That most of these ten 'ecclesiastical' notaries were priests and deacons, rather than monks, presumably points to origins within the diocesan ranks. Even still, they seem to have behaved not as agents of episcopal authority as such, but rather as free scribes or as notaries in the service of powerful patron groups. The notaries Ansgar and Heimo, for example, both self-described presbyters, appear only as notaries to the Etichonids, the ducal family in Alsace.[102] The priest and *emanuensis* Geroin was active in the Speyergau for the Ratbald-Wicbalds and appears in the Fulda charters as the notary to a Count Baugulf.[103] And the deacon Guntbert was busy in the Saargau on behalf of the Rodoins and Wolfoald-Gundoins.[104]

The remaining seventeen, however, were not professional clerics (at least no formal affiliations are mentioned). Their activities are traceable rather to the districts within which identifiable patron groups operated. Of these seventeen scribes, three were (lay) patrons of Wissembourg, each of whom also worked as a *notarius* or an *emanuensis* for the Wolfoald-Gundoin and Rodoin kin groups;[105] another self-identified *notarius* and *emanuensis* wrote on behalf of the same two groups;[106] two identified themselves as *cancellarii* and appear on the basis of their styles to have been local scribes;[107] one was in the service of a count;[108] one bears no self-designation as a notary, but appears as a scribe in both the Wissembourg and the Honau charters, thus pointing to the activities of a free notary;[109] and the rest are otherwise unidentifiable with respect to profession.[110] So far as one can tell from their self-identification (or

101 Ratker, deacon/*emanuensis* (*TW*, pp. 119–21); Desiderius, *presbiter* (p. 221); Gundbert, deacon/*cancellarius*/*emanuensis* (p. 128); Heimo, *presbiter* (pp. 128–9); Sindicho, deacon/*emanuensis* (pp. 130–1); Ansgar, *presbiter* (p. 131); Otricus, *presbiter* (p. 489); Basinus-Baldfrid, deacon (p. 132); Geroin, *presbiter*/*emanuensis* (pp. 133–5); and Bishop Hartbert (p. 346). Basinus might have been, on the basis of his field of activity, a monk, though he bears the same name as the bishop of Speyer. If he was the same bishop, he could have operated out of the cathedral; cf. *TW*, p. 132.

102 Ansgar's formulas are similar to those used in other Etichonid donations to Honau (*TW*, p. 131); and Heimo wrote up Etichonid transactions with both Wissembourg and Honau (cf. Bruckner, *Regesta Alsatiae*, nos. 103, 110, 126).

103 *TW*, pp. 133–5; *UF* 53.

104 *TW*, p. 128.

105 Chrodoin, *notarius* (*TW*, pp. 115–18); Hahicho, *notarius* (pp. 121–2); Chroccus, *emanuensis* (pp. 118–19). All wrote for the Wolfoald-Gundoins, and Hahicho also for the Rodoins.

106 Leudoin (*TW*, pp. 126–8).

107 Lantfrid (*TW*, p. 505); Wibald (p. 507).

108 Williulf (*TW*, p. 182).

109 Wanulf (*TW*, p. 371; Bruckner, *Regesta Alsatiae*, no. 167).

110 Heribert (*TW* 43), Gerhari (*TW*, p. 389), Faramund (pp. 129–30), Chudo (p. 390), Humbert (*TW* 14), Harbert (*TW*, p. 348), Grimoald (p. 345), Hildifrid (p. 342), Fruatolf (pp. 135–6).

lack thereof), in combination with their fields of activity, the location of the transactions, the location of the donated properties, or notarial styles, none of these yield any evidence of a formal affiliation with the monastery.

This is not to say that none of these lay notaries, or the priestly notaries, had no connection to the monastery at all. Some of them appear to have written either exclusively, or mostly, for Wissembourg, thus betraying a cordial, if informal, relationship. The 'ecclesiastical' *emanuenses* Ratker and Sindicho, for example, wrote up transactions involving properties donated in multiple districts almost exclusively at Wissembourg.[111] Two of the lay notaries, Chrodoin and Hahicho, when they were not both working on behalf of local groups, wrote on behalf of the monastery.[112] What this tells us, then, is that, early on, monks did not monopolize the production of charters. When the monks, or lay actors for that matter, wanted documents drawn up, they called upon a notariate, some of whom might have been in their service, but most of whom were independent of either the cloister or a secular patron.

In fact, local scribes dominated notarial activity in the late Merovingian period: of the seventy-six charters that date to the period before 751, thirty-six were drawn up by just five notaries from the Saargau.[113] By contrast, only twenty-two charters are traceable to the work of two monks and two putative monks, and seventeen of those were drawn up by a single scribe, the aforementioned Theutgar, who, as we have seen, seems to have become a monk only later.[114] The most intriguing of the five Saargau notaries is the self-described *notarius* Chrodoin, a prolific scribe among Wissembourg's late Merovingian charters and the same Chrodoin, son of Petrus, who was one of the progenitors of the Rodoins, the group responsible for many of the transactions in the Saargau section of the cartulary.[115] Between 695 and 718, Chrodoin drafted at least nine documents, appeared as donor or testator in five others, and appeared as a witness in six more.[116] In his capacity as a notary and a witness, he wrote and testified for a circle of people, the most prominent of whom were

[111] *TW*, pp. 120–1, 132. [112] See above, n. 105.

[113] Chrodoin (10), Chroccus (6), Hahicho (5), Leudoin (10), Faramund (5).

[114] See above, nn. 99–101.

[115] On the Rodoins, see Glöckner, 'Anfänge', 18–21; and F. Langenbeck, 'Probleme der elsässischen Geschichte in fränkischer Zeit', *Alemannisches Jahrbuch* (1957), 1–132, at 33–40. On the Rodoins and the cartulary of Wissembourg, see Hummer, *Politics*, 65–75, 190–207.

[116] *TW*, pp. 115–18. The editors cautiously credit him with a tenth charter whose copy is missing its notary yet whose formulas are evocative of Chrodoin's formulas. The donor in question was a certain 'priest Chrodoin', who the editors speculate is one and the same person. On the other hand, they also present compelling evidence that points to two separate individuals (*TW*, pp. 117, 215–16).

individuals of the Wolfoald-Gundoin group, the former mayoral family of Austrasia. Chrodoin's own transactions were drawn up not by himself, but by another prolific notary, the aforementioned Leudoin, the self-described *emanuensis*, *notarius* and *cancellarius*, and by all appearances a layperson, who was responsible for nine charters, among them transactions of the Wolfoald-Gundoins.[117] As the intertwined careers of these two notaries illustrate, in the early eighth century an impressive proportion of documentation arose from associative networks within localities.

More than one notary might be summoned to draft copies of charters for both parties to the transaction. In the purchase of property by Wissembourg in 715, the *notarius* Chrodoin claims that he 'wrote this sale and subscribed'.[118] A second draft reveals that 'Chrodoin wrote the charter, and I Gundbert also wrote and made a copy of the charter', presumably either for the seller Ermbert or for the monastery, although Gundbert himself seems not to have been a monk, but yet another local notary formally unconnected to Wissembourg.[119] In a donation of 705 or 706, and in the subsequent *precaria* of 706×7, two local notaries, Chroccus and Hahicho, indicate that they had each written a version of the same transaction. According to the donation charter, 'I Chroccus having been asked wrote [and] I Hahicho issued the original version ('autenticum relegi'), [wrote] the copy (*exemplaria*), and subscribed.'[120] In the *precaria* drafted the following year, the roles were reversed: 'I Hahicho wrote [and] I Chroccus issued the original version, wrote the copy and subscribed.'[121] The wording in these two documents again suggests the production of copies for the two parties, the patron and the institution, each presumably employing their own notaries.

By the end of the eighth century, the drafting of property transactions became centred emphatically on Wissembourg. From the 770s on, most of the extant documents were drafted by monks who, when they referred to themselves as *cancellarii*, clearly meant by that that they were monastic scribes.[122] The overlapping careers of two notaries responsible for drafting the lion's share of transactions between 760 and 785, Geroin (757, 764–84) and Kadwal (767, 774–82), neatly encapsulate the transition.[123] We have already met Geroin, who was both a priest and an *emanuensis* in the Speyergau and northern Alsace, and, judging from the documents he drafted, was closely tied to the prominent Ratbald-Wicbald group of donors.[124] I note here that the patterns of Geroin's activities evoke

117 *TW*, pp. 126–8. 118 *TW* 239. 119 *TW* 218 and p. 470; cf. p. 128.
120 *TW* 228. 121 *TW* 229. 122 *TW*, p. 137.
123 Of the sixty-seven transactions written up during this time, Geroin produced charters for twenty-seven and Kadwal fourteen (*TW*, pp. 538–46).
124 *TW*, pp. 133–5.

prevailing late Merovingian practices when notaries were frequently tied to patron groups. On the other hand, although Geroin appears not to have been a monk, he was also literally close to Wissembourg, perhaps having resided near or at the monastery: of the twenty-eight transactions he wrote up, twenty were conducted at Wissembourg, and two of those were said to have been done 'in the monastery' (*in ipso monasterio*).[125]

Kadwal, by contrast, was a monk of Wissembourg, was the first to identify himself as the monastic *cancellarius*, and stands at the beginning of an unbroken line of monastic *cancellarii* at Wissembourg. Although some of his style bears the influence of Geroin's, he introduced a number of changes to the formulas that shaped Geroin's later charters; these changes turned out to have had a lasting influence on his successors at Wissembourg, an indication that the monastery's *cancellarius* was harnessing the charters to a distinctive Wissembourg style.[126] Moreover, if Geroin's charters sometimes might refer to transactions conducted 'in the monastery', Kadwal's are the first charters to distinguish the act of transaction (*actum*) from the drafting of the charter itself and, beginning in 774, to indicate that the charter had been produced (*facta cartola*) at the monastic scriptorium.[127] Over the next several decades, between 782 and 811, three monks, Adalland, the dominant figure in Wissembourg's archive in the late eighth century;[128] Hildibodo and Wolfhart were responsible for drafting most of the charters in this, the most robust period for transactions.[129] The acts of donation recorded in these charters, when indicated, occurred overwhelmingly at Wissembourg: of the 128 transactions made between 770 and 811, only a dozen stipulate that they had been done elsewhere.[130] By all accounts, the more diverse notarial culture of the late Merovingian period had decisively come under the domination of Wissembourg and its notaries.

This reorganization of Wissembourg's scriptorium went hand in hand with an effort to systematize and preserve its records. Although Wissembourg's cartulary was not assembled until 860, it was preceded by other

[125] *TW*, pp. 135, 633. The number of transactions done at Wissembourg might have been higher since five do not reveal the location of the transaction. That is, in only three did he write somewhere other than Wissembourg. However, these three transactions, his activity on behalf of the Ratbald-Wicbalds and his serving as notary to Count Baugulf in the Fulda codices indicate that he worked independently of the monastery too.

[126] *TW*, pp. 136–7. [127] *TW* 54, 73, 90, 93, 95; cf. p. 137.

[128] H. Butzmann, 'Die Weißenburger Handschriften: Einleitung zum Katalog', in H. Butzmann, *Kleine Schriften: Festgabe zum 70.* Geburtstag, ed. Wolfgang Milde (Graz, 1973), 48–103, esp. 82–8.

[129] Of the ninety-four documents dated to this period, seventy-two were drafted by the three, and all but one of the seventy-two were conducted at the monastery (*TW*, pp. 546–55). On Adalland, Hildibodo and Wolfhart, see *TW*, 138–41, 142–4, 145–6.

[130] Cf. *TW*, pp. 540–57.

compilations. The oldest sections of the high medieval *Liber possessionum*, which convey aggregate figures of manorial holdings in the mid-Rhine region, were drawn up in the ninth century, perhaps in the 840s.[131] The *Brevium exempla*, a royal capitulary that dates to between 810 and 817 and advised monasteries on the organization of their records, issued as examples lists of those who held *precariae* and benefices in the Wormsgau from Wissembourg, an indication that the monastery had begun to formalize its record-keeping habits at least by the early ninth century.[132]

If charter production had come under Wissembourg's administration by the late eighth century, this is not to say that the monastery's role remained unchanged, or that all notarial activity had been monopolized by monastic scribes. After Wolfhart's tenure ended in 811, subsequent ninth-century transactions were more likely to be conducted away from Wissembourg at particular villages. Of the dozen charters drawn up down to 830 by Guntbert, the chief monastic scribe after Wolfhart, only five were conducted at Wissembourg.[133] And this seems not to have been a phenomenon particular to Guntbert: of the thirty-six transactions between 811 and 864, fewer than half (fifteen) are known to have been made at Wissembourg itself, a striking change from the last quarter of the eighth century.[134]

Indeed, a separate, albeit subordinate, line of notaries seems to have persisted for a time in the Saargau and the Saulnois. As we have seen, this trans-Vosges region was serviced in the late Merovingian period by a number of notaries, the most prominent of whom appear to have arisen from, or to have written for, the Rodoin and Wolfoald-Gundoin groups. Moreover, by contrast with transactions of property in Alsace, which were conducted almost always at Wissembourg even in the late Merovingian period,[135] those involving property in southern Lotharingia were just as likely to be conducted in local villages.[136] The Saargau's distinctiveness in this respect persisted into the Carolingian period. In 763 and 789, a certain *cancellarius* Lantfrid and a certain *emanuensis* Chrodoin, respectively, wrote up transactions in the Saargau.[137] In the latter case, Chrodoin redrafted a donation – originally made by a certain

[131] *Liber possessionum Wizenburgensis*, ed. C. Dette (Mainz, 1987); cf. A. Doll, 'Die Possessiones Wizenburgenses und ihre Neuedition', *Archiv für mittelrheinische Kirchengeschichte*, 41 (1989), 437–63, and M. Gockel, 'Kritische Bemerkungen zu einer Neuausgabe des Liber possessionum Wizenburgensis', *Hessisches Jahrbuch für Landesgeschichte*, 39 (1989), 353–80.

[132] MGH Capit. 1, no. 128.

[133] Gundbert: *TW*, pp. 147–9. [134] Cf. *TW*, pp. 557–63.

[135] The exceptions were Etichonid transactions, several of which were conducted at Strasbourg, an important centre of Etichonid lordship, *TW* 10–11, and 35/162.

[136] Cf. *TW*, pp. 629–33. [137] *TW* 263, 259/260.

Gunthart at Wissembourg and drawn up by *cancellarius* Adalland – when a certain Albrich wanted to join the donation. The fact that Chrodoin identified himself as an *emanuensis*, and that the transaction was made at Rieding near Saarbourg rather than at the monastery, strongly suggests that the joint transaction was drawn up, perhaps at Albrich's insistence, by a local notary. When we consider further that Lantfrid and Chrodoin bear names typical of those belonging to known members of the Rodoin group, which itself produced the earlier prolific lay notary Chrodoin, it appears that notaries continued to arise from within these patron groups throughout the eighth century.

Although there is no evidence that Rodoin notaries persisted into the ninth century, independent notaries did continue to operate exclusively in the Saargau, albeit under the general auspices of the monastery. Foremost among them was a certain John, who first appears in a charter of 807 as an *emanuensis* in the Saargau, and who proceeded to write up another six transactions down to 847.[138] Yet, the elaboration of the monastic notarial administration was not without consequences even here. In 846, on behalf of the monastic *cancellarius* Baldram ('ad vicem Baltramni cancellarii'), John wrote up three transactions made at Wissembourg by individuals of the Rodoin group.[139] John's responsibilities as a local notary were depicted as if they had been assigned to him by Wissembourg's *cancellarius*.

The phenomenon of monastic aggrandizement detectable at Wissembourg exhibited contrasting if complementary patterns elsewhere. The donation patterns at Fulda reveal that the monastery was supported first by patron groups in the better-developed mid-Rhine regions around Mainz and Worms, and then subsequently by patrons residing nearer to the monastery in the Grapfeld and the Saale basin as these regions were harnessed more thoroughly to Frankish rule during and after the Carolingian subjugation of Saxony.[140] As we have seen, most of the earliest charters were produced by non-monastic notaries operating within the dioceses of Strasbourg, Worms and especially Mainz. As at Wissembourg, hardly any of these early notaries were formally attached to Fulda. This is detectable in their fields of activity, which were limited to transactions performed mostly in the episcopal cities (e.g. *actum Mogontiae civitatis publice*) or at villages within the diocesan boundaries, but never

[138] *TW* 201, 230, 242, 268–71. [139] *TW* 268–71; cf. p. 147.

[140] For the period before 770, we have twenty charters from the mid-Rhine region beginning in 751 (*UF* 11, 18, 22–31, 33, 37, 40–2, 44, 48–9), a mere two from the Grapfeld beginning in 760 (*UF* 32, 39), and none from the Saalegau; cf. Stengel, 'Über die karlingischen Cartulare', 181–4.

at Fulda.[141] When they do invoke their professional status, they refer to themselves as *emanuenses*, and they often assert that that they had been asked (*rogitus*) to write. Half of these ten notaries identified themselves as priests; the other half by all appearances were laymen.[142] This figure, however, underplays the significance of the lay notaries, because the five self-identified priests authored just six of the seventy-four charters produced by the group of non-monastic notaries. To look at it another way, of the surviving fifty-six charters produced during the monastery's first four decades of existence down to 784, forty-one were drawn up by non-monastic scribes, thirty-four of which were produced by four notaries working out of Mainz, only one of whom was a priest, and he produced just one charter.[143] The most prolific of these was the *emanuensis*

141 On the non-monastic notaries, see Stengel, *UF*, pp. liii–lix, and Innes, *State and Society*, 114–17. There were ten non-monastic notaries; I have reproduced in parentheses their fields of activity, the numbers of charters they authored and their date(s) of service, after which I have listed the charters attributable to them. Anonymously composed charters believed on stylistic grounds to have been written by the notary are in [brackets]: Erlefrid, priest and *emanuensis*, Mainz, one, a. 751 (*UF* 11); Wolfram, *emanuensis*, Mainz, twenty-two, aa. 752–74 (*UF* 18, 22–4, 26, 28–33, 37, 40, 41, 44, 52, 54–5, 59, 61, 63, [64], 66); Winibald, Mainz, two, aa. 754–68 (*UF* 48–9); Weliman, Mainz, sixteen, aa. 775–88 (*UF* [70], 71–2, 76, 80–2, 87–8, 160–2, 177, [178], 179, [180]); Hiltibald, Mainz, fifteen, aa. 790–9 (*UF* 195–6, 231, 245, 248–53, 255–7, 260); Theotrich, *emanuensis*, Mainz, seven, aa. 800–15 (*UF* 263, 266–7, 270, 283–5); Hiaebo, priest and *emanuensis*, Worms, two, aa. 765–70 (*UF* 42, 50); Notbald, priest, Lobdengau/Worms, one, a. 763 (*UF* 38); Geroin, priest, Speyer, one, aa. 757–84 (*UF* 53); Erhard, southern Alsace/Basel, one, a. 785 (*UF* 163); Asaph, northern Alsace/Strasbourg, five, aa. 778–805 (*UF* 84, [176], 187, 254, 281); Uodalrich, priest, Alsace/Basel, one, a. 793 (*UF* 197); Sadrebald, Grabfeld, one, a. 762×3 (*UF* 39). Note: I have worked up here only the charters down to 802, where Stengel's edition ends. Asaph authored four more Alsatian charters after 802 (*CDF* 178–9, 208, 225); Theotrich authored six more in the region of Mainz (*CDF* 218, 222, 224, 244, 246, 270). The dates for Geroin's activity have been elaborated on the basis of his more extensive work at Wissembourg.

142 If any of the other five were priests, they neglected to say so, despite numerous opportunities. The Mainz scribe Hiltibald, for example, authored fifteen charters, served as witness in seven others, and was referred to as a neighbour by another donor, for a total of twenty-three chances to announce any clerical status (*UF*, p. lv).

143 Erlefrid, Wolfram, Winibald, Weliman; above, n. 141. The location of their transactions, and those of many other notaries, monastic or non-monastic, poses some problems because many of the charters in the Fulda codex do not reveal where the transaction had been performed. With respect to the non-monastic notaries, for example, Erlefrid's and Wolfram's activity in Mainz is well attested: the former's one, and eight of the latter's twenty-three, were done at Mainz. None of Wolfram's other fifteen charters divulge a place of transaction, but in the absence of any contrary information, we assume Mainz. None of Weliman's charters reveal a place of transaction, but his style is virtually identical to Wolfram's, he took a pen in 775 only after Wolfram's failed in 774, and a charter he drew up for the monastery at Honau was done at Mainz (Bruckner, *Regesta Alsatiae*, no. 275). Most of Theotrich's charters lack a place of transaction, but several of his later charters were transacted either at Mainz or in places nearby (*CDF* 218, 222, 224, 246). None of Hiltifrid's charters mentions a place of

Wolfram, who authored twenty-three charters between 752 and 774, and single-handedly was responsible for fourteen of the first seventeen surviving charters written up during the monastery's first two decades.[144] Fulda's earliest charters were generated overwhelmingly by a lay notariate based at Mainz.

Fulda itself became a centre for transactions and document production only after 775: property donated in 776 by a certain Ruduch signals the first recorded transaction made at Fulda (*actum in monasterio Fulda*).[145] This charter was written up by the priest and monk Asger (776–96), who is the first named monastic scribe to appear among the Fulda charters, as well as the most prolific of the monastery's late eighth-century scribes, having drafted charters for thirty-one transactions, and probably ten others that lack a notarial subscription.[146] The Fulda codices do convey six earlier charters written in a similar, monastic style, which were composed between 770 and 775, but these do not divulge the name of the notary and only one identifies the place of transaction.[147] These would appear to be the work of a priest named Rihelm, whose lone attested charter bears a similar construction, but his relationship to Fulda is unknown, and the one of the six unsigned charters that does mention the location of transaction purports to have been done at Mainz, not Fulda.[148]

Monastic notaries gained the upper hand among Fulda's charters only after 785 when Asger became most productive.[149] Of the 110 charters transacted between 785 and 802, seventy-four were put out by eight monastic scribes.[150] Fulda now became the major centre of activity: forty-six transactions were carried out there, thus overtaking Mainz as the

transaction, but again his style mimics that of the other Mainz notaries, and both he and Theotrich appear as witnesses for people donating property in the region around Mainz. Thus, all available evidence points without contradiction to Mainz as the field of activity for these scribes; or, to put it another way, not a scrap of positive evidence places them anywhere else. See *UF*, pp. lv–lvi.

144 Above, n. 141. 145 *UF* 75.

146 Cf. *UF*, pp. lx–lxiii. 147 *UF* 51, 56–8, 65, 69. 148 *UF* 86; cf. p. lx.

149 Asger put out just three charters before 785 (*UF* 75, 85, 144), and thirty-eight afterwards (*UF* 156, [167], 172, [181], 182–4, 186, 188, 190, 192, 200–10, [211], 212–13, [214], 215–18, [224–7], 229, 241–3). Charters in brackets refer to those lacking a notary but believed on stylistic grounds to have been drafted by Asger.

150 In addition to Asger (see previous note), these were Abraham, a. 785 (*UF* 157–8); Einhart, aa. 788–96 (*UF* 175, 189, 191, [219–20, 232–3], 234–5, 240); Hracholf, aa. 795–812 (*UF* [230, 233, 236–9, 244, 261, 265b, 269b], 275, [276–7], 279, [280, 282, 526–8]); Engilger, a. 798 (*UF* 258); Reccheo, aa. 800–19 (*UF* 264); Ramuolt, aa. 800–1 (*UF* 269, 278); and one anonymous notary (*UF* 259). Bracketed charters refer to those lacking a notary but believed on stylistic grounds to have been drafted by known notaries. On the monastic notaries, see *UF*, pp. lx–lxi.

most frequently mentioned location of transaction.[151] This business in turn necessitated a centre for the production of charters at the monastery. It perhaps is significant then that this period yields the first explicit statement that a transaction – the donation of a certain Gundacar in 796 – had been written up in the monastery: 'scripta haec [k]arta traditionis in monasterio Fulda'.[152]

The bulk of the work carried out by Fulda's notaries, however, was dependent upon transactions involving property east of the Rhine. If we single out the books of the cartulary devoted to transactions in the mid-Rhine region and Alsace, and examine their contents down to 802, we discover that non-monastic notaries, most of whom as we have seen operated out of Mainz, accounted for seventy-five transactions, and Fulda's notaries for just twenty-seven.[153] When Fulda's notaries did handle transactions of mid-Rhine properties, they did so overwhelming at Fulda, rather than at locations along the mid Rhine.[154] Conversely, the non-monastic notaries never appeared at Fulda, but always held forth in locations along the mid Rhine, mostly around Mainz.[155]

Now, if we examine the books of the cartulary dedicated to charters in Grapfeld and Saalegau, fifty-six of the fifty-eight charters down to 802 were drawn up by Fulda's notaries.[156] That is, just two transactions were drafted by non-monastic notaries in the right-Rhine regions. One of these was done by the aforementioned Wolfram, though he appears to have handled this donation of Grapfeld property at Mainz;[157] the other

[151] Those at Fulda were uniformly done by monastic scribes (*UF* 156–8, 172, 174–5, 181–4, 189–91, 200–4, 206–10, 212–13, 215–20, 230, 234–8, 240, 261, 265b, 269b, 276–7, 279–80, 282). Twenty-nine appear to have been done at Mainz; all but one, which was done by the monastic scribe Asger (*UF* 167), were drafted by three non-monastic notaries of the Mainz region, Weliman, Hiltigar and Theotrich (*UF* 161–2, 177–80, 185, 195–6, 231, 245, 248–53, 255–7, 260, 263, 266–7, 270, 283–5). None of these mentions the place of transaction; however, on the probable location of these transactions at Mainz or nearby, see above, n. 143.

[152] *UF* 230.

[153] These books correspond to the extant ninth-century portion of the cartulary. The non-monastic notaries were responsible for *UF* 11, 18, 22–4, 26, 28–31, 33, 37–8, 40–2, 44, 48–50, 52–5, 59–61, 63–4, 66, 70–2, 76, 80–2, 84, 87–9, 160–3, 177–80, 185, 187, 195–7, 231, 245, 248–57, 260, 263, 266–7, 270, 281, 283–5; and Fulda's notaries for *UF* 58, 69, 86, 89, 157–8, 167, 182, 184, 190–1, 210, 213, 215–20, 236–7, 259, 261, 268, 277–9.

[154] Mainz: *UF* 69, 167. Fulda: *UF* 157–8, 182, 184, 190–1, 210, 213, 215–20, 236–7, 261, 277, 279. No place of transaction is mentioned for *UF* 58, 86, 89, 259, 268, 278.

[155] See above, nn. 143, 151.

[156] These books correspond to the portions of the cartulary published by Pistorius in 1607. Fulda's notaries drafted *UF* 51, 56, 65, 75, 85, 156, 172, 175, 181, 183, 186, 188–9, 192, 200–9, 211–12, 224–7, 229–30, 232–5, 238–44, 258, 264, 265b, 269b, 275–6, 280, 282, 286–7, 526–8.

[157] *UF* 32. On Mainz as the probable locus of transaction, see above, n. 143.

by a certain Sadrebald *in villa publicus* Geldersheim, the centre of a royal estate in the Grapfeld, who was presumably a notary attached to the royals.[158]

This geographical bipolarity strongly suggests that the growth in Fulda's chancery was stimulated in large part by efforts to organize the underdeveloped and unruly lands east of the Rhine that, by contrast with the mid-Rhine region, required the importation of a documentary tradition, a tradition which would have to be supplied by the monastery itself. Yet these exertions had consequences for the development of Fulda's institutional consciousness as it continued to deal in mid-Rhine properties. If we compare the transactions undertaken in this region during the period before 785 to those undertaken between 785 and 802, we find that the monastery gradually began to assign its own notaries to donations of mid-Rhine properties, instead of relying so heavily on the Mainz notariate. Whereas before 785, monastic notaries accounted for just four out of forty-four mid-Rhine transactions,[159] between 785 and 802 they handled twenty-three out of fifty-eight.[160] Although the Mainz notariat remained a vibrant presence, and would continue to be so beyond 802,[161] an ever greater proportion of business gradually was taken up at Fulda by its own notaries. Thus, as at Wissembourg, we can detect patterns that testify to the elaboration of a distinctive and autonomous monastic archival consciousness in the late eighth century.

At first glance, the practices of the church of Freising appear to contrast sharply with those at Fulda and Wissembourg. One does not observe at Freising a transition from lay and diocesan notaries to a reliance on monks. From the earliest preserved charters, priests dominated the notarial culture of Bavaria and represent a significant proportion of the donors as well. This might be held up as evidence that the written word in Bavaria had been the exclusive preserve of the clergy. While these priests necessarily would have been canonically subordinate to the bishops of Freising, it is doubtful that they operated on behalf of the diocesan administration per se. Although Theodor Bitterauf, who edited Freising's charters, assumed

158 *UF* 39. On Geldersheim, see Weidinger, *Wirtschaftsstruktur*, 147.

159 *UF* 11, 18, 22, 23, 24, 26, 28–31, 33, 37, 38, 40–2, 44, 48–50, 52–5, *58*, 59–61, 63–4, 66, *69*, 70–2, 76, 80–2, 84, *86*, 87–8, *89*. Those undertaken by monastic notaries are in *italics*.

160 In the portions of the cartulary dedicated to the mid-Rhine region, the monastic notaries were responsible for these transactions made between 785 and 802: *UF* 157–8, 167, 182, 184, 190–1, 210, 213, 215–20, 236–7, 259, 261, 268, 277–9. The non-monastic notaries were responsible for *UF* 160–3, 177–80, 185, 187, 195–7, 231, 245, 248–57, 260, 263, 266–7, 270, 281, 283–5.

161 The Mainz notary Theotrich, for example, remained a prominent notary until 815 (*CDF* 218, 222, 224, 244, 246, 270).

that the earliest notaries were tied closely to Freising,[162] their behaviour points to a more subtle relationship between Freising, its patrons and the clerical writers.

The two earliest charters preserved in the Freising cartulary were composed in 744 and 748 by the priest Benignus, who appears to have operated as a free notary of sorts for the donors.[163] He tells us in the charter of a certain Moatbert that the donor 'asked this donation to be done', with 'his wife Totana consenting and affirming', and that he wrote 'with Duke Otilo confirming'. In the second, Benignus claims that he 'wrote, having been asked and sought out', presumably by the donor, Amilo, 'who asked this *traditio* to be done', though 'after this duke Tassilo confirmed this *epistula* with his own hand'. Arbeo, the future bishop of Freising, behaved similarly. He was 'asked and sought for' four times between 754 and 757, and in one of those, his notarial statement was followed by Duke Tassilo's confirmation of 'this *epistula*'.[164] Two years later in 759, Arbeo claims to have written at the 'command of the glorious duke'.[165] Who 'asked and sought for' his expertise is not always spelled out, but in yet another charter, which was transacted in 769 after he had become bishop, Arbeo reveals that he 'commanded this charter to be made from the petition' of the donor.[166] Arbeo's drafting of the donation of a certain Haholt in 758 underscores the joint agency of bishop and donors behind the production of Freising's charters: 'Arbeo priest wrote this charter at the command of Bishop Joseph and at the request of the donors Haholt and his son Arno.'[167]

The foregoing examples illustrate that early on the Bavarian dukes frequently were integral to the documentation of property transactions, sometimes literally so. Duke Tassilo strongly implies that he wrote and signed one of his own charters ('ego Tassilo propria manu mea scripsi et confirmavi'), and possibly a second.[168] It was more usual for the duke to appear in the document to bolster the transaction with his confirmation, in one case apparently by lending his own scribe. Sometime between 769 and 777, the priest Fater ostentatiously presented himself as a ducal scribe, 'the *capellanus* of lord Tassilo duke of the Bavarians', in the donation charter of a certain Rihhart. 'Having been asked by the

162 *TF*, pp. xxxviii–xxxix. 163 *TF* 1–2. 164 *TF* 7–10.
165 *TF* 14. 166 *TF* 31. 167 *TF* 11.
168 *TF* 35. See also *TF* 3: 'Imprimis Tassilo propria manu signum fecit'. Although neither charter bears any other indication of a notary, Bitterauf asserts that Tassilo did not write these charters, that the duke's statements mean only that he affirmed them. This might be the case for *TF* 3, but compare Tassilo's statement in *TF* 35 ('ego Tassilo propria manu mea scripsi et confirmavi'), with Alprich's, whom Bitterauf classifies as a Freising notary (*TF*, p. xxxix), in *TF* 6: '*Ego* indignus presbiter rogatus et petitus hanc donationem *scripsi manu mea*' (emphasis mine).

priest Isanhart and the layman Rihhart, he wrote this donation, so that it might remain stable and unshakable', a transaction that had been 'done in the home of St Pancratius'; that is, in the local church in the village of Steinhart.[169] According to the text of the charter, Rihhart gave the properties for the support of the church, so it might be that the priest Isanhart was his brother – as the last element of their names, *-hart*, hints – and possibly the pastor of St Pancratius. In any event, Rihhart's use of Fater as scribe signals his closeness to Duke Tassilo. On the other hand, Fater appears elsewhere among the retinue of the bishops of Freising,[170] thus underscoring the ways in which the dukes, the bishops and the patrons all might appeal to the services of clerics, whose roles could be redefined as the circumstances warranted. Indeed, the deployment of notaries could be startlingly *ad hoc*, as in the episode of a certain David, who made a donation sometime between 758 and 763 to a church in the Bavarian village of Puch. A priestly witness, Reginperht, was pressed into service as scribe, ostensibly because he was available and could write: 'Ego Reginperht rogatus fui ad scribendun. Non scripsi quomodo volui, sed sicut potui.'[171]

Other priestly notaries arose from the surrounding kin groups, presumably pastored local churches, and wrote up their own donations. The priest Willahelm, who was part of a nexus of groups tied to one another through the church of St Zeno at Isen, made a donation in 769 to St Zeno's and then wrote up the charter.[172] Sometime between 769 and 776, the brothers Alprich and the deacon Ascrich made a joint donation that was to pass to Freising's control only upon the deaths of Alprich; Ascrich; their two sisters, Marchraat and Uualtraat; and their three *nepotes*, Amiloni, Uuisurihhi and Angilrata. The transaction was then written up by Ascrich himself, who dated the charter not to the year of the ruler, but to the eternal reign of 'our Lord Jesus Christ'.[173] Similarly, the priest Oadalger made a donation in 770 of property inherited from his father Cello, a gift made, as with so many of the early charters of Freising, with the duke's consent. Oadalger drafted the charter and affirmed the witnesses ('ego Oadalger donator scripsi et subscripsi propria manu et testes firmavit'), though by all appearances a second draft was composed by his father Cello ('ego Cello manu propria scripsi et

[169] *TF* 37. [170] *TF* 7, 14a. [171] *TF* 12.

[172] *TF* 33. Willahelm stood as witness at the church of St Zeno when Haholt consecrated his son Arn, the future Carolingian *missus* and archbishop of Salzburg, to the church of Freising (*TF* 11). Willahelm's own donation to St Zeno's was witnessed by the priest Alpolt, who was among the donors to St Zeno's and a scribe for a donation to Freising transacted in the church of St Zeno (*TF* 4, 32).

[173] *TF* 36.

ipse tradidi').[174] And finally, the priest Uuatto seems to have been in the retinue, not of the bishop, but of a local lord, 'having been commanded by my lord Machelm' to write up his charter in 776.[175] These examples indicate that if the diocese was the probable source of scribal education, a demand for scribal talent arose from within patron groups too.

This more diverse group of notaries began to dwindle beginning in the 770s during Arbeo's episcopacy (764–83). The notaries henceforth almost always appear to be closely tied either to Freising, or its suffragan monastery, Schlehdorf.[176] This change can also be detected in notarial formulas now deployed to underscore episcopal agency. The notaries' claims that they had been 'asked and sought' ('rogatus et petitus') went extinct at the end of Bishop Joseph's tenure in 763.[177] That is, the usage was phased out by Joseph's successor, Arbeo. Moreover, although in charters up to 770 it was more common for the patrons to claim that they had 'asked this [charter of] donation to be made' ('hanc donationem/traditionem fieri rogavit'), than for the notaries to claim that the bishops had ordered them to write, nearly all references to patron requests vanish after 776.[178] Conversely, only after 772 – that is, at roughly the same time – do notaries consistently claim that they wrote at the command (*jussus*) or 'from the mouth' (*ex ore*) of the bishop.[179] Whether this development means that patrons were less assertive is impossible to say, though unlikely. The 'charter' of a certain Sigifried and his son Erchanfrid, for example, was 'ordered to be done' in 769 by Arbeo, but in response to the 'petition of the aforesaid' donor, an indication that donor agency probably persisted beneath the formulas.[180] But even this episode places the accent on the authority of the bishop, who is the recipient of a plea, after which he then orders the notary to act, thus underscoring the

174 *TF* 39. 175 *TF* 74. 176 Cf. *TF*, pp. xxxix–xl.

177 Or similar formulations, such as *rogitus* and *rogatione*. Patron rogation appears in *TF* 2, 6–8, 9b, 10–12, 19.

178 In the forty charters up to 770, patron requests appear in twelve transactions (*TF* 1–2, 6, 11–12, 13b, 15, 17, 25, 28, 30, 37), and episcopal commands in eight cases (*TF* 11, 19, 21, 23, 24c, 31–2, 38). A ninth episode occurs in *TF* 16; but see the following note.

179 The first of these occurred in 763 towards the end of Joseph's abbacy (748–64): *TF* 21. A second appeared in 760 (*TF* 16), but the record of this transaction is a *breve commemoratorii* and thus would appear to have been composed sometime later. In a third case, Joseph commanded a charter to be made, but at the request of the donor Haholt and his son Arn in 758 (*TF* 11). The phenomenon of episcopal command is much more indicative of charters transacted during Arbeo's tenure (764–83), but especially after 772. Beginning with *TF* 42 (a. 772), the episcopal command appears at a rate of every other transaction. The incidence is probably greater because many of the charters lacking the episcopal command were copied into the cartulary without their witness lists, immediately after which is where the episcopal command often appears.

180 *TF* 31.

transformation of the church of Freising's institutional consciousness in the late eighth century.

The examples of Wissembourg, Fulda and Freising illuminate lines of evidence detectable elsewhere and which also intersect in the late eighth and early ninth centuries. Some of the earliest attempts to book charters are traceable to the late eighth century in Bavaria and Rhaetia.[181] The pattern is also evident at St Gall where we do not encounter the organization of charters into codices, but whose records nonetheless reveal an initiative beginning around 770 to organize charters with dorsal notations and by 840 to group them by district.[182] The materials we have before us, therefore, are not accidents, documents that have arbitrarily survived the ravages of time and that we are somehow fortunate to have, but rather records present to us because of profound archival innovations that saw to their preservation.

Frankish cartularies weave a vivid tapestry of lay and ecclesiastical interests. They testify both to the production of charters for individuals, local churches and larger ecclesiastical institutions, and to the development of a radical archival consciousness within monasteries during the Carolingian era that ensured their preservation. If the charters bear witness to the eventual dominance of document production and preservation by monasteries beginning in the late eighth century, they also permit a tantalizing glimpse into the transitional era between the post-Roman period and the Carolingian period when multiple centres of notaries – local, court, diocesan and monastic – operated.

The observation that monasteries became crucial for the preservation of records is to be distinguished from the documentation that once existed beyond the cloister. Vestiges of that evidence in the cartularies demonstrate the movement of documents between patrons, village churches and monasteries, and between laypeople themselves, the incidence of whose sales and copies of transactions remained fairly uniform throughout the early medieval period. Moreover, courts and episcopal authorities certainly continued to generate documentation. The difference was the memorial ethos which compelled monks to preserve charters as memorial records *forever*, and which, more broadly, went hand in hand with the construction of the Carolingian political order.

This pivotal development in European history might explain the phenomenon of Cluny and its unmatched archive. If monasteries in the

[181] Geary, *Phantoms*, 88; P. Erhart and J. Kleindinst, *Urkundenlandschaft Rätien* (Vienna, 2004), 21–30.

[182] Above, Chapter 7, and Peter Erhart, '*Carta ista amalfitana est et nescitur legere*: The Charters of Cava dei Tirreni and St Gall and Their Evidence for Early Medieval Archival Practice', *Gazette du livre médiéval*, 50 (2007), 27–39.

Carolingian period had difficulty reconstructing their earliest holdings, the monastery of Cluny had little trouble at all. Looking back to the foundation in 910 from the eleventh century when the Cluniacs began to assemble their cartularies, the monks easily located founding documents and could assemble a dense record of donations from the foundation's first century, a stark contrast with, say, Fulda, Freising and Wissembourg.[183] Moreover, because monasteries had by then long become crucial to the perpetuation of aristocratic power, Cluny found itself the repository of a trove of sales between laypersons that had been transacted in the century before its founding.[184] The difference was that Cluny was founded at a time when the parameters of monastic records management had become firmly entrenched so that Cluny in effect was born with a memorial consciousness.

Perhaps it should not be a surprise then that the first extant independent lay record in the European tradition, the *Codex Falkensteinensis*,[185] emerged in the twelfth century after the Church reforms that distinguished clerical from lay authority, and bears witness not to a qualitatively distinct lay method for organizing property somehow submerged for centuries beneath an alien clerical culture. Rather, it was organized after the manner of a monastic cartulary, which had established the paradigm not merely for an enduring, albeit ever-evolving form of record-keeping, but also for the memorializing of property rights within an institutionalized family consciousness.

[183] See S. Barret, *La mémoire et l'écrit: L'abbaye de Cluny et ses archives (Xe–XVIIIe siècle)* (Münster, 2004), 27–144.

[184] See below, Chapter 11.

[185] E. Noichl, *Codex Falkensteinensis: Die Rechtsaufzeichnungen der Grafen von Falkenstein* (Munich, 1978); cf. J. Freed, *The Counts of Falkenstein: Noble Self-Consciousness in Twelfth-Century Germany* (Philadelphia, 1984).

# 9 The laity, the clergy, the scribes and their archives: the documentary record of eighth- and ninth-century Italy

*Marios Costambeys*

*Ecclesiastical institutions dominate the transmission of documents in the Lombard and Carolingian kingdoms of northern and central Italy, just as in the rest of the post-Roman West. While the Italian evidence shows straightforwardly that it was increasingly professional lay charter scribes who produced documents, analysis of surviving collections also uncovers other laypeople involved in the preservation of documents. Lay dossiers ended up in the hands of churches and monasteries in various ways, and not only because of those institutions' desire to reinforce their property claims; where such a desire was the object of preserving documents, other means were also available, such as the confirmation of property rights by a superior authority, or the validation of documents – and the production of new documents – by a law court. The Italian evidence shows how those who used charters, in a shifting legal landscape in which rights were never fixed or secure, provoked the development of these and other ways of managing documents on the part of both ecclesiastical and secular institutions.*

Every document that survives to us from the Lombard and Carolingian kingdoms of Italy has spent most of its life in a church or monastery.[1] This simple fact certainly sets apart those institutions from other entities, such as lay families, in one respect: they proved more successful at preserving documents through eras subsequent to when those documents were written. Whether they were also distinctive institutions in that initial, eighth- and ninth-century period is a more complicated question. The practical

[1] Additional abbreviations: *CDA*: *Codex diplomaticus Amiatinus: Urkundenbuch der Abtei S. Salvatore am Montamiata von den Anfängen bis zum Regierungsantritt Papst Innozenz III. (736–1198)*, ed. W. Kurze, 4 vols. (Tübingen, 1974–82); *CDV*: *Codice diplomatico veronese*, ed. V. Fainelli, 2 vols. (Venice, 1940–63); *CF*: *Il Chronicon Farfense di Gregorio di Catino*, ed. U. Balzani, 2 vols. (Rome, 1903); Manaresi: *I placiti del Regnum Italiae*, ed. C. Manaresi, 3 vols. (Rome, 1955–60).

existence of the Church as a single institution in Lombard and Carolingian Italy can very easily be questioned,[2] but the clergy continued to be what they had been for some time: an identifiable group with their own status, privileges and preoccupations. It was not simply the unique ability of consecrated priests to bring salvation closer through communion that automatically imbued them with this common charisma: every clerical grade – including monks – is generally held to have enjoyed the same, discrete, cachet.[3] The ninth century saw strenuous efforts to reinforce the lay–clerical distinction,[4] and while these may indicate contradictory trends – either that the barrier between the two was being eroded, or that its basic permeability was increasingly being recognized – they certainly affected the historical record that survives to us. As some communities of clerics – individual ecclesiastical institutions such as some monasteries – developed more robustly distinct characters, and clerical identities became increasingly solid, so improved both their capacity to preserve written records and their tendency to preserve those that best affirmed their identity. This is most evident in the beginnings in the ninth century of the 'cartulary tradition', but it also greatly affected archives of originals: ultimately, a significant role of both was that of repository of the institution's proofs of title.[5] In short, northern and central Italy in the eighth and ninth centuries saw decisive developments in the production and preservation of documents, developments that can best be understood by focusing on the lay–clerical divide.

In the same way that most manuscript codices have ecclesiastical provenances, single-sheet documents also survive because they were ultimately kept by ecclesiastical institutions. This is as true for Italy as for anywhere else in western Europe, as is clear from a brief perusal of the provenances in a printed collection such as the *Codice diplomatico longobardo*.[6] Just

2 E.g. M. de Jong, 'Charlemagne's Church', in J. Story (ed.), *Charlemagne: Empire and Society* (Manchester, 2005), 103–35, esp. 106.

3 Explicit treatment of clerical difference: R. Reynolds, 'The Organisation, Law and Liturgy of the Western Church, 700–900', in R. McKitterick (ed.), *New Cambridge Medieval History, II, c.700–c.900* (Cambridge, 1995), 589–622, at 605–13.

4 Most obviously evident in the Pseudo-Isidorian forgeries: see now the comprehensive texts and studies at www.pseudoisidor.mgh.de. See also K. Zechiel-Eckes, 'Pseudoisidorische Dekretalen', in *Lexikon der Kirchengeschichte*, 2 vols. (Freiburg, 2001), II, 1345–6, which modifies the classic survey of H. Fuhrmann, *Einfluss und Verbreitung der pseudoisidorischen Fälschungen*, 3 vols. (Munich, 1972–4). For succinct treatments uninformed by the most recent research, see H. Fuhrmann and D. Jasper, *Papal Letters in the Early Middle Ages* (Washington, DC, 2001), 135–95, and Reynolds, 'The Organisation, Law and Liturgy', 616–17.

5 Proof of title was of course not the only reason for the preservation or copying of charters: Geary, *Phantoms*, 81–114.

6 *CDL* I and II for non-royal documents from the Lombard kingdom proper down to 774; *CDL* III for royal diplomas to 774; *CDL* IV/1 for diplomas of the dukes of Spoleto to

as much as Francia, Italy exhibits a growing clerical self-consciousness, including a concern to shape institutional memory that is evident, for instance, in the canon law collection known as the *Collectio Anselmo dedicata*, compiled (if that is the right word) in Milan in 882×96, but that also affected archival practices.[7] Italian medievalists have not always been alive to the significance of this essential fact. Thus Armando Petrucci, while acknowledging the competence of numbers of laymen in subscribing charters in their own hand (which he equated with 'literacy'),[8] still saw literacy dominated by the clerical subscribers who are a distinct majority in those charters he examined, without recognizing that this predominance may be due to the charters' subject matter and places of preservation.[9] It is hardly surprising, to take the most egregious example, that the witness lists of charters concerning the cathedral of Lucca should be dominated by its clergy,[10] and this impression is confirmed if we look at subscriptions to the eighteen 'private' charters in our most easily identifiable 'lay' archive, the Campione dossier discussed below, in which

786×7; *CDL* IV/2 for diplomas of the dukes of Benevento; *CDL* V for private charters from the duchies of Spoleto and Benevento down to 787.

[7] On the *Collectio Anselmo dedicata*, see L. Kéry, *Canonical Collections of the Early Middle Ages (ca. 400–1140): A Bibliographical Guide to the Manuscripts and Literature* (Washington, DC, 1999), 124–8, and K. Zechiel-Eckes, 'Quellenkritische Anmerkungen zur "Collectio Anselmo dedicata"', in W. Hartmann and A. Grabowsky (eds.), *Recht und Gericht in Kirche und Welt um 900* (Oldenburg, 2007), 49–65.

[8] Petrucci's equation of literacy with the ability to sign one's name in this way has of course given way to an appreciation of the diversity of literate capability: for the point in relation specifically to late antique and early medieval Italy, see G. Cavallo, 'Dal segno incompiuto al segno negato: Linee per una ricerca su alfabetismo, produzione e circolazione di cultura scritta in Italia nei primi secoli dell'impero', in A. Bartoli Langeli and A. Petrucci (eds.), *Alfabetismo e cultura scritta nella storia della società italiana: Atti del Seminario tenutosi a Perguia il 29–30 marzo, 1977* (Perugia, 1978), 119–45, at 126–8; in general, McKitterick, *Carolingians*, 271–3.

[9] A. Petrucci, 'Libro, scrittura e scuola', in *La scuola nell'Occidente latino dell'alto medioevo*, Settimane 19 (Spoleto, 1972), 313–37, at 325–6 (trans. as 'Book, Handwriting and School', in A. Petrucci, *Writers and Readers in Medieval Italy*, trans. C. M. Radding [New Haven, CT, 1995], 59–76, at 67–8) examined 180 original charters from the Lombard kingdom dating between 720 and 774, containing 988 subscriptions, of which 326 are autograph (32.7%). Of the 988 subscriptions, 355 (35.9%) include clerical titles; assuming for the moment that all those who could designate themselves as clerics did so, this leaves 633 lay subscriptions. Of the latter, 93 are autograph: 9.4% of the total and 14.7% of the lay subscriptions; of the 355 clerical subscriptions, on the other hand, 233 are autograph: 65.6%, and 23.5% of the total. Of the 326 autograph subscriptions, 71.4% are by clerics, 28.6% by laymen. It is important to remember that the number of subscriptions is not the same as the number of subscribers, since the latter could, and in a few cases demonstrably did, witness more than one charter: see, e.g., P. Supino Martini, 'Le sottoscrizioni testimoniali al documento italiano del secolo VIII: Le carte di Lucca', *Bullettino dell'Istituto storico italiano per il medio evo e archivio muratoriano*, 98 (1992), 87–108.

[10] E.g. (among many) *CDL* I 99 (= *ChLA* XXXI 931).

only eleven of the seventy-one charter witnesses (15.5%, compared with Petrucci's average of 35.9%) give themselves or are given clerical titles (in a collection in which all but five witnesses have some sort of designation, mostly secular epithets like *vir devotus* or *vir honestus*).[11] The latter collection does show, however, that although the ecclesiastical colouring of our survivals exaggerates the absolute number of literate clergymen visible to us, the rate of clerical literacy may still have been somewhat higher than that among laymen: the twenty-eight autograph subscribers in the Campione charters include ten clerics; of the remaining forty-three, subscribing with *signa manus*, only one bears a clerical title. This should not surprise us, of course, given the straightforward requirements on the priesthood and monasticism as occupations, and it bears on the question of lay literacy that I shall consider shortly, but equally it should not detract from our recognition of the distorting effect that the circumstances of preservation exert on the documentary record. Its evidence makes society look more ecclesiastical than it really was.

A striking paradox appears when the clerical monopoly on preservation is set alongside another feature of the Italian documentary record: the growing dominance of laymen over the creation of documents. Increasingly through the ninth century, charter scribes were laymen. This is evident because they, along with the majority of others who set their hands to charters, took care to give themselves some kind of title, and in particular, it seems, to distinguish themselves as clerics when appropriate.[12] This becomes palpable in instances where we can trace promotion through the clerical hierarchy in the self-designations given by issuers and witnesses. Thus we can see Teudo graduate from *archipresbiter* of the see of Rieti to its bishop, or Audo progress from *subdiaconus* to *diaconus* to *archidiaconus* to bishop in Verona.[13] This attention to clerical identity extends to the

[11] A full breakdown is given in A. Bartoli Langeli, 'I documenti', in S. Gasparri and C. La Rocca (eds.), *Carte di famiglia: Strategie, rappresentazione e memoria del gruppo familiare di Totone di Campione (721–877)* (Rome, 2005), 237–64, at 256–61. I take a more optimistic view of the regularity and reliability of indications of clerical status than does N. Giovè, 'In margine al *dossier* di Totone di Campione', in Gasparri and La Rocca (eds.), *Carte di famiglia*, 265–82, at 275.

[12] For scribes' self-designations in the charters to 774, see N. Everett, *Literacy in Lombard Italy* (Cambridge, 2000), 200–1, who finds scribes giving themselves some kind of designation in 175 out of around 260 cases.

[13] Teuto: *CDL* V 3 (= *RF* V 1220, a.739) (*archipresbiter*); *CDL* V 20, 22 and *CDL* IV/I 14 (= *RF* II 34, 37, 46; a.753, 755, 761) (*episcopus*). Audo: *CDV* 131 (a.829: *subdiaconus*); *CDV* 153, 172 (a.839, 849: *diaconus*); *CDV* 197, 201 (a.855, 856: *archidiaconus*); *CDV* 217, 219, 226 (a.860, 860, 862: *episcopus*). Audo's episcopate lasted 860–9: see M. Miller, *The Formation of a Medieval Church: Ecclesiastical Change in Verona, 950–1150* (Ithaca, NY, 1993), 151 with n. 45.

writers of charters.[14] In the Farfa archive, for instance, scribes who were clerics all designated themselves as such, though sometimes alongside the term *notarius*, and variations in these designations are easily explicable by their progress from one grade to another (and/or their monachization).[15] The term *notarius*, unqualified, is the norm for a lay scribe in the Farfa archive, pointing towards the generally less regular use of designations by lay charter scribes.[16] Across northern and central Italy as a whole, there is enormous variety of titles for lay scribes: Costamagna's survey revealed twenty-three different designations.[17] It has nevertheless been generally accepted that in the absence of a qualifying clerical designation such titles *do* refer to *lay*men. The rising incidence of such terms through the course of the ninth century has been seen as the corollary of the widely observed decline of the clerical charter scribe in most parts of Italy in that period.[18]

At Lucca this change has been linked directly to the Frankish takeover: charter scribes who had belonged to the Lombard episcopal clergy gave way, it is suggested, to notaries serving the Frankish counts.[19] But in many parts of Francia itself the task of charter-writing was actually moving in the opposite direction – from secular to ecclesiastical scribes – in precisely this period.[20] In Lucca, meanwhile, the shift was still not complete more than two generations after the conquest, and in any case the association between the city's notaries and the bishop before 774 was unusually close. Comparison with the charters preserved at the abbey of S. Salvatore on Monte Amiata, fortunately all also extant in the original, reveals a gradual and likely quite complex development, in which the

[14] H. Zielinski, *Studien zu den spoletinischen 'Privaturkunden' des 8. Jahrhunderts und ihrer Überlieferung im Regestum farfense* (Tübingen, 1972), 137–41; H. Keller, 'Der Gerichtsort in oberitalienischen und toskanischen Städten', *Quellen und Forschungen aus italienischen Archiven und Bibliotheken*, 49 (1969), 1–72, esp. the table on 13.

[15] E.g. Palumbus in *CDL* V 5 (a.745: *diaconus*), 7 (a.746: *diaconus*), 25 (a.757: *monachus*), 27 (a.757: *presbiter et monachus*); or Theuferius in *CDL* V 52 (a.768: *presbiter notarius*), 63 (a.773, *presbiter notarius*), 75 (a.777: *presbiter*) – here he wrote his own charter offering himself to Farfa – which might explain 81 (a.778: *presbiter et monachus*) and 87 (a.778: *presbiter et monachus*); in the latter, though, he also calls himself *scriptor*. See Zielinski, *Studien*, 130, 135.

[16] Zielinski, *Studien*, 137–41.

[17] G. Costamagna, 'L'altomedioevo', in M. Amelotti and G. Costamagna, *Alle origini del notariato italiano* (Rome, 1975), 147–314, at 157, and, for the Lombard period, Everett, *Literacy in Lombard Italy*, 199–207.

[18] Zielinski, *Studien*, 140–1; Keller, 'Der Gerichtsort', 9–19, 31. Piacenza at least retained some kind of ecclesiastical notariate: F. Bougard, *La justice dans le royaume d'Italie de la fin du VIII^e^ siècle au début du XI^e^ siècle* (Rome, 1995), 69 and n. 11.

[19] A. Mailloux, 'Modalités de constitution du patrimoine épiscopal de Lucques, VIII$^{e}$–X$^{e}$ siècle', in *Les transferts*, 701–23, esp. 710–12.

[20] See above, Chapter 8.

turning point comes around 840. The 166 genuine acts datable from the collection's inception in 736 down to 900 were written by eighty-five scribes. Of these, twenty (23.5%) gave themselves clerical designations. But of the twenty-four scribes active in the period 840×900, only one did so (4.2%).[21] By comparison, three of the fifteen scribes (20%) of the Campione dossier, dating from 721 to 863, were clerics.[22] The laicization of the Italian charter scribe was uneven and drawn out, then, because of a number of factors: the deliberate encouragement of Frankish counts, certainly, but also a more general proliferation and professionalization of legal writing of this kind.

While there is little difference in terms of graphic ability between lay and clerical charter scribes, Petrucci and Romeo identified two basic levels of script among charter subscribers, characterized by competence in the new Italian cursive on the one hand, and in a more basic elementary minuscule on the other.[23] Part of their case was an interpretation of the subscriptions in the Campione dossier, though a recent detailed treatment of the same documents has shown that variations in graphic competence did not neatly follow the lay–clerical distinction.[24] Nevertheless, both studies show conclusively that education in a level of reading and writing necessary to engage in documentary culture was widespread and did not vary in its basics across those parts of Italy from which our evidence survives. Functional literacy in documents observed no obvious lay–clerical division.

The fact that endowments of monasteries could be recorded in quite humble documents – mere scribbled scraps, donating equally paltry pieces of land[25] – has been rightly interpreted as revealing the important social and economic roles of churches and monasteries in Italy, as in Francia.[26] It also incidentally reveals that written documents in general were deeply familiar and often very mundane. Just how familiar and mundane needs underlining. From northern and central Italy (down to and including the modern *regioni* of Lazio and Abruzzo), there survive to us dating from the years between *c.* 680 (when the run of documents

21 The data are recoverable from the lists and tables in *CDA* I, pp. xxiv–xxv, and *CDA* IV, pp. 178–86.

22 Bartoli Langeli, 'I documenti', 239.

23 A. Petrucci and C. Romeo, '*Scriptores in urbibus*': *Alfabetismo e cultura scritta nell'Italia altomedievale* (Bologna, 1992), 23.

24 Petrucci and Romeo, '*Scriptores in urbibus*', 57–63, and see now Giovè, 'In margine al *dossier* di Totone', 272–9.

25 E.g. *CDA* 36.

26 E.g. Mailloux, 'Modalités', and B. H. Rosenwein, 'Property Transfers and the Church, Eighth to Eleventh Centuries', in *Les transferts*, 563–75; see also Costambeys, *Power*.

really begins)[27] and 1000 some 7,500 documents that were not issued by a 'public' authority.[28] Two-thirds of these are single-sheet documents, 90 per cent of them originals, while the other third comes from a handful of monastic cartularies, principally those of Farfa and Casauria. Excluding the latter, plus the smattering of registers and extracts, the figure for survivals is broadly comparable with that for Catalonia.[29] There are two major differences, however: northern and central Italy covers a rather larger area, of course, but it nevertheless also preserves no significant archives of lay public figures to set alongside the comital records of Catalonia. The Italian survivals come from a minimum of fifty-three archives, all of them ecclesiastical. This fact is perhaps itself sufficient to explain why it has often been assumed that lay documents survive only rarely from Italy before the millennium. Moreover, we cannot benefit, as we can north of the Alps, from formula-books that indicate a prevalence of purely 'lay' documentary forms (at least in theory, as Brown argues). The earliest formula-book from north-central Italy, the *Cartularium Langobardicum*, dates from the late eleventh century.[30] But we do have a number of archives that are sufficiently substantial to include a diverse range of material, offering the possibility of discovering some of the documentary practices of laypeople.[31] The largest single repository by far is the archiepiscopal archive in Lucca, which contains over 1,800 pre-1000 documents, nearly all originals. There are also over 900 pre-1000 documents in the Casauria collection, and nearly that number in Farfa's cartularies. The abbey of S. Salvatore on Monte Amiata preserved about 180 pieces (now mostly in the Archivio di Stato in Siena). These mean that central Italy – Tuscany and Spoleto – is by far the best-represented area. Next best is Emilia-Romagna, with about 650 documents extant in Piacenza and about 300 in Ravenna. There are

27 The only original Italian documents dating from before 680 are the Ravenna papyri, edited in Tjäder and in *ChLA*: see the concordance in *ChLA* XXIX, p. 10. The earliest extant charters from Lombard Italy are copies: *CDL* I 4 (Siena vs. Arezzo); *CDL* III 1–3, 5 (Bobbio); 4, 6 (Piacenza vs. Parma).

28 The figure is that of F. Bougard, 'Actes privés et transferts patrimoniaux en Italie centro-septentrionale (VIII$^{e}$–X$^{e}$ siècle)', in *Les transferts*, 539–62, at 539. Definitions here are of course quite difficult, given the multiplicity of powers who could and did claim some sort of 'public' authority in Italy over this long period. So any number must remain approximate.

29 As Bougard points out ('Actes privés et transferts patrimoniaux', 540), this is even more the case if we exclude cartulary copies, regests and the like. For Catalan figures, see Kosto, 'Laymen', 52.

30 Above, Chapter 5; MGH LL 4:595–602. For the date, I follow the convincing arguments noted by Bougard, *La justice*, 308 with n. 4.

31 For what follows, full publication details down to 1995 are given in Bougard, *La justice*, 76–108. The principal change since then is the continuing publication of *ChLA*.

about another 600 from the whole of Lombardy (principally from Milan, with fewer in Brescia, Bergamo and Cremona), and about 200 from the Veneto (mostly from Verona).

## 'Lay' documents and their preservation in Italian archives

We do not have to penetrate far into this material to find abundant traces of lay documentary practices. I adopt here a definition of a 'lay document' as one in which neither party carries an explicit clerical designation. Thus I have not tried to separate documents involving secular officials because, while clerics are generally straightforward to identify, it is not always easy, in early medieval Italy's amorphous and shifting institutional context, to define where the official bureaucracy ended and 'private' lay families began. A similar problem exists with archives. There has been an assumption that where lay documents (as just defined) do exist, they survive because they were of interest to the ecclesiastical institution that absorbed them, with the corollary assumption that the landed property to which they generally relate followed the same trajectory. We shall see below that this can sometimes be demonstrated, but should underline here that the question does always need to be addressed, that we should be wary of drawing conclusions about the extent of the kind of competence with documents that was sufficient to commission, comprehend or preserve them simply from the places where those documents ended up (which in turn tends to have dictated how they are presented to us), and that a single explanation does not cover all instances of lay documents.

The need for complex and properly informed explanation becomes apparent as soon as we start to enumerate the number of documents in our archives that satisfy our basic definition of 'lay' status (both parties being non-clerical). Table 9.1 below shows the incidence of such lay documents in four archives of originals – Lucca, Monte Amiata, Verona and Bergamo – and one cartulary, that of Farfa, between the earliest survivals (*c.* 680) and 850.

The prominent exception of the Farfa cartulary simply emphasizes how important the process of selection was in the formation not just of cartularies but also of the ecclesiastical archives from which they were drawn: a point to which I will return. It should already be clear, though, that some surviving archives include lay documents in sufficient numbers to allow us to draw comparative conclusions. We can point not only to reasons why some lay documents were transmitted through ecclesiastical archives but also to differences in archival practices between the laity and ecclesiastical institutions.

Table 9.1 *Proportions of 'lay' documents in some Italian archives*

| | Non-royal, non-public[a] | Originals | 'Lay' documents | 'Lay' originals | Percentage 'lay' |
|---|---|---|---|---|---|
| Lucca | 625 | 625 | 31 | 31 | 5.0 |
| Monte Amiata | 112 | 111 | 31[b] | 31 | 27.7 |
| Verona | 44 | 24 | 8 | 7[c] | 18.2 |
| Bergamo | 13 | 11 | 5 | 4 | 38.5 |
| Farfa | 298 | 0 | 0 | 0 | 0 |

[a] I.e. not issued by rulers, and not court notices.
[b] One of these (*CDA* 41) includes as one party a *primicerius*, who, following Roman precedent, could have been either clerical or lay.
[c] One is an immediately contemporary copy.

A fortunate survival from Lombard-period Italy is particularly revealing in this regard. Some time in Desiderius' reign, the nun Ghittia was the recipient of a collection of over a hundred documents, only the list of which survives, giving, in most cases, the names of the issuers and recipients of each.[32] Some of these were wholly 'lay' documents; others related directly to the church of S. Pietro ai Sette Pini near Pisa; forty-four of them concerned a single individual, Alahis, possibly a relative of Ghittia. This is certainly a record of an 'archive', therefore, but one that was neither wholly lay nor entirely ecclesiastical. It may have come down to us because the references to the Pisan church led to its preservation in the episcopal archive of that city. But the number of types of legal document listed is much larger than the average ecclesiastical archive preserved. The largest number of types of transactions in the tables in François Bougard's survey of the private documents from the early medieval Italian kingdom is six (admittedly he runs a few types together);[33] among the seventy-two private documents in Ghittia's list, on the other hand, there are twenty different legal terms for transactions. The largest category by far (thirty-four) is the sale, but we also have acquisitions of *mundium*, deeds of *thingatio* (public confirmation of a legal contract) and declarations of fidelity, none of which are at all common among surviving documents.

The impression that collections of lay documents generally included different kinds of transaction from ecclesiastical ones is reinforced by the best-known and best-studied identifiable corpus associated with a lay

[32] *CDL* II 295. See Everett, 'Scribes and Charters', 39.
[33] F. Bougard, *La justice*, 65–108.

family, the dossier of the Totoni of Campione d'Italia.[34] These twenty-one charters, fourteen of which survive as originals, include ten different types of transaction. Even if we exclude the royal or imperial diplomas, we are left with records of the acquisition of free women's *mundia* (three), of the acquisition of slaves (three), of the loan of a slave (one), of a loan of money (one), of a betrothal and dowry (one), and of compensation for a killed slave (one), as well as the sales of land (three) and *pro anima* and *post obitum* donations (two each) that are familiar from ecclesiastical archives. What is perhaps most striking here is the emphasis on people rather than on landed property. Not only do they record the transfer of *mundium* (legal personality) of both free women and slaves (male and female), but they also enact the sale of the latter.

As has already been hinted, sales are one type of transaction that provides an index of difference between lay and ecclesiastical archives. Sales are consistently under-represented in ecclesiastical archives, apart from exceptional cases where an institution acquired much of its property through purchase, as did S. Clemente in Casauria, as examined below.[35] While a few ecclesiastical institutions did engage extensively in purchase and sale in building up and managing their patrimony, on the whole they stuck to the letter of the prohibition on the alienation of Church land,[36] utilizing legal devices including *ad tempus* transfers such as *precaria*, and often very unbalanced exchanges, as their principal means of parting with property.[37] But when we have records of archives of laymen's documents, they include large numbers of sales. A tabular arrangement of the incidence of documents of sale in some of the main collections from the period *c.* 680–850 reveals some striking patterns(Table 9.2).

Several features of Table 9.2 deserve notice. The first is simply that, taken together, these data reveal that sales and purchases of land, goods and people were numerous, and were activated by documents. We are coming to recognize the importance of an economy of sale and purchase in early medieval Europe, while at the same time appreciating that land, and other goods, can often not be regarded simply as commodities in a

34 Fully examined in Gasparri and La Rocca (eds.), *Carte di famiglia*.
35 Bougard, 'Actes privés et transferts patrimoniaux', 543.
36 On this very venerable and problematic prohibition, see now S. Wood, *The Proprietary Church in the Medieval West* (Oxford, 2006), 9–11, 19–20.
37 On *precaria*, see L. Morelle, 'Les "actes de précaire", instruments de transferts patrimoniaux (France du Nord et de l'Est, VIII^e^–XI^e^ siècle)', and P. Depreux, 'L'apparition de la précaire à Saint-Gall', and for the peculiarities of Italian precarial contracts, L. Feller, 'Précaires et livelli: Les transferts patrimoniaux *ad tempus* en Italie', all in *Les transferts*, 607–47, 649–73, 725–46; in general, see D. Ganz, 'The Ideology of Sharing: Apostolic Community and Ecclesiastical Property in the Early Middle Ages', in W. Davies and P. Fouracre (eds.), *Property and Power in the Early Middle Ages* (Cambridge, 1995), 17–30.

Table 9.2 *Proportions of documents of sale in some Italian archives*

| | Non-royal, non-public, documents | Sales | Percentage sales | lay documents | lay sales | Percentage lay sales |
|---|---|---|---|---|---|---|
| Lucca | 625 | 74 | 11.9 | 31 | 21 | 67.7 |
| Monte Amiata | 106 | 47 | 44.3 | 31 | 8 | 25.8 |
| Verona | 44 | 15 | 34.1 | 8 | 4 | 50.0 |
| Bergamo | 13 | 3 | 23.1 | 5 | 3 | 60.0 |
| Farfa | 191 | 28 | 14.7 | 0 | 0 | 0.0 |
| Campione dossier | 21 | 6 | 28.6 | 11 | 6 | 54.5 |
| Ghittia list[a] | 78 | 34 | 43.6 | – | – | – |

[a] Ghittia's list does not give sufficient information for us to be able to distinguish 'lay' documents. Nevertheless, the incidence of sales within it offers a useful comparator.

profit-driven market, but changed hands according to a social at least as much as an economic logic, in a society in which generosity, mutuality and reciprocal obligation were important determinants of wealth.[38] A second feature is that Table 9.2 gives a reason for historians' relative lack of attention to sales until recently: their smaller proportion in the larger collections of documents. That the larger proportion in smaller collections is not simply a statistical quirk of those numbers is shown by the percentage in Ghittia's list and, above all, in the Monte Amiata collection (on which, see below). The final notable feature is of course the huge proportion of lay documents that are sales. This simple analysis therefore reveals that sale and purchase, perhaps especially of land, needs to be woven into our view of economic relations that have often been dominated by a culture of gift-giving.

The imprint of land sales and purchases in ecclesiastical archives is arguably strongest where that archive absorbed groups of documents relating to properties that were eventually acquired by the institution. We can see this quite clearly in cases from both the Lucca and Monte Amiata collections. From Lucca we have charters revealing that between 742 and 752 a certain Crispinus bought land in several places, including twice from laymen at Pescia near Lucca.[39] With these he established the church of S. Martino in Lunata, the future of which he provided

[38] See now M. Innes, 'Framing the Carolingian Economy', *Journal of Agrarian Change*, 9 (2009), 42–58; Innes, 'Practices of Property in the Carolingian Empire', in J. Davies and M. McCormick (eds.), *The Long Morning of Medieval Europe: New Directions in Early Medieval Studies* (Aldershot, 2008), 243–69; Wickham, *Framing*, 216–18 and, in general, 694–708, with references.

[39] *CDL* I 80, 88, 102, 106 (the latter two not 'lay' documents).

for in 764: after the deaths of himself and his immediate heirs, it was to pass to the bishop of Lucca.[40] Similarly, the Monte Amiata archive includes charters of 765 and 791 by which a certain Walcari obtained from other laymen lands at Marano (near Sovana, southern Tuscany).[41] These, evidently, he attached to the church that he had founded there, half of the substance of which in 793 he gave to Monte Amiata.[42] In both these cases, the 'lay' documents passed through a limited series of fairly clear contexts, from production in an entirely lay environment, through an *Eigenkirche*, to a monastery. The creation of a dossier of documents was here, then, part of the process of consolidating property around a single focus, an *Eigenkirche*.

It is interesting to compare these cases with another evident in documents in the Monte Amiata collection. These relate to property at 'Agello' (mod. Gello, in the valley of the Orcia, quite close to Monte Amiata). Four charters record sales of land at 'Agello' between different sets of laymen in the period 750 to 786.[43] In 814 and 827, Monte Amiata itself bought land from laymen in the same place. Only one of these seems to have been related to the previous purchasers.[44] In other words, the abbey seems to have received not a single dossier of documents but a haphazard scatter of charters, some of which may have passed through several hands before reaching it. The time period here is also interesting, as Monte Amiata did not receive property at 'Agello' until much more than thirty years after some of the documents relating to it were issued, and therefore long after they would have had any legal force.[45] It is difficult to determine straightforward reasons for the retention of such documents. Initially, it is surely likely that they were brought into Monte Amiata's archive because the proprietary context was such that they might still be called upon to bolster rights of ownership. But they must soon have become obsolete, and their further retention is an interesting testimony to the archival culture at institutions like Monte Amiata. Perhaps it was simply that *any* document relating to important estates (and 'Agello' certainly became that) was regarded as worth keeping.

Both the complex forces driving the retention of documents and the importance of the traffic in landed properties emerge most clearly in the

[40] *CDL* II 179. [41] *CDA* 12, 39: the former was a purchase, the latter an exchange.

[42] *CDA* 42. *CDA* 91 reveals that this gift was evidently not unproblematic.

[43] *CDA* 7, 9, 10, 33. [44] *CDA* 74, 101.

[45] The 'thirty-year rule' in Lombard Italy: C. Wickham, 'Land Disputes and Their Social Framework in Lombard and Carolingian Italy, 700–900', in Wickham, *Land and Power: Studies in Italian and European Social History, 400–1200* (London, 1994), 229–56, with further references at n. 7 (orig. in *Settlement of Disputes*, 105–24); in general, E. Levy, *West Roman Vulgar Law: The Law of Property* (Philadelphia, 1951), 176–90.

records preserved by the monastery of Casauria.[46] Founded in 873 by the emperor Louis II near the frontier between the Carolingian domain and the southern, Lombard, principality of Benevento, Casauria preserved an extremely rich record of its fund of documents, latterly through the work of its exceptional twelfth-century archivist Giovanni di Berardo.[47] In the course of the 1170s, Giovanni transcribed into a single manuscript more than 2,000 documents, arranged into two sections.[48] First were the *munimina*: often abbreviated copies of documents that traced the proprietorship of landed properties before their acquisition by Casauria and were contracts mostly between two lay parties. They were arranged topographically, grouped according to the settlement boundaries of the ninth century (that is, before the dramatic settlement shifts of *incastellamento*); many evidently represent the remains of dossiers of documents belonging to a variety of lay families. In the second section were copied, usually in their entirety, the *instrumenta*: documents of which the monastery was either author or beneficiary, arranged in rigorously chronological order.[49] The *munimina* in particular therefore show signs of selection, edition and abbreviation, some of which can be ascribed to the initiative of Giovanni di Berardo; but we can also be fairly certain that there had been preceding collections and redactions of the original documentary material, perhaps in the form generally known as *Liber traditionum*.[50] A number of people intervened in the shaping of Casauria's archive; it is unlikely that all were pursuing the same motives or programme.

Layers of archiving serve to obscure the reasons why lay families' dossiers came into the abbey's hands, or why they were preserved in the form they were, abbreviated and often shorn of dating evidence. Laurent Feller's work has focussed on the ninety-seven documents, spanning the period *c.* 830 to 879, concerning the region of Vico Teatino, dominated by the dossier associated with the family of Karol, son of Liutprand.[51]

[46] L. Feller, *Les Abruzzes médiévales* (Rome, 1998), 63–84; L. Feller, A. Gramain and F. Weber, *La fortune de Karol: Marché de la terre et liens personnels dans les Abruzzes au haut moyen âge* (Rome, 2005).

[47] L. Feller, *Les Abruzzes*, 69–74; Feller, 'Le cartulaire-chronique de San Clemente a Casauria', in *Les cartulaires*, 261–77.

[48] BnF lat. 5411. Facsimile edition: *Liber instrumentorum seu chronicorum monasterii Casauriense*, ed. A. Pratesi (L'Aquila, 1982). On the structure of the codex, see C. Manaresi, 'Liber instrumentorum seu chronicorum monasterii Casauriensis della Nazionale di Parigi', *Rendiconti dell'Istituto lombardo di scienze e lettere*, Classe di lettere e scienze morali e storiche, 80 (3rd. ser., 11) (1947), 29–62.

[49] For a brief history of the ebb and flow of Casauria's landed wealth, see Feller, Gramain and Weber, *La fortune de Karol*, 19–24.

[50] On the distinction between cartularies and *libri traditionum*, see Geary, *Phantoms*, 81–2.

[51] On additions to and exclusions from the Karol dossier, see Feller, Gramain and Weber, *La fortune de Karol*, 149.

They document Karol's burgeoning landed estate, built up through purchases between about 850 and 870, made easier in at least one instance by a loan, secured against his land and lent at what seems to have been an exorbitant rate of interest. It may in part have been this acquisitiveness that forced his sons to sell to the monastery some, at least, of their estate, which they then leased back for an annual rent.[52] What is in doubt is the extent to which Casauria's Karol dossier represents the totality of the family's documents – and therefore documents the totality of its landed property – or constitutes simply the residue of an ordinary level of transaction between significant proprietors in the area. Put another way, did the presence of the monastery have a distorting effect either on the land market or on the documentary culture of the region?

The foundation of the monastery almost certainly affected the nature of transactions – we can only speculate as to what may have become of Karol's sons if they did not have the option of 'sale and re-lease' provided by Casauria – but had far less effect on the overall level of property transfers. 'Land market' seems an inadequate description of these, since it carries the baggage of modern economic definitions. While those linked by personal, familial and social ties in the 'Vico Teatino' could transact property between themselves through deeds of sale and purchase without significantly affecting their personal relationships, those relationships were often influential in determining the agreed price.[53] The 'Vico Teatino' dossier includes 'market exchanges' determined solely by the size and condition of the goods and a monetary evaluation of the compensating payment, but it also contains transaction records that do not state the quantity of the goods (the surface area of land) and/or its quality (the nature of its exploitation), and those that detail goods in kind, rather than money, as payment for land. Even a monetary payment could be subject to social pressures, but where it was absent, or where goods are not presented according to quantifiable criteria, there is plenty of scope for unwritten, informal, social elements to affect the transaction.[54]

Since our estimation of socio-economic relations depends as often on omissions as on inclusions of certain elements (like specified sums of money) in the transcribed records, the process of archiving becomes crucial. The regularity of the pattern of documentation in the 'Vico Teatino' dossier – those giving a surface area for transferred lands are

52 For differing interpretations of Karol's family's position, compare Feller, Gramain and Weber, *La fortune de Karol*, 93–115, with P. Cammarosano, 'Marché de la terre et mobilitié sociale dans les Abruzzes aux IX$^{e}$–XI$^{e}$ siècles: À propos d'un livre récent', *Revue historique*, 646 (2008), 369–82.

53 Feller, Gramain and Weber, *La fortune de Karol*, 6.

54 Feller, Gramain and Weber, *La fortune de Karol*, 90–1.

a group distinguishable also by other criteria – already suggests that both Giovanni di Berardo and previous generations of Casauria archivists retained the key substance of the dispositive clauses of the charters they were copying or abbreviating, even where they failed to copy the date clauses. The reliability of their work can be confirmed by comparison with originals. Those from Monte Amiata and Lucca have already been mentioned, but especially pertinent here is a small corpus of original charters in the cathedral archive of Piacenza documenting the activities of Peter 'de Niviano': twenty-six acts in which Peter and his wife built up their patrimony mostly through purchase.[55] They also demonstrate that Peter was able to liquidate his landed assets, both in order to make cash purchases and to offer loans to those in need. The latter look very similar to the 'help' delivered to the sons of Karol by Abbot Romanus of Casauria.

Lucca, Monte Amiata, Casauria and Piacenza all show that an ecclesiastical archive could become the repository of batches of lay documents. Often we have reason to assume that this was because the properties concerned ended up in these institutions' possession. A Veronese charter of 841 gives especially vivid testimony of this, because, although it is a lay document, by which a lay landowner sold land to a *sculdahis*, the dorse of the charter records the transfer of the properties described in the document, twenty or more years later and by an unknown donor, to the monastery of S. Maria in Organo.[56] Since the documents that we read in standard editions or in later cartularies are very often actually transcriptions of the recto side, the question arises how many more might in fact include such stipulations. The transfer of documentation to a monastery because of a transfer of land is also the obvious explanation in the case of Casauria, founded after Karol's major transactions. However, the examples of the estate dossier of 'Agello' at Monte Amiata and the personal dossier of Peter 'de Niviano' at Piacenza suggest an alternative: that these institutions functioned as convenient places of safe keeping for documents that, during their practical lifetime, had nothing to do with them.[57]

55 F. Bougard, 'Pierre de Niviano, sculdassius, dit le Spolétin, et le gouvernement du comté de Plaisance à l'époque carolingienne', *Journal des savants* (1996), 291–337, including editions of all documents in the dossier.

56 *CDV* 166; it names Abbot Romuald, abbot from August 860 (*CDV* 219) until 865×81 (*CDV* 232, 280).

57 For a list of documents from north of the Alps that included properties no longer in the abbey's hands, see the discussion of the earliest Passau cartulary by Geary, *Phantoms*, 90–3.

## An alternative to the archive: public validation of documents

The argument has been made that the increasing predominance of lay charter scribes indicates not only their professionalization but also the implication of the state in the process of charter redaction. According to the standard narrative, this resulted from the quest to give greater legal validity to documents. It envisages a fairly linear development in which a growing concern for the secure validation of activities and/or transactions led to the incorporation of a number of formal, public elements in the process of redaction, and ultimately to the formalization and public validation of the occupation of scribe (or, more narrowly, of notary – *notarius*) itself. This linear progression has been taken to imply that at its starting point in the Lombard period recourse to writing was relatively ineffective. Thus Paolo Delogu: 'in Lombard Italy . . . private acts were not publicly valid, even when written in the presence of witnesses'.[58] It is not clear what kind of public–private distinction is meant here. Everett has shown that the means of bestowing legal validity on charters in the Lombard period were identical to – and certainly inherited from – late and vulgar Roman practice.[59] Means of validation such as authentication by the correct number of witnesses reflect the emphasis on public performance – on the charter as capturing the moment of redaction – that was transmitted to, and even enhanced by, charter scribes of the Lombard period. In any case, if documents had no legal validity, in particular in court, then there would have been little point in drawing them up in the first place. In fact, however, there is substantial evidence that even documents commissioned by 'private' individuals had sufficient validity to be invoked as means of proof in formal, 'public', judicial hearings.[60] The *breve* lacked even those elements of formal enactment that the *carta* had[61] – including witness subscriptions – yet the term encompasses documents that were regularly advanced as proofs in court, not least the abbreviated records of court hearings themselves.[62] As elsewhere in the post-Roman West, Lombard Italy allowed legal validity to all sorts of documents.

58 P. Delogu, *An Introduction to Medieval History*, trans. M. Moran (London, 2002 [1994]), 174–5 (quotation at 175).

59 Everett, *Literacy in Lombard Italy*, 202–3 with references.

60 For examples, see Wickham, 'Land Disputes', and Costambeys, 'Disputes and Courts in Lombard and Carolingian Central Italy', *EME*, 15 (2007), 265–89.

61 The terms *carta, charta, cartula* and *chartula* used for single-sheet legal documents are interchangeable in this context.

62 E.g. Manaresi I 8, 16, 27, etc.

But to say this is not to deny the traditional narrative's central point that the Carolingian period witnessed a shift towards the authentication and validation of documents by the state. It is really this, surely, that Delogu had in mind when he wrote the words quoted above, and there is plenty of evidence to support such a view.[63] It falls into two categories: royal pronouncements about the appropriate activity of scribes, which taken together have been seen to have brought about their professionalization at the behest of the state; and the confirmation or revalidation of documents through public means. To take the former first, ninth-century royal acts focused on notaries in several noteworthy ways.[64] Capitularies about charter scribes involve the combination of exhortation and 'best practice' that has recently been identified as typical of Carolingian capitulary acts in general: it is in this sense that we should read the requirement that *notarii* be 'registered' by the royal *missi*, for instance.[65] The Italian capitularies, on the other hand, include stipulations that have been thought to reveal a more specific concern with procedure: notaries' redaction of *cartae publicae* was to be supervised by the count and his *scabini* and *vicarii*, they were to be required to forswear forgery or *colludium*, and maximum and minimum sums were set for their payment.[66] Yet, only the last, I suggest, is sufficiently precise to speak of any kind of system or verification, and it in fact looks to be quite anomalous.[67] The other clauses can be seen as establishing the general environment of notarial practice, rather than regulating specific activities. These therefore need to be set apart from the evidence for the laicization of charter scribes and cannot be seen as themselves aimed at or creating a notarial profession. It used to be argued that it was in the ninth century that notaries acquired *fides publica*: an authority bestowed by the state, through the law, to give validity to documents. But while it is true that by the late ninth century

[63] In what follows, I am drawing principally on Bougard, *La justice*, 66–76; see also the summary in Delogu, *An Introduction to Medieval History*, 175–6.

[64] MGH Capit. 1, no. 40, c. 3 (a. 803) ruled that *missi* should register the names of *notarii*; no. 43, c. 4 (a. 805) that each bishop, abbot and count should have 'his' *notarius*, a regulation that follows on from no. 90 (a. 781), specifically for Italy, which envisaged that the count would have a personal *notarius*. See Bougard, *La justice*, 66–7.

[65] C. Pössel, 'Authors and Recipients of Carolingian Capitularies, 779–829', in R. Corradini *et al.* (eds.), *Texts and Identities in the Early Middle Ages* (Vienna, 2006), 253–74; and M. Costambeys, M. Innes and S. Maclean, *The Carolingian World* (Cambridge, 2009), ch. 4. Interpretation of the nomination of *notarii* differs here from Bougard, *La justice*, 68.

[66] MGH Capit. 1, no. 158, cc. 12, 15 (a. 822×3) ('ut cancellarii [= notarii] ... veraces cartas publicas conscribant ante comitem et scabinis et vicariis eius'); MGH Capit. 2, no. 201, c. 13 (a. 832); no. 202, c. 5 (a. 832). For *cancellarius* as a synonym for *notarius*, see Bougard, *La justice*, 68–9.

[67] Bougard, *La justice*, 68 with n9.

some notaries were also judges, and therefore validated documents presented to them in court that they themselves, or their fellow notaries, had written, the notion that in doing so they possessed some recognized authority *qua* notaries is very anachronistic. When it came to validation, we can go along with François Bougard's observation that in the Carolingian period 'nothing has really changed in relation to the Lombard era: what gives the act force and validity is above all its redaction "in public". The adjective *publicus*, when it qualifies the scribe or the charter, most often has no other meaning than "not secret".'[68] True *fides publica*, and therefore the redundancy of the formal witness subscription, had to wait until the twelfth century.[69] The ninth-century *notarius* belonged to a profession only in an informal sense, his job description being set by practice and custom.

The use of 'public' instruments or mechanisms to confirm or validate documents points rather more directly to state involvement. The most obvious were the so-called *pancarte* confirmations: diplomas periodically issued by kings and emperors confirming, often, whole lists of 'private' documents.[70] Their preservation seems decisively to reinforce the notion that only Church institutions had the capacity to preserve title through generations. The fact that the surviving confirmation diplomas all concern the property acquisitions of monasteries raises an important question: was it only monasteries, or at any rate ecclesiastical institutions, that had the archival capacity that such documents required? We know that ecclesiastical institutions were not alone in receiving, and keeping, documents confirming the provisions of other documents: several are mentioned among Alahis' documents in the Ghittia list.[71] But the fact that these do not survive makes it hard to judge their shelf life, whereas ecclesiastical institutions' better archival capacity opened up different possibilities to them. Farfa, for instance, kept the confirmation diplomas of successive emperors and kings of Italy, even though each successive ruler's diploma only reiterated, and therefore in theory made redundant, that of his predecessor. What was the point of keeping a confirmation charter of Charlemagne if you had one, referring to the same properties,

68 Bougard, *La justice*, 69: 'rien n'a vraiment changé par rapport à l'époque lombarde: ce qui donne à l'acte force et validité, c'est avant tout sa rédaction "en public". L'adjectif *publicus*, lorsqu'il qualifie le scribe ou la charte, n'a le plus souvent pas d'autre signification que "non occulte".'

69 Bougard, *La justice*, 281–95; see also, e.g., C. La Rocca, *Pacifico di Verona: Il passato carolingio nella costruzione della memoria urbana* (Rome, 1995), 9.

70 *Pancartes* that included provisions for immunity must be read in the light of B. H. Rosenwein, *Negotiating Space: Power, Restraint and Privileges of Immunity in Early Medieval Europe* (Ithaca, NY, 1999), 99–134; in general, see Geary, *Phantoms*, 88.

71 *CDL* II 295.

from Otto III?[72] Was it simply that rights improved through sheer weight of documentation? The answer must in part be that Otto was presented with this pile of diplomas precisely in order that their provisions could be renewed: they were kept so that they could be shown to him. This speaks of a consciousness that the efficacy of such documents diminished with time, and that, in particular, their provisions needed confirmation by the reigning king or emperor. It reminds us that institutions as well as individuals had personal bonds with their lords, protectors, patrons, superiors and/or rulers that had to be renewed with each new incumbent.[73] In this respect, it must have impressed Otto that Farfa could demonstrate an association with every single one of his predecessors. Publicly displaying this part of its archive produced diplomas which in their turn could be, and were, displayed before judicial tribunals as proofs of title.[74] An archival capacity of this magnitude was something lay families struggled to match, and it allowed such institutions to strengthen their identity – and their socio-political clout – by selectively constructing their past.[75] Farfa's sheer longevity was one of the features that convinced rulers like Otto III that it was worth favouring (though we should not lose sight of others: the location, as well as the extent, of its properties, claimed or actual; its liturgical activity; its saintly associations).[76]

Lay families did, however, have access to the other form of public validation that ecclesiastical institutions used: the law courts. The ninth century saw the development of documentary forms apparently deliberately designed to validate existing charters through judicial proceedings. One such form was the *ostensio cartae*, first appearing in 880×1, in which a plaintiff's charter was copied out, other parties were asked if they wished to contradict it, and they declined to do so.[77] It was not the only such innovation. In the 870s, we get the first examples of a procedure known as *finis intentionis* (*finis intentionis terrae* or *finis intentionis*

72 *RF* III 413, issued in 996, not coincidentally the year of Otto's imperial coronation.

73 It would be inappropriate here to pursue further the crucial issue of vertical ties of dependence: see, e.g., A. Rio, 'Freedom and Unfreedom in Early Medieval Francia: The Evidence of the Legal Formulae', *Past and Present*, 193 (2006), 7–40. See also above, Chapter 5, and below, Chapter 10.

74 E.g. Manaresi I 38, 50 (= *RF* II 270, 286).

75 Geary, *Phantoms*, 81–114; W. Pohl, *Werkstätte der Erinnerung: Montecassino und die langobardische Vergangenheit* (Vienna, 2001).

76 Properties: Costambeys, *Power*; M. Stroll, *Medieval Abbey of Farfa: Target of Papal and Imperial Ambitions* (Leiden, 1997). Liturgy: S. Boynton, *Shaping a Monastic Identity: Liturgy and History at the Imperial Abbey of Farfa 1000–1125* (Ithaca, NY, 2006). Saints: E. Susi, 'Agiografia e territorio', in *I Longobardi dei ducati di Spoleto e Benevento: Atti del XVI congresso internazionale di studi sull'alto medioevo: Spoleto, 20–23 ottobre 2002, Benevento, 24–27 ottobre 2002* (Spoleto, 2003), 317–56.

77 Manaresi I 91; further examples until 900 are nos. 99, 105, 106, 107.

*status*).[78] Here, the plaintiff made a statement of his rights in a thing, declared himself ready to confront an opponent, and requested a formal recognition of his rights from a 'defendant' (often, this latter party would simply state that he had, or could make, no claim to rights in the thing). The main difference from the *ostensio cartae* was that the text of a charter was not included *in extenso* in the notice.[79] Precisely this method was used in 873 by Casauria to validate its ownership of the lands of Karol, son of Liutprand.[80] The third procedure, appearing first in 874 (but not again then until 896), was the *investitura salva querela*, in which the plaintiff stated his rights, no defendant appeared, and the court formally invested the plaintiff with possession, while leaving open the possibility that a defendant could press a claim to the property in the future, within a certain period.[81]

These forms give the impression of having been deliberately designed to provide plaintiffs with a new document to preserve or strengthen their title. The fact that not one of the earlier documents thus confirmed survives suggests quite strongly that these *notitiae* were in fact meant to *replace* those earlier documents. This in turn suggests that documents had shelf lives, and raises several questions. Were these time limits a function of the legal transactions that the documents contained (which may, for example, have been subject to the thirty-year rule),[82] of the materials from which they were made,[83] or of the limited archival capacity of the plaintiffs? Where did the initiative for these new forms lie: with those who employed charter scribes, or with the scribes themselves? It used to be thought that all three had their origins in the formula-book known as the *Cartularium Langobardicum*, in which they all appear. But, as we have seen, this text has now been firmly redated from the late ninth to the late eleventh century, so it must be seen as recording practice, not

78 Manaresi I 74–5, 79–80, 82–6 (all from Casauria). Compare the various Frankish processes for testing and validating a document discussed above, Chapter 5, and below, Chapter 11.

79 Bougard, *La justice*, 312–14, argues that this procedure was developed as a necessary response to the practice in which properties were initially occupied illegally and then successively alienated, or their usufruct granted and regranted, until the original owner's rights were lost sight of. The *finis intentionis* offered the opportunity to 'wipe the proprietorial slate clean', as it were: either the original owner could revindicate his rights, or he would lose them, and a new owner would be invested.

80 Manaresi I 75.

81 First in Manaresi I 77, then in 101–2. Bougard, *La justice*, 314–19, argues that this was simply the logical progression from a series of previous norms and procedures aimed at combating contumacy.

82 Note, though, that the rule made redundant more recent documents, not older ones.

83 Though note that by the ninth century almost everyone outside Rome seems to have been writing their charters on parchment.

setting it. The question of origins is a debate between *ad hoc* development and centralized direction. Chris Wickham has pointed to an increasing tendency in the Italian *notitiae* through the earlier decades of the ninth century for written documents to be taken uncritically as proof, and for their production in court to end the hearing. This would seem to be a first step on the road to the non-confrontational format of the *ostensio cartae*. On the other hand, the remarkably rapid spread of these three forms, once arrived at, seems to point to a controlling hand guiding their use. By the last decade of the tenth century, the vast majority of dispute *notitiae* were written in one of these three forms,[84] an increase so rapid as to suggest a very effective bureaucracy, centred on the legists attached to the royal court at Pavia.[85] The pressure to which they were responding is generally thought to have been generated by courts themselves, and in particular by judges' growing tendency to prefer charters as means of proof. This, it is argued, led them to develop a new set of practices, focused exclusively on the charter, that took over relatively quickly.

This goes some way to recognizing that the judicial system appears to us, through the *notitiae*, as concerned not with disputes at all, but with documents. Documents, that is, were not simply tools with which to argue, but very often appear to be reified as the thing in dispute: the dispute was either *about* the document or was intended to produce a document. Disputes could also lead to the destruction of documents: the (unlawful) destruction of documents is recorded in *notitiae* from the eighth and ninth centuries,[86] and their destruction as a result of court judgements in those from the eleventh.[87] The *ostensio cartae* form in particular seems to indicate that the court hearing had become *entirely* a matter of documents: the brandishing of one, and the writing of another (the *notitia*). Time and space were both important here. What has been said above suggests that even properly witnessed charters were not considered secure guarantors of title: their efficacy was limited by time (not

84 Wickham, 'Land Disputes', 237: 'The [north Italian] legists worked out formularies for the recording of *placita* in the late ninth century that caught on so fast that they covered nearly every formal *placitum* by 920, except in non-Carolingian southern Italy. (When the formulaic *placitum* became dominant, in fact, the usefulness of the formal court case for social historians drops dramatically.)' See also pp. 245–6.

85 While it is true that the *finis intentionis*, while common in Spoleto, really only got going in the north from the 960s, it still constitutes about a third of surviving cases from the last decade of the tenth century; the *investitura salva querela* makes up about a sixth of surviving *notitiae* from the 890s to the 1020s; and the *ostensio cartae* accounts for another third of survivals in the first half of the tenth century, rising to a half after about 950.

86 See below, Chapter 12, and A. Sennis, '"Omnia tollit aetas et cuncta tollit oblivio": Ricordi smarriti e memorie costruite nei monasteri altomedievali', *Bullettino dell'Istituto storico italiano per il medio evo*, 106 (2004), 93–135.

87 Manaresi II 294, 314bis; *RF* IV 658.

least by the lifetime of the witnesses) and by the narrow range of those they involved. As the civic institutions that had performed the function of validating titles (that is, *gesta municipalia*) atrophied between the seventh and ninth centuries, new mechanisms came to be needed.[88] It has often been noted that the decline of the *gesta* left a void, but suggestions for how it was filled have generally invoked vaguely individual or family enterprise.[89] The *notitia* obtained from the court might therefore either replace a document that was regarded as past its 'use by' date or strengthen one by broadening knowledge of it. Archiving was therefore not simply a question of once-and-for-all preservation. Archives had to be managed, and had to be accessible. Their management must therefore often have involved an element of turnover: documents had to be preserved in order to be brandished, but once the new court notice had been produced, the old document could be discarded (or the parchment reused).[90]

The development of the *notitia* through the ninth century therefore suggests that the judicial system was not simply a forum for settling disputes; it was also a mechanism for validating old documents and producing new ones. This may have been done in anticipation of disputes, rather than in response to them. But it may also have become necessary because other forms of validation and renewal were no longer available. Wickham, as we have seen, sees the appearance of the *ostensio cartae* and similar procedures as an essentially organic development then set in stone by some on-the-ball Pavese legists. For François Bougard, they were intended to confirm transactions already entered into (and in all cases already enacted by 'private' charters); and he notices that the majority seem to be especially important transactions, or those of a

[88] See above, Chapter 5.

[89] E.g. J. M. H. Smith, '*Aedificatio sancti loci*: The Making of a Ninth-Century Holy Place', in M. de Jong and F. Theuws (eds.), *Topographies of Power in the Early Middle Ages* (Leiden, 2001), 361–96, at 371: 'although the late Roman procedure of registering title in municipal archives, the *gesta municipalia*, lingered on here and there into the early seventh century, the onus for redacting and preserving texts gradually passed everywhere to individual or institutional proprietors', citing P. Johanek, 'Zur rechtlichen Funktion von Traditionsnotiz, Traditionsbuch und früher Sigelurkunde', in *Recht und Schrift*, 131–62, esp. 136–45.

[90] What we can see of their preservation indicates that it was their immediate beneficiaries who benefited from, and so preserved, *notitiae* employing *ostensio cartae* and similar forms: of the twenty-four surviving examples of these forms from the first thirty years of their existence (873–903), nineteen are preserved by the institution (always a church or monastery) that benefited from the document or by that institution's ultimate repository: Manaresi I 74–5, 77, 79–80, 82–6, 88, 91–2, 95, 99, 101–2, 105–7, 109, 111–13; of which nos. 77, 80, 91, 107 and 113 benefit parties other than those who preserved the document. By 'ultimate repository', I mean that, for instance, documents benefiting the monastery of S. Ambrogio in Milan are now in the Archivio di Stato there.

certain complexity. Some of these may have had real disputes behind them, and some not. What is equally important for Bougard is the simple fact that in switching to this more formulaic style, the notaries were setting the documentary record, the *notitia*, at one remove from the actual court case (if there was one).[91] For him, the *ostensio cartae* was the notaries' deliberate invention, prompted by a desire to make unnecessary the 'jeux d'écritures' that both lay and ecclesiastical parties had been engaging in previously: that is, the creative use of standard 'private' charter forms that were not individually sufficiently flexible to cover, for instance, the restructuring of a loan.[92] As he observes, 'A donation could hide a sale, a sale a loan.'[93] Recourse to the court apparatus also added a sought-after element to temporally limited or contingent transactions: donations that reserved usufruct for the donor's lifetime, or acts like manumissions that may have been initially provisional, could be confirmed by application to the court. One study indicates that the majority of *notitiae* employing new models like the *ostensio cartae* were produced only a short time after the documents they confirmed,[94] perhaps because they enabled the current possessor of a property to validate his right in a context in which traditional norms like the thirty-year rule tended to favour the residual rights of earlier possessors. This may have become especially important when time-limited leases were running out: it is surely significant, then, that the first such one- and two-generation leases appear in our records in the first half of the ninth century, and the first of these new forms some sixty or so years later.[95] These observations therefore confirm that the pressure for change may have come from the 'consumer' (that is, those who commissioned charters), and that it may have been a response to the growing inadequacy (rather, perhaps, than a fading away) of older means of preserving, validating, renewing or copying documents. The state looks to have been less of a driving force behind this change than is often argued; its only importance, in fact,

[91] Hence, if the term *placitum* refers first and foremost to the court hearing itself, it becomes ever less helpful to use it to refer to the document that that hearing eventually produced.

[92] See the example of A. R. Natale, *Il museo diplomatico dell'Archivio di Stato di Milano*, vol. I (Milan, 1968), nos. 82–3, in which S. Ambrogio in Milan had to perform all sorts of tergiversations of standard diplomatic simply in order to renew the loan of one of its debtors.

[93] Bougard, *La justice*, 328.

[94] S. H. Brunsch, 'The Authority of Documents in Early Medieval Italian Pleas', in B. Bolton and C. Meek (eds.), *Aspects of Power and Authority in the Middle Ages* (Turnhout, 2007), 277–87, at 285–6.

[95] See Bougard, 'Actes privés et transferts patrimoniaux', 551–5, on the chronological patterning of property concessions.

was that it provided the connections between notaries that enabled new documentary forms to be legitimized and disseminated.

Acknowledging the role of the courts in validating documents has a number of implications. First, it suggests that we should not restrict our definition of lay documents to what have traditionally been classed as 'private' acts. The *notitiae* of court cases bridged the divide between the traditional categories of 'public' and 'private', since they were very often simply a means of giving extra legal weight to transactions between 'private' individuals, families or institutions by having them confirmed by a recognized authority and, perhaps most importantly, by having them exposed to the scrutiny of the actors' peers: in other words, being no longer secret, they were now 'public'. Secondly, it reinforces the point that archiving was not a once-and-for-all procedure. A document could be periodically renewed, rendering redundant the previous document. But, of course, periodic renewal would only take place for as long as it was necessary and relevant to the parties concerned. Once the pattern of family property changed through death, inheritance and marriage – in other words generally after just a few generations – all trace of the title that had previously been renewed would be lost. Thirdly, as the *notitia* became more formalized, its function as a document of validation separated from its role as record of dispute, judgement and/or agreement. There had always been a necessity for *breves* recording negotiations not recorded in the court *notitia* (which can hardly be regarded as extra-judicial); that need only increased with the growing formality of the latter.[96]

## Ecclesiastical institutions and the preservation of documents

Was there, then, something special – something peculiarly ecclesiastical – about those ecclesiastical institutions that preserved documents? One reason above all why documents sometimes survived – and occasionally still survive – in the hands of ecclesiastical institutions is that those institutions did not undergo the kinds of changes that led to the dispersal and/or eventual disappearance of lay patrimonies – and the documents associated with them. They were entities that did not have to partition their patrimonies with every new generation, did not transfer property as part of marriage settlements, and, crucially, did not die. They have been subject to different acts of history. These may have led to

[96] E.g. *RF* II 205, 250, both *breves* (rather than official *notitiae*) recording dispute settlements; further, Bougard, *La justice*, 74–6.

the dispersal or destruction of their fund of documents and even extinguished the institutions themselves – how often have medievalists cursed Cromwell's commissioners, or the incendiary mobs of the French Revolution? – but such historical accidents were nowhere near as frequent, as routine – indeed, as inevitable – as those suffered by lay families. This contrast with the natural fragility of lay families makes it easy to assume that ecclesiastical institutions' superior durability is a peculiarly ecclesiastical quality, and to take it for granted. It is this, after all, that makes so many of them so much the obvious foci for local or regional studies across the entire early-to-high medieval period.[97] However, it needs to be underlined that institutions that managed to conserve their archives for posterity are *ipso facto* exceptional among the full complement of ecclesiastical institutions: most ecclesiastical archives did, in fact, have limited shelf lives. There are five broad reasons why ecclesiastical institutions' records might not remain *in situ*: natural accident (fire, decay); the disappearance or dramatic upheaval of the society that supported the institution (as with the bishoprics of northern Gaul and much of Britain in the fifth century); the absorption of the institution by another, with consequent transfer, and streamlining, of the record; the extinction of the institution with consequent dispersal of its archive; and (related to the latter) the extinction of the family that supported the institution. The latter three are those most relevant to the documents that survive from Italy, and the last reminds us that, among the total number of ecclesiastical institutions, those not dominated by a single family or interest group were the exception.[98] In particular, we can distinguish most (arguably not all) bishoprics in this respect, since their existence depended on a rather different basis (though they could, of course, be amalgamated and/or extinguished). Where monasteries are concerned, the provenances of the surviving documents reveal which of them had the most durable archives and suggest that their longevity depended on the ability of the institution to distinguish itself from the laity – that is, usually, from particular lay interest groups – to a sufficient extent to survive changes in those groups' fortunes.

[97] E.g. K. Schmid, *Die Klostergemeinschaft von Fulda im früheren Mittelalter*, 3 vols. in 5 (Münster, 1978); for Lucca, C. Wickham, *The Mountains and the City: The Tuscan Apennines in the Early Middle Ages* (Oxford, 1988), and now M. Stoffella, 'Aristocracy and Rural Churches in the Territory of Lucca Between Lombards and Carolingians: A Case Study', in S. Gasparri (ed.), *774: Ipotesi su una transizione* (Turnhout, 2008), 289–311.

[98] Wood, *The Proprietary Church*, esp. 221–30.

Broadly, therefore, the ecclesiastical institutions that were best at preserving documents were those that were most successful in defining themselves clearly and distinguishing themselves from the non-ecclesiastical. Indeed, the documents that they kept played a crucial part in this self-definition, because this was not simply a question of preservation for its own sake. These institutions had archival strategies involving selecting as well as retaining documents – strategies, moreover, that themselves shifted over time and according to circumstance. Perhaps the best example of this in Italy is Verona. Cristina La Rocca has made a strong case for the careful attention paid to shaping their past by Verona's episcopal clergy in the late eleventh and twelfth centuries.[99] The most striking aspect of this, she argues, is their selection of an obscure ninth-century archdeacon, Pacificus, whom they transformed into a Carolingian Renaissance man, the equal or superior of any such figure at the court of Charlemagne, making him responsible for all sorts of precocious initiatives that established a pioneering programme of documenting and record-keeping as the single most important distinguishing trait of Verona's clergy. La Rocca shows that this was achieved principally by the fabrication of a series of key documents that all argued for the independence of the cathedral chapter (Pacificus' institution) from the bishop. Elsewhere, cathedral chapters did not acquire such autonomy for another two centuries. She argues that the mid ninth century emerged as the point at which cathedral chapter and bishop could be portrayed as having separated because Verona tradition remembered genuine friction at that time between the cathedral clergy and the then bishop Ratold, an Aleman introduced into the diocese by the Carolingians. If she is right, then it is very likely that later generations of Veronese clergy not only added to their institutional tradition by forging charters but also shaped it through selecting what charters to keep. The question then arises of whether we can see some trace of archival selection (as well as augmentation through forgery) in the profile of the charters that have been preserved.

Although Verona's charter collection is not the easiest to study, because of the rather indiscriminate approach of its modern editor, La Rocca's work allows us to identify which of the later copies of charters are reliable and can therefore be added to the surviving originals. Of the resulting total of fifty-seven charters from the period 751–875, eight are 'lay' documents. All of these belong to dossiers associated with particular churches

[99] La Rocca, *Pacifico di Verona*, and La Rocca, 'A Man for All Seasons: Pacificus of Verona and the Creation of a Local Carolingian Past', in Y. Hen and M. Innes (eds.), *The Uses of the Past in the Early Middle Ages* (Cambridge, 2000), 250–77.

or estates, the most prominent among them being the monastery of S. Maria in Organo. This was jurisdictionally independent of the bishop of Verona throughout the period that concerns us here, falling under the purview of the patriarch of Aquileia. Only in the twelfth century, after the Concordat of Worms ensured that the bishopric was no longer part of the imperial power network in northern Italy, did the episcopate of Tebaldus (1135–57) see collaboration with the patriarch of Aquileia and a coming together of bishop and monastery.[100] It is to that period – precisely the time when the legend of Pacificus was in the making – that we can date an attempt to reshape and sift Verona's cathedral archive to exclude references to Bishop Ratold. Nearly all the documents preserved from the period of his episcopate (*c.* 814–40) are those concerning either the cathedral clergy or S. Maria in Organo. Only a handful of the bishop's own documents survive, and examination of their witness lists reveals the complete absence of the cathedral clergy; in the same way, the bishop is absent from the latter's charters. Crucial here is the unusual survival of a grant by Ratold, in which, in conjunction with the new Carolingian count of Verona, Hucpald, the bishop gave the estate of the late count, Ademar, to the church of S. Pietro in Castro.[101] Not only did this latter church belong to the episcopal and 'Carolingian' side of Verona's political division – by 871 it had come into the hands of the imperial monastery of S. Zeno, which from the start was antagonistic towards the much earlier foundation of S. Maria in Organo[102] – but also, here as elsewhere, the witness list shows Ratold having to turn to laymen, quite possibly Frankish immigrants, to help authenticate his act.[103] The cathedral clergy, on the other hand, often feature in the 'private' transactions that took place in Ratold's episcopate, often involving S. Maria in Organo.[104] Verona therefore shows quite palpably that in the ninth century documents were arranged and stored for reasons quite apart from any structural distinction between the ecclesiastical and the lay. In Verona, charter use followed political affiliation.

While ecclesiastical institutions' dominance of our documentary record for Italy looks at first sight to discourage any notion that we may be able to touch lay documentary culture, we have seen that this masks a variety of practices that cast doubt on the usefulness of the lay–clerical distinction in this context. Those who structured ecclesiastical archives may have preferred to preserve lay documents from early

[100] Miller, *The Formation of a Medieval Church*, 163–74.
[101] *CDV* 89. [102] *CDV* 241.
[103] La Rocca, *Pacifico di Verona*, 240, gives the example of Manaresi I 31 (*CDV* 121).
[104] E.g. *CDV* 124–5, 128, 131–2, 134–5, 144–6.

in – or before – the history of their institution because it reinforced its longevity. But this also implies that they often selected for omission or destruction later lay documents. Where these survive, as at Monte Amiata and Piacenza, they provide a precious indication that sometimes monasteries and episcopal centres offered the most practical repository for leaves of parchment that were valuable, at least to their owners. That those owners did not last down the generations may explain why many may later have been discarded. Family longevity affected the shelf life of a document. On the other hand, the need to preserve a document was felt less where mechanisms existed for reaffirming the provisions of a legal act, and often for thereby producing a new document. This was clearly one of the main functions of the law courts in eighth- and ninth-century Italy, and it pointed to a future in which the state – or at least those claiming its authority – would play a stronger role in documentary culture.

# 10 *Sicut mos esse solet*: documentary practices in Christian Iberia, *c.* 700–1000

*Adam J. Kosto*

*In Catalonia, an extraordinary number of documents survive: clear evidence of the continued vitality of the documentary culture that we have seen in the sources from the Visigothic kingdom. The evidence from the rest of Iberia shows that Catalonia was not exceptional, although here documents survive in ecclesiastical cartularies rather than originals. We can nonetheless see laypeople, even* servi *at the bottom of the social hierarchy, using documents for petty transactions, and not just land transfers. We can also spot signs of the earlier existence of lay family archives, in some cases of several stages of preservation by different lay families, and of dossiers of family documents being stored in churches. Overall, the Iberian evidence attests how the ways of producing and keeping documents, which had been as diverse as the patterns of landholding and transfer they recorded, tended to become more institutionalized from the tenth century, at the same time as the aristocracy consolidated their landed estates.*

In the mid tenth century, in the county of Portugal, Vermudo Pepiz granted to his wife Guntroda a villa called Fano. The grant was recorded in a document (*scriptura benefactis*), possibly along with other properties in a charter recording Guntroda's endowment (*dos*). Soon thereafter, Guntroda exchanged the villa for another in Salinas with Didaco, son of Menendo. This transaction, too, was recorded in a document, a 'charter of exchange' (*cartula commutacionis*). Neither of these two documents survives; both are mentioned in the prologue (*narratio*) of a grant made in 959 by Didaco and his wife, Ildonca, of the villa Fano, to the recently founded monastery of Guimarães. The couple granted Fano 'just as I exchanged it with lady Guntroda'. The presence of this document in the cartulary of Guimarães, the *Livro de Mumadona*, so called after the founder of the house, is no surprise, for one of the principal functions of a cartulary was to collect evidence of donations of property. The grant's mentions of these two earlier, lost, documents – *deperdita* – are more intriguing, for they offer evidence of transactions not involving an ecclesiastical institution, transactions solely between laypeople. Furthermore, Didaco's grant suggests the existence not just of two charters, but of many more, for it notes that his earlier exchange with Guntroda was recorded in duplicate *cartulae commutacionis* and that, furthermore, such record-making was the reigning custom: 'ex quibus utrorumque cartulas sibi commutacionis uicissim fecerunt sicut mos esse solet'.[1]

I have made the case elsewhere for the routine use of written records by laypeople in tenth-century Catalonia, as well as for the existence of lay archives, all in the context of a common (lay and clerical) culture of documentary practice.[2] The present chapter extends that investigation to the rest of the Iberian peninsula. Despite the fact that the eastern Pyrenean counties shared a common Visigothic heritage with the Christian kingdoms to the west, the much stronger and long-lasting Frankish influence on Catalonia led to cultural differences, notably (for present purposes) in areas such as linguistic development, palaeography and diplomatic practice. Original early medieval documents from Catalonia feature a version of caroline minuscule, while scribes from further west were using a Visigothic cursive. Similarly, scribes in Catalonia continued to date documents by the regnal year of French kings until 1180, while their Iberian counterparts elsewhere dated according to the Spanish era.[3] A hypothesis of the documentary exceptionalism of Catalonia would be reasonable. It proves, however, not to be valid. The evidence suggests that the regular use of documents by laypeople in the rest of Christian Iberia was very much the custom.

The dossier of documentary evidence for the Christian Iberian polities outside Catalonia – Aragon, Pamplona/Navarre, Castile, León, Asturias, Galicia and Portugal – is considerably more resistant to comprehensive analysis than the material from the Catalan counties, where scholars can

1 *PMH* 77 (additional abbreviations given at end of chapter). There is a facsimile edition of the Guimarães cartulary: *Livro de Mumadona: Cartulário medievo existente no Arquivo Nacional da Torre do Tumbo*, vol. I (only), *Reprodução facsimilada do códice*, ed. I. A. Pinto Ferreira (Lisbon, 1973). Other *deperdita* are indicated, for example, in *Sobrado* I 12 ('Ipsum uillare iam supradictum uobis uendimus atque concedimus sicut illum habuit mea auola iam supradicta per textus scripture incartatum de domna Unisco') and *PMH* 88 ('ego illa habui incartata cum uiro meo diue memorie Ranimirus Menendi secundum illa habuimus incartata de Rex domno ordonio'). My thanks to Wendy Davies and Roger Collins for comments on earlier versions of this chapter.

2 Kosto, 'Laymen'.

3 A. J. Kosto, *Making Agreements in Medieval Catalonia: Power, Order, and the Written Word, 1000–1200* (Cambridge, 2001), 5–7, and works cited there. See also the judgement of R. Collins, *Early Medieval Spain: Unity in Diversity, 400–1000*, 2nd edn (New York, 1995), 236: 'the Leonese and Asturian charters are less varied and more restricted in their style and contents than those of the contemporary counties of Catalonia'.

benefit from a single modern editorial project.[4] The Iberian material, surviving as original single-sheet documents as well as cartulary and antiquarian copies, is scattered among over two dozen modern, overlapping (and often competing) editions, all with different standards and practices with respect to dating, identification of likely forgeries, and, most importantly, judgements about what to label a single record. Only the most impressionistic arguments based on simple numerical analysis of the corpus as a whole are possible. Furthermore, the geographical range of the documents alone, with the concomitant differences in political, economic and social environments which gave rise to them, argues against an attempt at comprehensive study, although for the purposes of a comparison with Catalonia and other European regions, aggregation of the evidence is necessary and, it is hoped, instructive. For, taken together, the evidence is substantial: over 2,000 records from 1000 and earlier, with over 90 per cent from the tenth century. The single largest source is the composite archive of the cathedral of León (599 records), but there are other major collections, such as those of Celanova (241 records), San Millán de la Cogolla (119 records), Sahagún (360 records), Sobrado de los Monjes (119 records), the 'Fondo Antiguo' of La Coruña (100 records) and the remarkably under-utilized assemblage of Portuguese sources published by Herculano in the nineteenth century, in addition to many smaller dossiers.[5] This total is still only one-third the size of the complete corpus from Catalonia, although it is twice the size of the corpus from, for example, Anglo-Saxon England – a similarly heterogeneous area of similar size.[6]

The first part of this study discusses aspects of the evidence for the use of documents by laypeople to record their transactions. The second part examines the evidence for lay archival practices: the preservation

[4] Only the earliest documents have been edited as a coherent group (although even this has substantial gaps): *DEPA*. The project Regestalia, based at the Universidad de Alcalá de Henares, remains incomplete, and its website, previously at www2.uah.es/historia1/carlossaez/Regestos/default.htm, has been taken down.

[5] On the material generally, see Davies, *Acts of Giving*, esp. 22–6; E. Pastor Díaz de Garayo, 'Los testimonios escritos del sector meridional de Castilla (siglos X–XI): Ensayo de crítica documental', *Historia. Instituciones. Documentos*, 24 (1997), 355–79; L. Sierra Macarrón, 'Producción y conservación de la documentación altomedieval: Del Cantábrico al Duero (siglos IX–XI)', *Signo: Revista de historia de la cultura escrita*, 13 (2004), 99–120. J. Escalona Monge, P. Azcárate Aguiliar-Amat and M. Larrañaga Zulueta, 'A la ideología política: Los diplomas fundacionales de San Pedro de Arlanza y la construcción de una identidad para la Castilla medieval', in *Actas del VI Congreso internacional de historia de la cultura escrita*. I. *Libros y documentos en la Alta Edad Media: Los libros de derecho. Los archivos familiares* (Madrid, 2002), 159–206, is a model of the penetrating diplomatic scholarship that these sources demand.

[6] See below, Chapter 13.

and organization of documents outside and independent of ecclesiastical institutions. The arguments presented here, based as they are on an initial survey and entirely on printed sources, are necessarily preliminary; they are meant to provide a foundation for future work and a comparison to the material from Catalonia, but above all a basis for the inclusion of Christian Iberia as a whole in this broader survey of early medieval documentary practices across Europe and the Mediterranean.

## Lay documents

In the substantial corpus of evidence from the region of Osona-Manresa in Catalonia, the proportion of documents with no evident link to an ecclesiastical institution, cleric or monk was 39% (45% if counts and viscounts were included). The figure for the rest of Iberia is significantly lower, but still notable, around 20%, or about 400 of the roughly 2,000 documents.[7]

As other chapters in this volume suggest, the gap between Catalonia and the rest of the peninsula likely has less to do with a difference in early medieval documentary practices than with later decisions about preservation. While original single-sheet records constitute over half of the Osona-Manresa corpus, cartulary copies dominate the holdings elsewhere. The significance of the means of preservation can be demonstrated by an analysis of the one coherent edition that cuts across archival sources. The classic collection of Antonio C. Floriano, *Diplomática española del período astur (718–910)*, contains 225 documents (including fragments and *deperdita*), the bulk of the early medieval Iberian records from outside the Frankish March for those years.[8] Of the 225 documents, 20 per cent (44) are transactions between laypeople (excluding counts and kings) – a figure that matches the overall estimate above.[9] The proportion of *original*[10] documents that are transactions between laypeople, however,

[7] The incomplete database of documents being used currently includes 2,068 records, of which between 391 and 417 are lay documents according to the criteria used in the Osona-Manresa sample (Kosto, 'Laymen', 54–5).

[8] *DEPA*. Note that the main database includes only 163 records for this period. I include in the total the appendices of fragments and *deperdita*, as well as documents reputed false. I exclude the document at II, 398, which dates from after 910, as Floriano suspected; see *Sahagún* 152. For the Visigothic period, see Á. Canellas López, *Diplomática hispano-visigoda* (Zaragoza, 1979), and above, Chapter 4.

[9] *DEPA* 17, 26, 34, 43–4, 47, 66–8, 70, 72, 76, 81, 83, 94, 96, 111, 114, 117, 119, 121, 129–30, 139–40, 154–5, 163, 168–9, 172, 177, 183, 188, 190–1, 193–5, 199, 201, 203; also vol. I, appendix, 5, and vol. II, appendix, 9 and 12.

[10] I use the term as shorthand for 'document on a single sheet of parchment patently written around the time it claims to be written'. Some of these may be contemporary copies or forgeries, although it is worth exploring whether forgery was more common in documents related to ecclesiastical institutions than in documents generally.

is much higher: of the 225 documents, 39 are originals, and of these, 44 per cent (17) concern transactions between laypeople – a figure in line with the overall estimate for Osona-Manresa.[11] These figures underline the importance of transmission for our understanding of documentary practices in a given region,[12] and this type of analysis still needs to be applied to the Iberian corpus as a whole, and indeed beyond Iberia.[13]

If the surviving record understates the importance of the production of documents recording transactions between laypeople in numerical terms, early medieval formula-books, such as those surveyed by Brown, and sources such as the Ghittia list, discussed by Costambeys, lead us to suspect that the evidence is also skewed in terms of substance – that there were many more *types* of documents produced than have survived and that many of those were documents particularly relevant to transactions between laypeople.[14] The little-studied *Formulae Visigothicae* support such an argument.[15] The forty-five surviving formulas from this collection, which probably dates from the early seventh century, address the following topics: manumission (nos. 1–6 [of slaves] and 7 [of a son]), donations (7–10, 29–31), sales (11–13), nuptial endowments (14–20), testaments (21–6), exchanges (27–8), commendation (32), pact of division of property (33), judicial proceedings (36, 39–43), *precariae* (36–7), loans (38, 44) and monastic pacts (45–6). Of these, only fourteen explicitly concern churchmen or Church

[11] I follow Floriano's determination of the originality of various documents, although in most cases it is not a problem, as he is dealing with cartulary copies. The original documents (with lay documents in *italics*) are as follows: *DEPA* 9, 18, 24, *66*, 69, *72*, 73–5, *76*, *81*, *94*, *96*, 97, 103, 108, 112, *121*, 138, 141, 149, *154–5*, 159, *169*, *172*, 173–4, 176, 178, *183*, *191*, *193*, *195*, *203*; vol. II, appendix, 4–5, 8, *9*. Floriano does not seem to have confirmed the existence of an original for *DEPA* 97 and 103.

[12] The problem of transmission is, of course, complex. The surviving original documents *may* offer a more accurate reflection of the original documentary production than suviving documents of all types (originals and later copies, in and outside cartularies). But if, as Patrick Geary has suggested, documents relating directly to the interests of ecclesiastical institutions are *less* likely to have survived as originals once cartularies were created – if they were systematically destroyed, or, for institutional reasons, more likely to be lost – then the presence of lay documents among original charters is an exaggeration of the original documentary production. See Geary, *Phantoms*, 82.

[13] See esp. Kosto, 'Laymen', 73.

[14] Above, Chapters 6 and 9; see also Brown, 'Documents', 339.

[15] *Form. Vis.* Dedicated studies are rare: J. G. Bidermann, *Commentatio ad formulas Visigothicas novissime repertas* (Berlin, 1856); B. Martín Mínguez, *Las fórmulas tenidas por visigodas* (Madrid, 1920); K. von Schwerin, 'Sobre las relaciones entre las Fórmulas Visigóticas y las Andecavenses', *Anuario de historia del derecho español*, 9 (1932), 177–89; R. Mentxaka, 'En torno a *Formulae Visigothicae* 44', in S. Crespo Ortiz de Zárate and Á. Alonso Ávila (eds.), *Scripta antiqva in honorem Ángel Montenego Duque et José María Blázquez Martínez* (Valladolid, 2002), 827–40. See also Pastor Díaz de Garayo, 'Los testimonios', and above, Chapter 4.

business (6–10, 25,[16] 31 [?],[17], 45–6). The surviving Iberian documents themselves are dominated by donations of various types and sales; in her corpus of 1,960 tenth-century transactions, for example, Wendy Davies identified 980 gifts (50%) and 850 sales (43%), although, as she demonstrates well, the difference between the two is not always clear.[18] Exchanges and various records of judgement, types also found in the formula list, account for many of the remaining documents, although only a few of the types are completely absent from the corpus of early medieval Iberian charters in one form or another: the manumissions (1–7), a *gesta municipalia* protocol (25) and a series of judicial mandates (41–3).

Surviving sales, gifts, exchanges and even judgements record the disposition of land, which provides a clear incentive for their long-term preservation; the same is true of some of the less commonly attested documents, such as nuptial endowments.[19] Documents have survived, however, that are not even mentioned in the formula-book, and that offer tantalizing hints of a much broader world of document production. Consider profiliation, the process of transfer by adoption of an heir, usually (but not always) from outside the family. About half of the surviving *cartae profiliacionis* and other records referring to the process concern transfers between laypeople. In 875, for example, the couple Licerio and Fakilo made Adeit their heir (*in loco filio*) with respect to a villa; and in 905 the couple Severo and Recesinda made a second couple, Gundefredo and Basilia, their heirs (*in loco filios*) with respect to three villas.[20] In some cases, profiliation represented the submission of the humble to the more powerful, as when in 870, the *servus* Flaciano made his lord Nuño a co-heir of two villas.[21] This interpretation has borne much historiographical weight. But Davies has shown that profiliation was not just a means of domination, but in fact a very flexible instrument for the manipulation of social ties.[22] The next step is to examine profiliation in the context of *intrafamilial* transfers of land, which are not as rare for the early period and at apparently low social levels as has been assumed; again, this is not a problem limited to transactions between laypeople, but it is a problem dominated by them.[23]

[16] *Form. Vis.* 25, a model transcript of proceedings of a *gesta municipalia*, includes the passage 'per quam ecclesiabus sanctarum Dei aliqua concessit'.

[17] The address of this document hints at an ecclesiastical beneficiary.

[18] Davies, *Acts of Giving*, esp. 25; W. Davies, 'Sale, Price and Valuation in Galicia and Castile-León in the Tenth Century', *EME*, 11 (2002), 149–74.

[19] E.g. *Sobrado* I 119; *Otero* 50. [20] *DEPA* 114, 183.

[21] *León* 4; below, at n. 38. [22] Davies, *Acts of Giving*, 83–4, 160–1.

[23] Examples: *Liébana* 38, 69; *Corias* pp. 71, 106; *PMH* 14, 16, 61, 97; *Cardeña* 1; *Celanova* 11, 12, 27, 40, 158; *La Coruña* 9; *León* 22, 53, 97, 139, 204, 316, 396, 488, 525; *Sahagún*

Documents have also survived, however, that concern transactions *not* involving land. These sorts of transactions would again have been equally open to laymen, clerics, monks and ecclesiastical institutions alike, but it is the possibility of their use by laypeople that must be considered in reimagining the scope of early medieval document production.

Two texts reveal a documented trade in *servi*, a subject already seen in the chapters by Conant and Costambeys, above.[24] In 914, Silo granted to Muño and his wife, in a document that reads like a typical *carta donationis*, a *mancipella* by the name of Facquina, the daughter of Moderic.[25] Similarly, in 995, Rodrigo Guimirez and his wife Basselissa handed over, by means of a *scriptura donationis*, a 3-year-old *mancipia* by the name of Adosinda, the daughter of Ero and Munia, whom Rodrigo and Basselissa had inherited; they also granted, to another party, but by the same document, Adosinda's 15-day-old sister, Gossenda. For Adosinda (but not for Gossenda), they received a countergift of real property, which provides an explanation for the preservation of the document. But in the drafting of the document, the reference to real property is limited to the part of the text where one would expect to find the price or countergift. The penalty clauses, for example, refer simply to the *mancipiae*: 'Ita ut de odi [sc. *hodie*] tempore sic siant ipsas mancipias de iuri nostro abrasa et in uestro iuri uel dominio sint traditas adque confirmatas, et si aliquis omo proinde vos calomniare uoluerit de progenie nostre que nos in iudicio deuindicare non potuerimus aut autorigare noluerimus aut uos in uoce nostra tunc pariemus illas uobis duplatas uel quantum ad uos fuerint melioratas et uobis perpetim auiturum.' The *carta* protects the interests of the recipients of the *mancipiae*, not the the title to the lands.[26] Both of these are wholly lay transactions.

Even more surprising are two texts that record entry into servile status. The first is a *placitus* (*sic*) of 956, subscribed before eight witnesses, in which Astrulfo and Nomina undertook service in the house of the priest Zamario and his companion Farega: 'We promise that we will remain and live in your house and at your side and in your villa, and we will do there service (*servitio*) in the manner of good men (*homines bonos*). And if we should commit any fraud in your house or your villa, either with respect to your work or ours, or if we should attempt to go elsewhere ('in alia parte transire') without your permission or without your blessing, as it has been written we will remain as your *servi*, given over to your benefit and that of the church of St Martin, and furthermore we

1, 206; *Sobrado* I 82, 83. See Davies, *Acts of Giving*, 44; L. Feller and C. Wickham (eds.), *Le Marché de la terre au moyen âge* (Rome, 2005), e.g. 68–9, 169, 204–5, 328.

[24] See above, Chapters 3 and 9. [25] *Liébana* 19. [26] *PMH* 174.

will compensate you with ten oxen without delay and be held by you in perpetuity.'[27] This record, found in the cartulary of Guimarães, was perhaps initially preserved along with another from four years later in which the same couple ('Astrulfo et uxori mee Teodili congomento Nomina') sold to the same pair ('Zamarius et Farega deovota') a series of properties that ultimately passed to the monastery.[28] It is not unique. In 991, Argimirus and his wife Ermilla promised lady Trastala (in a document also called a *placitum*) that if he dared to transfer his services to someone else ('si ausatum fuerit me ad alia podestate proclamare') or left her villa without her permission or knowledge or orders, he would compensate her without delay with 5 *solidi* plus double damages ('de quo agitor dublato') . . . and he would lose his rights in his cows ('caread mea rationem de illas vacas que aveo').

This is something more than the entry into patronage networks evident in many contemporary charters,[29] but something distinctly less than the sort of submission-with-reciprocal-obligations evident in commendation contracts such as the much-studied example from the Tours formula-book or its analogue in the *Formulae Visigothicae*.[30] They are acknowledgements of dependence, with statements of fines for violation of that dependence. The function of such records is a bit of a puzzle. But the fact that Astrulfo and Nomina were simultaneously bound servants and capable of a substantial donation of land reminds us how poorly we understand the nature of personal service in the early Middle Ages. Like the records of sales of *servi* discussed, and like a *fidiatura* from Valpuesta that simply records the penalty for wrongs committed against the monastery, these documents are of only very temporary use.[31] They are not ephemera, like the famous tenth-century monastic cheese list from León,[32] but proof of uses of documents for more than the preservation of title to land. To the extent that this is one of the reasons given for an ecclesiastical monopoly on documentary practices, the Iberian evidence renders that argument weaker.

[27] *PMH* 70: 'conpromittimus quomodo sedeamus uel habitemus in uestra casa et apud uos et in uestra villa et faciamus ibidem seruitio sicut facent homines bonos. et si in uestra casa fraudem fecerimus aut in uestra villa aut in uestro labore aut de nostro aut si in alia parte transire uoluerimus sine uestro mando aut sine uestra beneditione sicut in scriptura resona que sedeamus uestros seruus traditus post parte uestra et parte ecclesia sancti martini et insuper pariemus uobis x boues extra aliqua dilatatione et uobis perpetim [habituri?]'. Presumably, Zamario served the church of St Martin.

[28] *PMH* 78. [29] Davies, *Acts of Giving*, 128–9, 149–54.

[30] *Form. Tur.* 47; *Form. Vis.* 32.

[31] *Valpuesta* 45. In this sense, they are analogous the lone *carta securitate* from Osona-Manresa (Kosto, 'Laymen', 44).

[32] *León* 480; cf. above, Chapter 4 at n.90.

A third way to think about the use of documents in early medieval Christian Iberia is to consider the sorts of people who used them. The low average value of sales and the absolute number of very low-value sales in a decade-long sample of documents in the Osona-Manresa corpus from Catalonia suggest that the majority of the actors were of modest social standing.[33] A comparable analysis is not possible for the remaining Iberian material for two reasons: first, we are dealing with data from a much wider geographical and chronological range, meaning that valuations are likely to be inconsistent; more importantly, price is not consistently recorded, if it is recorded at all, appearing variously in *solidi*, *modii* or (most commonly) in-kind units.[34] Nonetheless, Davies, in her study of these sources, came to the similar conclusion that many of the actors were not aristocrats: 'Some will have been relatively rich and some will have had relatively high status in their local communities; others will have been relatively poor.' She adopted the following convention: 'where properties of small scale were conveyed, where prices were low, where their donors and vendors were only associated with properties in one community, where these donors and vendors did not themselves appear across a wide area, and/or where witness lists do not include identifiable aristocrats, then it is a reasonable assumption that these actors were peasants'.[35] This is perhaps overly restrictive, but given the impossibility of numerical analyses and the difficulty of identifying individuals (a task complicated by a limited range of personal names), it is a sensible one, and one that allows us to consider a portion of the four hundred or so lay transactions as evidence of peasant document use. The argument is not a new one: Sánchez-Albornoz described the importance of small-time property holders in this region (although property holders under considerable seigneurial pressure), prefiguring the argument made by Bonnassie for Catalonia that an analysis of the Osona-Manresa corpus confirmed.[36] Scholars have now begun to discuss the extent to which the circulation of properties controlled by such individuals was or was not a 'market'.[37]

[33] Kosto, 'Laymen', 56. [34] For these problems, see Davies, 'Sale, Price and Valuation'.

[35] Davies, *Acts of Giving*, 16–22.

[36] C. Sánchez-Albornoz, 'Serie de documentos inéditos del Reino de Asturias', *Cuadernos de historia de España*, 1–2 (1944), 298–351, at 320–1, and Sánchez-Albornoz, 'Pequeños proprietarios libres en el reino asturleonés: Su realidad histórica', in Sánchez-Albornoz, *Investigaciones y documentos sobre las instituciones hispanas* (Santiago [Chile], 1970), 178–201; E. Sáez, 'Documentos gallegos inéditos del período asturiano', *Anuario de historia del derecho español*, 18 (1947), 399–431, at 404–6; P. Bonnassie, *La Catalogne du milieu du X^e^ à la fin du XI^e^ siècle: Croissance et mutations d'une société*, 2 vols. (Toulouse, 1975–6), I, 224–36, 307–43; Kosto, 'Laymen', 55–6.

[37] Feller and Wickham (eds.), *Le marché de la terre*; R. Pastor *et al.*, *Transacciones sin mercado: Instituciones, propiedad y redes sociales en la Galicia monástica, 1200–1300* (Madrid, 1999; trans. as *Beyond the Market: Transactions, Property and Social Networks in Monastic Galicia,*

It is possible, however, to go further. In two early documents, the juridical actors are identified as *servi*. In one, from 864, the *servus* Ausonio granted his lord (*domno*), Nuño, some orchard land. In 870, the *servus* Flaciano made this same Nuño a co-heir of two villas.[38] Sánchez-Albornoz asked the key question: 'What did men of the kingdom of Asturias mean by *servus*?' – although he went on to assume rather than argue his answer, that a *servus* was a slave.[39] The existence of servitude in Iberia in the eighth to tenth centuries is generally accepted, even if there is debate over the pace of its disapperance. Furthermore, in the case of domestic servants, *servi* could accumulate substantial property, enough even to purchase their own freedom.[40] The couples described in the previous section – Astrulfo and Nomina, and Argimirus and Ermilla – were not identified as *servi*, but they were certainly servile.[41] It is not implausible, therefore, that the documents of Ausonio and Flaciano are the documents of slaves. Indeed, slaves – or rather former slaves – would have been the parties most interested in the six manumission formulas that begin the *Formulae Visigothicae*, and the term 'chartermen' (*cartularii, cartulati*) that appears elsewhere in Europe as late as the tenth century may very well refer to freedmen.[42] The case remains unproven, but, combined with the acknowledgements of service, these two documents provide strong evidence for the use of documents by laymen at or very near the bottom of the social hierarchy – in the interest of their superiors, to be sure, in one case a cleric – but given the assumed difference in power between a servant and a master, the existence of such documents is a striking indicator of the routine nature of documentary practices.

*1200–1300* [Leiden, 2002]); L. Feller, A. Gramain and F. Weber, *La fortune de Karol: Marché de la terre et liens personnels dans les Abruzzes au haut moyen âge* (Rome, 2005). Much of the discussion focuses on later evidence, but as the latter volume – and many of the chapters in the present book – shows, there is an early medieval aspect to the story.

38 *León* 3, 4.

39 Sánchez-Albornoz, 'Serie de documentos', 321–2. He raises the possibility that this is a simple humility topos, starts discussing in the conditional the idea that *servus* means 'slave' ('Si *servus* equivalía a siervo . . . '), lists various points of evidence, and then asks, 'who, in view of these texts, will dare deny the advances made by *siervos*?' . . . without ever proving that a *siervo* is a slave. Cf. *León*, I, xlix–l.

40 Collins, *Early Medieval Spain*, 228; Bonnassie, *La Catalogne*, I, 299–300; Claudio Sánchez-Albornoz, 'Los siervos en el Noroeste hispano hace un milenio', in Sánchez-Albornoz, *Viejos y nuevos estudios sobre instituciones medievales*, 2nd edn, 3 vols. (Madrid, 1976–80), III, 1523–611; Davies, *Acts of Giving*, 18–19.

41 Above, at nn. 27–8.

42 J. L. Nelson, 'Literacy in Carolingian Government', in *Uses of Literacy*, 258–96, at 262; Niermeyer, *Lexicon*, s.v. *chartulatus*; but compare above, 134–5.

## Lay archives

Virtually all of the documentary evidence from the early Middle Ages comes down to us from collections that were for most of the period between the eleventh and eighteenth centuries, if not longer, in cathedral and monastic archives, whether in cartulary or single-sheet form. Still, many of the institutions that preserve these records were themselves founded only after the year 1000, or in the years just before. Where were the documents beforehand? The case of Sant Benet de Bages in Catalonia shows how the earliest records, in large part transactions between laypeople, documented the formation of the (lay) patrimony at the core of the institution's initial endowment. Monastic archives, in other words, could originate in the lay archives of their founders – a phenomenon seen above in the chapters by Hummer and Costambeys.[43] Individuals wealthy enough to found monasteries are clearly members of at minimum a local aristocracy. But their archives might contain obvious groupings of documents – dossiers within dossiers – that reflect the merger, or absorption, of archives well before the act of foundation, dossiers that might well have been assembled by less socially prominent individuals, even well-off peasants.[44] Analysis of the early content of several foundations from elsewhere on the Iberian Peninsula supports these findings.

One opportunity for such documentary archaeology is presented by the thirteenth-century cartulary of Sobrado de los Monjes. The formation and organization of the work have not been well studied, but it seems to contain traces of earlier efforts at cartularization.[45] The first volume, of 196 folios, includes some 645 entries, with documents dating from 803 through the thirteenth century; the second, with 176 folios, contains 541 entries, with documents from 787 through 1252.[46] The overall organization of the volumes is geographical, but of the 119 documents from the first millennium, all but three are found in the first volume. In that first volume, the 116 documents from the first millennium appear among the first 194 entries. If the last entry is discounted, the early grouping is confined to the first 137 entries, running to folio 58. Despite the overall geographical organization, then, 97 per cent (115/119) of the pre-1000 documents in the cartulary are confined to the first 58 folios of the first volume. In addition, the volume begins with a list of *capitula* corresponding to the Roman numerals in the rubrics of the first 106

43 Above, Chapters 8 and 9. 44 Kosto, 'Laymen', 60–2.

45 I am working simply from the printed edition. Direct examination of the manuscript might modify these hypotheses.

46 *Sobrado* I 220 (a. 1355) and II 334 (a. 1506) are clearly later additions.

documents,[47] although in the text the numerals continue through entry 144 on folio 59v, just before a rubric reading, 'Incipit Liber de Kartulis de Hereditatibus et possessionibus Graugie Guardianes'.[48] A break in the cartulary is thus evident around folio 59. Of the 115 documents from 1000 and before in this proposed early section, fully half record transactions involving only laymen.

The source of many of these documents is not hard to discern. The core of the monastery's endowment originated in a series of grants between 952 and 966 by Ermengildo and Paterna and their sons (Bishop) Sisnando and (Count) Roderic, along with the latter's wife Geloira.[49] All of the lay transactions date from 953 and earlier. From between 916 and 953, there are twenty-eight documents recording alienations by laypeople to the founding couple, plus three to Ermengildo alone and four to Paterna alone.[50] These include sales, gifts, exchanges, profiliations and fines, the latter category attesting to the power of the couple in the region. To these can be added two alienations by priests to the couple.[51] Most of the documents record the acquisition of land reflected in the initial endowment. The same is true of two grants by laypeople in 946 and 951 to Roderic and Geloira.[52] These thirty-nine documents are likely to have been part of the archive of a local aristocratic family that was turned over complete to the new institution when the estate became the monastery.

An inventory included in the archive may give us an even more precise glimpse of the moment of transformation.[53] The date with which the document starts ('In era [M$^{a}$ VIIII$^{a}$]'; that is, 971) is evidently a later addition. The text proper begins, 'Noticia uel inuentario de uillas et hereditates que in testamentos de monasterio Superato resonat, que

47 'Incipiunt capitula primi libri de hereditatibus et possessionibus que fuerunt antiquo tempore de monasterio Superaddi in diebus regis domini Ordonii et regis domini Ueremundi et regis domini Ranemiri et regine domine Tasarie et regis domini Adefonsi.'

48 The exceptions are *Sobrado* II 46 (s. X), 172 (a. 787), 278 (a. 996).

49 *Sobrado* I 1–6.

50 Couple: *Sobrado* I 10–12, 14, 16, 21–7, 29, 31, 60, 66–7, 70–1, 78–9, 95, 98–9, 101–3, 111. Ermengildo alone: *Sobrado* I 28, 53. Paterna alone: *Sobrado* I 15, 91–3. The documents to Paterna alone may instead be to the Paterna married to a Menendo, attested as a couple between 930 and 953 in the five lay alienations *Sobrado* I 54, 85, 87, 89, 100 (see also no. 105, a. 921, a grant from a priest) – unless Menendo is the same person as Ermengildo. *Sobrado* I 63 (Ermengildo and Paterna, a. 877) and 75 (Ermengildo alone, a. 858) are probably either different individuals or misdated.

51 *Sobrado* I 32, 61; see also 105, a sale by a priest to Menendo and Paterna.

52 *Sobrado* I 69, 90.

53 *Sobrado* I 112. Cf. below, at n. 72. Other tenth-century inventories include *Celanova* 177, 183–4, 239; *La Coruña* 87; *León* 505; *Sobrado* I 194; *PMH* 27.

fuerunt de Heremgildo et Paterna, et postea de filiis eorumdem, Sesnandi episcopi et germani sui Ruderici ducis et uxoris sue Giloire, et posuerunt illas insimul in ipso prefato monasterio.' The document lists over one hundred villas and churches, organized geographically. The grammatical antecedent of *illas* could be *villas et hereditates*, but the sense of the sentence suggests that it instead refers to *testamentos*: not all of the lands of Ermengildo and Paterna passed first to their children ('que fuerunt . . . postea de filiis eorumdem'), and it makes more sense to place documents than villas 'in' a monastery. Thus this may be as much an inventory of documents – of the family archive – as it is a record of the lands passed on to the Church. It might be argued that it is simply a collation of the properties named in the six founding documents, but although many of the place names in the inventory appear there, not all of them do (e.g. Abolim, Anobre, Auteiro, Aurioles, Avianco, Balio, Bavegio . . . ). If this hypothesis is correct, the geographical organization of the inventory may reflect a geographically organized archive of the sort seen at St Gall (described by Innes, above[54]), along the lines of what would later become standard monastic practice (shown in the predominantly geographical contemporary dorsal notations on surviving early medieval original charters).

Whether or not the contents of the Ermengildo/Paterna archive were inventoried in this manner, it is likely to have contained not just documents recording alienations to the family but also documents related to the earlier histories of those acquisitions. The villa Salamir, mentioned in the inventory and the founding documents, is the subject of a document recording a sale in 858; likewise, the villa Mundini, also in the inventory and the founding documents, is the subject of a document recording a sale in 905.[55] These are not yet direct links: documents recording the transfer to the person who ultimately transferred the property (and presumably the original document) to Ermengildo and Paterna. We come closer with the villa Marciani. A document of 927 records that Ermengildo and Paterna purchased the property there of one Lebora and her son Gisulfo. Gisulfo is said to have inherited the land from his father Aloito, who is in turn attested in a document of 895 purchasing lands at the villa Marciani (and elsewhere) from the priest Gundesindus.[56] The lands may in fact be different – Gisulfo claims to be selling land that had been in the family already with his grandfather – but the coincidence of person and place suggests a documentary link.

[54] Above, Chapter 7.
[55] Salamir: *Sobrado* I 72; cf. I 4, 6, 112. Mundini: *Sobrado* I 65; cf. I 3, 112.
[56] *Sobrado* I 79, 81.

In addition to working backward from the documents of Ermengildo and Paterna, one can work forward from the earliest documents preserved in the cartulary. Four of the ten oldest documents in the collection – indeed, some of the oldest surviving post-Visigothic documents from anywhere on the peninsula – are associated with the family of a certain Pompeyano. In 803, his children Ysilo and Fafila exchanged various properties. In 817, he granted to Fafila and Fafila's wife, Penetruda, a group of five villas. In 838, he sold to the couple Herfonsus and Hermildi a plot of land. Then, in 860, four of his grandchildren (Fafila's children) sold a plot of land to a certain Cenebrida.[57] The lands mentioned in the documents of 803, 817 and 860 overlap; the 838 sale seems to be separate. Many of the place names mentioned in the documents appear in the first endowment charter of 952, granted by Ermengildo and Paterna, and in the inventory from around 971,[58] but none of the names of the beneficiaries of these documents outside the family – that is, Herfonsus, Hermildi and Cenebrida – appear later in the Sobrado cartulary. There is no evidence, therefore, that any of these documents entered the Sobrado archive in connection with a family other than that of Pompeyano, further supporting the idea of these documents as a coherent group. The transactions of 803 and 817 were both documents that Fafila and his descendants would have kept to demonstrate title, but the other two are alienations from the Pompeyano family, and for a private individual to keep a duplicate parchment copy of an alienation – as proof, for example, that he or she was no longer subject to legal obligations attached to the property – would represent a level of document use not usually imagined for this period.

If the Pompeyano documents are the remnants of an archive – for they may just be a random collection of documents that happen to be interrelated – it is likely that it is not the archive of Pompeyano, but rather of a later individual who consolidated the lands in question. One candidate is Sisnando, the author of an endowment (*cartula dotis*) in 887: the thirty villas he granted to his wife in 887 (thus a generation after the last Pompeyano document) include at least three mentioned in the Pompeyano documents: Laureda, Mandeo and Codesosso.[59] Furthermore, Sisnando was likely related to Ermengildo or Paterna.[60] But some lands

[57] *Sobrado* I 82, 77, 18, 76. See also Sáez, 'Documentos gallegos inéditos'.
[58] *Sobrado* I 1, 112. [59] *Sobrado* I 119.
[60] The genealogy at M. del C. Pallares Méndez, *El monasterio de Sobrado: Un ejemplo de protagonismo monástico en la Galicia medieval* (La Coruña, 1979), 60, gives an Eldondia as a cousin of Ermengildo, and one of the children of the counts is named Sisnando. The dual coincidence of names suggests a family connection.

and documents of Pompeyano may have been granted directly to the latter couple: in 927, Segeredo, grandson of Fafila, granted them the villa 'que dicunt Pompeiani', with similar boundaries to the lands described in Pompeyano's grant of 817.[61] Again, the coincidence of names, places and documents is a strong indicator of a real documentary tradition behind the one represented in the cartulary.

The monastery of Santa Maria de Otero de las Dueñas offers a similar opportunity for this sort of approach, but with two important differences: in this case, the documents are preserved in large part as originals, but the monastery itself was not founded until the thirteenth century. Two of the great-great-grandfathers of the founder, María Núñez, were the eleventh-century counts Fruela Muñoz and Pedro Flaínez, whose families' acquisitions dominate the earliest holdings of the monastic archive. The lineages were joined by the marriage of the daughter of the former to the son of the latter, probably in the 1040s. Alfonso García Leal has identified 243 documents from the Otero collection presumably in the archives of these two counts when they were united shortly after the death of Pedro Flaínez in 1048 (Fruela Muñoz died in 1046), 72 recording acquisitions of Fruela Muñoz between 993×1003 and 1046, and 68 of Pedro Flaínez between 996 and 1047.[62] In the period of interest here, however, the two patrimonies, and thus their putative archives, would have existed separately. In fact, as the dates of the earliest documents of these two counts suggest, the tenth-century and earlier records offer instead a picture of the archives of their ancestors.

Of the fifty-one documents from 1000 and earlier in the Otero archive, thirty-one concern transactions between laypeople; in addition, there is one royal grant to a layperson and one sale from a priest to a layperson. Of these, three are the earliest acts of Pedro Flaínez and Fruela Muñoz, but most relate instead to the activity of their parents and grandparents: two sales and one grant to Muño Flaínez and Froileba (Pedro's paternal grandparents, discussed below in the context of Sahagún);[63] seven acquisitions by Flaín Muñoz, with and without his wife Justa (Pedro's parents),

61 *Sobrado* I 27: 'iuxta riuulo Mando et discurrit ipsa villa per terminos de Roadi et inde in terminos de Colimbrianos et inde in terminos de Sancto Iuliano, *et sunt ipsos terminos antiquos*' (my emphasis). Cf. *Sobrado* I 77: 'in riba de Mandeo . . . villa que est usque in terminos de Colimbrianos, et inde usque in terminos de Roadi'. See Pallares Méndez, *El monasterio de Sobrado*, 6n8.

62 A. García Leal, 'El archivo de los condes Fruela Muñoz y Pedro Flaínez (854–1048): Una visión nueva de viejos documentos', *Signo: Revista de historia de la cultura escrita*, 13 (2004), 121–47; García Leal, 'Los condes Fruela Muñoz y Pedro Flaínez: La formación de un patrimonio señorial', *Anuario de estudios medievales*, 36 (2006), 1–110. María Fruélaz was born after 1029 (Leal, 'Los condes', 10).

63 *Otero* 6, 11–12; below, 278–9.

six of which were directly linked to his judicial activity;[64] and five acquistions by Fruela Vimaraz, with and without his wife Adosinda (Fruela's maternal grandparents), three of which are linked to judicial activity, and one of which was a royal grant from Vermudo II.[65] The volume of records linked to judicial activity, which only increases under Pedro (19 records) and Fruela (17 records), might be seen as giving the collection a public or institutional character,[66] but these were very much *family* archives. They contain not only acts benefiting the counts themselves but also the endowment of Fruela's half-sister, Urraca (daughter of the first marriage of his mother, Jimena),[67] and an inventory of documents assembled by the parents of the second wife of Pedro Flaínez's father.[68] Most of the remaining lay transactions concern properties easily associated with one of the other families; several, for example, refer to Valdoré and the Esla River valley, one of the principal bases of the Flaínez, while two refer to Cirujales, in the territory dominated by the Fruélaz.[69] As in the Sobrado archive, direct links between early documents and later transmission are difficult to discern, but there are hints. Of the earliest records, three are sales to the couple Adriano and Eremesinda. One (a. 936) refers to Valdoré, and the other two (both a. 949) to El Montecillo; inherited property at the latter location was granted by Pedro's son to his own children in 1057.[70] A sale in 999 of property at Corniero is echoed in a transfer (for judicially ordered compensation) in 1048, and then again in Pedro's son's grant of 1057.[71]

The inventory merits further analysis.[72] It is a list of nine documents prepared by Fernándo Vermúdez and Elvira, likely the parents of the second wife of Pedro Flaínez's father.[73] The date with which the documents begin ('Era millesima XIIII', or 976) is plausible, but also evidently a later addition. It is labelled an 'Agutione [*recte* agnitione?] vel inventarium . . . de cartas de Villa Naptaulio'. The place in question has been identified as El Natahoyo, which also appeared in the 1057 grant by Pedro Flaínez. The documents themselves are not preserved in the

64 *Otero* 27, 33–4, 36, 38–9, 44.

65 *Otero* 30 (royal), 37, 40–1, 46.

66 Davies, *Acts of Giving*, 143–6; A. Prieto Prieto, 'Documentos referentes al orden judicial del monasterio de Otero de las Dueñas', *Anuario de historia del derecho español*, 44 (1974), 619–74; C. Estepa Díez, 'Poder y propiedad feudales en el período astur: Las mandaciones de los Flaínez en la montaña leonesa', in *Miscel.lània en homenatge al P. Agustí Altisent* (Tarragona, 1991), 285–327. For the difficulties of making such distinctions, above, 11, 15, 21–3, 50, etc.

67 *Otero* 50; García Leal, 'Condes', 8–9.

68 *Otero* 22; below, at n. 72.

69 *Otero* 3–4, 14, 24–5, 49 (Valdoré, Esla); 22, 28 (Cirujales).

70 *Otero* 3, 7–8; García Leal, 'Condes', 86–7.

71 *Otero* 45; García Leal, 'Condes', 86–7, 103.

72 *Otero* 22.

73 García Leal, 'Los condes', 66.

Otero archive; indeed, none of the individuals or place names appear earlier in the corpus. Of course, the grandchildren to whom the lands passed were not the direct ancestors of María Nuñez; if the charters passed with the land, they would have left the family archive. Around the year 1000, however, the land (and thus the documents) would have been in the possession of Pedro Flaínez.

Nine documents are listed and follow a general form: the *carta* of so-and-so, concerning such-and-such a type of property, located in such-and-such a place, such-and-such a portion. Thus the first is the charter of Donno, concerning an orchard (*pumare*) in Ramma, next to the house of Negella, for the whole of the enclosure (*clusa*). The second is the charter of Graciano, again concerning an orchard, in La Quintana, where Serpento lived, for a one-third portion. And so on through the ninth, the charter of Ranimiro Froilaniz, in Las Linares, bordering the lands of the sons of Abbatinus, for half of the lands. Documents 4 and 5 are charters of a Queen Uracca, one along with her son Ordono, another with her sons Ordono and Ramiro.[74] These descriptions reveal the author of the inventory working directly from the original documents, not bothering to clarify pronominal references: 'one property borders on the *strata kavallari*, and the second is above the house of Armentarius, and the third borders your lands'; 'the field that is next to your house'.

The contrast of this inventory with the Ermengildo/Paterna inventory is striking. Here there is no ambiguity: it is unquestionably a list of documents. And the scribe who drew it up was clearly interested in being able not just to identify the documents but also to digest their content; if the beneficiaries are assumed to be Fernándo Vermúdez and Elvira, who are after all named at the outset of the document, then the only key details missing from the point of view of a modern diplomatist are dates and (if sales) prices. In offering information about boundaries and the precise portions of property transferred, the scribe gives more information than would be required if the record were merely a finding list for the documents (compare, for example, the Ghittia list from Lombard Italy, which distinguishes various types of documents in phrases that recall dorsal notations).[75] What the Fernándo Vermúdez/Elvira list offers is the details of the legal acts; in that sense it is more of a miniature cartulary or *Traditionsbuch*, with a narrow geographical focus on a single

[74] This could be either Urraca, second wife of Fruela II of Asturias, who had sons by him of with those names between 917 and 925, or Urraca Fernández, who had a son named Ordoño by Ordoño III of León between 951 and 956, and a son named Ramiro by Sancho II of Pamplona after 970. Alternatively, the charters could be from two different Urracas. The first scenario seems most likely.

[75] *ChLA* XXVI 808; *CDL* II 295; above, 239.

villa. It is impossible to know how difficult it was to assemble these nine documents (How many others were with them in the *scrinium*? Were they already organized in labelled bundles, or was it a messy pile?), but the author of the list was clearly engaged in the preservation, organization and transmission of documentary records. The author was, in other words, working not with a mere collection of documents, but with an archive, and was doing so for laypeople.

Sobrado and Otero are examples of what might be called the 'founder phenomenon': monastic archives with their origins in the family archives of an aristocratic founder. San Toribio de Liébana offers a variation on this theme: the lay transactions that dominate the earliest holdings of the archive are not those of the founder, but rather of the family of an early abbot, Opila. The earliest forty-two documents in the archive (to 932) include twenty lay transactions, of which fourteen record the acquisitions of Opila's parents, Bacaudano and Faquilona.[76] This example of the integration of a lay archive into a monastic archive – rather than the wholesale transformation of one into the other – is fairly straightforward. Traces of lay archives in early institutional holdings are not always so obvious, as is shown by the case of Sahagún.

At least seven substantial dossiers survive among the ninth- and tenth-century documents of Sahagún, all of which look different from an archival perspective. Four of the five oldest documents are sales by laypeople to laypeople of properties at Piasca.[77] Of these, the three earliest are sales to the couple Argemundo and Recoire, one of a vineyard from Recoire's brother in 857, and two of various properties from the couple Daildi and David in 861. The daughter of one of the vendors in the fourth document, from 904, is named Daildi; given the rarity of the name, which appears nowhere else in the Sahagún corpus, a family connection is possible.[78] The monastery of Santa María de Piasca, which was incorporated into Sahagún in the twelfth century, is first recorded in 930,[79] well after all of these documents. A plausible hypothesis, then, is that the lands of Argemundo and Recoire – along with these documents – were at some point transferred to the monastery of Piasca, and then to Sahagún in the twelfth century.[80] Yet the coincidence of the place

[76] *Liébana* 18, 21, 23, 25–8, 32, 35–6, 39–42. The other lay transactions are *Liébana* 13–14, 19, 22, 31, 38.

[77] *Sahagún* 1–3, 5. The fifth document, *DEPA* 94 (a. 869), has no evident connections to any others in the corpus.

[78] See, however, *DEPA* 117 (a. 877), in which the donor's grandfather is named Daildi.

[79] *Sahagún* 39.

[80] Other documents from a hypothetical 'Santa María de Piasca dossier' include *Sahagún* 79, 96, 134–6, 153–4, 242, 288, 304–5.

name and the presence of these documents in the Sahagún archive are their only connections to the monastery of Piasca (although a grant to the community in 945 includes lands *iusta* [*domum*] *Require*),[81] so three alternatives remain: first, that there is no connection between the lands in question and the monastery of Piasca, and at some point the lands were transferred, along with the documents, directly to Sahagún; second, that the land was never transferred either to Piasca or to Sahagún, but that documents were stored in the archive of Piasca after its founding and later incorporated into the Sahagún archive; and third, that the land was never transferred either to Piasca or to Sahagún, but that the documents were stored at Sahagún itself from the beginning.

The survival of these four documents as originals has some relevance here. Most of the early charters of Sahagún survive not as originals, but in the early twelfth-century *Becerro gótico*.[82] Two-thirds of the originals before 950 (twenty-two of thirty-four) are royal or episcopal documents or transfers directly to Sahagún;[83] of the remaining third (twelve), seven relate to Piasca,[84] and two others are part of other groups of documents that probably represent archival dossiers.[85] Both of these dossiers offer instructive comparisons. The first concerns the monastery of Santiago de Valdávida. This monastery was endowed by Vermudo Nuñez, count of Cea, in 949, on confiscated lands that had been granted to him by Ramiro II in 943. The ninth- and tenth-century Sahagún corpus includes ten additional documents concerning Valdávida (without mentioning Sahagún). Of all these documents, only two, the endowment charter and a sale of 969, survive as originals, and all of the documents (including the two just mentioned) appear in the *Becerro gótico*.[86] Thus the Valdávida documents must have been incorporated into the Sahagún archive when the monastery was absorbed sometime before the composition of the cartulary in 1110. The second dossier concerns the priest

81 *Sahagún* 96.

82 Of *Sahagún* 1–129 (that is, the documents from 950 and earlier), ninety-three documents list the *Becerro* as the only or the earliest exemplar. This includes a number of document groups listed under a single number (*Sahagún* 34 [four acts], 36 [seven acts], 94 [twelve acts]).

83 Royal diplomas for Sahagún: *Sahagún* 6–8, 61, 70, 93, 98–9, 129. Royal diploma for another monastery: *Sahagún* 21. Transfers directly to Sahagún: *Sahagún* 18, 25, 29, 56, 80, 87, 120, 126, 128. Episcopal documents not mentioning Sahagún: *Sahagún* 33, 78. Episcopal confirmation for Sahagún: *Sahagún* 101.

84 *Sahagún* 1–3, 5, 39, 79, 96.

85 *Sahagún* 114 (Valdávida), 125 (Melic). The remaining three include two transfers between laypeople that I have not yet traced (*Sahagún* 4, 52) and a grant to the church of San Félix de Cisneros, which again I have not yet traced (*Sahagún* 105).

86 *Sahagún* 84 (grant to Vermudo), 113, 114 (endowment), 142, 157, 172–3, 208, 217, 252 (sale of 969), 254, 257.

Melic, whose documents include twelve sales and a profiliation (from 932 to 951) before his own grant to Sahagún and a testament of 959; only one of the thirteen earlier documents survives as an original, and it, too, is included in the *Becerro*.[87] The presence among the earliest Sahagún originals of two charters clearly linked to dossiers with demonstrable links to Sahagún might be used to support an argument that the Piasca documents are part of a similar dossier; that is, that the Pisaca originals, too, were preserved because they documented holdings of Sahagún. The fact that Piasca was not absorbed until after the composition of the *Becerro*, however, means that we cannot similarly test whether the compiler of the *Becerro gótico* judged those documents to be relevant to a picture of Sahagún's holdings. It remains possible, then, that these documents were stored in the archive despite having no formal connection to Sahagún.

A fourth substantial dossier (in addition to Piasca, Valdávida and Melic) appears to be a true lay archive, and from members of a family we have already seen to have archival habits: Muño Flaínez and Froileba, the grandparents of Pedro Flaínez of the Otero archive. Muño and his wife, and then Froileba alone after Muño's death, systematically acquired property at several locations: Valle de Laurenzo (by purchase in 947, 948 and 950, all drawn up by the priest Fredemundo),[88] Aleje (by purchase in 958, 959 and 961),[89] Noanca (by profiliation in 961; by purchase in 961, 962 and 963; by default on a loan in 962)[90] and Caso (by grant in 960 and by the same profiliation of 961).[91] Three other places appear in only one document each (Loides, profiliation, 960; Corniero, profiliation, 961;Vilasecos, purchase, 962); one sale, from 948, does not specify a location.[92] One output of this spree of acquisition was a set of fifteen documents produced over a fifteen-year period, all with Muño and/or his wife as beneficiaries. In 985, their daughter Jimena made a large donation to Sahagún, which mentions lands at Noanca and Valle de Laurenzo.[93] The correspondence is not perfect: the land at Noanca is said to have been purchased from the 'omes de Colle' rather than inherited from her parents; the *money* for the purchase of the land at Valle de Laurenzo, rather than the land itself, is said to have come from her parents; and the

[87] *Sahagún* 45 (profiliation), 69, 75, 81, 90, 103, 109, 111–12, 121, 125 (original), 131, 133, 167 (grant to Sahagún; original, not in *Becerro*), 168 (testament; original and in *Becerro*). *Sahagún* 183, a royal confirmation of the testament of Melic, which survives as a single sheet and in the *Becerro*, appears to be a forgery. An additional sale to Melic, in 951, survives in the *Tumbo* of the cathedral of León: *León* 232.

[88] *Sahagún* 107–8, 124. [89] *Sahagún* 161, 163, 189.

[90] *Sahagún* 191, 193, 198, 201, 213. [91] *Sahagún* 178, 191.

[92] *Sahagún* 110, 184, 191, 205. [93] *Sahagún* 328.

other place names do not appear. A subsequent grant by Jimena of lands at Valle de Laurenzo does mention her parents as previous owners, however, so we should not rule out still other donations of family lands that would cover the missing properties.[94] In contrast to the earliest dossiers, only one of the fifteen documents survives as an original;[95] the rest are preserved in the *Becerro gótico* of 1110.

A similarly sized dossier is more difficult to connect to Sahagún. Between 958 and 965, Ansur and his wife María made nine purchases of land at Tindal, Villanueva, León, Otereulo, Lampreana and Trejeco;[96] they also acquired by profiliation land at Villa Alva.[97] They granted the land at León, a field *(ferragine)* acquired in 961, to Sahagún in 963.[98] At some point between 965 and 970, Ansur acquired a new wife, Ilduara, and the new couple resumed the old couple's campaign, making six more purchases between 970 and 976 at Trobajo, Rebolare, León, Villa de Petro, Villa de Belone and Quintila.[99] The lands at Villa de Petro and Villa de Belone were purchased from the monasteries of San Martín de Valdepopulo and Santa María de León (?) and then immediately granted to San Salvador de Palazuelo; they then appear in a royal confirmation to Sahagún of 976 and in a dispute in 998.[100] The only grant directly to Sahagún other than of the field at León was made by Ilduara, now the widow of Ansur, of two villas not named in earlier documents.[101] In all, then, there are sixteen documents recording transactions in which Ansur and his wives are the beneficiaries that ultimately made their way into the Sahagún archive. All of them are preserved in the *Becerro*, while only three also survive as originals[102] – a good indication that even though few of the lands can be traced to the monastery (in the early documents, at any rate), they eventually became its property.

The dossier of Iscam and Filaura is slightly different, in that all but one of the surviving transactions concern a single place, Melgar de Foracasas, and the collection is preserved in a curious manner.[103] Twelve sales from between 945 and 954, totalling over 133 *solidi*,[104] are listed in abbreviated

94 *Sahagún* 345.

95 *Sahagún* 205. Jimena's grant of 985 also survives as an original, although the later grant does not.

96 *Sahagún* 158, 169, 182, 187, 194, 199, 210, 223, 237.

97 *Sahagún* 214. 98 *Sahagún* 194, 215. 99 *Sahagún* 260, 268, 278, 282.

100 *Sahagún* 269, 272–3. The sales are recorded in confirmations dated *after* the grant, and the second grant refers to the first – I have not yet sorted out this puzzle.

101 *Sahagún* 308.

102 *Sahagún* 214, 268, 272. The grant to San Salvador, Ansur's testament and Ildonza's grant also survive as originals (*Sahagún* 269, 284, 308).

103 *Sahagún* 94.

104 107 *solidi* in coin or kind, 26 *arenzos* (*solidi* in coin), 22 *modios* of wheat, a plot of land (*terra placabile*) and a cow (*vacca ruvia*); for one of the transactions, the price is missing.

form in a single document in the *Becerro*. Each item lists just the seller, the property, the price and the date. A sanction clause and subscriptions ('nos omnes supra scripti hoc confirmamus') follow the last document. Whether a multiple document was copied whole into the *Becerro* or the individual documents were synthesized for the purpose of the cartulary (the common subscription, absent in two other multiple documents in the corpus, may indicate the former solution[105]), at some point there was a collection of twelve charters relating to Melgar, which would have been transferred to the monastery at the time of two grants by Iscam, Filaura and Iscam's sister in 959, the second of which survives as an original.[106] The dossier of Iscam and Filaura is striking in that it brings us down to a quite modest social level: that of well-off peasants. The couple were landowners, to be sure, but they dealt with property in only a single place, and with small, low-value plots. If the twelve documents represent an archive or part of an archive, it was a peasant archive.

Muño Flaínez and Froileba were not, by contrast, just any laypeople, nor were Fernándo Vermúdez and Elvira, or Ermengildo and Paterna. They were local aristocrats – if not always counts themselves then moving in comital circles. Given the relative flatness and fragmented power structure of Iberian society in this period, comital designations and connections reveal more about their relative than their absolute power. Nonetheless, these were the families with the inclination and resources to amass the amount of property that could endow a monastic institution stable enough to last and thus to preserve their documents for posterity. But the Iberian dossiers just examined reveal that the archival habits of such families – accumulation, organization and transmission of documents – *preceded* their ties with ecclesiastical institutions, and furthermore drew on documentary habits of their social inferiors. Early medieval archives, like early medieval documentary practices generally, were not an ecclesiastical monopoly.

Uncovering the rhythms and logic – economic, social and cultural – of the massive transfer of property out of lay hands and into the hands of ecclesiastical institutions has been one of the great achivements of medieval historical scholarship. François Menant offers, however, a caution in the Italian context:

> There is a risk that the dominant impression is one of a permanent shift from lay property to Church property, an impression that is surely false, or at least very incomplete. On the other hand, the intermediate stages of concentration of small

105 *Sahagún* 34, 36.
106 *Sahagún* 162, 164. The first grant also includes lands in Valderaduey and Boñar.

peasant property, equally evident in the documentation, must take on greater importance: the concentration of small peasant property in the hands of more substantial landowners, rural but especially urban, whose holdings could pass in turn to the Church.[107]

The lay archives discussed in the second part of this chapter illustrate the validity of this model: the archival dossiers of lay monastic founders record clearly a process of concentration of smaller individual properties in the hands of substantial landholders. But this was merely the penultimate step, as even older records, the ones that record the transfers previous to the absorption of a property into a great estate, hint at the situation before: a world of modest aristocrats, small-time landowners and even humble servants, clerical *and* lay, buying and selling land, people and goods; paying fines; entering into agreements – and writing it all down frequently enough that to do so could be considered local custom.

Additional abbreviations:

| | |
|---|---|
| *Cardeña* | *Colección documental del monasterio de San Pedro de Cardeña*, ed. G. Martínez Díez (Burgos, 1998) |
| *Celanova* | *Colección diplomática del monasterio de Celanova* (842–1230), ed. E. Sáez and C. Sáez, vols. I–III (Alcalá de Henares, 1996–2006) |
| *Corias* | *El registro de Corias*, ed. A. García Leal (Oviedo, 2000) |
| *La Coruña* | *La Coruña: Fondo antiguo (788–1065)*, ed. C. Sáez and M. del V. González de la Peña, vols. I–II (Alcalá de Henares, 2003–4) |
| *DEPA* | *Diplomática española del período astur: Estudio de las fuentes documentales del Reino de Asturias (718–910)*, ed. A. C. Floriano, 2 vols. (Oviedo, 1949–51) |
| *León* | *Colección documental del archivo de la catedral de León (775–1230)*, ed. E. Sáez *et al.*, vols. I–III (León, 1987–90) |
| *Liébana* | *Cartulario de Santo Toribio de Liébana*, ed. L. Sánchez Belda (Madrid, 1948) |
| *Otero* | *Colección documental del monasterio de Otero de las Dueñas*, ed. J. A. Fernández Flórez and M. Herrero de la Fuente, vol. I (León, 1999) |

107 F. Menant, 'Les transactions foncières dans le Royaume d'Italie du X$^{e}$ à la fin du XII$^{e}$ siècle', in Feller and Wickham (eds.), *Le marché de la terre*, 147–60, at 151. In Iberia, Davies finds the increase in 'volume of peasant engagement with ecclesiastical landlords' – replacing relationships with lay lords – to be the main lesson of the tenth-century charters (Davies, *Acts of Giving*, 221).

| | |
|---|---|
| *PMH* | *Portugaliae monumenta historica* . . . , ed. H. de Carvalho e Araujo and J. J. Da Silva Mendes Leal, part 3, *Diplomata et Chartae*, vol. I (Lisbon, 1868) |
| *Sahagún* | *Colección diplomática del monasterio de Sahagún (siglos IX y X)*, ed. J. M. Mínguez Fernández (León, 1976) |
| *Sobrado* | *Tumbos del monasterio de Sobrado de los Monjes*, ed. P. Loscertales de García de Valdeavellano, 2 vols. (Madrid, 1976) |
| *Valpuesta* | *Cartulario de Valpuesta*, ed. M. Desamparados Pérez Soler (Valenica, 1970) |

# 11 On the material culture of legal documents: charters and their preservation in the Cluny archive, ninth to eleventh centuries

*Matthew Innes*

*Cluny has been central to the previous scholarship on lay documentary practices. In this chapter, however, and in the context of the rest of this volume, it appears now as a late tenth- and early eleventh-century manifestation of precisely the same processes we have seen elsewhere that generate our incomplete image of a common documentary culture. We note again the importance of intra-familial transactions, and the ongoing nature of the relationship between founding families and the institutions that eventually absorbed their documents. The case of Cluny also underlines that documents served purposes beyond storing and transmitting their content, in the same way that archives served purposes beyond storing and transmitting their documents.*

It may seem optimistic to devote an entire chapter of a book on the lay use of documents to the Cluny charter collection. After all, Cluny is probably the best studied monastery of the earlier medieval period: surely any charters preserved there can do no more than simply confirm the well-known maxim that our sources survive because of the institutional continuity of ecclesiastical archives? This chapter demonstrates that the contents of the Cluny archive, properly analysed, categorically refute this idea. Precisely because the Cluny charter collection was not only voluminous but also the subject of intensive early modern and modern interest, its remnants allow a detailed consideration of lay documentary and archival practices, and their relationship to the development of the institutional practices of the Church. Building on the other contributions to this book, this chapter sets out to sift through the contents of this institutional repository and to identify earlier layers of archival and documentary practice within the Cluny material. It goes on to argue that we can not only reconstruct archival and documentary practices that preceded and were subsumed by ecclesiastical institutions, but we can also reach a deeper understanding of the ways in which these practices were eventually pushed beneath the historiographical horizon by post-Carolingian archival reorganization and institutional memorialization. With the Cluny material it is possible not only to surmise the existence of a submerged iceberg of lay documentation but also to map the contours of the frozen matter hidden beneath the waves. The findings of this chapter also speak to two other crucial debates, the first epistemological and the second historiographical.

First of all, considering the transmission of the Cluny charters exposes the need to integrate classical diplomatic scholarship, with its emphasis on textual typologies, with a more contextualizing approach that embraces the material culture of legal documents: the physical traces, annotations and alterations that are the best evidence we have of how a document was received, used and understood.[1] After all, Jean Mabillon and the other early modern founders of diplomatic scholarship were concerned with establishing rules to ascertain the validity or otherwise of documents as a means to advance live legal and political arguments. The subsequent reception of their methods in the nineteenth and twentieth centuries and their adoption as the bedrock of national archives and the newly professionalized historical scholarship of the university curriculum owed much to the imperative of establishing an objectified narrative of identity shaped by the needs of the modern nation state.[2] Nonetheless, the criteria they established to test the reliability and date of particular texts have been indispensable in building an agreed evidential corpus and a set of methodological rules on which historical study can be based. The editions made possible by this work have brought the fruits of medieval archives to a wider constituency of modern

[1] Cf. G. Koziol, *The Politics of Memory and Identity in Carolingian Royal Diplomas: The West Frankish Kingdom (840–987)* (Turnhout, 2011). Like Koziol, I treat documents as material objects implicated in living social relationships that they helped to define, but I differ in my specific readings of the relationships between their embedded and ritual meanings, on the one hand, and their practical intent as written record on the other. I have benefited from the comments and observations of my colleagues in the Lay Archives Working Group, in particular Adam Kosto and Hans Hummer, whose own observations on Cluny sparked my own; from discussion with Jon Jarrett of work he undertook as a research assistant databasing *placita* and cartularies in work funded by Birkbeck College and the Leverhulme Trust; and from the comments and generosity of Wendy Davies, Barbara Rosenwein, Julian Swann, and Charles West. It is more than usually necessary, therefore, to emphasize that all conclusions and interpretations, and, above all, all errors and infelicities, in what follows are my own.

[2] Mabillon: D. Knowles, 'Jean Mabillon', in Knowles, *The Historian and Character* (Cambridge, 1964), 213–39, and Knowles, *Great Historical Enterprises* (Cambridge, 1962), 2–62. Functions of professionalized medievalism in the nation states of classical modernity: P. Geary, *The Myth of Nations: The Medieval Origins of Europe* (Princeton, NJ, 2003), 15–40; M. Innes, 'A Fatal Disjuncture? Medievalism and Medieval History in Britain', in J. Jarnut and H.-W. Goetz (eds.), *Mediävistik im 21 Jahrhundert: Stand und Perspektiven der internationalen und interdisziplinären Mittelalterforschung* (Munich, 2003), 73–100; R. J. W. Evans and G. P. Marchal (eds.), *The Uses of the Middle Ages in Modern European States: History, Nationhood and the Search for Origins* (London, 2010).

historians. Thus, documents as initially experienced by many modern scholars have undergone an ontological transformation, from material remains into standardized texts, divorced from the context of their storage and transmission. The establishment of canonical source-criticism has embedded a set of unwritten assumptions – some empirical and some epistemological – about what might constitute historical evidence and thus limited the perspectives of possible history.

The material culture of documents – their physical appearance, production and performance – was central to their reception by contemporaries, yet it is rarely considered in modern analysis.[3] Partly, this may be because many texts are transmitted through cartularies, but where original charters have been discussed as physical objects, this has tended to be framed by a 'strong thesis' positing a fundamental opposition between orality and literacy; the material presence of writing can be relegated to the status of an 'oral' hangover redolent of 'archaic' mentalities and so somehow alien and embarrassing to the progress of literacy; yet, the fact that writing is simultaneously both a physically present mnemomic and a means of communication, with the capacity to transcend the immediacies of time and place, is fundamental to its practical use in most pre-modern and indeed many modern social contexts.[4] Although there is a rich stream of recent scholarship on charter collections and their commemorative and legal functions, there has been next to no sustained study of the kinds of abbreviations, annotations and physical traces of preparation, storage and retrieval that – as we saw in the case of the St Gall documents discussed above – are crucial in reaching definitive conclusions about document use.[5] Moreover, by focusing attention on documents that can be reconstructed as 'first-order' historical phenomena – that is, as self-standing texts – documentary scholarship has diverted attention from a wider range of evidence that has been effectively if inadvertently excluded from serious historical analysis: references to documents – whether now lost or still surviving – embedded in surviving texts, for example, or evidence for the use of a surviving document

[3] It is particularly striking that even in facsimile reproductions of documents, the accompanying discussion focuses on the questions privileged by the traditional concern of diplomatic scholarship to establish an 'authoritative' text: see, e.g., D. Ganz and W. Goffart, 'Charters Earlier Than 800 from French Collections', *Speculum*, 65 (1990), 906–32. G. Koziol, 'A Father, His Son, Memory, and Hope: The Joint Diploma of Lothar and Louis V (Pentecost Monday, 979) and the Limits of Performativity', in J. Martschukat and S. Patzold (eds.), *Ritual, Inszenierung und Performanz vom Mittlelater bis zur Neuzeit* (Cologne, 2003), 83–103, takes materiality seriously.

[4] For a range of approaches to charters as evidence for literacy, see K. Heidecker (ed.), *Charters and the Use of the Written Word in Medieval Society* (Turnhout, 2000).

[5] See below, nn. 11, 87–8, for studies of charter collections and their functions.

after its initial production in the form of later additions or annotations.[6] In other words, the foundational agenda of modern historical scholarship has assumed a specific epistemology that has limited our engagement with medieval documents. While we respect the achievements of centuries of documentary scholarship, the need now is to treat documents as objects that, although they may now look like passive records of past social structures, were once material actors within the societies they purported to define. This will allow us not only to reframe some of the great set-piece questions of medieval scholarship but also to expand dramatically the evidential base from which they can be answered.

The second set of wider issues addressed by this analysis of the Cluny charters is historiographical. In recent scholarship, debate about the pace and nature of social transformation in post-Carolingian West and East Francia has been helpfully linked to a series of questions about archival and documentary transformations in the tenth and eleventh centuries. This connection between historiographies of social development and documentary change has achieved a high profile largely because of the revisionism championed by Dominique Barthélemy.[7] Questioning a dominant methodological presupposition of post-war Francophone medieval scholarship – the post-Carolingian 'feudal revolution' as first essayed by Marc Bloch and subsequently elaborated by Georges Duby's study of the Mâconnais and a host of other regional *thèses* – Barthélemy drew attention to the ways in which the texture of the documentary evidence changed in the tenth and eleventh centuries.[8] Documents – and in particular notices recording the progress of disputes – grew less laconic and tightly constrained by expectations about documentary form, and more likely to include the anecdotal and incidental details necessary to sustain an episodic narrative. So Barthélemy pointed out that they inevitably granted modern historians a fuller understanding of social bonds, in all their complexity and messiness, than did earlier, more formalized, documents. There were thus dangers in assuming that the kind of motivations and obligations made apparent by this new documentary *narrativité* directly reflected new forms of social relationship; rather, they might simply attest changing scribal conventions. From a complementary angle, other scholars have followed Patrick Geary's lead

[6] A 'forensic' as opposed to editorial approach has important epistemological and historiographical implications for traditional positivist methodologies, an issue which I hope to discuss elsewhere.

[7] D. Barthélemy, *La société dans le comté de Vendôme: De l'an mil au XIV$^e$ siècle* (Paris, 1993).

[8] M. Bloch, *Feudal Society*, trans. L. Manyon (London, 1961 [1937]); G. Duby, *La société au XI$^e$ et XII$^e$ siècles dans la région mâconnaise* (Paris, 1953). Of course, Bloch's agenda was not the same as Duby's, but it was via Duby's example that *annaliste* regional history became dominant. See T. N. Bisson, '*La terre et les hommes*: A Programme Fulfilled?', *French History*, 14 (2000), 322–45.

in emphasizing the agency and interests of ecclesiastical institutions, and in particular newly founded and reformed monasteries, Cluny foremost among them. For Geary, the establishment of these institutions as the primary repositories of social memory wrought significant cultural changes, not least in the ways aristocratic families remembered their pasts and so represented their presents: the picture of social transformation confidently identified by Duby half a century earlier might therefore be more apparent than real, first and foremost a result of changes in the realm of cultural representation.[9] Close examination of the narrative strategies of specific dispute notices, indeed, showed how these were not disinterested legal records but rather carefully constructed accounts that reflected the self-representation of ecclesiastical institutions as the stable central points of this society, and therefore presented aristocratic actions as wilfully and spontaneously violent, when the reality might have been rather more complex.[10]

Both Barthélemy and Geary drew on an older tradition of diplomatic scholarship that posed significant questions about the nature of the documentary record for post-Carolingian West Francia. A long tradition of studies of cartularies – compilations into which monastic institutions began to copy an edited and reordered version of their documentary holdings from the eleventh century onwards – reaches back through the central institutions of modern French medieval scholarship and the builders of national archives and collections in the nineteenth century to the antiquarians of the pre-Revolutionary era. Cartulary scholarship has increasingly demonstrated the danger of assuming that cartulary compilers of the eleventh century and later sought to present a direct and undistorted view of the contents of the archives from which they worked. They evidently made active choices about which documents to include and which to exclude, as well as improving texts and imposing their own editorial and organizational schemes, motivated by the interlocking imperatives of commemoration and the establishment of title.[11] As a result, students of post-Carolingian documentation have become aware of the ways in which cartularies effectively 'froze' a potentially more fluid and ambivalent archival situation, fixing a particular image of the documentary practices

[9] Geary, *Phantoms*, which in part built on the cultural turn in Duby's own work. For subsequent debate, see, e.g., L. Morelle, 'Histoire et archives vers l'an mil: Une nouvelle "mutation"?', *Histoire et archives*, 3 (1998), 119–41.

[10] P. Geary, 'Monastic Memory and the Mutation of the Year Thousand', in B. H. Rosenwein and S. Farmer (eds.), *Monks and Nuns, Saints and Outcasts: Essays in Honor of Lester K. Little* (Ithaca, NY, 2000), 19–36.

[11] *Les cartulaires*; A. Kosto and A. Winroth (eds.), *Charters, Cartularies and Archives: The Preservation and Transmission of Documents in the Medieval West* (Toronto, 2002); 'Pratiques de l'écrit documentaire au XI^e^ siècle', published as *Bibliothèque de l'École des chartes*, 155 (1997), 5–349.

of the earlier period. The stark judgements of previous generations, as passed down through handbooks on diplomatic, thus need wholesale revision.[12] Cartularies characteristically include only the selected highlights of available Merovingian and Carolingian documentation, solemn acts recording the merciful munificence of a charismatic and now legendary royal authority or commemorating the reckless piety of founders and celebrated benefactors. The comparison between the stately formality of such material and the more scrappy and often formless notices in which contemporary dealings were done need not, therefore, be indicative of a decline in documentary standards: where later cartularists chose to include more workaday material from the earlier material it is similarly pragmatic and eclectic.[13]

### Documentary practices before the monastic archive: the Cluny evidence

These interlocking questions frame our discussion of the Cluny archive. Cluny's is probably the best-known charter collection of the entire medieval period, one that has provided the empirical underpinnings for a series of paradigm-setting works on the social history of the post-Carolingian centuries.[14] The monumental six-volume edition of the surviving material prior to the thirteenth century, published by Bernard and Bruel over the last quarter of the nineteenth century, contains over 5,500 documents[15]; this has been supplemented by a range of subsequent studies correcting details (for example, of chronology)[16]; by fundamental

[12] O. Guyotjeannin, '*Penuria scriptorum*: Le mythe de l'anarchie documentaire dans la France du Nord (X$^{e}$–première moitié du XI$^{e}$ siècle)', *Bibliothèque de l'École des chartes*, 155 (1997), 11–44.

[13] D. Barthélemy, 'Une crise de l'écrit? Observations sur des actes de St-Aubin d'Angers (XI$^{e}$ siècle)', *Bibliothèque de l'École des chartes*, 155 (1997), 95–117.

[14] Most obviously, Duby, *La societé*, and Rosenwein, *Saint Peter*.

[15] *Cluny*, and for their sources, methods and subsequent scholarship, see S. Barret, 'Cluny, note sur le *Recueil des chartes de l'abbaye de Cluny* d'Auguste Bernard et Alexandre Bruel', *Bulletin du Centre d'études médiévales d'Auxerre*, 13 (2009): cem.revues.org/index11017.html. An indispensable research tool, comprising the searchable texts of the Cluny charters hyperlinked to a scanned *Cluny*, is the Cartae Cluniacensis Electronicae database hosted by the University of Münster: www.uni-muenster.de/Fruehmittelalter/Projekte/Cluny/CCE

[16] Most importantly, M. Chaume (and J. Marilier), 'Observations sur la chronologie des chartes de l'abbaye de Cluny', *Revue Mabillon*, 16 (1926), 44–8; 29 (1939), 81–9, 133–42; 31 (1941), 14–19, 42–5, 69–82; 32 (1942), 15–20, 133–6; 38 (1948), 1–6; 39 (1949), 41–3; 42 (1952), 1–4; and unpublished work by Maria Hillenbrandt. I am most grateful to the kindness of Barbara Rosenwein for sharing with me her collation of various corrections to Bernard and Bruel's datings suggested in subsequent scholarship: I have tried to integrate these into any quantifications in what follows. Obviously, any errors and anomalies that remain are my responsibility, but in any case the numbers provided in the discussion that follows are used indicatively, to demonstrate trends, and are not subjected to statistical analysis.

studies of the processes of archive formation and cartulary compilation by Atsma and Vezin, Barret and Iogna-Prat[17]; and by a series of studies on the palaeography of the surviving original charters, accompanied by their publication in facsimile by Atsma, Barret and Vezin,[18] while the electronically literate can enjoy a wealth of online resources hosted by the Institut für Frühmittelalterforschung at the University of Münster.[19]

It might be thought that this seam of documentation is so thoroughly worked as to be historiographically exhausted. However, we have the texts of 106 charters that predate Cluny's foundation in 909 or 910.[20] These pre-foundation documents do not consist of the familiar fare of donations to the Church, but instead are almost without exception secular exchanges of property. Six of these documents are royal diplomas, of which five give royal possessions (sometimes estates, sometimes churches) to various recipients, while the sixth confirms the swap of the Cluny estate between the bishop and count of Mâcon: the kind of material we commonly find in ecclesiastical cartularies of both Carolingian and post-Carolingian vintage. But the overwhelming majority of these documents are not royal, nor are they types of material routinely found elsewhere. Land sales involving laypeople account for well over half. Gifts from one layperson to another – evenly split between those where a kinship tie between vendor and buyer is explicitly recorded, and those between apparently unrelated parties – account for over a quarter, and include a significant number of transfers of dowry lands and morning-gifts from husband to wife (the vagaries of documentary form

17 H. Atsma and J. Vezin, 'Gestion de la mémoire à l'époque de saint Hugues (1049–1109): La génèse paléographique et codicologique du plus ancien cartulaire de l'abbaye de Cluny', *Histoire et archives*, 7 (2000), 5–29; S. Barret, *La mémoire et l'écrit: L'abbaye de Cluny et ses archives, X$^{e}$–XVIII$^{e}$ siècles* (Münster, 2004); D. Iogna-Prat, 'La confection des cartulaires et la historiographie à Cluny (XI$^{e}$–XII$^{e}$ siècles)', in *Les cartulaires*, 27–44.

18 *Les plus anciens documents originaux de l'abbaye de Cluny*, ed. H. Atsma, J. Vezin and S. Barret, 3 vols. to date (Paris, 1997–).

19 www.uni-muenster.de/Fruehmittelalter/Projekte/Cluny/. Other invaluable online resources are also being developed: see, e.g., the Chartae Burgundiae Medii Aevii project hosted by the Centre d'études médiévales at the University of Auxerre: cem.revues.org/index2372.html.

20 I have counted the documents chronologically prior to the foundation charter's stated date of 910, and excluded one outlying gift to Cluny from 909, which is problematic. For the foundation, see now D. Iogna-Prat, 'Cluny, 909–910, ou l'instrumentalisation de la mémoire des origines', *Revue Mabillon*, 11 (2000), 161–85. As explained above, n. 16, I have also endeavoured to take account of modern scholarship revising Bernard and Bruel's chronology. I have also excluded material transmitted via other institutions (e.g. the cartulary of the cathedral of St-Vincent at Mâcon), some of which is intimately intertwined with Cluny and was included by Bernard and Bruel. I thus count the following charters: *Cluny* 3, 5, 7–16, 18–28, 30–77, 79–111 (with 89bis), 219, 1095; no. 90, a single document recording both a sale and a *placitum*, is counted twice. Classification inevitably involves some degree of interpretation, but I have tried to follow the implicit typologies in scribal language and formulas as closely as possible.

making it difficult to make a hard and fast division between gifts and marriage agreements). In addition we have four records of dispute settlement (three heard before counts and one before imperial *missi*), two swaps of land, two swaps of unfree dependants and one poignant document in which an individual places himself in the servitude of another. Where churches do appear, they do so as the possessions of individual landowners, with the exception of two precarial grants made by bishops, another episcopal document confirming a grant to an abbot, one donation by a priest to his church and one transaction centred on a chapel. Hence, while there is the odd clerical actor or witness and a mixture of clerical and non-clerical scribes, the Church as an institution is far from hegemonic in determining these social practices or their documentary record.

This field of secular transactions and the documentary culture that it witnesses, moreover, continues to loom large among the surviving charters even after Cluny's foundation, through much of the tenth century. From the abbacy of the first abbot, Berno (910–27), almost 40 per cent of the transmitted documents – over sixty charters – are such secular transactions in which Cluny itself was not directly implicated, and under his successor Odo (927–42), in spite of a much thicker transmission of documents in which Cluny was the recipient as gift-giving took off, secular transactions in which neither the abbey nor the monks were involved still make up around 20 per cent of surviving documents – another haul of over fifty charters. In fact, through to at least the abbacy of Odilo (994–1049), we have a fairly steady rate of transmission of secular documents, with an average of three or four such charters surviving per year. The take-off of gifts to Cluny means that this constitutes a decreasing proportion of an increasing volume of surviving material, but in sum it gives us a sample of several hundred transactions in which local landowners bought and sold land from each other, contracted dowries, took each other to court and bought out each other's claims. Cluny's foundation does not mark a break in the nature, preservation or, apparently, the transmission of this material.[21]

These documents provide a priceless window onto the workings of a provincial society prior to the advent of a major monastery or aristocratic network, with all the changes that integration into a wider system of patronage brought. In fact, this rich seam of charters offers the possibility of complementing and testing the series of other regional studies that

[21] Here it has simply been used as a clean, convenient and unambiguous cut-off, prior to which a period of non-monastic preservation is a given and needs no further demonstration. Future research, indeed, might usefully separate tenth-century material that had an independent transmission prior to coming to the Cluny archive from that whose transmission was wholly monastic.

have had to work from the perspective of networks created around great monasteries, and adopt an indirect approach to reconstructing society before the advent of imperial aristocrats and the imperial Church; these documents directly record social phenomena that are normally inferred rather than demonstrated.[22] Given the formative influence on the historiography of post-Carolingian change of works whose empirical basis lay in the Mâconnais, it is striking that these late Carolingian documents have never been properly used to analyse social process on the ground; they have been oddly neglected by modern scholars.[23]

## The preservation of lay documents and the history of the Cluny archive

The vast majority of these pre-910 charters must therefore be categorized as 'lay documents' by any meaningful definition. With respect to archival and documentary practices, they therefore raise important issues.[24] The date of this material means that it must have been not only produced but also preserved, independently of Cluny, for a number of years; as we shall see, on occasion we can surmise how a document may have come to Cluny, but even for the mass of documents where this is not possible the chronological profile of the surviving sample indicates that it was possible for a secular document to survive without the archival agency of the Church for several decades.

The sheer volume of lay documentation transmitted via Cluny, and its presence so far into the abbey's history, is a brute fact that raises important questions of provenance and transmission. How and why did it come to be preserved? The keys to answering this question lie in the history of the Cluny archive. We are lucky that that history has recently been uncovered by Sébastien Barret, and that Barret's work itself was possible thanks to the work of the eighteenth-century antiquarian Louis-Henri Lambert de Barive.[25] Lambert worked in the Cluny archive in a series of visits over the course of the two decades before the French Revolution; he provided a priceless description of the thirteenth-century 'tower of the

[22] E.g. W. Brown, *Unjust Seizure: Conflict and Authority in an Early Medieval Society* (Ithaca, NY, 2001); Costambeys, *Power*; Hummer, *Politics*; Innes, *State and Society*.

[23] The Carolingian backdrop to Duby's Mâconnais was based on normative sources, and then interpreted as evidence for state institutions. For a powerful recent critique on both empirical and theoretical grounds, see S. D. White, 'Tenth-Century Courts at Mâcon and the Perils of Structuralist History', in W. Brown and P. Górecki (eds.), *Conflict in Medieval Europe: Changing Perspectives on Society and Culture* (Aldershot, 2003), 37–68.

[24] They have already been noted by several commentators, from Duby, *La societé*, xii, to Kosto, 'Laymen', 72, but I know of no extended discussion.

[25] Barret, *La mémoire et l'écrit*.

archives' on one side of the gatehouse, as well as many hundreds of transcripts of original documents he found within that tower.[26] Lambert's antiquarianism is clear from the care with which he made not merely transcriptions but almost mini-facsimiles, which attempted to reproduce aspects of the physical appearance and script of the documents.[27]

This antiquarianism, however, had very clear connections with wider currents in *ancien régime* cultural and political life. Lambert's activity at Cluny in the 1770s and 1780s coincided with a series of other initiatives in which archives were used for an immediate purpose. The records of the Cluniac order at the mother house, for example, had been extensively drawn on earlier in the century by scholars at St-Martin-des-Champs eager to assemble proofs for the monastery's rigorous observance and to defend the order against the laxness encouraged by the royal appointees who served as commendatory abbots of Cluny through this period; indeed, the vocation became a particularly live issue after the General Assembly of the Gallican Clergy in 1765, and the setting up of the Commission des Réguliers, which investigated the monastic orders right across the kingdom, reporting on standards of observance and winding up some houses.[28] Meanwhile, from 1774, a team of other antiquarians, like Lambert professional *avocats* from Autun, was hired by the local bishop and president of the Estates of Burgundy, Yves Marbeuf, to organize the records of the estates – this in the context of the continuing financial demands placed on the estates by the Crown, those same demands that made the fiscal privileges of the clergy as a whole, and the monastic orders in particular, such an issue of debate.[29] Lambert's own activity, however, was funded by the Cabinet des Chartes, founded in 1765 by the historiographer royal Jacob-Nicolas Moreau to create a national archival depository to underpin an unashamedly antiquarian and royalist history of France rich in useful precedent for his master.

26 S. Barret, 'La Tour des Archives de l'abbaye de Cluny', *Livraisons de l'histoire de l'architecture*, 10 (2005), 9–17.

27 On Lambert's antiquarianism, see above all S. Barret, 'Un avocat au service du Cabinet des chartes: Les travaux de Louis-Henri Lambert de Barive dans les archives de Cluny (v. 1770–v. 1790)', *Histoire et archives*, 15 (2004), 29–64.

28 See J. McManners, *Church and Society in Eighteenth-Century France*. I. *The Clerical Establishment and Its Social Ramifications* (Oxford, 1998), 141–73 (for 1765 and the issue of clerical taxation), 571–614 (for the commission and the monastic orders on the eve of Revolution); on Cluny at this date, see G. Chevron, 'L'abbaye et l'ordre de Cluny à la fin du XVIII^e^ siècle', *Revue Mabillon*, 39 (1949), 44–58; 40 (1950), 1–28; and on the impetus for the history of the order, G. Charvin, 'À propos d'un projet d'une histoire de l'ordre de Cluny au XVIII^e^ siècle', in *À Cluny: Congrès scientifique* (Dijon, 1950), 181–5. A revised constitution for the Cluniac order was finally approved in 1789.

29 See J. Swann, *Provincial Power and Absolute Monarchy: The Estates General of Burgundy, 1661–1790* (Cambridge, 2004).

Moreau's plan drew on the extensive labours undertaken by the Maurists over the previous century in collecting materials for unashamedly patriotic provincial and national histories, and built on the Maurist endeavour to institute a network of paid antiquarian helpers, each charged with ransacking the archives of a given province; Lambert's activity at Cluny needs placing in that context.[30]

The cultural, fiscal and political issues that framed Lambert's antiquarianism, in any case, fed through the period of the Revolution and the secularization of Cluny's estate, the dispersal of the archive and the destruction of the buildings.[31] It is normal to attribute the destruction of the archive to an episode of plundering and burning in 1793, and thus to invoke that random actor 'chance' in attributing survivals. In fact, the subsequent fate and shape of the archive suggests that as the abbey and its estates were dismembered, documents were falling into lay hands by various mechanisms. Historians who invoke 'chance', as so often, are actually adopting a shorthand for an unknown or uninvestigated process: mathematical and philosophical treatments of probability and truth may offer a better way to think about these problems.[32]

The Revolution and its aftermath, indeed, saw continued interest in the type of project masterminded by Moreau, alongside concern and controversy regarding control over initiatives that could not but be politically loaded, with the fate of royal and governmental archives and record collections the subject of vigorous debate. With the establishment of stability of a sort, however, it became increasingly clear that the concerns about precedent that had made archival control such a loaded issue in the unravelling of the *ancien régime* were no longer so pressing. Instead, a less immediately partisan political concern for the fate of documents and records disturbed in the Revolutionary and post-Revolutionary periods, and the need to preserve the monuments of the French past, emerged, evident in the foundation of the École des Chartes to create a centrally trained cadre of archivists who could classify and publish the

30 K. Baker, 'Controlling French History: The Ideological Arsenal of Jacob-Nicolas Moreau', in Baker, *Inventing the French Revolution: Essays on French Political Culture in the Eighteenth Century* (Cambridge, 1990), 59–85. Maurists: McManners, *Church and Society*, 594–600; Knowles, *Great Historical Enterprises*, 33–62; M. Lecomte, 'Les Bénédictins et l'histoire des provinces aux XVII$^{e}$ et XVIII$^{e}$ siècles', *Revue Mabillon*, 17 (1927), 237–46; 18 (1928), 39–58, 110–33, 302–23 (important for any early medievalist using Bouquet's *Recueil des historiens des Gaules et de la France* or Devic and Vaisette's *Histoire générale de Languedoc*).

31 B. Marguery-Melin, *La destruction de l'abbaye de Cluny, 1789–1823* (Cluny, 1985).

32 The best discussion of these issues, in the context of charter transmission in Lucca, is A. Esch, 'Überlieferungs-Chance und Überlieferungs-Zufall als methodisches Problem des Historikers', *Historische Zeitschrift*, 240 (1985), 529–70.

building blocks of the nation's history. Archives and archivalism were thus 'medievalized': it is striking that the various transcriptions and collections of documents made in the post-Revolutionary period contain only early and high medieval pieces. As the nation's historical imagination was fuelled by romantic essayists flirting with a glamorous and distant past, a gap opened between this endeavour and current controversy. At the same time, as the emerging French nation state devoted more and more energy to the cultivation of official records enabling it to rule its subjects, the ordering of the medieval past through public archives became a legitimating tool that expressed a grand narrative of French national identity rooted in the state.

The fate of cartularies and related documents thus became a major concern of archivists in Paris and beyond through the middle and late nineteenth century.[33] As regards Cluny in particular, it was the tireless efforts of Leopold Delisle at the Bibliothèque Nationale in the first half of the nineteenth century that led to so much of the material relating to the archive being reassembled in Paris. Delisle was able to purchase several sizeable collections of original charters from private individuals in Burgundy. These were to complement the abbey's surviving cartularies, which had been brought to Paris in the Revolutionary period, and Lambert's papers, which like most of the other material concerned with Moreau's endeavours had been seized to underpin the new national archives.[34] Bernard and Bruel's edition was really the culmination of Delisle's work in pulling back together as much material as could be identified; they also built heavily upon Lambert's work as they realized that his transcriptions were often closer to the original documents than the cartulary copies.[35]

The archival history of the Cluny charters thus in many ways exemplifies the transformation of archival cultures as the *ancien régime* was transformed into the nation state of classical modernity.[36] Similarly, the emergence of an archival culture less dependent on exigencies of access and place is clear in the late twentieth and early twenty-first centuries, with the growth of an international scholarly community devoted to the study of the records of Cluny, at first through conferences and papers but more recently through shared tools disseminated electronically on

[33] See I. Vérité, 'Les entreprises françaises de recensement des cartulaires (XVIII$^{e}$–XX$^{e}$ siècles)', in *Les cartulaires*, 178–213.

[34] See L. Delisle, *Inventaire des manuscrits de la Bibliothèque nationale, fonds de Cluny* (Paris, 1884).

[35] J. Richard, 'La publication des chartes de Cluny', in *À Cluny*, 155–60.

[36] Cf. above, 13.

the internet.[37] More immediately important for our purposes, however, is the fact that the disjuncture of the crucial Revolutionary and post-Revolutionary decades meant that the surviving material, as published by Bernard and Bruel, rests on three distinct vectors of transmission through the period of the abbey's suppression: via the abbey's cartularies, via those originals taken from Cluny in the Revolution but then sought out and bought up by Delisle, and via Lambert's papers.

Each of these distinct vectors of transmission privileges different kinds of material, creating a different image of the abbey's early medieval archive. The process of cartulary compilation, for example, had its origins in the later part of the abbacy of Odilo (994–1049) but reached fruition under Abbot Hugh (1049–1109), with the compilation of three independent but complementary collections, known to modern historians as cartularies A, B and C, but in fact best conceived as a single venture comprising three physically separate but conceptually interdependent parts.[38] The cartularies need to be contextualized alongside a range of other initiatives to provide written memorials of the abbey in its heyday: custumals and hagiographies designed to fix institutional memory and to preserve institutional identity drew on similar impulses to those evident in the cartularies.[39] The A cartulary organizes the abbey's documents in the form of a *gesta abbatum* of the first four abbots, beginning with a *chronologia* of the abbots and a dossier of foundational documents, and then evoking the history of the church and the memory of its benefactors, before giving the texts of the donations, purchases and privileges for Berno, Odo, Aymard and Maiolus in turn, with texts often embellished or improved for style, and context – including in many cases the date – elided. The B cartulary completes the process for the abbots under whom the cartularies were compiled, Hugh and his predecessor Odilo, and in so doing gives some clues as to the various stages of cartulary organization. The C cartulary, published on the occasion of the visit to Cluny of Pope Urban II – a former Cluny monk – in 1095–6, complements the two volumes of *gesta abbatum* in the A and B cartularies. It begins with the same evocation of the church and donors used in the A cartulary, but then organizes documents by a different principle: foundational material

[37] These developments differ from the 'postmodern' 'democratization of the archive' discussed by Derrida and other theorists; above, 13.

[38] H. Atsma and J. Vezin, 'Gestion de la mémoire à l'époque de saint Hugues (1049–1109): La génèse paléographique et codicologique du plus ancien cartulaire de l'abbaye de Cluny', *Histoire et archives*, 7 (2000), 5–29, with full references to earlier bibiliography.

[39] Iogna-Prat, 'La confection des cartulaires'; D. Iogna-Prat, 'La geste des origines dans l'historiographie clunisienne des XI$^{e}$–XII$^{e}$ siècles', *Revue bénédictine*, 102 (1992), 135–91.

is followed by papal and then royal diplomata, and then private charters grouped according to a geographical rationale. The momentous visit of the abbey's most illustrious 'old boy' was marked not only by the launch of a new kind of Christian warfare aimed at recapturing the Holy Places, but also by the consecration of the altars in the abbey's magnificent new church, and Urban's declaration of a 'sacred ban' – a zone of protected space – around this particular Holy Place. The publication of the C cartulary therefore both marked the culmination of decades of work aimed at establishing a definitive institutional memory and underpinned a programme of territorial sacralization.[40]

Comparison of the cartularized documents with surviving originals shows quite clearly that the process of cartulary compilation effected a series of changes to the charters included. Their texts were 'improved' by abridgement, correction and embellishment to fit the linguistic and literary expectations of this grand memorial project.[41] Inevitably, the act of recopying removed cues and markings that might guide the interpretation or aid the use of an original document. As we shall see below, such cues might be textual – dorsal notes summarizing a document, or annotations recording subsequent confirmations or contestations of a transaction – or non-textual – the fixing together of one document to another, earlier document relating to the same people or place, or the attachment of a legal staff or *festuca* whose exchange had symbolized the handover of property. Above all, cartularization involved the reorganization of the documents in terms of categories and classifications determined by the abbey's institutional needs: the commemoration of abbots and their patrons in the A and B cartularies, the geography of the estate and the need to preserve the abbey's liberties and privileges over that estate in the C cartulary.

The rich secular documentation of the late ninth and tenth centuries had no utility to the cartulary project, and is therefore almost wholly excluded from the cartulary tradition. Documents involving the circulation of estates within the family of the founder, Count William, were copied as necessary prologues to the foundational history of the abbey, but even these were not included uncritically or *en masse*, as the cartularists' exclusion of an exchange of unfree dependants between William

[40] E.g. B. H. Rosenwein, 'Visualising a Dispute Resolution: Peter of Albano's Protected Zone', in Brown and Górecki (eds.), *Conflict in Medieval Europe*, 85–108.

[41] A. Bruel, 'Note sur le transcription des actes privés dans les cartulaires antérieurement au XII$^{e}$ siècle', *Bibliothèque de l'École des chartes*, 6 (1875), 445–56, and, more broadly, Geary, *Phantoms*, 103–7; also now H. Atsma and J. Vezin, 'Originaux et copies: La reproduction des éléments graphiques des actes des X$^{e}$ et XI$^{e}$ siècles dans le cartulaire de Cluny', in Kosto and Winroth (eds.), *Charters, Cartularies and Archives*, 113–26.

and his sister Ava copied by Lambert shows.[42] The absorption of the family documents of aristocratic founders into monastic archives is a phenomenon widely paralleled, and it suggests a continuing give and take between founders and the institution which defined their family identity and memory and so was an obvious place to store family deeds; the phenomenon is well attested precisely because cartulary compilers right across the Carolingian and post-Carolingian world were anxious to commemorate pious founders, and indeed characteristically where secular documentation is copied into cartularies, it seems to consist of ancient muniments concerned with the founder's family.[43] Other than that, where Cluny received once royal estates or churches that had previously been granted out to favoured aristocrats, the royal documents recording those prior gifts – presumably stored at the estates or churches in question and passed over with them, often long after the abbey's foundation – were similarly favoured by cartulary compilers; again, this phenomenon is widely paralleled in cartularies right across the Frankish world.[44] But while those compiling these collections were interested in documents of charismatic antiquity that might commemorate near-legendary founders or add regalian lustre to their *codices*, they had no interest in records of sales or dowries between private individuals whose relationship to the abbey and its patrimony must by then, in most cases, have been long forgotten.

Had we the cartularies alone, any attempt to understand document use in ninth- and tenth-century Burgundy would run up against familiar evidentiary problems. We would be confident in demonstrating that the greatest aristocratic families – those of the abbey's founders, or the aristocratic *fideles* who received royal gifts – preserved documentary proofs relating to some of their patrimonies, particularly when dealing with the Church or with kings. We would have some tiny scraps of evidence for written documentation at a lower social level and end up asking whether this was the tip of the iceberg or the exception that proves the rule. The existence of a vigorous tradition of secular documentation by lesser local landowners in their dealings with each other would remain an unknowable unknown, as would the preservation of a significant volume of secular material within Cluny's archives. In and of itself, this serves as a sobering illustration of the dangers of taking a cartulary as a snapshot of a monastic archive at the point of compilation, rather than as a carefully crafted

42 *Cluny* 74; 89bis, a charter of William for one of his *fideles*, which was later passed with the property it concerned to Cluny, was similarly excluded; see below, n. 53.

43 As has been underlined by Jonathan Jarrett in an as yet unpublished work, which I am grateful to him for discussing with me; see also above, Chapters 8–10.

44 Though not all such documents were included in cartularies.

and consciously organized attempt to use archival materials for present purposes, to shape institutional memory.

The transmission of a significant number of originals, most retrieved or bought up by Delisle, has made clear the extent of reworking involved in copying original documents into cartularized form and proved invaluable in illuminating scribal practice and the processes of charter production. The surviving originals from Cluny provide further indirect evidence for the continuity of a broadly based documentary culture through the tenth century in this region. Palaeographical analysis has shown that charters subscribed by a single scribe are not necessarily all in the same hand, and suggests that the actual scribal subscription named the individual under whose authority a document was written, not the individual who physically wrote it. In other words, even as Cluny's monks were becoming important providers of literate services for the local community, they did so in the context of a complex scribal culture, a culture that rested on the notion that scribal office involved public trust, with the named scribe vouching for documents written up under his authority.[45]

Does the pattern of surviving originals hint at the scale of exclusion involved in cartulary compilation, or serve as a meaningful control on the cartularies?[46] Very few of our secular documents are preserved in original, rather than in antiquarian, copies: of the 106 pre-foundation documents, just thirteen. Of these thirteen originals, three were royal documents concerning property that later came to the abbey, including Louis the Pious' confirmation of the bishop of Mâcon's swapping of the *villa* of Cluny with Count Warin in 825, whence the estate came into the hands of Count William's family; a further charter records the gift of Cluny to William by his sister, Ava, abbess of St-Pierre-les-Nonnains. Of the remaining nine originals, no fewer than seven survive thanks to a remarkable, enigmatic and anonymous collection of more than fifty

[45] H. Atsma and J. Vezin, 'Autour des actes privés du chartier de Cluny (X$^{e}$–XIV$^{e}$ siècles)', *Bibliothèque de l'École des chartes*, 155 (1997), 45–60; Atsma and Vezin, 'Les responsables de la transcription des actes juridiques et les services de l'écriture au X$^{e}$ siècle: L'exemple de Cluny', in M.-C. Hubert, E. Poulle and M. Smith (eds.), *Le statut du scripteur au moyen âge* (Paris 2000), 9–20; B.-M. Tock, *Scribes, souscripteurs et témoins dans les actes privés en France (VII$^{e}$–début XII$^{e}$ siècle)* (Turnhout, 2005); Tock, 'Les actes entre particuliers en Bourgogne méridionale (IX$^{e}$–XI$^{e}$ siècles)', in P. Erhart, K. Heidecker and B. Zeller (eds.), *Die Privaturkunden der Karolingerzeit* (Zurich, 2009), 121–34.

[46] In analysing the distribution of originals, I have made use of the ARTEM database of original documents prior to 1121 in modern France: see B.-M. Tock *et al.*, *La diplomatique française du haut moyen âge: Inventaire des chartes originales antérieures à 1121 conservées en France*, 2 vols (Turnhout, 2001). The numbers in the following paragraph are based on the searchable online database at www.cn-telma.fr/originaux/index/, used in conjunction with the Münster Cartae Cluniacenses Electronicae database (above, n. 19), and with chronological adjustments made as outlined above, n. 16.

original charters made after Cluny's secularization and passed on to the Bibliothèque Nationale, where it still resides; the two remaining documents are the record of a judicial hearing at which Count Eblo of Poitiers found in favour of the abbey of Nouaillé, and a gift by Count William to one of his retainers, which was passed to Cluny with the estates it concerns.[47]

With Cluny's foundation, we have a far higher volume of surviving originals, as a significant number of donations to the abbey survive in the original as well as in cartulary copy: from the first four decades of the abbey's existence, in the period prior to 950, we have thirty-three original documents of which Cluny is the beneficiary, and of which just two are royal diplomata and the remainder 'private' donations covering the range of the social spectrum from Count William to small-scale local landowners. Through the tenth century, we continue to have a steady stream of originals in which Cluny is not directly implicated, preserved at a similar rate to that evident in the decades immediately before the abbey's foundation: from the period 910–50, fifteen originals in which Cluny is not involved, of which three are royal documents and eight are non-royal documents preserved in the same post-1789 collection that dominates the pre-910 originals.[48] Strikingly, the breakdown of transmitted originals of around one-third 'secular' transactions to two-thirds benefactions to Cluny is very similar to the overall ratio of all transmitted documents, including cartulary copies and early-modern antiquarian transcripts as well as originals. The similarity in the ratio of monastic to secular documentation in both original and all other vectors of transmission must confirm that the abbey's documentary traditions 'piggybacked' on and expanded an already rich documentary culture in the region. But, just as the activities of Lambert were crucial in preserving traces of the secular documents kept in the Cluny archive prior to its dispersal, so the seam of original lay documents would have vanished were it not for the antiquarian efforts evident in the charter collections now housed in the Bibliothèque Nationale in Paris: without the single collection in BnF lat. 17715, we would have just half a dozen non-royal secular documents prior to 950, two prior to the abbey's foundation and four from the

47 On the charter collection BnF lat. 17715, note the comments of Barret, 'Cluny, note', n. 17: this dossier eloquently shows the role of chance in transmission. For the transmission of *Cluny* 89bis, see below, n. 53; I am at a loss to explain the transmission of the Poitiers *placitum*, no. 81.

48 The non-Cluny documents from 910–50 are ARTEM nos. 1582–3, 1594–5, 1597, 1599, 1815–19, 1822, 1827, 1831, 2504. Of these, 1582–3 and 1599 are royal; the non-royal 1815–19, 1822, 1827 and 1831 are collected in BnF lat. 17715. Of the documents directly benefiting Cluny, four (ARTEM nos. 1821, 1824–5, 1830) are from BnF lat. 17715.

period 910–50. It is only if we strip out the efforts of antiquarian copyists like Lambert, and the collectors of original documents from departmental archives and the black market whose collections now grace the Bibliothèque Nationale, that the pattern of transmitted documents from Cluny matches that more familiar from other ecclesiastical foundations. At Cluny, however, we can move beyond an argument of implication and suggestion and directly demonstrate a significant documentary culture among lay landowners great and small. This is, above all, thanks to the work of Lambert and other eighteenth- and nineteenth-century antiquarians; without them, there would be no real clue to the volume of what Cluny once held, and the submerged part of this particular archival iceberg would remain invisible to the modern eye.

## Landowners and dossiers: documentary practices before and within the Cluny charter collection

How did this rich seam of secular material come to reach Cluny, and in what form was it 'archived' both before and after its acquisition by the monastery? Where secular documents are transmitted via cartulary traditions, it is normally in the form of 'dossiers' of title-deeds passed over to the monastery when it acquired an estate.[49] The effort to trace the contours of such groups of documents has been profoundly influenced by the Cluny material, and in particular by André Déléage's identification of a dozen such dossiers relating to the prehistory of an individual's gift to Cluny.[50] These dossiers normally contain between half a dozen and a dozen charters, documenting an individual's acquisition of properties later given to Cluny; they are not usually chronologically deep, characteristically dealing only with the activities of one conjugal couple rather than reaching back across the generations, and therefore potentially covering transactions spread over several decades but not more.[51]

[49] E.g. Kosto, 'Laymen', 72: 'The phenomenon of the integration of "dossiers" into ecclesiastical archives at the time of acquisition of a piece of land is perhaps best known from the Cluny *chartrier*.' The phenomenon has also been noted by Wendy Davies for Brittany and northern Iberia (W. Davies, *Small Worlds: The Village Community in Early Medieval Brittany* [London, 1989]; Davies, *Acts of Giving*), and Adam Kosto for Catalonia (Kosto, 'Laymen', which also includes a discussion of wider comparanda at 71–3).

[50] A. Déléage, *La vie rurale en Bourgogne jusqu'au début du onzième siècle*, 2 vols. (Macon, 1941), I, 234–40; Gratsianskii's work, noted by Kosto, 'Laymen', 72n134, is beyond my linguistic capacities.

[51] Compare, on this chronological-generational structure, above, 198, for the East Frankish evidence, and 269–81 for Iberia; on the Italian evidence and the possible influence of the 'thirty-year rule' based on the post-Roman development of vulgar law, see above, Chapter 9.

These parameters – dossiers of a relatively small number of linked documents typically reaching back three decades or so – are also suggested by the distribution curve of secular documents in the Cluny archive, which seems to mirror the pattern of growing gift-giving to the abbey, except three decades earlier. In other words, as the monks acquired land, they frequently acquired with it small collections of documents connected with that land and reaching several decades into the past.

Of the twelve identified dossiers, most are tenth-century in origin, with a couple spilling over into the eleventh; the earliest is that associated with Lilia. Lilia's dossier is larger than most of those identified, comprising up to a dozen documents that were passed on to Cluny when in 926 Lilia herself granted the abbey 'all that I have acquired with my husband in the county of Mâcon', naming three particular villages (*villae*).[52] Only one of these documents is transmitted in the original, a charter from 905 recording the gift of three fields and a clearance to Hugh and Lilia by Count William, who was to found Cluny just a few years later, and his sister Ava. This seems to have been preserved in the original on account of the lustre added by William's name: a dorsal note styles it as a record of the generosity of 'our lord William', suggesting that at some date after its passing into the Cluny archive with Lilia's other title-deeds, this charter was misunderstood as a record of William's munificence and so came to be treated differently from its fellows.[53] The only two documents transmitted via the cartulary are two charters recording Lilia's gifts to Cluny, the first from 916 and the second from 925; the former of these was also copied by Lambert, and the remaining nine texts survive thanks to the antiquarian endeavours of Lambert in the last decades of the abbey prior to its secularization in the Revolution.[54]

52 *Cluny* 275; Lilia had made a more limited, gift in 916 (no. 202) of holdings in a specific area within a single *villa*, but it makes more sense to see the totality of her title-deeds passing over with the totality of her estates following 926. *Villa*: F. Bange, 'L'*ager* et la *villa*: Structures du paysage et du peuplement dans la région mâconnaise à la fin du haut moyen âge (IX$^{e}$–XI$^{e}$ siècles)', *Annales ESC*, 39 (1984), 529–69; and in Carolingian sources generally, M. Costambeys, M. Innes and S. Maclean, *The Carolingian World* (Cambridge, 2011), 229–41, with references.

53 *Cluny* 89bis (V, 833–4). It is easy to see how on a superficial reading, in the context of the Cluny archive, this charter could have been interpreted as a pious gift to the abbey rather than to Hugh and Lilia – it was, however, not copied in the cartulary, presumably as its date preceded the foundation of the abbey, so it could not be linked to the *gesta* of any of the abbots. Its separation from its fellows might be implied by the fact that it was not used by Lambert.

54 *Cluny* 202, 275. The possibility must arise, given the transmission of the latter document via the cartulary alone, that the 925 charter represents a *post hoc* working-up of an earlier agreement negotiated at the time of the smaller 916 gift; the stress in no. 275 on William's relationship with Lilia might fit with this being the 'official' Cluny viewpoint.

These nine texts are all charters of sale in which Lilia and her husband Hugh are named as joint purchasers; they reach back three decades, to 897, and record a cluster of purchases of closely related – often contiguous – fields, meadows, vineyards and farmsteads over the period 897–908. Lilia and Hugh's activities were focused in Bierre, northwest of Cluny, and a handful of neighbouring settlements, some newly emerging and others longer established, but most notably Chateau, where the couple also seem, appropriately, to have had a residence. They underline the exceptional richness of this kind of material for the social historian. Purchase prices are given in *solidi*, or, on three occasions, other movables whose value is expressed in *solidi* and, once, *libri*; the prices vary from 1 to 50 *solidi*, with livestock being used instead of coin in the smaller transactions and 'silver and other goods' in the largest. There is the unmistakable bustle of sociability within this land market: these are local landowners dealing with the exigencies of the family fortunes by buying and selling smallholdings, and using documents to record those dealings, and Hugh and Lilia bought from both kin and neighbours. Hugh and Lilia, indeed, expended a large amount of movable wealth in both cash and kind over a decade, and for well-connected locals like them land appears to have been easily available for purchase – facts that sit uneasily with some received views of early medieval landed society.[55]

As Hugh and Lilia bought up property, they seem to have prospered and acquired a certain social cachet. Hugh in particular enjoyed important links with the high echelons of the aristocracy: charter scribes felt able to give Hugh the honorific title 'magnificent lord', and in the last donation in the series – the largest, from 908, in which Hugh and Lilia bought out another couple for 50 *solidi*'s worth of movables, acquiring the only demesne farm in the series – Count William, Cluny's founder, was among the witnesses. The couple's relationship with Count William was such that in 905 he and his sister had given Hugh and Lilia three fields that they owned in one quarter (*fine*) within the *villa* of Bierre, and a further smallholding in a clearance nearby. This charter – the only lay gift in the series and the only document surviving in the original – is unusual in the series in that there is a note of conscious self-representation that is lacking from the pragmatic records of Hugh and Lilia's ventures in the land market. Not only are both Hugh ('our beloved faithful [man]') and William

[55] Cf., in different contexts: Davies, *Acts of Giving*; W. Davies, 'Sale, Price and Valuation in Castile and Galicia-Leon in the Tenth Century', *EME*, 11 (2002), 149–74; L. Feller, A. Gramain and A. Weber, *La fortune de Karol: Marché de la terre et liens personnels dans les Abruzzes au haut moyen âge* (Paris, 2005).

('count, count of the palace[56] and margrave') given grand titulature, but also William, addressing Hugh, publicly states his motivation in giving 'on account of the love and benevolence we have towards yourselves'. As Barbara Rosenwein has recently shown, such expressions of love – present in around a fifth of the ninth- and tenth-century charters from Cluny – were consciously used by scribes to express the social and emotional ties that bound together the landowning class of the late Carolingian Mâconnais.[57] The dry pragmatism of Hugh and Lilia's other documents is thus dramatically juxtaposed with the more expressive note sounded to articulate the affective but also hierarchical relationship between the couple and their patron, who was simultaneously friend, benefactor and representative of a charismatic authority charged with ensuring divinely ordained regalian order. This charter indicates that the ideologies developed by Cluny's monks in the course of the tenth and eleventh centuries 'piggybacked' on shared ideas and expressions already current in the landowning communities out of which the abbey itself grew – and that the economy of gift-giving in land that grew up so rapidly around the tenth-century abbey did so precisely because gifts of land were already a crucial mechanism for creating and prolonging social relationships of patronage among the landowning classes.[58] Indeed, the existing relationship between William on the one hand, and Hugh and Lilia on the other,

[56] *Comes, conspalatius et marchio*, a titulature not untypical of the emerging 'territorial princes' of the decades around 900: generally, K. Brunner, 'Der fränkische Fürstentitel im neunten und zehnten Jahrhundert', in H. Wolfram (ed.), *Intitulatio*. II. *Lateinische Herrscher- und Fürstentitel im neunten und zehnten Jahrhundert* (Vienna, 1973), 179–340, and on William, J.-P. Brunterc'h, 'Naissance et formation des principautés au temps de roi Eudes: L'exemple de l'Aquitaine', in O. Guillot and R. Favreau (eds.), *Pays de Loire et Aquitaine de Robert le Fort aux premiers Capétiens* (Poitiers, 1997), 69–116, a reference I owe to Steve Robbie. On *conspalatius*, Adam Kosto has reminded me that Niermeyer, *Lexicon*, 257, has a handful of tenth-century charter references (from, e.g., Gorze and Montier-en-Der) for this title as a conflation of *comes palatii*, all of which postdate the Hugh gift; given the ease with which the language of the private documents in the Cluny archive slips from Latin into proto-Romance, it would make sense to see this as a vernacularization of the formal Latin title and so an indication of how William's standing was represented on a village level. See also *conpalatinus*: J. van de Straeten, 'Vie inédite de S. Hughes évêque de Rouen', *Analecta Bollandiana*, 87 (1969), 215–60, at 238–9 (a reference I owe to Stuart Airlie).

[57] B. H. Rosenwein, 'Circles of Affection in Cluniac Charters', in D. Bousseuil *et al.* (eds.), *Écritures de l'espace social: Mélanges d'histoire médiévale offerts à Monique Bourin par ses élèves et amis* (Paris, 2009), 397–415, esp. 408–10 (affection for *fideles*); also Rosenwein, 'Political Uses of an Emotional Community: Cluny and Its Neighbors, 833–965', in D. Boquet and P. Nagy (eds.), *Politiques des émotions au moyen âge* (Florence, 2010), 205–24.

[58] Rosenwein, *Saint Peter*, is fundamental; for gifts and Carolingian officials, see M. Innes, 'Practices of Property in the Carolingian Empire', in J. Davies and M. McCormick (eds.), *The Long Morning of Medieval Europe: New Directions in Early Medieval Studies* (Aldershot, 2008), 243–69.

so evident in 905, must raise the question of whether Hugh and Lilia's ability to buy up land so quickly was dependent on the material wealth and social support of their patron: was their building up of a local network part of the micropolitics by which aristocratic power was exercised in the localities, and was Cluny itself able to prosper precisely because it could take over these carefully built and painstakingly maintained networks on behalf of its founder?[59] Certainly, Lilia played on these links after her husband's death: in her gift of 926, she invoked the now dead Count William as her former lord (*senior*) and asked that both his soul and that of her current lord, his eponymous *nepos* and successor, benefit from her patronage of Cluny.

As Hugh and Lilia acquired property, their relationship with local churches appears to have grown closer: whereas their earlier transactions were written up by apparently lay scribes with no ecclesiastical affiliation, and publicly enacted in local meetings, five of their last six were written up by priests (three by the 'archpriest Josbert'), and one was staged at a local church. Other notable features of the documentation are the status enjoyed by wives as equal participants with their husbands in buying and selling land – though not in witnessing others' transactions – and their independent control over their acquisitions, as in Lilia's own donation to Cluny after her husband's death and several sales in the series in which women acted independently or alongside their sons. Lilia's activity on the land market appears to have stopped in 908; perhaps the last and largest acquisition, of a demesne farm in that year, had consolidated her status. Her first gift to Cluny of 916 appears to allude to a second husband, Walter, now apparently deceased, and this remarriage, along with the continued patronage and protection of successive counts claimed in the 926 donation, must have allowed her to secure her position.

The first of Lilia's gifts to Cluny, in 916, consisted of a smallholding (*curtilem*) within the *villa* of Bierre; it was made nearby at Chateau, where Lilia had acquired substantial interests in 908.[60] In contrast, Lilia's second gift to Cluny, from 926, was far less specific and more

59 The couple were probably local to the villages in which they operated, in that they appear only in the charters in which they acquired interests in those places, never as neighbours or witnesses elsewhere. The Hugh with interests in the *villa Caucilla* in the county of Vienne (*Cluny* 125, 137), and the landowner(s) of this name in *Cluny* 136, 145, 208, are different men with different interests and kin, as is the count Hugh in nos. 241, 256, active after our Hugh's death.

60 *Cluny* 202 is the 916 gift; was this gift to William's foundation based on William's gift to Hugh and Lilia, no. 89bis from 905? The two charters stipulate land in the same *ager* within the *villa*, but most of the couple's other acquisitions in Bierre were also in this *ager*, so the 916 gift was likely a composite estate of which William's fields formed just part.

open-handed in its terms, simply stipulating the granting to Cluny of all of her and her husband's acquisitions in the Mâconnais, and naming the three *villae* of Chateau, Bierre and *Rufiaco*,[61] which had been the focus of her activities. We cannot therefore be sure that the surviving dossier of sales documents the totality of her holdings – the 926 charter cannot be taken as an exhaustive list, and in any case is transmitted only through the cartulary, whose contents are known to have been 'touched up' so as to meet the dictates of institutional memory – or whether there were more acquisitions for which we now lack a charter record. Perhaps it was possible for a donation charter like that of 926 to be drafted in relatively generic terms, and to focus on pious motives and the identities of those who should benefit from the gift's salvific powers, precisely because its public witness of Lilia's wishes could be supported by title-deeds outlining her holdings; this would explain why the monks held onto Lilia's dossier. Equally, it does seem clear that some property covered in Lilia's dossier was not directly mentioned in either of the gifts to Cluny. The earliest document in the series, for example, concerns a smallholding in a perhaps embryonic settlement in the Autunois which – if it was still in Lilia's possession some thirty years later – is not explicitly alluded to in the text of her 926 gift to Cluny, which mentions only the three named places in the Mâconnais.[62]

While Lilia preserved the documents recording her acquisitions, and the Cluny monks felt that they needed keeping as title to their estates, within the surviving dossier there are embedded references to still more documents that do not survive: land bought by Hugh and Lilia in 900, for example, included one parcel that had been 'chartered' (the scribe used the verb *incartere* from the noun *carta*, 'charter') from husband to wife.[63] In other words, in this social circle it was assumed that the charter was the routine and usual mechanism for transferring dowry land or selling land, even to kin – so routine, indeed, that only those documents with

[61] The dossier vividly shows Hugh and Lilia building up a substantial estate in Bierre, and also acquiring land and residing at Chateau; *Rosiliago*, however, does not appear in the documents, and even if the land here were inherited or dowry land, we would expect documentation, given the profound penetration of written deeds evident in this society. The uncertainty underlines that even in a vivid case like this we must in all probability envisage lost documents that did not survive the dislocations of the Revolution.

[62] The *villa de Kasale Bertruda* in *Cluny* 60 would most likely be an emerging settlement, but it is in the Autunois, not the Mâconnais; if Lilia had sold or otherwise lost her holding here in the meantime, it is striking that she still had the charter. *Cluny* 84 concerns a small clearing, and a further small clearing is included with Bierre land in no. 89bis; nos. 64 and 100 involve land at *Rosiliago* (and no. 100 also identifies property in two other *villae* in addition to Chateau and Bierre): none of these places are mentioned in no. 275, although the clearings at least might easily be appendages of Bierre.

[63] *Cluny* 67; cf. above, 260n1.

immediate utility in terms of establishing title were passed on when land passed to a new owner. The evidently regular circulation of title to land among Lilia's class must have eased the rapid acquisition of property by Cluny after its foundation, not least because – as Lilia's own final gift reminds us – Cluny fitted snugly into the systems of patronage and power in tenth-century provincial society.

Of course, not all the deeds later piled up at Cluny were transmitted in this way. Within the documents, there are some clear subsets – the royal and episcopal documents granting local churches to individual aristocrats or churchmen, for example – for which we can posit alternative vectors of transmission, for such pieces presumably sat in the churches they concerned, possibly with related documents or those pertaining to a church's owners or patrons, until that church was passed on to Cluny and its documents absorbed into the monastery's archive; those royal diplomata preserved or copied precisely because of their illustrious glitter overwhelmingly fall into this class of document. But even on the most optimistic reading, such mechanisms can account for only a tiny share of the secular documentation preserved at Cluny: fewer than a dozen of the pre-foundation documents – that is, under 10 per cent or, perhaps more pertinently, a smaller share than that connected with Lilia. If we are to understand the nature of this material, then, it is on cases like Lilia's that we must base our model.

Dossiers like Lilia's ultimately suggest that Cluny ended up holding a large volume of secular deeds precisely because as it acquired land through the tenth century it also acquired the collections of title-deeds that went with that land. When Cluny began to acquire property and with it deeds to that property, it was drawing on well-established documentary practices rooted in the expectations of the landowning class. The monastery swept into its archive the folded packets of pierced parchment that patrons kept to document their holdings. This effect – the pull on the rich documentary traditions of its host society of an institution rapidly building up its holdings – probably also explains the variety of material acquired by the abbey's archives. For while it is possible to identify neat dossiers like Lilia's, directly related to property later handed over to the monks, it is also clear that a very significant proportion of the transmitted secular documents do not relate in a direct or obvious way to any subsequent gift.[64] Take the nine or so secular documents – three surviving in the original – from the late ninth century relating to the *villa* of *Caucilla*: these are not dominated by any single landowner in the way that Hugh and Lilia monopolize our secular documentation for Bierre, but show

[64] Cf. above, 269–81, on the Iberian evidence.

the circulation of property within a small but loosely connected group of landowners within the *villa*.[65] Cluny acquired land within *Caucilla* in the time of the first abbot, Berno, and its interests there were consolidated in 945, thanks to a gift by the viscount Ratburn that included a church; by 976, land parcels here were being let back as precarial grants, and by the end of the century, *Caucilla* was listed as one among the dozens of *villae* where Cluny's acquisitions were confirmed by King Raoul.[66] The connection between these tenth-century interests and the run of ninth-century charters is elusive – there is no explicit or direct link with the grant made by Ratburn half a century after the last transmitted secular document – and this encourages us at least to consider indirect mechanisms, such as the storage of local title-deeds whose utility was long since lost in a local church subsequently taken over by Cluny: a parallel state of affairs to those documented at Perrecy and Rankweil earlier in this book.

Of course, asserting a negative – in this case, demonstrating a lack of correlation between ancient title-deeds and current property interests – is always tricky for a historian, but the advent of electronically searchable databases of the Cluny material makes it possible to do so with reasonable confidence. In this bustling regional society, indirect and tangential connections of course abound, for, by the abbacy of Odilo at the latest, Cluny had a presence in most rural communities and a connection with most segments of the landowning class in the region. Even if we allow for some 'missing links', lost documents that would have tied apparently unconnected transactions together, we must admit the presence of a varied and multivalent documentary culture, and the possibility that as bundles were handed over to new owners, miscellaneous, stray or now redundant pieces of parchment were passed over also, rather like Lilia's 897 purchase, which ended up with Cluny three decades later even though the property itself seems to have passed into other hands.

## From dossier to archive: the social life of legal documents

How was an individual landowner's dossier organized, and what does the existence of such dossiers suggest about archival and documentary cultures? The surviving originals from Cluny give priceless clues to these otherwise intractable questions. Barret has drawn attention to the ways – evident in the originals – in which dossiers connected individual documentary texts relating to specific people or places: by the addition of subsequent notices, by the inclusion of documents on the same piece of

[65] *Cluny* 8, 23, 26, 32, 37, 42, 49, 79, 86. [66] *Cluny* 125, 137, 671, 1423, 2465–6.

parchment as an existing transaction, by the physical connection of separate parchments, and by the piercing through of one or more documents by the staff or *festuca* with which legal rituals of property transfer were performed.[67]

Such confections could be complex in structure, particularly when they related to an initial bequest to Cluny to which monks appended subsequent episodes relating to the same people or property. In the abbacy of Odilo, for example, Odalrich and Gauzfred made a donation to the monastery for the soul of their father Wicfred, which included some lands that had been previously been the object of a dispute with Cluny. The document records Odalrich and Gauzfred's subscription, and then, in a different hand, the consent of their family; a note of the gift of an unfree female dependant (*ancilla*) appears to have been inserted between the two groups of subscriptions, and a *festuca* driven through the lower corner of the parchment; a one-line notice recording a supplementary donation for the soul of Wichard is also recorded. A second parchment is sewn onto this mélange of documentary episodes. On the second parchment is an account of the events that took place in 1047, when Wichard, close to death and unable to talk, was taken to Cluny for burial: his relatives, after consultation, decided to make a gift and have a document drawn up, but contested the earlier gift of the *ancilla*, whose husband demanded to speak to Odilo for satisfaction, prior to the original charter being produced by the monks and the episode being concluded in high ritual involving the solemn reconfirmation of the first document and the paying off of the kin with 23 *solidi*.[68]

In Wichard's case, it is clear that 'dossierization' was undertaken by the monks, with the careful assemblage of the various material relating to his gifts, and its production when his kin at his deathbed contested earlier bequests. But there is good reason to think that as a strategy dossierization originated among the local landowning classes prior to the monastery's foundation. In 905, for example, Azo and Hildeard sold lands in the Lyonnais to Stephen and Gergergana, before witnesses. Lambert, thanks to whom we have the text of this act, also transcribed the notice of a quitclaim made by Azo and Hildeard in favour of Stephen and Gergergana, at Mâcon before the count and the *boni homines*, where witnesses attested to having seen the initial investiture (*vestitura*), the legal ritual whereby

[67] Barret, *La mémoire et l'écrit*, 96–107.

[68] *Les plus anciens documents* III 81–2 = *Cluny* 2008–9; see also Barret, *La mémoire et l'écrit*, 98–102, and K. Heidecker, '30 June 1047: The End of Charters as Legal Evidence in France?', in P. Schulte, M. Mostert and I. van Renswoude (eds.), *Strategies of Writing: Studies on Text and Trust in the Middle Ages* (Turnhout, 2008), 87–94.

property was symbolically passed from one individual to another normally through the handing over of a proxy such as a *festuca*.[69] The care taken in recording the quitclaim (*werpetitio*) here outweighs that given to documenting the original sale: the ritual performance of a quitclaim and its subsequent recording in writing were crucial strategies for the public demonstration of title, and the care taken by the abbey to maintain such records of quitclaim and to 'dossierize' them with original donations shows that it drew on and exploited these long-standing mechanisms for asserting title.[70] Because we are dependent on Lambert's transcription and the cartulary for the 905 case, we do not know exactly what this pair of documentary texts looked like on parchment, nor, indeed, whether there was a physical mnemonic of the *vestitura* that was the point of the second episode; what we can see clearly, however, is the creation of a mini-dossier to establish and publicly validate title.

This 905 case is suggestive of the pairing and grouping of documents in conflict-led dossiers, a phenomenon common in cartularies right across the Frankish world.[71] It also invites us to think of the other material traces of storage and use – dorsal notes, folding, uncut documents on a single piece of parchment – that we found in the St Gall archive. Many of the surviving originals from Cluny have dorsal notes, but we have less of a critical mass of such documents than at St Gall, so the reconstruction of monastic archiving systems and pre-monastic annotations has not yet been possible for Cluny. Nonetheless, because of Lambert's interest in recording the texts of dorsal notices where he found them, we do get a sense that some of our secular dossiers were organized and labelled with practical ends in mind. We have transcriptions of dorsal notes for around half of Lilia's dossier, for example, and these texts would tend to indicate that the documents were not classified as a single set of *cartae Ugonis et Lilianis* or titles to Bierre after their passing over to Cluny. The script of the only original dorsal note is roughly contemporary with that of the charter scribe, but we do not have dense enough evidence to draw firm conclusions about the when and why of dorsing, except to conclude that the dorsing was clearly not made on the entry of the charters into the Cluny archive – if it were, they would be consistently linked to Lilia.[72]

69 *Cluny* 90. 70 Cf. above, Chapter 9, for a parallel position in Italy.

71 See above, Chapters 7–8.

72 *Cluny* 60 ('the sale of Deodatus in *Kasal Bertrudo*), 67 ('Hugh's sale in Bierre'), 68 ('the sale of Raimbod'), 69 ('Hugh's sale in Bierre'), 82 ('Hugh's sale in Château'), 84 ('Ageda in Bierre'), 89bis ('The lord Count William in Bierre'), 93 ('Hugh's sale in Bierre'), 94 ('Theotrada's sale in Bierre'), 202 ('Lilia's donation in Bierre'). *Cluny* 89bis is an original; no. 275 is transmitted only by cartulary, so we have no such record.

These phenomena underline the extent to which we need to consider the materiality of the written word on parchment, and the interpenetration of written and oral in the legal rituals performed with and around charters. To older generations of historians, weaned on a strong contrast between literacy as a 'rationalizing' force and 'irrational' forms of legal ritual, the use of the charter as an object might be seen to militate against its 'common-sense' function as a written instrument, even to indicate its debasement; similarly, the existence of legal rituals of transfer led to questions about whether written documents were the 'real' dispositive mechanisms by which property ownership was transferred, or whether they served as written mnemonics of a dispositive oral ceremony; such worries were often linked in scholarship of a certain vintage to worries about 'Germanic' influence undermining 'Roman' legal principles.[73] These concerns indicate how, while it remains indispensable, traditional diplomatic scholarship's treatment of documents as disembodied texts, and its links to an equally weighty legal history rooted in strong oppositions between custom and written law, helped to shape an entire research agenda here. Yet, does it make any sense to compare the relative significance of oral testimony, performed legal ritual and written documentation in a context in which law and justice were conducted face to face, argued according to shared norms and reliant on local public opinion? The absence of any evidence indicating that early medieval people worried about issues of diplomatic or formal legalism must be telling. If our questions made sense to them, we would have cases turning on whether a written document or a legal ritual was the dispositive moment in a legal transaction; we do not. It must make more sense, in the context of the Cluny evidence, to stress the way in which a parchment was simultaneously a written document with probative value – one to which other documents or related notices might be added – and also an object that might be attached to other objects, with symbolic as well as legal functions.

As objects whose transfers between different members of a network defined that network, charters might be seen as acquiring a 'social life' of their own, playing a more active role in defining relationships than as mere passive records.[74] These annotations and attachments illustrate

[73] The bibliography on these issues is huge. For a convincing demonstration of the interpenetration of writing and ritual in a comparable legal culture, see J. Bowman, *Shifting Landmarks: Property, Proof and Dispute in Catalonia Around the Year 1000* (Ithaca, NY, 2004), and Bowman, 'Did Neo-Romans Curse? Law, Land and Ritual in the Midi (900–1100)', *Viator*, 28 (1997), 1–43.

[74] I owe this point to Charles West; the key reference is A. Appadurai, *The Social Life of Things* (Cambridge, 1988).

vividly that documents were used, interacting with the repertoire of legal rituals and oral testimony that were central to public meetings, even when the notices of those meetings do not mention the production of a charter: the 905 notice of quitclaim discussed above, for example, does not mention the existence of an earlier deed of sale, but its transmission context clearly indicates that an earlier deed informed the quitclaim. In working from cartulary copies, as we normally must, these elements are missing, for the documents have been ripped from the context of the network in which they had initially operated and recopied in a different register. In assessing the role of written documents in early medieval legal culture, then, we should take care before assuming that documents played a role only in cases where they are explicitly cited in records of court proceedings; we sould acknowledge the textuality of those records, especially where we are dependent on later cartulary copies that remove texts from their original contexts and prevent us from seeing the kind of linkages and usages clear from the processes of addition, annotation and dossierization apparent at Cluny.[75]

In and of itself, this must mean that we cannot attempt to examine the penetration of written documents in court proceedings simply by counting when and where they are explicitly mentioned in records of cases.[76] While documents such as the second parchment concerning Wichard's donation to Cluny can tell us much about how cited documents were used and received, early medieval scribal cultures were too fluid and the mechanisms by which documents might inform legal action too varied for us to assume that documents were routinely or regularly mentioned when used. In fact, in the case of Wichard's donation, considering a single document out of its archival context obscures a richer hinterland of archival and documentary practices.[77] Locating them in their original contexts shows us how documents acquired value and validity above all through their public authentication. The institutions and processes of the

[75] For *placita* texts as textual artefacts, see now W. Brown, 'Charters as Weapons: On the Role Played by Early Medieval Dispute Records in the Disputes They Record', *Journal of Medieval History*, 28 (2002), 227–48.

[76] Which does not, of course, mean that such endeavour is meaningless, just that it cannot be assumed to provide a definite or objective picture of document use. Cf. K. Heidecker, 'Communication by Written Texts in Court Cases: Some Charter Evidence (ca. 800–ca. 1100)', in M. Mostert (ed.), *New Approaches to Medieval Communication* (Turnhout, 1999), 101–26; Heidecker, 'Emploi de l'écrit dans les actes judiciaires: Trois sondages en profondeur: Bourgogne, Souabe et Franconie (VIII$^{e}$–début XII$^{e}$ siècle)', in M.-J. Gasse-Grandjean and B.-M. Tock (eds.), *Les actes comme expression du pouvoir au haut moyen âge* (Turnhout, 2003), 125–37.

[77] A point resoundingly made about the Wichard document – which in traditional diplomatic manuals had been seen as marking the end of the charter as a legal proof – by Heidecker, '30 June 1047'.

Roman state had provided precise contexts for the publication and validation of documents, but by our period these possibilities had receded. Instead, landowners sought to demonstrate that their documents had enjoyed a more generic form of public acceptance, one not bound to any institutional context or informed by firm legal rules so much as responding to norms and expectations shared by the charter-using classes.[78] The stress on scribal subscriptions and the confirmation of witnesses evident in original documents needs to be read in these terms, as demonstrations of a document's acceptance by the local 'public', not necessarily as indicating a particular institutional standing on the part of a scribe or a specific legal relationship to the transaction on the part of a witness. So, too, the tactics of annotation and linking documents to demonstrate their acceptability to a local public rested on a similar logic.

Dossierization through annotation, the copying of connected documents on a single parchment or the attachment of related parchments, was thus an archival practice that predated the monastery and was adopted by the monks simply because it was a practical and sensible strategy in this documentary culture. Through the tenth century, it remained the dominant archival strategy at Cluny, to the extent that we should probably think of the monastery's archive as a collection of dossiers each relating to dealings with a particular patron or kin group, or a particular estate.[79] Barret suggests that dorsal notices on the surviving originals indicate some attempt to classify and organize these documents to facilitate access by the beginning of Odilo's abbacy, at the end of the tenth century. It may be that these first stages of archival reorganization fed directly into, and perhaps anticipated, the process of cartulary compilation that began later in Odilo's abbacy. Although we have clear cases of dossierization well into the eleventh century and beyond, especially in cases like Wichard's where donations were contentious and contested, it does seem that cartulary compilation was one of a series of wider changes in archival organization designed to create an institutional memory that served both commemorative and practical purposes. In part, this was surely a simple necessity given the sheer scale of the abbey's holdings, in terms of both land and deeds documenting title to that land. In the tenth century, when the abbey had been in existence only one or two generations and the stories of the acquisition of specific estates were tied to the memory of the monks' dealings with particular benefactors, dossierization remained a viable – even a sensible – archival practice,

[78] Classen, 'Fortleben'; P. Johanek, 'Zur rechtlichen Funktion von Traditionsnotiz, Traditionsbuch und früher Siegelurkunde', in *Recht und Schrift*, 131–62; obviously, I read the post-Roman end differently. Cf. also above, Chapter 5.

[79] This is Barret's conclusion: *La mémoire et l'écrit*, esp. 103–7 on 'un "dossier" d'archives'.

facilitating as it did the documentation of episodic and oscillating relationships with patrons. By the end of the tenth century, however, the abbey's archive must have contained perhaps a thousand documents, and so probably well over a hundred groups of charters and dossiers, the earliest strata of which concerned the gifts of Lilia and her contemporaries, now beyond the horizon of living memory. The episodic relationships between Cluny and its patrons are so visible in the tenth-century documentation precisely because they defined archival practices and so determined the pattern of documentation at the abbey; by the second half of the eleventh century, as a different archival system established itself, the norms governing the 'gift economy' binding the monastery to its benefactors began to alter. The result was a shift from archival practices immediately identifiable to any lay landowner, which connected parchment to people to place to make sense of current relationships, to a new and deeper system of archival memory that underwrote institutional identity while enabling easy reference for those searching for documents relating to a particular privilege or specific estate. The case of Cluny thus shows how a monastery, in its early phases, might 'piggyback' on pre-existing archival and documentary practices. It also shows, however, how once an ecclesiastical patrimony had reached a certain scale, and an ecclesiastical institution a certain degree of self-consciousness, a fixed archival memory of a new kind, more distant from the practices of the landowning classes, might develop.

## Conclusions: charter collections, archival transformations and social change

Shifts in archival practice at Cluny, encapsulated in the compilation of the cartularies in the eleventh century, thus had their roots in the changing relationship between the monastery and its 'host' society in the first century and a half of its existence. These developments, however, were not unique to Cluny: they parallel a series of wider archival transformations right across the post-Carolingian kingdoms in the eleventh and twelfth centuries. In particular, major monastic houses sifted their charter collections as they had their traditions edited and reordered in cartularies and *pancartes*, technologies rapidly imitated by other ecclesiastical institutions and, in the course of the twelfth century, by major lay landowners too. In monasteries, the process seems to have had important links to wider currents of intellectual influence and to the spread of ideologies of 'reform' from centres like Cluny.[80] Initially motivated by the dual imperatives of institutional commemoration and tenurial protection, but

[80] Geary, *Phantoms*, 81–113; *Les cartulaires*.

increasingly tied up with the crystallization of new forms of seigneurial power over judicially defined territories, these eleventh-century compilations did have precedents in the 'books of traditions' of Carolingian times, into which some of the newly established churches in the recently conquered and Christianized provinces beyond the Rhine had copied records of donations. But ninth-century initiatives had been shaped by very specific impulses in particular contexts, above all by the tenurial disruption wrought by the 'Carolingianization' of these regions.[81]

While the records of Freising and Fulda have profoundly influenced modern historiographical expectations about Carolingian and post-Carolingian record-keeping, they should not be seen as representing a new archival template that swept aside the varied practices that had developed in the post-Roman centuries, nor did they replace the charter collections and dossiers that typified documentary practice within Frankish society.[82] The adoption of new forms of record-keeping right across eleventh- and twelfth-century western Europe, on the other hand, took place as landholding institutions – first ecclesiastical landowners and then the newly institutionalized secular lordships of the twelfth century – responded to far-reaching economic, social and tenurial changes.[83] Foremost among those imperatives in the earliest waves of cartulary compilation was a heightened awareness of the special status of ecclesiastical property and increased concern with identifying the dividing lines between the sacred and secular in this world – concerns very visible in the Cluny cartularies and their publication in concert with Urban II's promulgation of a 'sacred ban' around the heart of the monastery's territory. This sense that ecclesiastical possessions formed an inviolable patrimony interacted with notions of spiritual protection and immunity as norms about the interaction between churches and lay benefactors underwent fundamental revision.[84] Economic change – the increasing

[81] E.g. Hummer, *Politics*; M. Innes, 'Property, Politics and the Problem of the Carolingian State', in W. Pohl and V. Wieser (eds.), *Der frühmittelalterliche Staat: Europäische Perspektiven* (Vienna, 2009), 299–314; H. Wolfram, 'Die Notitia Arnonis und ähnliche Formen der Rechtssicherung im nachagilolfischen Bayern', in *Recht und Schrift*, 115–30; and above, Chapters 7–8.

[82] See above, Chapters 7–8.

[83] Chronology of cartulary compilation: I. Rosé, 'Panorama de l'écrit diplomatique en Bourgogne: Autour des cartulaires (XI–XVIII siècles)', *Bulletin du Centre d'études médiévales d'Auxerre* 11 (2007): www.cem.revues.org/index2352.html.

[84] See Rosenwein, *Saint Peter*, and Rosenwein, *Negotiating Space: Power, Restraint, and Privileges of Immunity in Early Medieval Europe* (Ithaca, NY, 1999), 156–83. On changing relationships between monks, benefactors and commemoration, see D. Iogna-Prat, 'The Dead in the Celestial Bookkeeping of the Cluniac Monks', in L. Little and B. H. Rosenwein (eds.), *Debating the Middle Ages: Issues and Readings* (London, 1998), 340–62, and on monks and laity, D. Iogna-Prat, *Order and Exclusion: Cluny and Christendom*

monetization and marketization of rural production, and the linked phenomenon of price inflation – led to the adoption of new techniques of estate management based on the more direct exploitation of possessions, as opposed to long-term fixed-rent arrangements embedded in social relationships.[85] Similarly, the crystallization of new forms of power in the countryside, rooted in the territorialized jurisdictional rights of the *seigneurie*, created a new layer of formal rule over and above the flux of sociable exchange.[86] For landowners – increasingly the great lay lords, now able to pass on institutionalized territorial power from generation to generation, as well as ecclesiastical institutions – new techniques of accountability and record-keeping were vital in facing these changes.[87]

As a result of these changes, earlier medieval documentary practices were effectively lost beneath our historiographical horizon as novel forms of archival organization reshaped earlier traditions.[88] Cartulary compilation involved both the selection and the reorganization of original documents which had been carefully ordered and preserved, in some cases for centuries, in institutional charter collections. While dorsal notes on surviving originals can, as we have seen, give some hint at the classification systems of early medieval charter collections, we can only access them indirectly, via the kind of methodology attempted above. We cannot know how much or how quickly old charter collections were dispersed or destroyed in the aftermath of cartulary compilation: at Cluny it is striking that the bundles of early charters selectively copied into or omitted from the cartularies seem to have remained, dormant and unused, with the monastery into the early modern period and the age of Lambert and his fellow antiquarians, but elsewhere there are hints at dispersal and reuse,

*Face Heresy, Judaism and Islam, 1000–1150*, trans. G. R. Edwards (Ithaca, NY, 2002 [1998]), 9–96.

85 G. Duby, 'Économie domaniale et économie monétaire: Le budget de l'abbaye de Cluny entre 1080 et 1155', in Duby, *Hommes et structures au moyen âge* (Paris, 1973), 61–82 (orig. *Annales ESC*, 7 [1952], 155–71).

86 The literature is huge, and intimately tied up with questions of causation that are hotly contested as part of the 'feudal revolution' debate; for a recent perspective, see T. N. Bisson, *The Crisis of the Twelfth Century: Power, Lordship and the Origins of European Government* (Princeton, NJ, 2008).

87 Monastic accounting: R. Berkhofer, *Day of Reckoning: Power and Accountability in Medieval France* (Philadelphia, 2004).

88 L. Morelle, 'The Metamorphosis of Three Monastic Charter Collections in the Eleventh Century (St.-Amand, St.-Riquier, Montier-en-Der)', in Heidecker (ed.), *Charters and the Use of the Written Word*, 171–204. Cf. S. Vanderputten, 'Transformations in Charter Production and Transmission during the "Iron Age" (Tenth–Early Eleventh Centuries): Some Evidence from Northern France and the Southern Low Countries', *Jaarboek voor Middeleeuwse Geschiedenis*, 7 (2004), 7–30; this paper is undermined by the fact that it adopts a quasi-quantitative methodology while failing to consider modes of transmission.

with some originals surviving precisely because they were recycled.[89] Once a donation was a century or more old, the practical utility of the dossier of title-deeds recording a property's prehistory and establishing the right of the donor to grant it must have receded. Cartularies were arguably more suited to documenting historical privileges, claims to immunity and rights of *seigneurie* – needs close to the hearts of many eleventh- and twelfth-century abbots and bishops – than were chests full of dossierized charters. Meanwhile, parchment remained in high – indeed increasing – demand, and new uses could always be found for old documents. More or less 'organic' turnover, with 'active' dossiers becoming dormant, gathering dust and perhaps eventually being lost or discarded, must have been common within early medieval charter collections; cartularies, on the other hand, fixed a very different kind of memory, shaped by the cultural and legal needs of a new social order, and in the long run that memory came to dominate institutions' understanding of their own past.

We certainly should not assume that the shift to cartulary copies was motivated by a 'crisis' that undermined the legal utility of original documents. The case of Wichard in 1047, discussed above, has been cited as an indication of the failure of such documents to be used as legal proof, but, in fact, in this case, negotiation between monks and their benefactors was structured around a dossier of documents and appended notices that was immediately fetched from the monastic archive when questions about the donation were raised. Transactions such as this, and the texts of the documents recording them, may be messy, and not comply to any formalized juristic rules about hierarchies of proof or any sense of a 'clean' legal process whereby rights were absolutely and irrevocably transferred, but that is precisely because at this date rights and norms remained embedded in social relationships in a world of 'substantive legalism' rather than subject to an abstracted 'formal law'.[90] In any case, the whole notion of a 'crisis' or 'decline' in written

[89] The extent of conscious archival destruction has been a major focus of debate following Geary, *Phantoms*.

[90] Rosenwein, *Saint Peter*, and, for formal law versus substantive legalism, S. D. White, *Custom, Kinship and Gifts to Saints: The Laudatio Parentum in Western France, 1050–1150* (Chapel Hill, NC, 1988), and White, 'Inheritance and Legal Arguments in Western France, 1050–1150', *Traditio*, 43 (1987), 55–103; on Wichard, Heidecker, '30 June 1047'. For the notion – inherited from diplomatic textbooks – of a decline in the use of written documents as proof, used to explain the move to cartularies, see G. Declercq, 'Originals and Cartularies: The Organisation of Archival Memory (9th–11th Centuries)', in Heidecker (ed.), *Charters and the Use of the Written Word*, 147–70; cf. P. Geary, 'Umgang mit Urkunden im frühen Mittelalter', in P. Erhart and L. Hollenstein (eds.), *Mensch und Schrift im frühen Mittelalter* (St Gall, 2006), 11–24, esp. 20–1.

documentation is itself an illusion created by changes in archival horizons. Because those Carolingian and earlier documents copied in the new cartularies of the eleventh and twelfth centuries overwhelmingly recorded the munificence of kings and founding benefactors and the disinterestedness of their justice, they create a backdrop of highly formalized acts of carefully formulated Latinity. From a certain perspective, searching for legal clarity and hierarchy, this backdrop might encourage criticism of the more episodic *narrativité* and breathless practicality of surviving documents: hence notions of a rising barbarity, even 'documentary anarchy'. But if we set aside the assumptions underpinning these judgements, a more continuous development of pragmatic legal writing becomes apparent.[91]

Cluny, because of its unique position in the high Middle Ages and the remarkable interest in its muniments in the eighteenth, nineteenth and twentieth centuries, offers a rare possibility of catching tantalizing glimpses of what lies beyond the evidentiary horizon set in the eleventh century. It is no accident that the only truly comparable case comes from St-Denis in Paris. St-Denis' continuing history through Merovingian and Carolingian times, and its close relationship with the Frankish Crown from the seventh century, mean that its early medieval archive must have looked very different in composition and chronological depth from that of Cluny. But, like Cluny, it was the subject of significant antiquarian interest through the *ancien régime* – modern diplomatic scholarship, indeed, was born from the St-Denis archive and Mabillon's efforts to prove the veracity of its traditions – and its contents fed directly into the national collections of the nineteenth-century French state, hardly surprisingly given the monastery's 'national' profile since medieval times. Thus the great cartulary compilations of the abbey – most especially the White Cartulary of the early thirteenth century – are complemented by a rich transmission of originals, and by the works of antiquarians, which may not be systematic efforts at transcription like Lambert's but nonetheless give a clear sense of what has been lost.[92] What is immediately clear is the extent to which the high medieval cartulary tradition was determined by current concerns. Remnants of a stream of donations by benefactors of the seventh to tenth centuries, ranging from members of the Carolingian family and the 'imperial aristocracy' to more local landowners, survive

[91] Guyotjeannin, '*Penuria scriptorum*'; Barthélemy, 'Une crise de l'écrit?'

[92] An indispensable study aid for anyone working on the St-Denis archive is the website directed by O. Guyotjeannin, 'Chartes de l'abbaye de St-Denis, VII–XIII siècle', saint-denis.enc.sorbonne.fr, with full transcriptions of the *Cartulaire blanc* and the early modern *Inventaire générale*; see also D. Sonzogni, *Le chartrier de l'abbaye de St-Denis en France au haut moyen âge: Essai de reconstruction* (Paris, 2003).

in the original, but the cartularies exclude most in a relatively systematic manner, with the exception of royal diplomata; our early modern inventories and antiquarian notes identify significant further numbers of now lost documents.[93] Within these traditions, there are tantalizing indications of now lost lay traditions similar to those we have analysed at Cluny: for example, a lone original document from 769 in which Aegefredus and Archesidana sold land in the *villa Pociollus* in the Pincerais to Nautlindo.[94] Famously, these survivals include a run of original papyri from the seventh century paralleled only at Ravenna in the West, which, along with a body of original royal diplomata on parchment from the last quarter of the seventh century, constitute the primary evidential basis for our knowledge of late Merovingian documentary culture. The fifty-nine surviving original Merovingian documents were transmitted outside the mainstream archival tradition, in that they were not copied in the cartularies, nor is there any evidence for their use at medieval St-Denis. Some of the magnificent ancient papyri were used to confect a series of eleventh-century forgeries: the medium evidently now had more value than the Merovingian message inscribed on it, as Abbot Suger sought to buttress the abbey's position by the production of allegedly ancient papal privileges. Others simply sat, excluded from the main monastic tradition rather like the secular material at Cluny. Others still – for example, twenty-two of the twenty-nine Merovingian documents used by the ninth-century author of the *Gesta Dagoberti* – were lost.[95] Significantly, very many of our surviving Merovingian documents do not directly relate to the abbey or its interests: some are royal privileges or judgements in favour of other beneficiaries, and some are the documents of wealthy private landowners from the Paris region, including an important run of last wills and testaments.

The close links between St-Denis, the Merovingian court at Paris, and the highest echelons of the Frankish elite doubtless explain how much of this came to end up at the abbey: as at Ravenna, there is a political nexus at work. But this specific context should not obscure the broader phenomenon of a church perhaps acting as a recognized store for significant and contestable documents, and so vacuuming up a significant quantity of papyrus and parchment in which its interests were not directly implicated. While elsewhere we simply do not have the weight

[93] E.g. D. Sonzogni, 'Un acte de vente inédit du chartrier de Saint-Denis (11 avril 702?)', *Bibliothèque de l'École des chartes* 159 (2002), 609–13.

[94] ARTEM no. 4488, *ChLA* XV 609.

[95] Geary, *Phantoms*, 107–13, with bibliography; H. Atsma and J. Vezin, 'La faux sur papyrus de l'abbaye de St-Denis', in J. Kerherve and A. Rigaudière (eds.), *Finances, pouvoirs et mémoire: Mélanges offerts à Jean Favier* (Paris, 1999), 684–99.

of antiquarian scholarship and rescued originals that typifies Cluny and St-Denis, we do have a constant murmur of hints that their cases were far from unusual. From Murbach, for example, our surviving originals focus on the abbey's founders and major benefactors, but we also have an original document from 762 in which Sighifrid gave a considerable portfolio of estates to his son Altmann, some of which later ended up in Murbach's hands; from Cambrai, a gift in 875 by Henry to his son Warmund; from Nouaillé, another gift between private individuals from 886 and a sale from 897 amidst a fascinating set of private dossiers; from Narbonne, two related sales from 912 and 925; from Poitiers, a sale from 923; from Limoges, a sale from 941; from La Grasse, a sale from 947; and so on.[96] The spread of this 'background noise' of chance survivals is evident from the database of original early medieval charters from modern France compiled by the ARTEM (Atelier de Recherche sur les Textes Médiévaux) project hosted by Nancy 2 University. In the ARTEM database, almost 60 per cent of the 672 surviving originals before 950 were issued by emperors, kings or popes; most of the remainder involve churches or priests as one of the actors, with only 56 where all parties were laymen.[97] But even if we acknowledge that 22 of these documents come from Cluny (almost all in the single charter collection in BnF lat. 17715), the scattering of other traditions does indicate that churches right across the Frankish world had contact with lay documentary traditions that they did not create or control.

Even cartularies – whose date and function mean that they are least likely to include lay documents – contain echoes of such traditions. It is almost normal for such collections to have a document or two concerning the families of founders or important early benefactors, and in a handful of cases specific impulses encouraged high medieval cartulary compilers to copy out whole dossiers of lay documents. At Perrecy – discussed above – our remarkable run of Carolingian estate documents and title-deeds survived on site through to the eleventh century, when they were copied in order to add ballast to a cartulary of the priory now founded on the Perrecy estate, which was concerned above all with the complex relationship between that priory and its mother house, the monastery of

[96] ARTEM no. 3873; *ChLA* XIX 676; ARTEM nos. 352, 1068, 1073, 2372–3, 1090, 647, 3785, respectively.

[97] The figures here are based on the discussion in Kosto, 'Laymen', 73–4, and in Tock, 'L'acte privé en France, VII$^{e}$–milieu du X$^{e}$ siècle', in *Les transferts*, 499–537, at 502–7, 534–5. Note that the majority of the St-Denis documents discussed above are excluded from these calculations as they are either royal or (in the case of many of the wills and 'private' documents) involve some property going to the Church. In any case the ARTEM search categories are not watertight when not backed up by a manual search.

Fleury.[98] At Redon in Brittany, an eleventh-century scribe came across dossiers of sales and exchanges similar to those we found at Cluny, was unable to fit them easily into his scheme of a cartulary in the guise of *gesta abbatum*, but copied them nonetheless.[99]

In all of these cases, we see a society in which documents were used and stored by landowners without defined public institutions of record, and without the Church enjoying hegemony as a provider of documentary services. In other words, we need to acknowledge the existence of a complex set of practices that cannot be understood as a mere staging post between the lost late antique world of public archives and the great ecclesiastical charter compilations of the eleventh and twelfth centuries, but needs evoking in its own terms. Crucial to these practices was the need to demonstrate that a document was a publicly validated record – hence the importance of scribes, subscriptions and witnesses, and the care taken to make public acceptance of a document physically tangible on the document itself, through annotation or the attachment of further documents or objects. This was a world in which establishing title through creating a convincing narrative that could mobilize public opinion was an important driver of document use, as late antique concerns about the registration of fiscal liabilities were no longer active, and the claims of the *seigneurie* had not yet developed. Our fragmentary dossiers show that documents were crucial episodes in ongoing narratives that linked land and landowners, and that were periodically debated, openly, in public. As pieces of parchment or papyrus they may be unremarkable, but their very scrappy materiality takes us to the heart of the archival and documentary culture of the early medieval centuries.

[98] See above, 176–82.

[99] W. Davies, 'The Composition of the Redon Cartulary', *Francia*, 17 (1990), 79–100; Davies, 'Intra-family Transfers in Southeastern Brittany: The Dossier from Redon', in *Les transferts*, 881–94; Davies, 'People and Places in Disputes in Ninth-Century Brittany', in *Settlement of Disputes*, 65–84; Davies, 'Priests and Rural Communities in Eastern Brittany in the Ninth Century', *Études celtiques*, 20 (1983), 177–97; Davies, *Small Worlds*.

# 12 Documentary practices, archives and laypeople in central Italy, mid ninth to eleventh centuries

*Antonio Sennis*

*The common documentary culture of tenth- and eleventh-century Italy is so highly visible in the sources as to have long been recognized, though we can now see that it was neither a recent development nor exceptional. Yet this chapter shows that active questions remain about laypeople's engagement with documents. The Italian evidence not only shows that lay families preserved documents but also hints at how they did so – for instance, through depositing them in chests and cupboards, sometimes apparently randomly. It also demonstrates how archives could be filtered by the deliberate destruction of documents that were considered redundant, irregular or forged. Conversely, when the provisions in documents needed to be maintained, they could be confirmed through the law courts. Once more, we see that it is not a distinction between clergy and laity that shaped documentary practices. Rather, lay families and their patrimonies, which shifted and fragmented with each generation, lacked the institutional mindset that ecclesiastical institutions developed, which encouraged them to preserve records for the long term.*

In the spring of 983, the emperor Otto II received a letter from Gerbert, the newly appointed abbot of the monastery of Bobbio. 'I would rather be bringing you good than sad news,' the monk wrote, 'but how could I keep silent, when I see my brethren consumed by hunger and degraded by nakedness? The situation would perhaps be bearable, had we not been deprived even of the hope that it might improve. By means of I do not know what documents, which here they call *libelli*, this church of God has been entirely sold. The money that was paid is nowhere to be found; our cupboards and granaries are empty; there is nothing in our pockets.'[1] The emperor died later in the year and never granted any privilege to Bobbio. We therefore do not know what, if anything, he had to say about the rather peculiar use that Gerbert's predecessors and their (mainly lay)

[1] Gerbert of Aurillac, *Epistolae* 2 (ed. P. Riché and J. P. Callu [Paris, 1993], 1:5).

counterparts seem to have made of a type of contract that was never meant to transfer permanently rights of property. For his part, Gerbert was quick to leave the Italian monastery and, in the course of time, was quite successful in grazing new, if by no means less troubled, pastures: first the see of Reims, then that of Ravenna and eventually the greenest of them all, Rome.[2] He did not, however, lose interest in the fortunes of Bobbio. Keeping, at least nominally, his abbatial title, Gerbert evidently kept an eye on how things were developing. On 1 October 998, Otto III intervened, at Gerbert's request, to put an end to the manipulation of *libelli*, or charters of lease.[3] Although highly contentious, the *Capitulare Ticinense*, issued on 20 September of the same year, sanctioned that, from then on, leases and emphyteuses granted by a church would expire with the death of the person who had granted them and would therefore not impinge on the will of his or her successor, who was completely free to confirm them or not. It is true that the fact that this capitulary was not included in the *Liber Papiensis* indicates that, most probably, it was never properly enforced.[4] Nevertheless, this episode and its legal results clearly remind us that, perhaps surprisingly for some contemporaries, the inhabitants of most parts of Italy, whether lay or cleric, indeed knew how important preserving written documents was to establish, claim and even abuse their rights.[5] Moreover, even if often many among them could not read what was written on the charters they owned, they knew how to use them well – at times, as in the case of Bobbio's counterparts, all too well.

When compared to other regions of Europe, Italy seems, at first glance, strikingly peculiar. If one looks at what are usually considered the fundamental elements in any written tradition – levels of literacy, social

[2] *Libelli*: P. Toubert, *Les structures du Latium médiéval: Le Latium méridional et la Sabine du IX^e^ siècle à la fin du XII^e^ siècle* (Rome, 1973), 516 ff.; C. Violante, 'La signoria rurale nel secolo X', in *Il secolo di ferro: Mito e realtà del secolo X*, Settimane 38 (Spoleto, 1991), 349 ff. Gerbert of Aurillac: M. Oldoni, 'Silvestro II', in *Enciclopedia dei Papi*, 3 vols. (Rome, 2000), II, 116–24.

[3] MGH DD Otto III, no. 303: 'iubemus . . . ut ea quae male his temporibus acta sunt sine abbatis Gerberti auctoritate et detinentur vel in precariis aut commutationibus rerum vel hominum sive in libellis aut aliquibus scriptis, nemo retineat, nullus ex eis se intromittere audeat, sed propria nostra auctoritate frustrentur et omnia destruantur, nisi ab eodem iterum melius ordinentur et restaurari videantur'.

[4] MGH Const. 1, no. 23; F. Bougard, *La justice dans le royaume d'Italie de la fin du VIII*[e] *siècle au début du XI*[e] *siècle* (Rome, 1995), 53; A. Visconti, 'Una legge feudale di Ottone III esclusa dal capitolare italico', *Reale istituto lombardo di scienze e lettere: Rendiconti*, 2nd ser., 60 (1927), 198–208. On the potentially destabilizing effects of this capitulary, see K. Görich, *Otto III. Romanus, Saxonicus et Italicus: Kaiserliche Rompolitik und sächsische Historiographie* (Sigmaringen, 1993), 269, 277; D. A. Warner, 'Ideals and Action in the Reign of Otto III', *Journal of Medieval History*, 25 (1999), 1–18, at 11.

[5] C. Wickham, 'Land Disputes and Their Social Framework in Lombard-Carolingian Italy, 700–900', in Wickham, *Land and Power: Studies in Italian and European Social History, 400–1200* (London, 1994), 229–56, at 242–3 (orig. in *Settlement of Disputes*, 104–24).

uses of writing, the development of a group of professionals who fulfil the documentary requirements of society – Italy has traditionally been considered to be an exception in medieval Europe. The (relatively) widespread use of writing and of written documents by the laity in early medieval Italy emerges as a fairly established fact, as Everett and Costambeys have already pointed out in their chapters above.[6]

Clearly, even in Italy, churches did have strong control over the production and circulation of written documents, and this fact had relevant consequences. For example, the relationship between a monastery and the notaries writing its charters tended to result in very strong, if not exclusive, control on the part of the institution over local social dynamics. Notaries could not only write acts; they could also, for example, testify in court in favour of the monastery or prove similarly useful in arbitrations.[7] Moreover, by conveying, often in an aggressive way, ideas about the right ordering of society, the undeniable liturgical dimension that any charter had was also used by churches to shape the relationships that they had with the outside world. When charters were placed beside the eucharistic species on a monastic altar, lay generosity was turned into a liturgical act, and the identification between the religious and material treasures of the community was thus reinforced.[8] Besides,

[6] A. Bartoli Langeli and A. Petrucci (eds.), *Alfabetismo e cultura scritta: Con alcuni contributi su psicologia e storia* (Bologna, 1978) (= *Quaderni storici*, 13 [1978], 437–796); F. H. Bäuml, 'Varieties and Consequences of Medieval Literacy and Illiteracy', *Speculum*, 55 (1980), 237–65; A. Bartoli Langeli, 'Storia dell'alfabetismo e storia della scrittura: Questioni di metodo', *Annali della Facoltà di lettere e filosofia dell'Università degli studi di Perugia*, 26, n.s. 12 (1988–9), 221–37; M. Banniard, *Viva voce: Communication écrite et communication orale du VI^e au IX^e siècle en Occident latin* (Paris, 1992); F. Cardini, 'Alto e basso medioevo', in G. Cavallo, C. Leonardi and E. Menestò (eds.), *Lo spazio letterario del medioevo: Medioevo latino* (Rome, 1992–8), 1.1:130–43, with bibliography; above, Chapters 4 and 9.

[7] E.g. the case of a Dominicus *tabellio* who, in the course of a long career spanning at least the period between 1068 and 1118, wrote almost all the charters related to the properties of the monastery of Fonte Avellana in the territory of Cagli (*Carte di Fonte Avellana. I. 975–1139*, ed. C. Pierucci and A. Polverari [Rome, 1972], index). Similarly, a certain Batalla, between 1152 and 1189, wrote 121 charters (practically all the surviving ones) regarding the properties of the Venetian monastery of S. Zaccaria in Monselice (*Codice diplomatico padovano dall'anno 1101 alla pace di Costanza (25 giugno 1183)*, ed. A. Gloria [Venice, 1879–81]; G. Tasini, 'I notai e le badesse: La gestione delle proprietà del monastero di San Zaccaria di Venezia in territorio di Monselice (secoli XII–XIII)', in *Chiese e notai (secoli XII–XV)* [Verona, 2004], 245–59). Medieval notaries who, in spite of a privileged relationship with a church, continued to write documents for other institutions or individuals: L. Fois, 'I notai del monastero di Sant'Ambrogio di Milano nel XIII secolo (una prima indagine)', in *Chiese e notai*, 261–84, at 273.

[8] F. Bougard, 'Trésors et *mobilia* italiens du haut moyen âge', in J.-P. Caillet (ed.), *Les trésors de sanctuaires, de l'Antiquité à l'époque romane: Communications présentées au Centre de recherches sur l'antiquité tardive et le haut moyen âge de l'Université de Paris X–Nanterre (1993–1995)* (Paris, 1996), 161–97, at 167 (and nn. 43–5 for a number of examples). Donations to monasteries performed in front of the altar: M. Ragnow, 'Ritual before

monasteries were communities whose members could suspend the celebration of sacraments for political gain and use sacred rites to invoke the eternal damnation of someone who had seized a piece of their land.[9] It is therefore not surprising that, for example, in the eleventh century the comparatively low literacy of laypeople rendered their religious life, in the eyes of clerics, inferior.[10]

Lay individuals, however, could prove to be quite at ease with the different stages (and values) of production, circulation and preservation of a charter. In late eighth-century Lucca, for example, the notary Filippus, on request of the donor Porphoreus, corrected the document from which it appeared that Porphoreus had given himself, as well as his properties, to the Tuscan church of S. Pietro di Castiglione.[11] Lay awareness of documentary practices progressed throughout the centuries. In the early twelfth century, the use of different systems of dating on the part of notaries writing charters for the abbey of Sassovivo frequently depended on precise requests of the parties (often lay donors).[12] And as for the liturgical dimension of documentary practices, it has to be said that it is not always easy to tell how effective all those frightening rituals were and whether the prospect of being excommunicated and damned was enough to keep people, especially lay outsiders, at bay. Although the survival of monastic communities largely depended on the spiritual function they performed, their members continually alluded to the suffering they had to endure from outsiders who evidently were not too worried about divine anger.[13] Benefactors could quickly change their minds and take back their charters of donation, at times cunningly exploiting just the elaborate liturgical setting that was supposed to bind them. This is, for

the Altar: Legal Satisfaction and Spiritual Reconciliation in Eleventh-Century Anjou', in J. Rollo-Koster (ed.), *Medieval and Early Modern Ritual: Formalized Behaviour in Europe, China, and Japan* (Leiden, 2002), 57–79, esp. 69–71.

[9] G. Constable, *The Reformation of the Twelfth Century* (Cambridge, 1996), 182; J. F. Romano, 'Julian of Vézelay, a Twelfth-Century Critic of His Monastery's Worldly Success', *Medieval Sermon Studies*, 50 (2006), 51–69, at 59–61; B. H. Rosenwein, 'Feudal War and Monastic Peace: Cluniac Liturgy as Ritual Aggression', *Viator*, 2 (1971), 129–57; L. K. Little, *Benedictine Maledictions: Liturgical Cursing in Romanesque France* (Ithaca, NY, 1993).

[10] Y. Congar, 'Clercs et laïcs au point de vue de la culture au moyen-âge: "laicus" = "sans lettres"', in *Studia mediaevalia et mariologica P. Carolo Balić... dicata* (Rome, 1971), 309–32.

[11] *CDL* II 250, 251: 'per uoluntate domni Peredei in Dei nomine episcopi et per rogitum Porphorei, ego Filippus clericus iscriptor huius cartule abstuli de hanc cartulam, persona ipsius Porphorei non esset offerta in ecclesia Sancti Petri; et iterum iuidem rescripsi, sicut ambarum partium placuit'.

[12] *Le carte dell'abbazia di S. Croce di Sassovivo*. II. *1116–1165*, ed. V. De Donato (Florence, 1975), p. xx, n. 37.

[13] J. Nightingale, *Monasteries and Patrons in the Gorze Reform: Lotharingia, c. 850–1000* (Oxford, 2001), 261.

example, the case of a certain Gaitelgrima, who, in the first decades of the twelfth century, argued that the donation with which her deceased husband had granted a *castrum* to S. Bartolomeo in Carpineto was not valid because he had not placed the charter on the altar.[14]

The most immediate answer to the question of why Italy would be so different from the rest of Europe is, usually, that the legacy of Roman traditions must have played some major role in determining this specificity. When new analyses have added nuance to this image of Italian exceptionalism, they have done so not by undermining what can be called the 'documentary awareness' of laypeople in Italy but, rather, by reappraising the spread and social distribution of documentary practices throughout the rest of Europe.[15] However, it remains a fact that until the eleventh century, even in Italy, documents – whether produced by and for the laity or the clergy – have been transmitted to us via ecclesiastical institutions.[16] This raises the question of whether laypeople, as individuals or as groups, ever felt the need for the intentional, organized, mindful preservation, over significant periods of time, of those documents we know they were using. In other words, since the use of documents was not restricted to clerics, and since laypeople, albeit with different degrees of intensity, were fully involved in the documentary practices of their respective social groups, were they also involved in their preservation? And, if so, in what ways, and to what extent?

To help explain the pre-eminence of churches in the conservation and transmission of texts and documents, some historians have tended to appeal vaguely to different lay and clerical attitudes towards writing. According to this view, the coexistence, not necessarily in conflict, of two separate spheres of culture, one related to writing (reserved to monks and clerics) and one to orality (peculiar to the laity), would have induced laypeople to preserve documents with much less care, if at all. When confronted with the entirety of documentary practices, lay individuals would have accessed some of them in ways that were structurally different from their ecclesiastical counterparts, ways that depended on their status, their aims and their education (or, better, lack thereof).[17] This

[14] Alexander the Monk, *Liber chronicorum monasterii sancti Bartholomei de Carpineto* 4 (ed. B. Pio [Rome, 2001], 154). On the problem of hypocritical submissions to churches by individuals who would then quickly renege, see also G. Koziol, *Begging Pardon and Favor: Ritual and Political Order in Early Medieval France* (Ithaca, NY, 1992), 316–21.

[15] *Uses of Literacy*, and the research that collection has inspired.

[16] P. Cammarosano, *Italia medievale: Struttura e geografia delle fonti scritte* (Rome, 1991), 39–111.

[17] H. Grundmann, '*Litteratus-illitteratus*: Der Wandel einer Bildungsnorm vom Altertum zum Mittelalter', *Archiv für Kulturgeschichte*, 40 (1958), 1–65; cf. the perceptive critiques of G. Severino Polica, 'Cultura ecclesiastica e culture subalterne: Rileggendo alcuni saggi di H. Grundmann', *Studi storici*, 23 (1982), 137–66.

would explain, at least in part, why archives that can be attributed to the activity of lay individuals or institutions before the twelfth century seem not to have survived in their original form – if they ever existed, some might be tempted to say. However, as seen in previous chapters, there is ample evidence that laypeople clearly did keep archives of documents of some sort; it is the processes of archival transformation that have masked the ways laypeople preserved and organized those documents.[18] Similar patterns will emerge in the following pages.

In revisiting the question of lay documentary practices in early medieval Italy, I concentrate here on three specific issues: the ways in which documents were originally preserved by laypeople and by churches; the destruction of charters as a sign that laypeople had a surprising familiarity with written documents; and the preservation of documents as a way of promoting group identity and awareness. Documents, in other words, were not just preserved; they were used self-consciously by their possessors.

## When and where were documents preserved?

On 1 February 968, in the presence of and with the consent of her husband Gratianus, the *nobilissima foemina* Theodora donated to Silvester, abbot of the Roman monastery of SS. Cosma and Damianus *in Mica aurea*, a field situated just outside the *Porta Portuense*, in the south-west quadrant of the city's *suburbium*. In doing so, Theodora and her husband specified that they could not actually give the abbot the documents, recent and old (*monimina novas et vetustas*), that attested their rights over that field. 'However,' they said, 'they seem to be somewhere *in arcibus nostris*, but once we have found them we promise that we, or our heirs, will give them to you and, if we refuse to do so, those documents will become void and invalid, and will forever remain deprived of any authority.'[19] It is difficult to understand what Theodora actually meant with the term *arx* – chests? a room? simply, 'the secure place where charters are kept'? – but this document does constitute explicit evidence of the fact that laypeople in tenth-century Italy preserved their documents in a specific place, presumably in their place of residence. It is negative evidence, because we cannot actually see Theodora retrieve the documents, yet it is quite revealing.

Moreover, unlike Demetrius and his *consortes* (see below), Theodora clearly refers to a complex of documents, some of which could have been

[18] See above, Chapters 7, 9–11.

[19] *Il regesto sublacense del secolo XI*, ed. L. Allodi and G. Levi (Rome, 1885), no. 52.

issued quite some time before. We may also notice that Theodora refers to herself as *nobilissima*, claiming membership in a very specific and self-distinctive social group in tenth-century Rome. We can therefore suppose that her patrimony was quite substantial, as would have been the number of documents related to its management. It is therefore possible to deduce that a system of keeping documents could be in place here.[20] We should, however, be careful not to overestimate how systematically those written records might have been kept and stored, as Theodora seems not to have been sure where exactly they were. Nevertheless, this is not specific to complexes of documents preserved by laypeople. At Subiaco in the tenth century, charters and other documents seem to have been kept, all together and without particular order, in chests and sacks, and finding a specific one might prove an impossible endeavour, as a document from July 993 reveals.[21]

The case of Theodora is not unique. The same thing happened, for example, in the context of a sale of some land in the Sublacense region in December 929, when the seller specified that he would keep all the documents related to those properties safe ('unde charte noue et uetuste aput me meosque heredes reiacent ad conseruandas et saluas faciendas'). And some years later, in November 935, in selling to the two brothers John and Peter a *fundus* just outside the Porta Salaria in Rome, a certain Peter specified that he would keep all the documents pertaining to that property safe, and added that he would give them to the buyers whenever they needed them.[22]

The practice of delivering the documents related to a piece of land that was being sold is quite widespread among both laypeople and clerics in central and southern Italy between the ninth and twelfth centuries.[23] However, these transfers of documents, evidence of a mentality predisposed to the preservation of documents, did not necessarily happen in a straightforward way. If the document included other properties excluded from the sale, then the seller – lay or cleric – could declare that he or she was not going to transfer the document as well, but promised to care for it

[20] Cf. the case of the *illustris vir* Kaloleus, whose landed patrimony is the only one for which management can be clearly documented (*Il regesto sublacense*, nos. 3, 93, 155).

[21] *Il regesto sublacense*, no. 78: 'post Georgi abbati appare libelli quę abuit. infra chartas monasterii iactauit, et minime eam inuenire potuit'.

[22] *Il regesto sublacense*, nos. 92, 61, respectively.

[23] Other examples: BnF lat. 5411 (*Liber instrumentorum de possessionibus, rebus, sive dignitatibus, quas Casauriense monasterium habuit, habet, vel habere debet*), fol. 112r–v (4 June 879) (ed. A. Sennis, *Strategie politiche, affermazioni dinastiche, centri di potere nella Marsica medievale* [Rome, 2002], appendix 1, doc. 29); *Il regesto sublacense*, no. 42 (20 June 967); *Codex diplomaticus Cavensis*, 10 vols. to date (Milan, 1873–93; Cava de' Tirreni, 1984–), VIII 1321 (July 1061).

and show it to the buyer, should it be necessary.[24] This practice, in which the careful keeping of the documents was a legal obligation, can be further clarified by some evidence from the *Codex Diplomaticus Cavensis*. In Salerno, as early as the mid ninth century and throughout the tenth and eleventh centuries, documents were read and copied, either integrally or in an abridged form, even long after their original date. For example, a *preceptum* of 846 was read out and copied during a sale of 995; a series of documents from 1019, 1027, 1036, 1043 and 1045 was copied in a sale of 1069; in June 1070, twenty documents issued between 1028 and 1054 were read and copied as part of the division of patrimony between two lay brothers; twenty-eight documents issued between 948 and 1040 were read out and copied during a dispute between two laymen in 1054.[25] The legal obligation, sometimes explicitly stated in a specific clause, to safeguard the other party's documents could even be part of the strategies of litigation in the course of a dispute. This is what happened in 1067, when Theophylact, abbot of the monastery of S. Nicola in Gallucanta near Salerno, accused a certain Constantinus and his mother Porpora of hiding and destroying some of the monastery's documents. Constantinus and Porpora were prepared to make the same accusation against the abbot. The judge made both parties promise to return to court with all the documents they possessed and swear not to have hidden or destroyed any other document related to their opponents.[26]

## Destroying documents

Destroying documents can indeed be considered a sign of a sophisticated capability to manipulate written culture. Traditionally, we are inclined to think that the need to safeguard documentary patrimony was

[24] The usual formula was (with irrelevant variations): 'Ipsa suprascripta venditionis charta apud me meosque heredes reiacunt ad conservandum et salvas faciendum pro alia res que nobis in eas continere videtur. Et pro hoc eam vobis minime contradere potui, sed quandoque vobis vestrisque successoribus necesse fuerit pro vestra defensione semper ostendere et demonstrare spondeo.' E.g. *Il regesto sublacense*, nos. 39–40, 43, etc.

[25] *Codex diplomaticus Cavensis* III 476 (a. 995); VII 1195 (a. 1054); IX 72 (a. 1069), 94 (a. 1070). Other examples: Salerno: II 338, 339, 368, 377, 395; V 725, 728, 731, 760, 797, 825; VII 1143, 1164, 1195; VIII 1265, 1281, 1292, 1297, 1316, 1321, 1322, 1325, 1361, 1373; IX 13, 53, 57, 94, 104. Capua: IV 621, 686; V 708, 779, 781, 845; VI, 1048; VII 1072, 1083, 1087, 1093, 1115–16, 1216, 1221, 1230; VIII 1235, 1241, 1245, 1261, 1271, 1278, 1282, 1323, 1335, 1348, 1352, 1355–6, 1358–9, 1366, 1379, 1381; IX 19, 38, 45, 55, 71, 78, 85, 89, 96–9, 102, 108, 132.

[26] *Codex Diplomaticus Cavensis* IX 36. The terms of the obligation (ten days to deliver the documents, one hundred days during which the recipient of the documents had to defend the other's rights on the basis of those documents, a penalty of 300 golden *solidi*) are fully specified, for example, in *Codex Diplomaticus Cavensis* VIII 1321.

peculiar to ecclesiastical institutions. Effectively, the prospect that the loss or destruction of documents could have serious effects on a community's rights, not only patrimonial, played a major role in the relations that various churches established with the holders of sovereign authority. Churches and monasteries could in fact explicitly request that the charters granting or confirming privileges include a specific clause according to which, in the event that their written titles were lost or destroyed, they were allowed to attest to the legitimacy of their claims by oath.[27] However, churches were not alone in doing so, as this clause was also included in documents possessed by laypeople. This is confirmed, for example, by a charter issued in 969 by Otto I in favour of his *fidelis*, Ingo, in relation to his patrimony *infra Regnum Italicum*, and by another conceded in 1038 by Conrad II to Raimbaldus, *comes* of Treviso.[28] As happened to churches, the rights of lay landowners were also protected when their validity could not be established because written evidence had been destroyed *before* the concession of a sovereign charter granting or confirming properties. This is what can be inferred from some examples included in formula-books.[29] At least in the Lombard principality of Benevento, by the mid ninth century the procedures for the certification of the status of property when the relevant documents (*munimina*) had been destroyed had already been turned into a general norm, applied to the whole of the society, as a law issued in 866 by Adelchis II indicates.[30]

Conversely, in Carolingian Italy documents that were considered worthless or in some way irregular had to be destroyed by law. This was the case for the *cartulae obligationis* related to men whose free status had in fact been acknowledged, or for goods sold at too high or too low a price due to necessity, or for donations whose value had been overestimated.[31] In the mid eleventh century, according to some formulas of the *Cartularium Langobardicum*, at the end of a dispute, the *incisio* or *capsatio chartarum* was required if the documents presented had been

27 See, for example, a charter issued by Otto III in 997 for the abbey of Nonantola (MGH DD Otto III, no. 237), another issued by Conrad II in 1026 for the monastery of Leno (MGH DD Conrad II, no. 57), and a third conceded by Conrad II, in the same year, to the monastery of S. Dionigi near Milan (MGH DD Conrad II, no. 58).

28 MGH DD Otto I, no. 371; MGH DD Conrad II, no. 277.

29 Among the numerous cases of intervention by a king or an emperor to remedy the loss of documents due to fire or flood, whether intentional or through negligence, see, for example, a charter issued in 967 by Otto II for the monastery of Subiaco (MGH DD Otto II, no. 336). Needless to say, this could be an opportune chance for the community to take advantage of the lack of written evidence in order to succeed in making groundless claims (a parallel for England is analysed in M. T. Clanchy, *From Memory to Written Record: England, 1066–1307*, 2nd edn (Oxford, 1993), 148–9; cf. 168); see also Brown, 'Documents'.

30 MGH LL 4:211–12 (c. 7).

31 MGH Capit. 1, no. 88, cc. 1–3.

judged to be false or, more simply, if their content had been superseded by new agreements or events. Moreover, the *traditio promissionis pro debito* required the *charta venditionis* with which someone had sold a piece of land to a creditor as warranty on the debt to be *capsata et taliata* once the debt had been fully repaid.[32] This practice became more and more common after the beginning of the eleventh century, when the documentary processes of private transactions started to include temporary acts that remained valid for a very short period of time.[33]

## Preservation and group dynamics

But how, and to what extent, can the preservation of charters be seen as one element of lay group dynamics, as a way of promoting group identity and awareness? On 17 August 942, in Rome, Alberic *princeps*, assisted by some Roman judges, presided over a case brought before him by Leo, abbot of the monastery of SS. Benedict and Scholastica in Subiaco. Leo complained that a group of inhabitants of Tivoli were making unlawful claims over the *fundus Paternu*, located some 20 miles from Rome. A certain Demetrius, apparently the spokesman of the group, responded, declaring that their claims were well grounded and that in fact they had a *charta* to prove it. Only, he said, they did not have it right there with them ('Demetrius cum supradictis litigantibus dixerunt, "habemus chartam sed non est hic"'). Alberic and the judges allowed Demetrius and his co-litigants some days to produce that document in court; they failed to do so and therefore lost the case.[34] This example might refer to a procedure quite common in Italian court cases between the 880s and the 1030s, a procedure that evokes the old Ravenna *gesta municipalia*. One of the litigants, usually the plaintiff, brought in front of the judges a document attesting to his (or sometimes her) rights that was then validated by the authority of the court. It is true that in this case it seems that the defendants, and not the plaintiff, are the ones to produce the charter, but this is probably due to the fact that the *narratio* of the document implies that the men from Tivoli had actually started the dispute.[35]

What this case anyway clearly reveals is that laypeople could at least claim that they were able to preserve documents attesting their rights. The fact that, according to the document copied in the cartulary of Subiaco, Demetrius came back before the judges empty-handed does not undermine this impression. Perhaps he was just bluffing and the judges

[32] MGH LL 4:597 (c. 9).
[33] Bougard, *La justice*, 71n20, 319–29. [34] *Il regesto sublacense*, no. 155.
[35] *Ostensio chartae*: Bougard, *La justice*, 319–30; above, 98–102, 249–54.

successfully called his bluff, but the tone of the document indicates that it was perfectly credible that those lay litigants had the document stored in a place from where it could be easily retrieved. Obviously, the use of a formulaic tone does not mean that the underlying events were, or were perceived to be, ordinary. However, and this is what interests me here, it seems to indicate that what was being followed was a quite standardized, evidently common procedure.

This document, however, also tells us something more. Demetrius was not alone, but was acting together with his *consortes*. Consequently this, and presumably every other, document attesting to the prerogatives of the group had to be handled in a way that guaranteed the rights of each member. Apart from their obvious patrimonial value, for *consortes* such as Demetrius and his co-litigants, documents could indeed be a way to define and emphasize their identity and solidarity as a group. This is confirmed, for example, albeit for a slightly later period, by a *memoratorium* transmitted by Gregory of Catino that relates how in 1066 (or 1077) a certain Teuto, an inhabitant of the *castellum* of Bibaro, went to Berardus, abbot of Farfa, begging him to return to him the document with which he and his kin had donated Bibaro to the monastery. Apparently, Berardus, moved to pity and acting 'sine consilio vel assensu congregationis' and 'contra legem et contra libertatem huius monasterii', gave the *cartula* to Teuto. Once he was back in Bibaro, Teuto summoned his kin and showed them the document. At this point, glad to have back the charter of donation, they tore it into pieces and burned it – but the fire went out of control and, *iudicio Dei*, the whole of Bibaro was destroyed.[36] It is clear that, in this case, the community's narrative of the events set the malicious destruction of this document in a framework of actions – the illicit (and preposterous) request to have the document back; the rash (and unbecoming) submissiveness demonstrated by the abbot; the sacrilegious (and ritually savage) rejection of the monastery's full rights – whose grand finale confirmed the community's absolute supremacy over the neighbouring society. Nevertheless, what is revealing is that, in this piece of propaganda, the adversaries of the monastery are shown as acting together as a group with respect to the document. Teuto brought it back and showed it to his kin, and every member of the group took part in its destruction, each tearing it, holding one piece and setting it on fire.[37]

36 *RF* V 1299; see A. Sennis, '"Omnia tollit aetas et cuncta tollit oblivio": Ricordi smarriti e memorie costruite nei monasteri altomedievali', *Bullettino dell'Istituto storico italiano per il medio evo*, 106 (2004), 93–135, at 107–8.

37 Rituals and symbolic values of the destruction of charters: A. Sennis, '"Omnia tollit . . ."', 101–14.

On the other hand, the configuration and articulation of these groups did not prevent each of their members from having patrimonial relations autonomous from, and external to, the ones maintained by the group as a whole.[38] Therefore, a single layperson could handle, and have to preserve, documents related to him or her both as an individual and as a member of a kin group. In other words, a system of preservation such as the one alluded to by Demetrius had to be structured enough to ensure the retraceability of each document according to its functions. This was obviously true when laypeople, as individuals or as members of a group, were involved in a dispute with a church. However, the use of documents could clearly take place outside the sphere of influence of a main monastery, as is demonstrated, for example, by the documentary dossiers from the cartulary of San Clemente a Casauria, dating between the ninth and the twelfth centuries and referring to donations, sales and exchanges in which the monastery did not take part, as discussed in the chapter by Costambeys.[39]

If laypeople, as I have argued, used and preserved documents in the early Middle Ages in the ways I have described, why have the vast majority subsequently disappeared while documents involving clerics and monks have survived? The preservation of documents by religious institutions – even documents that have lost any juridical value – may be explained by the theoretical ban on the alienation of the ecclesiastical patrimony of a church, which would have provided an ideological restraint on the alienation (or loss by other means) of *documents*. The contempt (and it is just one case among many) with which Gregory of Catino commented upon Abbot Berardus' decision to give the document back to the inhabitants of Bibaro could be a sign of this. Laypeople were not subject to such restraints. More importantly, however, churches and monasteries would have had the tendency to preserve documents because they operated with an *institutional* mindset. Gregory of Catino's own documents survived not because he was a monk *per se*, but because they were preserved in the archives of the institution to which he belonged: the monastery of Farfa.[40] An institutional mindset of this sort was largely absent among the laity in the early Middle Ages. Only in the late eleventh and twelfth centuries do we see lay institutions become generally present, and this

38 E.g. L. Feller, *Les Abruzzes médiévales: Territoire, économie et société en Italie centrale du IXᵉ au XIᵉ siècle* (Rome, 1998), 505–6. Social dimensions of the construction of landed patrimonies: Rosenwein, *Saint Peter* (Ithaca, NY, 1989).

39 BnF lat. 5411, fols. 6r–72v; above, Chapter 9.

40 A number of documents related to Gregory's family were copied by him in the Regestum (*RF* IV 948–75). They were probably attached to *RF* IV 948, which is a sale by Gregory's parents to Farfa.

is precisely when the laity regained a certain degree of control over the process of record-keeping.

Moreover, throughout the early Middle Ages, lay society in central Italy was characterized by a high degree of mobility. The highest strata did not constitute a compact order but, rather, a fluid group whose members were characterized by their wealth and power. The political fortune of a family could rapidly rise or be effaced, as could its patrimony. The patrimonies of lay elites became more stable in the twelfth century, when the number of prominent families decreased as they were integrated into larger political entities (namely the papal territories and the Norman, then Angevin, kingdom). This process had repercussions on lay documentary complexes while, at the same time, the *publica fides* that notaries had by then generally acquired made it possible, indeed necessary, for the documents of the laity to be preserved in the form of *inbreviaturae*.[41] We might add that it is only in the late eleventh and twelfth centuries that lay institutions return to general prominence in the region, and it is only then that the laity regain a certain control over the process of record-keeping. Thus the relevant comparison is not between clergy and laity, but between institutionalized and non-institutionalized juridical persons.

Laypeople in the early Middle Ages were not as successful at preserving documents; this was not because they were not part of the clergy, but because they were not grouped into institutions. By the time lay institutions emerged, however, churches had strongly established the institutional model of reference for medieval Italy. Besides, one of the hallmarks of the ideology and self-representation of medieval monasteries, the capability to control the dynamics through which written documents were produced and preserved by society, became an even more central element of their rhetoric after the mid eleventh century, when a new sense of historical development and therefore a different relationship between the present and the past began to emerge throughout Europe.[42]

I have argued elsewhere that, towards the end of the Middle Ages, at least some intellectuals outside the cloister considered monasteries as the custodians of the memorial patrimony of society. Moreover, monastic ideals became almost inextricably associated, by outside observers, with the fundamental function of preserving the material, written traces of the

[41] M. Lenzi, *La terra e il potere: Gestione della proprietà e rapporti economico-sociali a Roma tra alto e basso medioevo (secoli X–XII)* (Rome, 2000), 103.

[42] See above, Chapter 11; G. Constable, 'Past and Present in the Eleventh and Twelfth Centuries: Perceptions of Time and Change', in *L'Europa dei secoli XI e XII fra novità e tradizione: Atti della decima Settimana internazionale di studio (Mendola 25–29 agosto 1986)* (Milan, 1989), 135–70.

past.[43] We can now see that this was true not only for the very specific type of written memories – that is, the most precious legacies of classical culture, that I was discussing in that case.

Thus, in the first phase of their existence, Italian communes used local monasteries and convents to archive their documents. And this remained the case even after lay status had become a prerequisite for office holding.[44] For example, on 16 October 1244, *magister Acto Bentivolii*, *syndicus* of the commune of Cingoli, in the Marches, deposited four copies of the agreement that the commune had reached with the lords of Civitella. The copies were deposited as follows: one 'apud sanctum Franciscum, locum fratrum minorum; the second at the church of S. Esuperazio'; the third 'apud hospitale Spreti', where it was received by the abbess, Catherine; and the fourth 'apud dominum Rainaldum Glodii'.[45] Similarly, at Brescia, in 1252, the 'notae venditionum factarum sub extimatoribus seu consulibus iustitiae' were considered valid only if the corresponding *charta* 'inventa fuerit scripta in libris' which were given 'in deposito domino archipresbitero Brixiensi'.[46] At Verona, the originals of imperial charters issued by Frederick I were kept in the sacristy of the Friars Minor, while copies were kept in the sacristy of the commune and in that of the *capitanei*.[47]

The function of a church as a place where documents, both of an institution such as the commune and of individuals, could be put 'in salvamento' is also evident from a statute from Vicenza which mentions ten books of copies of charters: 'tempore compromissi perfidi Ecelini de Romano, qui libri sunt positi in salvamento in loco Sancte Corone in custodia Fratrum Predicatorum'.[48] Lay institutions and individuals in Italy continued to use churches to store their most precious documents well into the late medieval period. When Florentines had to escape the pestilence or political turmoil, they often deposited their 'scritture d'importanza' in monasteries.[49]

[43] A. Sennis, 'The Power of Time: Looking at the Past in Medieval Monasteries', in A. Müller and K. Stöber (eds.), *Self-Representation of Medieval Religious Communities: The British Isles in Context* (Berlin, 2009), 307–26.

[44] P. Torelli, *Studi e richerche di diplomatica comunale*, II (Mantova, 1915), 37.

[45] Cingoli, Archivio del comune, Pergamena 19, II; see also E. Sebastiani, 'Genesi, concetto e natura giuridica degli archivi di Stato in Italia', *Rivista italiana per le scienze giuridiche*, 37 (1904), 44.

[46] Statuti di Brescia, ed. F. Odorici, *Monumenta Historiae Patriae*, XVI (Turin, 1876), III, XXIII, 1726–7.

[47] A. M. Allen, *A History of Verona* (London, 1910), appendix I, CCXLVIII, p. 131.

[48] *Statuti del comune di Vicenza MCCLXIV* (Venice, 1886), 86.

[49] This is what Michele di Bindaccio Cerchi does in 1363 (Florence, Archivio di Stato, Dono Canigiani Cerchi, 310, fol. 6v) and Luca da Panzano in 1424 (Florence, Archivio di Stato, Strozziane II, 9, fols. 26v–27).

However, at such a late date, placing documents in the library or in the archive of a monastery was clearly an act meant to emphasize the memorialistic dimension of those written records, rather than to safeguard their immediately practical value. So, at Padua, only the chest containing 'omnia instrumenta, privilleia et rationes et statuta, que comune padue non operatur' was kept by the local Franciscans, and the podestà and the *anziani* kept its keys and a register of its contents. Similarly, when, still at Padua, the statutes were updated and four copies of the new version were distributed among four offices of the commune, the four outdated copies of the previous version of the statutes were sent to be kept 'unum penes monasterium sancti benedicti, aliud penes monasterium sancti iohannis de verdaria, tercium penes sanctam mariam de vancio, et quartum penes monaterium sancte marie de porcilia', possibly as a sort of documentary monument.[50]

It was, then, when new (mainly lay) institutions became mature and formalized enough to frame the complex of documentary practices in the society around them, that the role of churches and monasteries as overseers of the daily elements of those practices began to decline.

[50] *Libri statutorum communis Padue* 4.9/1133 (a. 1265), 4.15/1178 (a. 1263) (ed. A. Gloria [Padua, 1873], pp. 344, 360).

# 13 Archives and lay documentary practice in the Anglo-Saxon world

*Charles Insley*

*As previous chapters have traced continental documentary practices that moved fairly seamlessly between lay and ecclesiastical settings, it is instructive to examine the evidence from Anglo-Saxon England from this new perspective. Although it preserves no lay archive as such, England offers evidence substantial enough to allow us to detect some of the outlines of a cohesive documentary culture that included the laity. Exceptional survivals like the Fonthill Letter point to the intensive use of documents, as well as to historical developments that have shaped the surviving corpus, which is dominated by royal diplomas preserved by major monastic houses and bishoprics. Traces of the operation of documents in property disputes, coupled with the evidence for a lively traffic in land, indicate how common documents must have been; they also attest to a culture in which laypeople routinely handled and kept them. The elite probably had quite sophisticated archival methods. The forces shaping long-term preservation, especially after 1066, tended to preserve some types of document – such as Latin royal diplomas for major monasteries – and discouraged the retention of others – in particular, vernacular documents like leases – that must once have proliferated.*

In the early tenth century, probably in its second decade, a West Saxon ealdorman, Ordlaf, sat down and either wrote or dictated an account of the recent wrangling over an estate at Fonthill, in Wiltshire, and the crimes of a man called Helmstan.[1] The 'Fonthill Letter', as it has become

[1] Canterbury, Cathedral Archive, Dean and Chapter, Chartae Antiquae C 1282; P. H. Sawyer, *Anglo-Saxon Charters: An Annotated List and Bibliography* (London, 1968), since updated online by Susan Kelly and Sean Miller: www.trin.cam.ac.uk/chartwww/esawyer.99/eSawyer2.html (hereafter S) 1445. The Fonthill Letter is translated in D. Whitelock, *English Historical Documents*. I. *c. 500–1042*, 2nd edn (London, 1979) (hereafter *EHD*), no. 102; much the best modern edition and commentary is that of Simon Keynes (S. Keynes, 'The Fonthill Letter', in M. Korhammer with K. Reichl and H. Sauer (eds.), *Words, Texts and Manuscripts: Studies in Anglo-Saxon Culture Presented to Helmut Gneuss* [Cambridge, 1992], 53–97); a new edition is included in *The Charters of Christ Church, Canterbury*, ed. N. P. Brooks and S. E. Kelly (Oxford, forthcoming), no. 104. Keynes ('Fonthill', 56) argues for a date in the second decade of the reign of Edward the Elder;

known, now preserved in the archives of the Dean and Chapter of Canterbury Cathedral, is one of the great documentary treasures of the Anglo-Saxon period. As one might expect, it has seen the expenditure of a great deal of scholarly ink, for it is one of the best witnesses to the nuts-and-bolts functioning of criminal justice in Anglo-Saxon England, and so of quite exceptional importance in the effort to understand its culture of document use.[2]

In the simplest terms, the letter is an account of the recent history of the Fonthill estate by a third party to a litigation episode, in this case between a man called Æthelhelm *Higa* and the bishop of Winchester. The waters are muddied somewhat by the fact that Ordlaf, the probable author of the letter, had once owned the Fonthill estate before giving it to the bishop, and was the godfather of the Helmstan whose kleptomaniac behaviour had first sparked off the dispute at some point in the late 890s.[3] However, interesting as the legal exegesis of the document is, it does not directly concern us here, except insofar as it hints that documents were part and parcel of legal processes in late ninth- and tenth-century England, even those exclusively involving laymen, and so must have once been very common indeed.[4] The Fonthill Letter encapsulates many of the issues raised by thinking about archives and lay documentary practice in Anglo-Saxon England. First, there is the lay role in production, since the document was probably produced by a layman and almost certainly in a lay aristocratic household; second, since the interactions and processes it describes largely involved lay actors, it suggests that we may be able to access some of the functions of documents in lay society; third, it was written in the vernacular and forms part of a raft of vernacular documentation dealing with legal process and property ownership, pointing to language as a factor affecting document use and preservation; fourth, since it links documents, legal process and conveyancing, it highlights the relationship between documents and the operation of the law; and fifth, since it was preserved by a church, but one with no connection to either the property concerned or the events described, it testifies to the difficulty of discerning how and why documents were kept.

see also P. Wormald, 'A Handlist of Anglo-Saxon Lawsuits', *Anglo-Saxon England*, 17 (1988), 247–81, nos. 23–26a; P. Wormald, *The Making of English Law: King Alfred to the Twelfth Century*. I. *Legislation and Its Limits* (Oxford, 1999), 144–8; N. P. Brooks, 'The Fonthill Letter, Ealdorman Ordlaf and Anglo-Saxon Law in Practice', in S. Baxter *et al.* (eds.), *Early Medieval Studies in Memory of Patrick Wormald* (Aldershot, 2007), 301–17.

2 Keynes, 'Fonthill', 54.

3 See below, 346 and n33, for a discussion of the authorship of the letter.

4 As Brooks ('The Fonthill Letter', 306) has suggested.

## Literacy and lay documentary culture

In surveying and contextualizing the historiographical landscape of lay literacy in Anglo-Saxon England, Kathryn Lowe has argued for a 'change in attitude to the written document that was neither confined to the church or the state nor, indeed, to the centuries following the Norman Conquest'. This change, she suggests, is best exemplified by the chirograph, the name given to a form of charter, almost certainly originating in Anglo-Saxon England, in which two or three copies of the same document were made from the same sheet of parchment for safe keeping by interested parties, and where these counterparts could be easily matched and checked.[5] Lowe suggests that the key to understanding the role of the chirograph was that it was 'in form and function so attractive to the layman', seeming to respond to an audience that was not particularly literate but was interested in the possession and deployment of documents as part of the legal and conveyancing process. This impression of familiarity with documents is reinforced by Catherine Cubitt's reading of the eleventh-century Old English translation of the legend of the Seven Sleepers as showing that the late Anglo-Saxon judicial system made frequent reference to written texts. Cubitt is concerned here not simply to accept a degree of pragmatic literacy in late Anglo-Saxon lay society but also to argue that that pragmatic literacy might have reached some way down the social scale.[6] These persuasive demonstrations of the deep social penetration of documents contrast with earlier work that had regarded Anglo-Saxon England, right up until 1066, as what anthropologists in the mid twentieth century referred to as a 'traditional society', featuring only restricted literacy.[7] Such views had already been effectively countered by research indicating that literate practices, including the use of documents, were embedded within the norms and assumptions of Anglo-Saxon lay society.[8] The work of Lowe and Cubitt thus reinforces

[5] K. A. Lowe, 'Lay Literacy in Anglo-Saxon England and the Development of the Chirograph', in P. Pulsiano and E. M. Treharne (eds.), *Anglo-Saxon Manuscripts and Their Heritage* (Basingstoke, 1998), 161–204; quotations at 180.

[6] C. Cubitt, '"As the Lawbook Teaches": Reeves, Lawbooks and Urban Life in the Old English Legend of the Seven Sleepers', *English Historical Review*, 124 (2009), 1021–49, esp. 1048.

[7] P. Wormald, 'The Uses of Literacy in Anglo-Saxon England and Its Neighbours', *TRHS*, 5th ser., 27 (1977), 95–114, esp. 96–7; Wormald's conclusions are amplified in his *The Making of English Law*, 480–3; M. T. Clanchy, *From Memory to Written Record: England, 1066–1307*, 2nd edn (Oxford, 1993).

[8] S. E. Kelly, 'Anglo-Saxon Lay Society and the Written Word', in *Uses of Literacy*, 36–62; see also S. D. Keynes, 'Royal Government and the Written Word in Late Anglo-Saxon England', in *Uses of Literacy*, 226–57, and H. Collingridge, *Anglo-Saxon Literacy at Worcester: The Evidence of the Oswald Leases*, unpublished M.Phil. thesis, University of York (2002), 3–8, and, on Worcester's archive, F. Tinti, 'From Episcopal Conception to Monastic Compilation: Hemming's Cartulary in Context', *EME*, 11 (2002), 233–61.

the strong impression that laypeople, perhaps even at a relatively humble level, valued documents, used them in their business and, presumably, therefore, stored them in ways that meant that they could find them easily.[9] In this context, the Fonthill Letter shows how important informal lay document use may have been in a judicial process that English historiography of the early Middle Ages has often seen as underlying the importance of the state and the institutions of government.[10]

But the intention in the following discussion is not to reheat further the arguments over the importance and existence of socially or administratively significant lay literacy in England, but instead to look at the ways in which documents were used, stored and preserved by laymen as part of the relationship between lay society and document use – in other words, the documentary culture of Anglo-Saxon lay society. This is not to say that discussions about lay literacy are not important – quite the reverse. The apparent contradiction between the Fonthill Letter – a vernacular document written by a layman – and, for example, Patrick Wormald's rejection of a direct relationship between vernacular documentation and lay literacy shows that this letter may be very significant. Nevertheless, the *a priori* assumption adopted in this discussion is that a layman did not necessarily need to be able to read a document to understand its importance and place value on it as a piece of writing as well as an artefact with symbolic power.

It is perhaps worth qualifying at the outset some of the terms and concepts that have appeared elsewhere in this volume in the specifically Anglo-Saxon case. For the purposes of the present discussion, given that the vast majority, if not the entirety, of the extant corpus of Anglo-Saxon documentary material survives in an ecclesiastical context, 'lay archive' is understood very loosely as referring to a collection of documents that had been in lay hands at some point during their earlier history. While we cannot point to surviving 'lay archives' as such, it is possible to uncover their footprints, either in the surviving collections of documents in ecclesiastical hands, or in the processes in which documents were

9 The use of documents in legal procedure has been especially highlighted, in anglophone scholarship, by the two important collections of essays edited by Wendy Davies and Paul Fouracre: *Settlement of Disputes*, and *Property and Power in the Early Middle Ages* (Cambridge, 1995). Patrick Wormald's contribution to the former ('Charters, Law and the Settlement of Disputes in Anglo-Saxon England', pp. 149–68) is invaluable when considering the relationship between law, disputes and the deployment of charters; see also P. Wormald, 'A Handlist'.

10 J. Campbell, 'Observations on English Government from the Tenth to the Twelfth Century', *TRHS*, 5th ser., 25 (1975), 39–54; Campbell, 'Some Agents and Agencies of the Late Anglo-Saxon State', in J. C. Holt (ed.), *Domesday Studies* (Woodbridge, 1987), 201–18; Campbell, 'The Late Anglo-Saxon State: A Maximum View', *Proceedings of the British Academy*, 87 (1994), 39–65; Keynes, 'Royal Government and the Written Word'; Wormald, 'Uses of Literacy'.

deployed. Similarly, very few surviving Anglo-Saxon documents are genuinely 'lay documents', in the sense that there was no clerical involvement in their production or use – the Fonthill Letter is, as will be argued, perhaps the only surviving document where we can have some confidence of lay authorship, but, even then, the document was probably produced for use in a legal process where one of the parties was a bishop, and ultimately preserved in an ecclesiastical archive. Costambeys and Kosto adopt a definition whereby neither party to a document is explicitly identified as a cleric.[11] This is perhaps more helpful, since a significant number of our surviving Anglo-Saxon documents do not explicitly involve the Church as a party to the transaction or occasion recorded in the document, even if the Church was the ultimate repository of the relevant documentation.

## The evidence

England presents us with a corpus of a little over 1,600 documents that survive from before 1066, along with references to around 270 now-lost documents. In overall numbers, it fares badly in comparison with continental Europe, including Francia, physically and culturally the closest part of the continent. Even allowing for the depredations inflicted on ecclesiastical archives by the Henrician reformation of the mid sixteenth century and the civil wars of the mid seventeenth, the relatively small size of this corpus of documents may tell us something important about the extent to which documentary use was or was not a culturally embedded practice in Anglo-Saxon England. Certainly, the assumption of most scholars is that whatever level of documentary literacy there was in the eastern and southern parts of the Roman province of Britain it had completely vanished by the sixth century and was perforce reintroduced by the Augustinian mission in the 590s. It is possible that elite society in Kent, in some sense part of the wider cultural hegemony wielded by the Merovingian kings,[12] had some awareness of the potential and power of document use, but the overwhelming likelihood remains that, in what became the territories of Anglo-Saxon England, late Roman documentary culture, even in the ossified forms in which we see it in Merovingian Francia, had ceased to exist. This is an important point: in this respect England was qualitatively different from the rest of western Europe, where some bedrock of documentary culture seems to have survived the political and

[11] See above, 238, 259–60, 262. Cf. above, 3.

[12] I. N. Wood, *The Merovingian North Sea* (Ålingsas, 1983), 12–18; Kelly, 'Anglo-Saxon Lay Society', 41.

social traumas of the fifth and sixth centuries. This fissure in documentary culture may help to explain why we simply have fewer surviving documents from England before, say, 1000 than from anywhere else in the former Western Roman Empire. It may also account for the distinctive form much of that documentary evidence takes. Both Pierre Chaplais and Susan Kelly make the point that although the Anglo-Saxon solemn diploma, our most plentiful surviving document type, in its basics conforms to wider continental diplomatic norms, in important respects – in particular the absence of any internal or external validating structure – it remains highly unusual, a distinctiveness born of the circumstances of the reintroduction of documentary culture to southern and eastern England.[13]

Of our 1,600 or so surviving documents, a large majority, around 1,060, are in the form of Latin royal diplomas. A further 100 are Old English royal writs, largely dating from the reign of Edward the Confessor (1042–66). There are 80 documents that Peter Sawyer classified as grants by the laity, mostly in Latin with some wholly vernacular documents and many that contain both.[14] Another 150 documents are grants by bishops, while the remaining documents are an eclectic mixture of wills, leases, detached boundary clauses and other 'miscellaneous' documents, as Sawyer called them. These include records of law cases, agreements, lists of sureties and other notifications. The documentary record, then, is skewed towards the survival of the most prestigious documents, royal diplomas. Royal diplomas make up the major part of the vast majority of surviving Anglo-Saxon archives.[15] In an Anglo-Saxon context this preponderance is to some extent understandable, since diplomas functioned as title-deeds to property. But the contrast with the surviving bodies of charters from continental Europe, in which 'private' charters consistently

[13] P. Chaplais, 'Who Introduced Charters to England? The Case for Augustine', in F. Ranger (ed.), *Prisca Munimenta: Studies in Archival and Administrative History Presented to Dr A. E. J. Hollaender* (London, 1973), 88–107, at 100–1; Kelly, 'Anglo-Saxon Lay Society', 40–5; P. Wormald, *Bede and the Conversion of England: The Charter Evidence* (Newcastle upon Tyne, 1984), 5, 11–15. D. Howlett, *Sealed from Within: Self-Authenticating Insular Charters* (Dublin, 1999), 13–59, has controversially argued that the biblically derived numerical structure he has detected in the word ordering of a handful of early Kentish diplomas in effect constitutes an authenticating mechanism. For a robust rebuttal of Howlett's thesis, see, *inter alia*, H. McKee and J. McKee, 'Chance or Design? David Howlett's Insular Inscriptions and the Problem of Coincidence', *Cambrian Medieval Celtic Studies*, 51 (2006), 83–102, and 'The Problem of Coincidence: A Brief Final Response', *Cambrian Medieval Celtic Studies*, 56 (2008), 97–99.

[14] S.

[15] For example, of the thirty-two extant pre-Conquest documents that survive as part of the bishop of Exeter's archive, twenty-seven are diplomas. In contrast, the surviving archives of Worcester and Bury St Edmunds are dominated by vernacular material, mostly leases.

form a higher proportion than royal issues, is worth noting. In neither the English nor the continental cases are patterns of survival likely to reflect original levels of production at all closely. Something of what we have lost from England can be glimpsed in fragments: a layer of documentation concerning sales, leases and transfers of property and rights, often in the vernacular, of which only a few examples survive.[16] It should not be forgotten that one of the effects of the Norman Conquest of England was to eliminate Old English as a language of administration and business, and one can imagine a situation as early as the mid twelfth century in which documentation in Old English may have been perceived, for a variety of reasons, to be irrelevant. Indeed, at some point in the twelfth or thirteenth century, a Canterbury Christ Church archivist wrote 'inutile' on the dorse of the Fonthill Letter, a fact which makes its survival all the more remarkable.[17] In terms of our discussion about lay documentary culture and practice, this is an important caveat, since the documents that have survived are the most 'ecclesiastical' in their form; that is, they are often written in difficult and sometimes downright obscure Latin and shot through with religious symbolism and imagery, whose force, as Chaplais noted, is entirely spiritual.[18]

There are two other points to be made in conjunction with the evidence and the pattern of its survival. The first is that a significant proportion of it, somewhere between a third and a half of the surviving diplomas, is of questionable authenticity. The use of the word 'authenticity' is, of course, fraught with problems for the Anglo-Saxon diplomatist. Since the vast majority of documents lack the sort of marks of authentication we take for granted on the continent, such as autograph *signa* or subscriptions, it is unclear to what extent any Anglo-Saxon document, certainly any diploma, can be regarded as strictly 'authentic'.[19] The distinction between an original document and a single-sheet copy then becomes very hazy and may often hinge on detailed palaeographical analysis and dating of scripts. The reliability of the information in any given document becomes a test of patient textual and archival detective work. The phrase 'questionable authenticity' can therefore cover a multitude of sins,

[16] Much of the Worcester material exists in the only surviving pre-Conquest English cartulary, London, British Library, Cotton Tiberius A.VIII.

[17] It is possible that the uselessness of the letter was related to the fact that it concerned property in which Christ Church had no interest, rather than the language in which it was written.

[18] P. Chaplais, 'The Origin and Authenticity of the Royal Anglo-Saxon Diploma', *Journal of the Society of Archivists*, 3 (1965), 48–61, at 56.

[19] Wormald, *Bede*, 5. For the absence of authenticating marks, see Kelly, 'Anglo-Saxon Lay Society', 42–3.

ranging from documents that have been subtly altered but remain basically as produced, to elaborate but complete forgeries. This is an especial problem for early Anglo-Saxon diplomas (pre-*c.* 900), where perhaps half of the surviving corpus contains information that is hard to corroborate and might be regarded as untrustworthy, and where there has been a significant degree of later interference – often clerical – in the surviving documents.

The second point concerns the chronological distribution of our material, in particular the diplomas. The earliest surviving original diploma dates from 679, although, as Chaplais, Kelly and Wormald have all argued, given the already idiosyncratic diplomatic of these early charters, they were unlikely to have been the first to have been written in England, and it is possible that diplomas were produced much earlier in the seventh century.[20] It is tempting to posit a situation not unlike Merovingian Francia, where some of these early diplomas may have been written on papyrus, before a switch to the much more robust and readily available – in northern Europe – parchment.[21]

Something like 350 diplomas survive dated from the seventh, eighth and ninth centuries. A further 540 surviving diplomas date from the tenth century, with 160 from the period from 1000 to 1066. A similar, if less marked, shift in the pattern of survival can also be detected in the non-diploma material: writs, wills, bounds, lay charters, agreements and other memoranda. This jump in the number of surviving diplomas after 900 requires some thinking about, especially in relation to the notion of a growing dominance of monastic archives among centres of document preservation.[22] The simplest explanation for this great leap in survival is that many more diplomas were produced after around 925 than before. This is not inherently implausible. The tenth century saw a massive kingdom-building project launched by the West Saxon kings and their successors as kings of the English, and it seems likely that this political and military activity was attended by significant changes in landholding and landownership that required a large rise in the production of diplomas. For example, the political tension between the half-brothers Eadwig and Edgar in the years 955–7 saw the issuing of a large number of diplomas in the year 956, of which some eighty-five survive, as Eadwig presumably sought to use the granting of bookland, or heritable

[20] Chaplais, 'Who Introduced Charters into England?'; Kelly, 'Anglo-Saxon Lay Society', 40–3; Wormald, *Bede*, 11–15.

[21] The majority of scholarly opinion is sceptical about the existence of papyrus diplomas in England in the earlier seventh century, but it remains a possibility: Wormald, *Bede*, 11–15; Kelly, 'Anglo-Saxon Lay Society', 42.

[22] See the similar pattern in Iberia: Kosto, 'Laymen'; Davies, *Acts of Giving*.

land held by charter, as a means of securing backing from an English political and clerical establishment who were by no means universally enthusiastic about him.[23] As we also see elsewhere in this volume, political conflict here influenced document production and preservation: the coincidence of a complete lacuna in the run of documents for the years 910–24 with Edward the Elder's campaigns of conquest in the Danelaw might be another example.[24] The preponderance of royal diplomas in the Anglo-Saxon corpus of charters makes it inherently likely that changes in the activity and ambition of royal government might have affected the overall pattern of survivals.[25]

The influence of royal action on charter survival can be linked directly to the principal institutions in which documents survived: the major monasteries of the period. Since the tenth-century kingdom-building project in England also included extensive foundation, refoundation and patronage of monastic communities, the dominance of monastic centres for the preservation of documents should not be surprising. Increased activity, though, is not the only explanation for the great increase in post-900 survival. We might also point towards shifts in tenurial practice and perhaps towards a more aggressive attitude to ecclesiastical property fostered by the new monastic institutions founded or refounded in the tenth century. The notices of land transactions concerning Ely, compiled as part of the *Libellus Æthelwoldi* and copied into Book Two of the *Liber Eliensis*, are testament to the ruthlessness with which these tenth-century refoundations husbanded and expanded their properties, especially in terms of securing their title-deeds.[26] This is a question to which we will return.

## Fonthill and beyond: lay archives and legal process

To return to the document introduced at the beginning of this chapter, it is worth spending a little time with the Fonthill Letter and drawing

[23] P. Stafford, *Unification and Conquest: A Political and Social History of England in the Tenth and Eleventh Centuries* (London, 1989), 47–50; S. Keynes, *The Diplomas of King Æthelred 'The Unready' 978–1016* (Cambridge, 1980), 48–69.

[24] Compare Everett, above, 80–2, on the context of the *gesta municipalia* of Ravenna. For the lacuna in 910–24, see D. Dumville, 'Between Alfred the Great and Edgar the Peacemaker: Æthelstan, First King of England', in Dumville, *Wessex and England from Alfred to Edgar* (Woodbridge, 1992), 141–71, at 151–3.

[25] C. Insley, 'Where Did All the Charters Go? Anglo-Saxon Charters and the New Politics of the Eleventh Century', *Anglo-Norman Studies*, 24 (2002), 109–27; R. Fleming, *Kings and Lords in Conquest England* (Cambridge, 1991), 21–52.

[26] *Liber Eliensis*, ed. E. O. Blake (London, 1962), p. xxxiv; see also *Liber Eliensis* 2, esp. cc. 25, 27 (ed. Blake, 63–236; trans. J. Fairweather [Woodbridge, 2005], 84–284).

out some of its points of interest.[27] The letter is addressed to King Edward the Elder (899–924) and describes a dispute over a five-hide estate at Fonthill Magna in Wiltshire. The main actors in the story are a light-fingered king's thegn, Helmstan; another thegn, Æthelhelm *Higa*; and Ealdorman Ordlaf, the probable author of the letter.[28] The dispute hinges on the possession of Fonthill, initially claimed by Æthelhelm *Higa* against Helmstan. Helmstan, although clearly a man of some property and well connected – as well as Fonthill, the letter refers to a much larger estate belonging to Helmstan at neighbouring Tisbury – was also a rather incorrigible thief. The letter opens with a description of Helmstan's theft of a sword belt and the subsequent judgement made against him; the theft of a belt was not, perhaps, a trivial matter, given the status of sword belts as marks of rank and status.[29] This judgement seemed to have provoked Æthelhelm *Higa*'s suit: as Keynes suggests, Helmstan's law-worthy status may have been affected by the theft suit, thus making him vulnerable to further suits.[30] Helmstan's actions as a thief also arguably put him outside the law, since theft was regarded effectively as a breach of faith.[31] At this point, Helmstan, who presumably needed all the friends he could lay his hands on, sought the support of his godfather, Ealdorman Ordlaf, who interceded with King Alfred on Helmstan's behalf. This intercession, Keynes suggests, was to secure Helmstan the right to bring an oath to prove his title to the estate; in a meeting at Wardour, the case was heard and Helmstan adjudged to be in the right. The price of Ordlaf's intercession was that Helmstan then gave the land at Fonthill to Ordlaf, with a life interest in it for himself.

There matters should have rested, except for Helmstan's recidivist tendencies. Within eighteen months or perhaps two years of the initial lawsuit, Helmstan stole untended cattle at Fonthill and drove them to Cricklade. Once again, judgement was given against him, outlawry, and this time his property was forfeit, although Ordlaf secured exemption for Fonthill, which now belonged to him. By this time, Alfred the Great had died and the outlawry of Helmstan was lifted by his son, again after Ordlaf's intercession. At this point, Ordlaf then exchanged the five hides

27 Wormald, *The Making of English Law*, 144–8.

28 Brooks, 'Fonthill', 312–14, although see below, at n. 33.

29 C. Wickham, 'Rural Society in Carolingian Europe', in R. McKitterick (ed.), *The New Cambridge Medieval History*. II. *c.700–c.900* (Cambridge, 1995), 510–37, at 510.

30 Keynes, 'Fonthill', 73; Brooks, 'Fonthill', 310n16.

31 Wormald, *The Making of English Law*, 146–8. Wormald argues that Chapter 1 of Alfred's law code, which dealt with oaths, turned any criminal activity into a breach of faith. See *Die Gesetze der Angelsachsen*, ed. F. Liebermann, 3 vols. (Halle, 1898–1912), I, 29; *Ancient Laws and Institutes of England*, ed. B. Thorpe, 2 vols. (London, 1840), I, 60–1; *EHD*, no. 33.

at Fonthill for five hides at Lydiard with the bishop of Winchester. The penultimate act in this narrative was that Æthelhelm *Higa* renewed his claim to the estate, this time against the bishop of Winchester, at whose behest Ordlaf may have written his account. The final act is recorded in an endorsement of the letter, added not long after it was written, that records a meeting at Warminster where Æthelhelm *Higa* withdrew his suit.

The timescale of the events in the letter is unclear; Helmstan's initial theft of the belt happened no earlier than 897, since in the year or eighteen months that elapsed between this case and the cattle-rustling episode, King Alfred had died. The subsequent claim by Æthelhelm *Higa* against the bishop of Winchester may have happened considerably later; Keynes suggests a date in the second decade of the tenth century, a suggestion supported on philological grounds by Gretsch and palaeographical grounds by Dumville.[32] A date further away from belt-thieving and cattle-rustling is also suggested by the fact that Ordlaf could no longer remember the exact timescale between the two episodes, simply recording that he was not sure whether it was eighteen months or two years. Although Susan Reynolds and Mark Boynton have suggested an alternative author of the letter, most commentators seem satisfied that it was Ordlaf, notwithstanding the switch between the first- and third-person voice which occurs part-way through.[33] It has even been argued that Ordlaf physically wrote the letter; if he did, that would mark it as a very rare example of lay literacy in both reading and writing. If, on the other hand, Ordlaf had dictated the letter to a scribe, at whose status as layman or cleric we can only guess, this would raise the issue of what 'authorship' might have meant in this context: the letter might not then be a reliable indicator of laymen's possible command of the technology of writing, but it still shows clearly that many (at least of Ordlaf's status) could be deeply familiar with the use of documents in their everyday business.

Here we have, then, a letter dictated – if not written – by a layman, describing a world of legal processes into which the Church intrudes only at the end. The action takes place in both formal environments, clearly

[32] M. Gretsch, 'The Language of the Fonthill Letter', *Anglo-Saxon England*, 23 (1994), 57–102, at 90–2; D. N. Dumville, 'English Square Minuscule Script: The Background and Earliest Phases', *Anglo-Saxon England*, 16 (1987), 147–79, at 171.

[33] M. Boynton and S. Reynolds, 'The Author of the Fonthill Letter', *Anglo-Saxon England*, 25 (1996), 91–5; Brooks, 'Fonthill', 313–14, notes that shifts between the first and third person are not uncommon in other types of vernacular documents, such as wills. Elsewhere in Europe, the named scribe, while clearly taking overall responsibility for the production of the document, did not necessarily physically write the script; see above, 167, 298.

meetings of shire or hundred courts, and informal ones: in the first claim launched by Æthelhelm *Higa*, Ordlaf describes an occasion in the king's chamber at Wardour, where King Alfred was washing his hands. The legal processes referred to in the letter involve both the deployment of documents and non-documentary proofs, such as oath-takings. Indeed, the Fonthill Letter highlights some of the problems of creating a polarity between documentary and non-documentary culture in an early medieval context since the two are inextricably linked in this case.[34] The discussion in Alfred's chamber at Wardour concerned whether Helmstan should be allowed to proceed with a judicial oath to prove his title against Æthelhelm. What secured Helmstan this right was that some form of charter granting the land to Oswulf, from whom Helmstan had acquired Fonthill, was read out, along with the attestations of the king and others. As Keynes' translation of the letter puts it: 'then it seemed to all of those who were at that arbitration that Helmstan was nearer to the oath on that account'; in other words, possession of the charter improved Helmstan's chances of being able to clear his name by judicial oath.[35] The oath was crucial because it was a public declaration of the settlement reached at court, before the parties' peers, who were now implicated in making the settlement secure; only Helmstan's repeated criminality threw it back into dispute.[36]

Therefore, while the explicit object in dispute was the property at Fonthill, also at issue was Helmstan's trustworthiness, put in question by his indictment for theft, twice. Since the first item that he stole, the sword belt, was a traditional and typical badge of social standing, Helmstan's status may also have been a factor in the case: the extent of the property at issue at Fonthill, five hides, accords with the minimum holding associated in some sources with the rank of thegn.[37]

It is clear, though, for all the complex interplay of documentary and non-documentary proofs, that documents – charters, agreements, records of sales – were a vital part of this dispute and presumably of the whole process of transferring and conveyancing property in general.[38]

[34] Keynes, 'Royal Government', 256; Wormald, 'Charters', 167.

[35] Keynes, 'Fonthill', 75–6.

[36] For the significance of oaths in dispute settlement, see Innes, *State and Society*, 138–9, and M. Costambeys, 'Disputes and Courts in Lombard and Carolingian Central Italy', *EME*, 17 (2007), 265–89.

[37] Brooks, 'Fonthill', 314–15; for five hides and thegnly status, see the text christened by Liebermann *Geþyncðo* (ed. Liebermann, *Gesetze*, I, 456–69; trans. *EHD*, no. 51).

[38] Wormald, 'Charters', 167: 'what could be called the "oral-formulaic" approach to Anglo-Saxon litigation is not borne out by the records of actual pleas. Oaths mattered, but so, to a much greater extent than hitherto appreciated, did what modern justice would consider evidence, and such evidence was preferably in writing'.

As well as the letter itself, there are at least two other documents – and maybe more – floating around during the dispute. The first is the charter that one presumes accompanied the initial grant of Fonthill to a man called Æthelwulf, or one of his predecessors. Æthelwulf gave the land to his wife Æthelthryth as part of her dower, and she subsequently sold it to Oswulf. The second document concerns this purchase, since the letter refers, as noted above, to King Alfred giving his 'signature' (*hond-setene*) to Oswulf at this purchase: presumably some form of charter by Æthelthryth granting Fonthill to Oswulf, attested by Alfred. There may have been – probably were – more documents underlying Ordlaf's letter. When Helmstan gave the land to Ordlaf, he gave him the charter; whether this was a putative original diploma for the estate or a record of Oswulf's purchase from Æthelthryth is unclear. When Ordlaf subsequently exchanged the estate with the bishop of Winchester, one imagines that at least one charter changed hands, and it seems unlikely that the bishop of Winchester would not also have had some sort of record of the sale drawn up.

The Fonthill Letter seems, therefore, to stand as representative of a substantial documentary culture, in which sale agreements, conveyances and records of property transfers – possibly making extensive use of the vernacular – circulated more widely than is suggested by most of the surviving evidence, dominated as it is by documents from the top of the documentary hierarchy, such as royal diplomas. The events surrounding the composition of the letter also hint at a world where laymen were adept at manipulating charters and conveyancing, where a sharp operator like Ordlaf would smoothly offload disputed land in exchange for unencumbered property. An important point to note here is that the documents seemed to have circulated readily; in other words, laymen clearly kept their charters in a way that allowed their easy retrieval for use in such cases. While the Fonthill Letter is a unique survival, it seems very unlikely indeed that the sort of episode it describes was not common, and we should take seriously Brooks' suggestion that there were once many more documents like this in circulation.[39] Wormald's hand-list of Anglo-Saxon lawsuits, although small in comparison to lists of similar surviving Carolingian material such as *placita*, provides plenty of evidence of lay document use in dispute settlement, often interwoven with other forms of testimony.[40] Although Fonthill is not a *placitum* in

39 Brooks, 'Fonthill', 306.

40 Wormald, 'Charters, 151, makes the point that the records we have of Anglo-Saxon disputes are not formal *placita* in a continental sense, but usually descriptions of cases embedded in other documents.

the sense that a Carolingian aristocrat might understand the term – that is, as a type of document with distinctive formulation – it and the other narratives concerning lawsuits are to some extent analogous in function.

The well-known Kentish dispute over Snodland, for instance, was resolved by testing the boundaries detailed in the relevant charter.[41] The Snodland narrative, from the last quarter of the tenth century, also includes the theft of the relevant landbooks (charters) by priests, and their sale to the son of the man who had originally granted Snodland to the cathedral church of Rochester. It is a remarkably complex dispute and, like Fonthill, took place over a long period of time, in this case over the course of at least a generation. Although the surviving documentary record of the dispute is preserved in charters now part of the archive of Rochester Cathedral, the charters refer to the existence of other documents in lay hands during the earlier stages of the case. The widow of the man who had had the title-deeds stolen, Brihtwaru, surrendered them after being sued by the bishop of Rochester; she then, following King Edgar's death, recovered them in a counter-suit in which the bishop was compelled to hand them over. Again we have frequent document deployment in legal process and what appears to be a family archive.[42]

Another of the cases noted by Wormald, the dispute in 824 concerning Westbury between the church at Berkeley, in Gloucestershire, and the bishop of Worcester, hinged on the title-deeds originally possessed by the father of the lay donor of Westbury, a thegn called Æthelmund. The lay donor, Æthelmund's son Æthelric, had given the estate to Worcester, with a life interest for his mother, Ceolburh. To forestall any problems over his dispositions, the charter recording Æthelric's will notes that he had also given copies of the Westbury donation to 'friends'.[43] Wormald's interest in this dispute was to uncover the mechanism behind its resolution, but it is clear that whatever the process, it involved the deployment and preservation of documents by laypeople, including Æthelmund's widow Ceolburh, and again what may have been some sort of family 'archive'.

The consignment by Æthelric of copies of the donation to his friends points to the value attached to the charter as an object in its own right, an impression reinforced by further evidence for Æthelric's use of documents. He was party to the earliest surviving copy of a chirograph, a charter in which the same text was copied two or three times on a single membrane, which was then cut to produce congruent copies of identical texts; the chirograph in question documents an agreement of around 804

41 Wormald, 'A Handlist', no. 46 (S 1457).
42 Wormald, 'Charters', 157–60. 43 Wormald, 'Charters', 152–7.

between Æthelric and the bishop of Lichfield.[44] Counterparts were held by two of Æthelric's friends in this case too, explicitly as security, in addition to the parts held by Æthelric and the bishop.[45] The example of the chirograph suggests that these documents were not just put somewhere and forgotten, but that they could be retrieved and deployed if necessary: what would be the point of Æthelric giving copies to his friends ('amici necessarii mei et fidelissimi') if they were likely to lose them? To be of use, the charter had to be a recoverable object.

That laymen fully understood the value of documents is reinforced by an account of a transaction, dating from the later 970s or 980s, recorded in the *Libellus Æthelwoldi*, a twelfth-century Ely chronicle also used in the compilation of the better-known *Liber Eliensis*.[46] The account concerns a dispute over an estate at Hauxton and Newton, in which the relevant charters were in the possession of a man called Ælfwold, brother of the vendor Eadric.[47] So worried was Abbot Byrhtnoth of Ely about the 'claims and trickeries' that might arise from his abbey's failure to possess the charters – described in the *Libellus* as *cyrographi* – that he asked first Ealdorman Æthelwold and then Ealdorman Byrhtnoth to purchase the charters from Ælfwold, in return for charters for Ramsey and Sproughton, charters Ælfwold greatly desired ('quo cyrographo multum indiguit'). Again, the actors here all understood the value of the charters, even if they could not all read them, not just as symbolic of ownership but also as tools in dispute resolution.

Evidence like that for Snodland, Westbury and Hauxton and Newton shows a world where different modes of testimony happily coexisted but, significantly, one where the deployment of documents was commonplace, and where legal cases could run across a generation or two. It also seems likely that this document use did not include just diplomas but also an array of other documentary material: records of sales, conveyance notices and even memoranda such as the Fonthill Letter. The frequent use by laypeople of documents in judicial processes, sometimes with the Church, sometimes with other lay individuals, has implications for how we approach the question of lay archives. It would seem likely that if individuals expected to use their documents – title-deeds, notices of sale or whatever – then they would take steps to store them in places that were accessible and in a way that allowed for reasonably easy retrieval. The evidence of Æthelric suggests that laymen did indeed expect to have to use their documents and did expect their gifts and bequests to be

44 Lowe, 'Lay Literacy', 174; S 1187. 45 Lowe, 'Lay Literacy', 174.
46 *Liber Eliensis* 2.27 (ed. Blake, 100–1; trans. Fairweather, 122).
47 Keynes, 'Royal Government', 250–1; Lowe, 'Lay Literacy', 168–9.

challenged. Why else would Æthelric supply two copies of his agreement with the bishop of Lichfield to two close friends? Why else was the abbot of Ely so exercised about the charters held by Ælfwold?

What is also striking about many of the records of transactions in the *Libellus Æthelwoldi* is the extent to which purchases and exchanges were an essential part of the way in which a religious institution built up its endowments. The *Libellus* in fact attests to a busy traffic in land in tenth-century East Anglia, where estates, charters and money changed hands frequently and where both the abbey and its lay neighbours drove hard bargains. It seems unlikely that this was a phenomenon confined either to East Anglia or to the late tenth century. There is a strong argument that even in early Anglo-Saxon England a good number of estates changed hands for reasons other than straightforward inheritance and were often transferred in return for cash, payment in kind or other pieces of land, the quantities of which may have depended more on social factors than on a 'pure' market mechanism (that is, a payment in cash determined by supply and demand). It is overwhelmingly likely that the same exchanges occurred, perhaps even more frequently, in the later period too.[48] It is possible that the foundation or refoundation of land-hungry abbeys in East Anglia, such as Ely, Ramsey or Thorney, made the traffic in land in late tenth-century East Anglia particularly lively, but this does not alter the basic picture; indeed, if we return to Fonthill, the events described in the letter also describe the same piece of land changing hands several times. This, too, has implications for how we view the way in which laymen used and stored their documents. It is clear that diplomas functioned as title-deeds, and therefore possession of the diploma was key. Indeed, the *Libellus*' account of the acquisition of Bluntisham makes this quite clear: 'the person who had the charter was nearer to having the land than the one who did not have it'.[49] In other words, possession of the document did not guarantee possession of the land, but it helped enormously. This suggests a world where charters may have changed hands quite frequently and where additional documentation recording sales and transfers may have been drawn up to accompany such transfers. The *Libellus* episode concerning Hauxton and Newton referred to above also makes it clear that charters did change hands and that the new owners of a piece of property were very keen to have the title-deeds, often going to great lengths to secure them. This, in turn, suggests an environment where laypeople could organize and retrieve their title-deeds and other

48 J. Campbell, 'The Sale of Land and the Economics of Power in Early Anglo-Saxon England', *Haskins Society Journal*, 1 (1989), 23–37, at 25–6, 37.
49 *Liber Eliensis* 2.25 (ed. Blake, 99; trans. Fairweather, 122).

documents, and where the vernacular endorsements made on diplomas would have aided such organization. If we stray a little further into the realms of speculation, it is possible to imagine a situation in which a layman with a significant amount of property held by charter might have bundles of documents – diplomas, leases and notices of sale or exchange – stored in some sort of chest.

## Family archives

As well as the ready deployment of charters and chirographs in legal processes, both the Æthelric and Snodland cases also hint at the existence of family archives that operated across at least two generations. This is an important consideration; we might postulate an individual layman with the ninth- or tenth-century equivalent of the box under his bed, but for these collections to be transmitted across a number of generations of one family argues for something a little more systematic. Related to this is the question of whether such family archives or dossiers can be detected in the surviving record. There may be a number of such collections embedded in the surviving archives of Old English religious houses, but the archives of Burton Abbey in Staffordshire offer one of the clearest examples.

Although later medieval Burton traditions suggest an early community associated with St Modwenna on the site, the abbey as it was in the later Middle Ages was founded, or refounded, in the two decades before 1004, when its possessions and privileges were confirmed by King Æthelred II.[50] The founder was an influential and well-connected Midlands thegn called Wulfric Spot, whose surviving will shows him to have had a significant assemblage of estates stretching right across the Midlands, with a concentration in the counties of Staffordshire, Derbyshire, Warwickshire and Shropshire.[51] Wulfric was a 'king's thegn', that is, a senior member of the king's court, a connection emphasized by the fact that his brother Ælfhelm was ealdorman of York between 993 and 1006, and the fact that Wulfric, in his will, specifically commended his new foundation of Burton to King Æthelred's care.[52] That will also details Wulfric's extensive property bequests, and it is the connection of a number of these bequests to charters in the archive of Burton that allows us to identify a possible family archive embedded within the monastic archive.

[50] S 906.

[51] S 1536; *Charters of Burton Abbey*, ed. P. H. Sawyer (Oxford, 1979) (hereafter *Burton*), pp. xvi–xvii.

[52] S 1536; *Burton*, pp. xxxviii–xliii.

The Anglo-Saxon charters of Burton are preserved in a thirteenth-century cartulary incorporated into a manuscript now in the National Library of Wales, Peniarth 390.[53] The thirteenth-century copyist almost certainly had the original charters in front of him, since he went to the effort of copying into the cartulary some of the chrismons that open a number of them.[54] The ordering of the texts in Peniarth 390 does not help much in reconstructing the archive, since the cartularist opted to copy the texts in roughly chronological order, rather than in another way. Nevertheless, a number of the charters that can be plausibly connected to Wulfric's family predate the refoundation of the abbey at the very end of the tenth century or start of the eleventh, and what we have in Peniarth 390, therefore, is the sort of 'founder's archive' that we see in continental cartularies.[55]

Several of the charters in the Burton archive are grants directly to members of Wulfric's family, although there has been a degree of tampering with some of them. Two of the charters, dated 942, are grants to Wulfsige 'the Black' ('prenomine Maurus'), who was probably Wulfric's grandfather, covering lands in Derbyshire and Staffordshire.[56] A further grant, dated 951, of land at Marchington (Staffordshire) to the thegn Wulfhelm may be part of Wulfric's archive, as might a charter of King Eadwig for 'his man' Mæglsothen.[57] The grant to Mæglsothen is for land subsequently bequeathed by Wulfric to Burton Abbey, and the charter, therefore, may have been Wulfric's title-deed to the estate.

Wulfric himself was the beneficiary of several charters in the Burton archive, covering estates at Pillaton and Abbots Bromley in Staffordshire.[58] Other charters in the archive can be linked more tentatively to Wulfric's family. The ten-hide grant at Parwich made by King Edgar in 966 to the thegn Ælfhelm may have been to Wulfric's brother of that name.[59] More securely, the grant by Edgar to the thegn Wulfgeat of land at Arley in Warwickshire should also be regarded as part of Wulfric's family archive. Arley was among the gifts made by Wulfric's mother Wulfrun to her foundation of Wolverhampton, while Wulfgeat was named in Æthelred's confirmation of Wulfrun's bequests to Wolverhampton as her kinsman.[60] It is unclear how a bequest to one foundation,

53 Aberystwyth, National Library of Wales, Peniarth MS 390, fols. 173–84v; *Burton*, pp. xiii–xv.

54 *Burton*, p. xiv.

55 See above, Chapters 7, 8, 10–11.

56 *Burton*, p. xl, and nos. 5, 6; S 479, 484.

57 *Burton*, nos. 11, 15; S 557, 628.

58 *Burton*, nos. 26–7; S 878–9. S 879 is regarded as spurious, but Pillaton was among the estates bequeathed by Wulfric to Burton.

59 *Burton*, no. 21; S 739.

60 *Burton*, no. 20; S 720, 1380; *Anglo-Saxon Wills*, ed. D. Whitelock (Cambridge, 1955), 164–5.

Wolverhampton, ended up first being granted again to a member of the founder's family and then bequeathed by another member of the same family to a new foundation. Since at no point are the hidage assessments given, either for Wulfrun's initial bequest or in the 963 charter granting Arley to Wulfgeat, it is possible that the grants are separate, with Wulfrun bequeathing one portion of the estate and then another portion being booked to Wulfgeat.

Not all of these links are certain, and there is a degree of supposition about some of those posited between possible members of Wulfric's family.[61] It is also likely that the dossier of Wulfric's charters embedded in the Burton archive may have originally been larger than it was when Peniarth 390 was copied in the thirteenth century. Two charters now in the William Salt Library in Stafford, and not copied into Peniarth 390, also appear to have been part of Wulfric's collection.[62] What allows us to think of Wulfric's charters as a family archive is its multi-generational aspect. A number of charters in this collection were for beneficiaries other than Wulfric; one may have been from his brother and three from his grandfather, and there is also the possibility of grants from his mother. The evidence for Arley points to another strand of preservation by laymen, which may even indicate a different family archive. A grant by King Æthelred in 1001 of land in Arley and Itchington is extant on a single sheet that survived through much of the subsequent centuries at Coventry, but all the ecclesiastical institutions that might have preserved it there came into existence some time later (probably the earliest was Coventry abbey, founded in 1043).[63] So the charter must have spent at least the first generation after its creation in other hands, which must have included the initial beneficiary, the lay magnate Clofi. Whether he was receiving the estate that had previously belonged to Wulfgeat, or a different part of Arley, is not clear; but like Wulfric and his family, he seems to have had the desire and the means to preserve documents.

As already suggested, embedding lay collections in ecclesiastical archives raised the possibility that diplomas, in particular, could be amended, copied or interpolated after entering clerical hands. Since diplomas effectively conferred title, a perennial concern for a church was holding diplomas in which the church was not the beneficiary; something of these worries can be seen in the Hauxton and Newton case already encountered. One way in which a church could quite easily resolve this was to amend the charter to reflect the church's possession of the relevant estate. That this happened is clear; how often it happened, or in what particular circumstances, is much less clear. One example illustrates the

[61] *Burton*, pp. xxxviii–xliii. [62] S 878, 922. [63] S 898.

problem: Stoke Canon in Devon, a possession of the bishop of Exeter in 1066. Stoke was one of the estates that eleventh-century Exeter tradition believed had originally been given to the minster by King Æthelstan (924–39).[64] However, in 1031, Stoke was the subject of a grant by Cnut to a thegn called Hunuwine.[65] At some point between 1031 and 1066, Stoke passed to Exeter, as did Cnut's diploma, which is still preserved among the muniments of Exeter Cathedral. There is, though, another charter for Stoke preserved in the cathedral archives, one of a group of not-very-good forgeries produced at some point during the 1050s or 1060s.[66] This forgery was clearly based on Hunuwine's charter: it has the same hidage assessment – five – and exactly the same vernacular boundary clause. In this case, the desire of Bishop Leofric (bishop of Crediton and St Germans 1046–50, bishop of Exeter 1050–72) and his scribes seems to have been to make a recent acquisition from a layman appear to be a much more ancient grant direct to the minster. Fortunately for us, the original charter survives in this case, although why is unclear; had Hunuwine's charter vanished, we would have no idea that the estate had been in lay hands. This, of course, raises the question of the prevalence of this sort of practice. Where lay charters were copied into the twelfth-century chronicle-cartulary of Abingdon, they were attached to a statement that the layman named in the charter had made the church his heir.[67] The modern editor of Abingdon's charters, Susan Kelly, has suggested that the frequency with which this happens means that we must exercise great caution before taking such statements at face value.[68] As with the case of Hunuwine, the attachment of the simple statement of bequest may mask a more complicated mode of acquisition by the abbey. Such a process would also serve to break up collections of documents as they entered the abbey's archival landscape. The reasons for the preservation of embedded family documents in ecclesiastical archives must ultimately be various, some reflecting acquisitiveness on the part of the institution and its personnel, and some resulting more directly from the association of the institution with a lay family, and the position of both in the skein of local allegiances.

[64] Oxford, Bodleian Library, MS Auct. D. 2.16, fols. 8r–14r; Oxford, Bodleian Library, MS 579, fol. 6r–v (*Leofric Missal*, ed. N. Orchard, 2 vols. [London, 2002], II, 8–9); see C. Insley, 'Remembering Communities Past: Exeter Cathedral in the Eleventh Century', in P. Dalton, C. Insley and L. Wilkinson (eds.), *Cathedrals, Communities and Conflict in the Anglo-Norman World* (Woodbridge, 2011), 41–60, at 48–54.

[65] S 971. [66] S 387.

[67] *Charters of Abingdon Abbey*, ed. S. E. Kelly, 2 vols. (Oxford, 2000–1) (hereafter *Abingdon*), pp. cxxii–cxxiii.

[68] *Abingdon*, p. cxiii.

Related to the issue of family archives is the important but difficult question of whether Anglo-Saxon laymen used local churches or monasteries as their record repositories. The evidence here is, perhaps unsurprisingly, very unclear. We might start with the example of Ealdorman Æthelfrith, who, in the early tenth century, petitioned Edward the Elder, Æthelred and Æthelflæd, rulers of the Mercians, to replace charters he had lost.[69] According to one of these replacement charters, all of his charters of inheritance (*hereditarii libri*)[70] had been consumed by a ravaging fire. This raises some interesting issues. The first is that the mention of his 'books of inheritance' is clearly a reference to some sort of archive. Second, the charter states that Edward, Æthelred and Æthelflæd 'unanimously consented' to other charters being produced 'as far as he could relate them from memory' (*in quantum eos memoriter recordari potuisset*); this suggests not only that Æthelfrith had a number of diplomas, but also that he was familiar with their contents.[71] Third, there is the fire itself: given the date of Æthelfrith's petition, the first decade of the tenth century, it is tempting to see his archives as a casualty of the campaigns of the Vikings in Mercia in the late ninth century. If so, it is possible that his archives were burnt because they were in a church, often the targets of Viking attacks. This is, of course, speculation, and there is no reason why Æthelfrith's charters could not have been kept in his hall or some other such location. The history of the Fonthill Letter itself shows how preservation was often a matter of a series of personal choices. Since in the end the beneficiaries of the Fonthill dispute were the bishopric of Winchester, which got the estate at Fonthill, and Ordlaf, who got an estate in exchange for Fonthill, we would expect the letter initially to have resided with one of them. By the twelfth century, though, it was where it remains, in the archive of Christ Church, Canterbury, and where the later archivist's designation of it as 'useless' was, fortunately, ignored. It has been hypothesized that it reached Canterbury when one of the bishops of Winchester transferred to the archiepiscopal see of Canterbury, perhaps Ælfheah in 1006.[72] The other possibility is that Christ Church had a link to, or even provided a repository for the documents of, Ordlaf or one of his family; but it is less likely in this case simply because the known associations of Ordlaf and his son are with Winchester, Malmesbury and Wilton.[73] Nonetheless, both scenarios envisage that the letter spent time

[69] S 367; this incident is discussed by Lowe, 'Lay Literacy', 170–1.
[70] Here *liber* is a direct translation of Old English *boc*, 'book' or 'charter'.
[71] S 367. [72] Brooks, 'Fonthill Letter', 314–15.
[73] See S 354, 359, 362, 372–8, 381–3, 1286 (Ordlaf witnessing Winchester charters); 1284 (exchange of Fonthill for Lydiard between Ordlaf and bishop of Winchester);

in an archive associated with a person (ecclesiastical in one case, lay in the other), rather than an institution.

We are possibly on more concrete ground if we consider those archives that contain charters for property to which the Church had no claim. Cases in point are the so-called 'alien diplomas' in the Abingdon archive.[74] These are diplomas copied into the two twelfth-century Abingdon cartularies but concerning lands to which Abingdon seems to have had no claim at any point. Stenton suggested that these were charters that had been deposited for safe keeping with the abbey and then not retrieved (for whatever reason) and that had subsequently been merged with the abbey's archives.[75] As Kelly notes in her discussion of the Abingdon archive, this thesis is attractive on the face of it, since it might explain how Abingdon and, indeed, other houses such as the Old Minster Winchester or Glastonbury, came to be in possession of charters for estates that seem never to have been part of the monastic endowment. However, Kelly goes on to argue that most of the charters that apparently have no connection to the endowment were, in fact, related to estates the abbey had or still held in the twelfth century. She also raises the point that, since possession of a title-deed (that is, charter) conferred possession of the land, it would be a rash layman who would entrust his precious landbooks to monastic keeping, something that might have been especially pertinent given the much more rigid attitude to property displayed by many of the tenth-century foundations or refoundations, such as Abingdon, Ely or Ramsey.[76]

Keynes suggests that in some circumstances laymen might have deposited their diplomas with a monastery such as Abingdon for safe keeping in times of necessity, but such circumstances must have been rare, and there is precious little pre-Conquest evidence of such a practice. However, these reservations really concern diplomas, and it is likely that other sorts of records, such as agreements or wills, especially those drawn up in chirograph form, were deposited with churches. The *Libellus Æthelwoldi* contains an account of a will-making episode, in which Abbot Byrhtnoth of Ely had the will of a thegn called Siferth written as a tripartite chirograph before being read out and distributed to Siferth himself, Abbot Byrhtnoth and Ealdorman Æthelwine.[77] Once again we have the intersection of performance and text, since a key element of the process

1205 (exchange between Ordlaf and Malmesbury); 364, 368 (in the Wilton archive, granted to or witnessed by Ordlaf); 469 (grant to Wilton by Ordlaf's son Ordwald).

[74] *Abingdon*, pp. cxxxvii–cxlix.

[75] F. M. Stenton, *The Early History of the Abbey of Abingdon* (Reading, 1913), 43.

[76] *Abingdon*, pp. cxxxviii–cxlv.

[77] *Liber Eliensis* 2.11 (ed. Blake, 87; trans. Fairweather, 110).

was the reading out of the will, but the episode also underlines the close relationship of many local aristocrats to these foundations and the probability that they did entrust some of their documents to ecclesiastical keeping.

There remains the question of the extent to which the late tenth-century 'monastic reform' changed the archival landscape of Anglo-Saxon England. Much ink has been spilled on the nature of the monastic reform and the 'anti-monastic' reaction that followed the death in 975 of King Edgar, the most active proponent and patron of the reform.[78] What is relevant is that the reform appears to have redefined the relationship between monastery, benefactor and property, inasmuch as the houses founded or refounded during this period seem to have had a much more rigid and even aggressive attitude towards their property and the kin of their benefactors than older churches, which seem to have enjoyed a rather more cosy relationship with local aristocracies. Many of the episodes related in the *Libellus Æthelwoldi*, for instance, concern the thwarting by Ely of the claims made by relations of their benefactors.[79]

This attitude, in so far as it can be discerned, is especially important to keep in mind when we consider the nature of the corpus of surviving Anglo-Saxon charters. What survives is dominated by the archives of a handful of great houses: well over half of survivals, especially of diplomas, can be linked to the archives of Worcester, Abingdon, Old Minster Winchester and Christ Church Canterbury. It is very significant, therefore, that all of these institutions were, in some way, participants in the reform movement. How we are to regard this dominance or its implications is not at all certain, but a few lines of enquiry can be advanced. What is clear about the 'reform', even before its apogee in the reign of Edgar, is that it involved a significant transfer of landed wealth into the hands of the monastic Church.[80] This was a matter not simply of piety but of royal policy; the *Regularis Concordia*, promulgated under Edgar's auspices at a great council in Winchester, specified one rule for all monasteries, enjoined all monasteries to pray frequently for the king and the kingdom, and placed all monasteries under the king's lordship, while nunneries were subject to the queen.[81] These strictures, along with

78 See C. Cubitt, 'The Tenth-Century Benedictine Reform in England', *EME*, 6 (1997), 77–94.

79 See above, 351.

80 C. Cubitt, 'The Institutional Church', in P. Stafford (ed.), *A Companion to the Early Middle Ages: Britain and Ireland c. 500–c. 1100* (Oxford, 2009), 376–94, at 386–9.

81 T. Symons, '*Regularis concordia*: History and Derivation', in D. Parsons (ed.), *Tenth-Century Studies: Essays in Commemoration of the Millennium of the Council of Winchester and the Regularis Concordia* (Chichester, 1975), 37–59.

active promotion by Edgar of lay patronage of these institutions, turned these foundations, especially the Mercian and East Anglian ones, into a form of surrogate royal presence. These institutions were very like the abbeys founded by the Carolingians east of the Rhine, in that they functioned, in part, as centres of royal control in areas outside the West Saxon heartland of the kings of the English.

This transfer of landed wealth can be detected in the surviving archives, whether the *Abingdon Chronicle* or the *Liber Eliensis*, or even in those charters belonging to the family of Wulfric Spot that ended up in the hands of Burton Abbey.[82] Such a transfer also undoubtedly changed the relationship between these religious foundations and local aristocrats and landholders. It became at once closer, as lay patrons had a much larger stake in the Church, but also more rigid, as the Church in turn sought to loosen lay control over land in Church hands. This changing relationship affected the archival landscape; first, by generating an increase in the issuing of diplomas, as laymen sought permission to transfer land to the Church – an increase that can be seen in the pattern of survival of diplomas through the tenth century. Second, the new relationship also saw the transfer of diplomas and other documentation into the hands of the monastic Church, the sort of processes witnessed by the accounts in the *Libellus Æthelwoldi*. This in turn had implications for the way in which documents were preserved, and even for what documents were preserved.

The one part of England seemingly untouched by these developments was the North; that is, what had been the kingdom of Northumbria. Much of the preceding discussion has considered England south of the river Humber, with Burton Abbey in Staffordshire the northernmost outpost of the tenth-century expansion in monastic foundation and refoundation. The question of lay documentary and archival practice in the North is a very tricky one, not least because of the convoluted and violent history of Northumbria from the eighth century onwards. It is generally assumed that the archives of most northern houses were badly hit during the Viking attacks and settlements of the ninth and early tenth centuries, while the confused political situation that followed, until the extinction of the Viking kingdom of York in the 950s, was also hardly conducive to archival stability. Not that we should lay the blame solely at the feet of the Vikings: King Eadred's campaign in the North in 948, which saw the burning of the church at Ripon and the transfer to the South of the relics

82 See above, n. 46; *Burton*, pp. xliv–xlvii; *Abingdon*, pp. cxxxi–cxcii.

of Wilfrid, one of the North's most potent saints, presumably also had implications for whatever documents were stored there.[83]

What did laymen in the North do with their charters and other records? The much poorer survival of pre-Conquest material from northern England makes it tempting to posit – even allowing for Viking depredation – a much lower level of documentary use and culture than in the South. Tempting, but probably wrong; there is no reason to suggest that the same imperatives that drove lay document use and preservation in southern England were absent from the North. In southern England laymen collected and stored documents because they were useful, both in symbolic and practical ways. It is likely that these needs also obtained in northern England. We can, perhaps, detect glimpses of lay documentary culture in the twelfth-century corpus of writing from Durham Cathedral priory. These texts are generally regarded as drawing on earlier collections of annals, regnal lists and, possibly, documents such as charters. One episode, in particular, hints at a world of lay property transactions and collections of charters. Early in the first decade of the eleventh century, a prominent York thegn named Styrr Ulfson granted a large number of estates in North Yorkshire and County Durham to the community of St Cuthbert.[84] This episode is described in the *Historia de Sancto Cuthberto* – one of these twelfth-century Durham texts – in terms that suggest that the author had in front of him either the charter or some sort of written notice of it.[85] The episode is also described as having taken place under the witness of Archbishop Wulfstan and King Æthelred, so if the Durham scribe had a document in front of him it could have been either Styrr's charter or even a royal charter allowing Styrr to alienate the land.[86] Crucially, though, these estates had not been in Styrr's family for very long, since in the text he is described as having purchased them

83 *Anglo-Saxon Chronicle* (D), s.a. (ed. G. P. Cubbin [Cambridge, 1996], 44; trans. *EHD*, no. 1 [p. 223]).

84 *The Early Charters of Northern England and the North Midlands*, ed. C. R. Hart (Leicester, 1975), no. 130; W. Aird, *St Cuthbert and the Normans: The Church of Durham, 1071–1153* (Woodbridge, 1998), 47–8; H. H. E. Craster, 'The Red Book of Durham', *English Historical Review*, 40 (1925), 504–35, at 526. The estates concerned were Darlington, Coniscliffe, Cockerton, Haughton-le-Skerne, Normanby, Ketton and Lumley.

85 *Historia de sancto Cuthberto* 29 (ed. T. Arnold, Rolls Series 75.1:212–13).

86 Styrr's grant to the Cuthbert community seems to have been part of the complex interplay of regional political rivalries in what had been the kingdom of York; see Aird, *St Cuthbert*, 48–9; W. Kapelle, *The Norman Conquest of the North: The Region and Its Transformation, 1000–1135* (London, 1979), 17–24; C. Insley, 'Politics, Conflict and Kinship in Early Eleventh-Century Mercia', *Midland History*, 25 (2000), 28–42, at 35–7, for a discussion of these rivalries.

himself.[87] The question is then whether Styrr had charters, or at least memoranda of sale, for those transactions, charters that he then handed over to Durham. This seems to have been the sort of situation hinted at in texts such as the *Libellus Æthelwoldi*, and there is no reason to believe that property transaction did not happen in the same way north of the Humber.

Where the North might have differed, especially in terms of the contours of the archival landscape, is in the absence there of aggressive, archive-minded monasteries of the sort we see in East Anglia or Wessex; there were no 'Æthelwoldian' abbeys in the north. The imperatives of places such as Abingdon, Ely, the New Minster or Worcester shaped the archival landscape of southern England on the eve of the Norman Conquest, not least because they generated a significant shift of land into monastic hands. Their absence from the North might therefore be a major determinant of the much more exiguous survival of diplomatic evidence from northern England.

## Conclusions

The evidence surveyed here, perforce briefly and episodically, allows a number of conclusions to be drawn about lay documentary culture in England in the three and a half centuries before the Norman Conquest. The first is that those looking for lay archives in England will be disappointed; no such thing survives. However, it is also clear from what does survive that laypeople fully understood the importance of documents, not just as artefacts but also as texts, even if they could not read them; laypeople also involved documents in all sorts of transactions and social action, from an early date. The frequency with which documents appear in the fragmentary accounts that survive of disputes and conveyancing also suggests that lay individuals had mechanisms for accessing the necessary documentation. For a small-scale landholder, this may not have been difficult, since he or she may only have had a few charters; for larger-scale landowners, however, the ease with which documentation was deployed and the arenas in which it was deployed suggest some sort of rudimentary record-keeping beyond the proverbial box under the bed. Second, the likelihood that there was a lively traffic in landed property from an early date in England suggests a certain amount of documentation in circulation in addition to royal diplomas. This is hinted at by

87 *Historia de sancto Cuthberto* 29 (ed. Arnold, 212), 'Et ego emi propria pecunia et dedi Sancto Cuthberto iiii carucatas terrae.'

such lucky survivals as the Fonthill Letter. Third, the Fonthill Letter also illustrates how much material, especially in the vernacular, has now been lost. Only at Worcester and Bury St Edmunds does a significant body of Old English material – mostly leases – survive. However, it seems inconceivable that these were the only two institutions to lease land using vernacular documents.[88] Much of this additional documentation was probably lost in the centuries following the Norman Conquest. However, it is likely that this process of reshaping the archival landscape began before 1066, as religious institutions sought to control and organize their archives from the second half of the tenth century onwards and to prioritize the preservation, interpolation and copying of royal diplomas. We know what we have, but we can only guess at what we do not have but that once existed.

[88] See, for instance, S 1387, an Old English chirographic lease made by the bishop of Crediton in around 1018; also Lowe, 'Lay Literacy', appendix, 185–203.

# 14 Conclusion

Many more documents survive from the early Middle Ages than from the Roman Empire or its Byzantine successor, outside Egypt. Yet the view that Roman society at all levels was permeated with documents is persistent. Narrative sources assume routine documentation, and the fact of imperial unity has given ancient historians confidence in generalizing from scant direct evidence, like the papyri preserved in the unique conditions of Egypt, to provincial society as a whole. We might now be less likely to be swayed by the literature of the golden age than our predecessors; we might be more likely to stress the increasing prevalence of documents in third- and fourth-century legal procedure in the context of ever more ambitious attempts at social regulation on the part of the state; we might also point to the differing brands of *Romanitas* on offer in the provincial societies of the third, fourth and fifth centuries. Nevertheless, the general statement that Romans routinely resorted to documentation will be contested by few.

When we deal with the ever-thickening stream of surviving documentation from the last centuries of the first millennium, however, we are reluctant to generalize. Regional difference, a leitmotif of current early medieval studies, drives us to draw contrasts even between different provinces of the same kingdom when it comes to documentary practice or social structure.[1] More importantly, we are provoked to caution by the nature of our evidence. We have far more actual evidence from

[1] C. Wickham, 'Problems of Comparing Rural Societies in Early Medieval Europe', in Wickham, *Land and Power: Studies in Italian and Early Mediaeval Social History, 300–1100* (Rome, 1994), 201–26 (orig. *TRHS*, 6th ser., 2 [1992], 221–46); see, emblematically, Wickham, *Framing*, as well as J. M. H. Smith, *Europe After Rome: A New Cultural History* (Oxford, 2005). While there have been regional studies of the late Roman Empire, especially of Egypt, whence the bulk of documents survives for the period (R. S. Bagnall, *Egypt in Late Antiquity* [Princeton, NJ, 1996]; C. Adams, *Land Transport in Roman Egypt 30 BC–AD 300: A Study in Administration and Economic History* [Oxford, 2007]; P. Sarris, *Economy and Society in the Age of Justinian* [Cambridge, 2005]), these are taken as to some extent symptomatic of the imperial system as a whole. Studies of regions after *c*. 650, on the other hand, are generally taken to speak of diversity and difference.

the eighth and following centuries than we do for the Roman period precisely because the great churches and monasteries of early medieval Europe enjoyed a continuous archival history into early modern times, and because the records they held were therefore absorbed to a greater or lesser extent into the national and regional archives of modern governments. From there they entered into the documentary canons of the professionalized historical academies. We can debate what a Roman tax list looked like, in the absence of unambiguous direct evidence, but we know exactly how early medieval churches documented the dues of their tenants. Nevertheless, we are profoundly suspicious of this evidence because it represents only one institutional context, that of the Church. The legacy of nineteenth-century anticlericalism, and the corresponding assumption of a fundamental and structural antagonism between Church and State, has exerted a profound influence here, one that makes it far harder for us to accept ecclesiastical writings as representative of a culture as a whole than those of a Cicero or a Tacitus. The shadow of Gibbon's triumph of superstition and barbarism also looms large,[2] for in spite of now three generations of scholarship wrestling with the assumptions of cataclysm and decline, alternative characterizations of post-Roman change remain elusive. There is a striking historiographical comparison with early medieval China, where historical writing took place in a dedicated office at the imperial court and where the different mechanisms of transmission mean that practical and provincial documentation is more or less absent. Yet, in spite of political upheavals, the ideologies essayed in official historiography and their adaptation by early modern and modern regimes mean that the assumption of structural continuity remains unquestioned. Specialists are thus happy to generalize from exceptional survivals such as the archives of the Buddhist cave monastery of Tunhuang and assume a society in which the written instruments of imperial government penetrated deeply. Furthermore, the provenance of these remarkable but isolated documents is seen as unproblematic as there is little sense of a cultural divide between religious foundations and the wider populace.[3]

In the specific case of writing in early medieval Europe, the changing distributions of one particular form of writing – the inscribed word – have been used to shore up received views of a generalized decline of literacy, when in fact they relate to the shifting cultural, political and

[2] Edward Gibbon, *The History of the Decline and Fall of the Roman Empire*, ed. J. B. Bury, 7 vols. (London, 1898–1901), IV, 150: 'The progress of superstition and barbarism was rapid and universal.'

[3] D. Twitchett, 'Chinese Social History from the Seventh to the Tenth Centuries: The Tunhuang Documents and Their Implications', *Past and Present*, 35 (1966), 28–53.

ideological meanings of inscriptions.[4] In any case, in Byzantium the distribution of inscriptions likewise changes, and (outside Egypt) documents of practice from the early medieval period are far, far scarcer than in western Europe, but specialists have little doubt that documentation continued to play a significant role in the regulation of social relations.[5] In contrast, in western Europe, the thickening evidence for documents and document use from the eighth century onwards is generally understood in terms of revival and innovation, driven above all by the Church and by the imperatives of the Carolingian rulers who invested so heavily in it; debate turns on whether one takes a maximalist or minimalist view of the effects of this investment. As a result, scholars have tended to assume a gap between the documentary culture of Late Antiquity and that of the Carolingian and post-Carolingian world, a view underpinned by Pirenne's seizing on the move from papyrus to parchment in seventh-century Gaul as emblematic of a series of wider cultural and political changes.[6] A variety of grand narratives have been created to explain this perceived gap; the most familiar one describes a transition 'from public to private' in the shape of a shift from state to Church as the primary agency for document production and preservation.

This book has eschewed inherited grand narratives and instead has investigated the pattern and nature of the surviving documentation. And we have shown that we cannot infer changing documentary practices from changing patterns of documentary survival. We have demonstrated that people at all social levels used documents for a variety of purposes throughout Late Antiquity and the early Middle Ages. This is as true of laypeople as it is of the clergy. People with no ecclesiastical affiliation, ranging from the Apion family in fourth-century Egypt to prosperous peasants in tenth-century Iberia, deployed documents in ways that were unrelated to the needs of churches and monasteries. Incidental references to such documents suggest that their use was thoroughly mundane, while cases of their intentional destruction nevertheless reflect a sophisticated appreciation of their value. At the beginning of our story, in the fourth

[4] Cf. W. V. Harris, *Ancient Literacy* (Cambridge, MA, 2001), esp. 285–322, with M. Handley, *Death, Society and Culture: Inscriptions and Epitaphs in Gaul and Spain, 300–700* (Oxford, 2003).

[5] See above, Chapter 2, and C. Holmes, 'Provinces and Capital', in L. James (ed.), *A Companion to Byzantium* (Oxford, 2010), 55–66.

[6] H. Pirenne, 'Le commerce du papyrus dans la Gaule mérovingienne', *Comptes rendus des séances de l'Académie des inscriptions et belles-lettres* (1928), 178–91; Pirenne, *Mahomet et Charlemagne* (Brussels, 1937), 124–5. Cf. M. McCormick, *Origins of the European Economy: Communications and Commerce A.D. 300–900* (Cambridge, MA, 2001), 704–8.

century, the distinction between lay and ecclesiastical documentary cultures does not even apply; as we go forward, the distinction remains problematic. The ecclesiastical aspects of a shared documentary culture may become more visible, but a systematic comparison with lay practices indicates a continuum of values, imperatives and technologies. It is the differential histories of transmission, allied to modern assumptions about the Church as separate from and opposed to the state, that have created a historiographical divide.

When we examine this shared culture, we find that documentary practices – the production and use of documents as well as their preservation in archives – were shaped by the needs of institutions, but also by the needs of the people who resorted to them. These needs did not always overlap. The best-known examples of this phenomenon, and ones that have loomed large in the preceding chapters, are the lay patrons of the so-called proprietary monasteries, whose dossiers of title-deeds ended up in those monasteries' archives. The late antique *gesta municipalia*, although established to respond to the fiscal needs of the state by keeping track of tax obligations, also happened to meet the needs of local landowners by authenticating their documents, and therefore legally strengthening the transactions that those documents enacted.[7] Similarly, landowners in Italy from the Carolingian period onwards could and did take advantage of the judicial process to obtain documentary support for their property rights.[8] In other words, for us, writing with hindsight and attempting to tease out and then explain change over time, it is tempting to see shifting patterns of document production and storage as evidence for new institutions establishing cultural and social power. If we are theoretically minded, we might even invoke the processes of domiciliation and consignation, physical and interpretative control.[9] But post-Roman societies were multifaceted, and the wealth of evidence for lay documentary practice assembled in this book undermines a simplistic and misleading teleology of ecclesiastical takeover. We must therefore put the agency of those who needed documents and sought out archives into the picture and see institutions as responsive to social needs. Control of archives and control through archives need reading as complex and fundamentally contestable processes, not as raw facts.

The ultimate disappearance of the late Roman state in the West did not mean the disappearance of landowners and their needs; landowners simply found new ways to achieve old purposes. The language of the *gesta municipalia* continued to hold an attraction for some scribes in parts of the medieval West. Ongoing references to the registration of documents

[7] See above, Chapters 4 and 5. [8] See above, Chapter 9. [9] See above, 13.

in municipal archives in post-Roman contexts suggest that people were still seeking public validation of their transactions, despite the evident disappearance of the archives themselves.[10] A similar conclusion can be drawn from seventh-century estate accounts from Tours that still bear the imprint of Late Antique fiscal administration. The rare survivals of papyri in the ecclesiastical archives of the Merovingian monastery of St-Denis and the archbishopric of Ravenna also perpetuate recognizably late Roman forms.[11] While the language used in these documents may be archaic, the documents themselves are not fossils; they reveal practices with living roots in late Roman institutions that were evolving to meet changed circumstances. This evolution in documentary practices would continue throughout the early Middle Ages.

A core purpose of documents has always been to record and secure transactions and rights. This applies as much to a bureaucratic state as to an individual landowner. Late Roman documentary culture encompassed both, but it was essentially driven by the state's requirements both to register and to enforce its fiscal claims. Neither these requirements, however, nor the mechanisms through which they were achieved, were static. The need for documents in the Roman world actually increased in the third and fourth centuries as Roman government and Roman law grappled with the consequences of a reshaped empire.[12] One outcome was the abandonment of strictures on the formal aspects of documentary production, and a recognition that writing itself was a constitutive act, something that has profound implications for how we read early medieval documentary practices. In addition, the late Roman army also generated a significant amount of documentation. The direct needs of the Roman state, however, were not the only drivers of documentary production and use. The very existence of great estates promoted an intense circulation of documents.[13]

In this world, people used documents to meet their own needs. Estate records, designed in the first instance to register the income of landowners, also allowed peasants to document their creditworthiness.[14]

[10] See above, Chapter 5.

[11] Tours: W. Goffart, 'Merovingian Polyptychs: Reflections on Two Recent Publications', in Goffart, *Rome's Fall and After* (London, 1986), 233–53 (orig. *Francia*, 9 [1982], 55–77); J. Durliat, 'Qu'est-ce qu'un polyptyque? À propos des documents de Tours (*ChLA* 659)', in M. Sot (ed.), *Media in Francia: Recueil de mélanges offerts à Karl-Ferdinand Werner à l'occasion de son 65ᵉ anniversaire par ses amis et collègues français* (Paris, 1989), 129–38; S. Sato, 'The Merovingian Accounting Documents of Tours: Form and Function', *EME*, 9 (2000), 143–61. St-Denis: D. Ganz and W. Goffart, 'Charters Earlier Than 800 from French Collections', *Speculum*, 65 (1990), 902–36; Ravenna: above, Chapter 4.

[12] See above, Chapters 2–4. [13] See above, Chapters 2–3. [14] See above, 28–31.

The Ravenna papyri reveal that at least in Ravenna the *gesta municipalia* process, while clearly designed to help the state keep track of tax obligations, also gave owners the ability to validate transactions and secure their property.[15] These sorts of practices could only work in a society permeated by a more general use of documents at all social levels. The existence of writing of this kind is demonstrated not only by the Egyptian papyri but also by ephemeral documents such as receipts on *ostraca* or even curses on slate found in Visigothic Spain.[16]

The entry of Christians into the public sphere in the fourth century did nothing to change this situation. As already noted, the distinction between lay and clerical was not manifested on papyrus. Christians (and their developing institutions) simply participated in this fluid documentary culture like everyone else, whether as owners of and workers on great estates, commanders and soldiers in the army, or imperial bureaucrats and municipal functionaries. It would take centuries for Christian institutions to develop in a way that could affect broader documentary practices. In late sixth-century Gaul, for example, Gregory of Tours could compare his historiographical record of the *gesta* of the present to the public entry of titles and obligations into the *gesta* of the cities that still structured society; the great bishoprics that dominated Gregory's landscape may have had their own special archives, *gesta episcoporum*, but these were part of a common culture of document keeping that permeated both royal and local politics.[17]

As Gregory demonstrates, some aspects of late Roman documentary culture survived in many parts of the West at least into the sixth century. But by 700, document use was responding to a very different social order. In a state that rested on a regular cycle of tax assessment and registration, local documentation of fiscal liability was vital for both the operation of government and the security of local landowners; the underlying principle was well put by the Roman lawyer in the Burgundian kingdom who explained that no transfer of fields or lands could be effected unless the recipient was able to meet the tax liability and register his interests. In post-Roman times, however, assessment – always a potential flashpoint in local politics – became more and more vexed, as bishops rehearsed supposedly ancient liberties on behalf of their churches and cities, and ordinary landowners increasingly came to claim a new form of freedom, connected with the bearing of arms in the service of their king and

15 See above, 70–82 and Chapter 5.

16 See above, Chapter 3, and *Las pizarras visigodas: Edición crítica y estudio*, ed. I. Velázquez Soriano (Murcia, 1989), nos. 2–3, and pp. 613–14.

17 Ganz and Goffart, 'Charters Earlier Than 800'.

the adoption of barbarian ethnicity, but also encompassing claims to freedom from taxation. By the end of the seventh century, Marculf was able to equate a 'truly free' man with one who 'is not counted in the public register'. The late Roman fiscal system had atrophied, and while practices associated with it continued in places, at a local level they did so as custom, detached from any wider discourse of public obligation or fiscal law.[18]

Yet, although documents were no longer produced in direct association with this fiscal system, the documentary habit persisted. One of the ways that it persisted, and the best known, was among rulers. Thus, diplomas of the Merovingian Frankish kings predominate among the earliest charters in the archive of the abbey of St-Denis, to the extent that the latter may be seen as in some way a 'royal archive'. But this habit was not limited to rulers. The few extant non-royal charters and wills from this period (for example, the nine non-royal pre-Carolingian documents from the St-Denis archive that have no connection to St-Denis itself) show that the highest aristocracy also managed their affairs in writing and sought out the same forms of security and storage as their royal masters.[19] The earliest formula-books, meanwhile, indicate a much wider range of business carried out with documents: manumissions, powers of attorney, securities, receipts, quitclaims and so on. Similarly, the slate documents of Visigothic Iberia suggest that the basic business of running rural estates was being carried out in writing: the recording of oaths, professions of servitude and simple accounting.[20]

There was, then, no fundamental change in how people used documents. The scarcity of evidence for lay documentary practice, however, as well as the absence of the imprints of late Roman fiscality and above all the survival of what little evidence there is in ecclesiastical archives, has encouraged the view that laypeople in the West became marginalized from documentary culture. Historians have therefore looked to the Church as the ark in which late Roman documentary practices survived. Yet monks and clerics had not yet come to take leading roles in documentary culture; in many places major churches and monasteries

[18] This paragraph draws on W. Goffart's studies, collected in Goffart, *Rome's Fall and After*; also M. Innes, 'Land, Freedom and the Making of the Early Medieval West', *TRHS*, 6th ser., 16 (2006), 39–74, and Innes, University of London inaugural lecture, 2007: 'Roman Liberty and Gothic Freedom: From Late Antiquity to the Early Middle Ages' (forthcoming). The quotations are from the *Lex Romana Burgundionum* 60 (MGH LL nat. Germ. 2.1:159) and Marculf 1.19 (trans. Rio, *Formularies*, 153).

[19] The St-Denis records are edited in *ChLA* XIII–XIV; for bibliography and discussion, see above, 317–19.

[20] Formularies: Rio, *Legal Practice*. Slates: above, Chapter 4.

had not even begun routinely and systematically to store their own documents.[21]

In the Byzantine East, a bureaucratic, fiscal and military superstructure endured. The state, therefore, though it underwent profound transformations, continued to provide institutional frameworks within which documents circulated. The documentary practices and survival patterns visible in the Byzantine world differ correspondingly from those in the West.[22] Here, Marculf's famous seventh-century formula-book is a harbinger of the future. It reveals a broadly shared legal and documentary culture, but it also exemplifies a moment when the institutional resources available to landowners who wished to secure and preserve documents were beginning to change.[23] In Marculf's Neustria, churches were arguably becoming the institutions of record by default as alternatives receded, as the continued deposit of 'private' documents in the archive of St-Denis indicates. The remarkable run of early secular papyri, complete with *gesta municipalia* protocols, in the archives of the church of Ravenna immediately invites comparison. The chronology of change differed from region to region, depending on the range of local possibilities. Notably, churches were only one option among many for storing documents. Several early Frankish formulas assume that laypeople were keeping documents in their own homes.[24] As late as the reign of Charles the Bald, a lay aristocrat was able to resist the documentary claims of the local bishop by producing documents stored at the disputed estate.[25] Churches and monasteries themselves were subject to the same processes whereby a dominant church in a region became the institution of record. In Italy, the documents of the local churches in the relatively remote valley of the Garfagnana were deposited in the episcopal archive in Lucca.[26]

[21] See above, Chapter 8, as well as Hummer, *Politics*, 76–104; McKitterick, *Carolingians*, 77–126, esp. 122–4.

[22] See above, Chapter 2.

[23] Marculf; see above, Chapter 6.

[24] Brown, 'Documents'.

[25] See above, 176–9.

[26] For general comment on the 'registering' of charters at Lucca, see C. Wickham, *The Mountains and the City: The Tuscan Apennines in the Early Middle Ages* (Oxford, 1988), 9, 18, with nn. 5, 27. Dorsal notes on some of the Garfagnana charters confirm this, notably *ChLA* XXXVII 1074 (= *CDL* II 285), a charter concerning the church of S. Maria in Campori and written in 773, on which a dorsal note in an eighth-century hand reads '+ dos ecclesie Sancte Marie de Campulo'; in other words, the charter was already, within a few years of its issue, filed according to the name of the church it concerned, and therefore almost certainly not in that church. Since this charter in fact transferred future control of the church to the bishop of Lucca, it seems very likely that it was stored in the latter's archive. A similar note appears on the dorse of *ChLA* XXXVII 1094, equally important for the association of the church with the bishopric. Archiving according to the name of the estate is suggested by dorsal notes on the Garfagnana charter *ChLA* XXXII 951, issued in 759.

This phenomenon can also be seen at Wissembourg, where, for example, a series of transactions concerning the church at St Martin at Berg was ultimately deposited among the records of the great monastery.[27] In short, when people and institutions accumulated land and built relationships with each other, they accumulated documents and preserved them through the most convenient means available. Churches in particular were attractive for storage *not* because they controlled documentary culture, but because they were community centres and because they enjoyed supernatural and physical protection. In rural archaeological contexts, churches tend to be the first, and often the only, stone building. Even wooden churches such as proliferate in the seventh and eighth centuries were generally more substantial than the surrounding dwellings.

A long-standing paradigm in the historiography of this period connects a particular set of ecclesiastical institutions – bishoprics and large monasteries – to the rising Carolingian dynasty. As the Carolingians gained power, they established patronage over bishoprics and certain privileged monasteries in order to gain access to crucial material and social resources. Identifying churches and monasteries as especially convenient and potentially well-organized centres of documentary culture, they actively encouraged some of them to record and organize their relationships and income in writing in order to take advantage of local land and patronage networks. A number of monasteries drew their particular attention because they stood in strategically important locations: Nonantola and Farfa, for example, benefited in this way after Charlemagne's conquest of Lombard Italy in 774, as did several of their Aquitanian and East Frankish counterparts in the aftermath of conquest.[28] Some ecclesiastical institutions – for example, at St Gall and Salzburg – responded to the encroachment of Carolingian power by expanding their use and storage of documents.[29]

It is at precisely this point that we can see the great churches and monasteries in the Frankish heartland trying to locate old documents and to organize document storage and production in newly useful ways. The earliest polyptychs and cartularies are manifestations of this impulse, in part stimulated by the compact begun under Pippin whereby 'excess' land

[27] See above, 199–200.

[28] As is clear from F. Prinz's map of 'Schenkungen und Privilegien Karls des Großen', in W. Braunfels (ed.), *Karl der Große: Lebenswerk und Nachleben*, 5 vols. (Düsseldorf, 1965–8), I, 488. Cf. J. Semmler, 'Karl der Große und das fränkische Mönchtum', in Braunfels (ed.), *Karl der Große*, II, 255–89, here 267–70, 273–8.

[29] See M. Innes, 'Property, Politics and the Problem of the Carolingian State', in W. Pohl and V. Wieser (eds.), *Der frühmittelalterliche Staat: Europäische Perspektiven* (Vienna, 2009), 299–314, and H. Wolfram, 'Die Notitia Arnonis und ähnliche Formen der Rechtssicherung im nachagilolfischen Bayern', in *Recht und Schrift*, 115–30.

was distributed on the king's word.[30] So are ecclesiastical and monastic archives and staffs of clerical and monastic scribes. And it is only at this point that we can say with confidence that the overwhelming majority of scribes in the Frankish kingdoms – even those who served lay consumers – were clerical or monastic. This is evident from the patterns of charter production at St Gall and Wissembourg.[31] This is also the period in which churches and monasteries began compiling and copying on a large scale collections of formulas, many of which were relevant only to lay users. Gregory of Tours in the preface to his *Histories* had alluded to a multi-tiered and multivalent literate culture structured by the regular record of deeds (*gesta*) within cities that were increasingly dominated by bishops; Regino of Prüm, writing two centuries later, compared his work as a historian to the workaday task of a notary making a legal notice commemorating praiseworthy actions.[32]

In Francia, therefore, it appears as though the Church had in fact taken over documentary practice. The traditional picture of a clerical and monastic monopoly of documentary culture, however, generalizes to the entire early Middle Ages a reality that was in fact a consequence of Carolingian efforts to strengthen their regime in certain crucial regions. Furthermore, it ignores the continued and lively use of documents by laypeople both within and outside this ecclesiastical framework, as witnessed by the intensive record-keeping at Perrecy, Folkwine's anxiety to maintain documentary proof for his shady dealings, or the dozens of secular transactions that later found their way into the archives of the monasteries of Cluny and Redon.[33]

Our mental map tends to normalize and generalize the Carolingian story precisely because of the patterns of documentary survival. The Carolingian situation rests on the fact of large ecclesiastical institutions that serviced both their own needs and those of the imperial aristocracy and the royal court. As managers of estates, people and memory, Carolingian ecclesiastical institutions developed characteristic forms that they bequeathed to later centuries: estate registers, cartularies with a commemorative function, ecclesiastical notaries serving the wider community, and archives of ecclesiastical property records that might incorporate dossiers of lay documents. As it is the ecclesiastical cartularies and archives that have tended to survive, it is they that dominate the tractable

30 For the earliest stages of this impetus, see I. Heidrich, 'Das Breve der Bischofskirche von Mâcon aus der Zeit König Pippins (751–768): Mit Textedition', *Francia*, 24 (1997), 17–37.

31 See above, 155–73, 214–21.

32 Gregory of Tours, *Libri historiarum*, preface (MGH SRM 1.1:1); Regino of Prüm, *Chronicon*, preface (MGH SRG 50:1).

33 See above, Chapters 7 and 11.

record with which modern historians grapple. When, from the twelfth century onwards, secular institutions and aristocratic families did feel the need to create dedicated long-term archives on the model of those forms utilized by Carolingian and post-Carolingian ecclesiastical institutions, our picture of document use changes.[34]

The power of the traditional model has also tended to obscure both variation within the Carolingian heartland itself and the existence of different situations on its periphery. In areas with documentary habits continuing from Merovingian and ultimately late Roman times, lay landowners as well as churches had a variety of documentary resources on which to draw, even though it is the churches that loom large in the surviving evidence.[35] In those areas that experienced a distinct sub-Roman hiatus, and those that were never part of the empire, documentary practices had to be effectively reinvigorated or created *ab initio* by late Merovingian and early Carolingian churchmen. The emergent elites of the Carolingian period in these latter regions were induced to use documents in ways similar to their Neustrian and Burgundian cousins: they met their needs by piggybacking on the new ecclesiastical institutions to which they were so closely tied and on the documentary culture that had developed around them.[36] The formula evidence illustrates clearly the process of cultural translation that was often involved.[37] These differences are reflected in the contrasting documentary profiles of the regions of the Frankish world. Ninth-century cartularies were entirely a product of East Frankish churches that were newly founded in the eighth century and that rapidly amassed great quantities of landed wealth; although in many areas it is clear that these churches did not bring documentary practices into contexts where they were previously wholly lacking, the resulting picture is nonetheless one of churches and their scribes rapidly becoming the dominant institutions of record, preserving rich traditions

[34] E.g. E. Noichl, *Codex Falkensteinensis: Die Rechtsaufzeichnungen der Grafen von Falkenstein* (Munich, 1978), online with facsimile at www.bayerische-landesbibliothek-online.de/codexfalkensteinensisen, and W. Rösener, 'Codex Falkensteinensis: Zur Erinnerungskultur eines Adelsgeschlechts im Hochmittelalter', in Rösener (ed.), *Adelige und bürgerliche Erinnerungskulturen des Spätmittelalters und der Frühen Neuzeit* (Göttingen, 2000), 35–55; *Littere baronum: The Earliest Cartulary of the Counts of Champagne*, ed. T. Evergates (Toronto, 2003); A. J. Kosto, 'The *Liber feudorum maior* of the Counts of Barcelona: The Cartulary as an Expression of Power', *Journal of Medieval History*, 27 (2001), 1–22; H. Débax, 'Le cartulaire des Trencavel (*Liber instrumentorum vicecomitalium*)', in *Les cartulaires*, 291–9; *Liber instrumentorum memorialium ou cartulaire des Guillems de Montpellier*, ed. A. Germaine and C. Chabanneau, 3 vols. (Montpellier, 1884–6); A. Lewis, 'The Guillems of Montpellier: A Sociological Appraisal', *Viator*, 2 (1972), 159–70; also above, Chapter 12.

[35] See above, Chapters 7 and 11. [36] See above, Chapter 8.

[37] See, for example, the Bavarian formula derived from Marculf, in which a lay archive destroyed by fire was kept not in the plaintiff's home but rather in 'his' monastery: Brown, 'Documents', 351–2.

in which lay documents, while not wholly absent, are elusive. In West Francia, on the other hand, the Carolingian takeover reshaped the documentary and ecclesiastical landscape in more subtle ways, encouraging churches to marshal documents about their landholdings, for sure, but impinging less dramatically on long-standing documentary practices that had evolved from Roman times. Here, we have a more indirect insight into the entirety of Carolingian documentary culture, via the carefully selected acts favoured by eleventh- and twelfth-century cartulary compilers; only in exceptional contexts of transmission, as at Cluny or St-Denis, or where cartularists made unusual choices, as at Perrecy or Redon, do we get a glimpse of all aspects of Carolingian documentation.[38]

Anglo-Saxon England provides a control.[39] In many ways it parallels very well those areas of East Francia where documentary traditions were weak. In a similar fashion, it absorbed traditions from the continent already formed. However, even allowing for the distorting impact of Viking destruction and associated political changes, it is striking that many of the institutional forms we associate with the Carolingian and post-Carolingian heartlands were adopted late and intermittently in England: no polyptychs or cartularies survive from there until after 1066. In addition, the documentary forms of Anglo-Saxon charters have their own peculiarities deriving from the complex circumstances of their origins, and from the mid ninth century onwards they increasingly drew on the written vernacular.

In Italy, scribes were normally laymen throughout our period. That demonstrable fact is part of the evident continuity of institutions in the *civitas* centres, which may have been ecclesiasticized in the sense that they became focused on the cathedral church but in many fundamental respects remained late Roman. In their diplomatics, in their script, and in many areas in their use of papyrus, charters evolved directly from Roman predecessors.[40] Aristocracies in both Lombard and Byzantine Italy therefore had routine access to a variety of documentary resources. The social and material distance between those aristocrats and the more substantial landowning cultivators was less than in Francia.[41] As a consequence, documentary culture penetrated as far as the peasant class.

[38] East Frankish cartularies: see above, Chapters 7, 8 and 11; Geary, *Phantoms*, 81–113.

[39] See above, Chapter 13.

[40] See above, Chapter 4; Everett, *Literacy in Lombard Italy* (Cambridge, 2000), 197–234; A. Pratesi, *Genesi e forme del documento medievale* (Rome, 1979), 47–61. On the theme of the continuity of diplomatic, see the foundational L. Schiaparelli, 'Note diplomatiche sulle carte longobarde', *Archivio storico italiano*, 17 (1932), 3–34; 19 (1933), 3–66; 21 (1934), 3–55.

[41] See C. Wickham, 'Aristocratic Power in Eighth-Century Lombard Italy', in A. C. Murray (ed.), *Sources and Narrators of Early Medieval History* (Toronto, 1998), 153–70, with qualifications by Costambeys, *Power*, 165–6.

The social distance was even shorter in Iberia, where we have even more evidence for the use of documents by peasants. The Iberian evidence from the tenth century shows something of which we already have signs in eighth-century Italy, as well as in Francia: the formation of lay archives that were later absorbed into ecclesiastical institutions, sometimes institutions founded by the very families who assembled those archives. In Italy, the emergence of communes in the late eleventh century meant that there were institutions through which the laity might potentially regain a measure of control over record production and storage. Political and economic developments elsewhere in Europe around the same period would bring similar results.[42]

All of these observations tell us that we should contrast not clergy and laity, but rather institutionalized and non-institutionalized actors. This distinction is perhaps a better way to think about the nature of early medieval records and the patterns of their survival than the traditional lay–clerical divide, which, as we have consistently noted, is problematic. A priest who, along with four siblings, sold a plot of land to a lay couple can hardly be thought of as a representative of the institutional Church; that is, as a *clericus* in its twelfth-century sense. Though our evidence suggests that both he and his buyers would have wanted the sale recorded and validated by a document, that document would most likely not survive more than a few generations without the involvement of a long-lived, transpersonal institution that could preserve it. Only from the seventh century did some ecclesiastical institutions – churches and monasteries – develop that could perform this role. But the kinds of documents that an institution will preserve are determined by that institution's documentary interests. The primary *raison d'être* of the late antique *gesta municipalia* was to keep track of tax obligations. The documentary interests of early medieval churches and monasteries, in contrast, were largely driven by their own property, rights and privileges. Unlike the *gesta municipalia*, many early medieval churches and monasteries, and thus their archives, survived into modern times along with the institutional religion they represented. Yet, though our document of sale may well have been produced by a clerical or monastic scribe, it would not enter an ecclesiastical archive to be passed down to us unless the property involved ended up in a church's or monastery's possession, or unless the seller or the buyer decided to deposit it there for safe keeping. Even in an Italy with a thriving secular notariate, churches and monasteries were often the repositories of first choice for documents, very probably because they had institutional resources and operated with an institutional mindset that before the year 1000 was still largely absent within the laity. Such documents

[42] See also above, Chapters 9–12.

nevertheless still risked being thrown out at some future point unless the information they contained (or their age and suitability as the basis for forgeries) came to meet a clerical or monastic need.

We have shown that it is possible to study lay documentary practices, and, indeed, lay archives, in a period in which their very existence has been frequently doubted. We have presented evidence for the use of documents by people from all social strata, including those with no connection to churches or monasteries. It is clear that the ecclesiastical sources that continue to dominate perceptions of early medieval society were just one segment of a shared documentary culture. We have also offered a new narrative of institutional change that explains the patterns both of documentary production and of evidentiary transmission. One of the effects of vindicating a documentary culture that extended beyond the Church is to open up a range of new questions. For example, the evident volume of land sales adds new layers of complication to an economy usually seen as dominated by the gift. Similarly, the use of documents for the transfer of property *within* families, as visible in the lay dossiers preserved in monastic archives, invites us to reframe fundamental questions about early medieval social structures.[43]

Most importantly, however, we need to rethink archives. Our inherited model is tied up with the process of modern state formation. As we noted at the outset of this book, we tend to think about archives in terms of reference literacy and so as tools of governing institutions. Late antique and early medieval archives were different. Any attempt to assess them needs to avoid modern expectations. When we think of them, we should not imagine a giant central repository accessible only to experts, complete with index and classification systems. Instead, we should think of small collections of folded packets of charters, of related documents tied together or pierced with ritual sticks, of fragments of connected narrative linked by people and places. Stuffed into chests or boxes, kept in homes and local churches, most of these collections would only make sense to their possessor. As historians, we should respect their very scrappy materiality and their very local logic. This is how written documentation was experienced by late antique and early medieval people.

[43] L. Feller and C. Wickham (eds.), *Le marché de la terre au moyen âge* (Rome, 2005); W. Davies, 'When Gift Is Sale: Reciprocities and Commodities in Tenth-Century Christian Iberia', in W. Davies and P. Fouracre (eds.), *The Languages of Gift in the Early Middle Ages* (Cambridge, 2010), 217–37; Davies, *Acts of Giving*, esp. 44; Davies, 'Intra-Family Transfers in Southeastern Brittany: The Dossier from Redon', in *Les transferts*, 881–94.

# Index